EYEWITNESS TRAVEL GUIDES

PORTUGAL

Main consultant: MARTIN SYMINGTON

LONDON, NEW YORK,
MELBOURNE, MUNICH AND DELHI
www.dk.com

PROJECT EDITOR Ferdie McDonald
ART EDITOR Vanessa Hamilton
EDITORS Caroline Ball, Francesca Machiavelli
US EDITORS Mary Sutherland, Michael Wise
DESIGNERS Anthea Forlee, Carolyn Hewitson,
Nicola Rodway, Dutjapun Williams

MAIN CONTRIBUTORS
Susie Boulton, Christopher Catling, Clive Gilbert, Marion Kaplan,
Sarah McAlister, Alice Peebles, Carol Rankin, Norman Renouf,
Joe Staines, Robert Strauss, Nigel Tisdall,
Tomas Tranæus, Edite Vieira

PHOTOGRAPHERS
Joe Cornish, Paul Harris, Robert Reichenfeld,
Linda Whitwam, Peter Wilson, Francesca Yorke

ILLUSTRATORS
Richard Draper, Paul Guest, Stephen Gyapay,
Claire Littlejohn, Maltings Partnership, Isidoro Gonzàlez-Adalid
Cabezas/Acanto Arquitectura y Urbanismo S.L., Paul Weston,
John Woodcock, Martin Woodward

Reproduced by Colourscan (Singapore)
Printed and bound by South China Printing Co. Ltd., China

First American Edition, 1997
6 8 10 9 7

Published in the United States
by DK Publishing, Inc., 375 Hudson Street,
New York, New York 10014
Reprinted with revisions 1999, 2000, 2001, 2002, 2003, 2004

Copyright © 1997, 2004 Dorling Kindersley Limited, London
A Penguin Company

ISSN 1542-1554
ISBN 0-7894-9423-X

FLOORS ARE REFERRED TO THROUGHOUT IN ACCORDANCE WITH EUROPEAN USAGE,
I.E., THE "FIRST FLOOR" IS ONE FLIGHT UP

**The information in this
Dorling Kindersley Travel Guide is checked annually.**
Every effort has been made to ensure that this book is as up-to-date
as possible at the time of going to press. Some details, however,
such as telephone numbers, opening hours, prices, gallery hanging
arrangements and travel information, are liable to change. The
publishers cannot accept responsibility for any consequences arising
from the use of this book, nor for any material on third party
websites, and cannot guarantee that any website address in this
book will be a suitable source of travel information. We value the
views and suggestions of our readers very highly. Please write to:
Publisher, DK Eyewitness Travel Guides,
Dorling Kindersley, 80 Strand, London, Great Britain WC2R 0RL.

◁ **Palácio da Pena rising above the wooded Parque da Pena, Sintra**

CONTENTS

**Equestrian statue of José I
in Praça do Comércio, Lisbon**

INTRODUCING
PORTUGAL

LISBON

**Everyday scene in the Alfama,
the oldest quarter in Lisbon**

Typical blue-trim house near Beja in the Alentejo

Entrance to the chapterhouse at
Alcobaça monastery, Estremadura

17th-century tile decoration
on Palácio Fronteira, Lisbon

The great Gothic
monastery of Batalha

HOW TO USE THIS GUIDE

THIS GUIDE helps you get the most from a visit to Portugal, providing expert recommendations as well as detailed practical information. The opening chapter *Introducing Portugal* maps the country and sets it in its historical and cultural context. Each of the nine regional chapters, plus *Lisbon*, describe important sights, using maps, pictures and illustrations. Features cover topics ranging from architecture and festivals to beaches and food. Hotel and restaurant recommendations can be found in *Travellers' Needs*. The *Survival Guide* contains practical information on everything from transport to personal safety.

LISBON

Lisbon has been divided into five main sightseeing areas. Each of these areas has its own chapter, which opens with a list of the major sights described. All sights are numbered and plotted on an *Area Map*. Information on the sights is easy to locate as the order in which they appear in the chapter follows the numerical order used on the map.

Sights at a Glance lists the chapter's sights by category: Churches, Museums and Galleries, Historic Buildings, Parks and Gardens.

1 Area Map
For easy reference, the sights covered in the chapter are numbered and located on a map. The sights are also marked on the Street Finder *maps on pages 126–39.*

A locator map shows clearly where the area is in relation to other parts of the city.

All the pages relating to Lisbon have red thumb tabs.

2 Street-by-Street Map
This gives a bird's-eye view of the heart of each of the sightseeing areas.

A suggested route for a walk is shown in red.

Stars indicate the sights that no visitor should miss.

3 Detailed Information
All the sights in Lisbon are described individually. Addresses and practical information are provided. The key to the symbols used in the information block is shown on the back flap.

THE LISBON COAST

1 Introduction
A general account of the landscape, history and character of each region is given here, explaining both how the area has developed over the centuries and what attractions it has to offer the visitor today.

PORTUGAL REGION BY REGION
Outside Lisbon, the rest of Portugal has been divided into nine regions, each of which has a separate chapter. The most interesting cities, towns and sights to visit are located and numbered on a *Pictorial Map*.

Exploring the Lisbon Coast

2 Pictorial Map
This shows the main road network and gives an illustrated overview of the region. All entries are numbered and there are also useful tips on getting around the region.

Each area of Portugal can be identified quickly by its colour coding, shown on the inside front cover.

3 Detailed Information
All the important towns and other places to visit are described individually. They are listed in order, following the numbering given on the Pictorial Map. Within each entry, there is further detailed information on important buildings and other sights.

Story boxes explore specific subjects further.

For all the top sights, a Visitors' Checklist provides the practical information you need to plan your visit.

4 The Top Sights
These are given two or more full pages. Historic buildings are dissected to reveal their interiors; museums and galleries have colour-coded floorplans to help you locate the most interesting exhibits.

Palácio Nacional de Sintra

STAR FEATURES

Introducing Portugal

Putting Portugal on the Map

SITUATED IN THE EXTREME southwest corner of Europe, Portugal occupies roughly one-sixth of the Iberian Peninsula with a population of just over 10 million. To the north and east, a border measuring approximately 1,300 km (800 miles) separates Portugal from its only neighbouring country, Spain, and to the south and west, 830 km (500 miles) of coastline meets the Atlantic Ocean. The Atlantic archipelagos of Madeira and the Azores are included in Portugal's territory.

THE AZORES

Corvo
Flores
Graciosa
São Jorge   Terceira
Faial
Pico
São Miguel
Ponta Delgada
Santa Maria

0 kilometres   200
0 miles   100

The Azores
The Azores lie 1,300 km (800 miles) to the west of Lisbon in the Atlantic Ocean. Of volcanic origin, the islands are scattered over a distance of 650 km (400 miles).

MADEIRA

Porto Santo
Ilha do Porto Santo
Madeira
R101   R101
R101   Funchal

0 kilometres   20
0 miles   10

Madeira
Lying 965 km (600 miles) southwest of Lisbon in the Atlantic Ocean, the Madeiran archipelago has two inhabited islands, Madeira and Porto Santo.

KEY

✈	International airport
⛴	Ferry port
▬	Motorway
▬	Major road
=	Minor road
—	Main railway line
–•–	International boundary

ATLANTIC

OCEAN

0 kilometres   100
0 miles   50

(map of western Portugal)
Pontevedra
Vigo   Ourens
N525   A9 (E1)
N120   Minho
N13
Braga   N10
Guimarãe
Oporto   A4 (E82)
(Porto)   Dour
A1 (E1)
IP5 (E80)
Viseu
A1 (E1)   IP3 (E80)
Figueira   Coimbra
da Foz
N109   PORT
Zêzere
IP6 (E80
Tejo
N8
Santarém
A1 (E1)   N10
LISBON (Lisboa)
A6
Setúbal   Évora
A2 (E1)   Sado
IP
Beja
Sines   IP2 (E8
A2 (E1)   N2
N120
Portimão   N125
A22 (E1)
Far

◁ **Landscape near Lagos in the Algarve by Sir Cedric Morris (1889–1982)**

Greater Lisbon

The capital of Portugal is a hilly city on the Tagus estuary. The country's main port and business centre, Greater Lisbon has a population of around two million.

A PORTRAIT OF PORTUGAL

MOST VISITORS TO PORTUGAL *head for the sandy coves, rocky coastline and manicured golf links of the Algarve. But beyond the south coast resorts lies the least explored corner of Western Europe: a country of rugged landscapes, sophisticated cities, rural backwaters and sharply contrasting traditions.*

Portugal appears to have no obvious geographical claim to nationhood, yet this western extremity of the Iberian Peninsula has existed within borders virtually unchanged for nearly 800 years. Its ten million people speak their own language, follow their own unique cultural traditions, and have a centuries-old history of proud independence from, and distrust of neighbouring Spain.

For a small country, the regions of Portugal are immensely varied. The rural Minho and Trás-os-Montes in the north are the most traditional – some would say backward. Over the last few decades many inhabitants of these neglected regions have been forced to emigrate in search of work.

Horseman at festival in Vila Franca de Xira, Ribatejo

The south of the country could not be more different. The Algarve, blessed with beautiful sandy beaches and a wonderful, warm Mediterranean climate all year round, has been transformed into a holiday playground for North Europeans.

Two great rivers, the Tagus and the Douro, rise in Spain and then flow westwards across Portugal to the Atlantic Ocean. From the wild upper reaches of the Douro valley, comes Portugal's most famous product – port wine, from steeply terraced vineyards hewn out of the mountainsides. The Tagus, by contrast, is wide and languid, often spilling out over the flat, fertile, Ribatejo flood plain where fine horses and fighting bulls graze.

Crowded beach at high season at Albufeira in the Algarve

◁ **Traditional agriculture on smallholdings near Ponte de Lima in the Minho**

Rolling grassland of the Alentejo with village and medieval castle of Terena

At the mouths of the Tagus and Douro stand Portugal's two major cities, Lisbon and Oporto respectively. Lisbon, the capital, is a cosmopolitan metropolis with a rich cultural life and many national museums and art galleries. Oporto is a serious rival to Lisbon, especially in terms of commerce and industry. Most centres of population, however, are very much smaller: from the fishing communities on the Atlantic coast to the tiny medieval villages in the vast sunbaked plains of the Alentejo and the mountainous interior of the Beiras.

Woman stripping osiers for wickerwork in Madeira

Far out in the Atlantic Ocean lie two remote archipelagos that are self-governing regions of the Portuguese state: warm, luxuriant Madeira off the coast of Morocco, and the nine rainy, green, volcano tips that make up the Azores, about one third of the way across the Atlantic between Lisbon and New York.

POLITICS AND ECONOMICS

In the final quarter of the 20th century, a new era of Portuguese history began. From the late 1920s, under the long dictatorship of António Salazar, the country was a virtual recluse in the world community. The principal concern of foreign policy was the ultimately futile defence of Portugal's African and Asian colonies. Domestic industry and commerce were dominated by a few wealthy families, in an economic framework of extreme fiscal tightness.

The Carnation Revolution of 1974 brought this era to an end. At first the re-establishment of democracy was a painful process, but since the 1980s Portugal has assumed an increasingly confident Western European demeanour. Entry into the European Community in 1986 was welcomed at all levels of society, and led to an explosion of new construction,

Barredo quarter of Oporto, Portugal's second city

the like of which Portugal had never seen. Traditional exports, such as cork, resin, textiles, tinned sardines and wine, have been joined by new, heavier industries such as vehicle construction and cement manufacturing.

Grants and loans from the EU have funded the building of new roads, bridges and hospitals, and brought significant improvements in agriculture. Portugal's confidence in Europe is high since Oporto was the European Capital of Culture in 2001 and in July 2002 the euro became Portugal's currency.

Luxury yachts in the harbour at Vilamoura in the Algarve

THE PORTUGUESE WAY OF LIFE

Travellers in Portugal will find a mild-mannered, easy-going people. At the same time they have an innate sense of politeness, a quality they respect in others. The Portuguese also tend to dress well, if rather conservatively, and to use formal modes of address, calling new acquaintances by their Christian names, prefixed by Senhor, Senhora or Dona.

Collecting seaweed for fertilizer in the Ria de Aveiro lagoon

In spite of this, they are gregarious folk, often to be seen eating, drinking and making merry in large groups – at a *festa*, or in a restaurant celebrating a birthday or a first communion. There is a special weakness for children, who are cherished, indulged and welcomed everywhere. Visitors to the country who bring their youngsters with them will discover an immediate point of contact with their hosts. Nevertheless, behind the smiles and the good humour, there is a deep-rooted aspect of the national psyche which the Portuguese themselves call

View from the mountaintop village of Monsanto near the border with Spain

Farmworkers breaking for a picnic lunch in the fields of the Alentejo

The family is the bosom of Portuguese daily life. Although old customs are gradually changing, especially in the cities, it is quite common for three generations to live under one roof, and it is normal for both men and women to stay living in the family home until they marry. One thing that has changed dramatically is family size. A generation ago, families of ten or more children were commonplace – especially in remote, rural areas. Nowadays, one or two children constitute an average-sized family, often looked after by a grandmother while both parents go out to work.

saudade, a sort of ethereal, aching melancholy which seems to yearn for something lost or unattainable.

In so far as these generalizations hold true, so too do a couple of Portuguese characteristics which can prove irritating. The first is a relaxed attitude to time: no visitor should interpret lack of punctuality as a personal slight. The second is the fact that many Portuguese men tend to discard their native courtesy completely when they are behind the wheel of a car. Reckless driving, particularly high-speed tailgating, is a national pastime.

Catholicism is at the heart of Portuguese life, especially in the north, where you will see a crucifix or the image of a saint watching over most homes, cafés and

Tiled housefront in Alcochete, a small town on the Tagus estuary

barbers' shops. Weddings and first communion services are deeply religious occasions. Although church attendance is in decline, particularly in the cities, national devotion to Our Lady of Fátima remains steadfast, as does delight in festivals *(romarias)* honouring local saints, another tradition that is strongest in the north.

LANGUAGE AND CULTURE

There are few faux pas more injurious to national esteem, than to suggest that Portuguese is a mere dialect of Spanish. Great pride is taken in the language and literature. *Os Lusíadas*, the national epic by 16th-century poet Camões, is studied reverentially, while many Portuguese also delight in the

Town gate of Óbidos with shrine of Nossa Senhora da Piedade, lined with 18th-century tiles

Religious procession in the village of Vidigueira in the Alentejo

detached, ironic portrait of themselves in the 19th-century novels of Eça de Queirós. Pride too, is taken in *fado*, the native musical tradition which expresses the notion of *saudade*. In rural areas, especially the Minho, there is still an enthusiastic following for folk dancing.

There are several excellent newspapers, but the country's best-selling daily is *A Bola*, which is devoted exclusively to sport, football being a national obsession. Bullfighting too has its adherents, although with nothing like the passion found in Spain.

The Portuguese have long been avid watchers of television and are now producing many home-grown soap operas, films and documentaries. Up until just a few years ago, virtually all of these were imported from abroad.

Transport in the remote Beira Alta

The country has become more forward-looking in recent years, but most aspects of heritage hark back to the Discoveries. The best-loved monuments are those built in the one uniquely Portuguese style of architecture, the Manueline, which dates from this period. Many *azulejo* tile paintings, another cherished tradition, also glory in Portugal's great maritime past.

When the Portuguese joined the European Community in 1986, Commission President Jacques Delors solemnly warned them that they should think of themselves as "Portuguese first, and European second". Typically, the Portuguese were too polite to laugh out loud. How could anyone have imagined that this little country was in danger of suddenly throwing overboard centuries of culture nurtured in staunch independence?

Open-air café in Praça da Figueira in Lisbon's Baixa

Vernacular Architecture

Window in Marvão *(see p294)*

TRADITIONALLY, PORTUGAL'S rural architecture varied with climatic conditions and locally available building materials. Although light-weight bricks are now ubiquitous, many older houses still stand. There are the thick-walled granite houses of the north designed to keep out the cold and rain. The Beiras' milder climate means their houses are made of brick or limestone. In the Alentejo and the Ribatejo, the clay houses are long and low, to suit hot summers and chilly winters. The Algarve's gentler Mediterranean climate has led to houses of clay or stone.

Yellow-trimmed houses below walls of Óbidos *(see pp174–5)*

Chimneys are small or non-existent. Instead, smoke escapes through openings in the roof.

Roofs are constructed of slate or schist tiles, or occasionally thatch.

Village houses *in the Minho* (see p263) *and Trás-os-Montes regions* (see p233) *are two-storeyed and usually built with the staircase on the outside. The veranda is used for extra living space.*

Local granite is used for rustic stonework.

The ground floor is used to keep animals and for storage.

Fishermen's houses *found in the Costa Nova region south of Aveiro* (see p201) *are painted in brightly coloured stripes. Forests planted to prevent the sand dunes from encroaching on the land provide the raw material.*

Raised platforms guard against flooding.

Modern examples use tiles or painted façades to continue the tradition of striped houses.

Different coloured stripes painted onto the wood allowed the fishermen to identify their houses through the region's frequent mists.

Rooftops of Castelo de Vide in the Alentejo *(see p295)*

TILED ROOFS

Throughout Portugal, red clay roof tiles give towns and villages a memorable skyline. The most traditional and widely used type of roof tile is the *telha de canudo* or tubu-lar tile. Originating from the Moors, these half-cylindrical tiles are placed in two layers: the first is placed with the concave side facing up and the second with the concave side facing down, covering the joints of the first.

Telhados de quatro águas, the distinctive tiled roofs found in Tavira, the Algarve *(see p330)*

Telhas de canudo are used to cover the roof.

Verandas are glassed in and so can be used all year round.

Limestone used for the walls is usually stuccoed and whitewashed.

Houses in the Beiras (see pp194–221) *often have verandas, usually on the first floor. These are built to face the sun, at the same time affording protection from the cold north winds.*

PORTUGAL'S WINDMILLS

Windmills are thought to have existed in Portugal since the 11th century. Many pristine examples still dot the hillsides, particularly in coastal regions.

Most windmills *have a cylindrical brick or stone base. The upper section revolves to catch the wind in its canvas sails. Estremadura (see pp170–93) has good examples.*

Thatched houses *in the Sado Estuary (see p169) are now rare. Surviving examples have walls that consist of a wooden frame supporting woven sections made of straw and reed. The simple houses use only local materials.*

Wooden beams

Azorean windmills, *such as this example on Faial (see p370), are fairly similar to the Portuguese model, but show the clear influence of early Dutch and Flemish settlers in their sail design.*

Some roof tiles can be removed in summer for more light.

Wooden windows have a painted surround.

Huge chimneys provide spaces for smoking hams and sausages.

Colour-trimmed houses *of the Alentejo and Ribatejo regions are mainly constructed of clay. Long and oblong in shape, they have few openings, to ensure that the heat is trapped in winter and kept out in summer.*

Whitewashing protects the walls, deflects the hot summer sun and acts as a deterrent for pests and vermin. Many householders consider it a point of honour ro renew their whitewash each year.

CHIMNEYS OF THE ALGARVE

These are an important decorative feature of houses in the Algarve (see pp314–31). The Moorish influence can be seen in their cylindrical or prismatic shapes and the geometric designs perforating the clay. The chimneys are whitewashed and many have details picked out in colour to accentuate their ornamentation.

Manueline Architecture

THE STYLE OF ARCHITECTURE that flourished in the reign
of Manuel I *(see pp46–9)* and continued after his
death is essentially a Portuguese variant of Late Gothic. It
is typified by maritime motifs inspired by Portugal's Age
of Discovery, and by elaborate "all-over" decoration.
The artists behind it include João de Castilho and
Diogo Boitac, renowned for the cloister of the Mosteiro
dos Jerónimos *(see pp106–7)*, and Francisco and Diogo
de Arruda, designers of the Torre de Belém *(see p110)*.

**Twisted Manueline pillory
in Chaves *(see pp256–7)***

**Cross of the Order
of Christ *(see p185)***

***The portal** of the church of
Conceição Velha in Lisbon
(see p87) was commissioned
by Manuel in the early 16th
century. The king himself
appears in the carved relief
in the tympanum.*

**Armillary
sphere**

**Coat of Arms
of Manuel I**

Cables

**Swathes of
seaweed**

**Coral-encrusted
masts**

Anchor chains

Twisted ropes

***The ornate window** in
the Convento de Cristo at
Tomar (see pp186–7) was
commissioned by Manuel I
and designed by Diogo de
Arruda c.1510. It is the best-known
single motif of Manueline architecture, illustrating its exotic naturalism
and complex use of maritime detail.*

**Bust, probably of
the designer Diogo
de Arruda**

***Gil Vicente** created the
Belém Monstrance (1506)
from the first gold brought
back from India. Made for
Santa Maria de Belém (see
p107), its superstructure
echoes the south portal.*

DECORATIVE DETAILS

The most important motifs
in Manueline architecture
are the armillary sphere, the
Cross of the Order of Christ
and twisted rope. Naturalistic
and fantastic forms are often
used, as well as flatter, finely
crafted designs similar to
those found on contempo-
rary Spanish silverware. Later
Manueline schemes some-
times incorporate Italian
Renaissance ornamentation.

The armillary sphere was
a navigational device that
became the emblem of
Manuel I himself.

**The Cross of the
Order of Christ**
was the emblem of
a military order that helped to
finance early voyages. It also
emblazoned sails and flags.

REBUILDING THE MANUELINE PORTAL OF MADRE DE DEUS

The Manueline portal of the church of Madre de Deus in Lisbon *(see p123)* was destroyed in the 1755 earthquake, but it was not until 1872 that João Maria Nepomuceno was commissioned to rebuild it. For accuracy, he referred to an early 16th-century painting by an unknown artist, *The Arrival of the Relics of Santa Auta at the Church of Madre de Deus*, now in the Museu Nacional de Arte Antiga *(see pp96–9)*. The splendid procession in the picture is shown heading towards the Manueline portal of the church, which is clearly depicted. Like others of that period, it stands proud of the building and dominates the façade. The Manueline style favoured rounded rather than pointed arches and this one has an interesting trefoil shape.

Portal of Madre de Deus church today

The painting of *The Arrival of the Relics* showing the original 16th-century portal

Curving branches and crinkled exotic foliage recall Indian sculptural motifs.

Cross of the Order of Christ

In the Royal Cloister of Batalha (see pp182–3), *early 15th-century pointed Gothic arches incorporate exquisite Manueline screens on colonnettes, probably by Diogo Boitac, whose two designs alternate.*

Soft limestone allowed complex patterns to be carved in the tracery.

Armillary sphere

The colonnettes have all-over ornamentation, with repeated patterns of pearls, shells and coil motifs.

Pillars of plaited colonnettes were used by architects such as Boitac in the Igreja de Jesus in Setúbal *(see p168)*.

Twisted ropes decorate ceiling vaults, columns and arches, and girdle entire buildings inside and out.

The Buçaco Palace, *today a luxury hotel (see p210), was originally built as a royal hunting lodge about the end of the 19th century. An extraordinary building, the palace incorporates every conceivable element of Manueline architecture and decoration, illustrating the persistence of the style in Portuguese design, which continues to this day.*

Azulejos – Painted Ceramic Tiles

T HE IDEA OF COVERING walls, floors and even ceilings with tiles was introduced to Spain and Portugal by the Moors. From the 16th century onwards, Portugal started producing its own decorative tiles. By the 18th century, no other European country was producing as many tiles, for such a variety of purposes and in so many different designs; the blue and white tiles of the Baroque era are considered by many to be the finest. *Azulejos* became and still remain a very important addition to the interior and exterior architecture of Portuguese buildings.

1716 *Detail from Panel of Christ Teaching in the Temple*
Around 1690 blue and white story-telling tiles began to be produced. These figures are from a typical scheme by António de Oliveira Bernardes (c.1660–1732), the greatest master of the genre. The central panels are surrounded by a complex architectural border *(Igreja Da Misericórdia , Évora, see p303)*.

c.1520 *Frieze of Spanish-made Tiles*
These Moorish-style tiles were produced by compartmental techniques using raised and depressed areas to prevent the tin-glaze colours from running *(Palácio Nacional de Sintra, see pp158–9)*.

c.1680 *Hunting Cat*
Naturalistic panels of this period were often naively drawn, but used a wide range of colours *(Museu Nacional do Azulejo, see pp122–3)*.

1500	1600	1700
RENAISSANCE	**MANNERIST**	**BAROQUE**
1500	1600	1700

1565 *Susannah and the Elders*
The mid-16th century saw the introduction of the maiolica technique. This allowed artists to paint directly onto prepared flat tiles using several colours, as these did not run in the firing process. This panel of a biblical episode is one of the earliest produced in Portugal. The decorative details are typical of the Renaissance *(Quinta da Bacalhoa, see p167)*.

c.1650 *Carpet Tiles*
So-called because they imitated the patterns of Moorish rugs, these were produced mainly in blue, yellow and white. They often covered whole walls *(Museu Nacional do Azulejo, see pp122–3)*.

1736 *Capela de São Filipe*
The small chapel inside Setúbal's castle is a fine example of a complete decorative scheme using blue and white tiles. The panels, illustrating the life of St Philip, are signed by Policarpo de Oliveira Bernardes, son of the great António *(Castelo de São Filipe, see p168)*.

c.1670 *Tiled Altar Frontal*
The exuberant scheme incorporates Hindu motifs and other exotic themes inspired by the printed calicoes and chintzes brought back from India *(Museu Nacional do Azulejo, see pp122–3)*.

1865 *Viúva Lamego Tile Factory, Lisbon*
For the first half of the 19th century, relatively few tiles were produced. The fashion then returned for covering whole surfaces with tiles, and simple stylized designs were used to decorate shop fronts and residential areas. This naive, chinoiserie figure is part of a scheme dating from 1865 that covers the entire façade of the factory.

c.1970 *Tile Pattern*
The original design for this strikingly modern scheme by architect Raúl Lino dates from about 1910. Many of Portugal's leading modern artists have worked with *azulejos* (*Museu Nacional do Azulejo, see pp122–3*).

c.1770–84 *Corredor das Mangas*
The Rococo period saw the reintroduction of polychromatic *azulejos*. This antechamber in the royal palace at Queluz has tiled panels showing hunting scenes, the seasons and the continents (*Palácio de Queluz, see pp164–5*).

1927 *Battle of Ourique*
The early years of the 20th century saw a revival of large-scale historical scenes in traditional blue and white. This panel is by Jorge Colaço (*Carlos Lopes Pavilion, Parque Eduardo VII, Lisbon, see p115*).

1800	1900
NEO-CLASSICAL	**ART NOUVEAU** **MODERN**
1800	1900

c.1800 *The Story of António Joaquim Carneiro, Hatmaker*
Delicate Neo-Classical ornamentation surrounds the blue and white central subject matter in this charming tale of a shepherd boy who makes his fortune as a hatmaker in the big city. Sophisticated designs of this kind disappeared during the upheavals of the Peninsular War (*see p54*) at the beginning of the 19th century (*Museu Nacional do Azulejo, see pp122–3*).

c.1770 *Gatekeeper*
"Cut out" figures like this musketeer are an amusing feature of tile schemes in many palaces and mansions from the 18th century onwards. They stand guard at the entrance, on landings or on staircases (*Museu Nacional do Azulejo, see pp122–3*).

TILES IN DOMESTIC ARCHITECTURE

Art Nouveau friezes and decorations in deep colours enliven the façade of this early 20th-century house in Aveiro. To this day, tiles are used to cover façades of houses. They are relatively cheap to produce, long-lasting and need little maintenance. Tiled houses brighten up many Portuguese towns and villages. The town of Ovar (*see pp198–9*) is particularly striking. **Vila Africana, Aveiro (*see p200*)**

Decorated Ceramics

SMALL, TRADITIONAL local potteries *(olarias),* many of them family concerns, are found in most parts of Portugal. Different regions have their own distinct styles and attractive pottery can be bought from factories and local markets throughout the country. Choose from a variety of wares which include the excellent, practical brown earthenware, brightly coloured figurines *(bonecos),* intricate hand-painted designs and fine porcelain.

MINHO

Barcelos (see p273) *is the northern centre for pottery. Terracotta jars, vases, flowerpots and lanterns, and figurines in paintbox colours, are made in country workshops.*

The finest porcelain in Portugal, famous for its delicacy, is made at Vista Alegre (see p201). The factory is well worth visiting for its museum that charts the evolution of the art.

The faïence tradition of Coimbra (see pp202–5) and its environs continues today in numerous factories, such as Estrela de Conimbriga, south of the city, where this candlestick was made. Detailed Moorish, 17th- and 18th-century designs are painted by hand onto all kinds of domestic objects and artefacts.

ESTREMADURA AND RIBATEJO

Caldas da Rainha (see p175) *prides itself on its cabbage ware and other lookalike vegetable, fish and fruit ceramics, such as these "gourds". The factory also makes dinner sets with reliefs of flowers and foliage.*

LISBON

THE LISBON COAST

Ceramic art in Cascais (see p162) *was revived by Luís Soares in the 1970s. He used the ancient technique of drawing a free design on the soft clay with a sharp stiletto, so no two designs are the same. High-quality glazes and a hot firing give an excellent finish.*

| 0 kilometres | 50 |
| 0 miles | 25 |

Porches Pottery was founded in 1968 to revive a local craft and preserve ancient Iberian and Moorish patterns. Each piece is hand-glazed and painted in a free-flowing style, in blue, green and turquoise.

DOURO AND
TRÁS-OS-MONTES

BROWN EARTHENWARE

Matt and glazed earthenware, plain or painted with simple patterns, is widely used and sold at country fairs and markets throughout Portugal. The dishes make attractive and resilient cookware. They range from tall, lidded storage pots and sturdy, oven-proof casserole dishes to portable spirit-burners which are used for grilling *chouriço* sausages at the table.

Bisalhães *and other villages near Vila Real (see p255) make an unusual black or dark grey pottery, fired in pits and rubbed with moss and earth to achieve their colour. These tough pots can then be used for cooking.*

THE BEIRAS

White floral patterning *on plain terracotta is the hallmark of pottery from Nisa in the Alentejo. Shiny quartz or marble chips are painstakingly applied in lacy floral patterns reminiscent of embroidery.*

The red clay *of Estremoz (see pp300–1) is valued for its malleable qualities. Typical products are patterned in relief with bold decorative flourishes. Estremoz is also famous for its eccentric* bonecos.

The hand-painted pottery *of Redondo (see p300) has a distinctive homely style. Plates may be decorated with fresh floral designs or, as here, charming scenes of pastoral life.*

ALENTEJO

A potter *in São Pedro do Corval throws a jar "off the hump". This means she can produce, by eye, a number of equal sized jars from one large lump of clay. She is using a rib tool to shape and finish off the pot. Many small cooperative potteries can be found in the villages around Reguengos de Monsaraz (see p307).*

ALGARVE

Harvesting the Ocean

A VITAL INDUSTRY IN PORTUGAL, fishing employs about 25,000 men, trawling treacherous coastal waters for a huge variety of fish, destined for local consumption or export. Among the best places to see fishermen at work are Viana do Castelo, Peniche, Nazaré, Sesimbra and Ericeira in the west; and Sagres, Lagos and Olhão in the south.

Terracotta octopus pots

Viana do Castelo
MINHO
Póvoa de Varzim
Oporto
DOURO AND
TRÁS-OS-MONTES
Aveiro
THE BEIRAS
Figueira da Foz
Nazaré
ESTREMADURA
AND RIBATEJO
Peniche
Ericeira
LISBON   THE LISBON
COAST
Cascais   *Setúbal*
Sesimbra
ALENTEJO
Sines
ALGARVE
Portimão   *Tavira*
Olhão
Lagos
Sagres

Fishermen mend nets at Peniche (see p174), an important centre for sardines, which are at their best in the summer. About 250,000 tonnes are caught annually around the coast – for freezing, canning or eating fresh in seaside restaurants.

A quayside stall at Sesimbra (see p166) displays the local catch. In the foreground are several types of bream and bass. Traditionally, fishwives, or varinas, would sort the fish as it came in, ready for sale.

Ferragudo is a typical small Algarvian fishing community on the Arade estuary. Its tiny boats fish close to the coast mainly for local needs, leaving the heavy fishing to nearby Portimão, an important sardine centre on the Algarve.

FISHING BOATS

Of Portugal's 10,000 registered boats, many are ancient and weather-beaten. The largest, 24-m (80-ft) trawlers, have diesel engines and radios. Smaller trawlers are used for inshore fishing. At the other end of the scale is the oar-powered 5-m (16-ft) *meia-lua*, In some places this is hauled back up the beach by oxen.

*A typical Algarve fishing boat, a small trawler (*traineira*), is less than 12 m (40 ft) long. This means that fishermen cannot go far out to sea or gather very large hauls.*

The frail **meia-lua** *(half-moon) with its flat bottom and high prow, is still used on the west coast. It may be painted with a good luck symbol such as the Cross of the Order of Christ (see p185).*

The festival of Nossa Senhora da Agonia at Viano do Castelo (see pp274–5) *is one of several celebrations to honour the supreme guardian of fishermen. A statue of the Virgin is paraded through the streets, then carried out to sea in a flower-decked boat to bless the fleet.*

At Cascais on the Lisbon coast, an auction is held each evening at the fish market to sell the day's catch. It is a noisy, bustling affair, and a major attraction for locals and visitors alike.

Clamdiggers return from the shellfish beds at Cabanas, east of Tavira in the Algarve. Clams, cockles, whelks and razor shells all flourish here in the warm, shallow waters of the lagoon, and are gathered at low tide.

The trawler (traineira), *fishes furthest offshore, mainly for sardines. In a tradition dating back to the Phoenicians, trawlers are usually painted in bright colours, making them easily recognizable out at sea.*

TYPES OF FISH

The choice of fish in Portugal seems almost endless, from the ubiquitous, delicious sardine through bream, bass, mullet and tuna, to members of the eel and octopus families. Strangely, the national favourite is neither Portuguese nor eaten fresh: dried, salted cod *(bacalhau)* is known as *o fiel amigo*, the faithful friend, and has inspired countless recipes.

Sardines *(sardinhas)* or young pilchards are the leading fresh fish catch. Trawlers catch them with purse-seine nets as they swim in shoals 25–40 m (80–130 ft) below the surface.

Horse mackerel *(carapau)*, favoured for its cheapness and abundance, is baked, grilled or fried. It can also be marinated after cooking to improve flavour.

Tuna *(atum)* can reach 4 m (13 ft) and are found in schools near the Azores and the Algarve – the smaller the fish, the larger the school. Tuna is sold fresh, or canned for export.

Squid *(lulas)* occur plentifully all round the coast and are traditionally served in a stew, fried or grilled. The related cuttlefish *(chocos)* and octopus *(polvos)* are equally popular.

Red mullet *(salmonete)*, prized for its delicate flavour, frequents the coast around Setúbal, where the most famous recipes come from.

Scabbard fish *(peixe espada)* is a tasty, long, thin fish particular to Sesimbra and Madeira. It should not be confused with the similar-sounding but chunkier *espadarte* or swordfish, which tastes quite different.

The Wines of Portugal

ALTHOUGH STILL overshadowed by the excellence and fame of port, Portuguese table wine deserves to be taken seriously. After years of investment in the industry, many of the reds, such as the full-bodied wines from the Douro (made with some of the same grapes as port), have established an attractive style all their own. Great whites are fewer, but most regions have some. And of course there is *vinho verde*, the usually white, light, slightly carbonated wine from the north.

Sparkling rosés, *such as Mateus and Lancers, have been Portugal's great export success. But the country now has many excellent wines that reach beyond the easy-drinking charms of these.*

WINE REGIONS

Many of Portugal's wine regions maintain their individual style by specializing in particular Portuguese grape varieties. The introduction of modern wine-making techniques has improved overall quality, and as yet the increasing use of imported grape varieties seems no threat to Portuguese individuality.

KEY

☐	Vinhos Verdes
▨	Douro
☐	Dão
▨	Bairrada
▨	Estremadura
☐	Ribatejo
☐	Setúbal
☐	Alentejo

0 kilometres   50

0 miles   25

Vinho verde **vineyards in the village of Lapela, near Monção in the Minho**

Cellar of the Buçaco Palace Hotel, (*see pp210–11*), famous for its red wine

HOW TO READ A WINE LABEL

Tinto is red, *branco* is white, *seco* is dry and *doce* is sweet. Other essential information is the name of the producer, the region and the year. Wines made to at least 80 per cent from a single grape variety may give the name of that grape on the label. *Denominação de Origem Controlada* (DOC) indicates that the wine has been made according to the strictest regulations of a given region, but, as elsewhere, this need not mean higher quality than the nominally simpler *Vinho Regional* appellation. The back label often describes grape varieties and wine-making techniques used.

DOURO
DENOMINAÇÃO DE ORIGEM CONTROLADA

ENCOSTAS DO TUA
Reserva de 2000
VINHO TINTO

PRODUZIDO E ENGARRAFADO POR
SOCIEDADE AGRÍCOLA E COMERCIAL DOS VINHOS
VALE DA CORÇA, LDA
ABUNHEIRA · CARRAZEDA DE ANSIÃES · PORTUGAL
PRODUTO DE PORTUGAL

This wine is from the Douro and is made according to DOC regulations for the region.

The name of this wine means "banks of the River Tua", further specifying its geographical origin.

***Reserva* means** that the wine has been aged, probably in oak casks. It also implies that the wine is of higher quality than non-reserva wine from the same producer.

The Sociedade Agrícola e Comercial dos Vinhos Vale da Corça, Lda, produced and bottled this wine.

Vinho verde, *"green wine"* from the Minho region, can be either red or white, but the fizzy, dry reds are generally consumed locally. Typical white vinho verde is bone dry, slightly fizzy, low in alcohol and high in acidity. A weightier style of white vinho verde is made from the Alvarinho grape, near the Spanish border. Among the best brands are Soalheiro and Palácio da Brejoeira.

Bairrada *is a region where the small and thick-skinned Baga grape dominates.* It makes big, tannic wines, sometimes with smoky or pine-needle overtones and like the older Dão wines, they need time to soften. Modern winemaking and occasional disregard for regional regulations have meant more approachable reds (often classified as Vinho Regional das Beiras) and crisper whites. Quality producers include Luís Pato and Caves Aliança.

Ribatejo *is the fertile valley of the Tagus to the north and east of Lisbon.* After Estremadura, it is Portugal's biggest wine region measured by volume, but its potential for quality wines has only just begun to be realized. As in Estremadura, Vinho Regional bottlings are frequently better than DOC ones. Producers to look for include Quinta da Alorna, Casa Branco and Fiuza and Bright.

The Douro region is best known as the source of port wine, but in most years about half of the wine produced is fermented dry to make table wine, and these wines are now at the forefront of Portuguese wine-making. The pioneer, Barca Velha, was launched half a century ago and is both highly regarded and among the most expensive. Other quality producers include Calheiros Cruz, Domingos Alves de Sousa, Quinta do Crasto, Niepoort and Ramos-Pinto.

Picking grapes for *vinho verde*

Setúbal, to the south of Lisbon, is best known for its sweet, fortified Muscat wine, Moscatel de Setúbal. In addition, the region also produces excellent, mostly red, table wine. Two big quality producers dominate the region: José Maria da Fonseca (see p167) and J.P. Vinhos. The co-operative at Santo Isidro de Pegões makes good-value wines, while interesting smaller producers include Venâncio Costa Lima, Hero do Castanheiro and Ermelinda Freitas.

The Dão region now offers some of Portugal's best wines. Small producers, such as Quinta dos Roques, Quinta da Pellada and Quinta de Cabriz, and the large Sogrape company make fruity reds for younger drinking, fresh, dry whites and deeper, richer reds which retain their fruit with age – a far cry from the heavy, hard-edged, and often oxidized wines of the past.

Estremadura *is Portugal's westernmost wine area and has only recently emerged as a region in its own right.* Several producers now make modern Vinho Regional wines with character; look for wines by DFJ, Casa Santos Lima, Quinta de Pancas and Quinta do Monte d'Oiro. The most interesting DOC is Alenquer. Bucelas, to the south of the region, produces characterful white wines.

Alentejo produced wine has possibly made the biggest leap in quality in the last decade. Long dismissed by experts as a region of easy-drinking house reds for restaurants, this area now produces some of Portugal's most serious red wines and a surprising number of excellent whites. Among the best producers are Herdade do Esporão, Herdade dos Coelheiros, Cortes de Cima and João Portugal Ramos.

PORTUGAL THROUGH THE YEAR

Monção's Festa da Coca (June)

WHILE JULY and August are the most popular months for visiting, spring and autumn can be more rewarding if you want to tour and experience local culture. Free of excessive heat and crowds, the country is more relaxed. There is deep-rooted respect throughout the country for ancient traditions, which are most often reflected in religious festivals. *Festas* are held throughout the year, most frequently celebrating saints' days, but also marking the end of the harvest, or gastronomic and even sporting events. *Festas* call for prayers, processions, fireworks, eating and drinking, traditional folk dances and general merrymaking.

SPRING

FROM THE ALGARVE to Trás-os-Montes, the country erupts in wild flowers as warmer days set in. This is the time to see the countryside at its most beautiful, although rain can be expected until the end of May.

Easter is a time of great religious celebration, with Holy Week processions taking place all over the country.

MARCH

Open de Portugal de Golfe *(mid-Mar)*. Venue changes from year to year.
Festival Intercéltico do Porto *(end Mar or early Apr)*, Oporto. A festival of music from Portugal and Spain.

Funchal Flower Festival (April)

APRIL

Holy Week *(week before Easter)*, Braga. Events in the country's religious capital are particularly traditional and solemn. Torchlit processions are led by church authorities.

Fátima on 13 May, when 100,000 pilgrims gather every year

Easter Sunday is also the beginning of the bullfighting season throughout Portugal.
Mãe Soberana *(second Sun after Easter)*, Loulé, Algarve. Pilgrimage to Nossa Senhora da Piedade *(see p324)*.
FIAPE *(end Apr)* Estremoz. An international agricultural, cattle and handicrafts fair.

MAY

Festas das Cruzes *(early May)*, Barcelos. The Festival of the Crosses celebrates the day the shape of a cross appeared in the earth in 1504.
Flower Festival *(late Apr)*, Funchal, Madeira. Shops and houses are decorated with flowers. Ends with a parade of flower-covered floats.
Pilgrimage to Fátima *(12–13 May)*. Huge crowds make the pilgrimage to the place where the Virgin appeared to three children in 1917 *(see p184)*.
Queima das Fitas *(mid-May)*, Coimbra. Lively celebrations mark end of the university's academic year *(see p207)*.

Festa do Senhor Santo Cristo dos Milagres *(fifth Sun after Easter)*, Ponta Delgada, São Miguel, Azores. The largest religious festival in the Azores.
Festa do Espírito Santo *(Pentecost)*, Azores. High point of the festival of the Holy Spirit *(see p367)*.
Pilgrimage to Bom Jesus *(Pentecost)*, Braga. Penitents climb the spectacular staircase on their knees *(see pp278–9)*.
Algarve Music Festival *(May Jun–Jul)*, throughout region. Concerts and performances by the Gulbenkian Ballet.

Children carrying a cross at the Festas das Cruzes, Barcelos (May)

SUMMER

MOST VISITORS choose the summer months to visit Portugal. Since many businesses shut down in August, it is holiday time for locals too. Many families spend the entire summer by the seaside.

Summer is a good time to visit the cooler Minho, when the north is busy with saints' day festivals *(see pp226–7)*.

The famed horsemen of the Ribatejo, Vila Franca de Xira (July)

JUNE

Festa de São Gonçalo *(first weekend)*, Amarante. Young, unmarried men and women in the town swap phallus-shaped cakes as tokens of love.

Feira Nacional da Agricultura *(early Jun)*, Santarém. A combination of agricultural fairs, bullfighting and displays of folk dancing.

Santo António *(12–13 Jun)*, Lisbon. Celebrated in the Alfama district with singing and dancing, food and drink. Locals put up lanterns and streamers and bring out chairs for the thousands who arrive.

Festa da Coca *(Thu after Trinity Sun)*, Monção. Part of the Corpus Christi Day celebrations, the festival features scenes of St George in comic battle with the dragon.

São João *(23–24 Jun)*, Oporto. Mid-summer festivities include making wishes while jumping over small fires, and the *barcos rabelos* boat race *(see pp226–7)*.

São Pedro *(29 Jun)*, Lisbon. More street celebrations with eating, dancing and singing.

Festival de Música de Sintra *(Jun–Jul)*, Sintra. Classical music concerts and ballet.

JULY

Festa do Colete Encarnado *(first weekend)*, Vila Franca de Xira. Named after the red waistcoats of the Ribatejo horsemen, the festival consists of bullfights and bull running.

Festa dos Tabuleiros *(mid-Jul, every two or three years)*, Tomar. Music, dancing, fireworks and a bullfight *(see pp184–5)*. Four hundred women carry trays of decorated loaves on their heads.

Festa da Ria *(all month)* Aveiro. Folk dances, boat races and a best-decorated boat competition (see *p201*).

Festival da Cerveja *(late Jul)*, Fábrica do Inglês, Silves. This is a lively beer festival with folk dancing.

AUGUST

Festas Gualterianas *(first weekend)*, Guimarães. Three-day festival dating back to 1452. Torchlight procession, dancing, and medieval parade.

Madeira Wine Rally *(first weekend)*, Funchal, Madeira. Car enthusiasts flock to this challenging car rally, one of the stages of the European championships.

Festa da Nossa Senhora da Boa Viagem *(early Aug)*, Peniche. A crowd gathers at the harbour with lighted candles to greet a statue of the Virgin that

Festa dos Tabuleiros, Tomar

arrives by boat. Fireworks and dancing in the evening.

Jazz em Agosto *(early Aug)* Lisbon. Popular jazz festival with music in the gardens of the Gulbenkian Centre.

Semana do Mar *(1 week in Aug)*, Horta, Faial, Azores. Food, music, crafts, water sports and lively competitions in this sea festival.

Festival do Marisco *(mid-Aug)*, Olhão. A seafood festival, hosted by one of the big fishing ports in the Algarve.

Romaria de Nossa Senhora da Agonia *(weekend nearest to 20 Aug)*, Viana do Castelo. Religious procession, followed by display of floats, drinking, folk dancing, fireworks and bands. There is also

Girl in traditional dress, Viana do Castelo

a Saturday afternoon bullfight, and a ceremonial blessing of the town's fishing boats.

The sun-drenched Algarve, a major attraction for summer visitors

Procession at the Romaria de Nossa Senhora da Nazaré

AUTUMN

IN MANY WAYS, this is the best season for touring and sightseeing. From mid-September temperatures cool sharply, and autumn is usually drier than spring. This is a mellow, fruitful time of year with the countryside a collage of brown, gold and red.

September is also the start of the *vindima* (the vintage) season. Grapes are harvested and crushed to wine in a spirit of festivity, especially in the port-growing Douro region.

SEPTEMBER

Romaria da Nossa Senhora dos Remédios *(6–9 Sep)*, Lamego. The annual pilgrimage to this famous Baroque shrine is the main feature of three days of celebration. Activities include a torchlit procession and live bands.
Romaria da Nossa Senhora da Nazaré *(8 Sep and following weekend)*, Nazaré. Includes processions, folk dancing, and bullfights.
Feiras Novas *(mid-Sep)*, Ponte de Lima. A huge market with fairground, fireworks, carnival costumes and a brass band competition.
Festa da Senhora da Consolação *(throughout Sep)*, Sintra. A celebration of Portugal's patron saint with a month of parties, music and food in the Assafora area.

Portuguese Grand Prix, Estoril. This Formula One race is cancelled for the forseeable future.
National Folklore Festival *(mid-Sep)*, the Algarve. Colourful music and dance groups converge on the region's towns.
Wine Festival *(all month)*, Funchal and Estreito de Câmara de Lobos, Madeira. The Funchal festival is a lively, popular event, but the one in Estreito de Câmara de Lobos is more authentic.
Feira de São Mateus *(last week)*, Elvas. Festival offering a mixture of religious, cultural and agricultural events.

Musicians in regional costume at the National Folklore Festival in September

Damon Hill winning the Grand Prix at Estoril in 1995

OCTOBER

Feira de Outubro *(first or second week)*, Vila Franca de Xira. Bulls are run through the streets and bullfights staged.

Pilgrimage to Fátima *(12–13 Oct)*. Final pilgrimage of the year, on the date of the Virgin's last appearance.
Festival de Gastronomia *(last two weeks)*, Santarém. Sample the best of regional cooking at this food festival.
International Algarve Car Rally *(Oct–Nov)*, Algarve.

NOVEMBER

All Saints' Day *(1 Nov)*. Throughout the country candles are lit in churches and homes and flowers placed on graves to honour the dead.
Feira Nacional do Cavalo *(first 2 weeks)*, Golegã. Horse enthusiasts and bullfighters come to see horse parades and races. Included are celebrations for St Martin's Day *(11 Nov)* with a grand parade and running of bulls.
Encontros de Fotografia *(throughout-Nov)*, Coimbra. This is Portugal's biggest photography show and features exhibitions of the work of both world-famous and new photographers.

Horsemen at the Feira Nacional do Cavalo, Golegã

Wintry snow scene in the Serra de Montemuro, south of Cinfães *(see p249)*

WINTER

SEEKERS OF MILD, sunny climes fly south to the Algarve where many of the resorts remain alive in winter. For golfers too, the coolest months of the year are the most appealing. January and February also see the spectacular blossoming of almond trees right across southern Portugal.

Bolo rei, a cake enjoyed over the Christmas period

Other visitors migrate even further south to sub-tropical Madeira where winter, in particular Christmas and the New Year, is high season.

PUBLIC HOLIDAYS

New Year's Day (1 Jan)
Carnaval (Feb)
Good Friday
(Mar or Apr)
Dia 25 de Abril,
*commemorating 1974
Revolution* (25 Apr)
Dia do Trabalhador,
Labour Day (1 May)
Corpus Christi (6 Jun)
Camões Day (10 Jun)
Assumption Day
(15 Aug)
Republic Day (5 Oct)
All Saints' Day (1 Nov)
Dia da Restauração,
*commemorating
independence from Spain,
1640* (1 Dec)
**Immaculate
Conception** (8 Dec)
Christmas Day (25 Dec)

DECEMBER

Christmas *(25 Dec)*. Everywhere churches and shops display cribs. On Christmas Eve *bacalhau* (salted dried cod) is eaten. Presents are opened, and people go to midnight mass. In Madeira traditional *bolo de mel* (honey cake) is made, and children plant wheat, maize or barley in pots. The pots are placed around the crib to symbolize renewal and plenty.

JANUARY

New Year. Celebrations all over Portugal with spectacular firework displays welcoming in the New Year.
Festa dos Rapazes *(25 Dec – 6 Jan)*, around Bragança. Boys dress up in masks and rampage through their villages in an ancient pagan rite of passage. *(see p227)*.
Epiphany *(6 Jan)*. The traditional crown-shaped cake for

Epiphany, *bolo rei* (king's cake), is made with a lucky charm and a bean inside. The person who gets the bean must buy the next cake. *Bolo rei* is also made at Christmas.
Festa de São Gonçalinho *(2nd week)*, Aveiro. Festival in which loaves of bread are thrown to the crowds from the top of a chapel in thanks for the safe return of a fisherman, or for finding a husband.

Almond trees in blossom in February, the Algarve

FEBRUARY

Fantasporto *(2 weeks in Feb)*, Oporto. An important international film festival, showing many films by new directors, including science fiction films.
Carnaval *(varies according to Easter)*. Celebrated all over Portugal with spectacular costumes and floats; particularly colourful parades take place in Ovar, Sesimbra, Torres Vedras, Funchal and Loulé. Loulé's festivities are connected with the annual Almond Gatherers' Fair.

Men in Carnaval costume, Ovar

The Climate of Portugal

MAINLAND PORTUGAL has a pleasant climate with long, hot summers and mild winters. In the north winters are cool and wet; heading further south temperatures increase and rainfall decreases all the way down to the Algarve, where the climate is Mediterranean. Further inland a more Continental climate prevails with hotter summers and colder winters than on the coast. Madeira is rainy in the north, warmer and drier in the south, and the Azores are mild with year-round rainfall and strong winds.

MINHO

°C/F			
19/66	28/82	21/70	
8/46	15/59	10/50	12/54
			4/39
☀ 6 hrs	8.5 hrs	5 hrs	3 hrs
☂ 77 mm	20 mm	109 mm	113 mm
month Apr	Jul	Oct	Jan

Viana do Castelo
Oporto
Aveiro
BEIRA LITORAL

THE AZORES

Flores
São Jorge
Faial
Pico
Terceira
São Miguel

0 kilometres 200
0 miles 100

ESTREMADURA AND RIBATEJO

°C/F			
17/63	21/70	20/68	14/57
12/54	16/61	15/59	
			9/48
☀ 8 hrs	11 hrs	6.5 hrs	4.5 hrs
☂ 55 mm	2.5 mm	60 mm	92.5 mm
month Apr	Jul	Oct	Jan

Leiria
Santarém

THE AZORES

°C/F			
19/66	25/77	23/73	17/63
12/54	17/63	16/61	12/54
☀ 4.5 hrs	6 hrs	4.5 hrs	2.5 hrs
☂ 67 mm	27 mm	103 mm	120 mm
month Apr	Jul	Oct	Jan

THE LISBON COAST

°C/F			
20/68	28/82	23/73	
12/54	17/63	14/57	14/57
			8/46
☀ 9 hrs	12.5 hrs	7.5 hrs	5 hrs
☂ 47.5 mm	0 mm	65 mm	95 mm
month Apr	Jul	Oct	Jan

LISBON
Setúbal
Sines

MADEIRA

Porto Santo
Madeira
Funchal

0 kilometres 20
0 miles 10

MADEIRA

°C/F			
19/66	25/77	24/75	19/66
14/57	18/64	18/64	13/55
☀ 6 hrs	7.5 hrs	6 hrs	4.5 hrs
☂ 39 mm	2.5 mm	75 mm	103 mm
month Apr	Jul	Oct	Jan

Lagos

DOURO AND TRÁS-OS-MONTES

Douro

Average daily maximum temperature
Average daily minimum temperature
Average daily hours of sunshine
Average monthly rainfall

°C/F

	Apr	Jul	Oct	Jan
max	19/66	25/77	21/70	13/55
min	9/48	15/59	11/52	5/41
sun	8 hrs	12.5 hrs	6.5 hrs	4 hrs
rain	73 mm	15 mm	79 mm	149 mm
month	Apr	Jul	Oct	Jan

Trás-os-Montes

°C/F

	Apr	Jul	Oct	Jan
max	16/61	28/82	18/64	8/46
min	5/41	13/55	7/45	0/32
sun	7 hrs	9.5 hrs	6 hrs	4.5 hrs
rain	86 mm	20 mm	105 mm	159 mm
month	Apr	Jul	Oct	Jan

THE BEIRAS

Beira Litoral

°C/F

	Apr	Jul	Oct	Jan
max	21/70	29/84	23/73	14/57
min	10/50	15/59	12/54	6/43
sun	8 hrs	10.5 hrs	7 hrs	4.5 hrs
rain	76 mm	13 mm	87 mm	132 mm
month	Apr	Jul	Oct	Jan

Beira Baixa

°C/F

	Apr	Jul	Oct	Jan
max	19/66	31/88	21/70	11/52
min	10/50	18/64	12/54	5/41
sun	7.5 hrs	12 hrs	6 hrs	4.5 hrs
rain	48 mm	19 mm	52 mm	43 mm
month	Apr	Jul	Oct	Jan

ALENTEJO

Alto Alentejo

°C/F

	Apr	Jul	Oct	Jan
max	19/66	30/86	22/72	12/54
min	10/50	16/61	13/55	6/43
sun	8.5 hrs	12.5 hrs	7 hrs	5 hrs
rain	57 mm	5 mm	62 mm	96 mm
month	Apr	Jul	Oct	Jan

Baixo Alentejo

°C/F

	Apr	Jul	Oct	Jan
max	22/72	35/95	24/75	14/57
min	10/50	18/64	13/55	6/43
sun	8.5 hrs	12.5 hrs	7.5 hrs	5.5 hrs
rain	46 mm	2 mm	48 mm	49 mm
month	Apr	Jul	Oct	Jan

ALGARVE

°C/F

	Apr	Jul	Oct	Jan
max	20/68	28/82	23/73	16/61
min	13/55	20/68	16/61	9/48
sun	9 hrs	12.5 hrs	7.5 hrs	5.5 hrs
rain	31 mm	1 mm	51 mm	70 mm
month	Apr	Jul	Oct	Jan

Bragança

TRÁS-OS-MONTES

aga

Braga

● Vila Real

DOURO

BEIRA ALTA

● Viseu

● Guarda

Coimbra

BEIRA BAIXA

Castelo Branco ●

Portalegre ●

ALTO ALENTEJO

● Évora

● Beja

BAIXO ALENTEJO

Faro

0 kilometres   100
0 miles   50

OM MANVEL

per gratia de dz Rey de portugall z
dos algaruez. daquem z dale mar
em africa. senor de guinee z da conquista nauegaciam z co
mercio dethiopia arabia persia. z da India zc. A
quantos. esto aperpetua memoria feito buren fazemo
saber que assi como oproprio z principall cuydado dos q
tem algun cargo deue ser trabalhar como as cousas q
lhes sam encarregadas. seiam postas. no mais prospero
z melhorado estado que ser possa. assy tanto mais cabe
isto nos. Reis. z principes. fazello. quanto com mais. ex
cellente preeminencia sam per dz postos na terra peça
bem della z de seus bassallos. z pa toda exceuciam z exe
plo de virtude. E por que esta obrigaçam tam deuida

THE HISTORY OF PORTUGAL

PORTUGAL IS ONE of the oldest nation states in Europe: its foundation in 1139 predates that of its neighbour, Spain, by nearly 350 years. The Romans, who arrived in 218 BC, called the whole peninsula Hispania, but the region between the Douro and Tagus rivers was named Lusitania after the Celtiberian tribe that lived there. When the Roman Empire collapsed in the 5th century, Hispania was overrun first by Germanic tribes, then by Moors from North Africa in 711. Military reconquest by the Christian kingdoms of the north began in earnest in the 11th century and it was during this long process that Portucale, a small county of the kingdom of León and Castile, was declared independent by its first king, Afonso Henriques.

Portuguese ship (c.1500)

The new kingdom expanded southwards to the Algarve and Portuguese sailors began to explore the African coast and the Atlantic. Portugal's golden age reached its zenith in the reign of Manuel I with Vasco da Gama's voyage to India in 1498 and the discovery of Brazil in 1500. Eastern trade brought incredible wealth, but military defeat in Morocco meant that the prosperity was short-lived. Spain invaded in 1580 and Spanish kings ruled Portugal for the next 60 years.

After Portugal regained independence, her fortunes were restored by the discovery of gold in Brazil. In the second half of the 18th century, the chief minister, the Marquês de Pombal, began to modernize the country and to limit the reactionary influence of the church. However, Napoleon's invasion in 1807 and the loss of Brazil in 1825 left Portugal impoverished and divided. Power struggles between Absolutists and Constitutionalists further weakened the country, and despite a period of stability from the 1850s, the debt crisis worsened. In 1910, a republican revolution overthrew the monarchy.

The economy deteriorated until a military coup in 1926 led to the long dictatorship of António Salazar, who held power from 1928 to 1968. The Carnation Revolution ended his rule in 1974 and democracy was restored in 1976. Portugal's depleted economy was gradually revived by an influx of funds through joining the EU in 1986.

Portuguese mariners' chart of the North Atlantic drawn on parchment (c.1550)

◁ Illuminated frontispiece of the *Leitura Nova*, showing Portugal's coat of arms and portrait of Manuel I (c.1520)

The Rulers of Portugal

Afonso Henriques declared himself Portugal's first king in 1139, but his descendants' ties of marriage to various Spanish kingdoms led to dynastic disputes. João I's defeat of the Castilians in 1385 established the House of Avis which presided over the golden age of Portuguese imperialism. Then in 1580, in the absence of a direct heir, Portugal was ruled by Spanish kings for 60 years before the Duke of Bragança became João IV. A Republican uprising ended the monarchy in 1910. However, in the first 16 years of the Republic there were 40 different governments, and in 1926 Portugal became a dictatorship under the eventual leadership of Salazar. Democracy was restored by the "Carnation" Revolution of 1974.

1481–95 João II

1248–79 Afonso III

1211–23 Afonso II

1185–1211 Sancho I

1279–1325 Dinis

1438–81 Afonso V

1100	1200	1300	1400	1500
HOUSE OF BURGUNDY			AVIS	
1100	1200	1300	1400	1500

1325–57 Afonso IV

1357–67 Pedro I

1367–83 Fernando I

1223–48 Sancho II

1139–85 Afonso Henriques (Afonso I)

1433–8 Duarte

1521–5 João III

1385–1433 João I

1495–1521 Manuel I

1828–53 Maria II

57–78 Sebastião

1932–68 António
Salazar (prime minister)

1750–77 José I

1621–40 Felipe III
(Philip IV of Spain)

1853–61
Pedro V

1640–56 João IV

1816–26
João VI
(regent from
1792)

**1976–8 &
1983–5**
Mário
Soares
(prime
minister)

1656–83 Afonso VI

1861–89
Luís I

1683–1706
Pedro II (regent
from 1668)

1600	1700	1800	1900	2000
HAPSBURG	BRAGANÇA		REPUBLIC	
1600	1700	1800	1900	2000

1598–1621 Felipe II
(Philip III of Spain)

1985–95
Aníbal
Cavaco Silva
(prime
minister)

1580–98 Felipe I
(Philip II of Spain)

2002–
José Manuel
Durão
Barroso
(prime
minister)

1578–80 Henrique

1995–2002
António Guterres
(prime minister)

1777–1816
Maria I and Pedro III

1908–10
Manuel II

1826–28 Pedro IV

1706–50 João V

1889–1908 Carlos I

Prehistoric and Roman Portugal

Gold solidus (c.400 AD)

FROM ABOUT 2000 BC Portugal's Stone Age communities were supplanted by foreign invaders, most notably the Iberians and the Celts. When Rome defeated the Carthaginians in 216 BC and took over all their territories in eastern Spain, she still had to subdue Celtiberian tribes living in the west. One of these, the Lusitani, put up fierce resistance. After their defeat in 139 BC, their name was preserved in Lusitania, a province of Roman Hispania, corresponding roughly to present-day Portugal. Romanization led to four centuries of stability and prosperity, but as the Roman Empire collapsed, Lusitania was overrun by Germanic tribes, first the Suevi and then the Visigoths.

IBERIAN PENINSULA IN 27 BC

▨ *Roman provinces*

The amphitheatre probably dated from the building boom of the 1st century AD.

The forum and principal temple

Dolmen of Comenda
Dolmens such as this one near Évora were communal burial chambers. Many were built by the Neolithic peoples who lived in the Iberian Peninsula in the third millennium BC.

The main road led north to Aeminium (Coimbra).

Porca of Murça
Trás-os-Montes has preserved 16 statues of animals like this granite pig (see p257), probably used in Celtic fertility rituals.

Palestra (exercise area of the baths)

The Baths of Trajan had a spectacular view of the ravine below the city walls.

TIMELINE

c.2000 BC Iberian tribes arrive in the peninsula, probably from Africa

Iberian Gold gorget

139 BC Celtiberian resistance to Roman rule ends with the death of Viriatus, leader of the Lusitani tribe

3000 BC	2000 BC	1000 BC

2500 BC Portugal inhabited by late Stone Age people. Many megalithic tombs date from this time

Celtic stone warrior, 1st millennium BC

1000 BC Phoenicians set up trading stations and settlements along the southern coast

218 BC The Romans invade the Iberian Peninsula

c.700 BC Celtic invaders settle in Portugal

Floor Mosaic
Under Roman rule, the wealthy built lavishly decorated villas. This mosaic of a triton (1st century AD) comes from the House of the Fountains just outside the walls of Conimbriga.

WHERE TO SEE PREHISTORIC AND ROMAN PORTUGAL

The Alentejo is rich in Stone Age megaliths *(see p306)*, while the north has the two best examples of Celtiberian settlements at Sanfins *(p248)* and Briteiros. Many traces of the Roman period, including roads and bridges, are found throughout Portugal. Apart from Conimbriga, major sites, such as the villas at Pisões *(p311)* and Milreu *(p325)*, are mainly in the south. Faro's Museu Municipal *(p327)* has a good collection of local finds.

Roman Amphora
Garum, a popular, spiced sauce made of fermented fish, was manufactured at Tróia (see p169) and exported in 27-litre (6-gallon) amphorae like this one.

Aqueduct

Road east to Tomar

Visigothic Buckle
The Visigoths were warlike yet cultured people who strengthened the position of Christianity. However, their system of elective monarchy led to factional disputes.

A *domus*, private house with a garden

***Citânia de Briteiros**, a hilltop settlement founded around the 5th century AD, survived until well into the Roman period. It was discovered in 1874 (p281).*

RECONSTRUCTION OF CONIMBRIGA

The extensive remains of Conimbriga *(see p208)* give a vivid picture of how thoroughly Romanized Portugal became under the empire. The town expanded rapidly in the 1st century AD, when it achieved the self-governing status of a *municipium*. It fell to the Suevi in AD 468.

***Évora's temple** dates from the 2nd century AD (see p302). It is almost all that remains of an important Roman city.*

AD 73 Emperor Vespasian grants towns in the Iberian Peninsula same rights as Latin towns in Italy	415 Visigoths invade the peninsula and drive out the Vandals and the Alani	585 Visigoths take over the Suevian kingdom, fixing their capital at Toledo in Spain
	AD 200 Christianity becomes established in the peninsula	

AD 1	AD 200	AD 400	AD 600

27 BC During the rule of the Emperor Augustus the Iberian Peninsula is divided into three; Lusitania is the name given to the central province south of the River Douro	409 Invasion by "barbarian" tribes from central Europe: the Vandals, the Alani and the Suevi 411 Suevian kingdom established in Galicia and northern Portugal	*Visigothic chapel at São Frutuoso* (see p277)

Moorish Domination and Christian Reconquest

WHEN MUSLIMS from North Africa defeated the Visigoths in 711, the Iberian Peninsula became a province of the Caliphate of Damascus. Then, in 756, Abd al Rahman established the independent kingdom of Al Andalus, his capital Córdoba becoming one of the world's great centres of cul-

Bronze Moorish oil lamp in the shape of a bird

ture. Moorish control of the peninsula remained virtually undisputed for the next 300 years until the small Christian kingdoms in the north began the Reconquest. In the 11th century, as Moorish power waned, "Portucale" was just a small county of the Kingdom of León and Castile, centred on the Douro. It became independent after Afonso Henriques defeated the Moors at Ourique in 1139.

IBERIAN PENINSULA IN 1100

☐ *County of Portucale*

☐ *Kingdom of León and Castile*

☐ *Moorish kingdoms*

Without the Virgin to watch over them, the Faro fishermen's nets are empty.

Moorish Plate
Vivid depictions of a hunting dog, a falcon and a gazelle decorate this 11th-century plate found at Mértola, a river port on the Guadiana used by eastern traders.

The fishermen set off with new hope.

Coexistence
Under Moorish rule, co-operation between the faiths was common. This miniature from the 13th century shows the friendly meeting of two knights, one a Christian, the other a Moor.

TIMELINE

711 Large Muslim army of Berbers and Arabs (the Moors) conquers Iberian Peninsula following dispute over Visigothic succession

10th-century Hispano-Moorish ivory casket

722 Christian victory at Covadonga in Asturias marks start of gradual reconquest

868 Vímara Peres takes Oporto from the Moors

878 Christian forces recapture Coimbra

AD 700	AD 800	AD 900	AD 1000

756 Battle of Al Musara; Abd al Rahman defeats governor of Córdoba and founds kingdom of Al Andalus

Nora, a bucket wheel for raising water introduced by the Moors

955 Moorish leader Al Mansur retakes Coimbra, then forces Christian frontier back to the River Douro

1008–31 Civil war; Al Andalus divided into small kingdoms known as *taifas*

Stone Relief of São Tiago
In wars against the Moors, the apostle St James (São Tiago) assumed a special role. At Ourique in 1139, soldiers claimed to have seen him leading the Christian forces into battle.

WHERE TO SEE MOORISH PORTUGAL

The influence of the Moors is strongest in the south, in towns like Lagos *(see p320)*, Faro *(p326)* and Silves, where they ruled for longer and the architecture *(p19)* retains many Arab features. In Mértola *(p313)*, the church preserves much of the old mosque. Further north, the Castelo dos Mouros, in Sintra *(p157)*, and many other fortresses were taken over and rebuilt by the Christians.

12th-century Silver Dirham
This coin was minted at Beja by the Almohads, a Muslim sect even stricter than their forerunners, the Almoravids.

This cistern well was found on the site of the archaeological museum at Silves, a Moorish centre in the Algarve (p323).

The lost statue of the Virgin is recovered from the sea and restored to its rightful place on the walls.

Out at sea the fishermen's nets are full once more.

Capture of Lisbon
The Reconquest was given the status of a crusade by the pope. Lisbon was taken in 1147 with the aid of English troops bound for the Holy Land.

FARO UNDER MOORISH RULE

Christians who lived under Moorish rule were called Mozarabs. At Faro they placed a statue of the Virgin on the walls of the city, but resentful Muslims took the statue down. These four scenes from the *Cantigas de Santa Maria* tell the story of the miracle that followed.

1097 Alfonso VI of León and Castile entrusts Portucale to his son-in-law Henry of Burgundy	**1139** Battle of Ourique; Afonso Henriques declares himself King of Portugal	**1143** Treaty of Zamora establishes Portugal's independence	**1165–9** Geraldo sem Pavor captures a number of cities from the Almohads, including Évora and Badajoz
1086 Invasion of the Almoravids			
1050	**1100**	**1150**	
1064 Christians regain Coimbra	**1128** Battle of São Mamede; Afonso Henriques defeats his mother Teresa to win control of county of Portucale	**1153** Founding of Cistercian Abbey at Alcobaça	
Henry of Burgundy		**1147** Fall of Lisbon to Crusader army; Almoravid empire falls to the Almohads	

The New Kingdom

IBERIAN PENINSULA IN 1200

◻ *Kingdom of Portugal*

◻ *Spanish kingdoms*

◻ *Territory under Moorish rule*

THE PORTUGUESE RECONQUEST was completed in 1249 when Afonso III captured Faro in the Algarve. His successor, King Dinis, encouraged agriculture and commerce, earning the nickname of the "farmer king". He also built castles to defend the border from Castilian attack and expanded the navy. Territorial disputes with Castile came to a head in 1383 when King Fernando died and his son-in-law, Juan I of Castile, claimed the Portuguese throne for his wife Beatriz. Juan's opponents favoured Pedro I's illegitimate son, João of Avis, elected king by the *cortes* (parliament) in Coimbra in 1385.

14th-century statue of armed knight

Cancioneiro da Ajuda
King Dinis was a fine musician and poet. This illumination is from a collection of troubadour songs, many by the king himself.

Coat of arms of Portugal

The frieze shows scenes from the life of Pedro and Inês.

The aedicules contain finely carved scenes from the life of St Bartholomew, Dom Pedro's patron saint.

The faithful dog at the feet of the deceased was a common feature of Gothic tombs.

Fortifications of Serpa
King Dinis had a chain of fortified towns and castles built along the borders with Castile and Moorish Spain. This 16th-century drawing shows the medieval walls and towers of Serpa (see p310).

TIMELINE

Leiria Castle

Afonso III

1185 Sancho I becomes king; his victories in the Algarve are reversed by Al-Mansur, the Almohad caliph	**1211** First *cortes* (parliament) held at Coimbra	**1254** The *cortes* held at Leiria includes representatives of the towns

1200 — **1250**

1173 Remains of St Vincent brought from Cabo de São Vicente to Lisbon	**1179** Portugal recognized as kingdom by the pope	**1248** Anarchic reign of Sancho II ends in his deposition by his brother Afonso III **1249** Afonso III completes reconquest of the Algarve, but his claim to sovereignty is challenged by Castile	**1256** Lisbon becomes capital of Portugal in place of Coimbra

St Isabel (1271–1336)
King Dinis did not approve of his wife's acts of charity. A legend tells how the bread Queen Isabel was about to distribute to the poor turned into roses when she was challenged by her husband.

Six angels support the recumbent king.

Óbidos Castle, now a pousada, was rebuilt by King Dinis when he gave this fairy-tale town to his wife Isabel as a wedding present in 1282 (p172).

Cross of Sancho I
Sancho's reign (1185–1211) saw royal power and wealth increase despite disputes between the king and his bishops over papal authority.

Oporto's Sé (p240) has been much altered but the twin-towered west front retains its original 13th-century character.

St Bartholomew is martyred by being flayed alive.

TOMB OF PEDRO I
The Gothic carvings on the royal tomb at Alcobaça *(see pp178–9)* are the finest of their kind in Portugal. The forthright Pedro, who ruled from 1357–67, is remembered chiefly for the tragic tale of his murdered mistress, Inês de Castro, whose matching tomb stands facing Pedro's.

1279–1325 King Dinis consolidates Portugal's independence

1288 Portugal's first university founded in Lisbon

1297 Castile recognizes Portugal's sovereignty over the Algarve

Knight of the Order of Christ

1300

1319 Foundation of the Order of Christ *(see p185)*

1336 Death of St Isabel of Portugal

1349 Following Black Death, a law is passed enforcing compulsory rural labour

1355 After murder of Inês de Castro, Pedro takes up arms against his father Afonso IV

1350

1357 Accession of Pedro I, who has murderers of Inês de Castro brutally executed

1372 Fernando I's unpopular marriage to Leonor Teles leads to riots

1383 João of Avis ends regency of Leonor Teles and proclaims himself defender of the realm

1384 Juan I of Castile invades Portugal

The House of Avis

AFTER JOÃO OF AVIS had defeated the Castilians in 1385 to become João I of Portugal, he strengthened his position through an important alliance with England. His long reign saw the start of Portuguese imperialism and the beginning of maritime expeditions promoted by his son, Henry the Navigator *(see pp48–9)*. Further voyages of discovery in the reign of Manuel I "the Fortunate", led to trade with India and the East and, following Afonso de Albuquerque's capture of Goa, initially brought great wealth. So, too, did the colonization of Brazil. However, the lure of overseas adventure weakened mainland Portugal, which suffered serious depopulation. The age of expansion ended when a foolhardy military expedition to Morocco, led by King Sebastião, was soundly defeated in 1578.

IBERIAN PENINSULA IN 1500

▨ *Portugal*

▨ *Spain (Castile and Aragon)*

16th-century Porcelain Plate
In 1557 the Portuguese were granted Macao as a trading post in China. This Chinese plate bears the arms of Matias de Albuquerque, a descendant of the great Afonso, conqueror of Goa.

Arms of English royal family

John of Gaunt used the alliance with Portugal to pursue his own claim to the throne of Castile.

Troops Landing at Arzila
The kings of the Avis dynasty constantly sought to extend their domains to Morocco, where they established a small colony around Tangier. This Flemish tapestry celebrates Afonso V's capture of Arzila in 1471.

Luís de Camões
After serving in India and Morocco, where he lost an eye, the poet wrote Os Lusíadas *(see p188), an epic on the Discoveries.*

TIMELINE

1385 João I defeats Castilian army at Battle of Aljubarrota	**c.1425** *Leal Conselheiro*, a treatise on courtly behaviour written by King Duarte		**1496** Jews expelled from the country or forcibly converted
1415 Capture of Ceuta in Morocco		**1441** Lagos is site of first slave market in modern Europe	**1495–1521** Reign of Manuel I and great period of discoveries
1400	**1425**	**1450**	**1475**
1386 Alliance with England formalized by Treaty of Windsor	**1418** Henry the Navigator made governor of the Algarve	**1471** Conquest of Moroccan fortresses of Arzila and Tangier	**1494** Spain and Portugal divide the Atlantic region by Treaty of Tordesillas
		1482–3 João II successfully resists the Conspiracy of the Nobles	

King Duarte

Wedding of Manuel I
Manuel's reign marked the highest point in Portugal's golden age of discovery and conquest. His marriages were made to reinforce ties with Spain. Shown here is his third: to Leonor, sister of Carlos I of Spain, in 1518.

João I drew support from the merchants of Lisbon and Oporto rather than the nobles, many of whom sided with Castile.

Archbishop of Braga

Portugal's bishops took João's side after the pope had refused to legitimize the children of Inês de Castro *(see pp44–5)*.

JOÃO I AND THE ENGLISH
João's alliance with England against Castile led to his marriage in 1387 to Philippa of Lancaster, daughter of John of Gaunt, son of Edward III. This illustration from the chronicle of Jean de Wavrin shows the new king entertaining his father-in-law.

Battle of Alcácer-Quibir (1578)
King Sebastião saw his African expedition as a crusade against Islam. After Alcácer-Quibir, he and 8,000 of his troops lay dead, 15,000 captives were sold into slavery and the House of Avis dynasty was doomed.

Belém Monstrance (see p20)

1510 Beginning of Portuguese empire in Asia; Goa conquered by Afonso de Albuquerque

1531 Inquisition introduced into Portugal

1536 Death of Gil Vicente, Portugal's greatest dramatist

1572 Publication of *Os Lusíadas*, a verse epic celebrating Portugal's history by Luís de Camões

1500	1525	1550	1575

c.1502 Work starts on the Jerónimos monastery in Belém *(see pp106–7)*

1498 Vasco da Gama reaches India

1521–57 Reign of João III, known as "the Pious"

Gil Vicente

1559 Jesuit University established at Évora *(see p304)*

1578 King Sebastião's expedition to Morocco ends in his death and total defeat at the Battle of Alcácer-Quibir

The Age of Discovery

Portuguese *padrão*

PORTUGAL'S ASTONISHING PERIOD of conquest and exploration began in 1415 with the capture of the North African city of Ceuta. Maritime expeditions into the Atlantic and along the West African coast followed, motivated by traditional Christian hostility towards Islam and desire for commercial gain. Great riches were made from the gold and slaves taken from the Guinea coast, but the real breakthrough for Portuguese imperialism occurred in 1498 when Vasco da Gama *(see p108)* reached India. Portugal soon controlled the Indian Ocean and the spice trade, and established an eastern capital at Goa. With Pedro Álvares Cabral's "discovery" of Brazil, Portugal became a mercantile super-power rivalled only by Spain.

Armillary Sphere
This celestial globe with the earth in its centre was used by navigators for measuring the position of the stars. It became the personal emblem of Manuel I.

Magellan (c.1480–1521)
With Spanish funding, Portuguese sailor Fernão de Magalhães, known as Magellan, led the first circumnavigation of the globe (1519–22). He was killed in the Philippines before the voyage's end.

1500–1501 Gaspar Corte Real reaches Newfoundland.

1427 Diogo de Silves discovers the Azores.

1434 Gil Eanes rounds Cape Bojador (Western Sahara).

1460 Diogo Gomes discovers the Cape Verde archipelago.

1470s Discovery of island of São Tomé.

1482 Diogo Cão reaches the mouth of the Congo.

1485 On his third voyage Diogo Cão reaches Cape Cross (Namibia).

1488 Bartolomeu Dias rounds Cape of Good Hope.

1500 Pedro Álvares Cabral reaches Brazil.

The Adoration of the Magi
Painted for Viseu Cathedral shortly after Cabral returned from Brazil in 1500, this panel is attributed to Grão Vasco (see p213). The second king, Baltazar, is depicted as a Tupi Indian.

African Ivory Salt Cellar
This 16th-century ivory carving shows Portuguese warriors supporting a globe and a ship. A sailor peers out from the crow's nest at the top.

Japanese Screen (c.1600)
This screen shows traders unloading a nau, *or great ship. Between 1575 and their expulsion in 1638, the Portuguese monopolized the carrying trade between China and Japan.*

HENRY THE NAVIGATOR

Although he did not sail himself, Henry (1394–1460), the third son of João I, laid the foundations for Portugal's maritime expansion that were later built upon by João II and consolidated by Manuel I. As Master of the wealthy Order of Christ and Governor of the Algarve, Henry was able to finance expeditions along the African coast. By the time he died he had a monopoly on all trade south of Cape Bojador. Legend tells that he founded a great school of navigation either at Sagres *(see p320)* or Lagos.

1543 Portuguese arrive in Japan.

1513 Trading posts set up in China at Macau and Canton.

1510 Capture of Goa.

1498 Vasco da Gama reaches Calicut in India.

1518 Fortress built in Colombo (Sri Lanka).

1512 Portuguese reach Ternate in the Moluccas (Spice Islands).

KEY

– – – Discoverers' routes

Cloves

Pepper

Nutmeg

Cinnamon

The Spice Trade
Exotic spices were a great source of wealth for Portugal. The much-disputed Moluccas, or Spice Islands, were purchased from Spain in 1528.

PORTUGUESE DISCOVERIES

The systematic attempt to find a sea route to India, which led to a monopoly of the spice trade, began in 1482 with the first voyage of Diogo Cão, who planted a *padrão* (stone cross) on the shores where he landed.

Crow's nest

Square sail on foremast

Cross of the Order of Christ (see p185)

Lateen-rigged Caravel
These ships with three triangular sails were favoured by the first Portuguese explorers who sailed close to the African coast. For later journeys across the open ocean, square sails were found more effective.

Spanish Rule

Philip II of Spain

W HEN HENRIQUE, the Cardinal-King, died without an heir in 1580, Philip II of Spain successfully claimed the Portuguese throne through his mother, a daughter of Manuel I. Under Spanish rule, influential positions were held by Portuguese nobles, but a common foreign policy led to a steady loss of colonies to the Dutch. In 1640 a Portuguese revolt took place in Lisbon and the Duke of Bragança was chosen to become King João IV. Spain retaliated and the ensuing war continued until 1668. Meanwhile Portugal was forced to rely economically on her overseas territories.

Restoration of João IV
Two weeks after his supporters had ousted the Spanish in 1640, João was crowned on a platform outside the Royal Palace in Lisbon.

Spanish Armada
In 1588 Philip II of Spain hoped to invade England with his great fleet. It sailed from Lisbon where it had been equipped and provisioned.

The Graça fort was held by the Spanish.

António Vieira
Vieira (1606–97) was a Jesuit priest, writer and orator. He was sent on many diplomatic missions and clashed with the Inquisition over his support for Christianized Jews.

WAR OF INDEPENDENCE

Portugal's long war against Spain (1640–68) was fought mostly in the Alentejo. This *azulejo* panel from Palácio Fronteira in Lisbon *(see p125)* shows the Battle of Linhas de Elvas (1658). A Portuguese army besieged in Elvas *(see pp296–7)* was relieved by fresh troops from Estremoz, who soundly defeated the Spanish.

TIMELINE

1580 Battle of Alcântara; Spanish invade and Philip II of Spain becomes King of Portugal

1588 Spanish Armada sets sail from Lisbon to invade England

1583 Philip returns to Spain leaving his nephew, Cardinal-Archduke Albert of Austria, as viceroy

1581 The king invites Italian architect Filippo Terzi to Lisbon to remodel the Royal Palace and to build many churches

1580

Church of São Vicente de Fora (see p72) by Filippo Terzi and Baltasar Álvares, completed in 1627

1600

1614 Publication of the *Peregrinação* by Fernão Mendes Pinto, an account of his travels in Asia in the mid-16th century

1624 Dutch capture Portuguese colony of Bahia in Brazil

1620

1626 Jesuit missionary António de Andrade crosses the Himalayas into Tibet

1631 Birth of painter Josefa de Óbidos

Indo-Portuguese Contador
Luxury cabinets, known as
contadores, *were made from
teak and ebony in Portugal's
overseas colonies. Many came
from Goa. This fine 17th-
century example is from the
Museu Nacional de Arte
Antiga (see pp96–9).*

The besieged Portuguese
army at Elvas was retreating
from a previous unsuccessful
campaign in Spain.

Stout bastions deflected
the attackers' cannon fire.

WHERE TO SEE 17TH-CENTURY PORTUGAL

Under Spanish rule an austere
style of architecture prevailed,
typified by São Vicente de
Fora *(see p72)* in Lisbon, the
Sé Nova in Coimbra *(p204)*
and Santarém's Jesuit church
(p191). At Vila Viçosa the
style is evident in the long,
plain façade of the palace
of the Dukes of Bragança
(pp298–9). Colourful *azulejos*
from the period can be seen
at Palácio Fronteira *(p125)*
and the Museu Nacional do
Azulejo *(pp122–3)*.

***Palácio dos Biscainhos** in
Braga (p277) was built by rich
emigrants returning from Brazil.
Enlarged in later centuries, it
retains its 17th-century core.*

The relieving army
from Estremoz surprised
and routed the Spanish.

Josefa de Óbidos
*Born in Spain, Josefa
(1631–84) came to Óbidos
(see pp174-5) when young.
Trained by her father, she
painted religious subjects
and realistic still lifes.*

The Inquisition
*In the 16th and 17th centuries,
the Inquisition, set up by the
Catholic church, burned heretics
in Lisbon's Terreiro do Paço to
ensure religious conformity.*

The Age of Absolutism

Tightrope Walker
*This device, used at
Coimbra University
in the later 18th
century, shows the
centre of gravity
when an object
is in balance.*

THE 18TH CENTURY was a period of mixed fortune for Portugal. Despite vast revenues from Brazilian gold and diamonds, João V almost bankrupted the country with his extravagance. In contrast, Pombal, chief minister of João's successor José I, applied the ideas of the Enlightenment, reforming government, commerce and education. When Maria I succeeded in 1777, she reversed many of Pombal's decrees. The French invasion of 1807 forced Maria, by then mad, and the royal family into exile in Brazil.

**Gold coin
of João V**

The library contains
richly carved Baroque
bookcases and more
than 40,000 volumes.

Marquês de Pombal (1699–1782)
*After the 1755 earthquake (see pp62–3),
Pombal insisted that Lisbon be rebuilt
on strictly rational lines. Here he
proudly presents the new city.*

Queen's apartments

João V
*This miniature (1720) by
Castriotto shows João V drinking
chocolate, a fashionable drink
of the nobility, served to him
by the Infante Miguel.*

The basilica
contains many
marble statues made by
Italian masters set amid a
stunning scheme of yellow,
pink, red and blue marble.

TIMELINE

1703 Methuen Treaty with Britain secures market for Portuguese wines in Britain, and for British woollen goods in Portugal	**1723** Building of Baroque staircase of Bom Jesus near Braga (see pp278–9)	**1755** Earthquake devastates Lisbon and much of southern Portugal
	1730 Consecration of basilica at monastery-palace at Mafra	
1700	**1720**	**1740**
1706–50 Reign of João V "the Magnanimous", a period of great artistic extravagance	*Bom Jesus do Monte* **1733** First Portuguese opera, *The Patience of Socrates* by António de Almeida, performed at Royal Palace in Lisbon	**1748** First water flows along Águas Livres aqueduct in Lisbon
		1750 José I succeeds João V

Águas Livres Aqueduct
Opened in 1748, the aqueduct was paid for by the citizens of Lisbon. João V had it built across the Alcântara valley against the advice of his engineers.

WHERE TO SEE 18TH-CENTURY PORTUGAL

Baroque churches are found throughout Portugal, many with ornate interiors of gilded wood *(talha dourada)* such as São Francisco *(see p241)* and Santa Clara *(p239)* in Oporto. Tiled interiors are also very common *(pp22–3)*. Coimbra University houses the glittering Capela de São Miguel and a fine Baroque library. As well as the palaces at Mafra and Queluz, many elegant country houses, notably the Casa de Mateus, date from this era *(pp254–5)*.

Monks' refectory

18th-Century Dressing Chair
This richly gilded walnut chair has sturdy cabriole legs, showing the influence of the English Queen Anne style.

The belltowers contain a carillon of 114 bells.

Queluz Palace *(pp164–5), residence of Maria I, was begun in 1747. It is the finest example of Rococo architecture in Portugal.*

The Capela de São Miguel *at Coimbra University (pp206–7) was redecorated in Baroque style in the reign of João V.*

MONASTERY AT MAFRA

Begun in 1717, this vast monument to João V incorporates a royal palace, a church and a monastery *(see p152)*. It took 38 years to complete and contains some 880 rooms and 300 monks' cells.

The King's apartments are separated from the Queen's by a long gallery.

1756 Douro valley becomes world's first demarcated wine region

1759 Pombal expels Jesuits from Portugal

1760

1762 Spain declares war on Portugal

Statue of José I

1772 Pombal reorganizes Coimbra University, adding mathematics and natural sciences to the syllabus

1777 Accession of Maria I, who dismisses Pombal

1780

1775 Machado de Castro's statue of José I unveiled as centrepiece of reconstructed Lisbon

1789 Portuguese suppress Brazilian independence movement in Minas Gerais

Maria I

1799 Maria I's son João named Regent

1807 The French, under Junot, invade Portugal; royal family flees to Brazil

1808 French forced to retreat by Anglo-Portuguese force under Sir Arthur Wellesley; Treaty of Sintra

1800

Reform and Revolution

PORTUGAL SUFFERED many depredations during the upheavals of the Peninsular War, and after the loss of Brazil. A period of chaos culminated, in 1832, in civil war between the Liberal Pedro IV and the Absolutist Miguel: the War of the Two Brothers. Though the Liberals won, later governments were often reactionary. The second half of the century saw a period of stability and industrial growth, but attempts at expansion in Africa failed. By 1910, discontent with the constitutional monarchy was such that a Republican uprising forced King Manuel II into exile.

1820 Revolution
The revolution led to the royal family's return from Brazil and a new Liberal constitution. This proved unworkable and was revoked following an army coup in 1823.

Zé Povinho
This long-suffering, Everyman figure first appeared in 1875, created by artist and potter Rafael Bordalo Pinheiro. He expressed the concerns of the average Portuguese working man.

Priests are led away by Republican soldiers.

Republican ships shell the king's palace in Lisbon.

Personification of Portuguese Republic

Peninsular War (1808–14)
Napoleon tried twice to invade Portugal but was repulsed by an Anglo-Portuguese force led by Wellington. A key victory for the allies came at Buçaco (see pp210–11) in 1810.

THE BIRTH OF THE REPUBLIC

Republicanism spread among the middle classes and the army via a secret society called the Carbonária. The revolution took place in Lisbon in October 1910 and lasted less than five days. This contemporary poster celebrates the main events.

The Drunkards by José Malhôa
Malhôa (1855–1933) created a virtual social history of the period in genre paintings like this one, showing a group of peasants sampling new wine.

King Manuel II flees to England from Ericeira aboard the royal yacht.

Portugal and Africa
Captain Serpa Pinto's crossing of southern Africa in 1879 led to a plan to form a Portuguese colony from coast to coast.

Republican troops set up barricades at key points in Lisbon. They meet with little opposition.

Leading figures of the Republican party

Eça de Queirós
The great novelist (1845–1900) painted a scathing picture of the Portuguese bourgeoisie. He spent many years abroad as a diplomat.

WHERE TO SEE 19TH-CENTURY PORTUGAL

Neo-Classicism, which dominated the early part of the century, can be seen in Lisbon's Palácio da Ajuda *(see p111)*. More Romantic historical styles emerged later in the century, ranging from the fantastical Neo-Gothic of the Palácio da Pena *(pp160–61)* in Sintra to the subtle Orientalism of Monserrate *(p155)*. Notable stations associated with the spread of Portugal's railways include Lisbon's Rossio and São Bento in Oporto *(p239)*.

Rossio station (p82) in Lisbon has a striking façade in Neo-Manueline style by José Luís Monteiro. Completed in 1887, the station contains one of the first iron vaults in Portugal.

Ponte de Dom Luís I (p242) in Oporto dates from 1886. Its two-tier design by Teófilo Seyrig was inspired by the nearby railway bridge built by Gustave Eiffel.

1865–8 Coalition of two main parties

1869 Slave trade abolished in all Portuguese territories

1888 Publication of *Os Maias* by Eça de Queirós, a satirical examination of Portuguese lethargy

Manuel II

1910 Revolution: Manuel II abdicates and flees into exile

1870	1890	1910

1861–89 Reign of moderate Luís I

1877 Serpa Pinto sets out from Benguela in Angola to cross southern Africa

1886 Building of Ponte de Dom Luís I in Oporto

1908 Carlos I and his heir, Luís, assassinated by Republicans

1890 Plan to link African colonies of Mozambique and Angola is thwarted by ultimatum from the British

Modern Portugal

Modern tiles decorating a Lisbon metro station

THE EARLY YEARS of the new Republic were marked by political and economic crisis, until a military coup in 1926 paved the way for the New State of 1933. Under the oppressive regime of prime minister António Salazar, the country was freed of its debts, but suffered poverty and unemployment. Portugal's reliance on its African colonies led to costly wars, unrest in the army and the overthrow of the government in 1974. The painful return to democracy was rewarded by admission to the European Community in 1986.

1935 Death of poet Fernando Pessoa who wrote under four different names, in four distinct styles. This portrait by José de Almada Negreiros is in Lisbon's Centro de Arte Moderna *(see p120)*

1922 First flight across the South Atlantic by Gago Coutinho and Sacadura Cabral

1933 Founding of the *Estado Novo* (New State), harsh dictatorship led by Salazar. Government bans all strikes and censors the press, crushing opposition through brutal secret police force, the PIDE

1949 Portugal signs the North Atlantic Treaty and becomes a founder member of NATO

1911 Women given the vote

1910	1920	1930	1940	1950
1910	1920	1930	1940	1950

1916 Portugal enters World War I on side of the British and French

1918 Assassination of President Sidónio Pais; postwar years are period of social unrest with frequent strikes and changes of government

1928 António Salazar made finance minister; he imposes austerity measures, balancing the budget by 1929. In 1932 he becomes prime minister

1949 Neurosurgeon António Egas Moniz wins Nobel Prize for Medicine for his work developing the prefrontal lobotomy

1917 Three peasant children in Fátima claim to see Virgin Mary; site of vision becomes focus of major pilgrimage

1942 Salazar meets Spanish dictator Franco to confirm mutual policy of non-aggression

1926 Coup puts military in charge of Republic; General Carmona is new president, holding office until his death in 1951

1939–45 In World War II Portugal is theoretically neutral but, after threats to her shipping, is forced to sell minerals to Germany. From 1943 Portugal permits British and American bases in the Azores. Here Salazar *(centre)* talks to troops stationed there

1966 Opening of Ponte Salazar (now Ponte 25 de Abril) across the Tagus *(see p114)*

(see p114)

1986 Portugal joins European Community. Soares becomes the first civilian president of Portugal in 60 years

1998 Lisbon hosts Expo '98; the mascot Gil embodies the theme of water and the oceans

1966 National football team with brilliant Eusébio *(centre, kneeling)* reach quarter-finals of World Cup

1985 Social Democrats, under Aníbal Cavaco Silva, come to power

1955 Armenian oil magnate Calouste Gulbenkian dies leaving 2,355 million escudos (£55 million) to set up a foundation for the arts and education

1974 Carnation Revolution: in a near bloodless coup, Marcelo Caetano's regime is overthrown by the MFA (Armed Forces Movement), a group of discontented left-wing army officers

1995 António Guterres of the Socialist Party elected prime minister

1960	1970	1980	1990	2000
1960	1970	1980	1990	2000

1961 India annexes Portuguese colonies of Goa, Damão and Diu

1968 Salazar retires after stroke and is succeeded by the more moderate Caetano

1976 In the first free elections for nearly 50 years, the Socialist Mário Soares becomes prime minister

1988 Rosa Mota *(centre)* wins women's marathon at the Olympic Games in Seoul

1958 In the presidential elections, the opposition candidate General Delgado wins so much support that the result is rigged against him. He is later assassinated

1975 All of Portugal's remaining colonies except Macao are granted independence, putting an end to long, unwinnable wars in Africa. Troops, such as these on patrol in the Angolan bush, are hastily brought home

THE CARNATION REVOLUTION

The revolution of 25 April 1974 gained its popular name when people began placing red carnations in the barrels of soldiers' guns. Led by army officers disaffected by the colonial wars in Africa, the revolution heralded a period of great celebration, as Portugal emerged from decades of insularity. The political situation, however, was chaotic: the new government pushed through a controversial programme of nationalization and land reform in favour of the peasants, but in November 1975 the left-wing radicals were ousted by a short-lived counter-coup.

Newspaper headline announcing revolution

LISBON

Lisbon at a Glance

PORTUGAL'S CAPITAL sits on the north bank of the Tagus estuary, 17 km (10 miles) from the Atlantic. The city has a population of about 550,000, but the conurbation of "Grande Lisboa", which has engulfed many surrounding villages, has nearly two million people. Razed to the ground by the earthquake of 1755 *(see pp62–3)*, the city centre is essentially 18th century, with carefully planned, elegant streets in the Baixa. On the hills on either side of the centre, the narrow streets of the Alfama and Bairro Alto make it a personal, approachable city. Since its days of glory during the Age of Discovery, when the city was at the forefront of world trade, Lisbon has been an important port. Today the docks have moved; however, the great monuments in Belém still bear witness to the city's maritime past.

The Museu Nacional de Arte Antiga *houses paintings, decorative art and sculpture. Of particular interest are the Flemish-influenced Portuguese paintings such as this* Apparition of Christ to the Virgin *by Jorge Afonso (see pp96–7).*

The Mosteiro dos Jerónimos *is a magnificent 16th-century monastery. Commissioned by Manuel I, much of it is built in the peculiarly Portuguese style of architecture, known as Manueline. The extravagantly sculpted south portal of the church, designed by João de Castilho in 1516, is one of the finest expressions of the style (see pp106–7).*

BELÉM
(See pp100–111)

The Torre de Belém *was a beacon for navigators returning from the Indies and the New World, and a symbol of Portuguese naval power (see p110).*

◁ **Twin Romanesque towers of the Sé rising over the rooftops of the Baixa**

The Elevador de Santa Justa, built at the turn of the century, is a wrought-iron lift decorated with filigree that links the Baixa quarter with the Largo do Carmo (see p86).

FURTHER AFIELD
(See pp112–25)

The Museu Calouste Gulbenkian exhibits stunning art and sculpture bequeathed to Portugal by the millionaire, Calouste Gulbenkian, (see pp116–9).

The Museu Nacional do Azulejo, housed in the cloisters of the Convento da Madre de Deus, traces the history of Portuguese tiles and tile-making (see pp122–3).

0 kilometres   4

0 miles   2

BAIXA AND AVENIDA
(See pp80–87)

ALFAMA
(See pp68–79)

BAIRRO ALTO AND ESTRELA
(See pp88–99)

The Castelo de São Jorge, once a Moorish castle and then the abode of the Portuguese kings, was transformed in the 1930s into tranquil public gardens. The battlements afford spectacular views of the city (see pp78–9).

The Sé, Lisbon's greatly restored cathedral, is a sturdy Romanesque building noted for its beautiful rose window. Ecclesiastical robes and silver are among the many religious objects on display in the treasury (see p74).

0 metres   500

0 yards   500

The 1755 Lisbon Earthquake

Ex-voto tile panel offered by survivors

THE FIRST TREMOR of the devastating earthquake was felt at 9:30am on 1 November. A few minutes later there was a second, far more violent shock, reducing over half the city to rubble. Although the epicentre was close to the Algarve, Lisbon, as the most populated area, bore the worst. Over 20 churches collapsed, crushing the crowds who had assembled for All Saints' Day. A third shock was followed by fires which quickly spread. An hour later, huge waves came rolling in from the Tagus and flooded the lower part of the city. Most of Portugal suffered damage and the shock was felt as far away as Italy. Perhaps 15,000 people lost their lives in Lisbon alone.

This anonymous painting of the arrival of a papal ambassador at court in 1693 shows how Terreiro do Paço looked before the earthquake.

Some buildings that might have survived an earthquake alone were destroyed by the fire that followed.

The old royal palace, the 16th-century Paço da Ribeira, was utterly ruined by the earthquake and ensuing flood.

The royal family was staying at the palace in Belém, a place far less affected than Lisbon, and survived the disaster unscathed. Here the king surveys the city's devastation.

Ships crammed full of people fleeing the fire were wrecked and anchors thrown up to water level.

This detail is from an ex-voto painting dedicated to Nossa Senhora da Estrela, given by a grateful father in thanks for the sparing of his daughter's life in the earthquake. The girl was found miraculously alive after being buried under rubble for seven hours.

THE RECONSTRUCTION OF LISBON

Marquês de Pombal (1699–1782)

No sooner had the tremors abated than Sebastião José de Carvalho e Melo, chief minister to José I and later to become Marquês de Pombal, was outlining ideas for rebuilding the city. While philosophers moralized, Pombal's initial response is said to have been, "bury the dead and feed the living". He restored order, then began a progressive town-planning scheme. His efficient handling of the crisis gained him almost total political control.

REACTIONS TO THE DISASTER

French author, Voltaire

The earthquake had a profound effect on European thought. Eyewitness accounts appeared in the papers, many written by foreigners living in Lisbon. A heated debate arose as to whether the earthquake was a natural phenomenon or an act of divine wrath. Lisbon had been a flourishing city, famed for its wealth – also for its Inquisition and idolatry. Interpreting the quake as punishment, many preachers prophesied further catastrophes. Leading literary figures debated the significance of the event, among them Voltaire, who wrote a poem about the disaster, propounding his views that evil exists and man is weak and powerless, doomed to an unhappy fate on earth.

The ancient castle walls succumbed to the reverberating shock waves.

Flames erupted as the candles lit for All Saints' Day ignited the city's churches. The fire raged for seven days.

Some of Lisbon's finest buildings were destroyed, along with gold, jewellery, priceless furniture, archives, books and paintings.

At 11am, tidal waves rolled into Terreiro do Paço. The Alcântara docks, to the west, bore the brunt of the impact.

Churches, homes and public buildings all suffered in the disaster. The Royal Opera House, here shown in ruins, was only completed in March the same year.

A CONTEMPORARY VIEW OF THE EARTHQUAKE

This anonymous German engraving of 1775 gives a vivid picture of the scale of the disaster. Many who fled the flames made for the Tagus, but were washed away in the huge waves which struck the Terreiro do Paço. The human and material losses were incalculable.

The reconstruction of the centre of Lisbon took place rapidly. By the end of November the Marquês de Pombal had devised a strikingly modern scheme for a grid of parallel streets running from the waterfront to Rossio. The new buildings are shown in yellow.

Modern-day Lisbon holds many reminders of the earthquake. Pombal's innovative grid system is clearly visible in this aerial view of the Baixa (see pp80–87). The scheme took many years to complete, and the triumphal arch spanning Rua Augusta was not finished until over a century later, in 1873.

ENTERTAINMENT IN LISBON

FOR A SMALLISH European capital, Lisbon has a good and varied cultural calendar. Musical events range from classical and opera performances to intimate *fado* evenings, and large rock concerts. Dance, both classical and modern, is well represented in Lisbon. The Gulbenkian Foundation, long the only major arts patron, has been joined by other private funds as well as state institutions.

Football is a consuming passion of the Portuguese, and Lisbon's Sporting and Benfica teams play regularly at home. Lisbon outparties many larger capitals, with a nightlife known for its liveliness.

BOOKING TICKETS

TICKETS CAN BE reserved by phoning the Agência de Bilhetes para Espectáculos Públicos (**ABEP**). Pay in cash when you collect them from the kiosk. Some cinemas and theatres accept phone or credit card bookings – it is best to check first.

ABEP kiosk selling tickets on Praça dos Restauradores

LISTINGS MAGAZINES

PREVIEWS of forthcoming events and listings of bars and clubs appear weekly in major newspapers. English-language publications on offer include the monthly *Follow Me Lisboa* and the quarterly *Lisboa Step By Step,* which are available free from tourist offices. The monthly *Agenda Cultural* is in Portuguese.

CINEMA AND THEATRE

MOVIE-GOERS are very well served in Lisbon. Films are shown in their original language with Portuguese subtitles, and tickets are inexpensive. On Mondays most cinemas offer reductions. The city's older cinemas have now largely given way to modern multiplexes, usually in shopping centres such as Amoreiras or El Corte Inglés. While these screen mainstream

Hollywood fare, cinemas such as King Triplex show more European films. Classics and retrospectives can be seen at the **Cinemateca Portuguesa**, whose monthly programme is available at tourist offices.

Theatre performances are most often in Portuguese, but large institutions such as the **Teatro Nacional Dona Maria II** and the **Teatro da Trindade** occasionally stage guest performances by visiting companies. Less formally, **Chapitô** sometimes has open-air shows.

CLASSICAL MUSIC, OPERA AND DANCE

LISBON'S TOP CULTURAL centres are the modern **Centro Cultural de Belém** (*see p108*) and the **Fundação Calouste Gulbenkian** (*see pp116–19*). They host a variety of national and international events including concerts and ballet. **The Teatro Nacional de São Carlos** is Portugal's national opera, with a season that mixes its own productions with guest performances. The **Coliseu dos Recreios** has no institution attached and so offers a variety of events.

Performance at the Chapitô, circus school, Alfama

WORLD MUSIC, JAZZ, POP AND ROCK

LISBON'S MUSICAL SOUL may be *fado* (*see pp66–7*), but the city is no stranger to other forms of musical expression. African music, particularly that of former Portuguese colony Cape Verde, plays a big part in Lisbon's music scene. Venues include **B.Leza** and **Enclave**, both have frequent live performances.

The **Hot Clube** has been Lisbon's foremost jazz venue for as long as anyone can

The house orchestra playing at the Fundação Calouste Gulbenkian

Musician at Pé Sujo

remember, and has the right intimate atmosphere. **Speakeasy** is younger, slightly bigger, and varies live jazz with up-tempo blues, particularly at weekends.

Large rock and pop concerts are held at outdoor venues such as **Praça Sony** and football stadiums, or indoors at **Pavilhão Atlântico** or **Coliseu dos Recreios**.

NIGHTCLUBS

BAIRRO ALTO remains a lively area for Lisbon nightlife, although its mostly small bars don't usually have dance floors or keep very late hours. There are a exceptions, including the doyen of Bairro Alto clubs, **Frágil**, and the recent DJ club **V Imperium**.

Among the larger and more mainstream dance venues are **Kremlin** and **Kapital**; the first a nearly historic house club, the second a very middle-of-the-road disco.

Farther westward by the Doca de Santo Amaro marina is the attractively housed **Salsa Latina**, one of Lisbon's few salsa places. Inland, in the Alcântara area, are **W** and **Alcântara Club**, while

eastwards along the river near Santa Apolónia station, is **Lux**, the cream of Lisbon's current club scene.

SPECTATOR SPORTS

PORTUGAL IS HOSTING the 2004 European Football Championship, and Lisbon's two main teams, Sporting and Benfica, are both building new stadiums for the event. The Portuguese football cup finals, as well as other events such as the Estoril Open tennis tournament, are held at the **Estádio Nacional-Jamor**. The Pavilhão Atlântico is also used for indoor events such as tennis, volleyball and basketball. Estoril's **Autódromo** Fernanda Pires da Silva is a motor racing venue.

DIRECTORY

BOOKING TICKETS

ABEP
Praça dos Restauradores.
Map 7 A2.
[21-347 58 24.

CINEMA AND THEATRE

Cinemateca Portuguesa
Rua Barata Salgueiro 39.
Map 5 C5.
[21-359 62 62.

Chapitô
Costa do Castelo 7.
Map 7 C3.
[21-886 73 34.

King Triplex
Avenida Frei Miguel Contreiras 52a. **Map** 6 E1.
[21-848 08 08.

Teatro da Trindade
Rua Nova da Trindade 9
Map 7 A3.
[21-342 32 00

Teatro Nacional Dona Maria II
Praça Dom Pedro IV.
Map 7 B3.
[21-325 08 00.

CLASSICAL MUSIC, OPERA AND DANCE

Centro Cultural de Belém
Praça do Império. **Map** 1 C5. [21-361 24 00.

Coliseu dos Recreios
Rua das Portas de Santo Antão 92. **Map** 7 A2.
[21-324 05 80.

Fundação Calouste Gulbenkian
Avenida de Berna 45. **Map** 5 B2. [21-782 30 00.

Teatro Nacional de São Carlos
Rua Serpa Pinto 9. **Map** 7 A4. [21-325 30 00.

WORLD MUSIC, JAZZ, POP AND ROCK

B. Leza
Largo do Conde Barão 50.
Map 4 E3.
[21-396 37 35.

Enclave
Rua do Sol ao Rato 71A.
Map 4 D1.
[21-388 87 38.

Hot Clube
Praça da Alegria 38–9.
Map 4 F1.
[21-346 73 69.

Pavilhão Atlântico
Parque das Nações.
[21-891 84 09.

Praça Sony
Parque das Nações.
[21-891 90 00.

Speakeasy
Cais das Oficinas, Armazém 115, Rocha Conde d'Óbidos. **Map** 4 D4.
[21-395 73 08

NIGHTCLUBS

Alcântara Club
Rua da Colina Económica 11. [21-346 52 50.

Frágil
Rua da Atalaia 128.
Map 4 F2.
[21-346 95 78.

Kapital
Avenida 24 de Julho 68.
Map 4 E3.
[21-395 71 01.

Kremlin
Escadinhas da Praia 5.
Map 4 D3.
[21- 395 71 01.

Lux
Avenida Infante Dom Henrique.**Map** 8 D5.
[21-882 08 90.

Salsa Latina
Gare Marítima de Alcântara. **Map** 3 A5/B5.
[21-395 05 55.

V Imperium
Calçada do Tijolo 8.
Map 4 F2.
[96-743 03 03.

W
Rua Maria Luísa Holstein 13. **Map** 3 A4.
[21-363 68 30.

SPORTS

Autódromo Estoril
Alcabideche.
[21-469 14 62.

Estádio José Alvalade
(Sporting) Rua Francisco Stromp 2.
[21-756 79 30.

Estádio da Luz
(Benfica) Avenida General Norton Matos.
[21-726 61 29.

Estádio Nacional-Jamor
Cruz Quebrada
[21-419 72 12.

Fado: the Music of Lisbon

L IKE THE BLUES, *fado* is an expression of
longing and sorrow. Literally meaning
"fate", the term may be applied to an
individual song as well as the genre
itself. The music owes much to the
concept known as *saudade*, meaning
a longing both for what has been lost,
and for what has never been attained,
which perhaps accounts for its emotional
power. The people of Lisbon have nurtured
this poignant music in back-street cafés
and restaurants for over 150 years, and
it has altered little in that time. It is sung
as often by women as men,
always accompanied by the *guitarra*
and *viola* (acoustic Spanish guitar).
Fado from Coimbra has developed
its own lighter-hearted style.

**A *guitarra*
accompanist**

**A graphic depiction of the music's
low-life associations from the 1920s**

Argentina Santos is a legendary
singer and *fado* house owner. All
female *fadistas* wear a black shawl
in memory of Maria Severa.

The *guitarrista* plays
the melody and will
occasionally perform a
solo instrumental piece.

**FADO
DA ESPERA DE
TOIROS
DO FONOFILME
A SEVERA**

*Maria Severa (1810–36) was the
first great* fadista *and the subject
of the first Portuguese sound film
in 1931. Her scandalous life and
early death are pivotal to fado history, and her spiritual influence
has been enormous, inspiring
fados, poems, novels and plays.*

Most instruments have 12
paired strings, like this one.
The double strings produce a
resonant, silvery-sweet tone.

**Delicate mother-of-
pearl inlaid flower
motifs**

**Mother-of-pearl
finger plate**

THE GUITARRA

Peculiar to Portuguese culture, the
guitarra is a flat-backed instru-
ment shaped like a mandolin, with
eight, ten or twelve strings,
arranged in pairs. It has
evolved from a simple
19th-century design into
a finely decorated piece,
sometimes inlaid with mother-of-
pearl. The sound of the *guitarra*
is an essential ingredient of a good
fado, echoing and enhancing the
singer's melody line.

Alfredo Duarte (1891–1982) was a renowned writer of fado lyrics dealing with love, death, longing, tragedy and triumph. Affectionately known as O Marceneiro (the master carpenter) because of his skill as a joiner, he is still revered and his work widely performed.

All kinds of themes *may occur in* fado. *This song of 1910, for example, celebrates the dawning of the liberal republic. Such songsheets remained a favoured means of dissemination, even after the first records were made in 1904.*

A cultural icon for the Portuguese, Amália Rodrigues (1921–99) was the leading exponent of fado *for over 50 years. She crystallized the music's style in the postwar years, and made it known around the world.*

The viola provides rhythm accompaniment, but the player will never take a solo.

The music has long inspired *great writers and painters. O Fado (1910) by José Malhôa (see p55) shows it in an intimate setting with the* fadista *captivating his listener. The air of abandonment underlines the earthiness of many of the songs.*

THE FADO HOUSE

Lisbon's best *fado* houses are those run by *fadistas* themselves. Based on a love of the music and on relationships with other performers, such houses usually offer a truer *fado* experience than the larger, tourist-oriented houses. A good example is the **Parreirinha de Alfama**, owned by Argentina Santos (shown above). Less slick, but more emotionally charged, are performances of *fado vadio*, "itinerant" fado, in humbler restaurants and bars such as **Tasca do Chico** in Bairro Alto.

WHERE TO ENJOY FADO IN LISBON

Any of these fado houses will offer you good food, wine and music – or visit the Casa do Fado for a fascinating exhibition of the history of Fado.

Arcadas do Faia
Rua da Barroca 54–6.
Map 4 F2. [*21-342 67 42.*

Casa do Fado
Largo do Chafariz de Dentro 1.
[*21-882 34 70.* 8, 28, 50. 10am–6pm Wed–Mon.

Parreirinha de Alfama
Beco do Espírito Santo 1.
Map 7 E4. [*21-886 82 09.*

Senhor Vinho
Rua do Meio à Lapa 18.
Map 4 D3. [*21-397 74 56*

Tasca do Chico
Rua Diário de Notícias 39.
Map 7 A4. [*21-343 10 40.*

Taverna do Embuçado
Beco dos Cortumes.
Map 8 E4. [*21-886 50 88.*

ALFAMA

IT IS DIFFICULT TO BELIEVE that this humble neighbourhood was once the most desirable quarter of Lisbon. For the Moors, the tightly packed alleyways around the fortified castle comprised the whole city. The seeds of decline were sown in the Middle Ages when wealthy residents moved west for fear of earthquakes, leaving the quarter to fishermen and paupers. The buildings survived the 1755 earthquake (*see pp62–3*) and, although there are no Moorish houses still standing, the quarter retains its kasbah-like layout. Compact houses line steep streets and stairways, their façades strung with washing.

Portugal's coat of arms in the treasury of the Sé

Long-overdue restoration is under way in the most dilapidated areas, but daily life still revolves around local grocery stores and small, cellar-like tavernas.

Above the Alfama, the imposing Castelo de São Jorge crowns Lisbon's eastern hill. This natural vantage point, a defensive stronghold and royal palace until the 16th century, is today a popular promenade, with spectacular views from its reconstructed ramparts.

West of the Alfama stand the proud twin towers of the Sé. To the north-east, the domed church of Santa Engrácia and the white façade of São Vicente de Fora dominate the skyline.

SIGHTS AT A GLANCE

Museums and Galleries
Museu de Artes
  Decorativas **2**
Museu Militar **6**

Historic Buildings
Casa dos Bicos **7**
Castelo de São Jorge pp78–9 **10**

Churches
Santo António à Sé **9**

Santa Engrácia **5**
São Vicente de Fora **3**
Sé **8**

Belvederes
Miradouro da Graça **11**
Miradouro de Santa Luzia **1**

Markets
Feira da Ladra **4**

GETTING THERE

The 12 and 28 trams rattle up the narrow streets of the Alfama from the Baixa. Bus 37 does a circuit from the Castle to Rossio. Many buses run east along Avenida Dom Infante Henrique to Santa Apolónia station, and west to Belém.

KEY

	Street-by-Street: Alfama pp70–71
🚊	Railway station
🅿	Parking
🛈	Tourist information
—	Castle walls

0 metres 250
0 yards 250

◁ **Ironwork balconies on a house in Rua dos Bacalhoeiros, beside the Casa dos Bicos**

Street-by-Street: Alfama

A FASCINATING QUARTER at any time of day, the
Alfama comes to life in the late afternoon
and early evening when the locals emerge at their
doorways and the small tavernas start to fill. A
new generation of younger residents has resulted
in a small number of trendy shops and bars.
Given the steep streets and steps of the quarter,
the least strenuous approach is to start at the
top and work your way down. A walk
around the maze of winding alleyways will reveal picturesque
corners and crumbling churches
as well as panoramic views from
the shady terraces, such as the
Miradouro de Santa Luzia.

On Largo das Portas do Sol, café
tables look out over the Alfama towards
the Tagus estuary. Portas do Sol was one
of the entrance gates to the old city.

Statue of St. Vincent

The church of Santa Luzia
has 18th-century blue and
white *azulejo* panels
on its south wall.

Largo das Portas do Sol has its
own terrace viewpoint on a
converted rooftop on the east
side of the Santa Luzia church.

L. DAS PORTAS DO SOL

BECO DE SANTA HELENA

Castelo
de São
Jorge

R. DO CAS

RUA N. DE ARAÚJO

★ Museu de Artes Decorativas
*Set up as a museum by the banker
Ricardo do Espírito Santo Silva, the
17th-century Palácio Azurara houses
fine 17th- and 18th-century Portuguese furniture and decorative arts* **2**

KEY

– – –   Suggested route

0 metres	25
0 yards	25

STAR SIGHTS

**★ Miradouro de
Santa Luzia**

**★ Museu de Artes
Decorativas**

**★ Miradouro
de Santa Luzia**
*The view from this
bougainvillea-clad
terrace spans the tiled
roofs of the Alfama
toward the Tagus.
This is a pleasant
place to rest after
a walk around the
area's steep streets* **1**

Beco dos Cruzes, like most of the alleyways *(becos)* that snake their way through the Alfama, is a steep cobbled street. Locals often hang washing between the tightly packed houses.

LOCATOR MAP
See Lisbon Street Finder map 8

Rua de São Pedro is the scene of a lively early-morning fish market where the *varinas* sell the catch of the day. *Peixe espada* (scabbard fish) is one of the fish sold here.

Largo do Chafariz de Dentro is named after the 17th-century fountain *(chafariz)* that was originally placed within *(dentro)* rather than outside the 14th-century walls.

The church of Nossa Senhora dos Remédios was rebuilt after the 1755 earthquake *(see pp62–3)*. The pinnacled Manueline portal is all that remains of the original building.

São Miguel was rebuilt after it was damaged in the 1755 earthquake. It retains a few earlier features, including a fine ceiling of Brazilian jacaranda wood.

Popular restaurants hidden in the labyrinth of alleyways spill out onto open-air patios. The Lautasco *(see p404)*, in Beco do Azinhal, serves excellent Portuguese food.

Tile panel showing pre-earthquake Praça do Comércio, Santa Luzia

Miradouro de Santa Luzia ❶

Rua do Limoeiro. **Map** 8 D4. 🚌 28.

THE TERRACE by the church
of Santa Luzia provides a
sweeping view over the Alfama
and the River Tagus. Distinctive landmarks, from left to
right, are the cupola of Santa
Engrácia, the church of Santo
Estêvão and the two startling
white towers of São Miguel.
While tourists admire the
views, old men play cards
under the bougainvillea-clad
pergola. The south wall of
Santa Luzia has two modern
tiled panels, one of Praça do
Comércio before it was flat-
tened by the earthquake, the
other showing the Christians
attacking the Castelo de São
Jorge (see pp78–9) in 1147.

Museu de Artes Decorativas ❷

Largo das Portas do Sol 2. **Map** 8 D3.
📞 21-888 19 91/881 46 00. 🚋 37.
🚌 12, 28. 🕙 10am–5pm Sun–Fri.
⬤ 1 Jan, Easter, 1 May, 25 Dec. 🎫 ♿

ALSO KNOWN AS the Ricardo
do Espírito Santo Silva
Foundation, the museum was
set up in 1953 to preserve the
traditions and increase public
awareness of the Portuguese
decorative arts. The foundation
was named after a banker
who bought the 17th-century
Palácio Azurara in 1947 to
house his fine collection of
furniture, textiles, silver and

ceramics. Among the 17th- and
18th-century antiques displayed
in this handsome four-storey
mansion are many
fine pieces in exotic
woods, including
an 18th-century
rosewood back-
gammon and chess
table. Also of note
are the collections
of 18th-century
silver and Chinese
porcelain, and the
Arraiolos carpets
(see p301). The
spacious rooms still
retain some original
ceilings and azulejo panels.
　Workshops are housed in
the adjoining building, where
visitors can watch artisans
preserving the techniques of
cabinet-making, gilding, book-
binding and other traditional
crafts. Temporary exhibitions,
lectures and concerts are also
held in the palace.

**18th-century china
cutlery case, Museu
de Artes Decorativas**

**Stone figure of a woman praying by the
tomb of Carlos I in São Vicente de Fora**

São Vicente de Fora ❸

Largo de São Vicente. **Map** 8 E3.
📞 21-882 44 00. 🚋 12. 🚌 28.
🕙 9am–6pm Tue–Fri; 9am–7pm Sat;
9am–12:30pm, 3–5pm Sun.
🎫 📷 🎫 to cloisters.

ST VINCENT was proclaimed
Lisbon's patron saint in
1173, when his relics were
transferred from the Algarve
(see p319) to a church on this
site outside (fora) the city
walls. Designed by Italian
architect Filippo Terzi, and
completed in 1627, the off-
white Italianate façade is sober
and symmetrical, with towers
either side and statues of
saints Vincent, Augustine and
Sebastian over the
entrance. Inside, one is
drawn immediately to
Machado de Castro's
Baroque canopy over
the altar, flanked by
life-size wooden statues.
　The adjoining former
Augustinian monastery,
reached via the nave,
retains its 16th-century
cistern and vestiges of
the former cloister but
is visited for its 18th-
century azulejos.
Among the panels in the entrance hall off the first cloister
there are lively, though histori-
cally inaccurate, tile scenes of
Afonso Henriques attacking
Lisbon and Santarém. Around
the cloisters the tiled rural
scenes, surrounded by floral
designs and cherubs,
illustrating the fables of
La Fontaine. A
passageway leads
behind the church to
the old refectory,
transformed into the
Bragança Pantheon in
1885. The stone sarco-
phagi of almost every
king and queen are
here, from João IV,
who died in 1656, to
Manuel II, last king of
Portugal. Only Maria I
and Pedro IV are not
buried here. A stone
mourner kneels at the
tomb of Carlos I and
his son Luís Felipe,
assassinated in Praça
do Comércio in 1908.

Feira da Ladra ❹

Campo de Santa Clara. **Map** 8 F2. ☐ 7:30am–1pm Tue & Sat. 🚌 12. 🚋 28.

THE STALLS of the so-called "Thieves' Market" have occupied this site on the edge of the Alfama for over a century, laid out under the shade of trees or canopies. As the fame of this flea market has grown, bargains are increasingly hard to find amongst the mass of bric-a-brac, but a few of the vendors have interesting wrought-iron work, prints and tiles, as well as second-hand clothes. Evidence of Portugal's colonial past is reflected in the stalls selling African statuary, masks and jewellery. Fish, vegetables and herbs are sold in the central wrought-iron marketplace.

Bric-a-brac for sale in the Feira da Ladra

Santa Engrácia ❺

Campo de Santa Clara. **Map** 8 F2. ☐ 21-885 48 20. 🚌 12. 🚋 28. ☐ 10am–5pm Tue–Sun. ● public hols. 🖼 ♿

ONE OF LISBON'S most striking landmarks, the soaring dome of Santa Engrácia punctuates the skyline in the east of the city. The original church collapsed in a storm in 1681. The first stone of the new Baroque monument, laid in 1682, marked the beginning of a 284-year saga which led to the invention of a saying that a Santa Engrácia job was never done. The church was not completed until 1966.

The interior is paved with coloured marble and crowned by a giant cupola. As the National Pantheon, it houses cenotaphs of Portuguese heroes, such as Vasco da Gama *(see p108)* and Afonso de Albuquerque, Viceroy of India (1502–15) on the left, and on the right Henry the Navigator *(see p49)*. More contemporary tombs include that of the *fadista* Amália Rodrigues *(see p67)*. A lift up to the dome offers a 360-degree panorama of the city.

Museu Militar ❻

Largo dos Caminhos de Ferro. **Map** 8 F3. ☐ 21-884 25 69. 🚌 9, 25, 28, 39, 46. 🚋 28. ☐ 10am–5pm Tue–Sun. ● public hols. 🖼

APTLY LOCATED on the site of a 16th-century cannon foundry and arms depot, the military museum contains an extensive display of arms, uniforms and historical military documents. Visits begin in the Vasco da Gama Room with a collection of old cannons and modern murals depicting the discovery of the sea route to India. The Salas da Grande Guerra, on the first floor, display World War I related exhibits. Other rooms are devoted to the evolution of weapons in Portugal, from primitive flints through spears to rifles. The large courtyard, flanked by cannons, tells the story of Portugal in tiled panels, from the Christian Reconquest to World War I. The Portuguese artillery section in the oldest part of the museum displays the wagon used to transport the triumphal arch to Rua Augusta *(see p87)*.

The multicoloured marble interior beneath Santa Engrácia's dome

Casa dos Bicos ❼

Rua dos Bacalhoeiros. **Map** 8 D4. ☐ 21-881 09 00. 🚌 9, 28, 46, 76. 🚋 18, 25. ☐ 9:30am–5:30pm Mon–Fri (ground floor only). ● public hols.

THIS CONSPICUOUS house, faced with diamond-shaped stones *(bicos)*, was built in 1523 for Brás de Albuquerque, illegitimate son of Afonso, Viceroy of India and conqueror of Goa and Malacca. The façade is an adaptation of a style popular in Europe during the 16th century. The two top storeys, ruined in the earthquake of 1755, were restored in the 1980s, recreating the original from old views of Lisbon in tile panels and engravings. In the interim the building was used for salting fish (Rua dos Bacalhoeiros means street of the cod fishermen). The modern interior of the lower floors is used for temporary exhibitions.

The curiously faceted Casa dos Bicos, and surrounding buildings

The façade of the Sé, the city's cathedral

Sé ⑧

Largo da Sé. **Map** 8 D4. *21-886
67 52.* 37. 12, 28. *9am–
7pm Tue–Sat (cloister & treasury
10am–5pm), 9am–5pm Sun, Mon &
public hols.* to cloister
& treasury.

IN 1150, THREE YEARS after
Afonso Henriques recap-
tured Lisbon from the Moors,
he built a cathedral for the first
bishop of Lisbon, the English
crusader Gilbert of Hastings,
on the site of the old mosque.
Sé is short for Sedes Episco-
palis, the seat (or see) of a
bishop. Devasted by three
earth tremors in the 14th century, as well as the earthquake

of 1755, and
renovated over the
centuries, the
cathedral you see
today blends a
variety of archi-
tectural styles.
The façade, with
twin castellated
belltowers and a
splendid rose win-
dow, retains its
solid Romanesque
aspect. The gloomy
interior, for the most
part, is simple and
austere, and hardly
anything remains
of the embellish-
ment lavished
upon it by King
João V in the first
half of the 18th
century. Beyond
the renovated Romanesque
nave the ambulatory has nine
Gothic chapels. The Capela de
Santo Ildefonso contains the
14th-century sarcophagi of
Lopo Fernandes Pacheco,
companion in arms to King
Afonso IV, and his wife, Maria
Vilalobos. The bearded figure
of the nobleman, sword in

**Carved tomb of the 14th-century nobleman Lopo
Fernandes Pacheco in chapel in the ambulatory**

**Detail of the Baroque nativity scene
by Joaquim Machado de Castro**

hand, and his wife, clutching
a prayer book, are carved
onto the tombs with their
dogs sitting faithfully at their
feet. In the adjacent chancel
are the tombs of Afonso IV
and his wife Dona Beatriz.

The Gothic **cloister**, reached
via the third chapel in the ambulatory, has elegant double
arches with some finely carved
capitals. One of the chapels is
still fitted with its 13th-century
wrought-iron gate. Archaeological excavations in the
cloister have unearthed various
Roman and other remains.

To the left of the cathedral
entrance the
Franciscan chapel
contains the font
where the saint
was baptized in
1195 and is decor-
ated with a charm-
ing tiled scene of St
Antony preaching
to the fishes. The
adjacent chapel
contains a Baroque
nativity scene made of cork,
wood and terracotta by
Machado de Castro (1766).

The **treasury** is at the top
of the staircase on the right.
It houses silver, ecclesiastical
robes, statuary, illustrated
manuscripts and a few relics
associated with St Vincent,
which were transferred to
Lisbon from Cabo de São
Vicente in 1173 *(see p319).*
Legend has it that two sacred
ravens kept a permanent vigil
over the boat that transported
the relics. The ravens and the
boat became a symbol of the
city of Lisbon, still very much
in use today. It is also said
that the descendants of the
two ravens used to live in
the cloisters of the cathedral.

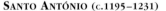

SANTO ANTÓNIO (c.1195–1231)

To the chagrin of the Lisboetas, their best-loved
saint is known as St Antony of Padua. Although
born and brought up in Lisbon, he spent
the last months of his life in Padua, Italy.
St Antony joined the Franciscan Order
in 1220, impressed by some crusading friars he
had met at Coimbra where he was studying.
The Franciscan friar was a learned and passionate preacher, renowned for his devotion
to the poor and his ability to convert heretics.
Many statues and paintings of St Antony depict
him carrying the Infant Jesus on a book, while
others show him preaching to the fishes, as
St Francis preached to the birds. He is also
often called upon to help find lost objects.
In 1934 Pope Pius XI declared St Antony
a patron saint of Portugal. The year 1995 saw
the 800th anniversary of his birth – a cause
for major celebrations throughout the city.

Santo António à Sé 9

Largo Santo António à Sé, 24. **Map**
7 C4. **[** 21-886 91 45. **▦** 37.
▦ 12, 28. **◯** 8am–7:30pm daily.
◐ public hols. **▮** **Museu Antoniano**
[21-886 04 47. **◯** 10am–1pm,
2–6pm Tue–Sun. **▨**

THE POPULAR LITTLE church
of Santo António allegedly
stands on the site of the house
in which St Antony was born.
The crypt, reached via the
tiled sacristy on the left of the
church, is all that remains of
the original church destroyed
by the earthquake of 1755.
Work began on the new
church in 1757 headed by
Mateus Vicente, architect of
the Basílica da Estrela *(see
p95)* and was partially funded
by donations collected by
local children with the cry
"a small coin for St Antony".
Even today the floor of the tiny
chapel in the crypt is strewn
with escudos and the walls
are scrawled with devotional
messages from worshippers.
  The church's façade blends
the undulating curves of the
Baroque style with Neo-
Classical Ionic columns on
either side of the main portal.
Inside, on the way down to the
crypt, a modern *azulejo* panel
commemorates the visit of
Pope John Paul II in 1982. In
1995 the church was given a
facelift for the saint's eighth
centenary. It is traditional for
young couples to visit the

The Miradouro and Igreja da Graça seen from the Castelo de São Jorge

church on their wedding day
and leave flowers for St Antony
who is believed to bring good
luck to new marriages.
  Next door the small **Museu
Antoniano** houses artefacts,
relating to St Antony, as well
as gold and silverware which
used to decorate the church.
The most charming exhibit is a
17th-century tiled panel of St
Antony preaching to the fishes.

Castelo de São Jorge 10

See pp78–9.

Tiled panel recording Pope John Paul II's visit to Santo António à Sé

Miradouro da Graça 11

Map 8 D2. **▦** 37. **▦** 12, 28.

THE WORKING-CLASS quarter
of Graça developed at
the end of the 19th century.
Today, it is visited chiefly for
the views from its *miradouro*
(belvedere). The panorama
of rooftops and skyscrapers is
less spectacular than the view
from the castle, but it is a
popular spot, particularly
in the early evenings when
couples sit at café tables
under the pines. Behind the
miradouro stands an Augustinian monastery, founded in
1271 and rebuilt after the
earthquake. Once a flour-
ishing complex, the huge
building is now used as
barracks but the church, the
Igreja da Graça, can still be
visited. Inside, in the right
transept, is the *Senhor dos
Passos*, a representation of
Christ carrying the cross on
the way to Calvary. This figure,
clad in brilliant purple clothes,
is carried on a procession
through Graça on the second
Sunday in Lent. The *azulejos*
on the altar front, dating from
the 17th century, imitate the
brocaded textiles usually
draped over the altar.

Castelo de São Jorge ⑩

Stone head of Martim Moniz

FOLLOWING THE RECAPTURE of Lisbon from the Moors in 1147, King Afonso Henriques transformed their hilltop citadel into the residence of the Portuguese kings. In 1511 Manuel I built a more lavish palace in what is now the Praça do Comércio and the castle was used variously as a theatre, prison and arms depot. After the 1755 earthquake the ramparts remained in ruins until 1938 when Salazar *(see pp56–7)* began a complete renovation, rebuilding the "medieval" walls and adding gardens and wild-fowl. The castle may not be authentic but the gardens and the narrow streets of the Santa Cruz district within the walls make a pleasant stroll and the views are the finest in Lisbon.

Torre de Ulisses has a camera obscura that projects views of Lisbon onto the inside walls of the tower.

RUA DAS COZINHAS

★ **Battlements**
Visitors can climb the towers and walk along the reconstructed ramparts of the castle walls.

Casa do Leão Restaurant
Part of the former royal residence can be booked for evening meals and parties (see p404).

A multimedia exhibit called Olisipónia recreates 16th-century Lisbon here.

★ **Observation Terrace**
This large shaded square affords spectacular views over Lisbon and the Tagus. Local men play backgammon and cards under the trees.

KEY

– – – Suggested route

◁ **Delightful hidden courtyard among the run-down houses in Santa Cruz, within the castle walls**

Porta de Martim Moniz is named after a knight who gave his life to keep the gate open for Afonso Henriques's troops in 1147. His bust is in a niche by the gate.

Porta de Santo André opens out into Largo Rodrigues de Freitas.

VISITORS' CHECKLIST

Porta de S. Jorge, Rua do Chão da Feira. **Map** 8 D3. ☎ 21-887 72 44. ☒ 37 ☒ 28.
☐ 9am–9pm daily Apr–Sep; 9am–6pm daily Oct–Mar. ☒
☐ ☒ **Torre de Ulisses.**
☐ 10am–12:30pm, 2–5pm Apr–Sep. Every half an hour, with a maximum of 15 people.
☒ **Olisipónia.** ☐ 10am–12:30pm , 2–5pm daily.
☒ Jan 1, May 1, Dec 25. ☒

Inside the 12th-century church of Santa Cruz do Castelo is a 17th-century statue of St George.

Santa Cruz square is a pleasant open space surrounded by the area's elegantly restored buildings.

RUA DAS FLORES DE SANTA CRUZ

LARGO DE SANTA CRUZ DO CASTELO

RUA DE SANTA CRUZ DO CASTELO

BECO DO RECOLHIMENTO

BECO DO FORNO DO CASTELO

RUA DO RECOLHIMENTO

RUA DO CHÃO DA FEIRA

Porta de São Jorge

Santa Cruz
The narrow, cobbled streets of the small quarter of Santa Cruz are tightly packed within the walls of the old castle.

0 metres		50
0 yards		50

Rua de Santa Cruz do Castelo
Peeling façades, potted plants and washing strung between window-sills characterize the pretty streets south of the Castelo de São Jorge.

STAR FEATURES

★ **Observation Terrace**

★ **Battlements**

BAIXA AND AVENIDA

ROM THE RUINS of Lisbon, devastated by the earthquake of 1755 *(see pp62–3)*, the Marquês de Pombal created an entirely new centre. Using a grid layout of streets, he linked the stately, arcaded Praça do Comércio beside the Tagus with the busy central square of Rossio. The streets were flanked by uniform, Neo-Classical buildings and named according to the shopkeepers and craftsmen who traded there.

Detail on statue of José I in Praça do Comércio

The Baixa (lower town) is still the commercial hub of the capital, housing banks, offices and shops. At its centre, Rossio is a popular meeting point with cafés, theatres and restaurants. The geometric layout of the area has been retained, but most of the buildings constructed since the mid-18th century have not adhered to Pombaline formality. The streets are crowded by day, particularly the lively Rua Augusta, but after dark the quarter is almost deserted.

SIGHTS AT A GLANCE

Museums and Galleries
Museu da Sociedade de Geografia **4**

Churches
Nossa Senhora da Conceição Velha **9**

Parks and Gardens
Jardim Botânico **1**

Lifts
Elevador de Santa Justa **7**

Historic Streets and Squares
Avenida da Liberdade **2**
Praça do Comércio **10**
Praça da Figueira **6**
Praça dos Restauradores **3**
Rossio **5**
Rua Augusta **8**

GETTING THERE

The area is extremely well served with buses from all directions, several Metro stations and Rossio mainline station. Trains from Sintra and the west arrive at Rossio station and ferries from Cacilhas and Barreiro arrive at Terreiro do Paço.

KEY

▩	Street-by-Street: Baixa *pp82–3*
Ⓜ	Metro station
🚉	Railway station
🚡	Funicular
⛴	Ferry boarding point
P	Parking
i	Tourist information

0 metres 250
0 yards 250

◁ **The triumphal arch in Praça do Comércio leading into Rua Augusta and the Baixa**

Street-by-Street: Restauradores

Tʜɪs ɪs ᴛʜᴇ ʙᴜsɪᴇsᴛ ᴘᴀʀᴛ of the city, especially the central squares of Rossio and Praça da Figueira. Totally rebuilt after the earthquake of 1755 (see pp62–3), the area was one of Europe's first examples of town planning. Today, the large Neo-Classical buildings on the wide streets and squares house business offices. The atmosphere and surroundings are best absorbed from one of the busy pavement cafés. Rua das Portas de Santo Antão, a pedestrianized street where restaurants display tanks of live lobsters, is more relaxing for a stroll.

Tiled panel on façade of the Tabacaria Monaco

Palácio Foz, once a magnificent 18th-century palace built by the Italian architect Francesco Fabri, now houses a tourist office.

The Elevador da Glória is a bright yellow funicular that rattles up the hill to the Bairro Alto as far as the Miradouro de São Pedro de Alcântara (see p94).

Praça dos Restauradores
This large tree-lined square, named after the men who gave their lives during the War of Restoration, is a busy through road with café terraces on the patterned pavements ❸

Restauradores

Rossio station, designed by José Luís Monteiro, is an eye-catching late 19th-century Neo-Manueline building with two Moorish-style horseshoe arches.

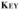
Kᴇʏ

– – – Suggested route

Sᴛᴀʀ Sɪɢʜᴛ

★ **Rossio**

Museu da Sociedade de Geografia
This collection from Portugal's former colonies is currently closed for refurbishment **4**

LOCATOR MAP
See Lisbon Street Finder map 7

Rua das Portas de Santo Antão recalls a 15th-century gate that once stood here. The lively street is now full of excellent seafood restaurants.

The Casa do Alentejo, restored in 1919, has a tranquil interior with a Neo-Moorish patio and fountain. It is a restaurant *(see p405)* and a meeting place for local Alentejans.

Church of São Domingos

Teatro Nacional Dona Maria II *(see p85)*

Praça da Figueira
Designed as the city's main marketplace in Pombal's reconstruction of the area, this square is now presided over by a 20th-century statue of João I **6**

★ Rossio
This attractively paved square is a social focal point with cafés, pastelarias and the National Theatre on the north side **5**

Café Nicola

Tabacaria Monaco

Rossio

Pastelaria Suiça

0 metres 50

0 yards 50

Bridge and pond shaded by trees in the Jardim Botânico

Jardim Botânico ❶

Rua da Escola Politécnica 58. **Map** 4 F1.
【 21-392 18 00. **📧** 58. **M**
Avenida. **Gardens** ⬭ 9am–6pm
(Apr–Sep: 8pm) Mon–Fri, 10am–6pm
(Apr–Sep: 8pm) Sat & Sun. **●** 1 Jan,
25 Dec. **▨** **㋮** **Museu de História**
Natural ⬭ for exhibitions only. **▨**
Museu da Ciência **【** 21-392 18
08. ⬭ 10am–1pm, 2–5pm Mon–
Fri, 3–6pm Sat. **●** public hols. **▨**

T HE COMPLEX, owned by the
university, comprises two
museums and four hectares
(10 acres) of gardens. The
botanical gardens, which slope
down from the upper level by
the main entrance towards Rua
da Alegria, have a distinct air
of neglect. However, it is worth
paying the entrance fee to
wander among the exotic trees
and dense shady paths of the
gardens as they descend to the
second entrance. A magnificent
avenue of lofty palms connects
the two different levels.

The **Museu de História
Natural** (Natural History
Museum) opens only for temporary exhibitions and these
are well advertised throughout
the city. The **Museu da
Ciência** (Science Museum),
whose exhibits demonstrate
basic scientific principles, is
popular with school children.

Avenida da Liberdade ❷

Map 7 A2. **📧** 2, 9, 36 & many other
routes. **M** Restauradores, Avenida.

F OLLOWING THE earthquake
of 1755 (see pp62–3), the
Marquês de Pombal created
the Passeio Público (public
promenade) in the area now
occupied by the lower part
of Avenida da Liberdade and
Praça dos Restauradores.

Despite its name,
enjoyment of the
park was restricted to
Lisbon's high society
and walls and gates
ensured the exclu-
sion of the lower
classes. In 1821,
when the Liberals
came to power, the
barriers were pulled
down and the
Avenida and square
became open to all.
The boulevard
you see today was
built in 1879–82
in the style of the
Champs-Elysées
in Paris. The wide
tree-lined avenue
became a focus for
pageants, festivities
and demonstrations.
A war memorial
stands as a tribute to
those who died in
World War I. The
avenue still retains
a certain elegance
with fountains and
café tables shaded by trees,
however, it no longer makes
for a peaceful stroll. The once
majestic thoroughfare, 90 m
(295 ft) wide and decorated
with abstract pavement patterns, is now divided by seven
lanes of traffic linking Praça
dos Restauradores and Praça
Marquês de Pombal to the
north. Some of the original
mansions have been preserved,
including the Neo-Classical
Tivoli cinema at No. 188, with
an original 1920s kiosk outside,
and Casa Lambertini with its
colourful mosaic decoration at
No. 166. However, many of
the Art Nouveau façades have
unfortunately given way to
newer ones occupied by
offices, hotels or shopping
complexes.

**19th-century monument in honour of the
Restoration in Praça dos Restauradores**

Praça dos Restauradores ❸

Map 7 A2. **📧** 2, 9, 36, 46 & many
other routes. **M** Restauradores.

T HE SQUARE, distinguished by
its soaring obelisk, erected
in 1886, commemorates the
country's liberation from the
Spanish yoke in 1640 (see
pp50–51). The bronze figures
on the pedestal depict Victory,
holding a palm and a crown,
and Freedom. The names and
dates inscribed on the obelisk
are those of the battles of the
War of Restoration.

On the west side, the Palácio
Foz houses a tourist office and
work premises. It was built by
Francesco Savario Fabri
in 1755–77 for the
Marquês de
Castelo-Melhor,
and renamed after
the Marquês de Foz,
who lived here in the
19th century. The smart
Avenida Palace Hotel (see
p381), on the southwest
side of the square, was
designed by José Lúis
Monteiro (1849–1942),
who also built Rossio
railway station (see p82).

**Detail from the memorial to the dead of
World War I in Avenida da Liberdade**

Museu da Sociedade de Geografia ❹

Rua das Portas de Santo Antão 100.
Map 7 A2. 🔲 *21-342 54 01.* 🚌 *9, 80, 90.* Ⓜ *Restauradores.* ⬤ *for renovation.* 🔲 *compulsory.*

L OCATED in the Geographical Society building, the museum houses an idiosyncratic ethnographical collection brought back from Portugal's former colonies. On display are circumcision masks from Guinea Bissau, musical instruments and snake spears. From Angola there are neckrests to sustain coiffures and the original *padrão* – the stone pillar erected by the Portuguese in 1482 to mark their sovereignty over the colony. Most of the exhibits are arranged along the splendid Sala Portugal, a large hall used also for conferences.

Rossio ❺

Map 6 B3. 🚌 *2, 36, 44, 45 & many other routes.* Ⓜ *Rossio.*

F ORMALLY CALLED Praça de Dom Pedro IV, this large square has been the nerve centre of Lisbon for six centuries. During its history it has been the stage of bullfights, festivals, military parades and gruesome *autos da fé (see p51).* However, today there is little more than an occasional political rally and the sober

Teatro Nacional Dona Maria II in Rossio illuminated by night

Pombaline buildings, disfigured on the upper level by the remains of neon adverts, are occupied at street level by small souvenir shops, jewellers and cafés. Centre stage stands a statue of Dom Pedro IV, the first emperor of independent Brazil *(see p54).* At the foot of the statue, the four female figures are allegories of Justice, Wisdom, Strength and Moderation – qualities dubiously attributed to Dom Pedro.

In the mid-19th century the square was paved with wave-patterned mosaics which gave it the nickname of "Rolling Motion Square". The hand-cut grey and white stone cubes were the first such designs to decorate the city's pavements. Today, only a small central section of the design survives.

On the north side of the square is the Teatro Nacional Dona Maria II, named after Dom Pedro's daughter. The Neo-Classical structure was built in the 1840s by the Italian architect Fortunato Lodi. The interior was destroyed by fire in 1964 and reconstructed in the 1970s. On top of the pediment is Gil Vicente (1465–1536), the founder of Portuguese theatre.

Café Nicola on the west side of the square was a favourite meeting place among writers, including the poet Manuel du Bocage (1765–1805), who was notorious for his satires.

Praça da Figueira ❻

Map 6 B3. 🚌 *14, 43, 59, 60 & many other routes.* 🚋 *15.* Ⓜ *Rossio.*

B EFORE THE 1755 earthquake *(see pp62–3)* the square next to Rossio was the site of the Hospital de Todos-os-Santos (All Saints). In Pombal's new design for the Baixa, the square took on the role of the city's central marketplace. In 1885 a covered market was introduced, but this was pulled down in the 1950s. Today, the four-storey buildings are given over to hotels, shops and cafés and the square is no longer a marketplace. Perhaps its most eye-catching feature is the multitude of pigeons that perch on the pedestal supporting Leopoldo de Almeida's bronze equestrian statue of João I, erected in 1971.

Bronze statue of King João I in Praça da Figueira

There are spectacular views of the Baixa from the platform.

Café

A walkway links the lift with Largo do Carmo (currently closed for renovations).

The two cars that travel up and down can hold 25 people each.

Filigree motifs decorate the wrought-iron shaft.

Rua do Carmo

Steps down to Rua de Santa Justa

Elevador de Santa Justa ❼

Rua de Santa Justa & Largo do Carmo.
Map 7 B3. 21-342 79 44.
8:30am–9:30pm Mon–Sat,
9am–9:30pm Sun.

ALSO KNOWN as the Elevador do Carmo, this Neo-Gothic lift was built at the turn of the century by the French architect Raoul Mesnier du Ponsard, an apprentice of Alexandre Gustave Eiffel. Made of iron and embellished with filigree, it is one of the more eccentric features of the Baixa. The ticket office is located behind the tower on the steps up to Rua do Carmo.

Passengers can travel up and down inside the tower in one of two smart wood-panelled cabins with brass fittings, but the walkway linking them to the Largo do Carmo in the Bairro Alto, 32 m (105 ft) above, is currently closed for works.

The very top of the tower, reached via a tight spiral stairway, is given over to café tables. This high vantage point commands splendid views of Rossio, the grid pattern of the Baixa, the castle on the opposite hill, the river and the nearby ruins of the Carmo church. The fire that gutted the Chiado district in 1988 (*see p92*) was extinguished very close to the lift.

Café on the top platform of the Elevador de Santa Justa

Rua Augusta ❽

Map 7 B4. Rossio. 2, 14, 36, 40 & many other routes.

A LIVELY PEDESTRIANIZED street decorated with mosaic pavements and lined with boutiques and open-air cafés, Rua Augusta is the main tourist thoroughfare and the smartest in the Baixa. Street performers provide entertainment, while vendors sell lottery tickets, books and souvenirs. The eye is drawn to the triumphal Arco da Rua Augusta framing the equestrian statue of José I in Praça do Comércio. Designed by the architect Santos de Carvalho to commemorate the city's recovery from the earthquake (*see pp62–3*), the arch was completed only in 1873.

The other main thoroughfares of the Baixa are Rua da Prata (silversmiths' street) and Rua do Ouro or Rua Aurea (goldsmiths' street). Cutting across these main streets full of shops and banks are smaller streets that give glimpses up to the Bairro Alto to the west and the Castelo de São Jorge (*see pp78–9*) to the east. Many of the streets retain shops that gave them their name: there are jewellers in Rua da Prata and Rua do Ouro, shoemakers in Rua dos Sapateiros and banks in Rua do Comércio.

The most incongruous sight in the heart of the Baixa is a small section of the Roman baths, located within the Banco Comercial Português in Rua dos Correeiros. The ruins and mosaics can be seen from the street window at the rear side of the bank; alternatively you can book ahead to visit the "museum" on 21-321 10 00.

Shoppers and strollers in the pedestrianized Rua Augusta

Nossa Senhora da Conceição Velha 🌑

Rua da Alfândega. **Map** 7 C4.
📞 21-887 02 02. 🚌 9, 46, 90.
🚃 18. 🕐 8am–6pm Mon-Fri, Sun
(services only). ⬤ Aug. 🚻 📷 ♿

THE ELABORATE Manueline doorway of the church is the only feature that survived from the original 16th-century Nossa Senhora da Misericórdia, which stood here until the 1755 earthquake. The portal is decorated with a profusion of Manueline detail including angels, beasts, flowers, armillary spheres and the cross of the Order of Christ (see pp18–19). In the tympanum, the Virgin Mary spreads her protective mantle over various contemporary figures. These include Pope Leo X, Manuel I (see pp46–7) and his sister, Queen Leonor, widow of João II. It was Leonor who founded the original Misericórdia (alms-house) on the site of a former synagogue.

Unfortunately, enjoyment of the portal is hampered by the stream of traffic hurtling along Rua da Alfândega and the cars that park right in front of the church. The gloomy interior has an unusual stucco ceiling; in the second chapel on the right is a statue of Our Lady of Restelo. This came from the Belém chapel where navigators prayed before embarking on their historic voyages east.

Detail from portal of Conceição Velha

Praça do Comércio 🌑

Map 7 C5. 🚌 2, 14, 40, 46 & many other routes. 🚃 15, 18.

MORE COMMONLY known by the locals as Terreiro do Paço (Palace Square), this huge open space was the site of the royal palace for 400 years. Manuel I transferred the royal residence from Castelo de São Jorge to this more convenient location by the river in 1511. The first palace, along with its library and 70,000 books, was destroyed in the earthquake of 1755. In the rebuilding of the city, the square became the pièce de résistance of Pombal's Baixa design. The new palace occupied spacious arcaded buildings that extended around three sides of the square. After the revolution of 1910 (see pp54–5) these were converted into government administrative offices and painted Republican pink. However, they have since been repainted royal yellow.

The south side, graced by two square towers, looks across the wide expanse of the Tagus. This has always been the finest gateway to Lisbon, where royalty and ambassadors would alight and take the marble steps up from the river. You can still experience the dramatic approach by taking a ferry across from Cacilhas on the southern bank. However, today the spectacle is spoilt by the busy Avenida Infante Dom Henrique, which runs along the waterfront. In the centre of Praça do Comércio is the equestrian statue of King José I erected in 1775 by Machado de Castro, the leading Portuguese sculptor of the 18th century. The bronze horse, depicted trampling on serpents, earned the square its third name of "Black Horse Square", used by English travellers and merchants. Over the years, however, the horse has acquired a green patina.

Shaded arcades along the north side of Praça do Comércio

The impressive triumphal arch on the north side of the square leads into Rua Augusta and is the gateway to the Baixa. Opened in January 2001, in the northwest of the square, the Lisboa Welcome Center has a tourist information service, gallery, restaurants and shops. In the opposite corner, stands Lisbon's oldest café, the Martinho da Arcada, formerly a haunt of the city's literati.

On 1 February 1908, King Carlos and his son, Luís Felipe, were assassinated as they were passing through the square (see p55). In 1974 the square saw the first uprising of the Armed Forces Movement which overthrew the Caetano regime in a bloodless revolution (see p57). For many years the area was used as a car park, but today this vast open space is occasionally used for cultural events and festivals.

The triumphal arch and statue of King José I in Praça do Comércio

BAIRRO ALTO AND ESTRELA

AID OUT IN A GRID pattern in the late 16th century, the hilltop Bairro Alto is one of the most picturesque districts of the city. First settled by rich citizens who moved out of the disreputable Alfama, by the 19th century it had become a run-down area frequented by prostitutes. Today, its small workshops and family-run *tascas* (cheap restaurants) exist alongside a thriving nightlife.

Tile panel in Largo Rafael Bordalo Pinheiro, Bairro Alto

Very different in character to the heart of the Bairro Alto is the elegant commercial district known as the Chiado, where affluent Lisboetas do their shopping. To the northwest, the Estrela quarter is centred on the huge domed basilica and popular gardens. The mid-18th century district of Lapa, to the southwest, is home to foreign embassies and large, smart residences.

SIGHTS AT A GLANCE

Museums and Galleries
Museu do Chiado **5**
Museu Nacional de Arte Antiga pp96–9 **11**
Museu Nacional da Marioneta **6**

Churches
Basílica da Estrela **13**
Igreja do Carmo **2**
São Roque **1**

Historic Buildings and Districts
Chiado **3**
Palácio de São Bento **10**
Solar do Vinho do Porto **7**
Teatro Nacional de São Carlos **4**

Gardens and Belvederes
Jardim da Estrela **12**
Miradouro de São Pedro de Alcântara **8**
Praça do Príncipe Real **9**

GETTING THERE
This area is reached via the Elevador da Glória from Praça dos Restauradores, the Elevador de Santa Justa from the Baixa, or by a steep, but pleasant walk. There is also a metro station on Largo do Chiado. Tram 28 passes Bairro Alto on its way between Graça and Estrela.

KEY
Street-by-Street: Bairro Alto *pp90–91*
M Metro station
R Railway station
Funicular
Ferry boarding point
P Parking
Railway line

◁ **Art Nouveau decoration in the Chiado's Café Brasileira, once popular with writers and intellectuals**

Street-by-Street: Bairro Alto and Chiado

THE BAIRRO ALTO (high quarter) is a fascinating area of cobbled streets, adjacent to the Carmo and Chiado areas, with peeling houses and tiny grocery shops. Since the 1980s, this has been Lisbon's best-known nightlife zone, with countless small bars and restaurants alongside the older *Casas de Fado*. While some gentri-

Baroque cherub, Igreja do Carmo

fication has taken place, it is still very much a modest residential district. In contrast, the Chiado is an area of elegant shops and old-style cafés that extends down from Praça Luís de Camões towards Rua do Carmo and the Baixa. Major renovation work has taken place since a fire in 1988 *(see p92)* destroyed many of the buildings.

Praça Luís de Camões

Once a haunt of writers and intellectuals, Chiado is now an elegant shopping district. The 1920s Brasileira café, on Largo do Chiado, is adorned with gilded mirrors.

Largo do Chiado is flanked by the churches of Loreto and Nossa Senhora da Encarnação.

The statue of Eça de Queirós (1845–1900), by Teixeira Lopes, was erected in 1903. The great novelist takes inspiration from a scantily veiled muse.

Baixa/Chiado

Rua Garrett is the main shopping street of the Chiado.

```
0 metres        50
0 yards         50
```

KEY

– – – Suggested route

Tavares, at No. 37 Rua da Misericórdia, first opened as a café in 1784. Today it is an elegant restaurant *(see p405)* decorated at the turn of the century with mirrors and elaborate stucco designs.

Elevador da Glória

The Museu de Arte Sacra has an interesting exhibition of religious artefacts and explains the history of the treasures in the church of São Roque next door.

BAIXA AND AVENIDA

BAIRRO ALTO AND ESTRELA

Tejo

LOCATOR MAP
See Lisbon Street Finder map 7

Cervejaria Trindade is a popular beer hall and restaurant decorated with *azulejo* panels.

★ São Roque
Opulent mosaics and semiprecious stones adorn the Baroque Capela de São João inside the 16th-century church of São Roque ❶

Teatro da Trindade

The tile decoration on the façade of this house, erected in 1864 on Largo Rafael Bordalo Pinheiro, features allegorical figures of Science, Agriculture Industry and Commerce.

RUA DA MISERICÓRDIA

RUA NOVA DA TRINDADE

RUA DA TRINDADE

TRAVESSA DO CARMO

LARGO DO CARMO

C. DO SACRAMENTO

★ Igreja do Carmo
The graceful skeletal arches of this Carmelite church, once the largest in Lisbon, stand as a reminder of the earthquake of 1755. The chancel, and main body of the church house an archaeological museum ❷

Elevador de Santa Justa is currently closed for works until mid-2003.

The shops in Rua do Carmo have been completely restored after the devastating fire in 1988 *(see p92)*.

STAR SIGHTS

★ São Roque

★ Igreja do Carmo

Ruins of the 14th-century Igreja do Carmo seen from the Baixa

São Roque ❶

Largo Trindade Coelho. **Map** 7 A3.
(21-323 53 83. **▨** 58, 100 &
Glória lift. **◯** 8:30 am–5pm Mon –
Fri; 9:30am – 5pm Sat, Sun; 9:30am –
1pm Saint's Days. **⚱** **Museu de
Arte Sacra (** 21-323 53 81. **◯**
10am–5pm Tue–Sun. **●** public hols.
✎ **◎**

S ÃO ROQUE's plain façade
belies a remarkably
rich interior. The
church was founded
at the end of the 16th
century by the Jesuit
Order, then at the
peak of its power. In
1742 the Chapel of
St John the Baptist
(last on the left) was
commissioned by the
prodigal João V from
the Italian architects
Luigi Vanvitelli and
Nicola Salvi. Con-
structed in Rome and
embellished with lapis lazuli,
agate, alabaster, amethyst,
precious marbles, gold, silver
and mosaics, the chapel was
given the Pope's blessing in
the church of Sant'Antonio
dei Portoghesi in Rome, dis-
mantled and sent to Lisbon in
three ships.
    Among the many tiles in the
church, the oldest and most
interesting are those in the
third chapel on the right, dating
from the mid-16th century
and dedicated to São Roque
(St Roch), protector against
the plague. Other features of
the church are the scenes of
the Apocalypse painted on
the ceiling, and the sacristy,
with its coffered ceiling and
painted panels of the life of St
Francis Xavier, the 16th-century

**Tile detail in the
Chapel of St Roch**

missionary. Treasures from the
Chapel of St John, including
the silver and lapis lazuli altar
front, are in the adjoining
Museu de Arte Sacra.

Igreja do Carmo ❷

Largo do Carmo. **Map** 7 B3. **(** 21-
346 04 73. **▨** 28 & Santa Justa lift.
▨ 58. **◯** May–Sep: 10am–6pm
Tue–Sun; Oct–Apr: 10am–
1pm, 2–5pm Tue–Sun. **●** 1
Jan, Easter, 1 May, 25 Dec. **✎**

T HE GOTHIC RUINS
of this Carmelite
church, built on a
slope overlooking the
Baixa, are evocative
reminders of the dev-
astation left by the
earthquake of 1755. As
the congregation was
attending mass the
shockwaves caused
the church to collapse,
depositing tons of masonry
on to the people below.

Founded in the late 14th
century by Nuno Álvares
Pereira, the commander who
became a member of the
Carmelite Order, the church
was at one time the biggest in
Lisbon.
    Nowadays the main body of
the church and the chancel,
whose roof withstood the
shock, house an **arch-
aeological museum** with a
small, heterogeneous
collection of sarcophagi,
statuary, ceramics and mosaics.
    Among the more ancient
finds from Europe are a
remnant from a Visigothic
pillar and a Roman tomb
carved with reliefs depicting
the Muses. There are also
finds from Mexico and
South America, including
ancient mummies.
    Outside the ruins, in the
Largo do Carmo, stands the
Chafariz do Carmo, an 18th-
century fountain designed by
Ângelo Belasco, elaborately
decorated with four dolphins.

Chiado ❸

Map 7 A4. **▨** 58. **▨** 28. **Ⓜ** Chiado.

H YPOTHESES abound for the
origin of the word Chiado,
in use since 1567. One of the
most interesting recalls the
creak (chiar) of the wheels of
the carts as they negotiated the
area's steep slopes. A second
theory refers to the nickname
given to the 16th-century poet
António Ribeiro, "O Chiado".
An area traditionally known

THE CHIADO FIRE

On 25 August 1988 a disastrous fire began in a store in
Rua do Carmo, the street that
links the Baixa with the Bairro
Alto. Fire engines were unable
to enter this pedestrianized
street and the fire spread into
Rua Garrett. Along with shops
and offices, many important
18th-century buildings were
destroyed, the worst damage
being in Rua do Carmo. The
renovation project, which is
now complete, has preserved
many original façades, and
was headed by Portuguese
architect, Álvaro Siza Vieira.

**Firemen attending the raging
fire in Rua do Carmo**

Stalls and circle of the 18th-century Teatro Nacional de São Carlos

for its intellectual associations, various statues of literary figures can be found here. Fernando Pessoa, Portugal's most famous 20th-century poet, is seated at a table outside the Café Brasileira. Established in the 1920s, this was a favourite rendezvous of intellectuals.

The name Chiado is often used to mean just Rua Garrett, the main shopping street of the area, named after the author and poet João Almeida Garrett (1799–1854). This elegant street, which descends from Largo do Chiado towards the Baixa, is known for its clothes shops, cafés and bookshops. Devastated by fire in 1988, the former elegance of this quarter has been recently restored.

On Largo do Chiado stand two Baroque churches: the Italian church, Igreja do Loreto, on the north side and opposite, Nossa Senhora da Encarnação, whose exterior walls are partly decorated with *azulejos*.

Teatro Nacional de São Carlos ❹

Rua Serpa Pinto 9. **Map** 7 A4. 📞 *21-325 30 45.* 🚌 *58, 100.* 🚊 *28.* Ⓜ *Baixa-Chiado.* ◯ *for performances..*

REPLACING a former opera house which was ruined by the earthquake of 1755, the Teatro de São Carlos was built in 1792–5 by José da Costa e Silva. Designed on the lines of La Scala in Milan and the San Carlo in Naples, the building has a beautifully proportioned façade and an enchanting Rococo interior. Views of the exterior, however, are spoiled by the car park, invariably crammed, which occupies the square in front. The opera season lasts from September to June, but concerts and ballets are also staged here at other times of the year.

Museu do Chiado ❺

Rua Serpa Pinto 4–6. **Map** 7 A5. 📞 *21-343 21 48.* 🚌 *58, 100.* 🚊 *28.* Ⓜ *Baixa-Chiado.* ◯ *10am–6pm Wed–Sun, 2–6pm Tue.* ● *1 Jan, Easter, 1 May, 25 Dec.* ♿

THE NATIONAL MUSEUM of Contemporary Art, whose collection of 1850–1950 paintings could no longer be described as contemporary, changed its name in 1994 and moved to a stylishly restored warehouse. The paintings and sculpture are arranged over three floors in 12 rooms. Each room has a different theme illustrating the development from

Romanticism to Modernism. The majority are works by Portuguese, often showing the marked influence from other European countries. This is particularly noticeable in the 19th-century landscape painters who had contact with artists from the French Barbizon School. The few international works of art on display include a collection of drawings by Rodin (1840–1917) and some French sculpture from the late 19th century. There are also temporary exhibitions which are held for "very new artists, preferably inspired by the permanent collection".

Grotesque puppet in Museu da Marioneta

Museu da Marioneta ❻

Convento das Bernardas, Rua da Esperança 146. **Map** 4 D3. 📞 *21-394 28 10.* 🚌 *6, 13, 27, 49, 60.* 🚊 *15.* Ⓜ *Cais do Sodré.* ◯ *10am–1pm, 2–6pm Wed–Sun.* ● *1 Jan, 1 May, 25 Dec.* ♿

THIS SMALL, ECCENTRIC puppet museum moved to this elegantly refurbished convent building in 2001. The collection includes characters dating from 17th-and 18th-century theatre and opera, among them devils, knights, jesters and satirical figures. The puppets are finely crafted but a substantial proportion of them possess gruesome, contorted features, which are unlikely to appeal to small children. The museum explains the history of the art form and runs videos of puppet shows. It is worth calling ahead to see if a live performance is being held on the small stage.

Art Nouveau façade of the popular Café Brasileira in the Chiado

The wide selection of port at the Solar do Vinho do Porto

Solar do Vinho do Porto ❼

Rua de São Pedro de Alcântara 45.
Map 4 F2. 🕻 21-347 57 07.
🚌 58. 🚋 28, Elevador da Glória.
🕐 2pm–midnight Mon–Sat.
⬤ public hols.

THE PORTUGUESE WORD *solar*
means mansion or manor
house and the Solar do Vinho
do Porto occupies the ground
floor of an 18th-century mansion. The building was once
owned by the German architect, Johann Friedrich Ludwig
(Ludovice), who built the
monastery at Mafra *(see p152)*.
The port wine institute of
Oporto runs a pleasant if
dated bar here for the
promotion of port. Nearly 200
types of port are listed in the
lengthy drinks menu, with
every producer represented
and including some rarities.
Unfortunately, many of
the listed wines are often
unavailable. All but the
vintage ports are sold by the
glass, with prices ranging
from one euro for the
simplest ruby to 70 euros for
a glass of 40-year-old tawney.

Miradouro de São Pedro de Alcântara ❽

Rua de São Pedro de Alcântara. **Map** 7
A2. 🚌 58. 🚋 28, Elevador da Glória.

THE BELVEDERE *(miradouro)*
commands a sweeping
view of eastern Lisbon, seen
across the Baixa. A tiled map,
conveniently placed against
the balustrade, helps you
locate the landmarks in the
city below. The panorama
extends from the battlements
of the Castelo de São
Jorge *(see pp78–9)*,
clearly seen surrounded
by trees on the hill to
the southeast, to the
18th-century church of
Penha da França in the
northwest. The large
monastery complex of
the Igreja da Graça *(see
p75)* is also visible on
the hill, and in the dis-
tance São Vicente de
Fora *(see p73)* is recognizable
by the symmetrical towers
that flank its white façade.

Benches and ample shade
from the trees make this
terrace a pleasant stop after
the steep walk up Calçada da
Glória from the Baixa. Alternatively, the yellow funicular,
Elevador da Glória, will drop
you off nearby.

The memorial in the garden,
erected in 1904, depicts
Eduardo Coelho (1835–89),
founder of the newspaper
Diário de Notícias, and below
him a ragged paper boy running with copies of the famous

daily. This area was once the
centre of the newspaper industry, however the modern
printing presses have now
moved to more spacious
premises west of the city.

The view is most attractive at
sunset and by night when the
castle is floodlit and the terrace
becomes a popular meeting
point for young Lisboetas.

Praça do Príncipe Real ❾

Map 4 F1. 🚌 58, 100.

Playing cards in Praça do Príncipe Real

LAID OUT IN 1860 as a prime
residential quarter, the
square still retains an air of
affluence. Smartly painted mansions surround a particularly
pleasant park with an open-air
café, statuary and some splendid robinia, magnolia and
Judas trees. The branches of a
huge cedar tree have been
trained on a trellis, creating a
wide shady spot for the locals
who play cards beneath it. On
the large square, at No. 26, the
eye-catching pink and white
Neo-Moorish building with
domes and pinnacles is part
of Lisbon university.

View across the city to Castelo de São Jorge from Miradouro de São Pedro de Alcântara

Museu Nacional de Arte Antiga ⓫

See pp96–9.

Jardim da Estrela ⓬

Praça da Estrela. **Map** 4 D2.
🚌 *9, 20, 38.* 🚋 *25, 28.*
🕐 *7am–midnight daily.*

Attractive wrought-iron music pavilion in Jardim da Estrela

Palácio de São Bento ⓾

Largo das Cortes. **Map** 4 E2.
📞 *21-391 90 00.* 🚌 *6, 49, 100.* 🚋
28. 🕐 *by appt only.*

Aᴌsᴏ ᴋɴᴏwɴ as the Assembleia da República, this enormous white Neo-Classical building is the seat of the Portuguese Parliament. It started life at the end of the 16th century as the Benedictine monastery of São Bento. After the dissolution of the religious orders in 1834, the building became the seat of Parliament, known as the Palácio das Cortes. The interior is suitably grandiose with marble pillars and Neo-Classical statues.

Lᴀɪᴅ ᴏᴜᴛ ɪɴ the middle of the 19th century, opposite the Basílica da Estrela, the popular gardens are a focal part of the Estrela quarter. Local families congregate here at weekends to feed the ducks and carp in the lake, sit at the waterside café or wander among the flower beds, plants and trees. The formal gardens are planted with herbaceous borders and shrubs surrounding plane trees and elms. The central feature of the park is a green wrought-iron bandstand, decorated with elegant filigree, where musicians strike up in the summer months. This was built in 1884 and originally stood on the Passeio Público, before the creation of Avenida da Liberdade (*see p44*).

The English Cemetery to the north of the gardens is best known as the burial place of Henry Fielding (1707–54), the English novelist and playwright who died in Lisbon at the age of 47. The *Journal of a Voyage to Lisbon*, published posthumously in 1775, recounts his last voyage to Portugal made in a fruitless attempt to recover his failing health.

Basílica da Estrela ⓭

Praça da Estrela. **Map** 4 D2.
📞 *21-396 09 15.* 🚌 *9, 38.*
🚋 *25, 28.* 🕐 *8am–1pm,
3–8pm daily.* 🚹 📷

The tomb of the pious Maria I in the Basílica da Estrela

Iɴ ᴛʜᴇ sᴇᴄᴏɴᴅ half of the 18th century Maria I (*see p165*), daughter of José I, vowed she would build a church if she bore a son and heir to the throne. Her wish was granted and construction of the basilica began in 1779. Her son José, however, died of smallpox two years before the completion of the church in 1790. The huge domed basilica, set on a hill in the west of the city, is one of Lisbon's great landmarks. A simpler version of the basilica at Mafra (*see p152*), the church was built by architects from the Mafra School in late Baroque and Neo-Classical style. The façade is flanked by twin belltowers and decorated with an array of statues of saints and allegorical figures.

The spacious, somewhat awe-inspiring interior, where light streams down from the pierced dome, is clad in grey, pink and yellow marble. The elaborate Empire-style tomb of Queen Maria I, who died in Brazil, lies in the right transept. Locked in a room nearby is Machado de Castro's extraordinary Nativity scene, composed of over 500 cork and terracotta figures. (To see it, ask the sacristan.)

Neo-Classical façade and stairway of Palácio de São Bento

Museu Nacional de Arte Antiga ⓫

PORTUGAL'S NATIONAL ART COLLECTION is housed in a 17th-century palace that was built for the counts of Alvor. In 1770 it was acquired by the Marquês de Pombal and remained in the possession of his family for over a century. Inaugurated in 1884, the museum is known to locals as the Casa das Janelas Verdes, referring to the former green windows of the palace. In 1940 a modern annexe (including the main façade) was added. This was built on the site of the St Albert Carmelite monastery, which was destroyed in the 1755 earthquake *(see pp62–3)*. The only surviving feature was the chapel, now integrated into the museum.

15th-century wood carving of St George

★ **St Jerome**
This masterly portrayal of old age by Albrecht Dürer expresses one of the central dilemmas of Renaissance humanism: the ephemeral nature of man (1521).

GALLERY GUIDE
The ground floor contains 14th–19th-century European paintings, as well as some decorative arts and furniture. Oriental and African art, Chinese and Portuguese ceramics and silver, gold and jewellery are on display on the first floor. The top floor is dedicated to Portuguese art and sculpture.

The Temptations of St Antony by Hieronymus Bosch

Stairs down to 🖥 🚻 ♿

St Augustine by Piero della Francesca

60 61 62 59 63 58 64 57 65 56 66 55 68 54 67 53 69 52 70 51 49 50

The Virgin and Child and Saints
Hans Holbein the Elder's balanced composition of a Sacra Conversazione *(1519) is set among majestic Renaissance architecture with saints in detailed contemporary costumes sewing or reading.*

Ecce Homo
Painted in the late 15th century by an artist of the Portuguese school, the unusual depiction of the accused Jesus, with the shroud lowered over his eyes, retains an air of dignified calm, despite the crown of thorns, the rope and the specks of blood.

KEY TO FLOORPLAN

- ☐ European art
- ☐ Portuguese painting and sculpture
- ☐ Portuguese and Chinese ceramics
- ☐ Oriental and African art
- ☐ Silver, gold and jewellery
- ☐ Decorative arts
- ☐ Chapel of St Albert
- ☐ Textiles and furniture
- ☐ Non-exhibition space

STAR EXHIBITS

★ **St Jerome by Dürer**

★ **Namban Screens**

★ **Adoration of St Vincent by Gonçalves**

★ Adoration of St Vincent
This polyptych, attributed to Nuno Gonçalves, dates from about 1470 (see p98).

First floor

Second floor

Faïence Violin
The museum's ceramics collection includes many decorative items made in Portugal for the royal family. This 19th-century objet d'art by Wenceslau Cifka is decorated with the royal coat of arms and portraits of the Italian Baroque composers, Scarlatti and Corelli.

★ Namban Screens
This detail from one of the museum's 16th-century Japanese screens illustrates a contemporary trading scene and the Portuguese fashion at the time.

Entrance

Ground floor

The Chapel of St Albert, dating from the 16th century, has a sumptuous Baroque interior decorated with blue and white *azulejos*.

Ivory Salt Cellar
Portuguese knights and dignitaries are carved on this 16th-century ivory salt cellar from Benin, West Africa.

Exploring the Collections of the Museu Nacional de Arte Antiga

THE MUSEUM has the largest collection of paintings in Portugal and is particularly strong on early religious works by Portuguese artists. The majority of exhibits came from convents and monasteries following the suppression of religious orders in 1834. There are also extensive displays of sculpture, silverware, porcelain and applied arts giving an overview of Portuguese art from the Middle Ages to the 19th century, complemented by many fine European and Oriental pieces. The theme of the discoveries is ever-present, illustrating Portugal's links with Brazil, Africa, India, China and Japan.

EUROPEAN ART

PAINTINGS by European artists, dating from the 14th to the 19th century, are arranged chronologically on the ground floor. Unlike the Portuguese art, most of the works were donated from private collections, contributing to the great diversity of works on display. The first rooms, dedicated to the 14th and 15th centuries, trace the transition from medieval Gothic taste to the aesthetic of the Renaissance.

The painters best represented in the European Art section are 16th-century German and Flemish artists. Notable works are *St Jerome* by Albrecht Dürer (1471–1528), *Salomé* by Lucas Cranach the Elder (1472–1553), *Virgin and Child* by Hans Memling (c.1430–94) and *The Temptations of St Antony* by the great Flemish master of fantasy, Hieronymus Bosch (1450–1516). Of the small number of Italian works, the finest are *St Augustine* by

the Renaissance painter, Piero della Francesca (c.1420–92) and a graceful early altar panel representing the Resurrection by Raphael (1483–1520).

Some Portuguese painters, including Josefa de Óbidos (*see p51*) and Gregório Lopes (1490–1550), are also displayed in the galleries of European art.

PORTUGUESE PAINTING AND SCULPTURE

MANY OF THE EARLIEST works of art are by the Portuguese primitive painters who were influenced by the realistic detail of Flemish artists. There had always been strong trading links between Portugal and Flanders and in the 15th and 16th centuries several painters of Flemish origin, for example Frey Carlos of Évora, set up workshops in Portugal.

Pride of place, however, goes to the São Vicente de Fora polyptych, the most important painting of 15th-century Portuguese art and one that has

Central panel of *The Temptations of St Antony* by Hieronymus Bosch

ADORATION OF ST VINCENT

Cistercian monks from Alcobaça (*see pp178–9*) | Friar

Fisherman

become a symbol of national pride in the Age of Discovery. Painted in about 1467–70, and generally believed to be by Nuno Gonçalves, the altarpiece portrays the *Adoration of St Vincent*, patron saint of Portugal, surrounded by dignitaries, knights and monks as well as fishermen and beggars. The accurate portrayal of contemporary figures makes the painting an invaluable historical and social document.

Later works include a 16th-century portrait of the young Dom Sebastião (*see pp46–7*) by Cristóvão de Morais and paintings by Neo-Classical artist Domingos António de Sequeira. The museum's sculpture collection has many Gothic polychrome stone and wood statues of Christ, the Virgin and saints. There are also statues from the 17th century and an 18th-century nativity scene by Machado de Castro in the Chapel of St Albert.

PORTUGUESE AND CHINESE CERAMICS

THE EXTENSIVE collection of ceramics enables visitors to trace the evolution of Chinese porcelain and Portuguese faïence and to see the influence of oriental designs on

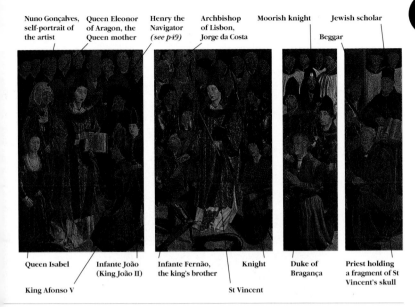

Nuno Gonçalves, self-portrait of the artist

Queen Eleanor of Aragon, the Queen mother

Henry the Navigator *(see p49)*

Archbishop of Lisbon, Jorge da Costa

Moorish knight

Jewish scholar

Beggar

Queen Isabel

Infante João (King João II)

Infante Fernão, the king's brother

Knight

Duke of Bragança

Priest holding a fragment of St Vincent's skull

King Afonso V

St Vincent

Portuguese pieces, and vice versa. From the 16th century Portuguese ceramics show a marked influence of Ming, and conversely the Chinese pieces bear Portuguese motifs such as coats of arms. By the mid-18th century individual potters had begun to develop an increasingly personalized, European style, with popular, rustic designs. The collection also includes ceramics from Italy, Spain and the Netherlands.

Chinese porcelain vase, 16th century

ORIENTAL AND AFRICAN ART

THE COLLECTION of ivories and furniture, with their European motifs, further illustrates the reciprocal influences of Portugal and her colonies. The 16th-century predilection for the exotic gave rise to a huge demand for items such as carved ivory hunting horns from Africa. The fascinating 16th-century Japanese Namban screens show the Portuguese trading in Japan. *Namban-jin* (barbarians from the south) is the name the Japanese gave to the Portuguese.

SILVER, GOLD AND JEWELLERY

AMONG THE MUSEUM'S fine collection of ecclesiastical treasures are King Sancho I's gold cross (1214) and the Belém monstrance (1506) *(see p20)*. Also on display is the 16th-century Madre de Deus reliquary which allegedly holds a thorn from the crown of Christ. Highlight of the foreign collection is a sumptuous set of rare 18th-century silver tableware. Commissioned by José I from the Paris workshop of Thomas Germain, the 1,200 pieces include intricately decorated tureens, sauce boats and salt cellars. The rich collection of jewels came from the convents, originally donated by members of the nobility and wealthy bourgeoisie on entering the religious orders.

APPLIED ARTS

FURNITURE, tapestries and textiles, liturgical vestments and bishops' mitres are among the wide range of objects on display. The furniture collection includes many Medieval and Renaissance pieces, as well as Baroque and Neo-classical items from the reigns of King João V, King José and Queen Maria I. Of the foreign furniture, French pieces from the 18th century are prominent.

The textiles include 17th-century bedspreads, tapestries, many of Flemish origin, such as the *Baptism of Christ* (16th century), embroidered rugs and Arraiolos carpets *(see p301)*.

Gold Madre de Deus reliquary inlaid with precious stones (c.1502)

BELÉM

AT THE MOUTH of the River Tagus, where the caravels set sail on their voyages of discovery, Belém is inextricably linked with Portugal's Golden Age *(see pp46–9)*. When Manuel I came to power in 1495 he reaped the profits of those heady days of expansion, building grandiose monuments and churches that mirrored the spirit of the time. Two of the finest examples of the exuberant and exotic Manueline style of architecture *(see pp20–21)* are the Mosteiro dos Jerónimos and the Torre de Belém.

Generosity, statue at entrance to Palácio da Ajuda

Today Belém is a spacious, relatively green suburb with many museums, parks and gardens, as well as an attractive riverside setting with cafés and a promenade. On sunny days there is a distinct seaside feel to the embankment.

Before the Tagus receded, the monks in the monastery used to look out onto the river and watch the boats set forth. In contrast today several lanes of traffic along the busy Avenida da Índia cut central Belém off from the picturesque waterfront, and silver and yellow trains rattle regularly past.

SIGHTS AT A GLANCE

Museums and Galleries
Museu de Arte Popular ⑩
Museu da Marinha ⑦
Museu Nacional de Arqueologia ⑤
Museu Nacional dos Coches ②
Planetário Calouste Gulbenkian ⑥

Parks and Gardens
Jardim Agrícola Tropical ③
Jardim Botânico da Ajuda ⑭

Churches and Monasteries
Ermida de São Jerónimo ⑫
Igreja da Memória ⑬
Mosteiro dos Jerónimos pp106–7 ④

Historic Buildings
Palácio de Belém ①
Palácio Nacional da Ajuda ⑮
Torre de Belém p110 ⑪

Monuments
Monument to the Discoveries ⑨

Cultural Centres
Centro Cultural de Belém ⑧

KEY

▦ Street-by-Street: Belém pp102–3

🚉 Railway station

⛴ Ferry boarding point

🅿 Parking

═ Railway line

GETTING THERE
The best way to reach Belém is to take tram 15 from Praça do Comércio along the busy waterfront. Buses 14, 27, 28, 43, 49, 51 and 112 also go to Belém. Slow trains from Cais do Sodré to Oeiras stop at Belém.

◁ Nave of Santa Maria de Belém, the church of the Jerónimos monastery

Street-by-Street: Belém

Stone caravel,
Jerónimos
monastery

PORTUGAL'S FORMER maritime glory, expressed in the imposing, exuberant buildings such as the Jerónimos monastery, is evident all around Belém. In Salazar's *(see p56)* attempted revival of awareness of Portugal's Golden Age, the area along the waterfront, which had silted up since the days of the caravels, was restructured to celebrate the former greatness of the nation. Praça do Império was laid out for the Exhibition of the Portuguese World in 1940 and Praça Afonso de Albuquerque was dedicated to Portugal's first viceroy of India. The royal Palácio de Belém, restored with gardens and a riding school by João V in the 18th century, briefly housed the royal family after the 1755 earthquake.

★ Mosteiro dos Jerónimos
Vaulted arcades and richly carved columns adorned with foliage, exotic animals and navigational instruments decorate the Manueline cloister of the Jerónimos monastery ❹

LARGO
DOS
JERÓNIMOS

PRAÇA DO IMPÉRIO

Museu Nacional de Arqueologia
Archaeological finds ranging from an Iron Age gold bracelet to Moorish artefacts are among the interesting exhibits on display ❺

Torre
de Belém
(see p110)

STAR SIGHTS

★ Mosteiro dos Jerónimos

★ Museu Nacional dos Coches

KEY

– – – Suggested route

Praça do Império, an impressive square that opens out in front of the monastery, is lit up on special occasions with a colourful light display in the central fountain.

Rua Vieira Portuense runs along a small park. Its colourful 16th- and 17th-century houses contrast with the typically imposing buildings in Belém.

Jardim Agrícola Tropical
Exotic plants and trees gathered from Portugal's former colonies fill these peaceful gardens that were once part of the Palácio de Belém ❸

LOCATOR MAP
See Lisbon Street Finder maps 1 & 2

Antiga Confeitaria de Belém, a 19th-century café, sells *pastéis de Belém*, rich custard in a flaky pastry cup.

TRAVESSA DOS FERREIROS

T. MARTA PINTO

RUA DE BELÉM

Central Lisbon

RUA VIEIRA PORTUENSE

Palácio de Belém
Also known as the Palácio Cor de Rosa (pink palace) because of its faded pink façade, the 16th-century former royal palace is the official residence of the President of the Republic of Portugal ❶

0 metres   50
0 yards   50

★ Museu Nacional dos Coches
This 18th-century coach used by the ambassador to Pope Clement XI is part of the collection in the old riding school of the Palácio de Belém ❷

Praça Afonso de Albuquerque is named after the first Portuguese viceroy of India. A Neo-Manueline column in the centre bears his statue, with scenes from his life carved on the base.

Palácio de Belém ①

Praça Afonso de Albuquerque.
Map 1 C4. 🕿 21-361 46 00. 🚌 14,
27, 28, 43, 49, 51. 🚋 15. 🚈 Belém.
🕐 9am–1pm, 3rd Sun of month. 📷

BUILT BY the Conde de
Aveiras in 1559 before the
Tagus had receded, this summer palace once had gardens
bordering the river. In the
18th century it was bought by
João V, who had acquired vast
wealth through gold from
Brazil *(see pp52–3)*. He radi-
cally altered the palace, added
a riding school and rendered
the interior suitably lavish for
his amorous liaisons.

When the great earthquake
struck in 1755 *(see pp62–3)*,
the king, José I, and his family
were staying here and thus
survived the devastation of
central Lisbon. Fearing another
earth tremor, the royal family
temporarily set up camp in
tents in the palace grounds
and the palace interior was
used as a hospital. Today the
elegant pink building, which
resembles a country estate, is
the residence of the President
of Portugal.

Pink façade of the Palácio de Belém, home of the President of Portugal

Museu Nacional dos Coches ②

Praça Afonso de Albuquerque.
Map 2 D4. 🕿 21-361 08 50. 🚌 14,
27, 28, 43, 49, 51. 🚋 15. 🚈 Belém.
🕐 10am–5:30pm Tue–Sun.
1 Jan, Easter, 1 May, 25 Dec. 💷 📷

THE MUSEUM'S collection of
coaches is arguably the
finest in Europe. Occupying
the east wing of the Palácio
de Belém, this was formerly
the riding school built by the
Italian architect Giacomo
Azzolini in 1726. Seated in
the upper

gallery, the royal family used to
watch their beautiful Lusitanian
horses *(see p296)* performing
in the arena. In 1905 the riding
school was turned into a museum by King Carlos's wife,
Dona Amélia, whose pink
riding cloak is on display.

Made in Portugal, Italy,
France, Austria and Spain, the
coaches span three centuries
and range from the plain to
the preposterous. The main
gallery, in Louis XVI style
with splendid painted ceiling,
is the setting for two straight,
regimented rows of coaches
created for Portuguese royalty.

The collection starts with
the comparatively plain 17th-
century red leather and
wood coach of Philip II
of Spain *(see pp50–51)*. The
coaches become increasingly
sumptuous, interiors lined
with red velvet and gold,
exteriors profusely carved
and decorated with allegories and royal coats of arms.
The rows end with three
huge Baroque coaches made
in Rome for the Portuguese
ambassador to the Vatican,
Dom Rodrigo Almeida e
Menezes, the Marquês de
Abrantes. The epitome of
pomp and extravagance,
but not necessarily of
comfort, these 5-tonne
carriages are embellished
with a plush interior and
life-size gilded statues.

The neighbouring gallery
has further examples of
royal carriages, including
two-wheeled cabriolets,
landaus and pony-drawn
chaises used by young
members of the royal
family. There is also a 19th-
century Lisbon cab, painted
black and green, the colours of

Rear view of a coach built in 1716 for the Marquês de
Abrantes, the Portuguese ambassador to Pope Clement XI

taxis right up to the 1990s. The 18th-century Eyeglass Chaise, whose black leather hood is pierced by sinister eye-like windows, was made during the era of Pombal *(see pp52–3)* when lavish decoration was discouraged. The upper gallery has a collection of harnesses, court costumes and portraits of members of the royal family.

Jardim Agrícola Tropical ❸

Largo dos Jerónimos. **Map** 1 C4. 📞 21-362 02 10. 🚌 27, 28, 43, 49, 51, 112. 🚊 15. 🕐 10am–5pm Tue–Fri, 11am– 6pm Sat & Sun. ● public hols. 🎫 Tue–Fri only. ♿ **Museu Tropical** 🕐 by appt only.

Aᴸsᴼ ᴋɴᴼᴡɴ as the Jardim do Ultramar, this peaceful park with ponds, waterfowl and peacocks, attracts surprisingly few visitors. Laid out at the beginning of the 20th century as the research centre of the Institute for Tropical Sciences, it is more of an arboretum than a flower garden. The emphasis is on rare and endangered tropical and subtropical plants. Among the most striking are dragon trees, native to the Canary Islands and Madeira, monkey puzzle trees from South America and a handsome avenue of lofty Washington palms. The oriental garden with its streams, bridges and hibiscus is heralded by a large Chinese-style gateway which represented Macau in the Exhibition of the Portuguese World in 1940 *(see p102)*.

Visigothic gold buckle, Museu de Arqueologia

The research buildings and **Museu Tropical** are housed in the Palácio dos Condes da Calheta, whose interior walls are covered with *azulejos* spanning three centuries. The museum has 50,000 dried plant specimens and 2,414 samples of wood.

Mosteiro dos Jerónimos ❹

See pp106–7.

Washington palms in the Jardim Agrícola Tropical

Museu Nacional de Arqueologia ❺

Praça do Império. **Map** 1 B4. 📞 21-362 00 00. 🚌 27, 28, 43, 49, 51, 112. 🚊 15. 🕐 10am–6pm Wed–Sun, 2pm– 6pm Tue. ● 1 Jan, Easter, 1 May, 25 Dec. 🎫 📷 ♿

Tʜᴇ ʟᴼɴɢ west wing of the Mosteiro dos Jerónimos *(see pp106–7)*, formerly the monks' dormitory, has been a museum since 1893. Reconstructed in the middle of the 19th century, the building is a poor imitation of the Manueline original. The museum houses Portugal's main archaeological research centre and the exhibits, from sites all over the country, include a gold Iron Age bracelet found in the Alentejo and Visigothic jewellery from Beja *(see p311)*, Roman ornaments and early 8th-century Moorish artefacts. The main Egyptian and Greco-Roman section is strong on funerary art, featuring figurines, tombstones, masks, terracotta amulets and funeral cones inscribed with hieroglyphics alluding to the solar system. The dimly-lit Room of Treasures has an exquisite collection of coins, necklaces, bracelets and other jewellery dating from 1800–500 BC. Along with other parts of the

museum, this room has been refurbished to allow more of the magnificent jewellery, unseen by the public for decades, to be shown.

Planetário Calouste Gulbenkian ❻

Praça do Império. **Map** 1 B4. 📞 21-362 00 02. 🚌 27, 28, 43, 49, 51, 112. 🚊 15. 🕐 for shows: 4pm & 5pm Sat & Sun (also school hols: 11am, 3pm & 4:15pm Wed & Thu). Special shows for children 11am Sun. ● public hols. 🎫 📷 ♿

Fɪɴᴀɴᴄᴇᴅ ʙʏ the Gulbenkian Foundation *(see p119)* and built in 1965, this modern building sits incongruously beside the Jerónimos monastery. Inside, the Planetarium reveals the mysteries of the cosmos. There are shows in Portuguese, English and French explaining the movement of the stars and our solar system, as well as presentations on more specialist themes, such as the constellations or the Star of Bethlehem (Belém).

The dome of the Planetário Calouste Gulbenkian

Mosteiro dos Jerónimos 4

Armillary sphere in the cloister

A MONUMENT TO THE WEALTH of the Age of Discovery *(see pp48–9)*, the monastery is the culmination of Manueline architecture *(see pp20–21)*. Commissioned by Manuel I in around 1501, after Vasco da Gama's return from his historic voyage, it was financed largely by "pepper money", a tax levied on spices precious stones and gold. Various masterbuilders worked on the building, the most notable of whom was Diogo Boitac, replaced by João de Castilho in 1517. The monastery was cared for by the Order of St Jerome (Hieronymites) until 1834, when all religious orders were disbanded.

Tomb of Vasco da Gama
The 19th-century tomb of the explorer (see p108) *is carved with ropes, armillary spheres and other seafaring symbols.*

Refectory
The walls of the refectory are tiled with 18th-century azulejos. The panel at the northern end depicts the Feeding of the Five Thousand.

The modern wing, built in 1850 in Neo-Manueline style, houses the Museu Nacional de Arqueologia *(see p105).*

The fountain is in the shape of a lion, the heraldic animal of St Jerome.

The west portal was designed by the French sculptor Nicolau Chanterène.

Entrance to church and cloister

Gallery

View of the Monastery
This 17th-century scene by Felipe Lobo shows women at a fountain in front of the Mosteiro dos Jerónimos.

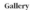

STAR FEATURES

★ **South Portal**

★ **Cloister**

★ **Cloister**
João de Castilho's pure Manueline creation was completed in 1544. Delicate tracery and richly carved images decorate the arches and balustrades.

VISITORS' CHECKLIST

Praça do Império. **Map** 1 B4.
21-362 00 34. 27, 28, 43, 49, 51, 112. 15. May–Sep: 10am–6pm Tue–Sun; Oct–Apr: 10am–5pm Tue–Sun. public hols. cloisters only.

Nave
The spectacular vaulting in the church of Santa Maria is held aloft by slender octagonal pillars. These rise like palm trees to the roof creating a feeling of space and harmony.

The chapterhouse holds the tomb of Alexandre Herculano (1810–77), historian and first mayor of Belém.

The chancel was commissioned in 1572 by Dona Catarina, wife of João III.

The tombs of Manuel I, his wife Dona Maria, João III and Catarina are supported by elephants.

★ **South Portal**
The strict geometrical architecture of the portal is almost obscured by the exuberant decoration. João de Castilho unites religious themes, such as this image of St Jerome, with the secular, exalting the kings of Portugal.

Tomb of King Sebastião
The tomb of the "longed for" Dom Sebastião stands empty. The young king never returned from battle in 1578 (see p47).

Façade of the Museu de Marinha

Museu de Marinha ⑦

Praça do Império. **Map** 1 B4. 🕻 *21-362 00 19.* 🚌 *27, 28, 43, 49, 51, 112.* 🚃 *15.* ⭘ *10am–6pm (Oct–Jun: 5pm) Tue–Sun.* ⬤ *public hols.* 📷 🅿 ♿

THE MARITIME MUSEUM was inaugurated in 1962 in the west wing of the Jerónimos monastery *(see pp106–7)*. It was here, in the chapel built by Henry the Navigator *(see p49)*, that mariners took mass before embarking on their historic voyages. A hall about the Discoveries illustrates the rapid progress in shipbuilding from the mid-15th century, capitalizing on the experience of the long-distance ex-plorers. Small replicas show the transition from the bark to the lateen-rigged caravel, through the faster square-rigged caravel, to the Portuguese *nau*. Also relating to the Discoveries are navigational instru-ments, astrolabes and replicas of 16th-cen-tury maps showing the world as it was known then. The stone pillars, carved with the Cross of the Knights of Christ, are replicas of the types of *padrão* set up as monuments to Portu-guese sovereignty on the lands discovered. Beyond the Hall of Discoveries a series of rooms displaying models of modern Portuguese ships leads on to the Royal Quarters where you can see the exquisitely furnished wood-panelled cabin of King Carlos and Queen Amélia from the royal yacht *Amélia*, built in Scotland in 1900.

The modern, incongruous pavilion opposite houses ori-ginal royal barges, the most extravagant of which is the royal brig built in 1780 for Maria I. The collection ends with a display of seaplanes, including the *Santa Clara* which made the first crossing of the South Atlantic in 1922.

VASCO DA GAMA (c.1460–1524)

In 1498 Vasco da Gama sailed around the Cape of Good Hope and opened the sea route to India *(see pp48–9)*. Although the Hindu ruler of Calicut, who received him wearing diamond and ruby rings, was not impressed by his humble offerings of cloth and wash basins, da Gama returned to Portugal with a cargo of spices. In 1502 he sailed again to India, establishing Portuguese trade routes in the Indian Ocean. João III nominated him Viceroy of India in 1524, but he died of a fever soon after.

16th-century painting of Vasco da Gama in Goa

Centro Cultural de Belém ⑧

Praça do Império. **Map** 1 B5. 🕻 *21-361 24 00.* 🚌 *27, 28, 29, 43, 49, 51, 112.* 🚃 *15.* **Exhibition Centre** ⭘ *11am–8pm.* 📷 ♿

THE CONSTRUCTION of a stark modern building directly between the Jéronimos mon-astery and the Tagus was clearly controversial. Built in 1990 as the headquarters of the Portuguese presidency of the European Community, it opened as a cultural and conference centre in 1993. It stresses music, performing arts and photography, with a large **Exhibition Centre** and design museum that displays choice pieces dating from 1937.

Both the café and restaurant spill out onto the ramparts of the building whose peaceful gardens of olive trees and geo-metric lawns mask the noise of the traffic below and look out over the quay and river.

The modern complex of the Centro Cultural de Belém

Monument to the Discoveries ⑨

Padrão dos Descobrimentos, Avenida de Brasília. **Map** 1 C5. 🕻 *21-303 19 50.* 🚌 *28, 29, 43, 49, 51, 112.* 🚃 *15.* ⭘ *9am–5pm (7pm Jul–Aug) Tue–Sun.* ⬤ *public hols.* 📷 *for lift.* 📷

STANDING PROMINENTLY on the Belém waterfront, this mas-sive angular monument, the Padrão dos Descobrimentos, was built in 1960 to mark the 500th anniversary of the death of Henry the Navigator *(see p49)*. The 52-m (170-ft) high monument, commissioned by the Salazar regime, commem-orates the mariners, royal patrons and all those who participated in the rapid devel-opment of the Portuguese Age

The huge pavement compass in front of the Monument to the Discoveries

Museu de Arte Popular ⑩

Avenida de Brasília. **Map** 1 B5. 21-301 12 82. 27, 28, 43, 49, 51, 112. 15. 10am–12:30pm, 2–5pm Tue–Sun. public hols.

THE DRAB BUILDING on the waterfront, between the Monument to the Discoveries and the Torre de Belém (see p110), houses the museum of Portuguese folk art and traditional handicrafts, opened in 1948. While the rooms housing the permanent collections are closed for alterations indefinitely, a temporary exhibition space is open. The exhibits, which are arranged by province, include local pottery, agricultural tools, costumes, musical instruments, jewellery and brightly coloured saddles. The display gives a vivid indication of the diversity between the different regions. Each area has its speciality such as the colourful ox yokes and ceramic cocks from the Minho, basketware from Trás-os-Montes, cowbells and terracotta casseroles from the Alentejo and fishing equipment from the Algarve. If you are planning to travel around the country the museum offers an excellent preview to the traditional handicrafts of the provinces.

Traditional costume from Trás-os-Montes

of Discovery. The monument is designed in the shape of a caravel, with Portugal's coat of arms on the sides and the sword of the Royal House of Avis rising above the entrance. Henry the Navigator stands at the prow with a caravel in hand. In two sloping lines either side of the monument are stone statues of Portuguese heroes linked with the Age of Discovery. On the western face these include Dom Manuel I holding an armillary sphere, the poet Camões with a copy of Os Lusíadas, the painter Nuno Gonçalves with a paint pallet as well as famous navigators, cartographers and kings.

On the monument's north side, the huge mariner's compass cut into the paving stone was a present from the Republic of South Africa

in 1960. The central map, dotted with galleons and mermaids, shows the routes of the discoverers in the 15th and 16th centuries. Inside the monument a lift whisks you up to the sixth floor where steps then lead to the top for a splendid panorama of the river and Belém. The basement level is used for temporary exhibitions, but not necessarily related to the Discoveries.

The rather ostentatious Padrão is not to everyone's taste but the setting is undeniably splendid and the caravel design is imaginative. The monument looks particularly dramatic when viewed from the west in the light of the late afternoon sun.

EASTERN FACE OF THE MONUMENT TO THE DISCOVERIES

Afonso V (1432–81), patron of the first explorers

Henry the Navigator (1394–1460)

Pedro Álvares Cabral (1467–1520), discoverer of Brazil

Vasco da Gama (1460–1524)

Fernão Magalhães (Magellan), who crossed the Pacific in 1520–21

Padrão erected by Diogo Cão in the Congo in 1482

Torre de Belém

VISITORS' CHECKLIST

Avenida da India. **Map** 1 A5.
📞 21-301 93 46. 🚌 27, 28,
29, 43, 49, 51, 112. 🚊 15. 🚢
Belém. ⬜ 10am–5pm Tue–Sun
(6pm Jun–Sep). ⬤ public hols.
📷 ⬤ ♿ ground floor only.

COMMISSIONED BY Manuel I, the tower was built as a fortress in the middle of the Tagus in 1515–21. Starting point for the navigators who set out to discover the trade routes, this Manueline gem became a symbol of Portugal's great era of expansion. The real beauty of the tower lies in the decoration of the exterior. Adorned with rope carved in stone, it has openwork balconies, Moorish-style watchtowers and distinctive battlements in the shape of shields. The Gothic interior below the terrace, which served as a storeroom for arms and a prison, is very austere but the private quarters in the tower are worth visiting for the loggia and the panorama.

Arms of Manuel I

Renaissance Loggia
The elegant arcaded loggia, inspired by Italian architecture, gives a light touch to the defensive battlements of the tower.

Armillary spheres
and nautical rope are symbols of Portugal's seafaring prowess.

Chapel

Royal coat of arms of Manuel I

Battlements are decorated with the cross of the Order of Christ *(see pp20–21).*

Virgin and Child
A statue of Our Lady of Safe Homecoming faces the sea, a symbol of protection for sailors on their voyages of discovery.

Governor's room

Gangway to shore

Entrance

Sentry posts

The vaulted dungeon
was used as a prison until the 19th century.

The Torre de Belém in 1811
This painting of a British ship navigating the Tagus, by JT Serres, shows the tower much further from the shore than it is today. In the 19th century land on the north bank was reclaimed, making the river narrower.

The simple Manueline chapel, Ermida de São Jerónimo

Ermida de São Jerónimo ⑫

Rua Pero de Covilhã. **Map** 1 A3. 🕿 21-301 86 48. 🚍 28, 43, 49, 51. 🞉 by appt only.

A LSO KNOWN AS the Capela de São Jerónimo, this elegant little chapel was constructed in 1514 when Diogo Boitac was working on the Jerónimos monastery *(see pp106–7)*. Although a far simpler building, it is also Manueline in style and may have been built to a design by Boitac. The only decorative elements on the monolithic chapel are the four pinnacles, corner gargoyles and Manueline portal. Perched on a quiet hill above Belém, the chapel has fine views down to the River Tagus and a path from the terrace winds down the hill towards the Torre de Belém.

Igreja da Memória ⑬

Calçada do Galvão, Ajuda. **Map** 1 C3. 🕿 21-363 52 95. 🚍 14, 27, 28, 32. 🚇 18. 🞉 4–6pm Mon–Sat. 🛉 🛆

B UILT IN 1760, the church was founded by King José I in gratitude for his escape from an assassination plot on this site in 1758. The king was re-turning from a secret liaison with a lady of the noble Távora family when his carriage was attacked and a bullet hit him in the arm. Pombal *(see pp52–3)*, whose power had now be-come absolute, used this as an excuse to get rid of his enemies in the Távora family,

accusing them of conspiracy. In 1759 they were savagely tortured and executed. Their deaths are commemorated by a pillar in Beco do Chão Salgado, off Rua de Belém.

The Neo-Classical domed church has a marble-clad in-terior and a small chapel, on the right, containing the tomb of Pombal. He died at the age of 83, a year after he had been banished from Lisbon.

Jardim Botânico da Ajuda ⑭

Calçada da Ajuda. **Map** 1 C2. 🕿 21-362 25 03. 🚍 14, 27, 28, 32. 🚇 18. 🞉 9am–5pm Thu–Tue. 🞉 public hols. 🞉 (free 9am–2pm Sun). 🛆

L AID OUT on two levels by Pombal *(see p15)* in 1768, these Italian-style gardens provide a pleasant respite from the noisy suburbs of Belém. The entrance (wrought-iron gates in a pink wall) is easy to miss. The park comprises tropical trees and box-hedge gardens sur-rounding neat flower beds.

19th-century throne from the Palácio Nacional da Ajuda

Notable features are the 400-year-old dragon tree, native of Madeira, and the flamboy-ant 18th-century fountain decorated with serpents, winged fish, sea horses and mythical creatures. A majestic terrace looks out over the lower level of the gardens.

Palácio Nacional da Ajuda ⑮

Calçada da Ajuda. **Map** 2 D2. 🕿 21-363 70 95. 🚍 14, 27, 28, 32, 42, 60, 73. 🚇 18. 🞉 10am–5pm Thu–Tue. 🞉 public hols. 🞉 🛆 🞉

T HE ROYAL PALACE, destroyed by fire in 1795, was re-placed in the early 19th century by the Neo-Classical building you see today. This was left incomplete when the royal family was forced into exile in Brazil in 1807 *(see pp52–3)*.

The palace only became a permanent residence of the royal family when Luís I be-came king in 1861 and married an Italian Princess, Maria Pia di Savoia. No expense was spared in furnishing the apart-ments. The ostentatious rooms are decorated with silk wallpaper, Sèvres porcelain and crystal chandeliers. A prime example of regal excess is the extraordinary Saxe Room, a wedding present to Maria Pia from the King of Saxony, in which every piece of furniture is deco-rated with Meissen porcelain. On the first floor the huge Banqueting Hall, with crystal chandeliers, silk-covered chairs and an allegory of the birth of João VI on the frescoed ceiling, is truly impressive. At the other end of the palace, Luís I's Neo-Gothic painting studio is a more intimate display of intricately carved furniture.

Manicured formal gardens of the Jardim Botânico da Ajuda

FURTHER AFIELD

THE MAJORITY of the outlying sights, which include some of Lisbon's finest museums, are easily accessible by bus or metro from the city centre. A ten-minute walk north from the gardens of the Parque Eduardo VII brings you to Portugal's great cultural complex, the Calouste Gulbenkian Foundation, set in a pleasant park. Few tourists go further north than the Gulbenkian, but the Museu da Cidade on Campo Grande is worth a detour for its fascinating overview of Lisbon's history.

***Azulejo** panel from Palácio Fronteira*

The charming Palácio Fronteira, decorated with splendid tiles, is one of the many villas built for the aristocracy that now overlook the city suburbs. Those interested in tiles will also enjoy the Museu Nacional do Azulejo in the cloisters of the Madre de Deus convent. Visitors with a spare half day can cross the Tagus to the Cristo Rei monument. Northeast of Lisbon is the vast oceanarium, Oceanário de Lisboa, in the Parque das Nações, which includes other family-oriented attractions, hotels and shops.

SIGHTS AT A GLANCE

Museums and Galleries
Centro de Arte Moderna **7**
Museu da Água **9**
Museu Calouste Gulbenkian pp116–19 **6**
Museu da Cidade **13**
Museu Nacional do Azulejo pp122–3 **10**

Modern Architecture
Amoreiras Shopping Centre **3**
Cristo Rei **1**
Parque das Nações **11**
Ponte 25 de Abril **2**

Historic Architecture
Aqueduto das Águas Livres **15**
Campo Pequeno **8**
Palácio Fronteira **16**
Praça Marquês de Pombal **4**

Parks and Gardens
Parque Eduardo VII **5**
Parque do Monteiro-Mor **17**

Zoos
Jardim Zoológico **14**
Oceanário de Lisboa **12**

KEY

▨	Main sightseeing areas
✈	Airport
⛴	Ferry boarding point
▬	Motorway
▬	Major road
=	Minor road

0 kilometres   4
0 miles   2

SIGHTS BEYOND THE CITY CENTRE

Vila Franca de Xira

A9 (CREL), IC17 (CRIL), Pontinha, Amadora, IC19, IC17 CRIL, N117, Carnaxide, Cascais, A9, N6, IC17 (CRIL), IP1 – A2 (E1), Porto Brandão, Setúbal, Almada, N10, Cacilhas, Seixal, Barreiro, Montijo, *Tejo*, Alcântara, N6, Graça, Xabregas, Benfica, Campo Grande, Praça Espanha, PARQUE FLORESTAL DE MONSANTO, IC15 - A5, IP1 – A1 (E1), Olivais, IC2

Cristo Rei ❶

Santuário Nacional do Cristo Rei, Alto
do Pragal, Almada. 📞 *21-275 10 00.*
🚢 *from Praça do Comércio & Cais do
Sodré to Cacilhas then* 🚌 *101.*
Lift ⬜ *9:30am–6pm daily.* ♿

M ODELLED ON the more
famous Cristo Redentor
in Rio de Janeiro, this giant-
sized statue stands with arms
outstretched on the south
bank of the Tagus. The 28 m
(92 ft) tall figure of Christ,
mounted on a huge pedestal,
was built by Francisco Franco
in 1949–59 at the instigation
of Prime Minister Salazar.

You can see the monument
from various viewpoints in
the city, but it is fun to take a
ferry to the Outra Banda (the
other bank), then a bus or
taxi to the monument. (Rush
hour is best avoided.) A lift,
plus some steps, takes you up
82 m (269 ft) to the top of the
pedestal, affording fine views
of the city and river.

**The towering monument of Cristo
Rei overlooking the Tagus**

Ponte 25 de Abril ❷

Map 3 A5. 🚌 *52, 53.*

O RIGINALLY CALLED the Ponte
Salazar after the dictator
who had it built in 1966,
Lisbon's suspension bridge
was renamed (like many other

monuments) to commemorate
the revolution of 25 April 1974
which restored democracy to
Portugal *(see p57).*

Inspired by San Francisco's
Golden Gate in the United
States, this steel construction
stretches for 2 km (half a
mile). The lower tier was

modified in 1999 to
accommodate a much-needed
railway across the Tagus.

The bridge's notorious
traffic congestion has been
partly resolved by the
opening of the 11-km
(7-mile) Vasco da Gama
bridge. Spanning the river
from Montijo to Sacavém,
north of the Parque das
Nações, this bridge was
completed in 1998.

Amoreiras Shopping Centre ❸

Avenida Engenheiro Duarte Pacheco.
Map 5 A5. 📞 *21-381 02 00.*
🚌 *11, 18, 23, 48, 51, 53, 58, 74, 83.*
⬜ *10am–11pm daily.* ● *25 Dec.* ♿

I N THE 18TH CENTURY, the
Marquês de Pombal *(see
pp52–3)* planted mulberry trees
(amoreiras) on the western
edge of the city to create food
for silk worms. Hence the
name of the futuristic shopping
centre that was built here in
1985. This massive complex,
with pink and blue towers,
houses 370 shops, ten cinemas,
and numerous restaurants.
Once an incongruous feature
of Lisbon, it now draws the
crowds, particularly the
young, and has been joined
by other new buildings and
shopping centres in the area.

Ponte 25 de Abril linking central Lisbon with the Outra Banda, the south bank of the Tagus

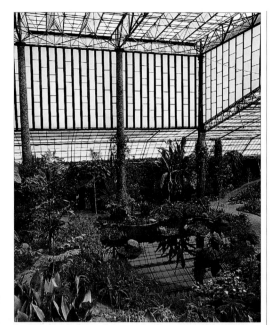

Tropical plants in the Estufa Quente glasshouse, Parque Eduardo VII

Praça Marquês de Pombal ❹

Map 5 C5. Ⓜ *Marquês de Pombal.* 🚌 *1, 2, 12, 20, 38 & many other routes.*

Aᴛ ᴛʜᴇ ᴛᴏᴘ of the Avenida da Liberdade *(see p84)*, traffic thunders round the "Rotunda" (roundabout), as the praça is also known. At the centre rises the lofty monument to Pombal, unveiled in 1934. The despotic statesman, who virtually ruled Portugal from 1750–77, stands on the top of the column, his hand on a lion (symbol of power) and his eyes directed down to the Baixa, whose creation he masterminded *(see pp62–3)*.

Allegorical images depicting Pombal's political, educational and agricultural reforms decorate the base of the monument. Standing figures represent Coimbra University where he introduced a new Faculty of Science. Although greatly feared, this dynamic politician propelled the country into the Age of Enlightenment. Broken blocks of stone at the foot of the monument and tidal waves flooding the city are an allegory of the destruction caused by the 1755 earthquake.

An underpass, which is not always open, leads to the centre of the square where the sculptures on the pedestal and the inscriptions relating to Pombal's achievements can be seen. Nearby, the well-tended Parque Eduardo VII extends northwards behind the square. The paving stones around the Rotunda are decorated with a mosaic of Lisbon's coat of arms. Similar patterns in small black and white cobbles decorate many of the city's streets and squares.

Detail representing agricultural toil on the base of the monument in Praça Marquês de Pombal

Parque Eduardo VII ❺

Praça Marquês de Pombal. **Map** 5 B4. 🄲 *21-388 22 78.* Ⓜ *Marquês de Pombal.* 🚌 *2, 11, 12, 22, 36.* **Estufa Fria** ⬜ *Apr–Sep: 9am–6pm daily; Oct–Mar: 9am–5pm daily (last adm 30 mins before closing).* ⬤ *public hols.* 📷

Tʜᴇ ʟᴀʀɢᴇsᴛ ᴘᴀʀᴋ in central Lisbon was named in honour of King Edward VII of England who came to Lisbon in 1902 to reaffirm the Anglo-Portuguese alliance. The wide grassy slope, that extends for 25 hectares (62 acres) was laid out as Parque de Liberdade, a continuation of Avenida da Liberdade *(see p84)* in the late 19th century. Neatly clipped box hedging, flanked by mosaic patterned walkways, stretches uphill from the Praça Marquês de Pombal to a belvedere at the top, which has its own landscaped garden and a pleasant café by the pond. From here there are fine views of the city. On clear days it is possible to see as far as the Serra da Arrábida *(see p167)*.

Located at the northwest corner, the most inspiring feature of this rather monotonous park is the jungle-like **Estufa Fria**, or greenhouse, where exotic plants, streams and waterfalls provide an oasis from the city streets.

There are in fact two greenhouses: in the Estufa Fria (cold greenhouse), palms push through the slatted bamboo roof and paths wind through a forest of ferns, fuchsias, flowering shrubs and banana trees; the warmer Estufa Quente, or hot-house, is a glassed-over garden with lush plants, water-lily ponds and cacti, as well as tropical birds in cages.

Near the estufas a pond with large carp and a play area in the shape of a galleon are popular with children. On the east side the **Pavilhão Carlos Lopes**, named after the 1984 Olympic marathon winner, is now a venue for concerts and conferences. The façade is decorated with a series of modern tiled scenes, mainly of Portuguese battles.

Museu Calouste Gulbenkian ⑥

THANKS TO A WEALTHY Armenian oil magnate, Calouste Gulbenkian *(see p119),* with wide-ranging tastes and an eye for a masterpiece, the museum has one of the finest collections of art in Europe. Inaugurated in 1969, the purpose-built museum was created as part of the charitable institution bequeathed to Portugal by the multimillionaire. The design of the building, set in a spacious park allowing natural light to fill some of the rooms, was devised to create the best layout for the founder's varied collection.

Mustard Barrel
This 18th-century silver mustard barrel was made in France by Antoine Sébastien Durand.

Lalique Corsage Ornament
The sinuous curves of the gold and enamel snakes are typical of René Lalique's Art Nouveau jewellery.

★ Diana
This fine marble statue (1780) by the French sculptor Jean-Antoine Houdon, was once owned by Catherine the Great of Russia but was considered too obscene to exhibit. The graceful Diana, goddess of the hunt, stands with a bow and arrow in hand.

Entrance

Stairs to

★ St Catherine
This serene bust of St Catherine was painted by the Flemish artist Rogier Van der Weyden (1400–64). The thin strip of landscape on the left of the wooden panel brings light and depth to the still portrait.

STAR EXHIBITS

★ **Portrait of an Old Man by Rembrandt**

★ **Diana by Houdon**

★ **St Catherine by Van der Weyden**

★ Portrait of an Old Man

Rembrandt was a master of light and shade. In this expressive portrait, dated 1645, the fragile countenance of the old man is contrasted with the strong and dramatic lighting.

VISITORS' CHECKLIST

Avenida de Berna 45. **Map** 5 B2.
[C] 21-782 32 45.
[M] Praça de Espanha or São Sebastião. 🚌 16, 18, 26, 31, 46, 56. 🕐 10am–6pm Wed–Sun, 2–6pm Tue.
🔴 Mon & public hols. ♿ 🅿
🔳 🍴 [W] www.gulbenkian.pt

Renaissance art

Vase of a Hundred Birds

The enamel decoration that adorns this Chinese porcelain vase is known as Famille Verte. *This type of elaborate design is characteristic of the Ch'ing dynasty during the reign of the Emperor K'ang Hsi (1662–1722).*

Gallery Guide

The galleries are laid out both chronologically and geographically, the first section (rooms 1–6) dedicated to Classical and Oriental art, the second section (rooms 7–17) housing the European collection of paintings, sculpture, furniture, silverware and jewellery.

Armenian art

Egyptian Bronze Cat

This bronze of a cat feeding her kittens dates from the Saite Period (8th century BC). Other stunning Egyptian pieces include a gilded mask of a mummy.

Persian faïence

Turkish Faïence Plate

The factories at Iznik in Turkey produced some of the most beautiful jugs, plates and vases of the Islamic world, including this 17th-century deep plate decorated with stylized animal forms.

KEY TO FLOORPLAN

- ☐ Egyptian, Classical and Mesopotamian art
- ☐ Oriental Islamic art
- ☐ Far Eastern art
- ☐ European art (14th–17th centuries)
- ☐ French 18th-century decorative arts
- ☐ European art (18th–19th centuries)
- ☐ Lalique collection
- ☐ Non-exhibition space

Exploring the Gulbenkian Collection

HOUSING CALOUSTE GULBENKIAN's unique collection of art, the museum ranks with the Museu de Arte Antiga *(see pp96–9)* as the finest in Lisbon. The exhibits, which span over 4,000 years from ancient Egyptian statuettes, through translucent Islamic glassware, to Art Nouveau brooches, are displayed in spacious and well-lit galleries, many overlooking the gardens or courtyards. The museum is quite small, however each individual work of art, from the magnificent pieces that make up the rich display of Oriental and Islamic art, to the selection of European paintings and furniture, is worthy of attention.

Late 16th-century Persian faïence tile from the School of Isfahan

EGYPTIAN, CLASSICAL AND MESOPOTAMIAN ART

PRICELESS TREASURES chart the evolution of Egyptian art from the Old Kingdom (c.2700 BC) to the Roman Period (1st century BC). The exhibits range from an alabaster bowl of the 3rd Dynasty to a surprisingly modern-looking blue terracotta torso of a statuette of *Venus Anadyomene* from the Roman period.

Outstanding pieces in the Classical art section are a magnificent red-figure Greek vase and 11 Roman medallions, found in Egypt. These are believed to have been struck to commemorate the Olympic games held in Macedonia in AD 242 in honour of Alexander the Great. In the Mesopotamian art section the large Assyrian

5th-century BC Greek vase

alabaster bas-relief represents the winged genius of Spring, carrying a container of sacred water (9th century BC).

ORIENTAL ISLAMIC ART

BEING ARMENIAN, Calouste Gulbenkian had a keen interest in art from the Near and Middle East. The Oriental Islamic gallery has a fine collection of Persian and Turkish carpets, textiles, costumes and ceramics. In the section overlooking the courtyard, the Syrian mosque lamps and bottles commissioned by princes and sultans, are beautifully decorated with coloured enamel on glass. The Armenian section has some exquisite illustrated manuscripts from the 16th to 18th centuries, produced by Armenian refugees in Istanbul, Persia and the Crimea.

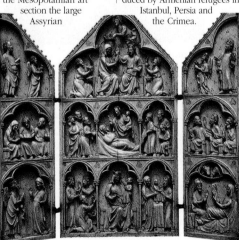

French ivory triptych of
Scenes from the Life of the Virgin **(14th century)**

FAR EASTERN ART

CALOUSTE GULBENKIAN acquired a large collection of Chinese porcelain between 1910 and 1930. One of the rarest pieces is the small blue-glazed bowl from the Yüan Dynasty (1279–1368), on the right as you go into the gallery. The majority of exhibits, however, are the later, more exuberantly decorated *famille verte* porcelain and the K'ang Hsi biscuitware of the 17th and 18th centuries. Further exhibits from the Far East are translucent Chinese jades and other semi-precious stones, Japanese prints, brocaded silk hangings and bound books, and lacquerwork.

EUROPEAN ART (14TH–17TH CENTURIES)

ILLUMINATED MANUSCRIPTS, rare printed books and medieval ivories introduce the section on Western art. The delicately sculpted 14th-century ivory diptychs and triptychs, made in France, show scenes from the lives of Christ and the Virgin.

The collection of early European paintings starts with panels of *St Joseph* and *St Catherine* by Rogier van der Weyden, leading painter of the mid-15th century in Flanders. Italian Renaissance painting is represented by Cima da Conegliano's *Sacra Conversazione* from the late 15th century and Domenico Ghirlandaio's *Portrait of a Young Woman* (1485).

The collection progresses to Flemish and Dutch works of the 17th century, including two works by Rembrandt: *Portrait of an Old Man* (1645), a masterpiece of psychological penetration, and *Alexander the Great* (1660), said to have been modelled on Rembrandt's son, Titus, and previously thought to have portrayed the Greek goddess Pallas Athena. Rubens is represented by three paintings, the most remarkable of which is the *Portrait of Hélène Fourment* (1630), the artist's second wife.

The gallery beyond the Dutch and Flemish paintings has tapestries and textiles from Italy and Flanders, Italian ceramics, rare 15th-century medallions and sculpture.

***View of the Molo with the Ducal Palace* (1790) by Francesco Guardi**

FRENCH 18TH-CENTURY DECORATIVE ARTS

SOME REMARKABLY elaborate Louis XV and Louis XVI pieces, many commissioned by royalty, feature in the collection of French 18th-century furniture. The exhibits, many of them embellished with laquer panels, ebony and bronze, are grouped together according to historical style with Beauvais and "chinoiserie" Aubusson tapestries decorating the walls.

The French silverware from the same period, much of which once adorned the dining tables of Russian palaces, includes lavishly decorated soup tureens, salt-cellars and platters.

Louis XV chest of drawers inlaid with ebony and bronze

EUROPEAN ART (18TH–19TH CENTURIES)

THE ART of the 18th century is dominated by French painters, including Watteau (1684–1721), Fragonard (1732–1806) and Boucher (1703–70). The most celebrated piece of sculpture is a statue of *Diana* by Jean-Antoine Houdon. Commissioned in 1780 by the Duke of Saxe-Gotha for his

gardens, it became one of the principal exhibits in the Hermitage in Russia during the 19th and early 20th centuries.

One whole room is devoted to views of Venice by the 18th-century Venetian painter Francesco Guardi, and a small collection of British art includes works by leading 18th-century portraitists, such as Gainsborough's *Portrait of Mrs Lowndes-Stone* (c.1775) and Romney's *Portrait of Mrs Constable* (1787). There are also two stormy seascapes by JMW Turner (1775–1851). French 19th-century landscape painting is well represented here, reflecting Gulbenkian's preference for naturalism, with works by the Barbizon school, the Realists and the Impressionists. The best-known paintings in the section, however, are probably Manet's *Boy with Cherries*, painted in about 1858 at the beginning of the artist's career, and *Boy Blowing*

Bubbles, painted about 1867. Renoir's *Portrait of Madame Claude Monet* was painted in about 1872 when the artist was staying with Monet at his country home in Argenteuil, in the outskirts of Paris.

LALIQUE COLLECTION

THE TOUR of the museum ends with an entire room filled with the flamboyant creations of French Art Nouveau jeweller, René Lalique (1860–1945). Gulbenkian was a close friend of Lalique's and he acquired many of the pieces of jewellery, glassware and ivory on display here directly from the artist. Inlaid with semi-precious stones and covered with gold leaf or enamel, the brooches, necklaces, vases and combs are decorated with the dragonfly, peacock or sensual female nude motifs characteristic of Art Nouveau.

CALOUSTE GULBENKIAN

Born in Scutari (Turkey) in 1869, Gulbenkian started his art collection at the age of 14 when he bought some ancient coins in a bazaar. In 1928 he was granted a 5 per cent stake in four major oil companies, including BP and Shell, in thanks for his part in the transfer of the assets of the Turkish Petroleum Company to those four companies. He thereby earned himself the nickname of "Mr Five Percent". With the wealth he accumulated, Gulbenkian was able to indulge his passion for fine works of art. During World War II, he went to live in neutral Portugal and, on his death in 1955, bequeathed his estate to the Portuguese in the form of a charitable trust. The Foundation supports many cultural activities and has its own orchestra, libraries, ballet company and concert halls.

Henry Moore sculpture in garden of the Centro de Arte Moderna

Centro de Arte Moderna ❼

Rua Dr Nicolau de Bettencourt.
Map 5 B3. 🄲 21-782 30 00.
Ⓜ São Sebastião. 🚌 16, 26, 31, 46, 56. ◯ 10am–6pm Wed–Sun, 2–6pm Tue. ⬤ public hols. ♿ &
ⓦ www.gulbenkian.pt

THE MODERN ART MUSEUM lies across the gardens from the Calouste Gulbenkian museum and is part of the same cultural foundation (see p119).

The permanent collection features paintings and sculpture by Portuguese artists from the turn of the 20th century to the present day. The most

famous painting is the striking portrait of poet Fernando Pessoa in the Café Irmãos Unidos (1964) by José de Almada Negreiros (1893–1970), a main exponent of Portuguese Modernism. Also of interest are paintings by Eduardo Viana (1881–1967), Amadeo de Sousa Cardoso (1887–1910), as well as contemporary artists such as Paula Rego, Rui Sanches, Graça Morais and Teresa Magalhães.

The museum is light and spacious with pleasant gardens and a cafeteria which attracts very long queues at weekends.

Campo Pequeno ❽

Map 5 C1. Ⓜ Campo Pequeno.
🚌 22, 45. **Bullring** 🄲 21-793 24 42.
◯ Easter–Oct: for bullfights. ♿ &

THIS SQUARE is dominated by the red-brick Neo-Moorish bullring built in the late 19th century. Temporarily closed, the building is undergoing major works to build an underground car park and leisure centre. Much of the bullring's distinctive architecture, such as keyhole-shaped windows and double cupolas will be

retained. Call the tourist office or the number listed above for information on this and other bullfight venues.

Renovated 19th-century steam pump in the Museu da Água

Museu da Água ❾

Rua do Alviela 12. 🄲 21-810 02 15.
🚌 35, 104, 105, 107. ◯ 10am–6pm Mon–Sat. ⬤ public hols.
♿ 📷

DEDICATED TO the history of Lisbon's water supply, this small but informative museum was imaginatively created around the city's first steam pumping station. It commemorates Manuel da Maia, the 18th-century engineer who masterminded the Águas Livres aqueduct (see p124). The excellent layout of the museum earned it the Council of Europe Museum Prize in 1990.

Pride of place goes to four lovingly preserved steam engines, one of which still functions (by electricity) and can be switched on for visitors. The development of technology relating to the city's water supply is documented with photographs. Particularly interesting are the sections on the Águas Livres aqueduct and the Alfama's 17th-century Chafariz d'El Rei, one of Lisbon's first fountains. Locals used to queue at one of six founts, depending on their social status.

Museu Nacional do Azulejo ❿

See pp122–3.

Neo-Moorish façade of the bullring in Campo Pequeno

The impressive Oriente Station, located next to Parque das Nações

Parque das Nações ⓫

Avenida Dom João II. 📞 *21-891 93 33.* Ⓜ *Oriente.* 🚌 *5, 10, 19, 21, 28, 44, 50, 68, 82.* 🚆 *Gare do Oriente.* ◯ *10am–8pm daily.* ♿ ⅄ ▣
Pavilhão do Conhecimento 📞 *21-891 71 00.* ◯ *10am–6pm Mon–Fri, 11am–7pm Sat & Sun.* 🔖

ORIGINALLY THE SITE of Expo '98, Parque das Nações has become a new focus for Lisbon. With its startling contemporary architecture, family-oriented attractions and modern living spaces, the park has renewed the eastern waterfront, an industrial wasteland as recently as 1990. Even from a distance, the soaring geometry of the platform canopies over Santiago Calatrava's Oriente Station set the architectural tone for the development. The impressive **Portugal Pavilion**, designed by the Portuguese architect Álvaro Siza Vieira has an enormous reinforced-concrete roof suspended almost miraculously, like a sailcloth, above its forecourt.

Families with children of any age will enjoy the **Pavilhão do Conhecimento** (Knowledge Pavilion), a modern museum of science and technology that houses several interactive exhibitions. Views can be had from the cable car that lifts visitors from one end of the park to the other or the **Torre Vasco da Gama**, Lisbon's tallest building. The promenade along the river, offers delightful views of the Tagus at its widest and the impressive Vasco da Gama bridge, is not to be missed.

The 10-mile (17-km) long Vasco da Gama bridge is the longest in Europe and was completed in 1998 for the Expo, to carry visitors from southern Portugal, Spain and elsewhere in Europe.

Oceanário de Lisboa ⓬

Esplanada D. Carlos 1, Parque das Nações. 📞 *21-891 70 02.* Ⓜ *Oriente.* 🚌 *5, 10, 19, 21, 28, 44, 50, 68, 82.* 🚆 *Gare do Oriente.* ◯ *Apr–Oct: 10am–8pm daily; Nov–Mar: 10am–7pm daily.* 🔖 ⅄

CENTREPIECE OF Expo '98 and now the main attraction at Parque das Nações, the somewhat aircraft carrier-like oceanarium was designed by American architect Peter Chermayeff, and is perched on the end of a pier, surrounded by water. It is the second-largest aquarium in the world, and holds an impressive array of species – birds and some mammals as well as fish and other underwater dwellers.

Four separate sea- and landscapes represent the habitats of the Atlantic, Pacific, Indian and Antarctic oceans, with suitable fauna and flora. The main attraction for most visitors, though, is the vast central tank with a dazzling variety of fish, large and small, swimming round and round. Hammerhead sharks co-exist peaceably with bream, barracudas with rays.

Museu da Cidade ⓭

Campo Grande 245. 📞 *21-751 32 00.* Ⓜ *Campo Grande.* 🚌 *1, 3, 33, 36, 47, 50, 101.* ◯ *10am–1pm, 2–6pm Tue–Sun.* ● *public hols.* 🔖 ⅄

PALÁCIO PIMENTA was allegedly commissioned by João V *(see pp52–3)* for his mistress Madre Paula, a nun from the nearby convent at Odivelas. When the mansion was built, in the middle of the 18th century, it occupied a peaceful site outside the capital. Nowadays it has to contend with the teeming traffic of Campo Grande. The house itself, however, retains its period charm and the city museum is one of the most interesting in Lisbon.

The displays follow the development of the city, from prehistoric times, through the Romans, Visigoths and Moors, traced by means of tiles, drawings, paintings, models and historical documents.

Visits also take you through the former living quarters of the mansion, including the kitchen, decorated with blue and white tile panels of fish, flowers and hanging game.

Some of the most fascinating exhibits are those depicting the city before the earthquake of 1755, including a highly detailed model made in the 1950s and an impressive 17th-century oil painting by Dirk Stoop (1610–86) of *Terreiro do Paço* (Praça do Comércio, *see p87*). One room is devoted to the Águas Livres aqueduct *(see p124)* with detailed architectural plans for its construction as well as prints and watercolours of the completed aqueduct.

The earthquake theme is resumed with pictures of the city amid the devastation and various plans for its reconstruction. The museum brings you into the 20th century with a large colour poster celebrating the Revolution of 1910 and the proclamation of the

18th-century Indian toy, Museu da Cidade

Museu Nacional do Azulejo ⑩

Pelican on the Manueline portal

D ONA LEONOR, widow of King João II, founded the Convento da Madre de Deus in 1509. Originally built in Manueline style, the church was restored under João III using simple Renaissance designs. The striking Baroque decoration was added by João V. The convent cloisters provide a stunning setting for the National Tile Museum. Decorative panels, individual tiles and photographs trace the evolution of tile-making from its introduction by the Moors, through Spanish influence and the development of Portugal's own style *(see pp22–3)*, up to the present day.

Panorama of Lisbon
A striking 18th-century panel, along one wall of the cloister, depicts Lisbon before the 1755 earthquake (see pp62–3). *This detail shows the royal palace on Terreiro do Paço.*

Hunting Scene
Artisans rather than artists began to decorate tiles in the 17th century. This detail shows a naive representation of a hunt.

KEY TO FLOORPLAN

- ☐ Moorish tiles
- ☐ 16th-century tiles
- ☐ 17th-century tiles
- ☐ 18th-century tiles
- ☐ 19th-century tiles
- ☐ 20th-century tiles
- ☐ Temporary exhibition space
- ☐ Non-exhibition space

STAR FEATURES

★ **Madre de Deus**

★ **Manueline Cloister**

★ **Nossa Senhora da Vida**

Level 2

Level 1

★ **Nossa Senhora da Vida**
This detail showing St John is part of a fine 16th-century maiolica altarpiece. The central panel of the huge work depicts The Adoration of the Shepherds.

Tiles from the 17th century with oriental influences are displayed here.

Café Tiles
The walls of the restaurant are lined with 20th-century tiles showing hanging game, including wild boar and pheasant.

VISITORS' CHECKLIST

Rua da Madre de Deus 4. 21-814 77 47. 18, 42, 104, 105. 2–6pm Tue, 10am–6pm Wed–Sun (last adm: 30 mins before closing). 1 Jan, Easter, 1 May, 25 Dec.

Level 3

Moorish Tiles
Decorated with a stylized animal motif, this 15th-century tile is typical of Moorish azulejo patterns.

Entrance

The Renaissance cloister is the work of Diogo de Torralva (1500–66).

★ Madre de Deus
Completed in the mid-16th century, it was not until two centuries later, under João V, that the church of Madre de Deus acquired its ornate decoration. The sumptuous Rococo altarpiece was added after the earthquake of 1755.

GALLERY GUIDE
The rooms around the central cloister are arranged chronologically with the oldest tiles on the ground floor. Access to the Madre de Deus is via level 2 of the museum. The front entrance of the church is used only during religious services.

The carved Manueline portal *(see p21)* was recreated from a 16th-century painting.

★ Manueline Cloister
An important surviving feature of the original convent is the graceful Manueline cloister. Fine geometrical patterned tiles were added to the cloister walls in the 17th century.

Jardim Zoológico ⑭

Estrada de Benfica 158–60. **【** 21-
723 29 00. **M** Jardim Zoológico.
🚌 16, 34, 54, 68 & other routes.
◯ 9am–6pm (Apr–Sep: 8pm)
daily. **🖼 ◎**

Dolphins performing in the aquarium of the Jardim Zoológico

THE GARDENS of the Jardim
Zoológico are as much a
feature as the actual zoo.
Opened in 1905, the zoo has
recently been revamped and
the majority of its aviaries
and cages now provide more
comfortable conditions for
the specimens. The most
bizarre feature is the dogs'
cemetery, complete with
tombstones and flowers.
Current attractions of the zoo
include a cable car which
tours the park, a reptile house
and dolphin shows. The area
is divided into four zones and
the admission charge is based
on how many you visit.

Aqueduto das Águas Livres ⑮

Best seen from Calçada da Quintinha.
◯ for guided tours by appt (Apr–Oct
only), phone Museu da Água. **【** 21-
813 55 22. **Mãe d'Água das Amoreiras**, Praça das Amoreiras. **【** 21-
325 16 46. **◯** 10am–6pm Mon–Sat.

CONSIDERED THE most
beautiful sight in Lisbon
at the turn of the century, the
impressive structure of the
Aqueduto das Águas Livres
looms over the Alcântara valley
to the northwest of the city.
The construction of an aqueduct to bring fresh water to the
city gave João V (see pp52–3)
an ideal opportunity to indulge

his passion for grandiose building schemes, as the only area
of Lisbon with fresh drinking
water was the Alfama. A tax
on meat, wine, olive oil and
other comestibles funded the
project, and although not
complete until the 19th century,
it was already supplying the
city with water by 1748. The
main pipeline measures 19 km
(12 miles), but the total length,
including all the secondary
channels, is 58 km (36 miles).
The most visible part of this
imposing structure are the 35
arches that cross the Alcântara
valley, the tallest of which
rise to a spectacular 65 m
(213 ft) above the city.
The public walkway along
the aqueduct, once a pleasant
promenade, has been closed
since 1853. This is partly due
to Diogo Alves, the infamous
robber who threw his victims
over the edge. Today, visitors
may take a lively, informative

guided tour over the
Alcântara arches. There are
also occasional tours of the
Mãe d'Água reservoir and trips
to the Mãe d'Água springs, the
source of the water supply.
These tours can be irregular,
so it is best to contact the
Museu da Água (see p120) for
details of the trip on offer.
At the end of the aqueduct,
the **Mãe d'Água das
Amoreiras** is a castle-like
building which once served
as a reservoir for the water,
supplied from the aqueduct.
The original design of 1745
was by the Hungarian architect,
Carlos Mardel, who worked
under Pombal (see pp62–3) in
the rebuilding of the Baixa.
Completed in 1834, it became
a popular meeting place and
acquired a reputation as the
rendezvous for kings and their
mistresses. Today the space is
used for art exhibitions, fashion
shows and other events.

Imposing arches of the Aqueduto das Águas Livres spanning the Alcântara valley

Palácio Fronteira 🔟

Largo São Domingos de Benfica 1.
📞 21-778 20 23. Ⓜ Jardim
Zoológico. 🚌 72. 🅁 Benfica. 🔘
Mon–Sat. 🔲 Jun–Sep: 10:30, 11, &
11:30am & noon; Oct–May: 11am &
noon. 🔘 public hols. 🔲

THIS DELIGHTFUL country
manor house was built as
a hunting pavilion for João de
Mascarenhas, the first Marquês
de Fronteira, in 1640. Although
skyscrapers are visible in the
distance, it still occupies a
quiet spot, by the Parque
Florestal de Monsanto. Both
house and garden have *azulejo*
decoration whose subjects
include battle scenes and
trumpet-blowing monkeys.

Although the palace is still
occupied by the 12th Marquis,
some of the living rooms and
the library, as well
as the formal gar-
dens, are included
in the tour. The
Battles Room has
lively tiled panels
depicting scenes
of the War of
Restoration *(see
pp50–51)*, with
a detail showing
João de Fronteira
fighting a Spanish
general. It was his
loyalty to Pedro II
during this war that earned him
the title of Marquis. Interesting
comparisons can be made between these naive 17th-century
Portuguese tiles and the Delft
ones from the same period in
the dining room, depicting
naturalistic scenes. The dining
room is also decorated with
frescoed panels and portraits
of Portuguese nobility by artists
such as Domingos António de
Sequeira (1768–1837).

The late 16th-century chapel
is the oldest part of the house.
The façade is adorned with
stones, shells, broken glass and
bits of china. These fragments
of crockery are believed to
have been used at the feast
inaugurating the palace and
then smashed to ensure no one
else could sup off the same set.
Visits to the **garden** start at the
chapel terrace, where tiled
niches are decorated with
figures personifying the arts
and mythological creatures.

**Bust of João I in gardens
of Palácio Fronteira**

Tiled terrace leading to the chapel of the Palácio Fronteira

In the formal Italian garden the
immaculate box hedges are
cut into shapes to represent
the seasons of the year. To
one end, tiled
scenes of dashing
knights on horse-
back, representing
ancestors of the
Fronteira family,
are reflected in the
waters of a large
tank. On either
side of the water,
a grand staircase
leads to a terrace
above. Here,
decorative niches
contain the busts
of Portuguese kings and colourful majolica reliefs adorn
the arcades. More blue and
white tiled scenes, realistic and
allegorical, decorate the wall
at the far end of the garden.

**Entrance to the theatre museum
in Parque do Monteiro-Mor**

Parque do Monteiro-Mor 🔟

Largo Júlio Castilho. 📞 21-759 03 18.
🚌 1, 3, 4, 7, 36, 101, 108. Park 🔘
10am–6pm Tue–Sun. 🔘 1 Jan,
Easter, 1 May, 25 Dec. **Museu
Nacional do Traje** 🔘 10am–6pm
Tue–Sun. **Museu Nacional do Teatro**
📞 21-756 74 10. 🔘 10am–6pm
Wed–Sun, 2–6pm Tue. 🔲 combined
ticket for park & museums. 📷 ♿

MONTEIRO-MOR PARK was
sold to the state in 1975
and the 18th-century palace
buildings were converted to
museums. Relatively few
visitors come here because
of the distance from the city
centre, but the gardens are
attractive and rather more
romantic than the manicured
box-hedge gardens so typical
of Lisbon. Much of the land
is wooded, though the area
around the museums has
gardens with flowering shrubs,
duck ponds and tropical trees.

The rather old-fashioned
Museu Nacional do Traje
(costume museum) has a
varied collection of costumes
worn by musicians, politicians,
poets, aristocrats and soldiers.

The **Museu Nacional do
Teatro** has two buildings, one
devoted to temporary exhibitions, the other containing a
very small permanent collection. Photographs, posters
and cartoons feature famous
20th-century Portuguese actors
and one section is devoted to
Amália Rodrigues, the famous
fado singer *(see pp66–7)*.

LISBON STREET FINDER

MAP REFERENCES given in this guide for sights and entertainment venues in Lisbon refer to the Street Finder maps on the following pages. Map references are also given for Lisbon's hotels *(see pp380–83)* and restaurants *(see pp404–7)*. The first figure in the map reference indicates which Street Finder map to turn to, and the letter and number which follow refer to the grid reference on that map. The map below shows the area of Lisbon covered by the eight Street Finder maps. Symbols used for sights and useful information are displayed in the key below. An index of street names and all the places of interest marked on the maps can be found on the following pages.

KEY TO STREET FINDER

- Major sight
- Place of interest
- **R** Railway station
- **M** Metro station
- Main coach stop
- Tram stop
- Funicular railway
- Taxi rank
- Ferry boarding point
- **P** Parking
- **i** Tourist information
- Hospital with casualty unit
- Police station
- Church
- Synagogue
- **C** Mosque
- Post office
- Viewpoint
- Railway line
- Motorway
- One-way street
- Pedestrianized street
- «45 House number

SCALE OF MAP PAGES 1–6

| 0 metres | 250 |
| 0 yards | 250 |

SCALE OF MAP PAGES 7–8

| 0 metres | 250 |
| 0 yards | 250 |

Street Finder Index

CENTRAL
PORTUGAL

Central Portugal at a Glance

BETWEEN PORTUGAL'S CAPITAL and its second city, Oporto, can be found some of the country's most impressive architecture and important historical sights. Near Lisbon are the fine palaces of Sintra and Queluz, and in Estremadura are several of Portugal's foremost religious sites. Estremadura and Beira Litoral mix empty beaches with quaint fishing villages and smart resorts, while the lush country stretching inland to the banks of the Tagus supports livestock and crops from grapes to fruit and rice. Further north, the Beiras are more varied, with the historic university town of Coimbra, the vine-clad valleys of the Dão wine region and the bleak highlands and fortress towns of Beira Alta and Beira Baixa. Dominating this remote region is the granite range of the Serra da Estrela.

Batalha *means "battle" and the monastery of Santa Maria da Vitória at Batalha was built to give thanks for victory over the Spanish at the Battle of Aljubarrota in 1385. Its delicate style makes it one of Portugal's finest Gothic buildings (see pp182–3).*

Alcobaça *is principally known for its abbey, founded in the 12th century by Portugal's first king, Afonso Henriques. The graceful, contemplative air of this great Cistercian house (see pp178–9) is exemplified by its huge vaulted dormitory.*

Beira Litoral

Sintra, *just west of Lisbon, is a cool wooded retreat from the heat of the capital. This is where the Portuguese monarchs chose to spend their summers. The Palácio Nacional is full of remarkable decorative effects, such as this painted "magpie" ceiling (see pp158–9).*

Estremadura

ESTREMADURA AND RIBATEJO
(See pp170–93)

LISBON
(See pp58–139)

THE LISBON COAST
(See pp148–69)

The Palácio de Queluz, *a masterpiece of Rococo architecture (see pp164–5), lies just outside Lisbon. The Lion Staircase leads up to the colonnaded pavilion named after its architect, Jean-Baptiste Robillion.*

| 0 kilometres | 50 |
| 0 miles | 25 |

◁ **Tomar's Templar fortress of Convento de Cristo overlooking the town**

Beira Alta

THE BEIRAS
(See pp194–221)

Beira Baixa

Ribatejo

Buçaco's *walled forest is an arboretum and a religious retreat. A Via Sacra winds among mossy trunks to stunning views from the hilltop Calvary* (see pp210–11).

The Serra da Estrela, *the highest mountain range in the country, offers startling contrasts of scenery, from bare ice-eroded peaks to green pastures dotted with shepherds' huts* (see pp218–19).

Coimbra University *is the oldest and most prestigious in Portugal* (see pp206–7). *Long ago it expanded beyond the royal palace which became its home in 1537, but the old palace, with its gilded Capela de São Miguel and spectacular library, are still at the heart of the campus.*

Tomar *was founded by the Knights Templar in the 12th century, when these warrior monks played a leading role in the campaigns to win back Portugal from the Moors. The Templars' fortress survives, as does the drum-shaped bulk of their Rotunda, or oratory. This forms the core of the Convento de Cristo which over the centuries was built up around the original church* (see pp184–7).

Horsemanship and Bullfighting

CLASSICAL DRESSAGE and bravura bullfighting in Portugal are linked to the Marquês de Marialva, the King's Master of the Horse from 1770 to 1799. He made famous the most advanced and difficult dressage techniques, including some in which the horse lifts itself off the ground like a ballet dancer. The Art of Marialva, as it is called, is of great use to horsemen in the bullring, and they will usually demonstrate some dressage movements for the entertainment of the crowd. The Ribatejo is the traditional centre of bullfighting, with events held from spring to autumn at annual fairs and towns such as Santarém, Vila Franca de Xira and Coruche. In Portugal, the bull is never killed in the arena.

Horseman at the national fair in Golegã

Advertising a summer bullfight in Santarém

Ribatejan herdsmen or campinos, *who round up the fighting bulls, here demonstrate their skills.*

Leading bullfighter João Moura salutes the crowd at a *tourada* with his tricorne hat.

The mane is plaited with ribbons for a beautifully groomed effect.

THE CAVALEIRO

The bullfighter or *cavaleiro* wears traditional 18th-century costume, including the satin coat of a grandee, and rides an elaborately adorned horse. He has to plant a number of darts *(farpas)* in the bull's shoulders, and his performance is judged on style and courage.

The costly saddle cloth is embroidered with João Moura's initials.

Box stirrups are traditional, stylish and secure.

Tail tidying and decoration go back to the ornate French style of Louis XV.

TRADITIONAL EQUESTRIAN SKILLS

Lisbon's Escola Portuguesa de Arte Equestre, and equestrian centres in the Ribatejo, today maintain the standards set by Marialva. The Lisbon school performs several times a year around the country. On Lusitanian horses of Alter Real stock *(see p296)*, riders in 18th-century costume give superb dressage displays. Their movements resemble these illustrations of 1790 from a book on equestrianism, dedicated to Dom João (later João VI), himself a keen horseman.

Plaque of Lezíria Grande Equestrian Centre (see p192)

The Marquês de Marialva trains his horse in the *croupade*, its hind legs tucked up beneath it, as it springs into the air.

THE BULLFIGHT

The *corrida* or *tourada* combines drama and daring. First, a team of bullfighters on foot (*peões de brega*) distracts the bull with capes, preparing it for the *cavaleiro*. He is followed by eight volunteer *forcados*, who aim to overcome the bull with their bare hands in what is known as the *pega*. Finally the bull is herded from the ring among a group of farm oxen.

At this opening ceremony in Montijo, *the two* cavaleiros *line up with the* forcados *on either side.*

The cavaleiro lodges long darts in the bull's shoulders.

The bull charges, provoked by the *cavaleiro* and the prancing horse. The bull's horns are blunted and sheathed in leather.

Partnership between man and horse is paramount. Most cavaleiros *ride a Lusitanian, the world's oldest saddle horse and a classic warrior steed, famed for its courage, grace and strength. Its agility and speed are essential in the ring, and defenders of bullfighting believe the spectacle has helped preserve the breed.*

The horse's lower legs are strapped for support.

The leader of the *forcados* tackles the bull head on, throwing himself between its horns and gripping it around the neck.

The next in line assists the front man, while the others prepare to lend support.

The bullfight ends with the *pega*. *The leader of the* forcados *challenges the bull to charge, then launches himself over its head. The others try to hold him in place and use their combined weight to bring the bull to a standstill, with one of the men holding onto its tail. Eight times out of ten the* forcados *get tossed in all directions, then re-form to repeat the challenge. The crowd laughs, but applauds the men's skill and courage.*

Dom João himself demonstrates the *galope*, a difficult exercise with a change of direction at each step.

The horse leaps from a standstill, back legs outstretched, in the dramatic *capriole*.

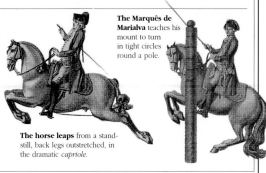

The Marquês de Marialva teaches his mount to turn in tight circles round a pole.

Regional Food: Central Portugal

Ceramic honey pot

GASTRONOMICALLY, the central region of Portugal is immensely varied. Aveiro specializes in eel stews and the sweet delicacy of *ovos moles (see p200)*, while sucking pig is a feature on menus around Coimbra. Along the coast, shellfish is varied and abundant; inland, kid and lamb are succulent, spiked with *colorau* (paprika) and cooked in the region's rich red wines. Milk from sheep and goats is turned into a variety of local cheeses, the most famous being Serra, from the Serra da Estrela. The Ribatejo's melons are renowned for their sweetness and Setúbal grows muscat grapes for the table and for wines.

Pataniscas *are tasty salt-cod fritters. Rissois, half-moons filled with a seafood sauce, are favourites as party snacks.*

Pãezinhos

Papo seco

Queijo de ovelha (ewe's milk cheese)

Requeijão

Sopa de pedra, *"stone soup", derives from a legend about a beggar monk. Full of vegetables and meats, it is tasty and filling.*

Fresh cheeses *made from ewe's or goat's milk are enjoyed with a variety of fresh rolls. Especially prized is Requeijão.*

Leitão à Bairrada, *roasted sucking pig with crisp crackling, is relished hot or cold, and can be bought in good delicatessens.*

Bife à café, *café-style steak, is tender steak with a creamy sauce, served with chips and topped with a fried egg.*

Frango à piri-piri, *a great favourite from Portugal's former colonies in Africa, is barbecued chicken with chilli.*

Bacalhau à Brás *binds shreds of salt cod (bacalhau), potato and onion with scrambled egg to make a highly esteemed dish.*

CHEESES

Most cheeses are made with ewe's or goat's milk or both. The best (and most expensive) is undoubtedly the buttery Serra, which becomes harder and more piquant as it ages *(see p215)*. Rabaçal is a mild cheese from Coimbra, while Azeitão, from near Setúbal, is quite pungent and Saloio, dried fresh cheese, is favoured for its milky taste. Individual small cheeses may be kept in oil.

Rabaçal   **Serra**

Azeitão   **Saloio**

Shellfish *is plentiful and much enjoyed in Portugal. Lisbon is full of specialist seafood restaurants with artistic displays of lobsters, prawns of all sizes, crayfish, oysters and crabs, including the spiny-shelled spider crab. Lesser-known delicacies such as goose barnacles will also appear on menus. Cockles and clams find their way into a variety of dishes, such as the rich seafood rice, arroz de marisco.*

Oysters

Crab

Shrimps

Lobster

Mussels

Prawns

Açorda de marisco *is a special and unusual dish: shellfish are added to a thick soup of mashed bread, oil, garlic and coriander.*

Salmonete grelhado, *grilled red mullet, is a speciality in Setúbal, where it is served with a lemony butter sauce.*

Mousse de chocolate *needs to be made with really good dark chocolate, but can be excellent.*

Arroz doce, *creamy rice pudding rich with egg, is flavoured with lemon rind and vanilla.*

Queijadas de Sintra (cheese tarts spiced with cinnamon)

Pastéis de nata (custard-cream tartlets)

Pastel de feijão (almonds, eggs and beans)

Broas (maize and almond)

Tartlets *such as* pastéis de nata *epitomize the region's infinite variety of cakes, many based on egg yolks, almonds and spices.*

LOCAL DRINKS

Central Portugal produces a number of wines *(see pp28–9)*, from which *aguardente* (brandy) is distilled. There are also local liqueurs, such as the herb-based Licor Beirão. From the region's many spas come a variety of mineral waters, of which Luso *(see p209)* is one of the most popular. Less known is the Lisbon area's beer-making tradition, and Lisbon itself has several *cervejarias* (beer houses).

Aguardente
Velha
Reserva

Mineral
water
from Luso

Licor
Beirão

Sagres
beer

THE LISBON COAST

W ITHIN AN HOUR'S DRIVE *northwest of Lisbon you can reach the rocky Atlantic coast, the wooded slopes of Sintra or countryside dotted with villas and royal palaces. South of Lisbon you can enjoy the sandy beaches and fishing towns along the coast or explore the lagoons of the Tagus and Sado river estuaries.*

Traders and invaders, from the Phoenicians to the Spanish, have left their mark in this region, in particular the Moors whose forts and castles, rebuilt many times over the centuries, can be found all along this coast. After Lisbon became the capital in 1256, Portuguese kings and nobles built summer palaces and villas in the countryside west of the city, particularly on the cool, green heights of the Serra de Sintra.

Across the Tagus, the less fashionable southern shore (Outra Banda) could be reached only by ferry, until the suspension bridge was built in 1966. Now, the long sandy beaches of the Costa da Caparica, the coast around the fishing town of Sesimbra and even the remote Tróia peninsula have become popular resorts during the summer months. Fortunately, large stretches of coast and unspoilt countryside are being protected as conservation areas and nature reserves.

Despite the region's rapid urbanization, small fishing and farming communities still remain. Lively fish markets offer a huge variety of fresh fish and seafood; Palmela and the Sado region are noted for their wine; sheep still roam the unspoilt Serra da Arrábida, providing milk for Azeitão cheese; and rice is the main crop in the Sado estuary. Traditional industries also survive, such as salt panning near Alcochete and marble quarries at Pero Pinheiro.

Though the sea is cold and often rough, especially on west-facing coasts, the beaches are among the cleanest in Europe. As well as surfing, fishing and scuba diving, the region provides splendid golf courses, horse riding facilities and a motor-racing track. Arts and entertainment range from music and cinema festivals to bullfights and country fairs where regional crafts, such as hand-painted pottery, lace and baskets, are on display.

Tiled façades of houses in Alcochete, an attractive town on the Tagus estuary

◁ Brightly painted fishing boats moored in the harbour at Sesimbra

Exploring the Lisbon Coast

NORTH OF THE TAGUS, the beautiful hilltown of Sintra
is dotted with historic palaces and surrounded by
wooded hills, at times enveloped in an eerie sea mist.
On the coast, cosmopolitan Cascais and the
traditional fishing town of Ericeira are both
excellent bases from which to explore
the rocky coastline and surrounding
countryside. South of the Tagus, the
Serra da Arrábida and the rugged
coast around Cabo Espichel can
be visited from the small port
of Sesimbra. Inland, the nature
reserves of the Tagus and Sado
estuaries offer a quiet retreat.

0 kilometres   10

0 miles   5

Cabo da Roca on the western edge of Serra de Sintra

KEY

�	Motorway
▬	Major road
▬	Minor road
▬	Scenic route
～	River
--	Ferry route
☆	Viewpoint

Torres Vedras

*VILA FRANCA DO
ROSÁRIO*

ERICEIRA **2**

1 *PALÁCIO DE MAFRA*

MONSERRATE **5**

COLARES **3**   **6** *SINTRA*

CABO DA ROCA

4

LOURES

IC19

*PALÁCIO DE
QUELUZ* **9**

LISBON

CASCAIS **7**   **8** *ESTORIL*

COSTA DA CAPARICA **11**

*Lagoa de
Albufeira*

CABO ESPICHEL
12

Convento da Arrábida in the hills
of the Serra da Arrábida

GETTING AROUND

Motorways give quick access from
Lisbon to Sintra, Estoril, Palmela and
Setúbal. Main roads are generally
well signposted and surfaced, though
traffic congestion can be a problem,
particularly at weekends and holidays.
Watch out for potholes on smaller
roads. Fast, frequent trains run west
from Lisbon's Cais do Sodré station to
Estoril and Cascais, and from Rossio
station to Queluz and Sintra. For trains
south to Setúbal, Alcácer do Sal and
beyond, take a ferry to Barreiro on
the southern bank of the Tagus. There
are good bus services to all parts of
the region, most of which leave from
Lisbon's Praça de Espanha.

Fishing boats
in the harbour
at Sesimbra

SEE ALSO

- **Where to Stay** pp384–6

- **Where to Eat** pp408–9

The stunning library in the Palácio de Mafra, paved with chequered marble

Palácio de Mafra ❶

Road map B5. Terreiro de Dom João V, Mafra. ☎ 261-817 550. 🚌 from Lisbon. ◐ 10am–4:30pm Wed–Mon. ● 1 Jan, Easter, 1 May, 25 Dec. ✝ free Sun am. ✔ compulsory.

THE MASSIVE BAROQUE palace and monastery *(see also pp52–3)*, which dwarfs the small town of Mafra, was built during the reign of Portugal's most extravagant monarch, João V. It began with a vow by the young king to build a new monastery and basilica, supposedly in return for an heir (but more likely, to atone for his well-known sexual excesses). Work began in 1717 on a modest project to house 13 Franciscan friars but, as wealth began to pour into the royal coffers from Brazil, the king and his Italian-trained architect, Johann Friedrich Ludwig (1670–1752), made ever more extravagant plans.

The king's bedroom in the Royal Palace

No expense was spared: 52,000 men were employed and the finished project housed not 13, but 330 friars, a royal palace and one of the finest libraries in Europe, decorated with precious marble, exotic wood and countless works of art. The magnificent basilica was consecrated on the king's 41st birthday, 22 October 1730, with festivities lasting for eight days.

The palace was only popular with those members of the royal family who enjoyed hunting deer and wild boar. Today, a wolf conservation project runs here. Most of the finest furniture and art works were taken to Brazil when the royal family escaped the French invasion in 1807. The monastery was abandoned in 1834 following the dissolution of all religious orders, and the palace itself was abandoned in 1910, when the last Portuguese king, Manuel II, escaped from here to the Royal Yacht anchored off Ericeira.

Allow at least an hour for the lengthy tour which starts in the rooms of the monastery, through the pharmacy, with fine old medicine jars and some alarming medical instruments, to the hospital, where 16 patients in private cubicles could see and hear mass in the adjoining chapel without leaving their beds.

Upstairs, the sumptuous palace state rooms extend across the whole of the monumental west façade, with the King's apartments at one end and the Queen's apartments at the other, a staggering 232 m (760 ft) apart. Halfway between the two, the long, imposing façade is relieved by the twin towers of the domed basilica. The interior of the church is decorated in contrasting colours of marble and furnished with six early 19th-century organs. Fine Baroque sculptures, executed by members of the Mafra School of Sculpture, adorn the atrium of the basilica. Begun by José I in 1754, many renowned Portuguese and foreign artists trained in the school under the directorship of the Italian sculptor Alessandro Giusti (1715–99). Further on, the Sala da Caça has a grotesque collection of hunting trophies and boars' heads. Mafra's greatest treasure, however, is its magnificent library, with a patterned marble floor, Rococo-style wooden bookcases, and a collection of over 40,000 books in gold embossed leather bindings, including a prized first edition of *Os Lusíadas* (1572) by the Portuguese poet, Luís de Camões *(see p46)*.

Statue of St Bruno in the atrium of Mafra's basilica

ENVIRONS: Once a week, on Thursday mornings, the small country town of **Malveira**, 10 km (6 miles) east of Mafra, has the region's biggest market, selling clothes and household goods as well as food.

At the village of **Sobreiro**, 6 km (4 miles) west of Mafra, Zé Franco's model village is complete with houses, farms, a waterfall and working windmill, all in minute detail.

Tractor pulling a fishing boat out of the sea at Ericeira

Ericeira ❷

Road map B5. 🕍 6,600. ☷
🛈 Rua Mendes Leal (261-863 122).
🅐 Apr–Oct daily.

ERICEIRA IS AN OLD fishing village which keeps its traditions despite an ever-increasing influx of summer visitors, from Lisbon and abroad, who enjoy the bracing climate, clean, sandy beaches and fresh seafood. In July and August, when the population leaps to 30,000, pavement cafés, restaurants and bars around the tree-lined Praça da República are buzzing late into the night. Red flags warn when swimming is dangerous: alternative attractions include crazy golf in Santa Marta park and an interesting museum of local history, the **Museu da Ericeira**, exhibiting models of traditional regional boats and fishing equipment.

The unspoilt old town, a maze of whitewashed houses and narrow, cobbled streets, is perched high above the ocean. From Largo das Ribas, at the top of a 30-m (100-ft) stone-faced cliff, there is a bird's-eye view over the busy fishing harbour below, where tractors have replaced the oxen that once hauled the boats out of reach of the tide. On 16 August, the annual fishermen's festival is celebrated with a candlelit procession to the harbour at the foot of the cliffs for the blessing of the boats.

On 5 October 1910, Manuel II, the last king of Portugal (see pp54–5), sailed into exile from Ericeira as the Republic was declared in Lisbon; a tiled panel in the fishermen's chapel

of Santo António above the harbour records the event. The banished king settled in Twickenham, southwest London, where he died in 1932.

🏛 Museu da Ericeira
Largo da Misericórdia. 🕻 261-864 079. ◻ Jun–Sep: Tue–Sun; Oct–May: Mon–Sat (pm only). ● public hols. 🗭

Colares ❸

Road map B5. 🕍 7,500. ☷
🛈 Praça da República 23, Sintra (21-923 11 57).

ON THE LOWER SLOPES of the Serra de Sintra, this lovely village faces the sea over a green valley, the Várzea de Colares. A leafy avenue, lined with pine and chestnut trees, winds its way up to the village. Small quantities of the famous Colares wine are still made, but current vintages lack the

character and ageing potential of classic Colares and growers face a financial struggle to survive. Their hardy old vines grow in sandy soil, with their roots set deep below in clay; these were the only vines in Europe to survive the disastrous phylloxera epidemic brought from America in the late 19th century with the first viticultural exchanges. The insect, which destroyed vineyards all over Europe by eating the vines, could not penetrate the dense sandy soil of the Atlantic coast. Wine can be sampled at the Adega Regional de Colares on Alameda de Coronel Linhares de Lima.

ENVIRONS: There are several popular beach resorts west of Colares. From the village of Banzão you can ride 3 km (2 miles) to **Praia das Maças** on the old tramway, which opened in 1910 and still runs from 1 July to 30 September. Just north of Praia das Maças is the picturesque village of **Azenhas do Mar**, clinging to the cliffs; just to the south is the larger resort of **Praia Grande**. Both have natural pools in the rocks, which are filled by seawater at high tide. The unspoilt **Praia da Adraga**, 1 km (half a mile) further south, has a delightful beach café and restaurant. In the evenings and off-season, fishermen set up their lines to catch bass, bream and flat fish that swim in on the high tide.

Natural rock pool at Azenhas do Mar, near Colares

Serra de Sintra Tour ❹

Tiled angels, Peninha chapel

THIS ROUND TRIP from Sintra follows a dramatic route over the top of the wooded Serra. The first part is a challenging drive with hazardous hairpin bends on steep, narrow roads that are at times poorly surfaced. It passes through dense forest and a surreal landscape of giant moss-covered boulders, with breathtaking views over the Atlantic coast, the Tagus estuary and beyond.

After dropping down to the rugged, windswept coast, the route returns along small country roads passing through hill villages and large estates on the cool, green northern slopes of the Serra de Sintra.

Atlantic coastline seen from Peninha

Colares ⑥
The village of Colares rests on the lower slopes of the wooded Serra, surrounded by gardens and vineyards *(see p153).*

Peninha ④
This 490-m (1,600-ft) high peak affords stunning views towards the coast. A 17th-century chapel decorated with *azulejo* panels is perched high on the grey rocks.

Cabo da Roca ⑤
A lighthouse at the top of an impressive cliff, 140 m (459 ft) high, marks the most westerly point of the European mainland.

0 kilometres   2

0 miles   1

KEY

━━ Tour route

— Other roads

�☀ Viewpoint

Seteais ⑧
The elegant, pink palace, now a luxury hotel and restaurant *(see p386 & p409)*, was built in the 18th century for the Dutch Consul, Daniel Gildemeester.

TIPS FOR DRIVERS

Length: 36 km (22 miles).
Stopping-off points: There are wonderful picnic spots in the forests and in the Parque da Pena, with cool springs of drinking water and fountains along the mountain roads. At Cabo da Roca you will find a café, restaurant and souvenir shops; at Colares there are several delightful restaurants and bars. (See also pp444–5.)

Monserrate ⑦
The cool, overgrown forest park and elaborate 19th-century palace epitomize the romanticism of Sintra.

Sintra ①
From the centre of the old town the road winds steeply upwards past magnificent *quintas* (country estates) hidden among the trees.

ERICEIRA
MAFRA
Palácio da Pena
N249
LISBOA
ESTORIL
CASCAIS

Parque da Pena ②
This huge, exotic park can be explored on foot *(see p157)*. It is also possible to drive as far as Cruz Alta, the highest point of the Serra de Sintra.

Convento dos Capuchos ③
Two huge boulders guard the entrance to this remote Franciscan monastery, founded in 1560, where the monks lived in tiny rock-hewn cells lined with cork. There are stunning views of the coast from the hill above this austere, rocky hideaway.

Palace of Monserrate

Monserrate ⑤

Road Map B5. Estrada de Monserrate.
☎ 21-923 73 00. ➡ to Sintra then taxi. ◯ 25 Mar–27 Oct: 9am–7pm; 28 Oct–24 Mar: 9am–6pm. ♿
W www.parquesdesintra.pt

THE WILD, ROMANTIC garden of this once magnificent estate is a jungle of exotic trees and flowering shrubs. Among the sub-tropical foliage and valley of tree ferns, the visitor will come across a waterfall, a small lake and a chapel, built as a ruin, tangled in the roots of a giant *Ficus* tree. Its history dates back to the Moors, but it takes its name from a small 16th-century chapel dedicated to Our Lady of Montserrat in Catalonia, Spain. The gardens were landscaped in the late 18th century by a wealthy young Englishman, the eccentric aesthete William Beckford. They were later immortalized by Lord Byron in *Childe Harold's Pilgrimage* (1812).

In 1856, the abandoned estate was bought by another Englishman, Sir Francis Cook, who built a fantastic Moorish-style palace (which now stands eerily empty) and transformed the gardens with a large sweeping lawn, camellias and sub-tropical trees from all over the world. These include the giant *Metrosideros* (Australian Christmas tree, covered in a blaze of red flowers in July), the native *Arbutus* (known as the strawberry tree because of its juicy red berries), from which the *medronheira* firewater drink is distilled, and cork oak, with small ferns growing on its bark.

The Friends of Monserrate is an organization that has been set up to help restore the sadly neglected house and gardens to their former glory.

Sintra ❻

Sintra's stunning setting on the north slopes of the granite Serra, among wooded ravines and fresh water springs, made it a favourite summer retreat for the kings of Portugal. The tall conical chimneys of the Palácio Nacional de Sintra *(see pp158–9)* and the fabulous Palácio da Pena *(see pp160–61)*, eerily impressive when on its peak the Serra is blanketed in mist, are unmistakable landmarks.

Today, the town (recognized as a UNESCO World Heritage site in 1995) draws thousands of visitors all through the year. Even so, there are many quiet walks in the wooded hills around the town, especially beautiful in the long, cool evenings of the summer months.

Exploring Sintra

Present-day Sintra is in three parts, Sintra Vila, Estefânia and São Pedro, joined by a confusing maze of winding roads scattered over the surrounding hills. In the pretty cobbled streets of the old town, Sintra Vila, which is centred on the **Palácio Nacional de Sintra**, are the museums and beautifully tiled **post office**. The curving **Volta do Duche** leads from the old town, past the lush **Parque da Liberdade**, north to the Estefânia district and the striking Neo-Gothic **Câmara Municipal** (Town Hall). To the south and east, the hilly village of São Pedro spreads over the slopes of the Serra. The fortnightly Sunday **market** here extends across the broad market square and along Rua 1° de Dezembro.

Exploring Sintra on foot involves a lot of walking and climbing up and down its steep hills. For a more leisurely tour, take one of the horse and carriage rides around the town. The **Miradouro da Vigia** in São Pedro offers impressive views, as does the cosy **Casa de Sapa** café, where you can sample *queijadas*, the local sweet speciality *(see p137)*.

The many fountains dotted around the town are used by locals for their fresh spring drinking water. Two of the most striking are the tiled **Fonte Mourisca** (Arab Fountain), named for its Neo-Moorish decoration, and **Fonte da Sabuga**, where the water spouts from a pair of breasts.

Fonte Mourisca on Volta do Duche

🏛 Museu do Brinquedo

Rua Visconde de Monserrate. **C** 21-924 21 71. ◯ Tue–Sun. ▓ &

This small museum has a fine international collection of toys, ranging from model planes, cars and trains, including 1930s Hornby sets, to battalions of toy soldiers, dolls and dolls' houses, tin toys and curious clockwork models of cars and soldiers. The museum is fun for a rainy day, particularly for nostalgic adults.

**Toy Alfa Romeo,
Museu do Brinquedo**

🏛 Museu de Arte Moderna

Avenida Heliodoro Salgado. **C** 21-924 81 70. ◯ Tue–Sun. ▓ & ▮▮ ▯

The Berardo Collection, accumulated by entrepreneur Joe Berardo, is regarded as one of the world's best private collections of 20th-century art and includes such big names as René Magritte, Jackson Pollock, Francis Bacon and Andy Warhol. Located at the north end of Sintra, it is a pedagogic exposé of movements and styles, particularly those of the post-war era.

🏚 Quinta da Regaleira

Rua Barbosa du Bocage. **C** 21-910 66 50. ◯ daily. ▓ mandatory; call to book. ▓ ▮▮ ▯

Built during the 1890s, this neo-Manueline palace and extensive gardens are a feast of historical and religious references, occult symbols and mystery. The obsession of the eccentric millionaire António Augusto Carvalho Monteiro, they are an absolute must for anyone interested in freemasonry, alchemy and other esoterica.

Chimneys of the Palácio Nacional de Sintra above the old town

♠ Castelo dos Mouros

Estrada da Pena. **[** 21-923 73 00.
○ daily. **●** 1 Jan, 25 Dec.
Standing above the old town,
like a sentinel, the ramparts
of the 8th-century Moorish
castle, conquered by Afonso
Henriques in 1147, snake
over the top of the Serra. On
a fine day, there are breathtaking views from the castle
walls over the old town to
Palácio da Pena, on a neighbouring peak, and far along

the coast. Hidden inside the
walls are a ruined chapel and
an ancient Moorish cistern. For
walkers, a steep footpath
threads up through wooded
slopes from the 12th-century
church of **Santa Maria**. Follow
the signs to a dark green swing
gate where the footpath begins.
The monogram "DFII" carved
on the gateway is a reminder
that the castle walls were
restored by Fernando II (see
p161) in the 19th century.

Battlements of the Castelo dos Mouros perched on the slopes of the Serra

VISITORS' CHECKLIST

Road map B5. ⛰ 25,000.
🚃 🚌 Avenida Dr Miguel
Bombarda. **ℹ** Praça da República
23 (21-923 11 57). 🎪 2nd & 4th
Sun of month in São Pedro.
🎵 Festival de Música (Jun–Jul).

♣ Parque da Pena

Estrada da Pena. **[** 21-923 73 00.
○ daily. **●** 1 Jan, 25 Dec. **♿**
A huge park surrounds the
Palácio da Pena where footpaths wind among a lush
vegetation of exotic trees and
shrubs. Hidden among the
foliage are gazebos, follies
and fountains, and a Romantic
chalet built by Fernando II for
his mistress in 1869. Cruz Alta,
the highest point of the Serra
at 530 m (1,740 ft), commands
spectacular views of the Serra
and surrounding plain. On a
nearby crag stands the statue
of Baron Von Eschwege, architect of the palace and park.

SINTRA TOWN CENTRE

Câmara Municipal ①
Casa de Sapa ②
Castelo dos Mouros ⑨
Fonte Mourisca ⑥
Fonte da Sabuga ⑦
Museu do Brinquedo ⑤
*Palácio Nacional de
    Sintra pp158–9* ③
Post office ④
Santa Maria ⑧

0 metres   200
0 yards   200

KEY

🚆 Railway station

🚌 Bus station

🅿 Parking

ℹ Tourist information

✝ Church

▪▪▪ Footpath

Palácio Nacional de Sintra

AT THE HEART of the old town of Sintra (Sintra Vila), a pair of strange conical chimneys rises high above the Royal Palace. The main part of the palace, including the central block with its plain Gothic façade

**Swan panel,
Sala dos Cisnes**

and the large kitchens beneath the chimneys, was built by João I in the late 14th century, on a site once occupied by the Moorish rulers. The Paço Real, as it is also known, became the favourite summer retreat for the court, and continued as a residence for Portuguese royalty until the 1880s. Additions to the building by the wealthy Manuel I, in the early 16th century, echo the Moorish style. Gradual rebuilding of the palace has resulted in a fascinating amalgamation of various different styles.

The Torre da Meca has dovecotes below the cornice decorated with armillary spheres and nautical rope.

The Sala das Galés (galleons) houses temporary exhibitions.

★ **Sala das Pegas**
It is said that King João I had the ceiling panels painted as a rebuke to the court women for indulging in idle gossip like chattering magpies (pegas).

★ **Sala dos Brasões**
The domed ceiling of this majestic room is decorated with stags holding the coats of arms (brasões) of 74 noble Portuguese families. The lower walls are lined with 18th-century Delft-like tiled panels.

Jardim da Preta, a walled garden

Sala de Dom Sebastião, the audience chamber

TIMELINE

		1495–1521 Reign	1683 Afonso VI	
10th century Palace becomes residence of Moorish governor	1281 King Dinis orders restoration of the Palácio de Oliva (as it was then known)	of Manuel I; major restoration and Manueline additions	dies after being imprisoned here for nine years by brother Pedro II	1755 Parts of palace damaged in great earthquake (*see pp62–3*)

800	1000	1200	1400	1600	1800

	1147 Christian reconquest; Afonso Henriques takes over palace	1385 João I orders complete rebuilding of central buildings and kitchens		1880s Maria Pia (grandmother of Manuel II) is last royal resident

8th century First palace established by Moors

Siren, Sala das Sereias (c.1660)

1910 Palace becomes a national monument

★ Sala dos Cisnes
The magnificent ceiling of the former banqueting hall, painted in the 17th century, is divided into octagonal panels decorated with swans (cisnes).

VISITORS' CHECKLIST

Largo Rainha Dona Amélia.
☎ 21-910 68 40. ◷ 10am–
5:30pm Thu–Tue. ● 1 Jan,
Easter, 1 May, 29 Jun, 25 Dec. ☒
☒ (free 10am–1pm Sun).
W www.ippar.pt

Sala das Sereias
Intricate Arabesque designs on 16th-century tiles frame this door in the Room of the Sirens.

The Sala dos Árabes
is decorated with fine *azulejos.*

The kitchens, beneath the huge conical chimneys, have spits and utensils once used for preparing royal banquets.

Entrance

Sala dos Archeiros,
the entrance hall

Manuel I added the *ajimece* windows, a distinctive Moorish design with a slender column dividing two arches.

Chapel
Symmetrical Moorish patterns decorate the original 14th-century chestnut and oak ceiling and the mosaic floor of the private chapel.

STAR FEATURES

★ Sala dos Brasões

★ Sala dos Cisnes

★ Sala das Pegas

Sintra: Palácio da Pena

ON THE HIGHEST PEAKS of the Serra de Sintra stands the spectacular palace of Pena, an eclectic medley of architectural styles built in the 19th century for the husband of the young Queen Maria II, Ferdinand Saxe-Coburg-Gotha. It stands over the ruins of a Hieronymite monastery founded here in the 15th century on the site of the chapel of Nossa Senhora da Pena.

Triton Arch Ferdinand appointed a German architect, Baron Von Eschwege, to build his summer palace filled with oddities from all over the world and surrounded by a park. With the declaration of the Republic in 1910, the palace became a museum, preserved as it was when the royal family lived here. Allow at least an hour and a half to visit this enchanting place.

Entrance Arch
A studded archway with crenellated turrets greets the visitor at the entrance to the palace. The palace buildings are painted the original daffodil yellow and strawberry pink.

Manuel II's Bedroom
The oval-shaped room is decorated with bright red walls and stuccoed ceiling. A portrait of Manuel II, the last king of Portugal, hangs above the fireplace.

In the kitchen the copper pots and utensils still hang around the iron stove. The dinner service bears the coat of arms of Ferdinand II.

★ Ballroom
The spacious ballroom is sumptuously furnished with German stained-glass windows, precious Oriental porcelain and four lifesize turbaned torchbearers holding giant candelabra.

★ **Arab Room**
Marvellous trompe-l'oeil frescoes cover the walls and ceiling of the Arab Room, one of the loveliest in the palace. The Orient was a great inspiration to Romanticism.

VISITORS' CHECKLIST

Estrada da Pena, 5 km (3 mile) S of Sintra. **[** 21-910 53 40. **▬** from Avenida Dr Miguel Bombarda, Sintra. **○** May–Oct: 9:30am– 6pm, Tue–Sun (Jun– Sept 7pm); Nov– Apr: 10am–5pm, Tue–Sun. **●** 1 Jan, Easter, 1 May, 29 Jun, 25 Dec. **☒** (free 10am–1pm Sun).

★ **Chapel Altarpiece**
The impressive 16th-century alabaster and marble retable was sculpted by Nicolau Chanterène. Each niche portrays a scene of the life of Christ, from the manger to the Ascension.

The Triton Arch is encrusted with Neo-Manueline decoration and is guarded by a fierce sea monster.

The cloister, decorated with colourful patterned tiles, is part of the original monastery buildings.

Entrance

STAR FEATURES

★ **Arab Room**

★ **Ballroom**

★ **Chapel Altarpiece**

FERDINAND: KING CONSORT

Ferdinand was known in Portugal as Dom Fernando II, the "artist" king. Like his cousin Prince Albert, who married the English Queen Victoria, he loved art, nature and the new inventions of the time. He was himself a watercolour painter. Ferdinand enthusiastically adopted his new country and devoted his life to patronizing the arts. In 1869, 16 years after the death of Maria II, Ferdinand married his mistress, the opera singer Countess Edla. His lifelong dream of building the extravagant palace at Pena was completed in 1885, the year he died.

Outdoor café in the popular holiday resort of Cascais

Cascais ⑦

Road map B5. 🕺 *33,000.* 🚊 🚌
ℹ️ *Rua Visconde da Luz 14 (21-486 82 04).* 🛒 *1st & 3rd Sun of month.*

HAVING BEEN A holiday resort for well over a century, Cascais possesses a certain illustriousness that younger resorts lack. Its history is most clearly visible in the villas along the coast, built as summer residences by wealthy *Lisboetas* during the late 19th century, after King Luís I had moved his summer activities to the 17th-century fortress here. The military importance of Cascais, now waned, is much older as it sits on the north bank of the mouth of the Tagus.

The sandy, sheltered bay around which the modern suburb has sprawled was a fishing harbour in prehistoric times. Fishing still goes on, and was recently given a municipal boost with the

decision to build a new quay for the landing and initial auctioning of the fishermen's catch. But Cascais today is first of all a favoured suburb of Lisbon, a place of apartments with a sea view and pine-studded plots by golf courses. It may sometimes seem more defined by its ceaseless construction boom than by any historic or even touristic qualities, but the beautiful, windswept coastline beyond the town has been left relatively undeveloped.

The Museu do Conde de Castro Guimaraes is perhaps the best place to get a taste of Cascais as it was just over a century ago. A castle-like villa on a small creek by a headland, its grounds are today part of a park. The house and its contents were bequeathed to the municipality.

Across the road from the museum is the new marina, one of the most emblematic new developments in Cascais. With its small shopping centre, restaurants and cafés it is becoming a weekend magnet for today's car-borne Cascais residents and tourists.

🏛 Museu do Conde de Castro Guimarães
Avenida Rei Humberto de Itália. ☎️ *21-482 54 07.* **Museum** ⏲ *10am–5pm Tue–Sun.* 📚 **Library** *Casa da Horta de Santa Clara.* ⏲ *10am–7pm Mon–Sat.* ⬤ *public hols.*

ENVIRONS: At **Boca do Inferno** (Mouth of Hell), about 3 km (2 miles) west on the coast road, the sea rushes into clefts and caves in the rocks making an ominous booming sound and sending up spectacular spray in rough weather. The place is almost obscured by a roadside market and cafés but a small platform gives a good view of the rocky arch with the sea roaring in below.

The magnificent sandy beach of **Guincho**, 10 km (6 miles) further west, is backed by sand dunes with clumps of umbrella pines, and a new cycle path. A small fort (now a luxury hotel) stands perched on the rocks above the sea. Atlantic breakers rolling in make this a paradise for experienced windsurfers and surfers, though beware of the strong currents.

Spectacular view of the weatherbeaten coastline at Boca do Inferno, near Cascais

Estoril ⑧

Road map B5. 🕺 *24,000.* 🚊 🚌
ℹ️ *Arcadas do Parque (214-664 414).*

DESPITE ONCE BEING the haunt of exiled royalty and obscure nobility fleeing European republicanism, the lovely resort town of Estoril does not rest on its historical laurels. Today, it is a tourist and business resort, and a place for comfortable retirement. As such, it relies equally on its historical reputation and on the natural attractiveness it has always possessed. There are also a number of good golf courses.

What separates Estoril from Cascais, besides a pleasant beach promenade of 3 km (2 miles) and a mansion covered ridge known as Monte Estoril, is its sense of place. The heart of Estoril is immediately accessible from the train station. On one side of the tracks, the riviera-like beach,

Sandy beach and promenade along the bay of Estoril

on the other, a palm-lined park flanked by grand buildings, stretches up past fountains to what is said to be Europe's biggest casino. Dwarfing the casino is the Estoril Congress Centre, a vast multipurpose edifice that speaks confidently of Estoril's contemporary role.

Palácio de Queluz **❾**

See pp164–5.

Alcochete **❿**

Road map C5. 🏘 *9,000.* ▦ ℹ *Largo da Misericórdia (21-234 26 31).*

THIS DELIGHTFUL old town overlooks the wide Tagus estuary from the southern shore. Salt has long been one of the main industries here, and saltpans can still be seen to the north and south of the town, while in the town centre a large statue of a muscular salt worker has the inscription: "Do Sal a Revolta e a Esperança" (From Salt to Rebellion and Hope). On the outskirts of town, is a statue of Manuel I *(see pp46–7),* who was born here on 1 June 1469 and granted the town a Royal Charter in 1515.

Statue of a salt worker in Alcochete (1985)

ENVIRONS: The **Reserva Natural do Estuário do Tejo** covers a vast area of estuary water, salt marshes and small islands around Alcochete and is a very important breeding ground for water birds. Particularly interesting are the flocks of flamingos that gather here during the autumn and spring migration, en route from colonies such as the Camargue in France and Fuente de Piedra in Spain. Ask at the tourist office about boat trips to see the wildlife of the estuary, which includes wild bulls and horses.

🐾 **Reserva Natural do Estuário do Tejo**
Avenida dos Combatentes da Grande Guerra 1. ⬛ *21-234 17 42.*

Pilgrims' lodgings, Cabo Espichel

Costa da Caparica **⓫**

Road map B5. 🏘 *12,000.* 🚆 *to Pragal then bus.* ℹ *Av. da República 18 (21-290 00 71).*

LONG SANDY beaches, backed by sand dunes, have made this a popular holiday resort for Lisboetas who come here to swim, sunbathe and enjoy the seafood restaurants and beach cafés. A railway, with open carriages, runs for 10 km (6 miles) along the coast during the summer months. The first beaches reached from the town are popular with families with children, while the furthest beaches suit those seeking quiet isolation. Further south, sheltered by pine forests, **Lagoa do Albufeira**, is a peaceful wind-surfing centre and camp site.

Cabo Espichel **⓬**

Road map B5. 🚌 *from Sesimbra.*

SHEER CLIFFS DROP straight into the sea at this windswept promontory where the land ends dramatically. The Romans named it Promontorium Barbaricum, alluding to its dangerous location, and a lighthouse warns sailors of the treacherous rocks below. Stunning views of the ocean and the coast can be enjoyed from this bleak outcrop of land but beware of the strong gusts of wind on the cliff edge.

In this desolate setting stands the impressive **Santuário de Nossa Senhora do Cabo**, a late 17th-century church with its back to the sea. On either side of the church a long line of pilgrims' lodgings facing inwards form an open courtyard. Baroque paintings, ex votos and a frescoed ceiling decorate the interior of the church. There are plans to fully restore the building and open it as a hotel. A domed chapel, tiled with blue and white *azulejo* panels, is located nearby.

The site became a popular place of pilgrimage in the 13th century when a local man had a vision of the Madonna rising from the sea on a mule. Legend has it that the tracks of the mule can be seen embedded in the rock. The large footprints, on Praia dos Lagosteiros below the church, are actually believed to be fossilized dinosaur tracks.

Spring flowers by the saltpans of the Tagus estuary near Alcochete

Palácio de Queluz ❾

IN 1747, PEDRO, younger son of João V, commissioned Mateus Vicente to transform his 17th-century hunting lodge into a Rococo summer palace. The central section, including a music room and chapel, was built, but after Pedro's marriage in 1760 to the future Maria I, the palace was again extended. The French architect, Jean-Baptiste Robillion, added the sumptuous Robillion Pavilion and gardens, cleared space for the Throne Room and redesigned the Music Room. During Maria's reign, the royal family kept a menagerie and went boating on the *azulejo*-lined canal.

A sphinx in the gardens

Corridor of the Sleeves
Painted azulejo panels (1784) representing the continents and the seasons, as well as hunting scenes, line the walls of the bright Corridor das Mangas (sleeves).

Neptune's Fountain

★ Sala dos Embaixadores
Built by Robillion, this stately room was used for diplomatic audiences as well as concerts. The trompe l'oeil ceiling shows the royal family attending a concert.

The Lion Staircase is an impressive and graceful link from the lower gardens to the palace.

STAR FEATURES

★ **Throne Room**

★ **Sala dos Embaixadores**

★ **Palace Gardens**

To canal

Lion Fountain

The Robillion Pavilion displays the flamboyance of the French architect's Rococo style.

Don Quixote Chamber
The royal bedroom, where Pedro IV (see p54) was born and died, has a domed ceiling and magnificent floor decoration in exotic woods, giving the square room a circular appearance. Painted scenes by Manuel de Costa (1784) tell the story of Don Quixote.

Music Room

Operas and concerts were performed here by Maria I's orchestra, "the best in Europe" according to English traveller, William Beckford. A portrait of the queen hangs above the grand piano.

VISITORS' CHECKLIST

Road map B5. Largo do Palácio.
21-434 38 60. Queluz-Belas or Queluz-Massama. from Lisbon, (Colégio Militar). 10am–5pm Wed–Mon. 29 Nov, Easter, 1 May, 25 Dec, 1 Jan. (free 10am–noon Sun). Cozinha Velha (see p409).

Chapel

The royal family's living rooms and bedrooms opened out onto the Malta Gardens.

★ Throne Room

The elegant state room (1770) was the scene of splendid balls and banquets. The gilded statues of Atlas are by Silvestre Faria Lobo.

Entrance

Malta Gardens

The Hanging Gardens, designed by Robillion, were built over arches, raising the ground in front of the palace above the surrounding gardens.

MARIA I (1734–1816)

Maria, the eldest daughter of José I, lived at the palace in Queluz after her marriage to her uncle, Pedro, in 1760. Serious and devout, she conscientiously filled her role as queen, but suffered increasingly from bouts of melancholia. When her son José died from smallpox in 1788, she went hopelessly mad. Visitors to Queluz were dismayed by her agonizing shrieks as she suffered visions and hallucinations. After the French invasion of 1807, her younger son João (declared regent in 1792) took his mad mother to Brazil.

★ Palace Gardens

The formal gardens, adorned with statues, fountains and topiary, were often used for entertaining. Concerts performed in the Music Room would spill out into the Malta Gardens.

Sesimbra ®

Road map C5. 🚶 *21,000.* 🚌
ℹ️ *Largo da Marinha 26–7 (21-228 85 40).* 🔄 *1st & 3rd Fri of month.*

A STEEP NARROW ROAD leads down to this busy fishing village in a sheltered south-facing bay. Protected from north winds by the slopes of the Serra da Arrábida, the town has become a popular holiday resort with Lisboetas. It was occupied by the Romans and later the Moors until King Sancho II *(see pp42–3)* conquered its heavily defended forts in 1236. The old town is a maze of steep narrow streets, with the **Santiago Fort** (now a customs post) in the centre overlooking the sea. From the terrace, which is open to the public during the day, there are views over the town, the Atlantic and the wide sandy beach that stretches out on either side. Sesimbra is fast developing as a resort, with holiday flats mushrooming on the surrounding hillsides and plentiful pavement cafés and bars that are always busy on sunny days, even in winter.

The fishing fleet of brightly painted boats is moored in the **Porto do Abrigo** to the west of the main town. The harbour is reached by taking Avenida dos Náufragos, a sweeping

Colourful fishing boats in the harbour at Sesimbra

promenade that follows the beach out of town. On the large trawlers *(traineiras)*, the catch is mainly sardines, sea bream, whiting and swordfish; on the smaller boats, octopus and squid. In the late afternoon, when the fishing boats return from a day at sea, a colourful, noisy fish auction takes place on the quayside. The day's catch can be tasted in the town's excellent fish restaurants along the shore.

High above the town is the **Moorish castle**, greatly restored in the 18th century when a church and small flower-filled cemetery were added inside the walls. There are wonderful views from the ramparts, especially at sunset.

Palmela ⑭

Road map C5. 🚶 *16,000.* 🚌 🚉
ℹ️ *Castelo de Palmela (21-233 21 22).* 🔄 *every other Tue.*

THE FORMIDABLE castle at Palmela stands over the small hilltown, high on a north-eastern spur of the wooded Serra da Arrábida. Its strategic position dominates the plain for miles around, especially when floodlit at night. Heavily defended by the Moors, it was eventually conquered in the 12th century and given by Sancho I to the Knights of the Order of Santiago *(see p43)*. In 1423, João I transformed the castle into a monastery for the Order, which has now been restored and converted into a splendid *pousada (see p385)*, with a restaurant in the monks' refectory and a swimming pool for residents, hidden inside the castle walls.

From the castle terraces, and especially from the top of the 14th-century keep, there are fantastic views all around, over the Serra da Arrábida to the south and on a clear day across the Tagus to Lisbon. In the town square below, the church of **São Pedro** contains 18th-century tiles of scenes from the life of St Peter.

The annual wine festival, the Festa das Vindimas, is held on the first weekend of September in front of the 17th-century Paços do Concelho (town hall). Traditionally dressed villagers, press the wine barefoot and on the final day of celebrations there is a spectacular firework display from the castle walls.

The castle at Palmela with views over the wooded Serra da Arrábida

Serra da Arrábida 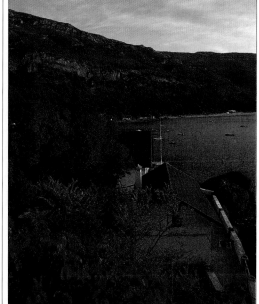❿

Road map C5. ▦ *Setúbal*.
ℹ *Parque Natural da Arrábida, Praça da República, Setúbal (265-54 11 40).*

THE PARQUE NATURAL da
Arrábida covers the small
range of limestone mountains
which stretches east-west along
the coast between Sesimbra
and Setúbal. It was established
to protect the wild, beautiful
landscape and rich variety of
birds and wildlife, including
eagles, wildcats and badgers.

The name Arrábida is from
Arabic meaning a place of
prayer, and the wooded hillsides are indeed a peaceful,
secluded retreat. The sheltered,
south-facing slopes are thickly
covered with aromatic and
evergreen shrubs and trees
such as pine and cypress, more
typical of the Mediterranean.
Vineyards also thrive on the
sheltered slopes and the town
of **Vila Nogueira de Azeitão** is
known for its wine, especially
the Moscatel de Setúbal.

The **Estrada de Escarpa**
(the N379-1) snakes across the
top of the ridge and affords
astounding views. A narrow
road winds down to **Portinho
da Arrábida**, a sheltered cove
with a beach of fine white sand
and crystal clear sea, popular
with underwater fishermen.
The sandy beaches of **Galapos**
and **Figueirinha** are a little
further east along the coast
road towards Setúbal. Just
east of Sesimbra, the Serra da
Arrábida drops to the sea in
the sheer 380-m (1,250-ft)
cliffs of Risco,
the highest
in mainland
Portugal.

Portinho da Arrábida on the dramatic coastline of the Serra da Arrábida

⌂ Convento da Arrábida

Serra da Arrábida. 【 *21-218 05 20.*
◐ *by appt only, via Fundação Oriente
(phone 21-352 70 02).* 📷
Half-hidden among the trees
on the southern slopes of the
Serra, this large 16th-century
building was once a Franciscan
monastery. The five round
towers perched on the hillside
were probably used for
solitary meditation.

🏛 Museu Oceanográfico

Fortaleza de Santa Maria, Portinho
da Arrábida. 【 *265-54 11 40.*
◐ *9am–noon, 2–5pm Tue–Fri.* 📷
This small fort, just above
Portinho da Arrábida, was
built by Pedro, the Prince
Regent, in 1676 to protect
local communities from
attacks by Moorish pirates.
It now houses a Sea Museum
and Marine Biology Centre
where visitors can see
aquaria containing many
local sea creatures,
including sea urchins,
octopus and starfish.

▮ José Maria de Fonseca

Rua José Augusto Coelho 11, Vila
Nogueira de Azeitão. 【 *21-219
89 40.* **FAX** *21-219 89 42.* ◐
*9am–noon, 2:15–4:15pm Mon–Fri;
10am–12:15pm, 2:15–4:30pm Sat.*
◑ *Dec 24–Jan 1.* 📷 🎫 ▯
The Fonseca winery produces
quality table wines and is
famous for its fragrant dessert
wine, Moscatel de Setúbal *(see
p29).* Tours of the winery
explain the process of making
moscatel and a visit to a series
of old cellars containing huge
oak and chestnut vats. Tours
last about 45 minutes and
include a wine tasting.

KEY

▬ Major road

▬ Minor road

═ Other road

0 kilometres 5

0 miles 3

Manueline interior of Igreja de Jesus, Setúbal

Setúbal ⑯

Road map C5. 🚶 *92,000.* 🚌 🚢
⛴ 🛈 *Casa do Corpo Santo, Praça do Quebedo (265-53 42 22).*

Although this is an important
industrial town, and the
third largest port in Portugal
(after Lisbon and Oporto),
Setúbal can be used to
explore the area. To the south
of the central gardens and
fountains are the fishing harbour, marina and ferry port,
and a lively covered market.
North of the gardens is the
old town, with attractive
pedestrian streets and squares
full of shops and cafés.

The 16th-century **cathedral**,
dedicated to Santa Maria da
Graça, has glorious tiled panels
dating from the 18th century,
and gilded altar decoration.
Street names commemorate
two famous Setúbal residents:
Manuel Barbosa du Bocage
(1765–1805), whose satirical
poetry landed him in prison,
and Luísa Todi (1753–1833),
a celebrated opera singer.

In Roman times, fish-salting
was the most important industry here. Rectangular tanks,
carved from stone, can be
seen under the glass floor of
the Regional Tourist Office at
No. 10 Travessa Frei Gaspar.

🏛 Igreja de Jesus
Praça Miguel Bombarda. 📞 *265-52
41 50.* ⏰ *9am–noon, 2–5pm Tue–
Sun.* ♿ **Museum** 📞 *265-52 47 72.*
⏰ *Tue–Sat.* ⬤ *public hols.*
To the north of the old town,
this striking Gothic church is
one of Setúbal's architectural
treasures. Designed by the

**Fisherman's boat on the shallow mud flats of
the Reserva Natural do Estuário do Sado**

architect Diogo Boitac in 1494,
the lofty interior is adorned
with twisted columns, carved
in three strands from pinkish
Arrábida limestone, and rope-
like stone ribs decorating the
roof, recognized as the earliest
examples of the distinctive
Manueline style *(see pp20–21).*

On Rua do Balneário, in
the old monastic quarters, a
museum houses 14 remarkable paintings of the life of
Christ. Painted in glowing
colours, the works are attributed to the followers of Jorge
Afonso (1520–30), influenced
by the Flemish school.

🏛 Museu de Arqueologia e Etnografia
Avenida Luísa Todi 162. 📞 *265-239
365.* ⏰ *Tue–Sat.* ⬤ *public hols.*
The archaeological museum
displays a wealth of finds from
digs around Setúbal, including
Bronze Age pots, Roman coins
and amphorae made to carry
wine and *garum*, a sauce
made from fish marinated in
salt and herbs considered a
great delicacy in Rome. The
ethnography display shows
local arts, crafts and industries,
including the processing of salt
and cork over the centuries.

♣ Castelo de São Filipe
Estrada de São Filipe. 📞 *265-52 38
44.* ⏰ *daily.*
The star-shaped fort was built
in 1595 by Philip II of Spain
during the period of Spanish
rule *(see pp50–51)* to keep a
wary eye on pirates, English
invaders and the local population. A massive gateway
and stone tunnel lead to the
sheltered interior, which now
houses a *pousada (see p385)*
and an exquisite small chapel,
tiled with scenes from the life
of São Filipe by Policarpo de
Oliveira Bernardes
(see p22). A broad
terrace offers mar-
vellous views over
the city and the
Sado estuary.

Environs: Setúbal is
an excellent starting
point for a tour by
car of the unspoilt
**Reserva Natural
do Estuário do
Sado**, a vast stretch
of mud flats, shallow

lagoons and salt marshes with patches of pine forest, which has been explored and inhabited since 3500 BC. Otters, water birds (including storks and herons), oysters and a great variety of fish are found in the reserve. The old tidal water mill at Mouriscas, 5 km (3 miles) to the east of Setúbal, uses the different levels of the tide to turn the grinding stones. Rice-growing and fishing are the main occupations today, and pine trees around the lagoon are tapped for resin.

▼ Reserva Natural do Estuário do Sado
🛈 *Praça da República, Setúbal (265-54 11 40).*

Península de Tróia 🄱

Road map C5. 🚌 ⛴ *Tróia.* 🛈 *Complexo Turístico de Tróia (265-49 43 12)*

Thatched fisherman's cottage in the village of Carrasqueira

HIGH-RISE HOLIDAY apartments dominate the tip of the Tróia peninsula, easily accessible from Setúbal by ferry. The Atlantic coast, stretching south for 18 km (11 miles) of untouched sandy beach, lined with dunes and pine woods, is now the haunt of sunseekers in the summer.

Near Tróia, in the sheltered lagoon, the Roman town of **Cetóbriga** was the site of a thriving fish-salting business; the stone tanks and ruined buildings are open to visit. To the south, smart new holiday villas and golf clubs are springing up along the lagoon.

Further on, **Carrasqueira** is an old fishing community where you can still see traditional reed houses, with walls and roofs made from thatch. The narrow fishing boats

View over Alcácer do Sal and the River Sado from the castle

moored along the mud flats are reached by walkways raised on stilts. From here to Alcácer do Sal, great stretches of pine forest line the road, and there are the first glimpses of the cork oak countryside typical of the Alentejo.

Cetóbriga
N253-1. 🕻 *265-49 43 18.* ⃝ *daily.*

Alcácer do Sal 🄱

Road map C5. 🏠 *9,000.* 🚍 🚌 🛈 *Rua da República 76 (265-610 070).* 📅 *1st Sat of month.*

BYPASSED by the main road, the ancient town of Alcácer do Sal (*al-kasr* from the Arabic for castle, and *do sal* from its trade in salt) sits peacefully on the north bank of the River Sado. The imposing castle was a hillfort as early as the 6th century BC.

The Phoenicians established an inland trading port here, and the castle later became a stronghold for the Romans. Rebuilt by the Moors, it was finally conquered by Afonso II in 1217. The restored buildings have now taken on a new life as a *pousada (see p384)*, with sweeping views over the rooftops and untidy storks' nests on the town's church roofs.

There are pleasant cafés along the riverside promenade and several historic churches. The small church of Espírito Santo now houses a **Museu Arqueológico** exhibiting local finds and the 18th-century **Santo António** holds a marble Chapel of the 11,000 Virgins. The bullring is a focus for summer events and hosts the agricultural fair in October.

🏛 Museu Arqueológico
Igreja do Espírito Santo, Praça Pedro Nunes. 🕻 *265-61 00 70.* ⃝ *daily.*

BIRDS OF THE TAGUS AND SADO ESTUARIES

Many waterbirds, including black-winged stilts, avocets, Kentish plovers and pratincoles are found close to areas of open water and mud flats as well as the dried out lagoons of the Tagus and Sado estuaries. Reed-beds also provide shelter for nesting and support good numbers of little bitterns, purple herons and marsh harriers. From September to March, the area around the Tagus estuary is extremely important for wildfowl and wintering waders.

Black-winged stilt, a wader that feeds in the estuaries

ESTREMADURA AND RIBATEJO

ETWEEN THE TAGUS *and the coast lies Estremadura, an area of rolling hills that tumble down to rugged cliffs and sandy beaches. In contrast, the Ribatejo is a vast alluvial plain stretching along the banks of the Tagus. Portugal's finest medieval monasteries bear witness to the illustrious, if turbulent past of these regions.*

The name Estremadura comes from the Latin *Extrema Durii*, "beyond the Douro", once the border of the Christian kingdoms in the north. As Portugal expanded southwards in the 12th century, land taken from the Moors *(see pp42–3)* was given to the religious orders. The Cistercian abbey at Alcobaça celebrates Afonso Henriques's capture of the town of Santarém in 1147, and the Knights Templar began their citadel at Tomar *(see p185)* soon after.

Spanish claims to the Portuguese throne brought more fighting: Batalha's magnificent abbey was built near the site of João I's victory over the Castilians at Aljubarrota in 1385. More recently, in 1808–10, Napoleonic forces sacked many towns in the region, but were stopped by Wellington's formidable defences, the Lines of Torres Vedras.

Nowadays, Estremadura is an area of expanding commerce, where vineyards, wheatfields and market gardens flourish. In the Ribatejo (the name means "Banks of the Tagus") the river's vast flood plain provides fertile soil for agriculture and grazing land for Portugal's prized black fighting bulls and fine horses.

The area around Tomar and the river towns along the Tagus have thriving industries, while on the River Zêzere, the dam built at Castelo de Bode in the 1940s heralded a new era of hydro-electric power. The Atlantic coast is a popular holiday destination, especially the fishing village of Nazaré and the sandy beaches along the Pinhal de Leiria forest. Visitors also flock to Portugal's most important religious shrine at Fátima, scene of celebrated visions of the Virgin Mary in 1917.

Posters advertising the local bullfighting events in Coruche

◁ Austere Gothic columns in the nave of the Cistercian abbey church at Alcobaça

Exploring Estremadura and the Ribatejo

THE IMPRESSIVE MONUMENTS in Estremadura recall the important role the region has played in Portugal's history. Tomar and Óbidos are convenient bases from which to visit the great abbeys at Batalha and Alcobaça or the modern shrine at Fátima. Leiria's charming old town is also a good place to stay and it is possible to make day trips from Lisbon. Those in search of more leisurely pursuits can enjoy boating on the Castelo de Bode lake or relaxing on the coast's stunning beaches. The fertile Lezíria plain of the Ribatejo is an area famous for bull- and horse-breeding. Here visitors can enjoy bullfights at Santarém and lively local festivals.

SIGHTS AT A GLANCE

Abrantes **14**
Alcobaça *pp178–9* **5**
Alenquer **22**
Alpiarça **18**
Barragem do
    Castelo de Bode **13**
Batalha pp182–3 **8**
Berlenga Islands **1**
Caldas da Rainha **4**
Castelo de Almourol **15**
Coruche **20**
Fátima **11**
Golegã **17**
Leiria **9**
Nazaré **6**
Óbidos **3**
Peniche **2**

Pombal **10**
Porto de Mós **7**
Santarém **19**
Tomar pp184–7 **12**
Torres Novas **16**
Torres Vedras **23**
Vila Franca de Xira **21**

GETTING AROUND

Although trains connect many of the major towns in the region, stations are often located outside the town. There are local bus services and coach trips from Lisbon to such destinations as Alcobaça and Tomar. Driving is the most convenient option. The A1 (E1) and A8 (IC1) allow easy north-south access. Avoid the NI (IC2) as it is often congested. The IP6 (E806) runs eastwards from the A1 (E1).

Colourful beach tents at São Martinho do Porto, near Nazaré

0 kilometres   25
0 miles   15

Bougainvillea overhanging the walls of a café in the well-preserved town of Óbidos

KEY

	Motorway
	Major road
	Minor road
	Scenic route
	River

SEE ALSO

- **Where to Stay** pp386–8
- **Where to Eat** pp410–11

The Renaissance bridge, Ponte Velha, over the River Nabão in Tomar, with the Convento de Cristo in the distance

Berlenga Islands ❶

Road map B4. ⛴ *from Peniche.*
ℹ *Peniche.*

Monks, a lighthouse keeper, fishermen and, recently, biologists have inhabited this rocky archipelago that juts out from the Atlantic Ocean 12 km (7 miles) from the mainland. Berlenga Grande, the biggest island, can be reached by ferry in about an hour. This island is a nature reserve with nesting sites for seabirds including guillemots and herring gulls.

On the southeast side of the island is the 17th-century pentagonal **Forte de São João Baptista**. This stark, stone fort suffered repeated assaults from pirates and foreign armies over the years. Today it is a basic hostel. Small boats can be hired from the jetty to explore the reefs and marine grottoes around the island. **Furado Grande** is the most spectacular of these; a 70-m (230-ft) tunnel, opening into the Covo do Sonho (Dream Cove) framed by imposing red granite cliffs.

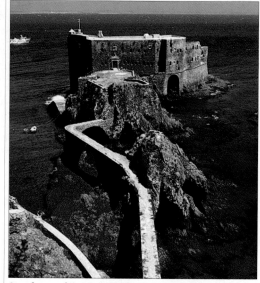

Stone fortress of São João Baptista on Berlenga Grande

Peniche ❷

Road map B4. 👥 *20,000.* 🚌
ℹ *Rua Alexandre Herculano (262-78 95 71).* 🏛 *Last Thu of the month (except Jul & Dec).*

Set on a peninsula, this small, pleasant town is partly enclosed by 16th-century walls. Totally dependent on its port, Peniche has good fish restaurants and deep-sea fishing facilities. At the water's edge on the south side of town stands the 16th-century **Fortaleza**, used as a prison during the Salazar regime *(see pp56–7)*. The fortress was made famous by the escape in 1960 of the communist leader, Álvaro Cunhal. Inside, the **Museu de Peniche** caters to popular interest with a tour that includes a look into the prison cells. In Largo 5 de Outubro, the **Igreja da Misericórdia** has 17th-century painted ceiling panels depicting the *Life of Christ,* and patterned *azulejo* panels from the same period.

🏛 **Museu de Peniche**
Campo da República. 【 *262-78 01 16.* ◯ *Tue–Sun.* ● *25 Dec.* 🎟

Environs: On the peninsula's western headland, 2 km (1 mile) from Peniche, **Cabo Carvoeiro** affords grand views of the ocean and the strange-shaped rocks along the eroded coastline. Here, the interior of the chapel of **Nossa Senhora dos Remédios** is faced with 18th-century tiles on the *Life of the Virgin* attributed to the workshop of António de Oliveira Bernardes *(see p22).*

Along the coast, 2 km (1 mile) east of Peniche, **Baleal** is a small community with gorgeous beaches and an idyllic fishing cove across a causeway.

Óbidos ❸

Road map B4. 👥 *3,000.* 🚉 🚌
ℹ *Rua Direita (262-95 92 31).*

This enchanting hilltown with pretty whitewashed houses is enclosed within 14th-century castellated walls. When King Dinis *(see pp44–5)* married Isabel of Aragon in 1282, Óbidos was among his wedding presents to her. At the time Óbidos was an important port, but by the 16th century the river had silted up and its strategic importance declined. It has since been restored and preserved as a picture-postcard town, popular with tourists.

Boats anchored in the old harbour at Peniche

The entrance into the town is through the southern gate, **Porta da Vila**, whose interior is embellished with 18th-century tiles. Rua Direita, the main shopping street, leads to Praça de Santa Maria. Here, a Manueline **pelourinho** (pillory) is decorated with a fishing net, the emblem of Dona Leonor, wife of João II. She chose this emblem in honour of the fishermen who tried in vain to save her son from drowning.

Opposite the pillory is the church of **Santa Maria**, with a simple Renaissance portal. The future Afonso V was married to his cousin Isabel here in 1441. He was ten years old, she eight. The interior of the church retains a simple clarity with a painted wooden ceiling and 17th-century tiles. In the chancel, a retable depicting the *Mystic Marriage of St Catherine* (1661) is by Josefa de Óbidos *(see p51)*. The artist lived most of her life in Óbidos and is buried in the church of **São Pedro** on Largo de São Pedro. Her work is also on display in the **Museu Municipal**.

Dominating the town is the **castle**, rebuilt by Afonso Henriques after he took the town from the Moors in 1148.

View of the castle over the whitewashed houses of Óbidos

Today it is a charming *pousada* *(see p387)*. The sentry path along the battlements affords fine views of the rooftops.

Southeast of town is the Baroque **Santuário do Senhor da Pedra**, begun in 1740 to a hexagonal plan. An early Christian stone crucifix on the altar remains a venerated item.

🏛 Museu Municipal
Praça de Santa Maria. **(** 262-95 50 10. **◯** daily. **●** 1 Jan, 25 Dec. 🖾

Caldas da Rainha ④

Road map B4. 🏠 22,000. 🚃 🚌
ℹ Praça da República (262-83 45 11). **◯** May–Nov. **●** Mon.

THE "QUEEN'S HOT SPRINGS" is a sprawling spa town. It owes its prosperity to successes in three quite different fields: thermal cures, fruit farming and ceramics. The queen who gave her name to the town was Dona Leonor, founder of the **Misericórdia** hospital on Largo Rainha Dona Leonor. The original hospital chapel later became the impressive Manueline **Igreja do Populo**, built by Diogo Boitac *(see pp106–7)*. Inside is the chapel of São Sebastião, built in the 15th century and faced with 18th-century *azulejos*.

The market in Praça da República and shops in Rua da Liberdade sell local ceramics, including the green cabbage-leaf majolica ware *(see pp24–5)* typical of the town. Examples of the religious and humorous work of the caricaturist and potter, Rafael Bordalo Pinheiro (1846–1905), can be seen in the **Museu de Cerâmica**, housed in the ceramics factory.

🏛 Museu de Cerâmica
Rua Dr Ilídio Amado. **(** 262-840 280. **◯** Tue–Sun. **●** public hols. 🖾

ENVIRONS: The saltwater **Lagoa de Óbidos**, 15 km (9 miles) west of Caldas, is a popular lagoon for sailing and fishing.

Pillory in front of the Igreja de Santa Maria in Óbidos

The fairytale town of Óbidos encircled by medieval crenellated walls ▷

Alcobaça ⑤

PORTUGAL'S LARGEST CHURCH, the Mosteiro de Santa Maria de Alcobaça, is renowned for its simple medieval architecture. Founded in 1153, the abbey is closely linked to the arrival of the Cistercian order in Portugal in 1138 as well as the birth of the nation. In March 1147, Afonso Henriques *(see pp42–3)* conquered the Moorish stronghold of Santarém. To commemorate the victory, the king fulfilled his vow to build a mighty church for the Cistercians. This massive task was completed in 1223. The monarchy continued to endow the monastery, notably King Dinis who built the main cloister. Among those buried here are the tragic lovers King Pedro and his murdered mistress Inês.

Sacristy Doorway
Exotic foliage and elaborate pinnacles adorn the Manueline doorway, attributed to João de Castilho (see p106).

Tomb of Inês de Castro

Dormitory

The chapterhouse was where the monks met to elect the abbot and discuss issues regarding the monastery.

The kitchen's huge chimney

The octagonal lavabo was where the monks washed their hands.

Refectory and Kitchen
Stairs lead up to the pulpit where one of the monks read from the Bible as the others ate in silence. In the vast kitchen next door, oxen could be roasted on the spit inside the chimney and a specially diverted stream provided a constant water supply.

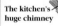

STAR FEATURES

★ **Cloister of Dom Dinis**

★ **Tombs of Pedro I and Inês de Castro**

★ **Cloister of Dom Dinis**
Also known as the Cloister of Silence, the exquisite cloister was ordered by King Dinis in 1308. The austere galleries and double arches are in keeping with the Cistercian regard for simplicity.

Death of St Bernard, late 17th-century ceramic sculpture by the monks

★ **Tombs of Pedro I and Inês de Castro**
Pedro's statue, attended by angels, lies opposite that of Inês. The king insisted that they face each other so that his first sight on Judgment Day would be of his beloved (see pp44–5).

VISITORS' CHECKLIST

Road map C4. Mosteiro de Santa Maria de Alcobaça, Praça 25 de Abril, Alcobaça. ☎ 262-50 51 20. ▦ from Lisbon, Coimbra & Leiria. ◷ 9am–7pm (Oct–Mar: 5pm) daily (last adm: 30 mins before closing). ● 1 Jan, Easter, 1 May, 25 Dec. ✟ 11:30am Sun. 🎦

Central Nave
The vaulted roof and soaring columns of the central nave create an impression of harmony and austere simplicity.

The façade is a richly decorated 18th-century addition. Marble statues of St Benedict and St Bernard flank the main doorway.

Main entrance

Sala dos Reis
Tiles from the 18th century depict the founding of the abbey and statues of Portuguese kings adorn the walls.

THE MURDER OF INÊS DE CASTRO

Reasons of state obliged Pedro, son and heir of Afonso IV *(see pp44–5)*, to marry Costanza, Infanta of Castile, despite the fact he was in love with a lady at court, Inês de Castro. When Costanza died, Pedro went to live with Inês in Coimbra. Persuaded that Inês's family was dangerous, Afonso IV had her murdered on 7 January 1355 *(see p203)*. On Afonso's death, Pedro took revenge on two of the killers by having their hearts torn out. Declaring that he had been married to Inês, Pedro had her corpse exhumed and crowned. In a final gruesome gesture, he compelled his court to kneel before Inês and kiss her decomposed hand.

The beach at Nazaré viewed from Sítio

Nazaré ❻

Road map C4. 🏠 *10,000.* 🚌
ℹ️ *Avenida da República 17 (262-56 11 94).* 🔵 *Fri.*

BESIDE A GLORIOUS BEACH in a sweeping bay backed by steep cliffs, this fishing village is a popular summer resort that has maintained some of its traditional character. Fishermen dressed in checked shirts and black stocking caps and fishwives wearing several layers of petticoats can still be seen mending nets and drying fish on wire racks on the beach. The bright boats with tall prows that once were hauled from the sea by oxen are still used, although now they have a proper anchorage south of the beach. According to legend the name Nazaré comes from

Baroque church of Nossa Senhora da Nazaré in Sítio

a statue of the Virgin Mary brought to the town by a monk from Nazareth in the 4th century.

High on the cliff above the town is **Sítio**, reached by a funicular that climbs 110 m (360 ft). At the cliff edge stands the tiny **Ermida da Memória**. According to legend, this is where the Virgin Mary saved Dom Fuas Roupinho, a local dignitary, and his horse from following a deer that leapt off the cliff in a sea mist in 1182. Across the square, the 17th-century church of **Nossa Senhora da Nazaré**, with two Baroque belfries and 18th-century tiles inside, contains an anonymous painting of the miraculous rescue. The church also contains the revered image of Our Lady of Nazaré. In September this statue is borne down to the sea in a traditional procession, a colourful reminder of the town's origins.

ENVIRONS: **São Martinho do Porto**, 13 km (8 miles) south of Nazaré, is a sandy beach on a curving, almost land-locked bay. The safe location makes it popular with families and children. The Visigothic church of **São Gião**, 5 km (3 miles) further south, has fine sculpting and well-proportioned arches.

Porto de Mós ❼

Road map C4. 🏠 *6,000.* 🚌
ℹ️ *Alameda D. Afonso Henriques (244-49 13 23).* 🔵 *Fri.*

ORIGINALLY A MOORISH fort, and rebuilt over the centuries by successive Christian kings, the rather fanciful **castle** perches on a hill above the small town of Porto de Mós. Its present appearance, with green cone-shaped turrets and an exquisite loggia, was the inspired work of King Afonso IV's master builders in 1420.

In the town below, the 13th-century church of **São João Baptista** retains its original

Romanesque portal. In the public gardens is the richly decorated Baroque church of **São Pedro**. Just off the Praça da República, the **Museu Municipal** displays a varied collection of local finds dating back to Roman remains and dinosaur bones. More modern exhibits include the local *mós* (millstones), as well as present-day ceramics and woven rugs.

🏛 **Museu Municipal**
Travessa de São Pedro. 📞 *244-49 96 15.* 🔵 *Tue–Sun.* ⚫ *public hols.*

Donkey in the Serra de Aire nature reserve, south of Porto de Mós

ENVIRONS: South of the town, the 38,900-ha (96,000-acre) **Parque Natural das Serras de Aire e Candeeiros** covers a limestone landscape of pastures, olive groves and stone walls and is a nesting place for the red-beaked chough.

The area is also dotted with vast and spectacular underground caverns with odd rock formations and festoons of stalactites and stalagmites. The **Grutas de Mira de Aire**, 17 km (10 miles) southeast of Porto de Mós, are the biggest, descending 110 m (360 ft) into tunnels and walkways around subterranean lakes. A tour through caverns with names such as the "Jewel Room", past bizarre rocks dubbed "Chinese Hat" or "Jellyfish", ends in a theatrical light and water show.

🦌 **Grutas de Mira de Aire**
Mira de Aire, E.N. 243. 📞 *244- 44 03 22.* 🔵 *daily.* 🎦

Batalha ❽

See pp182–3.

Leiria 9

Road map C4. 🏘 *13,000.* 🚗 🚌
ℹ *Jardim Luis de Camões
(244-82 37 73).* 🛒 *every second Tue
& Sat.* ⓦ *www.rt-leiriafatima.pt*

Episcopal city since 1545,
Leiria is set in attractive
countryside on the banks of
the River Lis. Originally the
Roman town of Collipo, it was
recaptured from the Moors by
Afonso Henriques *(see pp42–3)*
in the 12th century. In 1254
Afonso III held a *cortes* here,
the first parliament attended
by common laymen.

The resplendent hilltop
castle that crowns the city
houses a library and meeting
rooms. In the early 14th century, King Dinis restored the
castle and turned it into a
royal residence for himself
and his queen, Isabel of
Aragon. Within the castle
battlements stands the Gothic
church of **Nossa Senhora da
Pena**, today little more than a
roofless shell of dark granite
walls. A magnificent view from
the castle loggia overlooks the
wide expanse of pine forest,
the Pinhal de Leiria, and the
rooftops of the town below.

The old town below the
castle is full of charm, with
tiny dwellings over archways,
graceful arcades and the small
12th-century church of **São
Pedro** on Largo de São Pedro.
The Romanesque portal is all

that remains of the
original church. The
muted 16th-century
Sé above Praça
Rodrigues Lobo has
an elegant vaulted
nave and an altar-
piece in the chancel
painted in 1605 by
Simão Rodrigues.
From Avenida
Marquês
de Pombal, climbing
the hill opposite the
castle, an 18th-century stairway
takes you up to the elaborate
16th-century **Santuário de
Nossa Senhora da
Encarnação**. The small
Baroque interior is tightly
packed with colourful geometric *azulejo* panels and
17th-century paintings of the
Life of the Virgin.

⛪ Castle
Largo de São Pedro. 📞 *244-81 39 82.*
⭕ *daily.* ⬤ *1 Jan, 25 Dec.* 🎫

ENVIRONS: West of Leiria is
the long coastal pine forest, the
Pinhal de Leiria, planted by
King Dinis, "the farmer king",
to supply wood for ship building. "A green and whispering
cathedral", in the words of
the poet Afonso Lopes Vieira
(1878–1946), the forest extends
northwards to the beach of
Pedrogão. **São Pedro de Muel**,
22 km (13 miles) to the west
of Leiria, is a small resort on a
marvellous beach.

Exposed and rugged coastline west of Leiria

Pombal 10

Road map C4. 🏘 *12,500.* 🚗 🚌
ℹ *Viaduto Guilherme Santos (236-
213 230).* 🛒 *Mon & Thu.*

Closely associated with the
Marquês de Pombal *(see
pp52–3)* who retired here in
disgrace in 1777, this small
town of whitewashed houses
is overlooked by the stately
castle founded in 1171 by the
Knights Templar *(see p185)*.

The Marquis lived in what is
now Praça Marquês de Pombal.
Here the old prison and the
celeiro (granary) are adorned
with the Pombal family crest.
The former monastery of Santo
António contains the **Museu
Marquês de Pombal**. Its collection of documents and art
focuses on the Marquis.

**🏛 Museu Marquês
de Pombal**
Largo do Cardal. 📞 *236-212 018.*
⭕ *Mon–Fri.* ⬤ *public hols.* ♿

Arcaded loggia and castle towers guarding the town of Leiria

Batalha ❽

João I's coat of arms on portal

THE DOMINICAN ABBEY of Santa Maria da Vitória at Batalha is a masterpiece of Portuguese Gothic architecture, famous for its Manueline elements. The pale limestone monastery celebrates victory over Castile at Aljubarrota in 1385. João I had vowed that he would dedicate a magnificent church to the Virgin if he won the battle. Today, two unknown soldiers from World War I lie in the chapterhouse. The abbey was begun in 1388 under master builder Afonso Domingues, succeeded in 1402 by David Huguet. Over the next two centuries successive kings left their mark on the monastery: João's son, King Duarte, ordered a royal pantheon behind the apse, and Manueline additions include the Unfinished Chapels and much of the decoration of the abbey buildings.

Chapterhouse
Guards keep watch by the Tomb of the Unknown Soldiers beneath David Huguet's striking star-vaulted ceiling.

★ Royal Cloister
Gothic arches by Afonso Domingues and David Huguet around the cloister are embellished by Manueline tracery (see pp20–21) to achieve a harmony of form and decoration.

The lavabo, where monks washed their hands before and after meals, contains a fountain built around 1450.

Refectory

Main entrance

Portal
The portal was decorated by Huguet with religious motifs and statues of the apostles in intricate late Gothic style.

STAR FEATURES

★ Founder's Chapel

★ Royal Cloister

★ Unfinished Chapels

★ Unfinished Chapels
Begun under King Duarte, the octagonal mausoleum was abandoned by Manuel I in favour of the Jerónimos monastery in Belém (see pp106–7).

VISITORS' CHECKLIST

Road map C4. Mosteiro de Santa Maria da Vitória, Batalha. 244-76 54 97. from Lisbon, Leiria, Porto de Mós & Fátima. 9am–6pm (Oct–Mar: 5pm) daily. 1 Jan, Easter, 1 May, 25 Dec.

The stained-glass window behind the choir dates from 1514.

Manueline Portal
Most of the decoration of the Unfinished Chapels dates from the reign of Manuel I. This delicate portal was carved in 1509 by Mateus Fernandes.

Lofty nave by Afonso Domingues

The chapel is topped by an octagonal lantern.

★ Founder's Chapel
The tomb of João I and his English wife Philippa of Lancaster, lying hand in hand, was begun in 1426 by Huguet. Their son, Henry the Navigator, is also buried here.

João I's motto, *Por bem* (for good), is inscribed on his tomb.

THE BATTLE OF ALJUBARROTA

In 1383 Portugal's direct male line of descent ended with the death of Fernando I *(see pp44–5)*. Dom João, the illegitimate son of Fernando's father, was proclaimed king, but his claim was opposed by Juan of Castile. On 14 August 1385 João I's greatly outnumbered forces, commanded by Nuno Álvares Pereira, faced the Castilians on a small plateau near Aljubarrota, 15 km (9 miles) south of Batalha. João's spectacular victory ensured 200 years of independence from Spain. The monastery now stands as a symbol of Portuguese sovereignty and the power of the house of Avis.

Commander Nuno Álvares Pereira

Curved limestone gallery around the vast esplanade in front of the basilica at Fátima

Fátima ⓫

Road map C4. 👥 *4,000.* 🚌
ℹ️ *Avenida Dom José Alves Correia da Silva (249-53 11 39).* 🄰 *Sat.*

T HE SANCTUARY of Fátima is a devotional shrine on a prodigious scale, a pilgrim destination on a par with Santiago de Compostela in Spain or Lourdes in France. The Neo-Baroque limestone **basilica**, flanked by statues of saints, has a 65-m (213-ft) tower and an esplanade twice the size of St Peter's Square in Rome.

On 12 and 13 of May and October vast crowds of pilgrims arrive to commemorate appearances of the Virgin to three shepherd children (the three *pastorinhos*). On 13 May 1917, 10-year-old Lucia Santos and her young cousins, Jacinta Marta and Francisco, saw a shining figure in a holm oak tree. She ordered them to return to the tree on the same day for six months and by 13 October 70,000 pilgrims were with the children by the tree.

Only Lucia heard the "Secret of Fátima", spoken on her last appearance. The first part of the secret was a vision of hell; the second was of a war worse than World War I. The third part, a vision of papal assassination, was finally revealed by Pope John Paul II on the occasion of the Millennium. The Pope also beatified the two dead *Pastorinhos* in May 2000. Inside the basilica, begun in 1928, are the tombs of Jacinta and Francisco. Lucia, who became a Carmelite nun, is still alive today. The stained-glass windows show scenes of the sightings. In the esplanade, the **Capela das Aparições** marks the site of the apparition. Inside, the crown of the Virgin holds the bullet used in the assassination attempt on Pope John Paul II in 1981. East of the sanctuary, the childrens' homes have been preserved in the **Casa dos Pastorinhos**.

For most people, however, the most impressive sight is the intense emotion and faith of the penitents who approach the shrine on their knees. Wax limbs are burned as offerings for miracles performed by the Virgin and thousands of candles light the esplanade in the night-time masses.

🏠 **Casa dos Pastorinhos**
Aljustrel. 📞 *249-53 28 28.*
🄾 *daily.* ♿

ENVIRONS: The medieval town of **Ourém**, 10 km (6 miles) northeast of Fátima, is a walled citadel, dominated by the 15th-century castle of Ourém built by Afonso, grandson of Nuno Álvares Pereira (see p183). His magnificent tomb is in the 15th-century Igreja Matriz. The town's name is said to derive from Oureana, a Moorish girl who, before she fell in love with a Christian knight and converted, was called Fátima.

Ruined secret passage connecting the towers of the castle in Ourém

Tomar ⓬

Road map C4. 👥 *20,000.* 🚆 🚌
ℹ️ *Avenida Dr Cândido Madureira (249-32 24 27).* 🄰 *Fri.*

F OUNDED IN 1157 by Gualdim Pais, the first grand master of the Order of the Templars in Portugal, the town is dominated by the 12th-century castle containing the Convento de Cristo (see pp186–7). The heart of this charming town is a neat grid of narrow streets. The lively shopping street, Rua Serpa Pinto, leads to the Gothic church of **São João Baptista** on Praça da República, the town's main square. The late 15th-century church has an elegant Manueline portal and is capped by an octagonal spire. Inside, there is a carved stone pulpit and 16th-century paintings including a *Last Supper* by Gregório Lopes (1490–1550). A particularly gory beheading of John the Baptist is also attributed to Lopes.

The area outside the church is the focus of the spectacular Festa dos Tabuleiros, a festival with pagan origins held

Church and clocktower of São João Baptista in Tomar's main square

in July, every two or three years, in which girls in white carry towering platters of bread and flowers on their heads. The festival has similar roots to the Festa do Espírito Santo *(see p366)*, popular in the Azores.

Nearby, in Rua Dr Joaquim Jacinto, stands one of the oldest **synagogues** in Portugal, built in 1430–60 with four tall columns and a vaulted ceiling. The building was last used as a place of worship in 1497 after which Manuel I *(see pp46–7)* banished all Jews who refused to convert to Christianity. It has since been a prison, a hay loft and a warehouse. Today, it holds a small Jewish museum, the **Museu Luso-Hebraico de Abraham Zacuto**, named after a renowned 15th-century astronomer and mathematician.

Further south stands the 17th-century church of São Francisco. Its former cloisters now house the **Museu dos Fósforos**, a match museum proudly boasting the largest collection in Europe – over 43,000 matchboxes from 104 countries of the world.

On the east side of the River Nabão, just off Rua Aquiles da Mota Lima, is the 13th-century church of **Santa Maria do Olival**, with a distinctive three-storey belltower. Restored various times over the centuries, the church preserves its Gothic façade and rose window. Inside are the graves of Gualdim Pais (died 1195) and other Templar Masters, and an elegant Renaissance pulpit. The church once had significance far beyond Tomar as the mother church for mariners in the Age of Discovery.

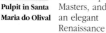
Pulpit in Santa Maria do Olival

Heading north, Rua Santa Iria takes you to the **Capela de Santa Iria**, beside the 15th-century bridge, **Ponte Velha**. This Renaissance chapel is said to have been built where the saint was martyred in the 7th century *(see p191)*. A powerful stone retable depicting *Christ on the Cross* (1536) stands

Tomar's main shopping street, Rua Serpa Pinto, overlooked by the castle

above the altar in the Capela dos Vales. On an island in the river the shaded **Parque do Mouchão** is a pleasant walk; an allegedly Roman water-wheel turns with the passing water. Continuing northwards, past the octagonal 16th-century **Ermida de São Gregório** with its wild Manueline doorway, a huge flight of steps leads to a 17th-century chapel, **Nossa Senhora da Piedade**.

On the slopes of the hill leading up to the Convento do Cristo is the Renaissance basilica, **Nossa Senhora da Conceição**, built between 1530 and 1550. Its exterior simpli-city contrasts with the elegantly proportioned and delicately carved Corinthian columns of the interior. The architect is believed to be Francisco de Holanda (1517–84), who worked for King João III.

🏛 **Museu Luso-Hebraico de Abraham Zacuto**
ℹ Rua Joaquim Jacinto. (249-32 24 27 *(for infol).* ⭘ *daily.* ● *public hols.*
🏛 **Museu dos Fósforos**
Largo 5 de Outubro. (*(as above).*
⭘ *daily.* ● *public hols.* ♿

THE ORDER OF CHRIST

During the 12th and 13th centuries, the crusading Order of the Knights Templar helped the Portuguese in their battle against the Moorish "infidels". In return they were rewarded with extensive lands and political power. Castles, churches and towns sprang up under their protective mantle. In 1314, Pope Clement V was forced to suppress this rich and powerful Order, but in Portugal King Dinis turned it into the Order of Christ, which inherited the property and privileges of the Templars.

Cross of the Order of Christ

Ideals of Christian expansion were revived in the 15th century when their Grand Master, Prince Henry the Navigator, invested the order's revenue in exploration. The emblem of the order, the squared cross, adorned the sails of the caravels that crossed the uncharted waters *(see pp46–7)*.

Tomar: Convento de Cristo

St Jerome,
south portal

Founded in 1162 by the Grand Master of the Templars, the Convent of Christ still retains some reminders of these monk-knights and the inheritors of their mantle, the Order of Christ (see p185). Under Henry the Navigator, the Governor of the Order from 1418, cloisters were built between the Charola and the Templars' fortress, but it was the reign of João III (1521–57) that saw the greatest changes. Architects such as João de Castilho and Diogo de Arruda, engaged to express the Order's power and royal patronage in stone, built the church and cloisters with dazzling Manueline flourishes, which reached a crescendo with the window in the west front of the church.

★ Manueline Window
Marine motifs entwine round this elaborate window. The carving at the base is thought to be either the architect (see p20) or the Old Man of the Sea.

Cloister of the Crows,
flanked by an aqueduct

★ Great Cloister
Begun in the 1550s, probably by Diogo de Torralva, this cloister reflects João III's passion for Italian art. Concealed spiral stairways in the corners lead to the Terrace of Wax.

The "Bread" Cloister
was where loaves were handed out to the poor who came to beg at the monastery.

The Terrace of Wax, where
honeycombs were left to dry

THE CHAROLA

The nucleus of the monastery is the 12th-century Charola, the Templars' oratory. Like many of their temples, its layout is based on the Rotunda of Jerusalem's Holy Sepulchre, with a central octagon of altars. In 1356, Tomar became the headquarters of the Order of Christ in Portugal, and the Charola's decoration reflects the Order's wealth. The paintings and frescoes (mostly 16th-century biblical scenes) and the gilded statuary below the Byzantine cupola have undergone much careful restoration. When the Manueline church was

The gilded octagon

built, an archway was created in the side of the Charola to link the two, making the Charola the church's main chapel.

STAR FEATURES

★ Charola

★ Manueline Window

★ Great Cloister

Manueline Church
Diogo de Arruda's church, begun in the early 16th century, is on two levels: this is the upper choir. The ornate ribbed vaulting incorporates the insignia and initials of Manuel I.

★ **Charola**
The original Templar church, sometimes called the Rotunda, was built in the shape of a 16-sided drum.

VISITORS' CHECKLIST

15 minute walk from Tomar centre. 249-31 34 81. from Lisbon, Coimbra & Leiria. Jun–Sep: 9am –6:30pm, daily; Oct–Apr: 9am–5:30pm, daily (last adm: 30 mins before closing). 1 Jan, Easter, 1 May, 25 Dec. (no flash/tripod).

Internal octagon of the Charola

Cemetery Cloister
Monks' tombstones pave the perimeter of this early 15th-century cloister, the first to be built here. In one corner stands a well.

The Laundry Cloister was built around a pair of large reservoirs, today planted with flowers.

Ruins of the former royal quarters

The south portal is initialled by João de Castilho.

Castle keep

Entrance

Templar Castle
In 1160 the Templars' Grand Master built this castle on land given to the Order for services in battle.

The defensive walls of the early 13th-century fortress at Abrantes

Barragem do Castelo de Bode ⓭

Road map C4. 🚌 to dam. 🚌 from Castanheira. 🛈 Tomar (249-32 24 27).

PERHAPS THERE ONCE was a "Castle of the Billygoat", but today the name refers to a large dam *(barragem)* that blocks the flow of the River Zêzere 10 km (6 miles) up-stream from its confluence with the Tagus. Construction of the dam began in 1946 to serve the first of Portugal's hydroelectric power stations. Above the dam, a long, sprawling lake nestles between hills covered in pine and eucalyptus forests in which lie small, isolated villages. The valley is a secluded area popular for boating, fishing and water sports and it is possible to hire equipment from centres along the lake shore. Canoes, windsurf boards and water skis can be found at the Centro Náutico do Zêzere,

in Castanheira on the western side of the lake, and yachting facilities are usually available from the lakeside hotels such as the peaceful Estalagem Lago Azul *(see p386)*. A cruise can also be taken from the hotel, stopping at the sandy beaches and the small islands.

Abrantes ⓮

Road map C4. 👥 15,000. 🚉 🚌 🛈 Esplanada 1° de Maio (241-362 555). 🛒 Mon.

GRANDLY SITUATED above the Tagus, the town was once of strategic importance. It had a vital role in the Reconquest *(see pp42–3)*, and during the Peninsular War *(see p54)* both the French General Junot and the Duke of Wellington made it a base. The ruined **fortress** that overlooks the town and the surrounding flatlands is a reminder of its status.

The 15th-century church of Santa Maria do Castelo, within the castle walls, is now the small **Museu Dom Lopo de Almeida**. Besides local archaeological finds, it houses the tombs of the Almeida family, counts of Abrantes. On Rua da República, the **Misericórdia** church, constructed in 1584, has six magnificent religious panels attributed to Gregório Lopes (1490–1550).

🏛 **Museu Dom Lopo de Almeida**
Rua Capitão Correia de Lacerda.
📞 241-37 17 24. 🕐 daily.

Whitewashed houses in Constância above the banks of the Tagus

ENVIRONS: The 16th-century church of São Tiago e São Mateus, in the unspoiled town of **Sardoal**, 8 km (5 miles) north of Abrantes, holds a compelling thorn-crowned Christ by the 16th-century painter, the Master of Sardoal. An 18th-century tile panel on the façade of the Capela do Espírito Santo, in Praça da República, honours Gil Vicente, the 16th-century playwright born here.

The pretty whitewashed town of **Constância**, 12 km (7 miles) west of Sardoal, nurtures the memory of the poet Luís Vaz de Camões. Sent away from court for misbehaving with a court lady, he lived here briefly after 1546. The **Casa Memória de Camões**, the poet's home on the river bank, can be visited.

🏚 **Casa Memória de Camões**
Rua do Tejo. 📞 249-739 536.
🕐 call for opening times.

LUÍS VAZ DE CAMÕES (1524–80)

The author of Portugal's celebrated epic poem, *Os Lusíadas*, had a passionate nature and was often in trouble. Banished from court, he enlisted in 1547 and set sail for North Africa, where he lost an eye. Imprisoned after another brawl, he agreed to serve his country in India, but his was the only ship from the fleet to survive the stormy seas. This experience gave his subsequent poem its vibrant power. A unique record of the Discoveries, this Classical-style epic charts the voyage of Vasco da Gama to India and recounts events and legends from Portuguese history. There was to be no success for Camões, however, and he passed bleak years in India yearning for Lisbon. His poem was published in 1572 but he died almost unnoticed.

Statue of Camões on the river bank at Constância

Castelo de Almourol 🕐

Road map C4. 🚌 *to Barquinha then taxi then ferry.* ☐ *daily during daylight hours.* 🛈 *Praça da República, Barquinha (249-72 03 50).*

D RAMATICALLY SET on a tiny island in the Tagus, this enchanting castle was built over a Roman fortress in 1171 by Gualdim Pais *(see p185)*. Legends of this magical place abound. A 16th-century verse romance called *Palmeirim de Inglaterra* weaves a tale of giants and knights and the fight of the crusader Palmeirim for the lovely Polinarda. Some say the castle is haunted by the ghost of a princess sighing for the love of her Moorish slave.

Over the centuries, the castle, surrounded by ramparts and nine towers, has never been taken by invading forces.

The evocative ruins of the island fortress of Almourol

Torres Novas 🕐

Road map C4. 🏃 *16,000.* 🚌 🛈 *Largo dos Combatentes 4–5 (249-81 30 19).* 🕐 *Tue.*

A NIMATED STREETS and many fine churches cluster beneath the castle walls of this handsome town. The ruins of the 12th-century **fortress**, scene of bitter fighting between Moors and Christians during the Reconquest, now enclose a garden. Just below the castle is the 16th-century **Misericórdia** church with a Renaissance portal and an interior lined with colourful "carpet" *azulejos* from 1674. The **Igreja de Santiago**, on Largo do Paço, was probably built in 1203, although tiles and a gilded retable with a wood carving of the young Jesus assisting Joseph in his carpentry are 17th-century additions.

In the centre of town is the **Museu Municipal de Carlos Reis**, named after the painter Carlos Reis (1863–1940) who was born here. The museum contains paintings by 19th- and early 20th-century artists, a 15th-century Gothic figure of Nossa Senhora do Ó, as well as coins and bronze and ceramic artefacts from the Roman ruins at Vila Cardílio.

🏛 **Museu Municipal de Carlos Reis**
Rua do Salvador. 📞 *249-81 25 35.* ☐ *Tue–Sun.*

ENVIRONS: Roman ruins dating from the 4th century AD at **Vila Cardílio**, 3 km (2 miles) southwest of Torres Novas, retain some superb mosaics and baths. On the northeast outskirts of town the **Grutas das Lapas**, large Neolithic caves, can be seen carved out of the rock. The small wetland **Reserva Natural do Paúl de Boquilobo**, 8 km (5 miles) south, between the Tagus and Almondo rivers, was declared a nature reserve in 1981. The willow trees and aquatic plants along the river shelter wildfowl in winter, and in spring it is an important nesting site for colonies of egrets and herons.

🛖 **Vila Cardílio**
Off N.3. ☐ *daily.* ♿
🛖 **Grutas das Lapas**
Rua José Mota e Silva, Lapas. ☐ *daily (ask for key at No. 16).*

Remains of the hypocaust, the Roman underfloor heating system, at Vila Cardílio outside Torres Novas

Portal of the Igreja Matriz in Golegã

Golegã ⑰

Road map C4. 👤 *9,000.* 🚌
ℹ️ *Largo do Parque de Campismo (249-976 742).* 🏪 *Wed.*

USUALLY A QUIET town, Golegã is overrun during the first two weeks of November by thousands of horse enthusiasts who throng to the colourful annual horse fair, the Feira Nacional do Cavalo. This coincides with the tasting of the year's new wine on St Martin's day (11 November). The fair attracts Portugal's finest horses, breeders and equestrians, while the atmosphere is enlivened by the joyful consumption of the young wine known as *agua-pé* (literally, foot water).

In the centre of town, the 16th-century **Igreja Matriz**, attributed to Diogo Boitac *(see pp106–7)*, has an exquisite Manueline portal and a calm interior. The small **Museu de Fotografia Carlos Relvas** is housed in the elegant Art Nouveau house and studio of the photographer (1838–94). A vivid modern art collection can be seen in the **Museu de Pintura e Escultura Martins Correia** in the old post office.

🏛 **Museu de Fotografia Carlos Relvas**
Largo Dom Manuel I. 📞 249-979 050. ⬤ *until further notice.* 🎫
🏛 **Museu de Pintura e Escultura Martins Correia**
Largo da Imaculada Conceição.
📞 249-979 050. ⬤ *Tue–Sun.*
⬤ *1 Jan, 25 Dec.* ♿ *to ground floor.*

Alpiarça ⑱

Road map C4. 👤 *8,000.* 🚌
ℹ️ *Parque de Campismo de Alpiarça (243-557 040).* 🏪 *Wed.*

SET IN THE VAST, fertile plain known as the Lezíria, which stretches east of the Tagus and is famous for horse breeding, Alpiarça is a small, neat town. The fine twin-towered parish church, on Rua José Relvas, is dedicated to **Santo Eustáquio**, patron saint of the town. Built in the late 19th century, it houses paintings from the 17th century, including a charming *Divine Shepherdess* in the sacristy in which the young Jesus is shown conversing with a sheep. The stone cross in the courtyard is dated 1515.

On the southern outskirts of town is the striking **Casa Museu dos Patudos** surrounded by vineyards. This was the residence of the wealthy and cultivated José Relvas (1858–1929), an art collector and diplomat as well as a politician and – briefly – premier of the Republic. The exterior of this eye-catching country house, built for him by Raúl Lino in 1905–9, has simple whitewashed walls and a green and white striped spire. The colonnaded loggia, reached via an outside staircase, is lined with colourful *azulejo* panels. The museum contains Relvas's personal collection of fine and decorative art. Renaissance paintings include *Virgin with Child and St John* by Leonardo da Vinci

and *Christ in the Tomb* by Albrecht Dürer. There are also paintings by Delacroix and Zurbarán as well as many works by 19th-century Portuguese artists, including 30 by Relvas's friend, José Malhôa *(see p55)*. Relvas also collected exquisite porcelain, bronzes, furniture and Oriental rugs, as well as early Portuguese Arraiolos carpets, including a particularly fine one in silk.

🏛 **Casa Museu dos Patudos**
2 km (1 mile) S, N.118. 📞 243-556 444. ⬤ *Tue–Sun.* ⬤ *public hols.* 🎫

Elegant façade of the country manor, Quinta da Alorna, outside Almeirim

ENVIRONS: **Almeirim**, 7 km (4 miles) to the south, was a favourite abode of the House of Avis *(see pp46–7)*. Today little of its royal past remains and most visitors come here to sample the famous *sopa de pedra* (stone soup) *(see p146)*.

Many large estates and fine stables extend across the vast flat plains of this fertile horse and cattle breeding area. The **Quinta da Alorna**, a handsome 19th-century manor house within walled gardens and well known for its wines, lies just outside Almeirim.

Tiled loggia of the Casa Museu dos Patudos, Alpiarça

The Tagus seen from the Jardim das Portas do Sol in Santarém

Santarém ⑲

Road map C4. 🏃 30,000. 🚍 🚌
🛈 *Rua Capelo e Ivens 63 (243-304 437).* 🅿 *2nd & 4th Sun of month.*

THE LIVELY DISTRICT capital of the Ribatejo, overlooking the Tagus, has an illustrious past. To Julius Caesar it was an important bureaucratic centre, Praesidium Julium. To the Moors it was the stronghold of Xantarim – from Santa Iria, the 7th-century martyred nun from Tomar *(see pp184–5)* whose body was thrown into the River Nabão and allegedly reappeared here on the Tagus shore. To the Portuguese kings, who ousted the Moors in 1147, Santarém was a pleasing abode and the site of many gatherings of the *cortes* (parliaments).

At the centre of the old town, in Praça Sá da Bandeira, is the vast **Igreja do Seminário**, a multi-windowed Baroque edifice built by João IV for the Jesuits in 1640 on the site of a royal palace. The huge interior has a painted wooden ceiling and marble and gilt ornamentation. From here, Rua Serpa Pinto runs southeast past a cluster of older buildings. The lofty **Igreja de Marvila**, built in the 12th century and later altered, has a Manueline portal and is lined with dazzling early 17th-century diamond-patterned *azulejo* panels. The medieval, although much restored 22-m (72-ft) high **Torre das Cabaças** was once a clock tower and now houses a small museum of time, **Núcleo Museológico do Tempo**. Opposite the tower, the **Museu Arqueológico** was formerly the Romanesque

church of São João de Alporão. Unfortunately, the museum has been closed because of unstable foundations, and has no reopening date as yet.

Rua Serpa Pinto leads into Rua 5 de Outubro and up to the **Jardim das Portas do Sol**, built on the site of a Moorish castle. The gardens are enclosed by the city's medieval walls, and a terrace affords a panorama of the river and its vast meadowlands.

Returning into town, on Largo Pedro Álvares Cabral, the 14th-century **Igreja da Graça** has a spectacular rose

window carved from a single stone. The church contains the tombstone of Pedro Álvares Cabral, who discovered Brazil *(see p48)*. Further south, the 14th-century **Igreja do Santíssimo Milagre**, on Rua Braamcamp Freire, has a Renaissance interior and 16th-century *azulejos*. A small crystal flask in the sacristy is said to contain the blood of Christ. The belief stems from a 13th-century legend in which a holy wafer intended to help persuade a husband to stop beating his wife was miraculously transformed into blood.

Santarém is an important bullfighting centre with a modern bullring at the southwest corner of town. During the first ten days of June, the town hosts the Ribatejo Fair, Portugal's largest agricultural fair, in which there are bullfights and contests between the colourfully dressed herdsmen, *campinos*. In the autumn (Oct/Nov) Portugal's biggest gastronomy festival is held here, with lots of informal eating at stands representing the country's regions and types of food.

Tomb of Duarte de Meneses in the Museu Arqueológico, Santarém

Fields and vineyards in the low-lying Lezíria extending beyond Coruche

Coruche ⓴

Road map C5. 🏚 *3,500.* 🚉 🚌
ℹ️ *Porto João Felicio (243-61 74 88).*
🛒 *last Sat of month.*

CORUCHE IS an attractive little town in the heart of the bullfighting country with a riverside location overlooking the Lezíria, the wide open plain that stretches east of the Tagus. The town, inhabited since Palaeolithic times, was razed to the ground in 1180 by the Moors as reprisal against the reconquering Christians.

In the central pedestrian street, Rua de Santarém, the **O Coruja** café is lined with vivid modern *azulejo* panels showing bulls in the Lezíria, the town's bullring and scenes of local life. A short walk up the street stands the tiny church of **São Pedro**. Its interior is completely covered with 17th-century blue and yellow carpet tiles. An *azulejo* panel on the altar front shows St Peter surrounded by birds and animals. Above the town

Chancel in the church of São Pedro covered in *azulejos*, Coruche

stands the simple 12th-century blue and white church of **Nossa Senhora do Castelo**. From here there are excellent views over the fertile agricultural land and cork oaks of the Sorraia valley and the Lezíria.

Bull-running *(largada)* in Vila Franca de Xira

Vila Franca de Xira ⓴

Road map C5. 🏚 *20,000.* 🚉 🚌
ℹ️ *Avenida Almirante Cândido dos Reis 147 (263-27 60 53).* 🛒 *Tue & Fri.*

SITTING BESIDE the Tagus, surrounded by the riverside industries that dominate this area, the town has a reputation larger than its modest appearance suggests. Traditionally the area has been the centre for bull and horse rearing communities. Twice a year crowds flock here to participate in the bull-running through the streets and watch the *tourada* and traditional horsemanship. The animated and gaudy Festa do Colete Encarnado (named after the red waistcoat worn by *campinos*, the Ribatejo

herdsmen) takes place over several days in early July. The festival is a lively occasion with folk dancing, boat races on the Tagus and sardines grilled in the street. A similar festival, the Feira de Outubro, takes place in October. The brightly coloured traditional costumes of the *campinos* and other exhibits related to bullfighting in Portugal are on display in the small **Museu Etnográfico**.

The town centre retains an exuberantly tiled covered **market** dating from the 1920s. Further east, on Largo da Misericórdia, striking 18th-century *azulejos* adorn the chancel of the **Misericórdia** church. South of town, the **Ponte Marechal Carmona**, built in 1951, is the only bridge across the River Tagus between Santarém to the north and Lisbon to the south.

🏛 **Museu Etnográfico**
Praça de Touros. 📞 *263-273 057.*
🕐 *Tue–Sun.* ⬤ *public hols.*

ENVIRONS: At the **Centro Equestre da Lezíria Grande** in Povos, 3 km (2 miles) south, you can watch stylish displays of dressage on thoroughbred Lusitanian horses *(see p296).*

🐴 **Centro Equestre da Lezíria Grande**
N.1. 📞 *263-285 160.* 🕐 *Tue–Sun.*
⬤ *1 Jan, Easter, 25 Dec.*

Alenquer

Road map C5. 🏘 *4,000*. 🚌
ℹ️ *Parque Vaz Monteiro (263-733 663).* 🗓 *2nd Mon of month.*

VILA ALTA, the old part of town, climbs steeply up the slopes of the hillside, high above the newer town by the river. In the central Praça Luís de Camões, the 15th-century church of **São Pedro** contains the tomb of the humanist chronicler and native son, Damião de Góis (1501–74). Pêro de Alenquer, a navigator for the explorers Bartolomeu Dias in 1488 and Vasco da Gama in 1497 *(see pp48–9)*, was also born here. Uphill, near the ruins of a 13th-century castle, the monastery church of **São Francisco** retains a Manueline cloister and a 13th-century portal. Founded in 1222, during the saint's lifetime, this was the first Franciscan monastery in Portugal.

ENVIRONS: At **Meca**, 5 km (3 miles) northwest, is the huge pilgrimage church of Santa Quitéria, where a blessing of animals takes place each May.

Defensive walls and the castle overlooking Torres Vedras

Torres Vedras ❷

Road map B5. 🏘 *30,000*. 🚉 🚌
ℹ️ *Rua 9 de Abril (261-31 40 94).* 🗓 *3rd Mon of month.*

THE TOWN IS CLOSELY linked with the Lines of Torres Vedras, fortified defenses built by the Duke of Wellington to repel Napoleon's troops during the Peninsular War *(see p54).* North of the town, near the restored fort of **São Vicente**, traces of trenches and bastions are still visible, but along most of the lines the forts and earthworks have gone, buried by time and rapid change.

Above the town, the restored walls of the 13th-century **castle** embrace a shady garden and the church of Santa Maria do Castelo. Down in the town, on Praça 25 de Abril, a memorial to those who died in the Peninsular War stands in front of the 16th-century Convento da Graça. Today the monastery houses the well-lit **Museu Municipal**. A room devoted to the Peninsular War displays a model of the lines; other interesting exhibits include a 15th-century Flemish School *Retábulo da Vida da Virgem*. Open for mass at weekends, the monastery church, **Igreja da Graça**, has a 17th-century gilded altarpiece. In a niche in the chancel is the tomb of São Gonçalo de Lagos *(see p320).*

Beyond the pedestrian Rua 9 de Abril, the Manueline church of **São Pedro** greets the visitor with an exotic winged dragon on the portal. The interior has a painted wooden ceiling, and colourful 18th-century *azulejo* panels depicting scenes of daily life adorn the walls. Behind the church, on Rua Cândido dos Reis, is a 16th-century water fountain, the **Chafariz dos Canos**.

🏛 **Museu Municipal**
Praça 25 de Abril. 📞 *261-31 04 84.*
🕐 *Tue–Sun.* ⚫ *public hols.* 🖼

THE LINES OF TORRES VEDRAS

Flintlock pistol from Peninsular War

In October 1809, to save Lisbon from Napoleonic invasion, Arthur Wellesley (later the Duke of Wellington) ordered an arc of defensive lines *(Linhas de Torres)* to be built. When complete, over 600 guns and 152 redoubts (masonry forts) lay along two lines stretching from the sea to the River Tagus. One was 46 km (29 miles) long, from the Sizandra river mouth, west of Torres Vedras, to Alhandra, south of Vila Franca de Xira. The second line, running behind the first as far as the sea, was 39 km (24 miles) long. A short third line covered the possibility of retreat and embarkation. Construction of the lines took place in extraordinary secrecy: rivers had to be dammed, earthworks raised, hills shifted and homes and farms demolished, but within a year the chain of hilltop fortresses was complete. On 14 October 1810, General Masséna, at the head of 65,000 French troops, saw with astonishment the vastly altered and fortified landscape and realized it was impregnable. In November, the invaders fell back to Santarém *(see p191)* and in 1811, suffering hunger and defeat, withdrew beyond the Spanish border.

Portrait of the Duke of Wellington, 1814

THE BEIRAS

STRETCHING FROM THE SPANISH FRONTIER *to the sea, the Beiras are a bulwark between the cool green north and the parched south. This diverse region encompasses the heights of the Serra da Estrela and the salt marshes of the Ria de Aveiro, and its towns vary from lively Figueira da Foz to the stately old university town of Coimbra.*

The three provinces of the Beiras may not be a hub of tourism, but their past commercial and defensive significance has left its mark. In Beira Litoral, the elaborate prows of Aveiro's seaweed boats are a legacy of trade with the Phoenicians. All over Beira Baixa, from its capital, Castelo Branco, to little granite villages, there are relics of early foreign occupations, and Viseu, Beira Alta's capital, grew up at a crossroads of trading routes used by the Romans.

The Romans were never as firmly entrenched here as further south, but the ruins of Conímbriga speak eloquently of the elegant city that once stood here, and which gave its name to Coimbra, the principal city of Beira Litoral. Afonso Henriques, as king of the new nation of Portugal *(see p42)*, moved his court to Coimbra, the young country's capital for over a century.

The upheavals of the nation's founding and a hard-won independence have left a rich heritage of castles and fortified towns. Conscious of Spain's proximity and claim on their land, successive Portuguese kings constructed a great defensive chain of forts along the vulnerable eastern border. The seemingly impregnable walls of Almeida still stand as a reminder of the region's unsettled history. These border fortresses continued to prove vital in the fight for independence from Spain in the 17th century, and again against Napoleon's forces *(see p54)*. Even Buçaco, revered for the peace and sanctity of its forest, is known also as the site of Wellington's successful stand against Masséna.

Despite the unforgiving terrain and 20th-century depopulation, the Beiras are the source of some gastronomic treats: Portugal's favourite cheese is made in the Serra da Estrela, and the lush Bairrada district around Mealhada is renowned for its *leitão*, sucking pig. The region's red wines are among Portugal's best known: elegant Bairradas and powerful Dãos *(see pp28–9)*.

Distinctive candy-striped beach houses in Costa Nova, between the Ria de Aveiro and the sea

◁ **A stone *pelourinho* (pillory) in a quiet corner of Castelo Mendo, one of the border towns in Beira Alta**

Exploring the Beiras

THE BEIRAS, ENCOMPASSING some of Portugal's finest scenery, comprise three regions. Along the Beira Litoral are the sleepy backwaters of the Ria de Aveiro and, in contrast, the busy seaside resort of Figueira da Foz. The stately old university city of Coimbra repays exploration, and is a convenient base for visiting the historic forest of Buçaco and several of Portugal's spas.

Inland lies Viseu, the charming capital of Beira Alta, on the route to the medieval strongholds of Guarda, Trancoso and the border castles. The country's highest mountains, the Serra da Estrela, separate the Beira Alta from the little-visited Beira Baixa, where Monsanto, voted "most Portuguese village", and the handsome little city of Castelo Branco are contrasting attractions.

Coimbra's Museu Nacional Machado de Castro, with a fine sculpture collection

SIGHTS AT A GLANCE

0 kilometres   25

0 miles   15

Summer at the seaside in popular Figueira da Foz

Dão vineyards between Viseu and Mangualde

GETTING AROUND

A rail network links the principal cities to smaller towns, but stations are often outside the town. Buses run from Coimbra to outlying areas, and local buses link villages and towns throughout the region. The most convenient way to explore the Beiras, however, is by car. The Oporto-Lisbon A1 (E2) motorway passes close to Coimbra and Aveiro, while the IP5 (E80) links Aveiro and the eastern uplands. Long inclines and bad bends make the IP5 Portugal's worst road for accidents. All but the major routes are relatively traffic-free and a pleasure to drive, but unpaved surfaces can still be expected.

Steep terraces in the Serra de Açor, around Piódão

KEY

▨▨▨	Motorway
▬	Major road
▬	Minor road
▨▨▨	Scenic route
〰	River
☀	Viewpoint

Arouca ❶

Road map C2. 🏃 *2,400.* 🚌
ℹ️ *Praça Brandão de Vasconcelos
(256-94 35 75).* 🗓️ *5 & 20 of month.*

THIS SMALL TOWN in a green
valley owes its principal
attraction, the great **Convento
de Arouca**, to its saintly royal
benefactor, Mafalda. Princess
Mafalda was born in 1195, the
daughter of Sancho I. She was
betrothed to the teenage Prince
Enrique of Castile, but when
he died in an accident, Mafalda
took the veil in Arouca. Under
her, the convent became
Cistercian and Mafalda's
wealth and dedication
made the house highly
influential. She died in
1256, and her incorrupt
corpse was discovered
in 1616, leading to her
beatification in 1793.

For over a thousand
years the convent has
stood beside Arouca's
church on the cobbled
main square. In the early 18th
century the church underwent
costly redecoration: 104 carved
choir stalls are surmounted by
paintings in sumptuous gilded
panels, and the organ and
chancel retable are also heavily
gilded. Honoured with its own
altar is a recumbent effigy of
Santa Mafalda in a silver and
ebony casket; her mummified
remains lie below the casket.

Guided tours take visitors
round the convent's museum,
in which are displayed some
exquisite silver monstrances,
furniture and religious works
of art, including two paintings

by 18th-century artist André
Gonçalves, showing Mafalda
saving the monastery from
fire. The Neo-Classical double
cloister, begun in 1781, the
large refectory and kitchen and
a chapterhouse covered with
cheerful Coimbra tiles of rural
scenes can also be visited.

🔒 Convento de Arouca
Largo de Santa Mafalda. 📞 *256-94
33 21.* ⏰ *Tue–Sun.* ⬤ *Wed am,
Jan, 2 May, 25 Dec.* 📷 ✓

**Silver and ebony casket in the convent church
at Arouca, containing the effigy of Santa Mafalda**

Santa Maria
da Feira ❷

Road map C2. 🏃 *10,000.* 🚉 🚌
ℹ️ *Praça da República (256-37 08
02).* 🗓️ *20 of month.*

PROSPEROUS FROM CORK and
its thriving markets, Santa
Maria derives its name from
long tradition – a document
from 1117 refers to "Terra de
Santa Maria, a place people
call Feira", after the fairs held
here. A large market each
month in the broad Rossio
upholds the town's reputation.

A double stairway leads from
the Rossio to the **Igreja dos
Lóios**, with blue 17th-century
tiles decorating the façades of
its two symmetrical belltowers.
On the opposite side of the
Rossio, winding streets of solid
merchants' houses from the
18th and 19th centuries lead
to a decorative stairway with
an ornamental fountain. This
rises up to the 18th-century
Misericórdia church.

Crowning a wooded hill on
the southern edge of the town
is the fairytale **castle**. Although
much is a 20th-century reconstruction, it follows the
15th-century design of a
local, Fernão Pereira, and
his son. They added
crenellations and towers
to an 11th-century fort
which in turn had been
built over a temple to
a local god. The title of
Conde da Feira was bes-
towed on Pereira, and
the castle remained in his
family until 1700. There
is not much inside the castle
now, but it retains its
romantic air.

⚓ Castle
Largo do Castelo. 📞 *256-37 22 48.*
⏰ *Tue–Sun.* 📷

Ovar ❸

Road map C2. 🏃 *14,000.* 🚉 🚌
ℹ️ *Rua Elias Garcia (256-57 22 15).*
🗓️ *Tue, Thu & Sat (general), 3rd Sun
of month (antiques).*

VARINAS, the hardworking
Portuguese fishwives, take
their name from Var, or O Var,
this small town which earned
its living from the sea and the
Ria de Aveiro that spreads out
to the south *(see p201)*. Industry has arrived in the shape of
foundries and steel mills, but
oxen still plod along the roads.

Gleaming tiles cover many
of the small houses, as well as
the twin-towered 17th-century
Igreja Matriz in Avenida do
Bom Reitor. In the town centre
the Calvary chapel of the 18th-
century **Capela dos Passos**
is adorned with woodcarvings
carrying a shell motif.

Ovar's Carnaval parade is
one of the most colourful in
Portugal, and its sponge cake,

The pinnacled and crenellated castle crowning Santa Maria da Feira

House façades in Ovar with their traditional eye-catching blue tiles

pão-de-ló, is highly esteemed. Tableaux in the **Museu de Ovar** recreate the lifestyle of a bygone era, alongside displays of regional costume and dolls. There are also mementoes of Júlio Dinis, a popular Portuguese novelist who lived in Ovar in the 19th century.

🏛 Museu de Ovar
Rua Heliodoro Salgado 11. 📞 256-57 28 22. ⬜ Mon–Sat. ● public hols. 🖼

Aveiro ❹

See pp200–1.

Praia de Mira ❺

Road map C3. 🏘 5,000. 🚌 ℹ *Praça da República (231-47 11 00).* 📅 *11 & 30 of month.*

Fishing boat on the beach at Praia de Mira

Tourism is only now making an impact on this stretch of coast backed by a wooded reserve, the Mata Nacional das Dunas de Mira. Praia de Mira, with the dunes and Atlantic on one side and the peaceful lagoon of Barrinha de Mira on the other, is a pretty fishing village developing as a resort. High-prowed fishing boats are still drawn up the spectacular beach by oxen, but leisure craft now cruise the shore and the inland waterways, and the fishermen's striped *palheiros* (*see p18*), popular as seaside cottages, are fast vanishing amid shops, bars and cafés.

Figueira da Foz ❻

Road map C3. 🏘 35,000. 🚆 🚌 ℹ *Avenida 25 de Abril (233-40 28 27).* 📅 *daily.*

Lively and rather cosmopolitan, this popular resort has a bustling marina, a casino and a wide, curving beach with breakers that attract intrepid surfers.

Although general jollity is the keynote, the town's **Museu Municipal Dr Santos Rocha** has a notable archaeological collection, and an eclectic display extending to Arraiolos carpets (*see p301*), a musical archive, fans and photographs.

The **Casa do Paço** has an amazing interior lined with 8,000 Delft tiles taken from a shipwreck in the late 17th century. Where the Mondego meets the sea stands the 16th-century fortress of **Santa Catarina**. The Duke of Wellington briefly made this little fort his base when he landed to retake Portugal from Napoleon in 1808 (*see p54*).

🏛 Museu Municipal Dr Santos Rocha
Rua Calouste Gulbenkian.
📞 *233-40 28 40.* ⬜ *9:30am–5:15pm Tue–Sun.* ● *public hols.*
🏛 Casa do Paço Largo Professor
Vitor Guerra. 📞 *233-42 21 59.*
⬜ *9am–5pm Mon–Fri.*
● *public hols.*

Montemor-o-Velho ❼

Road map C3. 🏘 2,600. 🚌
ℹ *Castelo de Montemor-o-Velho (239-68 03 80).* 📅 *every other Wed.*

This attractive and historic hillside town rises out of fields of rice and maize beside the River Mondego. Its **castle**, which served as a primary defence of the city of Coimbra (*see pp202–7*) is mostly 14th century, but it had previously been a Moorish stronghold, and the keep has fragments of Roman stonework. The church of **Santa Maria de Alcaçova** within its walls was founded in 1090. Restored in the 15th century, its naves and arches reflect the Manueline style.

Montemor was the birthplace of Fernão Mendes Pinto (1510–83), famous for the colourful accounts of his travels in the east. Another explorer, Diogo de Azambuja (died 1518), is buried here. Columbus is said to have sailed with Azambuja, who intrepidly navigated along the West African coast. His tomb, by the Manueline master Diogo Pires, is in the **Convento de Nossa Senhora dos Anjos** in the square of the same name (ask at the tourist office for key). Its 17th-century façade hides an earlier, more lavish interior, with Manueline and Renaissance influences.

⛪ Castle
Rua do Castelo. ⬜ *Tue–Sun.*

Enjoying café life in the spring sunshine of Figueira da Foz

Aveiro ❹

Wooden barrel of *ovos moles*

T HIS LITTLE CITY, once a great sea port, has a long history – Aveiro's salt pans were featured in the will of Countess Mumadona in AD 959. By the 16th century it was a considerable town, rich from salt and the *bacalhoeiros* fishing for cod off Newfoundland. When storms silted up the harbour in 1575 this wealth vanished rapidly, and the town languished beside an unhealthy lagoon, the *ria*. Only in the 19th century did Aveiro regain some of its prosperity; it is now ringed with industry and is home to an important university. The *ria* and canals give Aveiro its individual character.

Old Quarter

Tucked in between the Canal das Pirâmides and the Canal de São Roque are the neat, whitewashed houses of Aveiro's fishermen. In the early morning the focus of activity is the **Mercado do Peixe**, where the fish from the night's catch is auctioned.

Bridge across the Canal de São Roque

Skirting the Canal Central, along Rua João de Mendonça, are Art Nouveau mansions and some of the many *pastelarias* selling Aveiro's speciality: *ovos moles*. Literally "soft eggs", these are a rich confection of sweetened egg yolk in candied casings shaped like fish or barrels. As so often in Portugal, the original recipe is credited to nuns. *Ovos moles* are sold by weight or in little barrels.

Across the Canal Central

South of the Canal Central and the bustling Praça Humberto Delgado are the principal historic buildings of Aveiro. The **Misericórdia** church in the Praça da República dates from the 16th century, its façade of *azulejos* framing a splendid Mannerist portal. In the same square stands the stately 18th-century **Paços do Concelho**, or town hall, with its distinctive Tuscan-style pilasters.

Nearby, opposite the museum, is Aveiro's modest 15th-century cathedral of **São Domingos**. The figures of the Three Graces over the door on the Baroque façade were added in 1719.

A short walk south lies the **Igreja das Carmelitas**, its nave and chancel decorated with paintings of the life of the Carmelite reformer, St Teresa.

🏛 Museu de Aveiro

Ave de Santa Joana Princesa.
📞 234-423 297. ⏱ 10am–5:30pm Tue–Sun. ♿

The former Mosteiro de Jesus is full of mementoes of Santa Joana, who died here in 1490. The daughter of Afonso V, Joana retreated to the convent in 1472 and spent the rest of her life here. She was beatified in 1693 and her ornamental Baroque marble tomb, completed 20 years later, is in the lower choir. Simpler in style are the 18th-century paintings in the chapel, showing scenes of her life. This was once the needlework room where Santa Joana died. Among Portuguese primitive paintings is a superb 15th-century full-face portrait of the princess in court dress.

Also part of the museum are the superb gilded chancel (1725–9), 15th-century cloisters and refectory faced in Coimbra tiles. Between the refectory and chapterhouse lies the Gothic tomb of an armoured knight, Dom João de Albuquerque.

Colourful seaweed-collecting *moliceiros* moored along the Canal Central

Raking the salt as it dries in the pans fringing the Ria de Aveiro

ENVIRONS: Lying about 8 km (5 miles) south of Aveiro, at Ílhavo, is the modern block of the **Museu Marítimo e Regional de Ílhavo**, where the region's long seafaring history is told through displays of fishing craft and equipment, with maritime memorabilia from shells to model boats.

About 4 km (2 miles) further south a small sign points to the **Museu Histórico da Vista Alegre**. A name renowned in the world of porcelain (see p24), the Vista Alegre factory was established in 1824 and samples of its fine porcelain can be bought from the factory shop. The museum traces the history of the factory, and has displays of porcelain (together with some crystal glass) from the 1850s to the present day.

VISITORS' CHECKLIST

Map C3. 70,000. Avenida Dr Lourenço Peixinho. Avenida Dr Lourenço Peixinho. Rua João Mendonça 8 (234-423 680). 14 & 28 of month. Jul–Aug: Festa da Ria. Aveiro–Torreira: once daily (Jun–Sep).

Museu Marítimo e Regional de Ílhavo
Avenida Dr. Rocha Madail. 234-32 99 90. 10am–12:30pm, 2–5pm Tue–Fri, Sat & Sun pm (Jun–Sep: 2:30–6pm. public hols.
Museu Histórico da Vista Alegre 234-320 755. 9am–6pm, Tue–Fri public hols.

RIA DE AVEIRO

Old maritime charts show no lagoon here, but in 1575 a terrible storm raised a sand bar that blocked the harbour. Denied access to the sea, Aveiro declined, its population cut down by the fever bred in the stagnant waters. It was not until 1808 that the *barra nova* was created, linking Aveiro once more to the sea.

The lagoon which remains covers some 65 sq km (25 sq miles), and is nearly 50 km (30 miles) long, from Furadouro south past Aveiro's salt pans and the *Reserva Natural das Dunas de São Jacinto* (nature reserve of São Jacinto) to Costa Nova. The reserve includes beaches, dunes and woods as well as the lagoon, and is home to a large and varied bird population, including pintails and goshawks. Of the boats seen here the most elegant is the *moliceiro*. Despite the bright, often humorous, decoration on its high, curving prow, this is a working boat, harvesting *moliço* (seaweed) for fertilizer. Chemical fertilizers have drastically cut demand for *moliço*, but a few of the stately craft survive; the Festa da Ria is a chance to see them in full sail.

Intricately painted prow of a *moliceiro* in the Ria

KEY

	Motorway
	Major road
	Minor road
	Other road
	Salt marsh

The seaward waterfront at the fishing village of Torreira

Coimbra

The birthplace of six kings and the seat of Portugal's oldest university, Coimbra arouses an affection in the Portuguese shared by no other city. To the Romans the town founded on Alcaçova hill was Aeminium, but as its importance grew it took on the mantle and name of nearby Conímbriga *(see p208)*. Coimbra was wrested from the Moors in AD 878, only to come under their control again a century later, until finally freed by Ferdinand the Great of Castile in 1064. When Afonso Henriques, the first king of Portugal, decided to move his capital south from Guimarães in 1139 *(see pp42–3)*, his choice was Coimbra, an honour it retained until 1256. For the Portuguese, Coimbra carries the roots of nationhood and, for visitors, a wealth of fascinating historic associations.

Student in May celebrations

Orientation

In the historic heart of the city, high above the Mondego, lie the cathedrals, university and a fine museum, but a first impression of Coimbra is likely to be of commerce, not culture. Shops, traffic and the railway rule the riverside and around the Praça do Comércio. The Largo da Portagem is a useful starting point, and river trips depart from nearby, alongside the Parque Dr Manuel Braga.

Tomb of Portugal's first king, Afonso Henriques, in Santa Cruz

The Lower Town

From Largo da Portagem, Rua Ferreira Borges leads past shops, lively bars, restaurants and *pastelarias* to the Praça do Comércio. In one corner of this bustling square stands the church of **São Tiago**. Its plain façade is a restoration of the 12th-century original, but inside is an exuberant Rococo altarpiece in gilded wood.

Running north of the Praça do Comércio, Rua Visconde da Luz leads to the Praça 8 de Maio and the historic church of **Santa Cruz** *(see p205)*. Portugal's first two kings are buried here, and monks from the adjacent monastery of Santa Cruz tutored the first students at Coimbra university.

Beyond Praça 8 de Maio is Rua da Sofia, the "street of wisdom", named after the theological colleges that once stood here. The convent churches to which they were attached remain: the **Igreja do Carmo** (1597), with a 16th-century retable, and the **Igreja da Graça**, founded by João III in 1543. The nearby Pátio da Inquisição is a reminder that Coimbra, like Lisbon and Évora, was a seat in the 16th century of the fiercely intolerant Inquisition *(see p51)*.

Café tables in the Praça do Comércio, overlooked by São Tiago

Pátio das Escolas, at the heart of Portugal's oldest university

VISITORS' CHECKLIST

Road map C3. 🏠 150,000.
🚆 Coimbra A, Avenida Emídio
Navarro; Coimbra B, N of city,
on N.11. 🚌 Avenida Fernão de
Magalhães. ℹ️ Praça da República
(239-83 32 02). 🛒 Mon–Sat.
📅 early May: Queima das Fitas;
early Nov: Festa das Latas (a feast
to celebrate new students).

are from the workshop of the 16th-century sculptor, Jean de Rouen. The tower now houses an arts and crafts gallery.

Among the houses lining the maze of steep alleys that wind up to the top of the hill are a number of *repúblicas*, student lodgings since medieval times. Coimbra's two cathedrals, **Sé Velha** and **Sé Nova** *(see p204)*, lie in the shadow of the hilltop **university** *(see pp206–7)*. Beyond is the upper town's main square, Praça da República.

Across the Mondego
It is worth crossing the river just to admire the view of old Coimbra. The two convents of **Santa Clara** *(see p205)* on the southern bank have close ties with Santa Isabel, and with Inês de Castro, Pedro I's luckless lover, who was stabbed to death here in 1355 *(see p179)*. A romantic legend tells how a spring, the **Fonte dos Amores**, rose on the spot. This can be seen in the garden of the 18th-century Quinta das Lágrimas, now a hotel *(see p389)*, just south of Santa Clara-a-Velha.

| 0 metres | 200 |
| 0 yards | 200 |

COIMBRA CITY CENTRE

The Upper Town
The altered and restored 12th-century **Arco de Almedina**, off the Rua Ferreira Borges, is the gateway to the old city (in Arabic *medina* means town). Steps lead up past the **Torre de Anto**, whose Renaissance windows and medallions

KEY

🚆	Railway station
🚌	Bus station
⛴	River boat service
🅿	Parking
ℹ️	Tourist information
✝	Church
▬	Aqueduct
▥	Steps

The Arco de Almedina arching over the steps to the upper town

Exploring Coimbra

THAT THE CITIZENS of Coimbra fondly call their river, the Mondego, "O Rio dos Poetas" gives a clue to the affection they have for their vibrant and beautiful city. From the university *(see pp206–7)* at the top of Alcáçova hill, down the narrow streets and stairways to the lower town, the city is crammed with historic buildings and treasures (and, all too often, slow-moving traffic). Most sights are within walking distance of each other, and despite its steep hill, Coimbra is a city best appreciated on foot. Across the Mondego there are further historic sights and an unusual theme park for children.

Elaborate façade of the Sé Nova

The Sé Velha's gilded altarpiece

🔒 Sé Velha
Largo da Sé Velha. 📞 *239-82 52 73.* ⏰ *10am–1pm, 2–6pm Mon–Sat, 10am–1pm Fri.* 💰 *to cloister.*

The fortress-style Old Cathedral is widely regarded as the finest Romanesque building in Portugal, a celebration in stone of the triumph over the Moors in 1064. The nation's first king, Afonso Henriques, made the

city of Coimbra his capital and his son, Sancho I, was crowned here in 1185, soon after the cathedral was completed.

Inside, square piers lead the eye up the nave to the flamboyant retable over the altar. This was the work of Flemish woodcarvers in about 1502 depicting the birth of Christ, the Assumption and many saints. A 16th-century altarpiece in the south transept is also highly decorated, as is the Manueline font, thought to be by Diogo Pires the Younger. In contrast is the quiet restraint of the cloister, built in 1218 but restored in the 18th century.

The tomb of the city's first Christian governor, Sisinando (a Moslem convert who died in 1091), lies in the chapterhouse, and in the north aisle is the tomb of the Byzantine Dona Vetaça (died 1246), who was companion and tutor to the wife of King Dinis, the saintly Queen Isabel *(see p45).*

🔒 Sé Nova
Largo da Feira. 📞 *239-82 31 38.* ⏰ *9am–noon, 2–5:30pm Tue–Fri.* 💰 *public hols except for mass.*

New is a relative term, as this church, a short walk from the university, was founded by the Jesuits in 1598. (Their adjacent Colégio das Onze Mil Virgens is today part of the sciences faculty.) The Jesuit Order was banned by the Marquês de Pombal in 1759 *(see p52)* but their church became the episcopal seat in 1772. Jesuit saints still look out from the façade.

The interior, more spacious than the Sé Velha, is barrel-vaulted, with a dome over the crossing. To the left of the entrance is a Manueline-style octagonal font brought, like the choir stalls, from the Sé Velha. The paintings above the stalls are copies of Italian masters. The altarpiece in the 17th-century chancel, featuring more Jesuit saints, is flanked by a pair of 18th-century organs.

Coimbra seen from the Mondego, with the university's landmark belltower crowning Alcáçova hill

🏛 Museu Nacional Machado de Castro

Largo Dr José Rodrigues. 239-82 37 27. 9:30am–12:30pm, 2–5:30pm Tue–Sun.

The elegant 16th-century loggias and lovely courtyards of the former bishops' palace are the setting for the display of some of Portugal's finest sculpture – Joaquim Machado de Castro (1731–1822) was himself a master sculptor. Among the medieval pieces is an endearing knight holding a mace. Also in the collection, together with furnishings and vestments, are paintings from the 12th to 20th centuries, including an early 16th-century work, *The Assumption of Mary Magdalen*, by the Master of Sardoal. An intriguing feature of the museum is the Cripto-portico de Aeminium, a maze of underground Roman passages containing a collection of Roman sculpture and stelae and Visigothic artefacts.

Claustro do Silêncio (Cloister of Silence) in the monastery of Santa Cruz

🏛 Santa Cruz

Praça 8 de Maio. 239-82 29 41. 9am–noon, 2–5:45pm Mon–Sat, 4–6pm Sun. to cloister.

Founded in 1131, the church and monastery of Santa Cruz are rich in examples of the city's own early 16th-century school of sculpture. Carvings by Nicolau Chanterène and Jean de Rouen adorn the church's Portal da Majestade, designed by Diogo de Castilho in 1523. The chapterhouse by Diogo Boitac is Manueline in style, as are the Claustro do Silêncio and the choir stalls, carved in 1518 with a frieze on the theme of exploration. The first two kings of Portugal, Afonso Henriques and Sancho I, were reinterred here in 1520. Their elaborate tombs are thought to be by Chanterène, also buried here.

🌿 Jardim Botânico

Calçada Martim de Freitas. 239 822 897. daily.

These, Portugal's largest botanical gardens, were created in 1772 when the Marquês de Pombal introduced the study of natural history at the University of Coimbra.

The entrance, near the 16th-century aqueduct of São Sebastião, leads into 20 ha (50 acres) devoted to a remarkable collection of some 1,200 plants, including many rare and exotic species. The gardens are used for research, but are laid out as pleasure gardens, with greenhouses and a wild area overlooking the Mondego.

Open-air study in the Jardim Botânico

🏛 Santa Clara-a-Velha

Santa Clara. for restoration.

Santa Isabel, the widow of King Dinis, chose to rebuild the convent of Santa Clara for her retreat. She died in 1336 in Estremoz *(see p300)*, but was buried here in the convent church. The murdered Inês de Castro was also laid to rest here 20 years later, but was re-entombed at Alcobaça *(see pp178–9)*.

Almost from the day it was built, Santa Clara suffered from flooding from the river and was finally abandoned in 1677. In 1696 Santa Isabel's remains were moved to safety in the Convent of Santa Clara-a-Nova. The original Gothic church has been in silted ruins since the end of the 17th century, but is now at last being restored.

🏛 Santa Clara-a-Nova

Alto de Santa Clara. 239-44 16 74. 9am–noon, 2–5pm Tue–Sun. to cloister.

The vast "new" convent of the Poor Clares was built between 1649 and 1677 to house the nuns from Santa Clara-a-Velha on drier land uphill. The building was designed by a mathematics professor, João Turriano, and although intended as a convent, now serves in part as a barracks for the army. In the richly Baroque church, pride of place is given to the silver tomb of Santa Isabel, installed in 1696 and paid for by the people of Coimbra. The saint's original tomb, a single stone, lies in the lower choir and polychrome wooden panels in the aisles tell the story of her life. The convent's large cloister, built by the Hungarian Carlos Mardel, was contributed in 1733 by João V, a generous benefactor who was well-known for his charity to nuns.

🏰 Portugal dos Pequenitos

Santa Clara. 239-80 11 70. daily. 25 Dec.

Markedly different in mood from the rest of Coimbra, Portugal dos Pequenitos is a children's wonderland. Here, set in a pretty park, is a world in miniature and children and adults alike can explore scaled-down versions of Portugal's finest national buildings, whole villages of typical regional architecture, and pagodas and temples representing the far-flung reaches of the former Portuguese empire.

Child-sized model of an Algarve manor house in Portugal dos Pequenitos

Coimbra University

An Atlas on the Via Latina

IN RESPONSE to an ecclesiastical petition, King Dinis founded a university, one of the world's oldest and most illustrious, in 1290. Vacillating between Lisbon and Coimbra, it was finally installed in 1537 in Coimbra's royal palace. Study was mostly of theology, medicine and law until the much-needed reforms by the Marquês de Pombal in the 1770s broadened the curriculum. A number of 19th-century literary figures, including Eça de Queirós *(see p55)*, were alumni of Coimbra. Many buildings were replaced after the 1940s, but the halls around the Pátio das Escolas echo with 700 years of learning.

Museu de Arte Sacra
As well as works of art on religious themes, the four rooms of the museum display vestments, chalices and books of early sacred music.

★ **Capela de São Miguel**
Although begun in 1517 the chapel's interior is mostly 17th and 18th century. The azulejos, ornate ceiling, even the fine Mannerist altar, are eclipsed by the dazzling organ, angels trumpeting its Baroque glory.

The portal of Capela de São Miguel is Manueline in style, the work of Marcos Pires before his death in 1521.

Portrait of João V (c.1730)

★ **Biblioteca Joanina**
Named after its benefactor, João V (whose coat of arms is over the door), the library was built in the early 18th century. Its rooms, rich in gilt and exotic wood, are lined with 300,000 books.

STAR FEATURES

★ Biblioteca Joanina

★ Capela de São Miguel

The belltower, symbol of the university, can be seen from all over the city. The best-known of its three bells, called *a cabra*, the goat, has summoned generations of students to lectures since the tower was completed in 1733.

VISITORS' CHECKLIST

Universidade de Coimbra, Paço das Escolas. 239-85 98 00. 1 from Largo da Portagem. Nov–Mar: 10am–5:30pm; Apr–Oct: 9am–7:20pm. 25 Dec.

Sala Grande dos Actos
Also known as the Sala dos Capelos, this is where major events such as investitures are celebrated. Dons' benches line the walls below portraits of Portuguese monarchs.

The Via Latina is a colonnaded walkway added to the original palace in the 18th century. The Portuguese coat of arms above the double staircase is crowned by a statue of Wisdom, while below, figures of Justice and Fortitude flank José I, in whose reign (1750–77) the Marquês de Pombal modernized the university.

To ticket office

Sala do Exame Privado
José Ferreira Araújo's exuberant ceiling, painted in 1701, arcs above a frieze of portraits of past rectors in the private examination hall.

STUDENT TRADITIONS

When the university was first founded, the only subjects studied were canon and civil law, medicine and letters – grammar and philosophy. To indicate which faculty they belonged to, students began to pin coloured ribbons to their gowns: red for law, yellow for medicine, dark blue for letters. Much has changed in 700 years, but students are still initiated in rites whose origins are long forgotten, and in May, as the academic year ends, there is a ceremonial burning of ribbons, the Queima das Fitas.

Burning faculty ribbons in best scholastic tradition

Porta Férrea
Built in 1634, this heavy iron gate to the university pátio is flanked by figures representing the original faculties.

Conímbriga ❾

Road map C3. 2 km (1 mile) S of
Condeixa-a-Nova. 🚌 from Coimbra.
Site 🔲 9am–1pm, 2–8pm (Sep–Mar:
6pm) daily. ⬤ 25 Dec. **Museum**
📞 239-94 11 77. 🔲 10am–1pm,
2–7pm (Sep–Mar: 6pm) Tue–Sun.
⬤ 25 Dec. 📷 ♿ museum only.

THIS, THE LARGEST and most
extensively excavated
Roman site in Portugal *(see
pp40–41)*, was on the Roman
road between Lisbon (Olisipo)
and Braga (Bracara Augusta).
There is evidence of Roman
habitation as early as the 2nd
century BC, but it was under
Augustus, from
about 25 BC,
that Conímbriga
became a sub-
stantial town:
baths, a forum
and the aque-
duct have been
uncovered from
this era. The
finest buildings,
however, date
from the 2nd and 3rd centuries
AD, and they provide a vivid
image of a prosperous city.

**Detail of a bedroom floor in
a house near the entrance**

The site is approached along
a section of Roman road that
led into the city from the east.
Just to the left cluster the out-
lines of shops, baths and two
once-luxurious houses, both
with exquisite mosaic floors.

At Conímbriga is one of the
largest houses discovered in
the western Roman empire.
This opulent villa, known as
the Casa de Cantaber, is built
around ornamental pools in
superb colonnaded gardens,
with its own bath complex and
a sophisticated heating system.
Some of the fine mosaics in
the museum probably came
from this huge residence.

The Casa das Fontes, dating
from the first half of the 2nd
century, is under a protective
cover but walkways provide a
good view. Its pictorial mosaics
and fountains, rare survivals,
which give the house its name,
form a strong image of the
Roman taste for good living.
The city's pools, and the baths
and steam rooms of Trajan's
thermae, were fed by a spring
3.5 km (2 miles) away via an
aqueduct, mostly subterranean,
built in the time
of Augustus.

Official exca-
vation was begun
here in 1912, but
a considerable
part of the 13-ha
(32-acre) site has
yet to be fully ex-
plored, including
an amphitheatre
north of the city.

In the 3rd or early 4th century,
buildings were plundered for
stone as defensive walls were
hastily raised against Barbarian
hordes. In a successful assault
in AD 468, the Suevi burned
the city and murdered the inhabitants. Excavated skeletons
may date from this episode.

Just outside the ruins is an
informative museum which
explains the history and layout
of the site, and has exhibits
of Roman busts, mosaics and
coins alongside more ancient
Celtic artefacts. There is also
a restaurant and picnic site.

**View of the church of São Miguel
within the castle walls at Penela**

Penela ❿

Road map C3. 🚶 620. 🚌
🅸 Praça do Município (239-56 11
32). 🏪 Thu.

PENELA'S THICKSET **castle** was
built in 1087 by Sisinando,
governor of Coimbra, as part
of the line of defences of the
Mondego valley. Its squat
towers provide wonderful
views over the village and, to
the east, of the wooded Serra
da Lousã. The church within
the castle walls, **São Miguel**,
dates back to the 16th century.
Below, in Penela itself, **Santa
Eufémia**, dated 1551 above
its decorative doorway, has a
Roman capital used as a font.

ENVIRONS: Among walnut and
olive groves 5 km (3 miles) to
the west, is the tiny village of
Rabaçal, whose tasty cheese,
made with a mixture of sheep's
and goat's milk, is a regional
speciality *(see p146)*. Some
village women still mature the
cheese rounds in darkened
rooms in their homes.

Lousã ⓫

Road map C3. 🚶 9,000. 🚉 🚌
🅸 Câmara Municipal, Rua Dr João de
Cáceres (239-99 03 76). 🏪 Tue & Sat.

THE PAPER FACTORY at Lousã,
on the forested banks of
the River Arouce, was opened
in 1716 and is still working.
Skilled papermakers imported
from Italy and Germany by the
Marquês de Pombal *(see p52)*
brought prosperity, still evident
in the handsome 18th-century

The central garden of the Casa das Fontes in Conímbriga

The castle at Arouce, near Lousã, oddly defenceless in its deep valley

houses. Most elegant of these is the **Palácio dos Salazares**, a private home in Rua Viscondessa do Espinhal. Also notable is the **Misericórdia**, with a 1568 Renaissance portal, in Rua do Comércio.

ENVIRONS: Deep in a valley, 3 km (2 miles) south of Lousã, is the **Castelo de Arouce**. Legend says it was built in the 11th century by a King Arunce who took refuge in the valley when fleeing from raiders. Permission to visit the castle is available from the town hall. Near the castle are the three shrines of the **Santuário de Nossa Senhora da Piedade**.

A viewpoint on the tortuous road south towards Castanheira de Pêra gives a splendid view across the valley. A turning east leads up to **Alto do Trevim** which, at 1,204 m (3,950 ft), is the highest point in the Serra de Lousã.

Buçaco ⑫

See pp210–11.

Luso ⑬

Road map C3. 3,000.
Rua Emidio Navarro (231-93 91 33).
Mon–Sat.

I N THE 11TH CENTURY Luso was just a village linked to a monastery at Vacariça, but it developed into a lively spa town in the 18th century as

its hot-water springs became a focus for tourism. The thermal waters, which originate from a spring below the **Capela de São João**, are said to be of therapeutic value in the treatment of a wide range of conditions, from bad circulation and muscle tone to renal problems and rheumatism.

There are a number of grand, if somewhat faded, hotels here, and an elegant Art Nouveau lobby adorns the former casino, but the main reason for visiting the resort is to enjoy its spa facilities. An additional attraction of Luso is the proximity of the treasured national forest of Buçaco, which is a powerful presence above the town.

ENVIRONS: Between Luso and Curia, **Mealhada** is an attractive small town in the heart of a region famous for *leitão*, sucking pig *(see p146)*. This enormously popular dish is prominently advertised at numerous hotly competing restaurants in the area.

Arganil ⑭

Road map D3. 3,000.
Avenida das Forças Armadas (235-20 48 23). Thu.

T RADITION SAYS that this was a Roman city called Argos. In the 12th century, Dona Teresa, the mother of Afonso Henriques *(see pp42–3)*, gave the town to the bishopric of Coimbra, whose incumbent also acquired the title of Conde de Arganil. Most of the town's architecture is unremarkable, but the church of **São Gens**, the Igreja Matriz in Rua de Visconde de Frias, dates back perhaps to the 14th century.

ENVIRONS: One of the most curious local sights is kept in the sanctuary of Mont'Alto, 3 km (2 miles) above the town. Here, the **Capela do Senhor da Ladeira** harbours the Menino Jesus, a Christ Child figure in a bicorne hat (part of a full wardrobe). He comes out for *festas* but the chapel key is otherwise available from the last house on the right.

Menino Jesus in Mont' Alto sanctuary, Arganil

Taking the spa waters at the Fonte de São João, Luso

THERMAL SPAS

In response to the Portuguese enthusiasm for thermal waters and health-orientated holidays, spa resorts have developed across the northern half of the country, with several of them in the Beiras, near Luso. All offer extensive sports facilities and a calm ambience as well as treatments for all the body's major systems. Most spas close for the winter, but Curia, 16 km (10 miles) northwest of Luso, is open all year for relaxation and treatments. Luso itself produces the country's best-known bottled mineral water.

Buçaco ⑫

Viewpoint of Cruz Alta

Part ancient woodland, part arboretum, the National Forest of Buçaco is a magic place. As early as the 6th century it was a monastic retreat, and in 1628 the Carmelites built a house here, walling in the forest to keep the world at bay (women had already been banned by the pope in 1622). In their secluded forest the monks established contemplative walks, chapels – and trees. The trees, added to by Portuguese explorers, gained papal protection in 1632, and the 105 ha (260 acres) contain some 700 native and exotic species, including the venerable "Buçaco cedar". The peace of the forest was disturbed in 1810 as British and Portuguese troops fought the French on Buçaco ridge. In 1834 the monastery closed, but the forest endures, with its shady walks, hermits' grottoes and the astonishing Buçaco Palace Hotel at its centre.

★ Fonte Fria
This impressive cascade, fed by the greatest of the forest's six springs, tumbles down to a magnolia-fringed pool.

Porta dos Degraus and steps leading to Luso

Vale dos Fetos
Leading down to a small lake, the Valley of Ferns is lined with luxuriant specimens collected worldwide. The magnificent tree ferns give the valley a tropical air.

The Portas de Coimbra incorporate the papal bulls defending the trees and forbidding entry to women.

BUÇACO PALACE HOTEL

King Carlos, who commissioned this extravaganza in 1888, never lived to see his creation. His son, Manuel II, visited only briefly before his exile in 1910 *(see p55)* – he is said to have brought the French actress, Gaby Deslys, here for a romantic interlude. Its rebirth as a luxury hotel, serving its own renowned wines, was the inspiration of the royal chef and it became a fashionable rendezvous for socialites; in World War II it was also rumoured to be frequented by spies. It is now one of the great hotels of Portugal *(see p388)*.

Gaby Deslys, with whom Manuel II reputedly had a brief romance

KEY

▬	Wall
•••	Route of Via Sacra
P	Parking
⛪	Chapel
🌿	Viewpoint

STAR SIGHTS

★ Buçaco Palace Hotel

★ Fonte Fria

Monastery

Only the cloisters, chapel and a few monks' cells of the Carmelite monastery remain. A plaque records that Wellington slept in one of the cork-lined cells.

VISITORS' CHECKLIST

Road map C3. 3 km (2 miles) SE of Luso. ▣ ⓘ Luso (231-93 91 33). **Monastery** ◯ Sat–Thu. **Forest** ◯ daily. 🚗 for vehicles (May–Oct). **Museu Militar** Almas do Encarnadouro. 📞 231-93 93 10. ◯ Tue–Sun. ● 1 Jan, Easter, 25 Dec. 🎉 ♿ 📷 27 Sep: Anniversary of Battle of Buçaco.

Porta da Rainha was made for Catherine of Bragança, but when her visit in 1693 was cancelled the gateway was sealed up for 11 years.

Tasmanian eucalyptus (1876)

Museu Militar, devoted to the Peninsular War

N234

RUA DA RAINHA

★ Buçaco Palace Hotel

Completed in 1907, the Neo-Manueline folly of a hunting lodge built by Luigi Manini includes murals and tiles by prominent artists. Azulejos in the hall feature scenes of the Battle of Buçaco.

The Monument to the Battle of Buçaco marks Wellington's victory on the ridge of Buçaco on 27 September 1810. As the nearby Museu Militar explains, this decisive battle halted the French march on Coimbra.

Cruz Alta, the forest's highest point, has glorious views as far as the sea

Porta da Cruz Alta

The Buçaco cedar, now 26 m (85 ft) high, is believed to have been planted in 1644.

0 metres	250
0 yards	250

Via Sacra

Chapels containing life-size figures mark the Stations of the Cross along this winding pathway. They were installed by the Bishop of Coimbra in 1693.

The village of Piódão, blending with the granite of the surrounding Serra de Açor

Piódão ⓯

Road map D3. ⚐ *60*. ⬛ *to Coja 20 km (12 miles) away.* ⓘ *Arganil (235-20 48 23).*

As its name suggests, the Serra de Açor, hills of the goshawk, is a place of bleak beauty, where solitary villages cling to precipitous terraces. Piódão, nestling in its valley, is the most striking of these dark schist and slate hamlets. Seemingly remote, Piódão was, until the late 19th century, on the main commercial route from Coimbra to Covilhã, but with newer roads the village was forgotten. With help from EU funds, it is now coming back to life: shops are opening, houses are being repainted with traditional blue trim, and in the main square the bright white **Igreja Matriz** stands out against the surrounding dark stone. Happily, Piódão still retains its old-world charm.

Oliveira do Hospital ⓰

Road map D3. ⚐ *3,500*. ⬛ ⓘ *Casa da Cultura, Rua do Colégio (238-609 269).* ⚑ *2nd Mon of month.*

These lands once belonged to the Knights Hospitallers, a gift in 1120 from the mother of Afonso Henriques. The 13th-century **Igreja Matriz** in Largo Ribeira do Amaral, houses a magnificent reminder of the era of these warrior monks. One of the founders of the

town, Domingues Joanes, lies in a large tomb surmounted by a charming equestrian statue.

Today, this lively industrial town is perfectly situated for exploring the valleys of the Mondego and the Alva.

Environs: At Lourosa, 12 km (7 miles) to the southwest, the 10th-century church of **São Pedro** reflects the changing fate of Portugal over the centuries. A cemetery excavated beneath the church dates from the Roman era; the porch is Visigothic, while inside are ten impressive Roman arches and an *ajimece* (Moorish window).

Caramulo ⓱

Road map C3. ⚐ *1,700*. ⬛ ⓘ *Avenida Dr. Jerónimo de Lacerda (232-86 14 37).*

In a grassy rolling serra west of Viseu, this small town was once, with its clear mountain air, a centre for sanatoria.

Interior of São Pedro at Lourosa, near Oliveira do Hospital

It is better known today for two very disparate museums in a single institutional block.

In the art collection of the **Museu do Caramulo**, the exhibits on show range across 16th-century Flemish tapestries, sculpture, porcelain, silver and ivory to Egyptian bronzes from 1580 to 900 BC. The paintings are as varied: from Portuguese primitives to the 20th century. Chagall and Dalí are represented, as is the Portuguese Maria Helena Vieira da Silva (1908–92). One of Picasso's haunting still lifes was donated by the artist in 1947.

The collection in the **Museu do Automóvel** is just as eclectic: a working 1899 Peugeot, Bugattis and Rolls-Royces, and a bullet-proof 1938 Mercedes-Benz ordered for Salazar when he was prime minister *(see pp56–7)* but never used.

🏛 **Museu do Caramulo (Fundação Abel de Lacerda) and Museu do Automóvel** Caramulo. 📞 *232-86 12 70.* 🕐 *10am–6pm daily.* ● *Easter, 24 & 25 Dec.* 🌀

Environs: From the museum the road winds southwest up to two viewpoints and picnic spots in the Serra do Caramulo. About 4 km (2 miles) from Caramulo are the wild-flower pastures of **Cabeça da Neve**, at 970 m (3,200 ft). A little further on, signposted to the west, is the boulder-strewn upland of **Caramulinho**, rising to 1,074 m (3,524 ft). The views from here are magnificent.

Viseu

Road map D3. 🏘 *19,500.* 🚌
ℹ️ *Avenida de Gulbenkian (232-42 09 50).* 🛍 *Tue.*

A<small>N ENTHRALLING</small> old town is at the heart of this lively regional capital. Viseu has been a major northern crossroads since the time of the Romans and is the centre of the Dão wine-growing region *(see p29).*

On a visit to Viseu it is hard to miss that this was the home town of one of Portugal's great 16th-century artists. The name of Grão Vasco graces a hotel, a museum, even a wine label.

On the western side of the old town is the striking 15th-century **Porta do Soar de Cima**, a remnant of the original walls. In the Rossio, the main square, the **Igreja dos Terceiros de São Francisco** (1773) has an Italianate façade and gilded interior. The 1887 town hall on the west side has a grand stairway and *azulejos* featuring the history of Viseu and its personalities. Just north is Rua Augusto Hilário, named after the originator of Coimbra-style *fado (see pp66–7)* who was born here.

The two-towered 17th-century façade of Viseu's cathedral

🔒 Sé

Largo da Sé. ☎ *232-42 29 84.*
🕐 *9am–noon, 2–7pm daily.* .

Viseu's cathedral still retains a few Romanesque features, but it has been altered over the centuries in a variety of styles which work together surprisingly well. The façade is a 17th-century replacement of a Manueline frontage that fell down in 1635. Inside, the vaulted roof is supported by 16th-century knotted ribs on 13th-century columns. In the north chapel are fine *azulejos* from the 18th century, while those in the two-storey cloister date from a century earlier. The sacristy has a lavishly painted ceiling and early "carpet" tiles *(see p22).* In the chancel, choir stalls in Brazilian jacaranda contrast with a startling modern altar, an inverted pyramid in polished granite and steel.

The Sé's treasury, housed in the chapterhouse, includes a 12th-century Gospel and a 13th-century Limoges coffer.

Facing the cathedral is the **Misericórdia** church, with its 18th-century Rococo façade. It houses a temporary exhibition from the Museu de Grão Vasco.

🏛 Museu de Grão Vasco

Largo da Sé. ☎ *232-42 20 49.*
🕐 *Tue–Sun.* ⬤ *until May 2004.* 📷

In the 16th-century former bishops' palace abutting the cathedral is the Museu de Grão Vasco, Viseu's "great Vasco". The paintings of Vasco Fernandes (c.1475–1540) and his fellow artists of the Viseu School are highly esteemed for their naturalism, background landscapes, drapery and attention to detail. Their treatment of light betrays the marked influence of Flemish painters.

On the upper floor of the three-storey museum are exhibited the masterpieces that once adorned the chancel altarpiece in the cathedral. Predominant are Grão Vasco's monumental *St Peter* and, from a series of 14 panels on the life of Christ, *The Adoration of the Magi.* Painted in about 1503–5, it is memorable for the inclusion of a Brazilian Indian among those paying homage to the newborn Christ *(see p48).* Some of the other panels are thought to be by fellow artists in the Viseu School.

Among other masterpieces hung here are works by Grão Vasco's great rival, Gaspar Vaz, including a *Last Supper.* On the lower floors are works by Portuguese artists from the 19th and 20th centuries, including the brilliant Columbano Bordalo Pinheiro.

The graceful Rococo façade of the church of the Misericórdia, Viseu

St Peter (1503–5) by Vasco Fernandes in the Museu de Grão Vasco, Viseu

Sernancelhe

Road map D2. **1,100.**
Avenida das Tilias (254-595 226).
every other Thu.

SMALL WHITEWASHED houses
cluster around the granite
heart of this modest Beira
town which was established
on the banks of the Távora in
the 10th century. In the central
Praça da República stands the
Romanesque **Igreja Matriz**.
The granite statues in its façade
niches, survivors from the
12th century, flank a notable
arched portal embellished by
a semicircle of carved angels.
The pillory that stands across
the square is dated 1554.

The grandest house here is
the Baroque **Solar dos
Carvalhos** behind
the church. Long
and low, with
carved granite
portals against
whitewashed
walls, it is where
the local noble
family lived in
the 18th century.
It is still a private house.

**Carved arch over the portal of
the Igreja Matriz, Sernancelhe**

Only a few stubs of castle
wall remain on the rocky outcrop overlooking the square,
but a small battlemented house
has been built into them.

ENVIRONS: In the Serra da
Lapa, which rises to the south
of Sernancelhe, stands a popular shrine known as the
**Santuário da Nossa
Senhora da Lapa**. The
story tells of a dumb
shepherd girl, Joana,
who found a statue of
the Virgin Mary on a
great boulder and took
it home. Irritated, her
mother threw it on the
fire, at which moment
the child miraculously
spoke: "Don't burn it,"
cried Joana. "It is the
Senhora da Lapa."

A chapel was built
to enshrine the boulder,
and the image, now
with a slightly scorched
face, looks down from
an ornamental recess.
The space below her
niche is packed with
images and offerings
left by pilgrims.

The main gateway into the old walled town of Trancoso

The castle at **Penedono** is captivating. Perched on rocks in
the middle of this small town
17 km (11 miles) northeast of
Sernancelhe, it has survived
since at least the 10th century.
The castle is mentioned
in the medieval tale of
a knight known as
O Magriço, who
went to England
with 11 other
knights to joust
in honour of 12
English ladies.
There is little to
see inside the
castle – if closed, the key is in
the store beside the *pelourinho*
(pillory), but there are splendid
views from the walls.

**Santuário da Nossa
Senhora da Lapa**
Quintela da Lapa, 11 km (7 miles)
SW of Sernancelhe.
232-68 89 93. daily.

**The castle of Penedono, near Sernancelhe,
with its imposing medieval battlements**

Trancoso

Road map D2. **6,000.**
**Avenida Heróis de São Marcos
(271-81 11 47).** Fri.

WHEN KING DINIS married
Isabel here in 1283 (see
pp44–5), he gave her Trancoso
as a wedding gift. He was also
responsible for the impressive
walls that still encircle the town
and, in 1304, established here
the first unrestricted fair in Portugal. Left in peace after 1385,
the town became a lively commercial centre. Trancoso once
had a large Jewish population,
and in the old Judiaria, houses
survive with one broad and
one narrow door, separating
domestic life from commerce.

From the southern gate, Rua
da Corredoura leads to **São
Pedro**, restored after 1720. A
tombstone in the church commemorates Gonçalo Anes,
a local shoemaker who, in the
1580s, wrote the celebrated
Trovas under the name of
Bandarra. These prophesied
the return of the young King
Sebastião (see p107).

ENVIRONS: Tumbledown ruins
above a humble village are all
that remain of the medieval
citadel of **Marialva**, 14 km
(9 miles) to the northeast of
Trancoso. Granite walls, fragments of stone carvings and
a striking 15th-century pillory
emanate an aura of lost grandeur. Probably founded by
Ferdinand of León and Castile
early in the 11th century and
fortified by Sancho I, it is not
known why Marialva fell into
ruin. No battle destroyed it
and it seems merely to have
been abandoned as townsfolk
moved to more fruitful lands.

SERRA CHEESE

Serra, made from the milk of ewes grazing in the Serra da Estrela *(see pp218–19)*, is Portugal's finest cheese. It is made in the winter – its success was once governed by the temperature of the women's hands as they worked in their cool granite kitchens – and traditionally the milk is coagulated with *flor do cardo*, thistle. Now the small factories producing the cheese, in rounds of 1.5–2 kg (about 3–5 lb), are certified to ensure quality and authenticity (fakes are not uncommon). At room temperature Serra becomes runny. The cheese is scooped out with a spoon through a hole cut into the top.

A shepherd with his flock on the slopes of the Serra da Estrela

Celorico da Beira ㉑

Road map D3. ♦ 3,000. 🚃 🚌
🛈 Estrada Nacional 16, Forno Telheiro (271-74 21 09). 🛒 Tue, Dec–May: alternate Fri.

IN THE LEE OF the Serra da Estrela, the pastures around Celorico da Beira have long been a source of the region's famous Serra cheese. From December to May the cheese market is held in the Praça Municipal and every February there is a cheese fair.

Around Rua Fernão Pacheco, running from the main road up to the castle, is the old centre of Celorico, a cluster of granite houses with Manueline windows and Gothic doors. Of the 10th-century **castle**, battered by a long succession of frontier disputes with Spain, only a tower and the outer walls remain. Its stark silhouette is less dramatic at close quarters. The **Igreja Matriz**, restored in the 18th century, has a painted coffered ceiling. During the Peninsular War, the church served briefly as a makeshift hospital for the English forces.

Almeida ㉒

Road map E2. ♦ 1,600. 🚌
🛈 Portas de São Francisco (271-57 42 04). 🛒 8th day & last Sat of month.

FORMIDABLE defences in the form of a 12-pointed star guard this small, delightfully preserved border town.

Almeida was recognized by Spain as Portuguese territory under the Alcañices Treaty on 12 September 1297, but this did not stop further incursions. The present Vauban-style stronghold *(see p297)* was designed in 1641 by Antoine Deville after Spain's Philip IV, in post-Restoration rage, destroyed the earlier defences protecting the town and its medieval castle.

From 1742 to 1743 Almeida was in Spanish hands again, and then during the Peninsular War was held in turn by the French under Masséna and the British under the Duke of Wellington. In 1810, a French shell lit a powder trail that destroyed the castle.

To breach the town's fortifications today, it is necessary to cross a bridge and pass through a tunnel. The underground **casamatas**, soldiers' barracks, can be visited and an armoury in the main gateway, the Portas de São Francisco, holds further mementoes of Almeida's military past. In the town itself are a 17th-century parish church and a **Misericórdia** church of a similar age, attached to one of Portugal's oldest almshouses. A walk around the grassy walls gives rewarding views of the town.

Almeida's complex fortifications, still discernible despite the incursion of grass and wild flowers

Border Castles Tour ㉓

D EFENDING PORTUGAL'S FRONTIERS was a vital priority
of the nation's early kings. The greatest period of
castle-building was in the reign of King Dinis (1279–
1325). All along the shakily held border, Spanish
incursions were frequent and loyalties divided. Castles
were constantly being assaulted, besieged and rebuilt,
and those that survived are a lasting reminder of this
long period of dispute. Much of the terrain, especially
in the Serra da Marofa, is bleak and rocky, but near
Pinhel and beyond Castelo Mendo
the scenic valley of the
River Côa provides a
dramatic backdrop.

Castelo Rodrigo ②
This tiny fortified village still
has its encircling walls built
by King Dinis in 1296. But
the fine palace of its lord, the
Spanish sympathizer Cristóvão
de Moura, was burnt down
at the Restoration in 1640
(see pp50–51).

Almeida ①
The town's star-shaped
defences are a finely
preserved example of
the complex but effec-
tive style of fortifications
developed by the French
engineer, Vauban, in the
17th century (see p297).

Figueira de
Castelo Rodrigo ③
From the 18th century,
Castelo Rodrigo was
largely abandoned in
favour of less isolated
Figueira, now a flourish-
ing little town known
for its almond blossom.
Just to the south, topped
by a huge stone Christ
the King, is the highest
point of the Serra da
Marofa, 977 m (3,205 ft).

Pinhel ④
Part of the region's defences
since Roman times, Pinhel
formed the fulcrum for a
network of fortresses, and in
the early 14th century King
Dinis built it up into an
impressive citadel. Much of
this ring of walls survives, as
do two towers.

*VILA NOVA
DE FOZ
CÔA*

*SERRA DA
MAROFA*

Côa

*Vale
Verde*

*Aldeia
Nova*

*Ribeira
de Tourões*

*Vale
Verde*

*Vilar
Formoso*

GUARDA

SABUGAL

*Fuentes
de Oñoro*

SALAMANCA

TIPS FOR DRIVERS

Length: 115 km (72 miles).
Stopping-off points: Most
villages have cafés, and Pinhel
and Almeida have restaurants.
Road conditions: The tour uses
well-surfaced roads but short cuts
are deceptive and are not recommended. (See also pp444–5.)

KEY

▬▬   Tour route
═══   Other roads
–·–·   International boundary
⁂   Viewpoint

0 kilometres   10
▬▬▬▬▬▬
0 miles   5

Castelo Mendo ⑤
Beyond the main gate, guarded
by two stone boars, little survives of the castle here, but the
distant views make its role as a
frontier fort easy to appreciate.

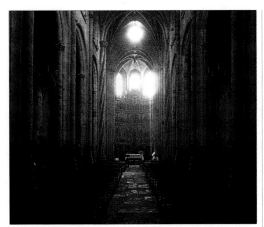

The soaring triple-aisled interior of Guarda's Gothic cathedral

Guarda ㉔

Road map D3. 🏚 20,000. 🚉 🚌
ℹ️ *Praça Luís de Camões (271-205 530).* 🏛 *1st & last Wed of month.*

SPREAD OVER a bleak hill on the northeast flank of the Serra da Estrela, Guarda is Portugal's highest city, at 1,056 m (3,465 ft). Founded in 1197 by Sancho I, the city's original role as frontier guard explains its name and its rather forbidding countenance. Some of its arcaded streets and squares are lively and interesting, but the great fortress-like **Sé**, with its flying buttresses, pinnacles and gargoyles, could never be described as lovely. Master architects who worked on the cathedral, begun in 1390 and completed in 1540, included Diogo Boitac (from 1504 to 1517) and the builders of Batalha *(see pp182–3)*. The interior, by contrast, is light and graceful. The 100 carved figures high on the altarpiece in the chancel were worked by Jean de Rouen in 1552.

On display in the nearby **Museu de Guarda** are two floors of paintings, artefacts, archaeological discoveries and a section on the city's own poet, Augusto Gil (1873–1929).

From the cathedral square, Rua do Comércio leads down to the 17th-century **Miseri-córdia** church. Inside the ornamental portal are Baroque altars and pulpits. Just north of the cathedral, in the historic town centre, is the 18th-century church of **São Vicente**, which has 16 elaborate *azulejo* panels depicting the life of Christ.

Guarda used to support a thriving Jewish community and in Rua Dom Sancho I is a key shop that may once have served as a synagogue. History records that João I, on a visit to Guarda, was smitten by Inês Fernandes, the beautiful daughter of a Jewish shoemaker. From their liaison a son, Afonso, was born. In 1442 the title of first Duke of Bragança was bestowed on Afonso, and 200 years later his descendant would take the throne as João IV, first of the Bragança monarchs *(see p299)*.

Cabral family crest in the chapel, Belmonte

Centum Cellas, a curious Roman landmark near Belmonte

🏛 Museu de Guarda

Rua Alves Roçadas 30. 📞 *271-21 34 60.* 🕐 *Tue–Sun.* ⬤ *public hols.* 📷

Serra da Estrela ㉕

See pp218–19.

Belmonte ㉖

Road map D3. 🏚 3,600. 🚉 🚌
ℹ️ *Castelo de Belmonte (275-91 14 88).* 🏛 *1st & 3rd Mon of month.*

BELMONTE was for generations the fiefdom of the Cabral family, a name associated with heroic exploits. Pedro Álvares Cabral, who in 1500 was the first navigator to land in Brazil, had forebears who fought at Ceuta *(see p48)* and Aljubarrota *(see p183)*. Fernão, an earlier ancestor known as the Giant of the Beiras, was famed for his feats of strength. The family crest, incorporating a goat *(cabra)* as a play on words, can be seen in the castle and adjacent chapel. The **castle**, begun in 1266, retains its keep and, a later addition, an ornate Manueline window. The little church of **São Tiago** nearby has preserved its Romanesque simplicity: the frescoes above the altar and, in a tiny side chapel, a serene granite pietà date from the 13th century. Beside the church is the 15th-century **Capela dos Cabrais** which holds the Cabral family tombs.

On the opposite side of the village is the modern **Igreja da Sagrada Família** (1940). It is the repository for a treasured statue of Nossa Senhora da Esperança, which, according to tradition, accompanied Cabral on his voyage to Brazil.

ENVIRONS: Just northeast of Belmonte is a Roman tower, **Centum Cellas**, also called Torre de Colmeal. The role of this square, three-storeyed structure is uncertain and archaeologists' theories have suggested a range of functions from hostel or military base to mansion and temple.

Serra da Estrela ㉕

Haymaking near the town of Linhares

Tʜᴇsᴇ "ꜱᴛᴀʀ ᴍᴏᴜɴᴛᴀɪɴꜱ" are the highest range on mainland Portugal, with much of the Serra over 1,500 m (5,000 ft). The highest point rises to 1,993 m (6,539 ft) but is topped by a small stone tower – the Torre – to "stretch" it to 2,000 m. The exposed granite of the upper slopes is good for little but grazing sheep, and stone shepherds' huts form part of the landscape, their thatched roofs renewed each year after the harsh winter. Sheep have shaped the fortunes of the area, providing wool for a textile industry and supplying milk for Portugal's best-known cheese. A designated nature reserve, the Serra's long-distance paths and stunning flora attract walkers and nature enthusiasts, while a winter snowfall brings skiers to the slopes around Torre.

Cabeça do Velho
The granite of the mountain tops has been eroded into many weird shapes, such as this "old man's head" near Sabugueiro. It is matched by an "old woman's head" south of Seia.

Valezim
In Valezim are several old water mills of a type not often found in Portugal. Two of them are still used to grind grain.

Seia is one of the main entry points to the Parque Natural da Serra da Estrela.

Viseu

Seia

Alva

Cabeça do Velho

Sabugueiro

Curral dos Martins

Valezim

N339

Rodeio Grande

N231

Coimbra

Vide

Muro

Ribeira de Alvoco

Penha dos Abutres

Torre

Penhas da Saúde

N230

N231

Unhais da Serra

Alto da Pedrice

N230

N230

N338

Serra Cheese Shop
The best Serra cheese, prized for its rich flavour (see p215), is still made by hand. Farmers sell their produce at cheese fairs and at stalls or small shops such as this one near the summit of Torre.

Penhas de Saúde, once a health spa, is now popular with skiers.

Torre
Despite the unpredictability of snow, the slopes below Torre are used for skiing, tobogganing or just fun in the snow.

STAR SIGHTS
★ Zêzere Valley
★ Linhares

★ **Linhares**
Guarded by the towers of its medieval castle, Linhares is like a living museum. The forum, from which medieval justice was dispensed, survives, as do many fine houses from its 15th-century heyday.

VISITORS' CHECKLIST

Road map D3. 🚹 *Mercado Municipal, Rua Pinto Lucas Marrão, Seia (238-317 762); Covilhã (275-319 560); Gouveia (238-492 185); Manteigas (275-981 129).* 🚉 *Covilhã, Guarda.* 🚌 *to Covilhã, Seia & Guarda. Limited local service within park.* 🏪 *Sat in most towns.* 🎭 *Feb: Carnaval & annual cheese fairs; Dec: Santa Luzia.*

KEY

🟫	Major road
══	Minor road
🚹	Tourist information
☀	Viewpoint

Manteigas, at the heart of the Serra, is a textile centre. Just to the west there is a *pousada (see p390).*

★ **Zêzere Valley**
The Zêzere eventually joins the Tagus, but here, near its source, the young river flows through a classic glacier-cut valley. The golden broom growing here is used to thatch mountain huts.

Covilhã, the largest and liveliest town in the area, has a busy morning market. It is also known for its fine textiles woven from locally produced wool.

Poço do Inferno
This cascade in a gorge of the River Leandros is a spectacular sight, especially when it freezes in winter.

SHEEPDOG OF THE SERRA

Intelligent, loyal and brave, the Serra da Estrela sheepdog embodies all the qualities required in this wild region. Its heavy coat, as shaggy as its charges, helps it survive the bitter high-altitude winters and in the past its strength was called upon to defend the flock from wolves. Pedigree Serra da Estrela dogs (reputedly with some wolf's blood introduced in their breeding) are raised at kennels near Gouveia and west of Manteigas.

Sabugal ㉗

Road map E3. 🕌 *2,500.* 🚌
ℹ️ *Câmara Municipal, Praça da República (271-75 10 40).*
🗓️ *1st Thu & 3rd Tue of month.*

IN 1296, WHEN THIS small town beside the River Côa was confirmed as Portuguese in the Treaty of Alcañices, the **castle** was refortified by the ever-industrious King Dinis *(see p44)*. Its imposing towered walls and unusual five-sided keep survive from this era, although the castle suffered in peacetime from villagers raiding it for building stone.

Peopled since prehistoric times, Sabugal still has part of its medieval walls, reinforced in the 17th century and now ringed by newer houses. In the Praça da República stands a granite **clocktower**, reconstructed in the 17th century.

ENVIRONS: Wrapped in its ring of walls, **Sortelha**, 20 km (12 miles) west, is enchanting. It sits on a granite outcrop and the views from the high keep of its gem of a 13th-century castle are stunning. In front of the arched castle entrance is a 16th-century pillory with an armillary sphere on top. In the tiny citadel are a school and stony lanes of granite houses, some discreetly converted into restaurants *(see p413)*.

The local fondness for bullfights *(see pp144–5)* is reflected in names of nearby villages

The castle at Sabugal, with its distinctive five-sided keep

such as **Vila do Touro**. In a local variation, the *capeia*, bulls were taunted into charging into a huge fork of branches.

Penamacor ㉘

Road map D3. 🕌 *3,200.* 🚉 🚌
ℹ️ *Ave 25 de Abril (277-39 43 16).*
🗓️ *1st & 3rd Wed of month.*

FOUGHT OVER by successive waves of Romans, Visigoths and Moors, this frontier town was fortified in the 12th century by Gualdim Pais, Master of the Knights Templar *(see pp184–5)*. Today the weather-beaten castle walls rise above a quiet town at the heart of hardy, sparsely inhabited country where the main attraction is the hunting of small game.

From the main square, the road up to the old town passes beside the former town hall,

built over a medieval archway. Beyond lie the restored **castle keep** and the 16th-century **Igreja da Misericórdia**, with an elegant Manueline portal capped by armillary spheres, the emblem of Manuel I.

ENVIRONS: Penamacor is the headquarters of the **Reserva Natural da Serra da Malcata**. These 20 sq km (8 sq miles) of forested wilderness shelter wolves, otters and, most importantly, are one of the last refuges of the Iberian lynx. Visitors should first call at the information centre for advice.

🦌 **Reserva Natural da Serra da Malcata**
🚌 *to Penamacor or Sabugal.* ℹ️ *Rua dos Bombeiros Voluntários, Penamacor (277-39 44 67).* 📷 *by appt.*

Monsanto ㉙

Road map E3. 🕌 *1,500.* 🚌
ℹ️ *Rua Marquês de Graciosa (277-31 46 42).* 🗓️ *3rd Sat.*

AN ODD FAME hit Monsanto in 1938 when it was voted "most Portuguese village in Portugal". The village is at one with the granite hillside on which it perches: its lanes blend into the grey rock, the houses squeezed between massive boulders. Tiny gardens sprout from the granite and dogs drink from granite bowls.

The ruined **castle** began as a *castro*, a Lusitanian fortified settlement, and suffered a long history of sieges and battles for its commanding position. It was finally destroyed by a 19th-century gunpowder

Monsanto's houses, dwarfed by immense granite boulders

explosion. Cars cannot venture beyond the village centre, but the view alone is worth the walk up to the ruined walls.

A story is told of how a long siege by the Moors drove the hungry villagers to a desperate ploy. They threw their last calf, full of their last grain, over the walls, a show of profligacy that convinced the Moors to give up. Each May there is a mock re-enactment of this victory amid much music and singing.

Idanha-a-Velha ③

Road map D3. ⚐ 90. ▦ ⓘ *Rua da Sé (277-91 42 80).*

THIS MODEST HAMLET among the olive groves encapsulates the history of Portugal. Discreet signposts and explanations in Portuguese, French and English guide visitors round the landmarks of this fascinating living museum.

Idanha-a-Velha was, it is said, the birthplace of the Visigothic King Wamba, and had its own bishop until 1199. The present appearance of the **cathedral** comes from early 16th-century restoration, but in the echoing interior are stacked inscribed and sculpted Roman stones.

In the middle of the village stand several historic monuments: a 17th-century pillory and the Renaissance **Igreja Matriz**, while near an early 20th-century olive press is a ruined **Torre dos Templários**, a relic of the Templars. This order of religious knights held sway in Idanha until the 14th century *(see pp184–5).*

Statue-lined Stairway of the Apostles in the unusual Jardim Episcopal, Castelo Branco

Castelo Branco ③

Road map D4. ⚐ 35,000. ▣ ▦ ⓘ *Alameda da Liberdade (272-33 03 39).* ● *Mon.*

THIS HANDSOME, busy old city, overlooked by the vestiges of a Templar castle, is the most important in the Beira Baixa.

Much the greatest attraction is the extraordinary **Jardim Episcopal** beside the former bishops' palace. Created by Bishop João de Mendonça in the 18th century, the garden's layout is conventionally formal; its individuality lies in its dense population of statues. Baroque in style and often bizarre in character, stone saints and apostles line the box-edged paths, lions peer at their reflections in pools and monarchs stand guard along the balustrades – the hated kings of the 60-year Spanish rule *(see p50)* conspicuously half-size.

The 17th-century Paço Episcopal itself now houses the **Museu Francisco Tavares Proença Júnior**. Its wide-ranging collection includes archaeological finds, displays of 16th-century tapestries and Portuguese primitive art. Castelo Branco is also well known for its fine silk-embroidered bedspreads, called *colchas*, and examples of these are also exhibited in the museum.

In the mainly 18th-century Convento da Graça opposite there is a small **Museu de Arte Sacra** with a varied collection of religious art, including an ivory Christ. Beside the road back to the town centre stands a 15th-century cross known as the **Cruzeiro de São João**.

♣ Jardim Episcopal
Rua Bartolomeu da Costa. ◐ *daily.* ▨
▥ Museu Francisco Tavares Proença Júnior
Rua Bartolomeu da Costa.
⒞ 272-34 42 77. ◐ 10am–12:30pm, 2–5:30pm Tue–Sun.
▥ Museu de Arte Sacra
Rua Bartolomeu da Costa. ⒞ 272-34 84 20, ext. 237. ◐ 9am–12:30pm, 2–6pm Mon–Fri. ● *public hols.* &

The historic little village of Idanha-a-Velha, among its olive groves beside the River Ponsul

NORTHERN
PORTUGAL

Northern Portugal at a Glance

PORTUGAL NORTH of the River Douro is rural and unspoilt, yet offers splendid opportunities for cultural sightseeing, walking and water sports. Beyond the cultivated valley of the Douro and the fertile Minho rises the remote and romantically named Trás-os-Montes ("Behind the Mountains"), with its tracts of wilderness and tiny medieval townships. It could be said the nation was conceived between the Minho and the Douro, and historic cities such as Oporto, Bragança and Braga give fascinating insights into the country's past.

In the Parque Nacional da Peneda-Gerês scenery ranges from dramatic forested valleys to flowery meadows. Local farmers store their grain in curious stone espigueiros *(see pp270–71).*

Viana do Castelo, at the mouth of the River Lima, is elegant and relaxed (see pp274–5). The stately buildings in the Praça da República, including the arcaded Paços do Concelho *(the old town hall), reflect the town's wealthy past.*

MINHO
(See pp262–81)

Douro Litoral

***Bom Jesus do Monte**, near Braga, attracts worshippers, penitents and tourists, who all come to climb 116 m (380 ft) up the Baroque staircase (see pp278–9). This is the Staircase of the Five Senses, with fountains depicting each of the senses.*

Oporto, set on Penaventosa Hill above the River Douro, is Portugal's second city (see pp236–47). Alongside a wealth of historic sights and sophisticated shopping, it offers the charm of its steep medieval alleys tumbling down to the lively riverside quays, and a chance to taste port at its point of origin.

◁ *Azulejos* on the Igreja do Carmo in Oporto, depicting the founding of the Carmelite Order

The Casa de Mateus, familiar to many from the Mateus Rosé wine label, lies in the hills above the valley of the Douro. This Baroque solar, or manor house, is set in beautifully manicured formal gardens, its distinctive pinnacles rising above the orchards and vineyards that surround it (see pp254–5).

Bragança, capital of Trás-os-Montes, gave its name to Portugal's last and longest-ruling royal dynasty. The keep and walls of this remote citadel, founded in the 12th century, look out over the valley of the River Fervença (see pp258–9).

Trás-os-Montes

DOURO AND TRÁS-OS-MONTES
(See pp232–61)

Alto Douro

0 kilometres   25

0 miles   10

Port Country, as the scenic valley of the Upper Douro is commonly called, is the nursery of Portugal's port industry. A tour of a quinta, or wine estate, with its steeply terraced riverside vineyards, is highly recommended (see pp252–3).

The Festivals of the North

PORTUGUESE CITIES, towns and villages all have their own particular saints' days. These are primarily religious occasions, particularly in the Minho and across the devout north, but are also a chance to put aside the cares of life for a day or two. It is a popular maxim that a holy day is best celebrated by eating, drinking, dancing and merrymaking, as well as worshipping and giving thanks. The most solemn and spectacular celebrations of Holy Week, Semana Santa, can also be seen in the north, especially in Braga *(see pp276–7)*, Portugal's ecclesiastical capital.

Dressing up for Holy Week

A solemn moment as Easter candles are lit in Braga

EASTER

HOLY WEEK, culminating in Easter Sunday, is the major religious festival of the year. In Braga, processions snake round the city walls to the great cathedral, and every village has its own ceremonies.

The start of Holy Week is heralded by Palm Sunday, when branch-waving faithful line the streets to commemorate the entry of Christ into Jerusalem. Good Friday evening is palpably solemn, as innumerable processions follow the 14 Stations of the Cross, many believers doing public penance as they recall Christ's suffering. In some villages an effigy of the lifeless and bleeding Christ is carried through the streets.

On Easter Sunday, after an uplifting mass proclaiming the risen Christ, every parish priest processes around his village with a crucifix on a tall staff for parishioners to kiss the feet of Jesus. While the priest takes a customary glass of wine, his entourage ecstatically let off rockets. Families then traditionally lunch on roast kid *(cabrito)*.

After Easter, in early May, the passion of Christ is recalled in Barcelos *(see p273)*. Crosses are erected the length of a petal-strewn route for the **Festa das Cruzes**.

Street procession during the Festa das Cruzes in Barcelos

SÃO JOÃO

OPORTO's celebration of São João *(23–24 Jun)* is one of Portugal's most exuberant festivals. It coincides with the summer solstice, and to celebrate, people eat, drink and dance all night, playfully hitting each other over the head with giant garlic-leeks (or sometimes, even more strangely, with squeaky plastic hammers). Bonfires are lit and a spectacular display of fireworks explodes over the Douro.

Wielding a São João hammer

COSTUME IN THE MINHO

Festivals are important vehicles for keeping alive tradition, particularly regional costume. These days, rock music and designer clothes are as much part of young people's life in Minho villages as elsewhere in western Europe, but traditional dress is worn with pride on days of celebration. The Minho's costume is the most colourful in Portugal, with exquisitely embroidered scarves and aprons in colours denoting village loyalties. Messages of love and friendship are stitched on to pockets, and bodices are half-lost under tiers of gold filigree.

Gold necklets

Embroidered apron pockets

A new tradition, which has become a part of São João over the last decade, is the annual regatta of the *barcos rabelos*, the boats in which port used to be shipped down the Douro *(see p252)*.

ROMARIAS

ANY KIND of celebration or party can be described as a *festa*, but one billed as a *romaria* implies a religious dimension. Most *festas* in the north are *romarias*; they begin with a special mass, then saints' statues are brought from the church to be paraded through the streets on litters. Blessings are dispensed in all directions – fire engines and ambulances frequently also getting the treatment – followed by a spraying with some Raposeira sparkling wine. Many *romarias* take place in the summer, and in August few days go by without a celebration. **Assumption Day** *(15 Aug)*

STICK DANCING

Stick dancers, or *pauliteiros*, can still be seen at village festivals in Trás-os-Montes. The dances are of ancient origin, probably associated with fertility rites, and the sticks may once have been swords. The most famous troupe comes from the village of Duas Igrejas, near Miranda do Douro *(see p260)*.

Dancers performing at a *festa*

Nossa Senhora da Agonia, Viana do Castelo

is fêted all over Portugal with dancing and music. *Gigantones*, grotesque giants of pre-Christian origin, join street processions and fireworks light the sky. A few days later, around 20 August, one of the year's most spectacular *romarias* takes place in Viana do Castelo *(see pp274–5)*. The festivities celebrating **Nossa Senhora da Agonia** include a bullfight and an afternoon devoted to a kaleidoscopic display of regional costume, which may include more than a thousand participants. As a finale, fireworks are let off from the bridge over the River Lima to cascade down into the water as a fiery waterfall.

On the coast just to the west of Braga, villagers in São Bartolomeu do Mar mark the end of their *romaria (22–24 Aug)* by dipping their children in the sea, as a mock sacrifice to the waves.

Outlandish costumes and masks donned for the Dia dos Rapazes

CHRISTMAS AND WINTER

ON CHRISTMAS EVE, families gather to enjoy enormous quantities of *bacalhau* (salt cod) and mulled port, and to exchange presents, before attending midnight mass.

Between Christmas and Epiphany, Trás-os-Montes village boys dress in crazy, fringed suits to take part in the rite-of-passage **Dia dos Rapazes**. The Christmas season ends on **Dia de Reis** *(6 Jan)*, when the *bolo rei*, or "king cake", rich with crystallized fruit "jewels", is eaten *(see p33)*.

Comical giants leading an Assumption Day parade in Peso da Régua

The Story of Port

THE "DISCOVERY" OF PORT dates from the 17th century when British merchants added brandy to the wine of the northern Douro region to prevent it souring in transit. They found that the stronger and sweeter the wine, the better flavour it acquired. Methods of maturing and blending continue to be refined by the main port producers. Croft was one of the first big shippers, followed by other English and Scottish firms. Despite the consolidation of the global drinks industry, much of the port trade is still in British hands, and some firms are still family-run.

Barco rabelo ferrying port down the Douro river

OPORTO

Vila Real

Peso da Régua

Pinhão

Lamego

Corgo

Pinhão

Tua

Douro

Sabor

Douro

THE PORT REGION

Port comes only from a demarcated region of the upper Douro valley, stretching 100 km (62 miles) to the Spanish border. Régua and Pinhão are the main centres of production, but most top-quality vineyards lie on estates or *quintas* in the harsh eastern terrain.

STYLES OF PORT

There are essentially two categories of port: red and wood-aged. The former are deeper in colour and will develop after bottling; the latter, which include tawney ports, are ready to drink when they are bottled. White port is in a category of its own.

Vintage, the star of any shipper's range, is made from wines of a single year, from the best vineyards. It is blended and bottled after two years in wood, and may then mature for a very long time in the bottle.

Vintage

Late Bottled Vintage (LBV) is wine of a single year, bottled between four and six years after the harvest. Filtered LBV does not require decanting but may have less flavour than unfiltered, "traditional" LBV.

LBV

Aged tawny port is blended from top-quality wines that have been aged in wood for a long time. The age on the label is not precise, but the older it is, the paler, more delicate, less fruity and more expensive the port is likely to be.

Aged Tawny

Tawny port without indication of age may not have been in wood for long enough to develop the complex flavours of aged tawny; its style is light and its price fairly low. It may be a blend of red and white ports.

Tawny

Ruby port is deep red and should be full of lively fruit flavour. It has been aged for two or three years, sometimes in wood, sometimes not. It is less complex than either LBV or Vintage, but costs considerably less.

Ruby

White port is made from white grapes and may be sweet or not so sweet. It is mainly drunk chilled as an aperitif. Some types of white port have a slightly lower alcohol content than the normal 20% for port.

White

Collecting grapes in tall wicker baskets for transport to the wineries

How Port is Made

The climax of the Douro farmers' year comes in late September when bands of pickers congregate to harvest the grapes. More than 40 varieties are used for making port, but there are five recommended top varieties.

Treading the grapes in stone tanks or lagares to extract the juice is a feature of very traditional quintas. Some shippers believe it adds a special quality.

Fermentation in cement or steel tanks is a more common method. Carbon dioxide builds up within the tank, forcing the fermenting must (juice from the grapes) up a tube into an open trough at the top. The gas is released and the must sprays back over the pips and skins, in a process similar to treading.

In the fortification process, the semi-fermented must is run into a second vat where brandy – actually grape spirit – is added. This arrests the fermentation, leaving the wine sweet from natural grape sugar.

Thousands of bottles of Graham's vintage port from 1977 await full maturation in the cellars of the Vila Nova de Gaia lodge.

Quality tawny port is matured in oak casks in the port lodges. Once bottled, it is ready for drinking and does not require decanting.

Vintage Port

In the interests of maintaining the highest standards of quality – and of not saturating the market – port producers do not "declare" a vintage every year. Each year, the wine from the best vineyards is closely monitored for 18 months, other producers are consulted about their quality, and then a decision is taken. If a vintage is not declared, the wine may remain in wood to be blended as tawny or LBV in future, or it may be bottled as a "single quinta" port – a kind of second-label vintage. On average, producers declare a vintage three times in a decade, though not always in the same years.

A good vintage needs time in bottle to reveal itself. Fifteen years is seen as a minimum, although many impatient drinkers do not actually wait that long; there is even a fashion for drinking young vintage port. The nature of vintage port's aging process results in a continuously evolving list of great vintages. Most experts agree, however, that no recent vintage has yet equalled that produced in 1963.

Pre-war vintages
1927, 1931, 1935:
All great and now very rare.

Post-war vintages
1945, 1947, 1948, 1955:
    For the very rich and extremely lucky.
1963 Perhaps the greatest post-war vintage.
1970 Its reputation has been rising and is now on par with 1963.
1994 A fine vintage, particularly from producers Dow, Taylor and Quinta do Noval.
1997 Another fine vintage.
2000 A very promising year.

Taylor's 1994 vintage

Regional Food: Northern Portugal

Walnuts

THE LUSH MINHO IS CREDITED with the invention of many recipes which have been adopted nationally, the ubiquitous *caldo verde* soup being just one example. The coast is rich in fish, although salt cod *(bacalhau)* is actually imported. Once common in the Minho's rivers, much of the lamprey is now imported and the trout farmed. Cumin, unusually, is used to spice dishes. The robust diet of Trás-os-Montes echoes the austere landscape: pork, both fresh and cured, features widely, and nuts and dried beans often add body to dishes. The local sweet tooth ensures the *pastelarias* have delicious pastries.

Broa *is a golden, close-textured maize bread with a thick, crunchy crust.*

Paio, a sausage made with pork loin

Highly spiced *chouriço* sausage

Cured ham from Lamego

Monte*, from Trás-os-Montes, is a smooth, creamy cheese made with cow's and ewe's milk.*

Cured meats *play an important role in northern dishes. The best hams are from Lamego, and Trás-os-Montes produces fine* chouriços, *flavoured with paprika and often wine.*

Bola *is popular at Easter and for picnics. A rich bread dough is layered with a mixture of cured meats into a kind of pie.*

Pastéis de bacalhau *are a national addiction. These little salt-cod cakes are eaten cold as a snack or hot as a main dish.*

Caldo verde*, Portugal's most famous soup, gets its vibrant colour from its main ingredient:* couve galega, *a type of kale.*

Sopa de castanhas piladas*, a winter soup from Trás-os-Montes, is made with dried chestnuts, beans and rice.*

Bacalhau à Gomes de Sá *is a creation from Oporto of salt cod, potato and onion layers, topped with egg and olives.*

Truta de Barroso *uses local trout stuffed with ham and then fried in bacon fat. It is served with boiled potatoes.*

Feijoada, *popular throughout Portugal, is a stew of kidney or butter beans and cured meats, with many local variations.*

Vitela no espeto *is loin of veal barbecued (ideally on a spit), then sprinkled with oil and covered to draw out the juices.*

Rojões, *a widely popular and variable dish, uses cumin to spice pork which is then cooked in wine and garlic to a rich stew.*

Chouriço — Morcela

Pork

Chicken — Beef

Cozido à portuguesa *is a national dish with its origins in Trás-os-Montes, where it is a Carnaval speciality. A variety of meats, sausages and vegetables are served in their own broth.*

Morcela

Farinheira

These sausages *are two of the many types of cured meats used in dishes such as* cozido à portuguesa. *Farinheira is made from pork, wine and flour, while morcela is a well-seasoned blood sausage. It is good sliced and fried or barbecued.*

Torta de Viana *is a sponge roll with a sweetened egg filling.*

Toucinho do céu *is a rich almond and cinnamon cake; it means "bacon from heaven".*

Papos de anjo *(angel's breasts) take their curious name from their delicate shape.*

Sopa dourada, *sponge cake under a blanket of ground almonds and egg yolk, was created in Viana do Castelo.*

Cakes *fulfil the Portuguese passion for sweet things. Northern specialities are rich and velvety smooth, addictively sugary, and often flavoured with cinnamon.*

DRINKS

Northern grapes also produce *bagaceira*, a clear distillation of the remains of wine pressing, and Portuguese spirit, *aguardente*. The region has many spa towns, such as Pedras Salgadas, that provide excellent mineral waters.

Mineral water from Pedras Salgadas

Aguardente

Pudim Abade de Priscos, *named after the abbot who invented it, is flavoured with port, spices and lemon.*

DOURO AND TRÁS-OS-MONTES

O N ITS WAY TO THE ATLANTIC, *the Douro or "Golden River" weaves its scenic path through deep-cleft gorges, terraced with thousands of vineyards, to the historic city of Oporto, home of port.* To the northeast, the high plateaus and mountain ranges of Trás-os-Montes, "Behind the Mountains", form Portugal's wildest region.

As early as the 9th century BC, Phoenician merchants arrived in the Douro estuary to trade. The Romans later developed the settlements of Portus and Cale on either side of the river, and the names subsequently united, as Portucale, to denote the region between the Minho and Douro rivers. This was the nucleus of the kingdom of Portugal *(see pp42–3)*. The estuary and coastal strip, or Douro Litoral, is now a mix of fishing ports, beach resorts and industrial zones, while Portus, at the river's mouth, became Oporto, the regional capital and Portugal's second city.

Rich from centuries of trade, cosmopolitan Oporto is at once modern and steeped in the past, its waterfront and higgledy-piggledy streets a delight to explore. From its hillside, Oporto looks across the Douro to the lodges which nurture the precious wine to which the city gave its name: port.

The upper reaches of the river are devoted to the cultivation of grapes for port, the landscape shaped by endless vineyards and wine estates *(quintas)*.

In contrast with the thriving Douro valley, Trás-os-Montes is remote and untamed, a refuge in the past of religious and political exiles. The hard life and lack of opportunity to better it have depopulated the land; those who remain till the fields and herd their flocks in the unforgiving climate, according to the rhythm of the seasons.

The rural north clings closely to tradition and local *festas* are some of the country's most colourful *(see pp226–7)*. Outside influences are beginning to make an impact on Trás-os-Montes, but for the visitor it remains a land of quiet stone villages amid fields of rye and moorland, where the wild Parque Natural de Montesinho stretches from Bragança to the Spanish border.

Terraced vineyards covering the hillsides between Pinhão and Alijó, in the valley of the Upper Douro

◁ **Oporto's Barredo district, where houses are squeezed into the steep maze of ancient alleys**

Exploring the Douro and Trás-os-Montes

O PORTO ITSELF IS SO FULL OF INTEREST that many visitors venture no further. But to follow the Douro upstream is to discover a world of neat terraced vineyards and prosperous *quintas* all dedicated to producing wine and port. Oporto apart, either Peso da Régua or the pilgrimage town of Lamego would make a convenient base from which to explore the area.

Trás-os-Montes is Portugal's poorest and least-known region. Its isolated capital, Bragança, is full of historic associations, and lies on the edge of the wild terrain of the Montesinho reserve. Between here and Chaves is spectacular country seldom visited by tourists.

Rocky outcrops of the Parque Natural do Alvão

SIGHTS AT A GLANCE

KEY

▀▀	Motorway
▬	Major road
▬	Minor road
▀▀	Scenic route
∼	River
☀	Viewpoint

Oporto's quayside, the Cais da Ribeira, in the early morning

Port country near Pinhão, where vineyards clothe the banks of the Douro

Orense

RIO DE ONOR

PARQUE NATURAL DE MONTESINHO ⑱

BRAGANÇA ⑰

VINHAIS

Zamora
Valladolid

CHAVES

VALPAÇOS

N206

IP4 (E82)

N213

MURÇA

MIRANDELA ⑯

VILA FLOR

ALIJÓ

N214

N215

TUA

VILA NOVA DE FOZ CÔA

TORRE DE MONCORVO ㉑

FREIXO DE ESPADA À CINTA ㉒

Guarda

Sabor

MOGADOURO ⑳

SERRA DE MOGADOURO

VIMIOSO

N218

MIRANDA DO DOURO ⑲

DUAS IGREJAS

Douro

N221

N219

N316

N221

N230

N221

Douro

SEE ALSO

- *Where to Stay* pp390–93
- *Where to Eat* pp413–16

| 0 kilometres | 25 |
| 0 miles | 10 |

GETTING AROUND

With the frenetic tempo of traffic in Oporto, it is best to negotiate the inner city by bus, taxi or on foot. Boat trips from Oporto are a good way to see the varied Douro landscape at a relaxed pace. Trains link Oporto to the major towns of the north and also run along the Douro valley. Services are less frequent beyond Peso da Régua, but a trip alongside the Douro is highly recommended. In Trás-os-Montes, public transport is minimal and driving is the most convenient way to explore this remote region, especially now the IP4 (E82) links Vila Real and Bragança. However, the state of repair of many minor roads leaves a lot to be desired.

The Sabor near Bragança, on the southern edge of the Parque Natural de Montesinho

Oporto ●

E VER SINCE THE ROMANS built a fort here, where their trading route crossed the Douro, Oporto has prospered from commerce. Quick to expel the Moors in the 11th century and to profit from provisioning crusaders en route to the Holy Land, resourceful Oporto took advantage of the wealth generated by Portugal's maritime discoveries in the 15th and 16th centuries. Later, the wine trade with Britain compensated for the loss of the lucrative spice trade. Still a thriving industrial centre and the country's second largest city, Oporto, known locally as Porto, blends industry with charm. In 2001 the city was the European Capital of Culture, and hosted an array of events throughout the year.

Lion and eagle statue, Rotunda da Boavista

The cathedral (Sé) and statue of Vímara Peres (see p42)

The Cathedral District

Oporto's cathedral (see p240) crowns the city's upper level and in the surrounding streets are a variety of monuments to the city's past, including the Renaissance church of Santa Clara (see p239) and the turn-of-the-century railway station of São Bento (see p239), alongside bustling street markets.

Beneath the towering cathedral lies the crowded Barredo, a quarter seemingly unchanged since medieval days, where balconied houses cling to each other and to the vertiginous hillside, forming a maze of ancient alleys; some are no more than outside staircases.

Ribeira

This riverside quarter is a warren of narrow, twisting streets and shadowy arcades. Behind brightly tiled or pastel-painted façades, many in faded glory, a working population earns its living, hangs out the washing, chats and mixes in lively street scenes. Restoration of this atmospheric district is attracting a growing number of restaurants and nightclubs.

Washing hanging out to dry in a typical street in the Ribeira district

Cordoaria

The Cordoaria gardens lie in the lee of the hilltop landmark of the Torre dos Clérigos (see p241). Nearby streets are full of interesting shops.

A shop specializing in Bacalhau (dried salted cod)

Looking north up the Avenida dos Aliados to the Câmara Municipal

Central and Baixa

The civic centre of Oporto ranges along the Avenida dos Aliados, leading up to the modern Câmara Municipal, or town hall. Along this broad double avenue are to be found the city's banks and offices, and thriving outdoor cafés. To the east, the Baixa or "lower level" district attracts shoppers, especially to the fashionable

Boavista

The busy Avenida da Boavista is lined with hotels, residential blocks and shops. In the centre of the Rotunda da Boavista, as Praça de Mouzinho de Albuquerque is known locally, a statue of a lion (the Luso-British forces) crushing an eagle (the French) marks the victory in the Peninsular War. South of the rotunda is some of the best shopping in the city.

OPORTO CITY CENTRE

Casa do Infante ⑫
Casa-Museu Guerra Junqueiro ⑭
Igreja do Carmo ⑤
Igreja dos Clérigos ⑥
Igreja dos Congregados ⑦
Igreja da Misericórdia ⑧
Igreja Românica ①
Jardim do Palácio de Cristal ③
Museu Românico ②
Museu Soares dos Reis ④
Museu dos Transpotes e
    Comunicações ⑨
Palácio da Bolsa ⑩
Ponte de Dom Luís I ⑯
Santa Clara ⑮
São Francisco ⑪
Sé ⑬

KEY

🟪	Cathedral District pp238–9
🚉	Railway station
🚌	Main terminal for coaches
🚢	River boat service
🅿️	Parking
ℹ️	Tourist information
✝️	Church

leather and jewellery shops in and around the pedestrianized Rua de Santa Catarina and the parallel Rua Sá da Bandeira. Between them lies the two-tier covered Bolhão market. Noisy and exuberant, it provides an entertaining view of Oporto daily life. Everything can be bought here, from fresh fruit and vegetables to household goods and pets.

Fresh fruit and vegetables in the colourful Bolhão market

Street-by-Street: Oporto's Cathedral District

Aᴿᴄʜᴀᴇᴏʟᴏɢɪᴄᴀʟ ᴇxᴄᴀᴠᴀᴛɪᴏɴꜱ show that Penaventosa Hill, now the site of Oporto's cathedral, or Sé, was inhabited as early as 3,000 years ago. In its elevated position, the cathedral is a useful landmark and its terrace provides an excellent orientation point. The broad Avenida de Vímara Peres, named after the military hero who expelled the Moors from the city in AD 868, sweeps south past the huddle of steep alleys and stairways of the Barredo. The view to the north is towards the extraordinarily embellished São Bento station and the busy commercial heart of the city.

Rua das Flores
Behind the traditional shop-fronts in the Street of Flowers are many of the city's best jewellers and goldsmiths.

A semi-covered market
near the Sé offer fresh fish, fruit and vegetables alongside household goods, bric-a-brac and souvenirs.

Terreiro da Sé
This broad open terrace offers a wonderful panorama of the city. In one corner stands a Manueline pillory, complete with hooks.

Former bishops' palace

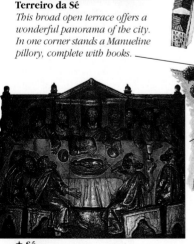

★ Sé
Although imposing and perhaps a little forbidding, Oporto's cathedral contains many small-scale treasures. This 17th-century gilded painting of the Last Supper is in the Capela de São Vicente (see p240).

The Casa-Museu Guerra Junqueiro is a charming museum in a house that once belonged to the 19th-century poet *(see p240).*

Ponte de Dom Luís I

Praça da Liberdade

Praça de Almeida Garrett
Traffic hurries by oblivious to the architectural diversity of this busy square in the centre of Oporto.

PRAÇA DE ALMEIDA GARRETT

RUA DO LOUREIRO

AVENIDA DOM AFONSO HENRIQUES

RUA CHÃ

RUA SARAIVA DE CARVALHO

★ São Bento Station
Oporto's central railway station, on the site of an earlier monastery, was completed in 1916. Inside is a feast of azulejos by Jorge Colaço (see p23), depicting early modes of transport, rural festivities and historic scenes.

The Fernandine Walls, named after Fernando I, were built in the 14th century; only fragments here and along the Cais da Ribeira *(see p236)* remain.

Santa Clara
The Renaissance church of Santa Clara presents a strong contrast between its simple external façade and the opulent gilded woodwork of its interior.

0 metres   50
0 yards   50

KEY

– – – Suggested route

STAR SIGHTS

★ Sé

★ São Bento Station

Exploring Oporto

THROUGHOUT OPORTO THERE IS EVIDENCE of the wealth that flowed into the city from the 15th century onwards. Trade in the commodities from Portugal's newly claimed lands *(see pp48–9)* brought Brazilian gold and exotic woods to embellish Oporto's churches, and prosperous merchants spent prodigiously on paintings and *azulejos*. Recently the city authorities restored footpaths, cobbled streets and stone steps to create five historical walks between the Jardim do Palácio de Cristal and the river.

The magnificently gilded Arabian Room in Oporto's Palácio da Bolsa

Sé

Terreiro da Sé. **22-205 9028.** 8:30am–12:30pm; 2:30pm–7pm daily. **cloisters** 9am–12:30pm, 2:30–6pm daily.

Built as a fortress church in the 12th and 13th centuries, the cathedral has since been so modified that it lacks a unified style. The only noteworthy survival from the 13th century is the beautiful rose window in the west front. In the small chapel to the left of the chancel is a silver retable of dazzling workmanship, saved from invading French troops in 1809 by means of a hastily raised plaster wall. The south transept gives access to the 14th-century cloisters and the Capela de São Vicente. Niccolò Nasoni's 18th-century staircase leads to the upper levels, where *azulejo* panels depict the life of the Virgin and Ovid's *Metamorphoses*.

Portuguese water jug, Museu Guerra Junqueiro

Casa-Museu Guerra Junqueiro

Rua de Dom Hugo 32. **22-205 3644.** Tue–Sun. public hols.

The former home of the poet and fiery Republican activist, Guerra Junqueiro (1850–1923), is an 18th-century Baroque gem. From the tranquil courtyard, visitors enter the poet's private collection, which ranges from Portuguese furniture and rare ceramics to Flemish tapestries and a remarkable set of English alabaster sculptures. On elegant tables in the Dom João V Room there is a colourful parade of Chinese dogs.

Casa do Infante

Rua da Alfândega 10. **22-205 60 25.** 8:30am–5pm Mon–Fri. public hols. Compulsory guided tours, booked in advance.

Legend has it that Prince Henry the Navigator was born in this house on Oporto's riverfront. Today the building houses Oporto's city archives, which include historical documents, among them Prince Henry's christening certificate, photographs and recent archaeological finds.

Palácio da Bolsa

Rua Ferreira Borges. **22-339 9000.** 9am–7pm daily. special events. compulsory.

Where the monastery of São Francisco once stood, the city's merchants built the stock exchange, or Bolsa, in 1842. The Tribunal do Comércio, where Oporto's mercantile law was upheld, is full of historic interest, and has a small adjoining picture gallery. But the glittering highlight is the Arabian Room. This galleried salon, its convoluted blue and gold arabesques inspired by Granada's Alhambra, makes a setting fit for Scheherazade.

Museu dos Transportes e Comunicações

Rua Nova da Alfândega, Edifíco da Alfândega. **22-340 30 00.** 10am–noon; 2–6pm Tue–Fri, 3–7pm Sun and public hols.

Housed in the vast Neo-Classical customs building on the riverfront, this museum includes a permanent exhibition about the automobile and interactive exhibitions on media, science, new technologies and art. The building also houses a restaurant, various spaces for cultural events and the customs service.

Casa da Misericórdia

Rua das Flores 15. **22-207 4710.** Mon–Sat. public hols.

This religious hospice, alongside its imposing church, was founded in the 16th century. Its most precious possession is the masterful *Fons Vitae* (Fountain of Life), donated by Manuel I in about 1520. The artist's identity remains unproven, but Van der Weyden and Holbein have both been suggested. The picture shows the king with his family and nobles kneeling before the crucified Christ.

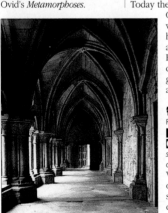

The Gothic cloisters on the south side of the Sé

São Francisco's Tree of Jesse

Illustrating biblical episodes, either in stained-glass windows or as elaborate carvings, was a common form of "Bible teaching" before literacy became widespread. A popular subject was Christ's genealogy, showing his descent from the kings of Judah and Israel. This was commonly rendered as an actual tree, tracing the family line back through Joseph to the father of King David, Jesse of Bethlehem.

São Francisco's Tree, in gilded and painted wood, was carved between 1718 and 1721 by Filipe da Silva and António Gomes. Its sinuous branches and trunk, sprouting from a reclining Jesse, support a dozen expressive figures, culminating in Christ flanked by His mother, Mary, and St Joseph.

Virgin Mary

Jesus Christ

Joseph

Solomon, who succeeded his father, David, was famed for his wisdom and for the building of the Temple in Jerusalem.

Jesse is shown with the roots of the Tree springing from his loins. His youngest son was David, the slayer of Goliath, who became king of Israel and Judah.

King David, identified by his harp

São Francisco

Rua do Infante D.Henrique. 22-206 2100. 9am–5pm daily. Catacombs included.

Construction of São Francisco began in the 14th century, but it is the 18th-century interior that amazes visitors. Over 200 kg (450 lb) of gold encrusting the high altar, columns and pillars is wrought into cherubs, garlands and cavorting animals, reaching a crescendo with the Tree of Jesse on the north wall. A tour includes the catacombs and treasures from the church's monastery, destroyed in 1832.

Igreja dos Congregados

Rua da Sá da Bandeira 11. 22-200 29 48. daily. public hols

The modern tiles clothing the façade of this 17th-century church are by Jorge Colaço (see p23). They depict scenes from the life of St Antony, and provide a dignified presence amid the traffic that clogs this part of the city.

Igreja dos Clérigos

Rua São Filipe de Nery. 22-200 17 29. daily. **Tower** daily.

This hilltop ensemble of church and tower is an unmistakable landmark. Built in the 18th century by Niccolò Nasoni, the church's oval interior was the first in Portugal.

The soaring Torre dos Clérigos with which the architect complemented his design is, at 75 m (246 ft), still one of the tallest buildings in Portugal. The dizzying 240-step climb is worth it for the superb views of the river, the coastline and the Douro valley.

São Francisco's extravagant interior

Torre dos Clérigos, Oporto's landmark and panoramic viewpoint

Detail of the *azulejo* panel on the side wall of the Igreja do Carmo

🔒 **Igreja do Carmo**
Praça Carlos Alberto 32. ☎ 22-207
8400. ◯ *daily.* ♿

This characteristic example of Portuguese Baroque architecture was constructed by José Figueiredo Seixas between 1750 and 1768. Its most notable feature is the immense *azulejo* panel covering one outside wall. Designed by Silvestro Silvestri, it depicts the legendary founding of the Carmelite order on Mount Carmel.

The earlier Igreja das Carmelitas next door was completed in 1628 in a combination of Classical and Baroque styles. It is now part of a barracks.

🏛 **Museu Soares dos Reis**
Rua Dom Manuel II. ☎ 22-339 37 70.
◯ *Tue–Sun.* ◯ *public hols.* ♿

The elegant Carrancas Palace, built in the 18th century, has been a Jewish textile workshop, a royal abode and, in the Peninsular War, a military headquarters. In 1809 Oporto was in French hands, and Marshal Soult and his troops were quartered here. They were ousted in a surprise attack by Arthur Wellesley, later Duke of Wellington, who then calmly installed himself at the marshal's dinner table.

Today, the palace provides an appropriate setting for an outstanding museum, named after António Soares dos Reis, the country's leading 19th-century sculptor. Pride of place goes to the display of Portuguese art. This includes paintings by the 16th-century master, Frey Carlos, and the Impressionist, Henrique Pousão. Also hung here are landscapes of Oporto by the French artist, Jean Pillement (1728–1808). The star sculpture exhibit, *O Desterrado* (The Exile), is Soares dos Reis's own marvel of pensive tension in marble, completed in 1874. Further sections display

***O Desterrado* by Soares dos Reis**

A River View of Oporto

Flowing over 927 km (576 miles) from its source in Spain to the Atlantic, the Douro has been linked with the fortunes of Oporto since time immemorial. There is an unsubstantiated story that Henry the Navigator, patron of Portuguese explorers, *(see p49)*, was born in the waterfront Casa do Infante. The days are long since gone when ships laden with port or goods from overseas would moor here, but the river continues to be a focal point of the city. A river cruise is a chance to appreciate Oporto from a different viewpoint.

Most river-boat operators are based in the shadow of the swooping curve of the splendid two-tier Ponte de Dom Luís I, built in 1886 by an assistant of Gustave Eiffel, to link the city to Vila Nova de Gaia on the southern bank. The city is in the process of constructing a largely above ground metro system. When finished it will use the upper level of the Dom Luís I bridge. Just upriver, the new Infante Dom Henrique bridge is for cars.

Vila Nova de Gaia
is home of the port lodges *(see p247)*.

Ponte da Arrábida

Quayside of the Cais da Estiva

Portuguese pottery, Limoges enamels, porcelain and decorative art. Historical exhibits in the museum include an appealing 15th-century silver bust of São Pantaleão, patron saint of Oporto, and a sword which was once owned by the first king of Portugal.

🔒 Igreja Românica de Cedofeita

Largo do Priorado. 📞 22-200 0635. ⏱ phone to check. 🅿

Constructed in Romanesque style in the 12th century, this plain little church is thought to be the oldest in the city. It is said to have been built on the site where Theodomir, the King of the Suevi (a Germanic tribe who occupied the area), was converted to Christianity in the 6th century by Saint Martin.

🏛 Museu Romântico

Rua de Entre-Quintas 220. 📞 22-605 70 33. ⏱ Tue–Sun. ⬤ public hols. 📷

The Quinta da Macieirinha was briefly the residence of the abdicated King Carlo Alberto of Sardinia (1798–1849), who lived here for the final two months of his life. In 1972 the upper floor of the mansion

Temporary exhibits in the billiards room of the Museu Romântico

was converted into a museum. The well-proportioned rooms looking out over the river display to advantage delicately finished French, German and Portuguese furniture, as well as rugs, ceramics and miscellaneous exhibits. Among the oil paintings and watercolours displayed here are portraits of Baron Forrester *(see p252)* and Almeida Garrett, the great Portuguese Romantic poet, playwright and author.

On the ground floor of the Quinta da Macieirinha, the Port Wine Institute operates the Solar do Vinho do Porto. In this unexpected bar it is possible to

choose from a tasting list of over 150 varieties of port, then relax in the secluded garden and enjoy the view across the Douro.

🌺 Jardim do Palácio de Cristal

Rua Dom Manuel II. ⏱ daily.

Inspired by the Crystal Palace of London's Great Exhibition in 1851, Oporto's own crystal palace was begun in 1861. The steel and glass structure of the original was replaced in the 1950s by the Pavilhão Rosa Mota, an ungainly shape dubbed "the half-orange" by local wits. Concerts are occasionally held here and the leisure gardens are enlivened by a fair at *festa* time.

Cyclists in the Jardim do Palácio de Cristal

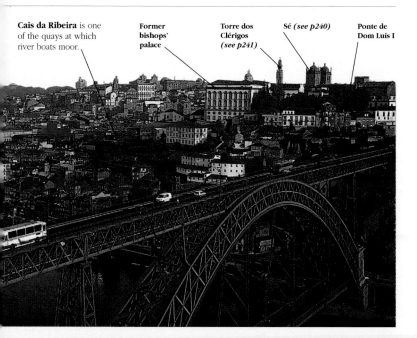

Cais da Ribeira is one of the quays at which river boats moor.

Former bishops' palace

Torre dos Clérigos *(see p241)*

Sé *(see p240)*

Ponte de Dom Luís I

Oporto: Further Afield

Away FROM THE CITY CENTRE, Oporto has many additional places of interest. Crossing the Ponte de Dom Luís I brings you to Vila Nova de Gaia, the home of port, and the Mosteiro da Serra do Pilar, with one of the finest views of the old city. In the northern and western suburbs are several fascinating attractions, from the great church of the Hospitallers at Leça do Bailio, north of Oporto, to the latest developments in Portuguese art exhibited in the beautifully modern setting of the Museu Serralves.

Along the coast, beyond the river-mouth castle at Foz do Douro, lies Matosinhos which, despite its industrial port, is renowned for its seafood. The beaches, such as Espinho, are the main draw along the coast south of Oporto.

A tram, once such a feature of Oporto, in the Museu do Carro Eléctrico

🏠 Mosteiro da Serra do Pilar

Serra do Pilar. [22-375 22 98. ○ Jun–Sep (cloisters by appt only).
It is a steep walk up to this circular 16th-century church, but worth it. From the terrace, the future Duke of Wellington planned his surprise attack on the French in 1809. It is easy to see the advantage gained, for the panoramic view takes in the port lodges below, the sweep of the River Douro and the old city on the far side.

🏛 Fundação de Serralves Museu de Arte Contemporânea

Rua Dom João de Castro 210. [22-615 65 00. ○ 10am–7pm Tue–Sun (Apr–Sep; 10pm Sat, Sun & hols; Oct–Mar 10pm Thu). ◑ 1 Jan, 25 Dec. 🖼 ⛔ Ⓦ www.serralves.pt
Created in 1989 as the country's main institution for contemporary art, the foundation is responsible for both the Art Deco Casa de Serralves and the Museu de Arte Contemporânea. The museum occupies a long white ship of a building and houses a permanent collection dating from the 1960s. There are works by Christian Boltanski, Bruce Nauman and Julião Sarmento.

🏛 Museu do Carro Eléctrico

Alameda Basílio Teles 51. [22-615 81 85. ○ Tue–Sun. 🖼
Trams, once the backbone of the city's transport system, have been trundled into retirement at the tram museum. Among the gleaming beauties on show are No. 22, introduced in 1895 as the first electric tram on the Iberian Peninsula.

A ride on No. 18, Oporto's last tram, takes a scenic route along the river to Rua Infante Dom Henrique and back.

🏛 Casa-Museu Fernando de Castro

Rua Costa Cabral 716. ○ by appt only. [22-509 46 25. 🖼
The former residence of the businessman, collector and poet, Fernando de Castro (1888–1950), was donated to the state by his sister in 1951. His collection ranges from religious sculpture saved from disbanded churches to works by modern artists, and includes a painting of the infant Jesus attributed to Josefa de Óbidos (*see p51*). Also of special interest are figurines from the 19th and 20th centuries by Teixeira Lopes, both father and son.

Environs: Forts around the river mouth, such as **Castelo da Foz** at Foz do Douro and **Castelo do Queijo** just to the north, are reminders that for centuries the coast and ships were under constant threat from the Spanish and pirates.

The church of **Bom Jesus**, near Matosinhos, was reconstructed by Niccolò Nasoni in the 18th century. Each June, pilgrims come here to honour a wooden statue of Christ. Found on the beach in the 10th century, it was allegedly carved by the disciple Nicodemus.

The 14th-century fortified **Igreja do Mosteiro** at Leça do Bailio, 8 km (5 miles) north of Oporto, was Portugal's first headquarters of the Order of Hospitallers. The church is graced with elegant Gothic arches, finely sculpted capitals and a splendid rose window.

The Art Deco Casa de Serralves

◁ **Barcos rabelos** moored beside the quay at Vila Nova de Gaia

Vila Nova de Gaia

AFONSO III, IN DISPUTE with the Bishop of Oporto over shipping tolls, established a rival port at Vila Nova de Gaia. In 1253, they reluctantly agreed to share the levies. Today the heart of Vila Nova de Gaia is devoted mostly to the maturation and shipping of port *(see pp252–3)*. Although the regulation that port could be made only in Vila Nova de Gaia was relaxed in 1987, this is still very much the centre of production. Every alley is lined with the lodges or *armazéns* (there are no cellars here) in which port is blended and aged.

Taylor's port

Guided tours are a chance to see how port is made (see pp228–9) and often end with a tasting to demonstrate the different styles.

The port lodges dominate Vila Nova de Gaia. Over 50 port companies are based in these narrow streets, ageing and blending most of the world's supply of port beneath a sea of red roofs emblazoned with world-famous names.

KEY

🚢 Boat trips
🅿 Parking
ℹ Tourist information
✝ Church

0 metres 250
0 yards 250

PORT LODGES

Barros ④	Graham ①
Borges ⑩	Ramos Pinto ⑥
Cálem ⑨	Sandeman ⑧
Cockburn ③	Taylor ⑦
Ferreira ②	Vasconcelos ⑤

VISITING THE LODGES

Joining a tour: Lodges listed here are among those offering tours. Booking is not usually necessary, but contact a lodge beforehand to confirm times, the tourist office at Avenida Diogo Leite 242 (22-377 30 80) can supply addresses and telephone numbers.
Opening times: Variable. Usually Mon–Fri; some also at weekends. Most close on public holidays.

The former monastery of São Bento at Santo Tirso, now a college

Santo Tirso ②

Road map C2. 🏛 *12,000.* 🚊 🚌
🅸 *Praça 25 de Abril (252-830 411).*
📅 *Mon.*

S ANTO TIRSO, a major textile
centre, lies beside the River
Ave. The town's most notable
building is the former monastery of **São Bento**. Founded
by the Benedictines in the
8th century, the monastery was
later rebuilt, then modified in
the 17th century. The pairs of
columns in the 14th-century
Gothic cloister are graced
with richly carved capitals.

The monastery is now an
agricultural college, but houses
the **Museu Abade Pedrosa**,
featuring local archaeological
finds, including stone axes,
bronze armlets and ceramics.

🏛 Museu Abade Pedrosa
Rua Unisco Godiniz 100. 📞 *252-83
04 00.* 🕐 *Tue–Sun.* 📅 *public hols.*

The sanctuary of Nossa Senhora
da Piedade in Penafiel

ENVIRONS: At Roriz, 13 km
(8 miles) east of Santo Tirso,
the Romanesque church of
São Pedro perches above the
Vizela valley. A date of 1228 is
carved in the porch, although
there are claims that a church
may have stood here as early
as the 8th century. Above the
portal is a fine rose window.
Set apart from the church are
an attractive belltower and the
ruins of the monastic cloister.
Sanfins de Ferreira, 5 km
(3 miles) further east, is the
hilltop site of a *citânia*, an Iron
Age citadel, probably inhabited
from around the 6th century
BC. Traces remain of a triple
ring of defensive walls around
about 100 huts, and there is
also a small museum on the
site. The guard next door will
let you in on public holidays.

⛪ Sanfins de Ferreira
Sanfins, signposted off N209.
📞 *255-86 20 29.* 🕐 *by appt only.*

Penafiel ③

Road map C2. 🏛 *8,000.* 🚌
🅸 *Avenida Sacadura Cabral 90 (255-
71 25 61).* 📅 *10 & 20 of month.*

T HE GRANITE TOWN of Penafiel
stands on a hilltop above
the River Sousa. Apart from
an elegant Renaissance-style
Igreja Matriz, there is also a
sanctuary, **Nossa Senhora da
Piedade**, built in 1908 in a
curious medley of Neo-Gothic
and Byzantine styles. Penafiel
is chiefly known, however, as
the regional centre for *vinho
verde* production *(see pp28–9).*

ENVIRONS: One of the region's
foremost estates producing
vinho verde is the picturesque
Quinta da Aveleda, which
lies just north of Penafiel.

Boelhe, around 17 km
(11 miles) south of Penafiel,
merits a detour for the 12th-
century church of São Gens.
Only 10 m (33 ft) high, and a
mere 7 m (23 ft) in width and
length, it is claimed to be the
smallest Romanesque church in
the country. Its simple design
enhances the aesthetic appeal.

In the 13th-century church of
São Salvador at **Paço de Sousa**,
8 km (5 miles) southwest of
Penafiel, is the tomb of Egas
Moniz. A figure of legendary
loyalty, he was counsellor to
Afonso Henriques (1139–85),
the first king of Portugal.

🍷 Quinta da Aveleda
Signposted from N115. 📞 *255-71
10 41.* 🕐 *Mon–Fri.* 📅 *public hols.*
🅿 ♿ 📷 *compulsory.*

The tiny church of São Gens at
Boelhe, south of Penafiel

Amarante ④

Road map D2. 🏛 *10,000.* 🚊 🚌
🅸 *Alameda Teixeira de Pascoães
(255-420 246).* 📅 *Wed & Sat.*

T HE PRETTY, RIVERSIDE town
of Amarante is one of the
gems of northern Portugal.
Rows of 17th-century mansions
with brightly painted wooden
balconies line Amarante's
narrow streets, and restaurants
seat diners on terraces overhanging the river. The origins
of the town are uncertain but
the first settlement here was
probably around 360 BC.
Much of the town was burnt
down in 1809, after a two-
week siege by the French
forces under Marshal Soult.

A recurring name in Amarante is that of São Gonçalo, a very popular saint born at the end of the 12th century. There are many stories of the dancing and festivities he organized to keep ladies from temptation by finding them husbands, and he has become associated with matchmaking and fertility. On the first weekend in June, the Festa de São Gonçalo begins with prayers for a marriage partner, followed by dancing, music and the giving of phallic-shaped São Gonçalo cakes.

When the old Roman bridge across the Tâmega collapsed during floods in the 13th century, it was São Gonçalo who was credited with replacing it. The present Ponte de São Gonçalo crosses to the 16th-century **Igreja de São Gonçalo**, where his memory lives on. In the chapel to the left of the chancel, the image on his tomb has been eroded through the embraces of thousands of devotees in search of his intercession.

The **Museu Amadeo de Sousa-Cardoso** is housed in the old monastery cloister next to the church. One of the exhibits describes a fertility cult that predates even São Gonçalo. The *diabo* and *diaba* are a pair of bawdy devils carved in black wood, and are 19th-century replacements for a more ancient duo destroyed in

The Ponte de São Gonçalo across the Tâmega at Amarante

the Peninsular War. They gradually became the focus of a type of local fertility rite, and were threatened with burning by an outraged bishop of Braga; the *diabo* was "castrated" instead.

The museum's other prized possession is the collection of Cubist works by the artist after whom the museum is named. Amadeo de Sousa-Cardoso (1887–1918), one of Portugal's leading 20th-century artists, was a native of Amarante.

🏠 Igreja de São Gonçalo
Praça da República.
📞 255-42 20 50. ⬜ daily.
🏛 Museu Amadeo de Sousa-Cardoso
Alameda Teixeira de Pascoães.
📞 255-420 272. ⬜ Tue–Sun.
⬤ public hols. 🖼

Cinfães ❺

Road map D2. 🏘 *4,000.* 🚌
ℹ *Rua Dr Flávio Resende 43 (255-560 571).* 🎣 *10 & 26 of month.*

CINFÃES LIES just above the Douro, tucked below the foothills of the Serra de Montemuro whose peaks rise over 1,000 m (3,300 ft). The town is a gateway to Lamego and the Upper Douro to the east *(see pp252–3)* and is surrounded by verdant scenery. Cinfães itself is an agricultural centre and local handicrafts include weaving, lacework, basketry, and the production of miniature *rabelos*, the boats that used to ship port down the river to Oporto *(see p250).*

ENVIRONS: Around 16 km (10 miles) west of the town, at Tarouquela, is the 12th-century church of **Santa Maria Maior**. Romanesque columns flank the portal, while later additions include the 14th-century Gothic mausoleum beside the chancel.

In the village of **Cárquere**, between Cinfães and Lamego, stands another church dedicated to the Virgin Mary. Legend tells how the sickly young Afonso Henriques, future king of Portugal, was healed at Cárquere by his devoted aide, Egas Moniz. In about 1110, guided by a dream, Moniz unearthed a buried statue of the Virgin and built a church for her. Miraculously, his young charge was cured overnight. The present church dates from the 14th or 15th century, but the finest of its treasures is a minute ivory carving of the Virgin, of unknown date.

The 12th-century church of Nossa Senhora de Cárquere, near Cinfães

Painted ceiling panels in São Nicolau, Mesão Frio's Igreja Matriz

Mesão Frio ⑥

Road map D2. 🏘 *700.* 🚌
ℹ *Avenida Conselheiro José Maria Alpoim (254-89 01 00).* 🛒 *Fri.*

THIS SCENIC GATEWAY to the port wine-growing region enjoys a fine setting above the River Douro. Around it, the majestic tiers of the Serra do Marão rise to form a natural climatic shield for the vineyards to the east. Mesão Frio itself is known for its wickerwork and a culinary speciality, *falachas* or chestnut cakes.

The Igreja Matriz of **São Nicolau** was rebuilt in 1877, but has fortunately retained its magnificent late 16th-century ceiling panels, each one featuring an individual portrait of a saint. The tourist office and town hall are housed in the 18th-century **cloisters** of a former Franciscan monastery.

On the western edge of the town, the lavish Baroque **Casa da Rede** can be seen from the roadside, but not visited.

Peso da Régua ⑦

Road map D2. 🏘 *5,500.* 🚃 🚌
ℹ *Rua da Ferreirinha (254-31 28 46).*
🛒 *Wed.*

DEVELOPED from the villages of Peso and Régua in the 18th century, Peso da Régua is the major hub for rail and road connections in the region.

In 1756, Régua, as the town is invariably called, was chosen by the Marquês de Pombal as the centre of the demarcated region for port production. From here, *rabelos*, the traditional wooden sailing ships, transported the barrels of port through hazardous gorges to Vila Nova de Gaia (*see p247*). They continued to ply the river even after the advent of the Douro railway in the 1880s offered a faster and safer means of transport. Régua suffered frequently in the past from severe floods, and these are still a threat, although they have lessened since dams were built across the Douro in the 1970s and 1980s.

Visitors to Régua usually pause only briefly on their way to explore the "port country" (*see pp252–3*), but it is worth seeking out the **Casa do Douro**, the administrative headquarters of the Port Wine Institute. Its modern stained-glass windows, created by Lino António, vividly depict the history and production of port. Also displayed is a fine map of the Douro valley drawn in the mid-19th century by Baron Forrester (*see p252*).

🏛 **Casa do Douro**
Rua dos Camilos. 📞 *254-32 08 11.*
⭕ *Mon–Fri.* ⬤ *public hols.*

ENVIRONS: In the surrounding countryside are some beautiful *quintas*, the country estates where port is produced. One of the nearest to Régua is the attractive **Quinta da Pacheca** at Cambres, 4 km (2 miles) to the southwest. The **Enoteca de Granjão**, in a village on the road to Mesão Frio, will organize visits to this and other port lodges, and can collect visitors from hotels or the bus or train station in Régua.

🍷 **Enoteca de Granjão**
Granjão (on N108). 📞 *254-32 27 88.*
⭕ *10am–7pm daily.* ⬤ *public hols.*

Stained-glass window of the Casa do Douro, Peso da Régua, showing loaded *rabelos*

Lamego ⑧

Road map D2. 🏘 *12,000.* 🚌
ℹ *Avenida Visconde Guedes Teixeira (254-61 20 05).* 🛒 *Thu.*

AN ATTRACTIVE TOWN within the demarcated port area, Lamego also produces wines, including Raposeira, Portugal's premier sparkling wine. This fertile region is also known for its fruit and choice hams.

In its more illustrious past, Lamego claims to have been host in 1143 to the first *cortes*, or national assembly, to recognize Afonso Henriques as first king of Portugal. The town's later economic decline was halted in the 16th century, when it turned to wine and textile production, and handsome Baroque mansions from this prosperous period are still a feature of the town. Today, the main focus of Lamego is as a pilgrimage town.

Vineyards on the slopes of the Serra do Marão around Mesão Frio

The grand staircase leading up to Nossa Senhora dos Remédios, Lamego

🔒 Nossa Senhora dos Remédios

Monte de Santo Estêvão. ⬜ *daily.*

A small hilltop chapel, originally dedicated in 1391 to St Stephen, became the focus of pilgrims devoted to the Virgin, and in 1761 Nossa Senhora dos Remédios was built on the spectacular site. The church is reached via an awe-inspiring double stairway, similar to Braga's even larger Bom Jesus *(see pp278–9).* Its 686 steps and nine terraces, embellished with *azulejos* and urns, rise to the Pátio dos Reis, a circle of noble granite figures beneath the twin-towered church. The church itself is of marginal interest, but there is a well-earned view across the town to the Douro and its tributaries.

In early September pilgrims arrive in their thousands for Lamego's Romaria de Nossa Senhora dos Remédios *(see p32),* many of them climbing the steps on their knees.

🔒 Sé

Largo da Sé. 🛈 *254-612 766.*
⬜ *daily.*

Lamego's Gothic cathedral, founded in 1129, retains its original square tower, while the rest of the architecture reflects modifications between the 16th and 18th centuries, including a Renaissance cloister with a dozen arches.

🏛 Museu de Lamego

Largo de Camões. 🛈 *254-600 230.*
⬜ *Tue–Sun.* 🔴 *public hols.* 🖼

One of the country's best local museums is housed in the former bishops' palace. Pride of place goes to the strikingly original *Criação dos Animais* (Creation of the Animals), part of a series of masterly altar panels attributed to the great 16th-century Portuguese artist, Grão Vasco *(see p213).* Finely worked 16th-century Flemish tapestries include a vividly detailed life of Oedipus.

ENVIRONS: At the foot of the valley 4 km (2 miles) east, the **Capela de São Pedro de Balsemão** is said to be the oldest church in Portugal. Although much modified, the 7th-century sanctuary, of Visigothic origins, remains. Here, in an ornate tomb, lies Afonso Pires, a 14th-century bishop of Oporto. A statue of Nossa Senhora do Ó, the pregnant Virgin, is from the 15th century.

The 12th-century monastery of **São João de Tarouca,** the first Cistercian house in Portugal, lies 16 km (10 miles) south of Lamego. The interior of the church has many fine 18th-century *azulejo* panels, notably those in the chancel depicting the founding of the monastery, and in the sacristy, where none of the 4,709 tiles has the same design. The church also contains a remarkable *St Peter* by Grão Vasco. The Count of Barcelos, bastard son of King Dinis, is buried here, his tomb adorned with vigorous scenes of a boar hunt.

Just to the northeast, **Ucanha** is famed for its fortified tollgate and bridge, imposing survivals from the 12th century.

🔒 São João de Tarouca

Signposted from N226. ⬜ *Tue–Sun.*
🔴 *3rd weekend of month.* ♿

The monastery church of São João de Tarouca in its peaceful setting

Port Country Tour ⑨

Bottles of
Graham's port

THE BARRELS OF PORT maturing in the port lodges of Vila Nova de Gaia *(see p247)* begin their life here, on the wine estates *(quintas)* of the Upper Douro *(see pp228–9)*. Centuries of toil on the poor schist have created thousands of terraces along the steep river banks, many no wider than a person's outstretched arms. Recently, many vineyards have had their terraces widened to allow tractor access, but some of the oldest ones are protected as part of the cultural heritage. Many *quintas*, including those shown on the map, welcome visitors. Early autumn is the most rewarding time to tour; workers sing as they pick, and celebrate a good *vindima* or harvest.

The village and vineyards of Vale de Mendiz just before sunset

Peso da Régua ①
Régua's role as an administrative centre for port and, later, for the wines of the region, goes back to 1756. The *rabelos* moored here are a reminder of how port used to be transported down to the lodges of Vila Nova de Gaia.

VILA REAL

São Martinho

Paradela de Guiães   N322

Estrada

Galafura

PORTO   *Quinta São Domingos*   *Quinta do Crasto*   *Ferr*

N108   ①   *N108*

Duoro   *Quinta São Luís*

N222   N2   *N313*   *Folgosa*

IP3   *Corgo*   *IP3*

0 kilometres	5
0 miles	3

KEY

■ Tour route

= Other roads

— Railway

✻ Viewpoint

JOSEPH JAMES FORRESTER, PORT BARON

In 1831, Joseph Forrester arrived from Britain to join his uncle's wine company in Oporto, and enthusiastically set about reforming the port trade. In his 1844 treatise, *A Word or Two on Port*, he waged war on shippers who adulterated the wine. He also studied the vine blight, *Oidium tuckeri*, drew up remarkably detailed maps of the Douro valley and found time to become a talented watercolourist. His contribution was such that in 1855 Pedro V bestowed on him the title of Barão. In 1862, Forrester's boat capsized at Cachão de Valeira. Dragged down by his moneybelt, he drowned, but the ladies in his company survived, buoyed up by their crinolines.

Pinhão ②

Many of the most famous names in port production have *quintas* close to this small town. Its railway station is decorated with 24 dazzling *azulejo* panels depicting local scenes and folk culture.

TIPS FOR DRIVERS

Tour length: 125 km (78 miles).
Beyond Pinhão, steep, narrow roads can make the going slow.
Stopping-off points: The drive beside the Douro has several fine viewpoints. Alijó, Régua and Sabrosa make good overnight stops (see pp390–93) and many quintas offer tours and port-tasting. (See also pp444–5.)

Sabrosa ③

The village of Sabrosa, set among vineyards above the River Pinhão, has a wealth of 15th-century houses. It was in one of these that the explorer Magellan *(see p48)* was born in about 1480.

Alijó ④

Alijó was officially founded in 1226, but a number of *castros* (hill forts) in the area tell of habitation from a much earlier date. The name of the *pousada* here, the Barão de Forrester *(see p390)*, recalls the famous reformer.

São João da Pesqueira ⑦

From São João da Pesqueira's viewpoint, São Salvador do Mundo, there are fine views of the valley and its vineyards. In early spring the landscape foams with almond blossom.

Tua ⑤

Tua, in a region famous for its luscious oranges and figs, has long been a junction on the Douro railway line. Travelling on one of the infrequent trains is an enjoyable way of seeing the valley's terraced vineyards.

Barragem de Valeira ⑥

Until the end of the 18th century the Douro was unnavigable beyond Cachão de Valeira. Even when engineers had bypassed the worst of the rapids, this stretch of water remained treacherous – it was here that Baron Forrester met his death – until the water was tamed by the Valeira dam in 1976.

Casa de Mateus ⑩

The wood-panelled library, repository of many valuable works

English 17th-century cupboard in the Tea Salon

THE SPLENDID MANOR HOUSE, or *solar*, depicted on the labels of Mateus Rosé *(see p28)* epitomizes the flamboyance of Baroque architecture in Portugal. It was built in the early 18th century, probably by Niccolò Nasoni, for António José Botelho Mourão, among whose titles was 3rd Morgado de Mateus. His descendants still live here, but visitors can tour the gardens and part of the house, and buy the estate's produce (but not Mateus wine, which is a separate concern).

The Manor House

Inside and out, the Casa de Mateus was conceived to present carefully created vistas and series of mirror images. A formal pool added in the 1930s continues this spirit of harmonious repetition, reflecting the main façade and its two wings.

Tours start in the first-floor entrance salon, a well-proportioned room graced by a pair of sedan chairs and with a magnificent wooden ceiling featuring family coats of arms. Doorcases and ceilings throughout the house are of richly carved chestnut. The Tea Salon has a 17th-century William and Mary cupboard and

Coat of arms on the entrance hall ceiling

matching longcase clock from England, while the Salon of the Four Seasons gets its name from the large 18th-century paintings on its walls. Many of the paintings in the house were contributed by the 4th Morgado's uncle, an archdeacon in Rome who was also responsible for the original gardens. The library, remodelled in the mid-20th century, contains volumes dating back to the 16th century, but the rarest book is in the small museum: an 1817 copy of *Os Lusíadas* *(see p188)*, with engravings by leading artists. It is one of a

limited edition produced by the colourful diplomat grandson of the 3rd Morgado (his tomb is in the family chapel beside the house). Also on display in the museum is family correspondence with famous figures of the era, including Frederick the Great and Wellington.

The Gardens

Beneath the entrance staircase a dark passageway leads between the stables to an inner courtyard and out to the formal gardens on the far side of the house. Little remains of the original gardens planted by the horticultural archdeacon, and the present gardens were laid out in the 1930s and 1940s. The style, however, is of an earlier, romantic era and the complex parterres and formal beds edged with tightly clipped dwarf box hedges form a living tapestry which

The principal façade of the Casa de Mateus, its pinnacled symmetry reflected in a rectangular pool

Immaculate box-edged flower beds in the Casa de Mateus gardens

reflects perfectly the ornate symmetry of the house. In winter the grand old camellias, relics from the 19th century, are a highlight of the gardens, but for most visitors the lasting memory is of the vast cedar tunnel, greatest among the many pieces of topiary here.

Beyond the formal gardens lie the well-ordered orchards and fields of the estate.

THE CEDAR TUNNEL

This celebrated feature in the Casa de Mateus garden was formed from cedars planted in 1941. It is 35 m (115 ft) long and 7.5 m (25 ft) high, the tight-knit greenery providing an aromatic walk in summer. To keep it in shape, gardeners have to scale specially fashioned outsize ladders.

Vila Real ⓫

Road map D2. ⍟ 14,000.)))) Avenida Carvalho Araújo 94 (259-32 28 19).) Tue & Fri.

PERCHED OVER a gorge cut by the confluence of the Cabril and Corgo rivers, Vila Real is a busy commercial centre. As the communications hub of the Upper Douro, it makes a convenient starting point from which to explore the valley of the Douro to the south and the Parque Natural do Alvão to the northwest. Vila Real also has a motor-racing circuit, which hosts major events each year during June and July.

Midway along the broad main street, Avenida Carvalho Araújo, is the 15th-century **Sé**. This fine Gothic cathedral was originally the church of a Dominican friary. The other monastic buildings burnt down in suspicious circumstances in the mid-19th century.

At the southern end of the avenue, a plaque on the wall at No. 19 marks the birthplace of Diogo Cão, the explorer who discovered the mouth of the Congo in 1482 (see pp48–9).

The **Igreja dos Clérigos**, in nearby Rua dos Combatentes da Grande Guerra, is also known as Capela Nova. It presents a pleasing Baroque façade attributed to Niccolò Nasoni and an interior of fine blue and white azulejos.

ENVIRONS: The small village of **Bisalhães**, 6 km (4 miles) to the west, is famed for its boldly designed black pottery (see p25). Examples can be

seen displayed for sale at the annual Festa de São Pedro, celebrated in Vila Real each year on 28–9 June. Also seen at this time is the fine linen from nearby Agarez.

Parque Natural do Alvão ⓬

Road map D1.) to Ermelo via Campeã.) Praceta do Tronco, Cruz das Almas, Vila Real (259-302 830).

The scenic Parque Natural do Alvão

WITHIN THE 72 sq km (28 sq miles) of the nature reserve between the Corgo and Tâmega rivers, the scenery ranges from verdant, cultivated lowlands to bleak heights that reach 1,339 m (4,393 ft) at **Alto das Caravelas**. Despite hunters and habitat encroachment, hawks, dippers and otters can still be spotted. Between the picturesque hamlets of **Ermelo** and **Lamas de Olo**, where maize is still kept in espigueiros (see p271), the Olo drops in a spectacular cascade, the **Fisgas de Ermelo**. From **Alto do Velão**, just southwest of the park, are splendid views west over the Tâmega valley.

Vila Real seen across the deep gorge of the Corgo and Cabril rivers

A farmer and his grazing ox near Carvalhelhos, Serra do Barroso

Serra do Barroso ⑬

Road map D1. 🚌 *to Montalegre or Boticas.* ℹ️ *Praça do Município, Montalegre (276-51 02 00).* 🌐 www.rt-atb.pt

JUST SOUTHEAST of the Parque Nacional da Peneda-Gerês *(see pp270–71)* is the wild and remote Serra do Barroso. The landscape of heathery hillsides is split by the immense Barragem do Alto Rabagão, the largest of many reservoirs in the area created by the damming of rivers for hydroelectric power. Water is a mainstay of the local economy: a high rainfall enables farmers to eke out an existence on the poor soil, and the artificial lakes attract fishing and watersports enthusiasts. The source of one of the country's most popular bottled mineral waters is at **Carvalhelhos**.

The village of **Boticas** nearby produces a beverage with a more original claim to fame. In 1809, the locals buried their wine rather than have it fall into the hands of the invading French. When the enemy departed, the wine was retrieved and found to have improved. The bottles were colloquially termed *mortos* ("dead"), hence the name of the wine – *vinho dos mortos*. The practice continues and bottles are usually buried for up to two years.

The area's principal town is **Montalegre**, on a plateau to the north. Its most notable feature is the imposing keep, 27 m (88 ft) high, of the ruined 14th-century castle.

Oxen are bred in the Serra, and inter-village *chegas dos bois* (ox fights) are a popular pastime. The contest is usually decided within half an hour, when the weaker ox takes to its heels.

Chaves ⑭

Road map D1. 🏛 *18,000.* 🚌 ℹ️ *Terreiro da Cavalaria (276-34 06 61).* 🗓 *Wed.* 🌐 www.rt-atb.pt

BESIDE THE UPPER REACHES of the Tâmega stands historic Chaves, attractively sited in the middle of a fertile plain.

Thermal springs and nearby gold deposits encouraged the Romans to establish Aquae Flaviae here in AD 78. Its strategic position led to successive invasion and occupation by the Suevi, Visigoths and Moors, before the Portuguese gained final possession in 1160. The name Chaves ("keys") is often associated with the keys of the north awarded to Nuno Álvares Pereira, hero of Aljubarrota *(see p183)*. A likelier but more pedestrian explanation is that Chaves is simply a corruption of the Latin "Flaviae".

Today Chaves is renowned for its spa and historic centre, and for its smoked hams. A curiosity of the north, the distinctive black pottery *(see p25)*, is made in nearby Nantes.

The old town focuses on the Praça de Camões. The 14th-century **keep** overlooking this pleasant medieval square is all that remains of the castle given to Nuno Álvares Pereira by João I. On the south side of the square stands the **Igreja Matriz** with its fine Romanesque portal. The Baroque

Tiled and gilded Misericórdia church at Chaves

Misericórdia church opposite has an exquisite interior lined with 18th-century *azulejos*. Attributed to Policarpo de Oliveira Bernardes *(see p22)*, the huge panels depict scenes from the New Testament.

The 14th-century keep of Chaves castle, set in formal gardens

🏛 Museu Militar and Museu da Região Flaviense
Praça de Camões. 📞 276-34 05 00. 🕐 *Tue–Fri, Sat & Sun pm.* ● *public hols.* 🎟 *joint ticket.*

Within the castle keep is a small military museum, where suits of armour, uniforms and associated regalia are on display. Also exhibited are military memorabilia from the city's defence against the attack by Royalists from Spain in 1912.

In the flower-filled garden surrounding the keep are a few archaeological finds from Chaves's long history, but most are to be found in the Museu da Região Flaviense behind the keep. Here, in the Paço dos Duques de Bragança, are displayed a variety of local archaeological discoveries. Items of interest include souvenirs of the Roman occupation, such as milestones and coins, alongside an oxcart and a straw mantle of the type worn by shepherds for protection in the rain or the hot sun.

🚩 Ponte Romana

The 16-arch Roman bridge across the Tâmega was completed around AD 100, at the time of the Emperor Trajan. Its construction brought added importance to Chaves as a staging post on the route between Braga and Astorga (in northwestern Spain). On the bridge are Roman milestones which record that funds to build it were raised locally.

🚩 Thermal springs

Largo Tito Flávio Vespasiano.
📞 276-33 24 45. ⬜ daily. ♿
A few minutes on foot from the city centre is one of the hottest springs in Europe. Water here bubbles up at a temperature of 73°C (163°F) and the spa's facilities attract both holiday-makers and patients seeking treatment *(see p209)*. Chaves water is recommended for the treatment of ailments as diverse as rheumatism, kidney dysfunction and hypertension.

The huge cleft Pedra Bolideira near Chaves

ENVIRONS: Close to the village of Soutelo, 4 km (2 miles) northwest of Chaves (the route is signposted), is the strange **Outeiro Machado Boulder**. It measures 50 m (165 ft) in length and is covered with mysterious hieroglyphs and symbols of unknown meaning. These may be Celtic in origin.

Another gigantic boulder, the **Pedra Bolideira**, lies near Bolideira, 16 km (10 miles) east of Chaves. Split in two, the massive larger section balances lightly, needing only a gentle push to rock it to and fro.

The spa town of **Vidago**, 17 km (11 miles) southwest of Chaves, is well known for its therapeutic water. The Vidago Palace Hotel *(see p393)*, once the haunt of royalty, has been renovated in recent years, but retains the regal charm of its park, lakes and pump room.

Murça's **Misericórdia** chapel, with its vine-embellished pillars

Murça ⑮

Road map D2. 🏠 3,000. 🚌
ℹ️ Alameda do Paço (259-51 01 20).
🗓️ 13 & 28 of month.

THE MARKET TOWN of Murça is famed for its honey, goat's cheese and sausage. Its major attraction, and the focal point of the garden in the main square, is its **porca**, an Iron Age granite pig with a substantial girth of 2.8 m (9 ft) *(see p40)*. The role of *berrões*, as beasts such as these are called, is enigmatic, but they may have been linked to fertility cults. Smaller versions survive in Bragança, Chaves and elsewhere. In more recent times the Murça *porca* has been pressed into service at elections, when the winning political parties would paint her in their colours.

The **Misericórdia** chapel on the main street is notable for its early Baroque façade, attractively ornamented with designs of vines and grapes.

Mirandela ⑯

Road map D1. 🏠 8,000. 🚉 🚌
ℹ️ Praça do Mercado (278-20 02 72).
🗓️ 3, 14 & 25 of month.

MIRANDELA, at the end of the Tua narrow-gauge railway line, has pretty gardens running down to the River Tua and an elegant Roman bridge with 20 asymmetrical arches. Built for the deployment of troops and to aid the transport of ore from local mines, it was rebuilt in the 16th century and is now for pedestrians only.

Displayed in the **Museu Municipal Armindo Teixeira Lopes** are sculpture, prints and paintings, including views of Lisbon and Mirandela by the local 20th-century artist after whom the museum is named.

The 17th-century **town hall** once belonged to the Távoras, but the family was accused of attempted regicide in 1759 and all trace of them was erased.

🏛 Museu Municipal Armindo Teixeira Lopes

Rua Coronel Sarmento Pimentel.
📞 278-20 15 90. ⬜ Mon–Fri;
Sat & Sun pm. ⬤ public hols.

ENVIRONS: In a pretty valley 15 km (9 miles) northeast of Mirandela lies **Romeu**. Its **Museu das Curiosidades**, as the name implies, is a hotch-potch of exhibits from the turn of the century onwards. The collection of the local Menéres family, it includes Model-T Fords, musical boxes and early photographic equipment. Next door is the famed Maria Rita restaurant *(see p415)*.

🏛 Museu das Curiosidades

Jerusalém do Romeu. ⬜ noon–4pm Tue–Sun. ⬤ public hols. ♿

The River Tua at Mirandela, with its Roman bridge and waterside parks

Bragança: the Citadel ⑰

THIS STRATEGIC HILLTOP was the site of a succession of forts before Fernão Mendes, brother-in-law to King Afonso Henriques, built a walled citadel here in 1130. Like several predecessors, it was named Brigantia. Within the walls still stand Sancho I's castle, built in 1187, with its watchtowers and dungeons, and the pentagonal 12th-century Domus Municipalis beside the church of Santa Maria.

The town gave its name to Portugal's final royal dynasty, descended from an illegitimate son of João I who was created first Duke of Bragança in 1442 *(see p299)*.

Bragança's walled citadel on its isolated hilltop

Porta da Traição

The Museu Militar in the robust Gothic keep includes memorabilia from the Africa campaigns (1895) of a local regiment. The keep is 33 m (108 ft) high.

The medieval pillory has the appearance of skewering a hapless *porca*, an ancient stone pig *(see p40)*, to the pedestal.

★ **Castle**
The castle's Torre da Princesa, scene of many tragic tales, was refuge to Dona Sancha, unhappy wife of Fernão Mendes, and prison to other mistreated wives.

Porta da Vila

RUA DOM FERNÃO O BRAVO

To town ←

Porta de Santo António

Santa Maria
The church's elaborately carved portal dates from its 18th-century restoration.

★ **Domus Municipalis**
This, the only surviving example of Romanesque civic architecture in Portugal, served as a hall where the homens bons *("good men") settled disputes. Below was the town's cistern.*

VISITORS' CHECKLIST

Road map E1. 🏠 *35,000.*
🚌 *Agência de Viagens e Turismo
Sanvitura, Avenida João da Cruz.*
ℹ️ *Avenida Cidade de Zamora
(273-38 12 73).* 🚐 *3, 12 & 21
of month.* 🎭 *mid-Aug: Nossa
Senhora das Graças.* **Castle** and
Museu Militar 📞 *273-322 378.*
🕐 *Fri–Wed.* ⚫ *public hols.* ♿

KEY

– – – Suggested route

0 metres   50

0 yards   50

Porta do Sol

Houses within the Citadel
*Bragança had outgrown the
citadel by the 15th century,
but streets of small houses
still cluster within the walls.*

Museu Abade de Baçal gardens, where archaeological finds are displayed

Beyond the Citadel

By the 15th century, Bragança
had expanded west along the
banks of the River Fervença.
The Jewish quarter in Rua dos
Fornos survives from this era,
when Jews from North Africa
and Spain settled here and
founded the silk industry.

Despite its royal links, the
town never overcame its isolation, the Bragança monarchs
preferring Vila Viçosa *(see
pp298–9).* Only now are the
investments of returning emigrants and the completion of
the Oporto-Spain motorway
reviving trade. A new cathedral "for the millennium" was
inaugurated in 1996, another
indicator of the city's rebirth.
Near the modest old cathedral in the town centre is a
lively covered market where
delicacies such as smoked
hams and *alheiras* (chicken
sausages) are sold.

🏛 Museu Abade de Baçal

Rua Abílio Beça 27. 📞 273-33 15 95.
🕐 *Tue–Sun.* ⚫ *public hols.* ♿
The Abbot of Baçal (1865–
1947) was a prodigious scholar
whose definitive researches
into the region's history and
customs, including its Jewish
connections, were published
in 11 volumes. Bragança's
museum is named after him.

Highlights among the paintings are *The Martyrdom of St
Ignatius,* an unsigned triptych
of the 16th century, and watercolours by Aurélia de Sousa
(1865–1922), including her impressionist *A Sombra* (In the
Shade). In another section are
displayed colourful *pauliteiros*
costumes *(see p227)* and gruesome instruments of torture.

In the garden are a variety
of archaeological discoveries
including *porcas* and tablets
with Luso-Roman inscriptions.

⛪ São Bento

Rua de São Francisco.
🕐 *variable hours.* ♿
Founded in 1590 by Bishop
António Pinheiro, São Bento
has two startlingly contrasting
ceilings: a splendid canopy of
Moorish-influenced geometric
carving in the chancel, and a
richly coloured 18th-century
trompe l'oeil over the nave.

⛪ São Vicente

Largo do Principal. 🕐 *variable hours.*
The secret wedding between
Inês de Castro and Dom Pedro
is reputed to have taken place
here in 1354 *(see p179).* The
original 13th-century church
was reconstructed in the 17th
century with the addition of a
great deal of sumptuous gilt-
work. The *azulejo* panel to the
right of the main door depicts
General Sepúlveda exhorting
the citizens of Bragança to
free themselves from French
occupation in 1809.

Street in the old Jewish quarter,
sloping steeply down to the river

The sparsely inhabited landscape of the Parque Natural de Montesinho

Parque Natural de Montesinho ⑱

Road map E1. 🚌 *to Rio de Onor & Vinhais.* 🛈 *Bairro Salvador Nunes Teixeira 5, Bragança (273-381 234).*

ONE OF THE WILDEST areas in Europe, the reserve covers 70,000 ha (175,000 acres) between Bragança and the border with Spain. The region, understandably, is known as Terra Fria (Cold Land). Bleak mountains rise to 1,481 m (4,859 ft) above heather and broom, descending to oak forests and valleys of alder and willow.

Spectacular views of the park can be enjoyed from **Vinhais**, on its southern fringe, and the wilderness attracts walkers and riders – mountain bikes and horses can be hired locally.

The population clusters in farming communities on the lowlands, leaving much of the Serra an undisturbed habitat for rare species such as wolves and golden eagles, as well as boars, otters and falcons.

Little changed from medieval times, villages such as **França** and **Montesinho** are typical

in their stone houses, wooden balconies and cobbled streets. Ancient practices such as herbal cures and reverence for the supernatural linger, and ties are communal rather than national: in **Rio de Onor** Spanish and Portuguese have been welded into a unique dialect, Rionorês.

Farm parlour, Museu da Terra de Miranda

Miranda do Douro ⑲

Road map E1. 🏠 *3,000.* 🚌 🛈 *Largo do Menino Jesus da Cartolinha (273-43 11 32).* 🗓 *1st of month.*

THIS MEDIEVAL OUTPOST stands on top of the Douro gorge, which here forms an abrupt border with Spain. Its key position and the establishment of a bishopric here in 1545 paved the way for the town's development into the cultural and religious centre of Trás-os-Montes. But in 1762, during the Seven Years' War against France and Spain, the powder store exploded, claiming 400 lives and destroying the castle (only the keep remains). This mishap, compounded by the transfer of the bishopric to Bragança, led the town into a deep economic decline, only recently halted by new trade links with the coast and Spain.

The lovely twin-towered **Sé** was founded in the 16th century. The graceful wood-carvings of the chancel retable depict, among other themes, the Apostles and the Virgin attended by angels. But the cathedral's most original feature is a wooden figure of the Boy Jesus in the south transept. The Menino Jesus da Cartolinha represents a boy who, legend tells, appeared during a Spanish siege in 1711 to rally the demoralized Portuguese to miraculous victory. Devotees dressed the statue in 17th-century costume and later gave him a top hat *(cartolinha)*.

The excellent **Museu da Terra de Miranda** houses an eclectic display of archaeological finds, folk costume, a reconstruction of a Mirandês farmhouse parlour and curious rural devices such as an inflated pig's-bladder cosh.

🏛 Museu da Terra de Miranda
Largo Dom João III. 🛈 *273-43 11 64.* ◑ *Tue–Sat & Sun am.* ● *public hols.* 🖾

ENVIRONS: Just southwest of Miranda, the village of **Duas Igrejas** is famed for its stick dancers, or *pauliteiros*, who perform at local festivals and overseas *(see p227)*. The tradition is in decline, but for the Festa de Santa Bárbara, on the third Sunday in August, the dancers don their distinctive black and white costumes and are accompanied in their energetic display by drums and *gaita de foles* (bagpipes).

A distinctive *pombal* or dovecote still found around Montesinho

THE DOVECOTES OF MONTESINHO

Doves supply not only food, but also droppings, which are highly prized as fertilizer. In this part of Trás-os-Montes the traditional horseshoe-shaped dovecote or *pombal* is still a familiar sight, although many are now disused. The birds nest in rough cells inside the whitewashed schist walls and enter and leave through gaps in the tile or slate roof. They are fed via a small raised door at the front of the *pombal*.

The church and town of Mogadouro, viewed from beside the ruins of its 13th-century castle

Mogadouro ⑳

Road map E2. ⍟ *3,000.* ☒
ℹ *Largo de Santo Cristo, Bemposta
(279-343 756).*

APART FROM the hilltop tower, little remains of the great castle founded here by King Dinis and presented to the Templars in 1297. From the top there are fine views over the drowsy little market town known for its handicrafts, particularly leather goods.

Mogadouro's 16th-century **Igreja Matriz** features a 17th-century tower, while lavishly gilded retables from the 18th century decorate the altars.

Torre de Moncorvo ㉑

Road map E2. ⍟ *2,500.* ☒
ℹ *Travessa Dr. Campos Monteiro 21
(279-25 22 89).* ☒ *8 & 23 of month.*

FAMED FOR the white mantle of almond blossom that fleetingly covers the valleys in early spring (egg-shaped *amêndoas cobertas*, sugared almonds, are an Easter treat), Moncorvo also offers an atmospheric stroll through its maze of medieval streets. Its name is variously attributed to a local nobleman, Mendo Curvo, or perhaps to his raven *(corvo)*.

The ponderous 16th-century **Igreja Matriz**, the largest in Trás-os-Montes, boasts a 17th-century altarpiece depicting scenes from the life of Christ.

ENVIRONS: The fate of the Côa valley, south of Moncorvo, was finally decided in 1996 when plans for a dam were dropped to preserve the world's largest collection of open-air Stone Age rock art. Discovered in 1933 and estimated to be 20,000 years old, it features bulls, horses, fish and a naked man, the Homem de Pisco. Vila Nova de Foz Côa, Castelo Melhor and Muxagata offer several guided tours a day into the **Parque Arqueológico do Vale do Côa**, and visits must be booked in advance.

⋔ Parque Arqueológico do Vale do Côa
Avenida Gago Coutinho 19a, Vila Nova de Foz Côa. ☎ *279-768 260.* ☐ *by appt only.* ⬤ *public hols.* 🖭 🖊

Rich interior of the Igreja Matriz at Freixo

Freixo de Espada à Cinta ㉒

Road map E2. ⍟ *2,300.* ☒
ℹ *Avenida do Emigrante (279-65 34 80).* ☒ *5th of every month.*

SEVERAL STORIES try to explain the curious name of this remote border town. "Ash tree of the girt sword" may derive from the arms of a Spanish nobleman, or a Visigoth called Espadacinta, or from a tale that, when founding the town in the 14th century, King Dinis strapped his sword to an ash.

Dominating the skyline is the heptagonal **Torre do Galo**, a relic from the 14th-century defences. Views from the top are splendid, especially in spring when the almond blossom attracts a great many tourists. A newer cultivation is that of silkworms, revival of an 18th-century industry.

The intricate 16th-century portal of the **Igreja Matriz** leads into a splendid small-scale version of Belém's Mosteiro dos Jerónimos *(see pp106–7)*. Panels of the altarpiece, attributed to Grão Vasco *(see p213)*, include a fine *Annunciation*.

♣ Torre do Galo
Praça Jorge Álvares. ☐ *Tue–Fri.* ⬤ *public hols.*

MINHO

NOWN AS THE BIRTHPLACE *of the nation, the Minho has two of Portugal's most historic cities: its first capital, Guimarães, and Braga, the country's main religious centre. Life in the province is still firmly rooted in tradition. Agriculture thrives thanks to abundant rainfall that makes this the greenest area in Portugal.*

The province of Minho occupies land between the River Douro in the south and the River Minho in the north. Fortified hilltop stone forts *(castros)* remain as evidence of the Neolithic history of the region. When Celtic peoples migrated into the area in the first millennium BC, these sites developed into *citânias* (settlements) such as Briteiros.

During the 2nd century BC, advancing Roman legions conquered the land, introduced vine-growing techniques and constructed a network of roads. Roman milestones are still visible in Peneda-Gerês National Park. When Christianity became the official religion of the Roman empire in the 4th century AD, Braga became an important religious centre, a position it holds to this day. The Suevi swept aside the Romans in the 5th century, followed by the Visigoths, who were ousted in turn by the Moorish invasion of 711. The Minho was won back from the Moors in the 9th century. The region rose to prominence in the 12th century under Afonso Henriques *(see pp42–3)*, who proclaimed himself the first king of Portugal and chose Guimarães as his capital.

The Minho's fertile farms and estates have been handed down within families for centuries, each heir traditionally receiving a share of the land. This custom results in plots of land too small to support their owners, many of whom emigrate in search of work. The economy of the Minho, under pressure from high local unemployment, concentrates on medium-scale industry around Braga and Guimarães. Agriculture in the valleys includes production of the area's distinctive *vinhos verdes* or "green wines". Despite the growth of tourism, the Minho has maintained its strong folk traditions. Carnivals and street markets pervade everyday life and ox-drawn carts are still in use.

Cows being herded across a bridge near the Brejoeira Palace, south of Monção

◁ **The sanctuary of Nossa Senhora da Peneda, in the Parque Nacional da Peneda-Gerês**

Exploring the Minho

I N THE SOUTH of the Minho lie Braga and Guimarães, the two major cities of the region, both rich in historic sights. From Braga, the Baroque splendour of Bom Jesus or the ruins of Citânia de Briteiros, the country's largest Iron Age site, are within easy reach. Between Braga and the coast lies Barcelos, the ceramics centre of the region, famed for its weekly market. Travelling north, the pretty town of Viana do Castelo is a useful base from which to explore the coast. Turning inland again, the picturesque market town of Ponte de Lima, beside the River Lima, is one of many places in the Minho that provide accommodation in traditional manor houses. In the north of the Minho, the River Minho forms the border with Spain. Along the river, fortified towns offer magnificent views into Spain. To the northeast, walkers and wildlife enthusiasts should not miss the dramatic mountain ranges of the Parque Nacional da Peneda-Gerês.

Foal grazing in the Parque Nacional da Peneda-Gerês

SEE ALSO

- *Where to Stay* pp393–4
- *Where to Eat* pp416–17

Manueline portal on the 16th-century parish church, Vila do Conde

MONÇÃO

VALENÇA DO MINHO

VILA NOVA DE CERVEIRA

PAREDES DE COURA

CAMINHA

ARCOS DE VALDEVEZ

PONTE DA BAR

BRAVÃES

PONTE DE LIMA

VILA PRAIA DE ÂNCORA

VIANA DO CASTELO

ESPOSENDE

BARCELOS

BRAG

POVOA DE VARZIM

VILA DO CONDE

VILA NOVA DE FAMALICÃO

Vigo
Pontevedra

Minho

Lima

Cávado

Ave

Porto

Porto

SIGHTS AT A GLANCE

Vinho verde **vineyards near Monção**

GETTING AROUND

The road system is efficient, with motorways joining Oporto with Braga, Guimarães, Valença on the Spanish border and Viana do Castelo along the coast. Elsewhere in the region, potholes are a common hazard, and motorists need to allow time for the scenic routes winding through the mountains in the east. Train routes link Oporto to Barcelos and Viana do Castelo, en route to the border with Spain; separate lines run to Guimarães and Braga from Oporto. A bus network provides frequent service to the main towns, but it is reduced for more isolated destinations, especially those in the east.

| 0 kilometres | | 10 |
| 0 miles | 5 | |

KEY

▬▬	Motorway
▬▬	Major road
▬▬	Minor road
▬▬	Scenic route
▬▬	River
☀	Viewpoint

Popular cafés in Praça do Conselheiro Silva Torres, Caminha's attractive main square

Caminha ❶

Road Map C1. 🏠 *2,000*. 🚂 🚌 🚌
🛈 *Rua Ricardo Joaquim de Sousa (258-92 19 52)*. ◐ *Wed.*

THIS ANCIENT FORTRESS town perches beside the Minho with fine views across the river to Spain. Occupied in Celtic and Roman times for its strategic position, Caminha developed into a major port until the diversion of its trade to Viana do Castelo in the 16th century. Today it is a small port, with a daily ferry connection to A Guarda in Spain.

On the main square is the 15th-century **Torre do Relógio** clock tower, once a gateway in the medieval defensive walls, and the 17th-century **Paços do Concelho** with its attractive loggia supported by pillars. Cross to the other side of the square, past the Renaissance fountain, to admire the seven Manueline windows on the upper storey of the **Solar dos Pitas** mansion (15th century).

The Rua Ricardo Joaquim de Sousa leads to the Gothic **Igreja Matriz**. Begun in the late 15th century, it has a superb inlaid ceiling of panels carved in Mudéjar (Moorish) style. Renaissance carvings above the side doors depict the Apostles, the Virgin, and several figures in daring poses, including one man with his posterior bared towards Spain.

ENVIRONS: Foz do Minho, the mouth of the Minho, lies 5 km (3 miles) southwest of town. From here local fishermen will take groups (by prior arrangement) to the ruined island fortress of **Forte da Ínsua**.

The small walled town of **Vila Nova de Cerveira**, 12 km (7 miles) northeast of Caminha on the road to Valença, has a 16th-century castle, refurbished as the luxurious Pousada Dom Dinis (*see p394*). The tranquil atmosphere is ideal for a stroll in narrow streets lined with 17th- and 18th-century mansions, or along the riverfront, where a car ferry runs to the Spanish town of Goián.

Valença do Minho ❷

Road Map C1. 🏠 *3,000*. 🚂 🚌
🛈 *Avenida de Espanha (251-823 329)*. ◐ *Wed.*

SET IN A COMMANDING position on a hilltop overlooking the River Minho, Valença is an attractive border town with an old quarter set in the narrow confines of two double-walled forts, shaped like crowns and linked by a causeway. During the reign of Sancho I (1185–1211), the town was named *Contrasta*, due to its position facing the Spanish town of Tui.

The **forts** date from the 17th and 18th centuries and were designed according to the principles of the French architect, Vauban. There are fine views from the ramparts across the river into Galicia. Although the town was briefly captured by Napoleonic troops in 1807, its formidable bastions resisted subsequent shelling and attacks from across the river in 1809.

Lining the cobbled alleys of the old quarter are shops full of linen, wickerwork, pottery and handicrafts to tempt the thousands of Spanish visitors who stroll across the bridge to shop. South of the ramparts is the newer part of town.

In Praça de São Teotónio, **Casa do Eirado** (1448) boasts a crenellated roof and late Gothic window, adorned with the builder's signature. The 18th-century **Casa do Poço** presents symmetrical windows and wrought-iron balconies.

A quiet sunlit corner in the old quarter of Valença do Minho

ENVIRONS: The **Convento de Ganfei**, 5 km (3 miles) east of Valença on the N101, was reconstructed in the 11th century by a Norman priest. It retains pleasing Romanesque features, including ornamental animal and plant motifs and vestiges of medieval frescoes. To visit the chapel, ask for the key at the house opposite.

Part of the walls and ramparts surrounding Valença do Minho

Monção **❸**

Road Map C1. 🏘 *2,500.* 🚌
ℹ️ *Largo do Loreto (251-65 27 57).*
🗓 *Thu.*

A REMOTE and charming town, Monção once formed part of the string of fortified border posts standing sentinel on the River Minho. Both the town's main squares are lined with old houses, and decorated with chestnut trees, flowerbeds and mosaic paths.

The 13th-century **Igreja Matriz** in Rua João de Pinho boasts an outstanding Romanesque doorway of sculpted acanthus flowers. Inside, to the right of the transept is the cenotaph of the valiant Deu-la-Deu Martins, the town's heroine, erected in 1679 by a descendant. A leafy avenue east of the town leads to the hot mineral springs used for the treatment of rheumatism.

A colourful element in the June Corpus Christi festival is the Festa da Coca, when St George engages the dragon *(coca)* in comic ritual combat before giving the final blow.

ENVIRONS: The countryside around Monção produces excellent *vinho verde (see p29)*; one of the best-known estates is the privately owned Neo-Classical Palácio de Brejoeira, 5 km (3 miles) south of town.

About 5 km (3 miles) southeast of Monção, the monastery of **São João de Longos Vales** was built in Romanesque style

Bridge across the Lima at Ponte da Barca, with the town behind

in the 12th century. The exterior capitals and interior apse have fantastical sculpted figures, including serpents and monkeys. Visits are arranged by the tourist office in Monção.

The town of **Melgaço,** 24 km (15 miles) east of Monção provides a useful gateway to the Peneda-Gerês National Park.

Parque Nacional da Peneda-Gerês **❹**

See pp270–71.

Ponte da Barca **❺**

Road Map C1. 🏘 *2,000.* 🚌
ℹ️ *Largo da Misericórdia 11 (258-45 28 99).* 🚌 *every other Wed.*

THE TOWN OF Ponte da Barca derives its name from the graceful 15th-century bridge that replaced the boat once used to ferry pilgrims across the River Lima *(ponte* means

bridge, and *barca* means boat). A stroll through the tranquil town centre leads past the pillory (crowned with sphere and pyramid), the graceful arcades and noble mansions from the 16th and 17th centuries. The Jardim dos Poetas (Poets' Garden) and riverside parks are ideal for picnics, and the huge open-air market along the river is well worth a visit.

Carved relief on the tympanum of the small parish church at Bravães

ENVIRONS: Some of Portugal's finest Romanesque carvings are on the 13th-century church at **Bravães**, 4 km (2 miles) west of Ponte da Barca. Sculpted monkeys, oxen, and birds of prey decorate the columns of its main portal; the tympanum shows Christ in majesty flanked by two angels.

The town of **Arcos de Valdevez**, 5 km (3 miles) north of Ponte da Barca, nestles by the banks of the River Vez and lies within convenient reach of Peneda-Gerês National Park. The impressive church of **Nossa Senhora da Lapa** was built in 1767 by André Soares. This Baroque showpiece has an oval exterior, yet transforms the interior into an octagon.

Hiking enthusiasts should ask the tourist office for directions to follow the circuit of elevated viewpoints and local villages from the hamlet of **São Miguel**, 11 km (7 miles) east of Ponte da Barca.

DEU-LA-DEU MARTINS

In 1368, when a Spanish army had besieged Monção to the verge of starvation, Deu-la-Deu Martins used the last of the town's flour to bake rolls that she flung over the walls to the Spaniards, with taunts that there were plenty more

The heroic Deu-la-Deu Martins on Monção's coat of arms

to throw at them. Thinking their time was being wasted in a futile siege, the troops soon withdrew. In gratitude for saving the town, Deu-la-Deu (the name means "God gave her") is remembered on the town's coat of arms, where she is shown with a loaf of bread in each hand. *Pãezinhos* (bread rolls) *de Deu-la-Deu* used to be baked to honour her memory, but the tradition is no longer followed.

Vinho verde **vineyards near Monção** ▷

Parque Nacional da Peneda-Gerês ➍

Broom in Peneda Mountains

Peneda-Gerês National Park, one of Portugal's greatest natural attractions, stretches from the Gerês Mountains in the south to the Peneda range and the Spanish border in the north. Established in 1971, it extends over about 700 sq km (270 sq miles) of wild, dramatic scenery, with windswept peaks and wooded valleys of oak, pine and yew. It also hosts rare wolves and golden eagles among its rich variety of fauna. In the park's villages, everyday life remains firmly rooted in tradition.

Lamas de Mouro, at the northern entrance to the park, serves as an information centre and offers accommodation.

Castro Laboreiro is best known for the breed of sheepdog to which it gives its name. The ruins of a medieval castle can be seen in the village.

Castelo Lindoso, in the frontier village of Lindoso, is a fine 13th-century castle which has now been renovated to house an art gallery.

★ **Nossa Senhora da Peneda**
Surrounded by massive rocks, this elaborate sanctuary is a replica of Bom Jesus (see pp278–9). The site is visited in early September by pilgrims from all over the region.

Soajo
The traditional village of Soajo, surrounded by terraced hillsides, is known for its collection of espigueiros. *The village's local festival takes place in the middle of August.*

| 0 kilometres | | 5 |
| 0 miles | 2 | |

Vilarinho das Furnas
Beautifully set in a rocky landscape, the Vilarinho das Furnas reservoir was formed by the damming of the River Homem. The reservoir is good for swimming as well as hikes along its shores.

Caldas do Gerês, known since Roman times for its spa, now serves as an information centre and base for excursions from the centre of the park.

Pitões das Júnias Monastery
Dating to 1147, the picturesque ruins of this monastery lie approximately 3 km (2 miles) south of the road leading into Pitões das Júnias village.

VISITORS' CHECKLIST

Road map C1. 🚌 *from Braga to Caldas do Gerês; from Arcos de Valdevez to Soajo & Lindoso; from Melgaço to Castro Laboreiro & Lamas de Mouro.* 🅷 *Caldas do Gerês: on main road (253-39 01 10); Lamas do Mouro: next to camp site; Arcos de Valdevez: Rua Padre Manuel Himalaia (258-515 338). Information on camp sites, hiking & pony trekking is available at these offices and at Montalegre (see p256).* **Castelo Lindoso** ⬜ *Tue–Sun.* ⬤ *public hols.* ▨

Inverneiras in Sedra
Migration during the summer from these solidly built winter houses to brandas, stone shelters high in the mountains, is still practised in some villages.

★ Roman Road
Sections of the old Roman road that ran from Braga to Astorga in Spain, can still be seen at points along the Homem river valley.

STAR SIGHTS

★ Nossa Senhora da Peneda

★ Roman Road

ESPIGUEIROS

The tomb-like architecture of *espigueiros* (granaries) appears in several areas of the park, especially in the villages of Lindoso and Soajo. Constructed either of wood or granite, they are raised on columns and slatted for ventilation. The design keeps grain and maize at the right humidity as well as off the ground, out of reach of hens and rodents. Topped with an ornamental cross or pyramid, the design of *espigueiros* has scarcely changed since the 18th and 19th centuries.

Granite *espigueiro*, Lindoso

KEY

═══	Road
▬ ▬	Long-distance footpath
▬ ·	National boundary
🅷	Tourist information
☆	Viewpoint

Ponte de Lima ⑥

Road Map C1. 🏛 *3,200.* 🚌
🏨 *Praça da República (258-94 23 35).*
🛒 *every other Mon.*

THIS ATTRACTIVE riverside town takes its name from the ancient bridge over the River Lima. During the Middle Ages, the town played a pivotal role in the defence of the Minho against the Moors.

The Roman **bridge** has only five of its original stone arches; the rest were rebuilt or restored in the 14th and 15th centuries. The 15th-century church of Santo António now houses the **Museu dos Terceiros**, a museum of sacred art. The **Museu Rural** has antique farming equipment, an authentic regional kitchen and gardens.

The remaining medieval fortifications of Ponte de Lima include the 15th-century **Palácio dos Marqueses de Ponte de Lima**.

The town's market, a tradition dating back to 1125, takes place on the river's wide and sandy left bank. In mid-September crowds gather in the town to celebrate the *Feiras Novas* (new fairs), a combined religious festival and folkloric market.

Stone carving of a musician, Museu dos Terceiros

🏛 **Museu Rural**
Largo da Arnado. 📞 *258-900 414.*
🕐 *2–6pm Tue–Sun.* 🌑 *public hols.*

Viana do Castelo ⑦

See pp274–5.

Ponte de Lima's Roman bridge, leading to the church of Santo António

Former dormitory of the Mosteiro de Santa Clara, Vila do Conde

Vila do Conde ⑧

Road map C2. 🏛 *21,000.* 🚉 🚌
🏨 *Rua 25 de Abril 103 (252-24 84 73).* 🛒 *Fri.*

THE SMALL TOWN of Vila do Conde enjoyed its boom years as a ship-building centre in the Age of Discovery *(see pp46–7)*; today it is a quiet fishing port. By the river, in the historic centre, the main attraction is the **Mosteiro de Santa Clara**, founded in 1318. The principal dormitory building, dating from the 18th century, is now a correctional institution for teenagers. The church and cloisters, however, are open to the public. The Gothic church has Renaissance additions and contains the tombs of the nunnery's founders, Dom Afonso Sanches (son of King Dinis) and his wife Dona Teresa Martins. By the Mosteiro de Santa Clara are parts of the imposing 5-km (3-mile) **aqueduct**, built in 1705–14, with 999 arches.

At the heart of the historic centre is Praça Vasco da Gama, with an unusual pillory in the shape of an arm with thrusting sword – a vivid warning to potential wrongdoers. Bordering the square by the pillory is the 16th-century **Igreja Matriz**, notable for its wonderfully ornate Manueline portico, attributed to João de Castilho.

The town is a centre for lace-making (bone lace or *rendas de bilros*). Visitors can buy samples and see the skills at the **Escola de Rendas** (lace-making school). The same building also houses the Museu de Rendas (lace museum).

🏠 **Mosteiro de Santa Clara**
Largo Dom Afonso Sanches. 📞 *252-63 10 16.* 🕐 *Mon–Fri.* 🌑 *public hols.*
🏛 **Escola de Rendas**
Rua de São Bento 70. 📞 *252-248 470.* 🕐 *mid Jun–Sep: daily; Oct–mid-Jun: Mon–Fri.* 🌑 *public hols.*

ENVIRONS: The town of **Póvoa de Varzim**, 3 km (2 miles) north of Vila do Conde, is a resort with sandy beaches, amusements and nightlife.

In the village of Rates, 10 km (6 miles) northeast, the 13th-century church of **São Pedro de Rates** boasts a portal surmounted by gracefully sculpted statues of saints, and a rose window. Its nearby counterpart at Rio Mau, the church of **São Cristóvão de Rio Mau**, was finished in 1151. Above the door is a bishop (possibly St Augustine) flanked by helpers.

THE LEGEND OF THE BARCELOS COCK

A Galician pilgrim, as he was leaving Barcelos en route to Santiago de Compostela, was accused of stealing silver from a landowner, and sentenced to death by hanging. As a final plea to save himself, the prisoner requested a meeting with the judge, who was about to tuck into a meal of roast cockerel. The Galician vowed that as proof of his innocence the cockerel would stand up on the plate and crow.

The judge pushed aside his meal and ignored the plea. But as the prisoner was hanged, the cockerel stood up and crowed. The judge, realizing his mistake, hurried to the gallows and found that the Galician had miraculously survived thanks to a loose knot. According to legend, the Galician returned years later to carve the Cruzeiro do Senhor do Galo, now housed in the Museu Arqueológico in Barcelos.

Traditional Barcelos cock

Azulejos of St Benedict's miracle of the sickle, Nossa Senhora do Terço

Barcelos ❾

Road map C1. 🏛 *10,000.* 🚉 🚌
🛈 *Torre de Menagem, Largo da Porta Nova, (253-81 18 82).* 🛒 *Thu.*

A PLEASANT riverside town, Barcelos is famed as the country's leading ceramics and crafts market and the source of the legendary cock that has become Portugal's national symbol. From its origins as a settlement in Roman times, the town of Barcelos developed into a flourishing agricultural centre and achieved political importance during the 15th century as the seat of the First Duke of Bragança. The town's star attraction is the Feira de Barcelos, a huge weekly market held on Campo da República. Anything from clothes to livestock can be bought here. Pottery enthusiasts can browse amongst bright designs including clay figurines and the famous clay cockerels.

North of the square stands **Nossa Senhora do Terço**, the 18th-century church of a former Benedictine nunnery. In contrast to its plain exterior, the interior is beautifully decorated with panels of *azulejos* illustrating St Benedict's life.

In the southwest corner of the square, a graceful cupola crowns the **Igreja do Senhor da Cruz**, built around 1705 on the site where two centuries earlier João Pires, a cobbler, had a miraculous vision of a cross etched into the ground. The Festa das Cruzes (festival of crosses), the town's most spectacular event, is held at the beginning of May to celebrate the vision. During the celebrations thousands of flowers are laid on the streets to welcome a procession to the church, and events include magnificent displays of local folk costumes, dancing and fireworks.

The other historic attractions in the town are clustered together in a tranquil setting beside the 15th-century granite bridge that crosses over the River Cávado. The privately owned **Solar dos Pinheiros** is an attractive mansion on Rua Duques de Bragança, built in 1448. The sculpted figure plucking his beard on the south tower is known as Barbadão, the "bearded one". So incensed was this Jew when his daughter bore a child to a gentile (King João I) that he vowed never to shave again, hence his nickname.

A rich Gothic pillory stands in front of the ruined Counts' Palace or Paço dos Condes, destroyed by the earthquake of 1755. The ruins provide an open-air setting for the **Museu Arqueológico**, which displays stone crosses, sculpted blazons, sarcophagi, and its famous exhibit, the Cruzeiro do Senhor do Galo, a cross paying tribute to the Barcelos cock legend. Next to the palace, the **Igreja Matriz** is Romanesque with Gothic influences, and dates from the 13th century. There are 18th-century *azulejos* inside as well as an impressive rose window. The nearby **Museu de Olaria** illustrates the history of ceramics in the region.

🏛 **Museu Arqueológico**
Paço do Duque. 📞 *253-80 96 00.* ⏰ *daily.* ● *public hols.*
🏛 **Museu de Olaria**
Rua Cónego J. Gaiolas. 📞 *253-82 47 41.* ⏰ *Tue–Sun.* ● *1 Jan, Easter, 15 Aug, 1 Nov, 25 & 26 Dec.* 🎫 ♿

16th-century pillory on terrace overlooking the River Cávado at Barcelos

Street-by-Street: Viana do Castelo ❼

Viana do Castelo lies in a beautiful setting on the Lima estuary. During the 15th century, the town gained prominence as a fishing centre and provided ships and seafarers for the great maritime discoveries of the 16th century (*see pp48–9*). From here João Velho set off to explore the Congo, and João Álvares Fagundes charted the rich fishing grounds of Newfoundland. Wealth derived from trade with Europe and Brazil funded the town's many opulent mansions built in Manueline, Renaissance and Baroque styles. Today the main interest lies in the winding streets and intimate squares of the city centre, easily explored on foot.

The fountain, constructed in 1553 by João Lopes the Elder, forms the focal point of the square.

Casa dos Lunas was once the home of the Luna family

Railway and bus stations

Palacete Sá Sotto Mayor dates from the Renaissance.

Misericórdia
Built in 1598, this unique Renaissance building features arcades supported by magnificent caryatids.

Museu Municipal, Nossa Senhora da Agonia

PRAÇA DA REPÚBLICA

PRAÇA DA ERVA

RUA DA PICOTA

VIELA DOS FORNOS

B. DOS FORNOS

RUA SACADURA CABRAL

RUA DO POÇO

RUA DO TOURINHO

RUA HOSPITAL VELHO

T. DO HOSPITAL VELHO

VIELA DA PARENTA

★ **Praça da República**
The Gothic arches of the restored Paços do Concelho, formerly the town hall, dominate the head of Viana's main square. Manueline motifs include the arms of João III.

The Hospital Velho
was originally a pilgrims' hospice. It now houses the Alto Minho tourist office.

STAR SIGHTS

★ **Igreja Matriz**

★ **Praça da República**

---

0 metres   50

0 yards   50

KEY

– – – Suggested route

Casa da Praça, a magnificent Baroque mansion

Casa de João Velho
is a 15th-century
house, said to
have belonged
to the town's
most famous
navigator.

The fountain in Praça da República, the centre of daily life in Viana

★ Igreja Matriz
*The arch surrounding the
west door of Viana's 15th-
century, fortress-like parish
church is adorned with
Gothic reliefs of the apostles.*

Exploring Viana do Castelo
Both a busy fishing port and
holiday resort, Viana is overlooked by the peak of Monte
de Santa Luzia. The town is
the capital of Minho folk culture, playing host to lively
festivals and supporting a
thriving handicrafts industry.

🏛 Museu Municipal
Largo de São Domingos. 🕿 258-82
03 77. ◻ Tue–Sun. ● public hols.
📷 ♿ new wing only.
Viana's Museu Municipal
is housed in the 18th-
century Palacete dos
Barbosas Maciéis
and has an excellent
collection of rare
ceramics, furniture,
archaeological
finds and paintings.
In one of the upstairs
rooms, the walls are
tiled with animated
allegorical depictions
of the continents,
while the chapel is
lined with tiles signed
by the 18th-century
artist Policarpo de
Oliveira Bernardes,
(see p22). Among
the exhibits are a
17th-century Indo-
Portuguese cabinet
magnificently deco-
rated with inlaid ivory, and
pieces of Oporto faïence from
the Massarelos district, embellished with fine brushwork.

**Early 19th-
century ceramic,
Museu Municipal**

🔒 Nossa Senhora da Agonia
Campo de Nossa Senhora da Agonia.
🕿 258-824 067. ◻ daily. ♿
Northwest of the centre, the
mid-18th century chapel of
Nossa Senhora da Agonia
houses a statue of Our Lady of
Sorrows *(agonia)*. The chapel,
with façade and altar designed
by André Soares, draws enormous crowds for the *romaria*
of Nossa Senhora da Agonia,
a three-day festival held each
year in the month of August
(see p227). The statue is carried in procession through
the town amid much feasting
and celebration.

ENVIRONS: In order to enjoy
exceptional views, take the
zig-zag road to **Monte
de Santa Luzia**, 5 km
(3 miles) north of the
town centre. (A funicular
runs on winter weekends
from the station.) The
basilica, completed in
1926 and modelled on
the Sacré Coeur in Paris,
is a pilgrimage site with
little aesthetic appeal.
The steep climb, how-
ever, is well rewarded
by the superb views from
the top of the dome. Be-
hind the church you can
wander along woodland
paths or visit the
Pousada de Santa Luzia
(see p394). From the
pousada it is a short
walk to the top of the
hill, where there are
traces of a Celtiberian
settlement *(citânia)*.
The excellent beach of
Praia do Cabedelo lies to
the south of the town. The
beach is accessible by road
via the bridge or by a five-
minute ferry crossing from
the riverside dock on Avenida
dos Combatentes da Grande
Guerra. To the north lies **Vila
Praia de Âncora**, another
popular beach resort.

Braga ⑩

CHURCHES, GRAND 18TH-CENTURY HOUSES and pretty gardens provide the focus for the charm and interest of Braga's centre, once past the urban development on the city outskirts.

Known in Roman times as Bracara Augusta, Braga has a long history as a religious and commercial centre. In the 12th century, it became the seat of Portugal's archbishops, and the country's religious capital. The city lost some influence in the 19th century, but today continues as the ecclesiastical capital of Portugal and main city of the Minho.

Symbol of the city, Our Lady of the Milk

Not surprisingly, Braga hosts some of Portugal's most colourful religious festivals. Semana Santa (Holy Week) is celebrated with dramatic, solemn processions, while the lively festival of São João in June sees dancing, fairs and fireworks.

The west façade of the Sé, with its 15th-century galilee, or porch

Exploring Braga

The compact historic centre borders **Praça da República**, the central square. Within the square stands the 14th-century **Torre de Menagem**, all that remains of the city's original fortifications.
A short walk leads to Rua do Souto, a narrow pedestrian street lined with elegant shops and cafés, including the **Café Brasileira**, furnished in 19th-century salon style. Towards the end of the road stands the impressive **Sé**, the cathedral of Braga. Other churches worth a visit include the small, 16th-century **Capela dos Coimbras**, and the 17th-century Baroque **Santa Cruz**. Many of the finest mansions in Braga also date from the Baroque period, such as the **Palácio do Raio** and the **Câmara Municipal** (the town hall). Both buildings are attributed to the 18th-century architect André Soares da Silva.

The blue-tiled façade of the Palácio do Raio, also known as the Casa do Mexicano

🔒 Sé

Rossio da Sé. ⬭ *daily.*
Museu de Arte Sacra 🔔 *253-26 33 17.* ⬭ *daily.* 📷
Braga's cathedral was begun in the 12th century, when Henry of Burgundy decided to build on the site of an older church, destroyed in the 6th century. Since then the building has seen many changes, including the addition of a graceful galilee (porch) in the late 15th century. The church now exhibits a range of styles from Romanesque to Baroque. Outstanding features include the chapel to the right, just inside the west door, housing the ornate 15th-century tomb of the first-born son of João I (*see pp46–7*), Dom Afonso, who died in childhood. Also of interest are the upper choir

with its elaborately carved wooden stalls, and the ornate, gilded, Baroque organ cases.

The cathedral also houses the Treasury or **Museu de Arte Sacra**, which contains a rich collection of ecclesiastical treasures as well as, statues, carvings and *azulejo* tiles.

Several chapels can be seen in the courtyard and cloister. The Capela dos Reis houses the tombs of the founders, Henry of Burgundy and his wife Dona Teresa, as well as the preserved body of the 14th-century archbishop Dom Lourenço Vicente.

From Rua de São João you can admire a statue of Nossa Senhora do Leite (Our Lady of the Milk), symbol of the city of Braga, sheltered under an ornate Gothic canopy.

🏛 Antigo Paço Episcopal

Praça Municipal. 🔔 *253-60 11 35.*
Library ⬭ *Mon–Fri.*
Near the Sé is the former archbishops' palace. The façades date from the 14th, 17th and 18th centuries, but

The Jardim de Santa Bárbara by the walls of the Antigo Paço Episcopal

a major fire destroyed the interior in the 18th century. The palace is now used as a library and archives. Beside it are the immaculate gardens of the Jardim de Santa Bárbara.

🏛 Palácio dos Biscainhos

Rua dos Biscainhos. **C** 253-20 46 50. **○** Tue–Sun. 🎫

To the west of the city centre is the Palácio dos Biscainhos. Built in the 16th century and modified over the centuries, this imposing aristocratic mansion features ornate, terraced gardens and grand salons with lavish stucco ceilings. It now houses the city's Museu Etnográfico e Artístico (Ethnography and Arts Museum) with displays of foreign and Portuguese furniture. An unusual detail is the ribbed, paved ground floor, designed to allow carriages inside the building to deposit guests and drive on to the stables beyond.

ENVIRONS: The attractively simple chapel of **São Frutuoso de Montélios**, 3.5 km (2 miles) northwest of Braga, is one of the very few remaining examples of pre-Romanesque architecture to be found in Portugal. Built around the 7th century, it was destroyed by the Moors and rebuilt in the 11th century.

West of Braga, 4 km (2.5 miles) from the centre and on the road to Barcelos, is the former Benedictine **Mosteiro de Tibães**. Dating back to the 11th century, this magnificent architectural complex with its gardens and cloisters, was rebuilt in the 19th century and is being refurbished to house a historical centre.

At Falperra, 6 km (4 miles) southeast of Braga, stands the church of **Santa Maria Madalena**. Designed by André Soares da Silva in 1750, it is known for its ornate exterior, perhaps the country's finest expression of the Rococo.

🛈 São Frutuoso de Montélios

Av. São Frutuoso. **C** (Tourist office) 253-26 25 50. **○** 9am–12:30pm, 2–5pm Wed–Sun, 2–5pm Tue.

🏛 Mosteiro de Tibães

Lugar de Tibães. **C** 253-62 26 70. **○** Tue–Sun. 🎫 to museum. 🔃

Interior of the old coach stable at the Palácio dos Biscainhos

BRAGA CITY CENTRE

Antigo Paço Episcopal ⑤
Câmara Municipal ③
Capela dos Coimbras ⑧
Jardim de Santa Bárbara ⑥
Market ①
Palácio dos Biscainhos ②
Palácio do Raio ⑩
Santa Cruz ⑨
Sé ④
Torre de Menagem ⑦

KEY

🚌 Bus station

P Parking

🛈 Tourist information

✝ Church

0 metres 250

0 yards 250

Bom Jesus do Monte ⑪

O N A FORESTED SLOPE east of Braga stands Portugal's most spectacular religious sanctuary. In 1722 the Archbishop of Braga devised the giant Baroque Escadaria (stairway) of Bom Jesus as the approach to a small existing shrine. The stairway and the church of Bom Jesus were completed by Carlos Amarante in 1811. The lower section features a steep Sacred Way with chapels showing the 14 Stations of the Cross, the scenes leading up to Christ's crucifixion. The Escadório dos Cinco Sentidos, in the middle section, depicts the five senses with ingenious wall-fountains and statues of biblical, mythological and symbolic figures. This is followed by the similarly allegorical Staircase of the Three Virtues.

Fountain on Staircase of the Three Virtues

At the summit, an esplanade provides superb views and access to the church. Close by are several hotels, a café and a boating lake hidden among the trees. Both a pilgrimage site and tourist attraction, the sanctuary attracts large festive crowds at weekends.

★ Escadaria
The staircase is built of granite accentuated by whitewashed walls. The steps represent an upward spiritual journey.

Chapel of the Crucifixion

Chapel of Jesus before Pilate

Chapel of the Road to Calvary

Chapel of the Flagellation

Entrance Portico
At the foot of the giant stairway stands a portico bearing the coat of arms of Dom Rodrigo de Moura Teles, the archbishop who commissioned the work.

★ Funicular Railway
The funicular (elevador) dates back to 1882. Hydraulically operated, it makes the ascent to the terrace beside the church in three minutes.

Chapel of Christ's Agony in the Garden

Chapel of the Last Supper

Chapel of the Kiss of Judas

Chapel of Darkness

The Hotel do Elevador (*see p393*) stands near the top of the funicular.

Hotel do Parque

Pelican fountain

VISITORS' CHECKLIST

Road map C1. 5 km (3 miles) E of Braga. **(** 253-67 66 36. *funicular to the top.* *daily.* *daily.*

The church of Bom Jesus was built on the site of a 15th-century sanctuary. In front of it stand eight statues of people who condemned Christ, including Herod and Pilate.

Chapel of the Descent from the Cross
Each chapel has a tableau of life-size terracotta figures in a scene from Christ's last journey.

On the Staircase of the Five Senses are five fountains, each representing a bodily sense: sight, hearing, smell, taste and touch.

Statues, symbols and inscriptions elaborate on the theme of the senses.

Staircase of the Three Virtues
The final stretch of staircase represents the gaining of Faith, Hope and Charity, symbolized by fountains and various allegorical figures.

Chapel of Simon the Cyrenian

Chapel of the Crown of Thorns

Fountain of the Five Wounds of Christ
The fountains positioned at various points on the long ascent symbolize the water of life and purification of the body and spirit. In the fountain at the foot of the Staircase of the Five Senses, water spills from the five bezants on the Portuguese coat of arms, a symbolic reference to Christ's wounds.

0 metres 25
0 yards 25

STAR FEATURES

★ **Escadaria**

★ **Funicular Railway**

Guimarães

Baroque candle-holder, Paço dos Duques

FRAMED BY GENTLY RISING HILLS, the town of Guimarães is celebrated as the birthplace of the nation. When Afonso Henriques proclaimed himself king of Portugal in 1139 (*see pp42–3*), he chose Guimarães as his capital, and the distinctive outline of its proud castle appears on the Portuguese coat of arms. In the well-preserved city centre, the narrow streets of the medieval quarter are ideal for exploration on foot. The cobbled Rua de Santa Maria, lined with old town houses embellished with ornate statuary, leads up from the main square, the Largo da Oliveira, past the Paço dos Duques to the castle. To feel the hustle and bustle of the Middle Ages, visit the town in the first week of August for the Festas Gualterianas, a festival of medieval art and costume.

♠ Castelo de Guimarães
Rua Conde Dom Henrique. 253-41 22 73. ☐ daily. ● 1 Jan, Easter, 1 May, 25 Dec.

The castle's huge square keep, encircled by eight crenellated towers, dominates the skyline. First built to deter attacks by Moors and Normans in the 10th century, it was extended by Henry of Burgundy two centuries later and, according to tradition, was the birthplace of Portugal's first king, Afonso Henriques. The font where he was reputedly baptized is kept in the tiny Romanesque chapel of **São Miguel**, situated at the western end of the castle.

♛ Paço dos Duques
Rua Conde Dom Henrique. 253-41 22 73. ☐ daily. ● 1 Jan, Easter, 1 May, 25 Dec.

Constructed in the 15th century by Dom Afonso (first Duke of Bragança), the Burgundian style of the Paço dos Duques reflects Dom Afonso's taste acquired on his travels through Europe. The palace fell into disuse when the Bragança family moved to Vila Viçosa (*see pp298–9*). In 1933, under the Salazar dictatorship (*see pp56–7*), it was renovated as an official residence for the president.

On view in a small museum inside the palace, are lavish displays of Persian rugs, Flemish tapestries and paintings, such as the impressive *O Coreiro Pascal* (Paschal Lamb) by Josefa de Óbidos (*see p51*). Paying unusual homage to the nation's maritime exploits, the chestnut ceiling in the banqueting hall imitates the upturned hull of a Portuguese caravel.

⛫ Museu de Alberto Sampaio
Rua Alfredo Guimarães. 253-423 910. ☐ Tue–Sun. ● 1 Jan, Easter, 1 May, 25 Dec.

This museum, housed in the beautiful Romanesque cloister and adjoining rooms of Nossa Senhora da Oliveira, displays some outstanding religious art, *azulejos* and ceramics, all from local churches.

The star exhibits, donated to the church by João I, are his tunic worn at the battle of Aljubarrota in 1385 (*see p183*), and a 14th-century silver altarpiece, comprising a triptych of the Visitation, Annunciation and Nativity, reportedly taken from the defeated Spanish king. The Santa Clara room contains gilt carving, the work of local craftsmen, taken from the former convent of Santa Clara, now the town hall.

Largo da Oliveira, centre of old Guimarães

⛪ Nossa Senhora da Oliveira
Largo da Oliveira. 253-41 61 44. ☐ daily.

This former monastery lies on the square's east side. Founded by Afonso Henriques, the church was restored by João I in gratitude to Our Lady of the Olive Tree for his victory at Aljubarrota (*see p183*). The Manueline tower is from 1515.

In front of it is the Padrão do Salado, a 14th-century Gothic shrine housing a cross. It commemorates the legend of how the church and square acquired their name. An olive tree was transplanted here to supply the altar lamp with oil, but it withered. In 1342, the merchant Pedro Esteves placed the cross on it, whereupon the tree flourished. The tree that stands in the square today dates only from 1985.

The massive battlements surrounding the keep of Castelo de São Miguel

Road map C1. 🕌 60,000.
🚉 Avenida Dom João IV.
🚌 Alameda Mariano Felgueiras.
ℹ️ Praça de Santiago (253-518
790). 🛍 Fri. 🎭 first weekend
in Aug: Festas Gualterianas.

🏛 **Museu Martins Sarmento**
Rua Paio Galvão. 📞 253-41 40 11.
⏰ Tue–Sun. 🎫 public hols. 📷
Named after the archaeologist
who excavated major Iron
Age sites in the north, notably
Citânia de Briteiros, the museum is housed in the Gothic
cloister of the 14th-century
convent of São Domingos. Specializing in finds from these
sites, some dating to the Stone
Age, the museum contains
a wealth of archaeological,
ethnological and numismatic
exhibits. These include a rare
pair of Lusitanian granite
warriors, a bronze votive oxcart, and the Pedras Formosas,
two stone slabs inscribed with
human figures. The most striking exhibit is the Colossus of
Pedralva, a stone figure that
stands 3 m (10 ft) tall.

🏛 **São Francisco**
Largo de São Francisco. 📞 253-51
25 17. ⏰ Tue–Sun. 🎫 public hols.
Built in 1400 in Gothic style,
the elegant church of São Francisco was reconstructed in the
18th century. The interior of
the church boasts a chancel
covered in magnificent 18th-
century *azulejos* with scenes
from the life of St Antony.

ENVIRONS: The former monastery of **Santa Marinha da
Costa** is one of Portugal's top
pousadas (see p379). It stands
5 km (3 miles) southeast of
Guimarães, and was founded
in 1154. The gardens and
chapel are open to the public.

Renaissance stone fountain at Santa
Marinha da Costa monastery

Reconstructed huts at the Iron Age site of Citânia de Briteiros

Citânia de Briteiros 🔞

Road map C1. 15 km (9 miles) N of
Guimarães, off N101. 📞 253-41 59
69. 🚌 from Guimarães & Braga.
⏰ Apr–Sep: 9am–7pm daily;
Oct–Mar: 9am–6pm daily. 📷

THE IRON AGE settlement
of Citânia de Briteiros
is one of Portugal's most
impressive archaeolo-
gical sites. Excavated by
Martins Sarmento (1833–
99), who devoted his life
to the study of Iron Age
sites, are the foundations
of 150 stone dwellings,
a number of which have
since been reconstructed.

From about the 4th
century BC to the
4th century AD, the
site was inhabited by
Celtiberians, but was
most probably under
Roman rule from c.20
BC. A network of
paths leads visitors
past paved streets,
subterranean cisterns,
sewers and water supply ducts.
The Museu Martins Sarmento
in Guimarães displays various
excavated artefacts.

**The basto statue
of Cabeceiras
de Basto**

Cabeceiras de Basto 🔞

Road map D1. 🕌 17,000. 🚌
ℹ️ Paços do Concelho, Praça da
República (253-66 91 00). 🛍 Mon.

THE TERRAS DE BASTO, once
a region of refuge from
Moorish invasion, lie east of
Guimarães among mountains

and forests. Statues known as
bastos, believed to represent
Celtic warriors, are found in
various parts of the Terras de
Basto where they served as
territorial markers. In the main
town, Cabeceiras de Basto,
the prime attraction is the
Baroque **Mosteiro de
Refojos**, with its splendid
dome 33 m (108 ft) high,
surrounded by statues of
the Apostles, and sur-
mounted by a statue of
the archangel Michael.

The town also owns the
best of the *basto* statues,
albeit with a French
head; it was changed by
troops as a joke during
the Napoleonic Wars.

ENVIRONS: The fine
hiking country of
the Terras de Basto,
carpeted with flowers
in spring, has other
villages worth visiting.
Mondim de Basto,
overlooking the River
Tâmega some 25 km
(15 miles) south of
Cabeceiras, is a convenient
base for climbing **Monte
Farinha** which, at 966 m
(3,169 ft) is the highest peak
in the region. Then climb the
steps to the top of the church
of Nossa Senhora da Graça on
the summit, for splendid views.

Over the Tâmega, the village
of **Celorico de Basto** has a
small castle and several manor
houses in the surrounding area.
Most are private but some,
such as the **Casa do Campo**
(see p393), are part of the
Turismo de Habitação scheme
(see p376) and take in guests.

SOUTHERN
PORTUGAL

Southern Portugal at a Glance

SOUTH OF THE TAGUS the vast wheatfields and rolling plains of the Alentejo stretch almost uninterrupted to the horizon. There is a rich legacy of early civilization here, dating back to prehistory, but visitors to Elvas, Beja or even the World Heritage city of Évora will usually be untroubled by mass tourism – until reaching the southern coast. Many visitors know nothing of Portugal except the tourist playground of the Algarve, yet it is least typical of the country. The sandy beaches are a year-round attraction but the historic town centres such as Faro, and the quieter hinterland, are well worth exploring.

***Évora**, the Alentejo's historic university city, has monuments dating back to the Roman era. Gleaming white arcades and balconies of finely wrought ironwork are reminders that for over 450 years, until 1165, Évora was inhabited by the Moors (see pp302–5).*

***Beja** flourished under the Moors and its museum is housed in a former convent resplendent with Hispano-Arab tiles, such as these in the chapter-house (see p311).*

Baixo Alentejo

ALGARVE
(See pp314–31)

***Lagos**, principal town of the western Algarve, is flanked by inviting cove beaches, such as Praia de Dona Ana, which make it easy to understand why sunseekers flock here (see pp320–21).*

0 kilometres   25

0 miles   10

◁ **Sandy beach and calm waters at the popular resort of Albufeira**

Alto Alentejo

***Marvão**, within a stone's throw of the Spanish border, sits like a miniature fortress high in the Serra de São Mamede. The granite walls which protect the tiny town merge imperceptibly with the rock and have kept Marvão safe through centuries of dispute (see p294).*

***Elvas** has some of the best-preserved fortifications in Europe (see p297). At the centre of the walled old town lies the Praça da República, where Elvas's former cathedral looks out over the square's striking geometric mosaics.*

ALENTEJO
(See pp290–313)

***Vila Viçosa** was chosen in the 15th century as the seat of the dukes of Bragança. Here they built their vast Paço Ducal (see pp298–9), in front of which stands a bronze equestrian statue of the 8th Duke, who became King João IV in 1640.*

***Faro**, the gateway to the Algarve thanks to its international airport, is nevertheless bypassed by many visitors. Much was destroyed by the 1755 earthquake, but the town still has a pleasant historic centre beside the harbour. In spring the streets and squares are scented with the sweetness of orange blossom (see pp326–8).*

The Beaches of the Algarve

FACING NORTH AFRICA to the south, and exposed to the force of the Atlantic in the west, the Algarve has a varied coastline. The Barlavento (windward side) includes the west coast and the south coast as far as Faro.

Sunbathing on the beach

Beaches around the promontory of Sagres are backed by cliffs and on the west coast many beaches are deserted. The sea here is colder and rougher than on the south coast, with dangerous currents. Between Sagres and Lagos is the start of a series of beautiful sandy coves, punctuated with grottoes, overlooked by tightly packed holiday resorts. East of Faro, the *Sotavento* (leeward side) has long, sandy beaches washed by warmer calmer water.

Arrifana ①
The gracefully curving beach of Arrifana is one of the most stunning on the west coast. Sheltered below high cliffs, the approach by road offers dramatic views *(see p318)*.

Beliche ③
Despite being at the "world's end", Beliche is sheltered by Cabo de São Vicente. The sandy beach is backed by fascinating caves and rock formations *(see p320)*.

Castelejo ②
This long, deserted beach of soft sand can only be reached via a dirt road by bicycle, car or jeep. Its remote location, however, ensures peace and quiet *(see p319)*.

Aljezur

Vila do Bispo

Lagos

Portimão

Lagoa

Armação de Pêra

Albufeira

Sagres

0 kilometres   10

0 miles   5

KEY

Motorway

Major road

Minor road

For key to symbols see back flap

Martinhal ④
Martinhal is a wide, sheltered expanse of sand east of Sagres. The area is popular for water sports of all kinds, and the beach boasts an aquatic school with parasailing, water-skiing and windsurfing *(see p320)*.

Dona Ana ⑤

A tiny cove on the way to Ponta da Piedade, Dona Ana is one of the prettiest beaches in the Algarve, although crowded during the summer. A boat trip to see nearby caves and grottoes is highly recommended (see p321).

Meia Praia ⑥

A vast expanse of sand stretching for 4 km (2 miles), the sheltered Meia Praia is the longest beach in the Algarve. Easily reached by road, there is also a boat trip from Lagos during the summer months (see p321).

Praia da Rocha ⑦

Framed by ochre cliffs and lapped by calm water, this spacious beach is justifiably famous – and crowded in high season. Water sports can be practised here in a gentler sea than the extreme southwest and visitors are well catered for (see p322).

Ilha de Tavira ⑪

In summer, boats go from Quatro Águas to the sandy Ilha de Tavira. The beach facing the coast has calm water, whereas the beaches on the ocean side, that run the length of the island, offer good swimming and windsurfing (see p330).

Carvoeiro ⑧

Carvoeiro is a fishing village with a diminutive cove. The whole area is great for cove beaches, and a boat trip or a walk along the cliff will take you to spectacular sandy beaches with excellent swimming and snorkelling.

Monte Gordo ⑫

The warm water and balmy climate, combined with vast stretches of clean sand backed by pine woods, make Monte Gordo a very popular resort.

Senhora da Rocha ⑨

Senhora da Rocha, named after a small chapel on its eastern promontory, is actually three small, sheltered beaches. Typical of this part of the coast, these half-moons of sand tucked below eroded yellow cliffs are reached via steep steps.

São Rafael ⑩

The small, popular beach of São Rafael offers soft sand and shallow water, with spectacular caves and eroded rock formations to explore. For those without a car, it is a steep walk down from the bus stop on the main road (see p323).

Regional Food: Southern Portugal

THE TUNA AND SARDINES on offer in the Algarve are unrivalled, but every type of seafood, from cod to clams, is excellent. Inland, fish is replaced by goat, lamb and, above all, acorn-fed pigs, cooked into delicious stews with local wine. A feature of southern cooking is the *cataplana*, a kind of tightly sealed wok in which the food steams in its own juice. Bread is enjoyed, not just as a snack, but to soak up the herby juices in fish and meat dishes *(ensopados)*. Almonds, oranges, figs and olives grow in abundance throughout the south.

Peppers

Nisa   Évora

Ewe's milk cheeses come from all over the Alentejo. Among the best are Évora and the piquant Nisa.

Spicy **linguiça**

Presunto

Chouriço

Salpicão, made with pork loin

Empadas de Galinha (chicken pies)

Pão alentejano, *the peasant loaf of the Alentejo, is served at most meals and used in many bread-based dishes.*

Pork *is used in many guises in the Alentejo, which produces sausages and cured hams* (presunto) *in delicious variety. Chicken pies are a speciality of Évora.*

Sopa alentejana, *fragrant with garlic, coriander and olive oil, is a bread-based soup topped with a poached egg.*

Gaspacho, *always served cold, is a garlic-laden tomato soup, incorporating cucumber, sweet peppers and olive oil.*

Salada mista *usually means a simple salad of lettuce leaves, tomatoes and onions dressed with olive oil and vinegar.*

Atum de cebolada, *from the Algarve, is a fresh tuna steak which is cooked on a bed of onions with tomato sauce.*

Sardinhas assadas, *charcoal-grilled sardines, are a seaside tradition – a feast in summer when they are at their best.*

Lulas recheadas *are succulent squid stuffed with cured meats and rice, then cooked in an onion and tomato mixture.*

Caldeirada *is a stew made with a variety of fish layered with potato. It is extremely popular all along the coast.*

Porco à alentejana, *a curious marriage of pork and clams, is usually cooked in a cataplana, which seals in the flavours.*

Ensopado de Borrego, *a favourite in the Alentejo, is a stew of young lamb served on bread to mop up the gravy.*

Coelho em vinho *is an Alentejan recipe for rabbit, a meat popular all over Portugal. This version is cooked in wine.*

Cabrito assado *is a small kid, roasted whole, with a covering of paprika, garlic, wine and lard to keep it moist.*

Olive oil (azeite) *enriches dishes from gaspacho to salads.*

Bolo podre ("rotten cake"), a dark, spiced honey cake

Queijada, a cheesecake from the Alentejo

Selection of marzipan *doces de amêndoa*

Ameixas de Elvas, **the preserved greengages known as Elvas plums**

Figos cheios, figs studded with almonds

Almonds

Dried figs

Sweetmeats *in the south reflect the rich harvest of figs and almonds from the Algarve, fashioned into mouthwatering honeyed treats.*

FRUIT

As well as the ubiquitous grape, the climate favours greengages, apricots and citrus fruits. Mild winters help the Algarve grow the best figs, oranges and strawberries in the country.

Oranges

Grapes

LIQUEURS

The south's best wines are from the Alentejo *(see pp28–9)*, but the Algarve has two local liqueurs: the bitter-almond *amarguinha*, splendid on ice, and *medronheira*, made from the pretty fruit of the strawberry tree *(Arbutus unedo)*.

Amarguinha, an almond liqueur

Medronheira sweetened with honey

ALENTEJO

THE SUN-BAKED ALENTEJO *occupies nearly one-third of Portugal, stretching all the way from the Tagus south to the Algarve. Its vast rolling plains, golden with wheat or silver with olive trees, its whitewashed villages, megaliths and castles, and above all the space and tranquillity, are the Alentejo's great attractions for visitors.*

Stone circles, dolmens and other relics of Stone Age life pepper the Alentejan plain, particularly around Évora, a historical gem of a city at the region's geographical centre.

Évora, like Beja, Vidigueira and other towns, was founded by the Romans, who valued this land beyond the Tagus – *além Tejo* – for its wheatfields. Introducing irrigation systems to overcome the soil's aridity, they established enormous farms to grow grain for the empire. Worked by peasant farmers, these huge estates, or *latifúndios*, still exist, some of them now being run as co-operatives.

Grain apart, the vast plains yield cork from the bark of cork oaks and olives – Elvas is prized for these as well as its candied greengages *(see p289).* Vineyards around Reguengos and Vidigueira have long produced powerful wines, and the Alentejo has a number of demarcated wine regions *(see pp28–9).* Since 1986, Portugal's membership of the European Union has increased the rate of investment and modernization, although the region is still sparsely populated, supporting only ten per cent of the population. Land tenure has always been a concern here, and communism has a strong appeal – the Alentejans were solid supporters of the 1974 revolution *(see p57).*

Many towns and villages, especially in the south, carry echoes of the long Moorish occupation in the cube-like white houses, while to the north and east the plains give way to a rocky terrain of fortified villages and scrubland grazed by flocks of sheep.

Portuguese from other regions mock the amiable *alentejanos* for their slow ways, but they are widely admired for their singing and their handicrafts.

An Alentejan house in Odemira, with the traditional blue trim typical of the region

◁ Cork oaks and olive trees breaking up the wheatfields of the Alentejo plains

Exploring the Alentejo

Fá

THE ANCIENT CITY of Évora, with its exceptional historic centre and location in the heart of the Alentejo, is an obvious starting point for exploring this varied and beautiful region.

To the northeast lie the white towns of Estremoz and Vila Viçosa, where local marble has been used in the construction of some fabulous façades, and Alter do Chão, home of Portugal's royal horse, the Alter Real. Nearer the formerly-disputed Spanish frontier, towns and villages still shelter within massive fortifications, while travelling south the legacy of the Moors becomes ever more apparent; Beja and Mértola, especially, are full of Moorish history.

On the west coast there are some lovely beaches, with many stretches still relatively untouched by tourism.

The cromlech of Almendres, one of many prehistoric sites around Évora

SIGHTS AT A GLANCE

The fertile farmland and orchards of the northern Alentejo, seen from Estremoz

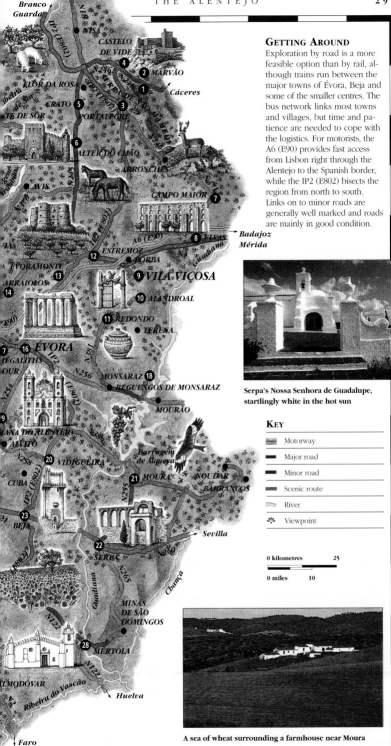

GETTING AROUND

Exploration by road is a more feasible option than by rail, although trains run between the major towns of Évora, Beja and some of the smaller centres. The bus network links most towns and villages, but time and patience are needed to cope with the logistics. For motorists, the A6 (E90) provides fast access from Lisbon right through the Alentejo to the Spanish border, while the IP2 (E802) bisects the region from north to south. Links on to minor roads are generally well marked and roads are mainly in good condition.

Serpa's Nossa Senhora de Guadalupe, startlingly white in the hot sun

KEY

▩▩▩	Motorway
▬▬▬	Major road
▬▬▬	Minor road
▨▨▨	Scenic route
∿	River
⁂	Viewpoint

0 kilometres   25

0 miles   10

A sea of wheat surrounding a farmhouse near Moura

Serra de São Mamede ❶

Road map D4. 🚌 *to Portalegre.*
🚪 *Portalegre.*

THE DIVERSE GEOLOGY and capricious climate of this remote range, caught between the Atlantic and the Mediterranean, encourage a fascinating range of flora and fauna. In 1989, 320 sq km (120 sq miles) of the Serra were designated a *parque natural*, and griffon vultures and Bonelli's eagles soar overhead. Red deer, wild boar and the cat-like genet live among the sweet chestnut trees and holm oaks, and streams attract otters and amphibians, such as the Iberian midwife toad. The reserve is also home to one of the largest colonies of bats in Europe.

The Serra's apparent emptiness is deceptive: megaliths suggest that it was settled in prehistoric times, and in the south of the reserve, rock paintings survive in the Serra de Cavaleiros and Serra de Louções. Below Marvão is the Roman town of Amaia (São Salvador de Aramenha), and the Roman network of roads still winds among the trim white villages, offering grand views at every curve.

From Portalegre, the road climbs for 15 km (9 miles) to the Pico de São Mamede at 1,025 m (3,363 ft). A minor road leads south to Alegrete, a fortified village crowned by its ruined 14th-century castle.

Sheep in the summer pastures of the Serra de São Mamede

Marvão ❷

Road map D4. 🏠 *650.* 🚉 🚌
🚪 *Largo de Santa Maria (245-99 38 86).* 🔺 *Thu.*

THIS SERENE MEDIEVAL hamlet is dramatically set at 862 m (2,828 ft) on a spectacular escarpment facing Spain. Its 13th-century walls and 17th-century buttresses blend seamlessly into the granite of the mountains, making it an impregnable stronghold. The Romans, who called the outcrop Herminius Minor, were followed by the Moors – the name may have come from Marvan, a Moorish leader – whom the Christians evicted with difficulty only in 1166.

The walls completely enclose the little collection of whitewashed houses, a *pousada* *(see p395)* and the 15th-century **Igreja Matriz**. Rua do Espírito

Santo leads past the former governor's house (now a bank) with its 17th-century iron balcony, and a Baroque fountain, up towards the **castle**.

Built by King Dinis in about 1299, the castle dominates the village. Its walls enclose two cisterns, a museum displaying historic weapons and a keep. The castle offers spectacular views south and west towards the Serra de São Mamede and east to the Spanish frontier.

The **Museu Municipal**, in the former church of Santa Maria, retains the main altar, and has an interesting exhibition of traditional remedies and local archaeological finds dating from Palaeolithic to Roman times.

🏛 **Museu Municipal**
Largo de Santa Maria. 📞 *245-909 132.* ⭕ *daily.* ⬤ *25 Dec.* 📷

Portalegre ❸

Road map D4. 🏠 *15,000.* 🚉 🚌
🚪 *Rossio (245-331 359).* 🔺 *Wed & Sat (food); 2nd Wed of month (clothes).* 🌐 *www.rtsm.pt*

STRATEGICALLY POSITIONED on a low plateau of the Serra de São Mamede amid fertile country, Portalegre is of Roman origin. Fortified by King Dinis *(see pp44–5)*, it acquired city status in 1550.

Textile, tapestry and silk industries brought prosperity in the 16th and 17th centuries, reflected in the city's fine Renaissance and Baroque mansions. These are to be

Looking out over the plain from the heights of Marvão's castle

found along Rua 19 de Junho, the main street of the old town. Near the new town's central square, the Rossio, a former Jesuit monastery is now the only tapestry factory still in use. Cork production is also a tradition here, and the tall chimneys of cork factories on the edge of the city indicate a continuing industry.

Uphill lies the cathedral or **Sé**. Built in 1556, it acquired its Baroque façade and twin pinnacles in the 18th century. The late Renaissance interior has paintings by anonymous Portuguese artists and a sacristy lined with striking *azulejo* panels. These blue and white tile pictures, dating from the first years of the 17th century, depict scenes from the life of the Virgin Mary and the flight of the Holy Family into Egypt.

In an adjacent 18th-century mansion is the small **Museu Municipal**, where the eclectic collection on display ranges from religious art to Portuguese ceramics.

The home of José Régio (1901–69), the eminent Portuguese poet and dramatist, is near the Praça da República. Now the **Museu José Régio**, it contains some fascinating folk art objects in a variety of media as well as his collection of crucifixes and a recreated Alentejan kitchen.

🏛 **Museu Municipal**
Rua José Maria da Rosa.
📞 245-300 120. 🕐 Wed–Mon. ▨
🏛 **Museu José Régio**
Rua José Régio. 📞 245-203 625.
🕐 Tue–Sun. ▨

The crenellated monastery, now a *pousada*, of Flor da Rosa, near Crato

Castelo de Vide ❹

Road map D4. 🏠 *3,000.* 🚉 🚌
ℹ️ *Rua Bartolomeu A. da Santa 81 (245-901 361).* 🛍 *Fri (clothes).*

SPRAWLED ON a green slope of the Serra de São Mamede, this pretty spa town enjoyed by the Romans has worn well. It is fringed by modern development but the lower town, around Praça Dom Pedro V, retains its Baroque church of **Santa Maria**, the 18th-century town hall and pillory, and handsome mansions from the same era. In the Largo Frederico Laranjo is one of several sources of the town's curative waters: the **Fonte da Vila**, a carved stone fountain with a pillared canopy. Just above is the maze-like **Judiaria**, where small white houses sprout vivid pots of geraniums. Its cobbled alleys conceal a 13th-century **synagogue** and are lined with fine Gothic doorways. The town's oldest chapel, the 13th-century **Salvador do Mundo** on the Estrada de Circunvalação, has a much admired *Flight into Egypt* by an unknown 18th-century artist.

Folk crucifix, Museu José Régio, Portalegre

In the upper town, the tiny **Nossa Senhora da Alegria** offers a feast of 17th-century polychrome floral tiles. It stands within the walls of the **castle** that gave the town its name. This was rebuilt in 1310 by King Dinis, who negotiated here to marry Isabel of Aragon. Much of the castle was lost in an explosion in 1705.

Red-tiled roofs of Castelo de Vide

Crato ❺

Road map D4. 🏠 *2,000.* 🚉 🚌
ℹ️ *as for Portalegre (245-331 359).*
🛍 *3rd Thu of month.*

MODEST HOUSES under outsize chimneys give no hint of Crato's past eminence. Part of a gift from Sancho II to the powerful crusading Order of Hospitallers, Crato was the Order's headquarters by 1350. Its prestige was such that Manuel I and João III were both married here, and João III's nephew was Grand Prior.

In 1662, invading Spanish forces sacked and burned the town, a catastrophe from which it never recovered. The Hospitallers' **castle** remains, in ruins, and in the Praça do Município the 15th-century **Varanda do Grão-Prior** marks the entrance to what was the Grand Prior's residence.

Rua de Santa Maria leads, via an avenue of orange trees, to the **Igreja Matriz**, much altered since its 13th-century origins. In the chancel, 18th-century *azulejos* depict fishing, hunting and travelling scenes.

ENVIRONS: Just north of Crato are the imposing monastery and church of **Flor da Rosa**. Built in 1356 by the Grand Prior of Crato, father of Nuno Álvares Pereira (*see p183*), the monastery was restored and in 1995 opened as a *pousada* (*see p395*). A tapestry in the dining room shows the monastery surrounded by pine forests, as it was until the 20th century.

Alter do Chão 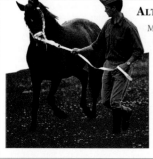 ❻

Road map D4. 🏛 *2,700.* 🚌
ℹ *Temporarily in: Edifício Cine-Teatro Largo os Doze Melhore de Alter (245-61 00 04).* 🎪 *1st Thu of month.*

THE ROMANS founded Elteri (or Eltori) in 204 BC, but razed it under the Emperor Hadrian after the inhabitants were accused of disloyalty. The town was re-established in the 13th century.

Dominating the town centre is the five-towered **castle** (closed for restoration). It has a Gothic portal built in 1359 by Pedro I. The flower-filled market square, the Largo Doze Melhores de Alter, lies at its feet.

Several streets northwest of the castle are graced by fine Baroque town houses, many trimmed with Alentejan style yellow paintwork. The 18th-century **Palácio do Álamo** (closed until 2004), houses an art gallery and library.

♦ Castle
Largo Barreto Caldeira. ◯ *Jun–Sep: variable hours.* ● *until further notice.*

ENVIRONS: Alter is best known for the **Coudelaria de Alter**, founded in 1748 to breed the Alter Real. The stud extends to 300 ha (740 acres) around attractive stables painted in the royal livery of white and ochre.

Spanning the Seda 12 km (7 miles) west along the N369 is the robust six-arched **Ponte de Vila Formosa**. This bridge carried the Roman road from Lisbon to Mérida in Spain.

Ⓤ Coudelaria de Alter
3 km (2 miles) NW of town. 📞 *245-61 00 60.* ◯ *Tue–Sun.* 📷 ♿

Campo Maior's macabre but compelling Capela dos Ossos

Campo Maior ❼

Road map E5. 🏛 *8,500.* 🚌
ℹ *Praça da República (268-68 03 00).* 🎪 *2nd Sat of month.*

ACCORDING TO LEGEND, this town got its name when three families settled in *campo maior*, the "bigger field". King Dinis fortified the town in 1310 and the monumental Porta da Vila was added in 1646.

Disaster struck in 1732 when a gunpowder magazine, ignited by lightning, destroyed the citadel and killed 1,500 people. It seems likely that after a decent period, the victims provided the material for the morbid **Capela dos Ossos**, entirely faced in human bones. Dated 1766, it bears an inscription on mortality spelt out in collar bones.

Each September the streets are dressed with paper flowers for the joyful Festa das Flores.

⛪ Capela dos Ossos
Largo Dr. Regala 6. 📞 *268-686 168.* ◯ *daily (if closed, ask priest to open).*

Elvas ❽

Road map D5. 🏛 *15,000.* 🚉 🚌
ℹ *Praça da República (268-62 22 36).* 🎪 *2nd & 4th Mon of the month.*

ONLY 12 KM (7 miles) from the Spanish border, Elvas feels like a frontier town. The sprawl of modern Elvas caters for busy cross-border traffic, but the old town's fortifications are among the best preserved in Europe. Within the walls a few architectural features and many of the street names are reminders that for 500 years the town was in Moorish hands.

Elvas was liberated from the Moors in 1230, but for another 600 years its fate was to swing between periodic attacks from Spain and the witnessing of numerous peace treaties.

Despite its dramatic history, Elvas is nowadays associated in Portuguese minds with Elvas plums *(see p289)*.

Summer roses brightening an Elvas street

ALTER REAL: HORSE OF KINGS

Most Lusitano horses – Portugal's national breed – are grey, but those called Alter Real ("real" means royal) are purebred bay or brown. King José (1750–77), who yearned for a quality Portuguese horse, imported a stock of Andalusian mares, from which the gracious, nimble Alter Real was bred. The equestrian statue in Lisbon's Praça do Comércio *(see p65)* is of José astride his beloved Alter, Gentil. The stud prospered until the Napoleonic Wars (1807–15), when horse stealing and erratic breeding sent the Alter into decline. By 1930, the royal horse was practically extinct, but years of dedication have ultimately revived this classic breed.

THE FORTIFICATIONS OF ELVAS

A walk around the top of the battlements gives a fine view of the old town and a vantage point from which to appreciate the ingenious design of the fortifications. Using the principles of the French military architect, the Marquis de Vauban, a series of pentagonal bastions and free-standing angled ravelins form a multi-faceted star, protecting the walls from every angle. What survives dates mostly from the 17th century, when the defences held off Spanish troops in the War of Independence *(see pp50–51)*. Elvas also served as Wellington's base to besiege Badajoz across the Guadiana.

Two surviving satellite forts indicate the strategic importance of Elvas: just to the south-east lies **Forte de Santa Luzia** (1641–87), and 2 km (1 mile) to the north is the 18th-century **Forte de Graça**, which is still a military post.

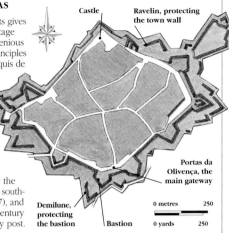

Castle

Ravelin, protecting the town wall

Portas da Olivença, the main gateway

Demilune, protecting the bastion

Bastion

0 metres   250
0 yards   250

♣ Castle
Parada do Castelo. ○ *daily.*
Romano-Moorish in origin, the castle which crowns the steep Elvas streets was rebuilt by Sancho II in 1226. It has been subjected to further remodelling over the years, principally by King Dinis and then in the late 15th century under João II, whose arms, which incorporate a pelican, can be seen above the entrance. The great keep was erected in 1488. Until the end of the 16th century the castle was used as the residence of the mayors of Elvas.

♠ Nossa Senhora da Assunção
Praça da República. ☎ 268-62 59 97. ○ *Mon–Fri.* ♿ *(via side door).*
Until 1882, this was the cathedral of Elvas. Built in the early 16th century, its architect was Francisco de Arruda, who also designed the town's impressive aqueduct. His Manueline south portal survives, but much of the church has been modified. The *azulejos* in the nave date from the early 17th century.

⛪ Museu Arqueológico and Biblioteca
Largo do Colégio. ☎ 268-62 24 02. ○ *Tue–Sun (library: Mon–Sat).* ● *1 Jan, Easter, 25 Dec.* 🎟 *to museum.*
This archaeological museum is set to move to a new site in Rua do Açolges (no date as yet). The cool rooms in the present building display a collection which ranges from

Roman water pots to prehistoric artefacts. The associated library, which is entered by a tiled porch, contains more than 50,000 books, including a number of rare early works.

♠ Nossa Senhora dos Aflitos
Largo do Pelourinho. ○ *Tue–Sun.*
The plain exterior belies the wealth within the walls of this little 16th-century church. The octagonal floor plan originates from the layout of an earlier Templar church, but its appeal is in the fine marble columns and spectacular yellow and blue *azulejos* added in the 17th century. These line the walls and reach up into the cupola.

Just behind the church is the archway of the Arab Porta da Alcáçova, a vestige of Elvas's Moorish fortifications. In the

Largo do Dr. Santa Clara, with its pillory

adjacent Largo do Dr. Santa Clara is a pillory, carved in typically exuberant Manueline style *(see pp20–21)* and still armed with its hooks.

The arches of the great aqueduct

♠ Aqueduto da Amoreira
Until the 16th century the only source of drinking water in Elvas was the Alcalá well in the west of the town. When this began to fail, alarmed citizens conceived the notion of an aqueduct to bring water from the spring at Amoreira, some 8 km (5 miles) away. Work, begun in 1498, was not finished until 1622. The great round buttresses and arches of architect Francisco de Arruda march across the valley and still deliver water to the fountain in the Largo da Misericórdia. The aqueduct has a total of 843 arches in up to five tiers and in places towers to over 30 m (100 ft).

Vila Viçosa: Paço Ducal

THE DUKES OF BRAGANÇA owned vast estates, but the lavish palace at Vila Viçosa, begun by Dom Jaime in 1501, became their favoured residence.

When the 8th Duke became king in 1640, many of the furnishings accompanied him to Lisbon, but the long suite of first-floor rooms is still splendid, from the Sala de Cabra-Cega, where royal parties played blind man's buff, to the heroic Sala de Hércules. More intimate are the rooms of King Carlos and his wife, which are much as he left them the day before his assassination in 1908.

Chapel
Despite later additions, the chapel has retained its coffered ceiling and other features from the early 16th century. It was here, on 3 December 1640, that the 8th Duke learnt that he was to become king.

Dining room

First floor

★ Sala dos Duques
Lining the ceiling of the Room of the Dukes are portraits of all the dukes of Bragança by the Italian Domenico Dupra (1689–1770), commissioned by João V. On the walls are Brussels tapestries of scenes from the life of Achilles.

The vast kitchen, which once regularly fed several hundred people, gleams with over 600 copper pots and pans, some large enough to bathe in.

Sala de Cabra-Cega

The armouries, in a series of vaulted rooms, display swords, crossbows, halberds and suits of armour.

Ground floor

The library is contained in several rooms and includes precious early works collected by King Manuel II in exile *(see p57)*.

Formal Gardens
The Jardim da Duquesa and the Jardim do Bosque are partly enclosed by palace walls, but can be seen from the dining-room windows. Their geometric formality reflects the palace's architectural style.

Entrance

STAR FEATURE

★ Sala dos Duques

VISITORS' CHECKLIST

Terreiro do Paço. [C] 268-
980 659. ☐ 9:30am–1pm,
2–5pm Tue–Fri; 9:30am–1pm,
2:30–6pm Sat–Sun. (Last
admission one hour before
closing.) ● 1 Jan, Easter, 25
Dec, 1 May. 📷 🎟 compulsory.

KEY TO FLOORPLAN

☐	Royal rooms
▨	Library
☐	Chapel
▨	Armouries
☐	Kitchen
▨	Treasury
☐	Public areas

PALACE GUIDE

*Guided tours, which last
about an hour, take in the
royal rooms ranged along the
first floor and ground-floor
areas such as the kitchen and
the treasury. Entry to the coach
museum, on the north side of
the palace, and armoury is
by separate tickets. From
time to time areas may
be closed for restora-
tion and rooms
can be shut off
without notice.*

Vila Viçosa ❾

Road map D5. 🏘 10,000. 🚌
ℹ️ Praça da República (268-88
11 01). 🛒 Wed.

AFTER THE EXPULSION of the
Moors in 1226, this hill-
side town was named Val
Viçosa – "fertile valley". In the
15th century it became the
country seat of the dukes of
Bragança, and when the 8th
Duke became King João IV,
Vila Viçosa was expanded to
meet the needs of nobles
and visiting ministers. Substantial houses, built from the
local white marble, in streets
lined with orange trees, reflect
its prosperous royal past.

The town is full of reminders
of the Braganças. Dominating
the west side of the Terreiro do
Paço is the long façade of the
Paço Ducal, which stretches
for 110 m (360 ft). Visitors to
the palace emerge through the
Porta do Nó, a marble and
schist gateway formed into the
knot symbol of the Braganças.

In the centre of the square a
statue of João IV on horseback
looks across to the **Igreja dos
Agostinhos** (not open to the
public). Founded in 1267 but
rebuilt in the 17th century, the
church was intended as the last
resting place of the dukes, but
despite their affection for Vila
Viçosa, most Bragança monarchs are buried in Lisbon, at
São Vicente de Fora *(see p72)*.

**View from the castle at Vila Viçosa,
looking towards the Paço Ducal**

In the Renaissance **Convento
das Chagas**, on the south side
of the square, are the tombs of
the Bragança wives. Founded
by the 4th Duke's second wife
in 1530, the convent is being
converted to a *pousada*.

Alongside the Paço Ducal, an
18-km (11-mile) wall rings the
tapada real, or royal chase.
Uphill from the Terreiro do
Paço is the **castle**, where an
exhibition explains the history
of the hunt. The castle, built by
King Dinis, was the Braganças'
residence from 1461 until the
Paço Ducal became habitable.

In the nearby 14th-century
church of **Nossa Senhora da
Conceição** stands a Gothic
image of the Virgin, said to be
from England. During the 1646
cortes João IV crowned her as
patron saint of Portugal, after
which no Portuguese monarch
ever wore a crown.

♠ **Castle**
Avenida Duques de Bragança.
[C] 268-980 128. ☐ Tue–Sun.
● public hols. 📷

**The Porta do Nó, its carved knots
the symbol of the Braganças**

THE ROYAL HOUSE OF BRAGANÇA

**Catherine, born at
Vila Viçosa in 1638**

Afonso, illegitimate son of João I, was
created Duke of Bragança in 1442,
first of an influential but bloodstained
dynasty. Fernando, the 3rd Duke, was
executed in 1483 by his cousin, João
II, who feared his power. Jaime, the
unstable 4th Duke, locked up his wife
in Bragança castle *(see p258)*, then
killed her at Vila Viçosa. It was Dom
Jaime who initiated the building of
the palace at Vila Viçosa, an ambitious
work embellished by later dukes to
reflect their aspirations and affluence.

The 8th Duke only reluctantly relinquished a life of music
and hunting here to take up the throne *(see p50)*.

The Braganças ruled Portugal for 270 years, accumulating
wealth and forging alliances (João IV's daughter, Catherine,
married Charles II of England), but inbreeding enfeebled the
bloodline *(see p165)*. The last monarch, Manuel II, fled to
exile in 1910, two years after his father and brother were shot
by Republicans. The present duke farms quietly near Viseu.

Alandroal, surrounded by groves of cork oaks

Alandroal ❿

Road map D5. 🏘 *2,100.* 🚌
ℹ️ *Largo da Misericordia (268-440 045).* 🅿️ *Wed.*

THE LOW-LYING little town of Alandroal, wrapped tidily around its **castle** ruins, was built by the Knights of Avis, who settled here from 1220. Little remains inside, but a surviving inscription shows it was completed in 1298. The **Igreja Matriz** within its walls dates from the 16th century.

The **Misericórdia** church near the castle walls contains beautiful *azulejos* reputed to be the work of Policarpo de Oliveira Bernardes (1695–1778).

ENVIRONS: Terena, 10 km (6 miles) south of Alandroal, is well known for its pottery. The 14th-century sanctuary of **Nossa Senhora de Boa Nova** has frescoes covering its walls and ceiling; dating from 1706, these depict saints and Portuguese kings. For access ask at the house opposite the church.

MARBLE: ALENTEJO'S WHITE GOLD

Portugal is the world's second largest exporter of marble, and even Italy, the biggest producer, buys Portugal's quality stone. Around 90 per cent – over 500,000 tonnes a year – is quarried around Estremoz. The marble from Estremoz and nearby Borba is white or pink, while the quarries at Viana do

Quarrymen near Estremoz, working on elephantine blocks of prized marble

Alentejo yield green stone. Marble has been used for construction since Roman times and in towns such as Évora *(see pp302–5)* and Vila Viçosa *(see pp298–9)*, palaces and humble doorsteps alike gleam with the stone often referred to as Portugal's "white gold".

Redondo ⓫

Road map D5. 🏘 *3,600.* 🚌
ℹ️ *Praça da República (266-909 100).* 🅿️ *2nd Thu of month.*

THE CENTRE OF ONE of the Alentejo's wine regions *(see p29),* medieval Redondo is also renowned for its pottery. Whole families work to produce Roman-style water jugs, casseroles and bowls painted with humorous folk-art motifs *(see p25).* These are sold from the tiny white houses leading up to the ruins of the **castle** founded by King Dinis.

ENVIRONS: The **Convento de São Paulo** in the Serra de Ossa, 10 km (6 miles) north, was built in 1376; Catherine of Bragança stayed here on her return home in 1692 after the death of her husband, King Charles II of England. It is now a luxury hotel *(see p396),* but retains its wonderful 16th- to 18th-century *azulejos.*

Estremoz ⓬

Road map D5. 🏘 *8,000.* 🚌
ℹ️ *Largo da República 26 (268-33 35 41).* 🅿️ *Sat.*

A KEY STRONGHOLD in the War of Restoration *(see p50)* and then in the War of the Two Brothers *(see p54),* Estremoz looks out from its hilltop over groves of gnarled olive trees.
The medieval upper town, set within stout ramparts, is dominated by a 13th-century marble keep, rising to 27 m (89 ft). This is the **Torre das Três Coroas**, the Tower of the Three Crowns, recalling the kings (Sancho II, Afonso III and Dinis) in whose reigns it was built. The adjoining castle and palace complex, built for Dona Isabel, is now restored as a *pousada (see p395).* The saintly Isabel *(see p45),* wife of King Dinis, died here in 1336 and the **Capela da Rainha Santa** dedicated to her is lined with *azulejos* recording her life.
Today the bustling weekly market in the Rossio, the main square in the lower town, is a reflection of local farming life. Across the square are the remains of King Dinis's once-fine

palace and the town's **Museu Municipal**, with a display of archaeological finds, restored living rooms and a parade of *bonecos*, the charming pottery figurines for which Estremoz is famous *(see p25)*.

🏛 **Museu Municipal**
Largo Dom Dinis. 📞 *268-33 92 00.*
⭕ *Tue–Sun.* ⚫ *public hols.* 📷
⛪ **Capela da Rainha Santa**
Largo Dom Dinis. (Entrance through adjacent Design Gallery.) ⭕ *Design Gallery staff will open on request.*

Évoramonte ⓫

Road map D5. 🏘 *1,000.* 🚌
ℹ *Junta de Freguesia (268-95 02 00).*

Stone "rope" embellishing the castle walls at Évoramonte

ABOVE THE DOORWAY of No. 41, along Évoramonte's single street, is a historic plaque. It records that here, on 26 May 1834, Dom Miguel ceded the throne, ending the conflict with his older brother *(see p54)*.

Évoramonte's eye-catching **castle**, its walls bound by bold stone "ropes", largely replaced an earlier castle that fell in an earthquake in 1531. The 16th-century walls, however, have been controversially "restored" with concrete. An exhibition explains the castle's history.

⛫ **Castle**
⭕ *Tue–Sun.* 📷

Arraiolos ⓮

Road map D5. 🏘 *2,400.* 🚌
ℹ *Praça Lima e Brito (266 490 254).*
📅 *1st Sat of month.*

THE FOUNDATION of Arraiolos is attributed either to Celts or perhaps to local tribes in about 300 BC. Its 14th-century **castle** seems overwhelmed by the town walls and

looming 16th-century **Igreja do Salvador**. Typically, houses in Arraiolos are low and white, and are painted with a blue trim to ward off the devil.

The principal sight in Arraiolos, however, is of women stitching at their bright wool rugs in the shadowy rooms behind the main street. Carpets have been woven in Arraiolos since the 13th century and decorate countless manor houses and palaces throughout Portugal. The craft may have begun with the Moors, but floral designs of the 18th century are thought to be the finest. At the many carpet shops here it is also possible to see a range of contemporary designs with their bright colours and less elaborate patterns.

ENVIRONS: At **Pavia**, 18 km (11 miles) to the north, is the startling sight of a tiny chapel built into a dolmen. It is signposted as Anta de São Dinis; if closed, ask at the café nearby.

Montemor-o-Novo ⓯

Road map C5. 🏘 *7,000.* 🚌
ℹ *Largo Calouste Gulbenkian (266-898 103).* 📅 *2nd Sat of month.*

MONTEMOR WAS fortified by the Romans and then by the Moors – the Arab warrior Al-Mansur is remembered in the name of the nearby River

The view down the nave of the Igreja Matriz in Montemor-o-Novo

Almançor. The town, regained from the Moors in the reign of Sancho I, was awarded its first charter in 1203. The **castle**, rebuilt in the late 13th century, is now a ruin crowning the hill.

Montemor's 17th-century **Igreja Matriz** stands in Largo São João de Deus, named after the saint who was born nearby in 1495. The Order of Brothers Hospitallers that St John of God founded evolved from his care for the sick, especially foundlings and prisoners.

A former convent in the upper town is now the **Museu de Arqueologia** and **Museu Regional**. The former has local archaeological finds and antique farming tools, the latter has a series of themed rooms on pottery and sacred art.

🏛 **Museu de Arqueologia**
Convento de São Domingos, Largo Professor Dr Banha de Andrade.
📞 *266-890 235.* ⭕ *Tue–Sun.* 📷

Arraiolos, crowned by its castle and the Igreja do Salvador

Street-by-Street: Évora ⑯

RISING OUT OF the Alentejan plain is the
enchanting walled city of Évora. The
town rose to prominence under the Romans
and flourished throughout the Middle Ages
as a centre of learning and the arts. It was a
popular residence of Portuguese kings, but
fell out of favour after Spain's annexation
of Portugal in 1580. Its influence waned
further when the Jesuit university closed in
the 18th century. Students once again throng
Évora's streets, joined by visitors who come
to discover its many historical sites and enjoy
the atmosphere of the old town. The city's
historic legacy was officially recognized in
1986, when UNESCO declared Évora
a World Heritage Site.

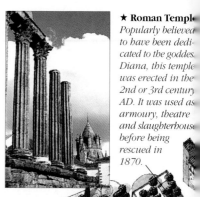

★ Roman Temple
*Popularly believed
to have been dedi-
cated to the goddess
Diana, this temple
was erected in the
2nd or 3rd century
AD. It was used as
armoury, theatre
and slaughterhouse
before being
rescued in
1870.*

Rua 5 de Outubro
*The shops along this street sell
curios and handicrafts, from
painted chairs to carved cork.*

```
0 metres        50
0 yards         50
```

KEY

– – – Suggested route

PRAÇA DO
GIRALDO

Tourist
information

Praça do Giraldo
*The fountain in Évora's main square was erected in
1571. Its marble predecessor received the first water
delivered by the town's aqueduct (see p305).*

RUA DO SALVADOR
RUA DE DONA ISABEL
RUA DAS CASAS PINTADAS
PRAÇA DO SERTÓRIO
RUA DE VASCO DA GAMA
RUA JOÃO DE DEUS
RUA NOVA
RUA 5 DE OUTUBRO
RUA DA REPÚBLICA

To
railway
and bus
stations

STAR SIGHTS
★ Sé
★ Roman Temple
★ Museu de Évora

Convento dos Lóios

This 15th-century monastery is now a luxurious pousada, where guests sleep in cells and dine in the cloisters (see p395). The convent's white-fronted church, known as Os Lóios or São João Evangelista, contains some notable 18th-century azulejos.

VISITORS' CHECKLIST

Map D5. 55,000. Largo da Estação. Estrada de Lisboa. Praça do Giraldo (266-730 030). Sat & 2nd Tue of month. Jun: Festa de São João; beg. Sep in odd years: the notable Evora air show.

Old University *(see p304)*

Roman walls

★ Museu de Évora

The city's museum (see p304) includes works by artists who painted in Évora, such as the early 16th-century Two Bishop-Saints by the Master of Sardoal.

Casa de Garcia de Resende

The house of the Renaissance poet and diplomat, Garcia de Resende (1470–1536), is distinguished by a remarkable Manueline window.

★ Sé

Évora's cathedral (see p304), which took over 50 years to complete, has the look of a fortress about it. The portal is flanked by a pair of unmatched towers.

Largo do Marquês de Marialva

The Igreja da Misericórdia is noted for its panels of early 18th-century *azulejos (see p22).*

Nossa Senhora da Graça

Above the Palladian façade of this 16th-century church loom four muscular figures supporting globes. They are quaintly nicknamed Os Meninos, "the children".

Exploring Évora

SQUEEZED WITHIN ROMAN, medieval and 17th-century walls, Évora's web of streets is an architectural and cultural cornucopia. From the forbidding cathedral, a stroll down past the craft shops of Rua 5 de Outubro leads to Praça do Giraldo, the city's lively main square, whose arcades are a reminder of Moorish influence. Évora's religious dedication is reflected in the number and variety of its churches – over 20 churches and monasteries, including a grisly chapel of bones. On a happier note, Évora's restaurants are excellent and the pleasure of wandering the historic streets is enhanced by evocative names such as Alley of the Unshaven Man and Street of the Countess's Tailor.

Azulejos at the Old University, depicting Aristotle teaching Alexander

⛪ Sé

Largo do Marquês de Marialva.
📞 266-759 330. ◯ daily (museum Tue–Sun). 🖼 to cloister & museum.
Begun in 1186 and consecrated in 1204, the granite cathedral of Santa Maria was completed by 1250. Romanesque melds with Gothic in this castle-like cathedral whose towers, one turreted, one topped by a blue cone, give the façade an odd asymmetry. Flanking the portal between them are superb 14th-century sculpted Apostles. The 18th-century high altar and marble chancel are by JF Ludwig, the architect of the monastery at Mafra (see pp52–3). A Renaissance portal in the north transept is by Nicolau Chanterène. In the cloisters, which date from about 1325, statues of the Evangelists stand watch at each corner.

A glittering treasury houses sacred art. The most intriguing exhibit here is a 13th-century ivory Virgin whose body opens out to become a triptych of tiny carved scenes: her life in nine episodes.

🏛 Museu de Évora

Largo do Conde de Vila Flor.
📞 266-702 604. ◯ Tue–Sun. ● some public hols. 🖼
This 16th-century palace, once the residence of governors and bishops, is now the regional museum. Évora's long history is represented here, from Roman columns to modern sculpture in creamy local marble. A beautiful Moorish window came from the old town hall, and a stone frieze probably from the Roman temple. Notable upstairs are *The Life of the Virgin*, a 16th-century

Carved figures of the Apostles decorating the Gothic entrance to the Sé

Flemish polyptych in 13 panels and works by the Portuguese painter known as the Master of Sardoal, especially his *Two Bishop-Saints* and a *Nativity*.

🏛 University

Largo dos Colegiais. 📞 266-740 800. ◯ daily. ● public hols. 🖼 Sat & Sun.
With the establishment of the Jesuits' Colégio do Espírito Santo, Évora, already noted for its architecture and sacred art, became a seat of learning. The school, which was inaugurated in 1559 by Cardinal Henrique, brother of João III, flourished for 200 years, but was closed in 1759 when the reforming Marquês de Pombal banished the Jesuits (see p53).

Today part of the University of Évora, the school still has a graceful cloister and notable *azulejos* – in the classrooms they depict suitably studious themes such as Plato lecturing to disciples (1744–9). The 18th-century Baroque chapel, now the Sala dos Actos, is used for graduation ceremonies.

🏛 Praça do Giraldo

Évora's bustling main square is bounded along its eastern side by a series of graceful Moorish arcades. The name Giraldo, some say, stems from Geraldo Sem-Pavor (the Fearless), an outlaw who in 1165 ousted the Moors for King Afonso Henriques.

The square has witnessed some bloody acts: João II watched the beheading of his brother-in-law, the Duke of Bragança, here in 1483, and it was the site in 1573 of an Inquisitional burning. Today, it is a favourite meeting-place, especially on market days.

⛪ São Francisco

Praça 1° de Maio. 📞 266-704 521. ◯ daily. 🖼 to Capela dos Ossos.
The principal fascination of this 15th-century church is its Capela dos Ossos. This gruesome chapel of bones was created in the 17th century from the remains of 5,000 monks. Two leathery corpses, one of a child, dangle from a chain, and a mordant reminder at the entrance reads: *Nós ossos que aqui estamos, pelos vossos esperamos* (We bones that are here await yours).

Largo da Porta de Moura, with its striking Renaissance fountain

🏛 Largo da Porta de Moura

The western entrance to this square is guarded by the vestiges of a Moorish gateway. Both the domed Casa Soure and the double arches of the belvedere on Casa Cordovil at the opposite end, show the Arab influence on architecture in Évora. The central fountain, looking like some futuristic orb, surprisingly dates back to 1556. Just south of the square, the portal of the Convento do Carmo features the knot symbol, denoting it once belonged to the Braganças (*see p299*).

🌿 Jardim Público

🕐 *daily.* ♿

On the southern edge of the old town, Évora's public gardens are set out on the site of the grandiose Palácio de Dom Manuel, built for Afonso V (1438–81) and embellished by successive kings. It was the venue for grand banquets and ceremonies but fell into disrepair and finally disappeared in 1895. All that remains is the graceful Galeria das Damas, a 20th-century reconstruction of a walkway and pavilion built for Manuel I (1495–1521).

⚔ Walls

The fortifications that have protected Évora down the centuries form two incomplete concentric circles. The inner ring, of which only fragments are discernible, is Roman, from perhaps as early as the 1st century AD, with Moorish and medieval additions – the two stubby towers that give the Largo da Porta de Moura its name mark an Arab gate.

In the 14th century, new walls were built to encompass the growing town. Completed under Fernando I, these had 40 towers and ten gates, including the Porta de Alconchel, which still faces the Lisbon road.

When João IV was defiantly declared king in 1640 (*see p50*), major fortifications were erected on this outer ring in anticipation of Spanish attack, and it is these 17th-century walls which are most evident today. The fear of attack was not unfounded, and the walls withstood much battering from the besieging Spanish in 1663.

Surviving arches of Évora's 16th-century aqueduct

⛲ Aqueduto da Água de Prata

Évora's aqueduct, evocatively called "of the silver water", was built between 1531 and 1537 by the town's own eminent architect, Francisco de Arruda. The construction was regarded with wonder, and is even described in Os Lusíadas, the epic by Luís de Camões (*see p188*). It originally carried water as far as the Praça do Giraldo. Like the walls, it was damaged in the 17th century during the Restoration War with Spain, but a surviving stretch, some 9 km (5 miles) long, can still be seen approaching from the northwest: there is a good view of it from Rua Cândido dos Reis.

THE ROMANS IN THE ALENTEJO

Once the Romans gained dominance over Lusitania (*see pp40–41*), they turned the Alentejo into a vast wheatfield: their very name for the principal town – Ebora Cerealis (Évora) – reflects the importance of the region's grain supply. *Latifúndios*, large farms instigated by the Romans, survive to this day, as do Roman open-cast copper and iron mines. Local marble was used in the construction of the finest villas, and Roman remains are to be found scattered throughout the region, particularly in Évora and Beja (*see p311*) and in more isolated sites such as São Cucufate, near Vidigueira (*see p310*) and Miróbriga, near Santiago do Cacém (*see p312*).

Roman bridge over the Odivelas, near Vidigueira

Megaliths Tour ⑰

ARCHAEOLOGISTS DATE the *pedras talhas*, hewn stones, near Évora to between 4000 and 2000 BC. Their symbolism remains mysterious. Dolmens are thought to be where Neolithic communities buried their dead, together with their possessions – more than 130 have been found in the region. Tall phallic menhirs jutting from olive groves immediately suggest fertility rites, while cromlechs, carved stones standing in regulated groups, probably had religious significance. This tour includes examples of each; more can be found further east, near Monsaraz, and the museum in Montemor-o-Novo *(see p301)* has finds related to the area.

Menhir of Almendres ②
Standing 2.5 m (8 ft) tall, this solitary stone is located away from the cromlech, in an olive grove behind a row of tall Cooperativa Agrícola storage bins.

Cromlech of Almendres ③
This oval, made up of 95 ellipitical stones, is believed to have been a temple dedicated to a solar cult. The route to the cromlech is signposted from the N114.

Grutas do Escoural ⑥
Discovered in 1963, these caves contain paintings about 15–20,000 years old.

Évora ①
In the undulating farmland around the historic city of Évora *(see pp302–5)* at least 150 megalith sites have been found.

MONTEMOR-O-NOVO   ARRAIOLOS

N370

Aiesteira

São Matias

Guadalupe

N114

MONTEMOR-O-NOVO

Senhora da Boa Fé

③ ②

④

N380

①

Santiago do Escoural

São Brissos

Valverde

ALCÁÇOVAS

Dolmen of Zambujeiro ④
This, the largest dolmen in Portugal, has an entrance passage 14 m (46 ft) long leading to a chamber built of enormous stones. It is off the beaten track; the route from Valverde leads across farmland.

Dolmen-chapel of São Brissos ⑤
Beyond the hamlet of Brissos, this tiny chapel has been created from an *anta* or dolmen. Another is to be found at Pavia *(see p301)*.

KEY

▰▰▰ Tour route

═══ Other roads

0 kilometres   5

0 miles   3

TIPS FOR DRIVERS

Tour length: 80 km (50 miles).
Access to sites: The only guarded site is Escoural. The caves are closed at lunchtime, on Mondays and at some other times. Access roads to the sites are often no more than tracks, and signposting can be erratic. (See pp444–5.)

Riding through the narrow streets of Monsaraz on the day of a bullfight

Monsaraz ⑱

Road map D5. 🏠 *150.* 🚌
🛈 *Largo Dom Nuno Álvares Pereira 5 (266-557 136).*

THE TINY MEDIEVAL walled town of Monsaraz perches above the River Guadiana on the frontier with Spain. Now a pretty backwater, it has known more turbulent times. Regained from the Moors in 1167 by the intrepid adventurer Geraldo Sem-Pavor (the Fearless), the town was handed over to the militant Knights Templar. Its frontier position continued to expose it to Spanish attack, but in 1381 assault came from an unexpected quarter. Troops of the Earl of Cambridge, Portugal's ally, were enraged by lack of pay and the annulment of the earl's betrothal to Fernando I's daughter, and unleashed their wrath on Monsaraz.

Principal access to the town is through the massive Porta da Vila. Rua Direita, the main street, leads up to the **castle**. Built by Afonso III and Dinis in the 13th century as part of the border defences, it was reinforced in the 17th century. The keep commands glorious views in all directions and at its foot is the garrison courtyard which today serves on occasion as a bullring.

The 16th-century **Igreja Matriz** in Rua Direita is worth visiting for its tall gilded altars and painted pillars. The 17th- and 18th-century houses along here display coats of arms. In the Gothic Paços da Audiência, now the **Museu de Arte Sacra,** is a collection of vestments, religious books and sculpture. Its earlier role as a law court is reflected in an unusual secular fresco: *O Bom e o Mau Juiz* (The Good and Bad Judge).

🏛 Museu de Arte Sacra
Largo Dom Nuno Álvares Pereira.
⭘ *Tue–Sun.* 🈂

ENVIRONS: Surrounded by vineyards, **Reguengos de Monsaraz**, 16 km (10 miles) west, lies at the heart of one of the region's demarcated wine areas *(see p29)*. Its 19th-century church, Santo António, was built in flamboyant Neo-Gothic style by the architect of Lisbon's bullring *(see p120)*.

A number of striking megaliths are found near Monsaraz. The spectacular **Menhir of Outeiro**, 5.6 m (18 ft) tall, and the strangely inscribed **Menhir of Bulhôa** are signposted in Telheiro, just north of Monsaraz. About 4 km (2 miles) south is the **Cromlech of Xerez**, a menhir in a square of lesser stones.

The tiny houses of **Mourão**, some 8 km (5 miles) further on, have huge chimneys. The town's 14th-century castle looks out over the River Guadiana and vast new Alqueva Dam.

Viana do Alentejo ⑲

Road map D6. 🏠 *3,500.* 🚌
🛈 *Praça da República (266-93 01 12).* 📅 *2nd & last Thu of month.*

THE NATURAL SPRINGS of Viana do Alentejo have offered an abundant water source in the Alentejo's dry heartland since Roman times. Its **castle**, begun in 1313, was built to the design of King Dinis, the height of the outer wall exactly calculated to protect soldiers from attacking lancers. The unusual cylindrical towers show a Moorish influence and much of the later remodelling dates from João II, who held a *cortes* here in 1481–2.

Mirroring the castle walls are the crenellations and pinnacles of the adjacent 16th-century **Igreja Matriz**. The highly carved Manueline entrance to this splendid fortified church leads into a majestic triple-naved interior.

Ten minutes' walk east of the town stands the vast pilgrimage church of **Nossa Senhora de Aires**, rebuilt in the 1700s. Inside, the chancel's golden canopy contrasts with pilgrims' humble ex votos.

ENVIRONS: The Moorish-style castle at **Alvito**, 10 km (6 miles) south of Viana, was built in 1482 for the newly ennobled Barão de Alvito; it now operates as a *pousada (see p395).*

The low roofs and distinctive pepperpot chimneys of Mourão, near Monsaraz

A bullfight in the shadow of the 13th-century keep of Monsaraz castle ▷

The vineyards around Vidigueira caught in the evening light

Vidigueira ⑳

Road map D6. 👥 *2,800.* 🚌
🛈 *Piscinas Municipais (284-434 492).*
🗓 *2nd Sat of month.*

Fine wines from Vidigueira make it a leading centre of wine production in the Alentejo. Less well known is the fact that the explorer Vasco da Gama was Conde de Vidigueira. His remains, now in the Mosteiro dos Jerónimos (*see pp106–7*), lay from 1539 to 1898 in the Convento do Carmo, now private property. A mediocre statue of the town's most famous son stands in the flowery square named after him. The main features of this unpretentious little town are a **Misericórdia** church dated 1620, and a clocktower from Vasco da Gama's time.

Environs: One of Portugal's most notable Roman sites, **São Cucufate**, named after a later monastery, lies 4 km (2 miles) west. The vaulting belonged to a 4th-century villa, but excavations have revealed the baths of a 2nd-century house, whose wine presses, reservoir and temple indicate a sumptuous Roman residence.

Moura ㉑

Road map D6. 👥 *12,000.* 🚌
🛈 *Largo de Santa Clara (285-25 13 75).* 🗓 *1st Sat of month.*

Legend mingles with history in this quiet town among oak and olive trees. Salúquia, daughter of a Moorish governor is said to have thrown herself from the castle tower on learning that her lover had been killed. From this tragedy the town acquired its name – Moura, the Moorish girl. The town's old Moorish quarter is an area of narrow streets and low, whitewashed houses.

Even after the Reconquest in the 12th century, Moura's frontier position left it open to attack. A siege in 1657, during the War of Restoration (*see pp50–51*), levelled much of it. The 13th-century **castle** survived, only to be blown up by the Spanish in 1707 – just a skeletal keep and wall remain. **Nossa Senhora do Carmo**, near the castle, was founded in 1251, the first Carmelite convent in the country. Its two-storey cloister shows Gothic and Renaissance influence and the chancel ceiling frescoes are early 18th century.

View over Moura's quaint Moorish quarter

Serpa ㉒

Road map D6. 👥 *4,800.* 🚌
🛈 *Largo Dom Jorge de Melo 2–3 (284-54 47 27).* 🗓 *last Tue of month.*

After peaceful vistas of olive trees, Serpa's stout walls, topped by an arched aqueduct, come as a surprise. Beside the monumental **Porta de Beja** is a *nora*, or Arab water wheel. Won from the Moors in 1232, Serpa successfully resisted foreign control until a brief Spanish occupation in 1707.

Today, Serpa is a quiet agricultural town that produces an esteemed ewe's-milk cheese. Pleasing squares and streets of houses that dazzle with the brilliance of their whitewash are overlooked by a **castle** of Moorish origin, rebuilt by King Dinis in the late 13th century. The **Convento de Santo António** in Rua da Ladeira was founded in the 15th century and is noted for its flamboyant 18th-century *azulejos*.

Serpa's great Porta de Beja

Environs: Serpa is just 35 km (22 miles) from the Spanish border. The Moors, and later Spain, fought for control of the region, which was finally ceded to Portugal in 1295. Continued disputes have left the legacy of a chain of watchtowers and a peppering of fortresses across these hills. One of the most notable, the deserted fort at **Noudar**, was built in 1346, but even in this isolated corner, evidence of pre-Roman habitation has been uncovered.

On the border at **Barrancos**, an incomprehensible mix of Spanish and Portuguese is spoken. A speciality here is *pata negra* (black trotter), a ham from the local black pigs.

LOVE LETTERS OF A HEARTSICK NUN

Mariana's window

Lettres Portugaises, published in French in 1669, are celebrated for their lyric beauty. They are the poignant letters of a nun whose French lover deserted her: she was Mariana Alcoforado, born in Beja in 1640; he was the Comte de Saint-Léger, later Marquis de Chamilly, fighting in the Restoration wars with Spain. The true authorship of the five letters may be in doubt, but the story of the lovelorn nun endures – Matisse even painted her imaginary portrait. Sentimental visitors to the convent of Nossa Senhora da Conceição (now the Museu Regional) in Beja still sigh over "Mariana's window".

Beja ㉓

Road map D6. 🏛 18,000. 🚊
🚌 🛈 Rua Capitão João
Francisco de Sousa 25 (284-31
19 13). 🗓 Sat.

CAPITAL of the Baixo (lower) Alentejo, Beja is a city of historic and social importance. It is also a major centre for the production of wheat, olives and cork, which are grown on the Bejan plains and provide the city's lifeblood.

The town became a regional capital under Julius Caesar, who called it Pax Julia after the peace made here with the Lusitani *(see p40)*. The Praça da República marks the site of the Roman forum. The Moors arrived in AD 711, giving the town its present name and a lively, poetic culture until they were forced out in 1162.

More recently, Beja has been the scene of struggles against oppressive regimes. In 1808, occupying French troops

massacred the inhabitants and sacked the city, and in 1962, during the Salazar regime *(see pp56–7)*, General Delgado led an unsuccessful uprising here.

Beja's old town, an area of narrow, often cobbled, streets, stretches from the castle keep southeast to the 13th-century convent of São Francisco, now a superb *pousada (see p395)*.

🏛 Museu Regional Rainha Dona Leonor

Largo da Conceição. 📞 284-32 33 51.
🕐 Tue–Sun. 🌑 public hols. 🎫
In the heart of the old town, the former Convento de Nossa Senhora da Conceição houses the regional museum. A little marble ossuary near the entrance contains the bones of the convent's first abbess. Exhibits are mostly paintings and coats of arms, but the building itself is a remarkable blend of architectural styles, with a Gothic church portal, Manueline windows and a dazzling Baroque chapel. Its

azulejos are especially beautiful, the most notable being the Hispanic-Arab tiles in the chapterhouse and the early 16th-century examples in the cloister. Upstairs is a section on local archaeology and the romantic "Mariana's window".

♣ Torre de Menagem

Largo do Lidador. 📞 284-31 18 00.
🕐 Tue–Sun. 🌑 public hols. 🎫
The unmistakable landmark of the castle keep marks the northwest limit of the old quarter. This work of King Dinis in the late 13th century towers 36 m (118 ft) high. The 183-step climb up through its three storeys provides a rewarding panorama from the top.

Beja's landmark castle keep

🏛 Museu Visigótico

Largo de Santo Amaro. 📞 284-323
351. 🕐 Tue–Sun. 🌑 public hols.
🎫 joint ticket with Museu Regional.
Just beyond the castle keep stands Beja's oldest church, Santo Amaro, its columns surviving from its Visigothic origins. Appropriately, the church now serves as an exhibition area for the Museu Regional's collection of relics from this early but important period of Portugal's history.

ENVIRONS: The remains of the luxurious **Roman villa** at Pisões, 10 km (6 miles) southwest of Beja, date from the 1st century AD. Excavation is far from complete, but extensive floor mosaics and fragments of decorated walls, baths, a bathing pool and hypocaust have been uncovered.

🏛 Roman villa

Herdade de Almocreva, Estrada de
Aljustrel (follow signs). 🕐 Tue–Sun.

Chapterhouse of the former convent, now Beja's Museu Regional

Igreja Matriz, Santiago do Cacém

Santiago do Cacém ❷

Road map C6. 🏠 6,000. 🚌
ℹ️ *Largo do Mercado (269-82 66 96).*
📅 *2nd Mon of month.*

Santiago do cacém's Moorish castle was rebuilt in 1157 by the Templars *(see pp184–5)*. Its walls, which enclose the cemetery of the adjacent 13th-century **Igreja Matriz**, afford panoramic views of the Serra de Grândola to the northeast. The attractive main square is enhanced by the elegant 18th-century mansions built by rich landowners who came here to escape the heat of the plains.

The **Museu Municipal** still retains some cells from its days as a Salazarist prison *(see p56)*. Exhibits here include Roman finds from nearby Miróbriga.

🏛 Museu Municipal
Largo do Município. 📞 *269-82 73 75.*
🕐 *Tue–Fri, Sat & Sun (pm only).*
⬤ *public hols.*

ENVIRONS: On a hill just to the east of Santiago do Cacém lies the site of the Roman city of **Miróbriga**. Excavations, still in progress, have uncovered a forum, two temples, thermal baths and a circus which had seating for 25,000 spectators.

⋔ Miróbriga
Signposted off N121. 📞 *269-825 148.*
🕐 *Tue–Sun.* ⬤ *public hols.* ♿

Sines ❷

Road map C6. 🏠 9,300. 🚢 🚌
ℹ️ *Castelo de Sines (269-63 44 72).*
📅 *1st Thu of month.*

The birthplace of Vasco da Gama *(see p108)* is now a major industrial port and tanker terminal ringed with refinery pipelines. Once past this heavy industrial zone visitors reach the old town with its popular sandy beach, but it is not always possible to escape the haze of pollution.

A prominent landmark above the beach is the modest medieval **castle**, restored in the 16th century by King Manuel. It was here that Vasco da Gama, son of the *alcaide-mor*, or mayor, is reputed to have been born in 1469, and a museum dedicated to the great navigator is to be housed in the castle keep. A modern statue of Vasco da Gama stands looking out over the bay.

The **Museu Arqueológico** in the town displays striking jewellery, perhaps Phoenician, found on a nearby estate.

🏛 Museu Arqueológico
Rua Francisco Luis Lopes 38. 📞 *269-63 23 30.* 🕐 *Tue–Sun.* ⬤ *public hols.*

ENVIRONS: North and south of Sines are attractive beaches. About 10 km (6 miles) south, **Porto Covo** is a picturesque village with an old fort above a cove beach. A little further to the south and a short boat ride offshore is the low hump of **Ilha do Pessegueiro**, Peach Tree Island. Treeless and windswept, with the ruins of a fort, the little island is rather less romantic than it sounds.

More appealing are two sea-blue lagoons, **Lagoa de Santo André** and **Lagoa de Melides**, set in a long stretch of sandy coast about 20 km (12 miles) north of Sines. The lagoons attract a commune of campers, but vast open spaces remain for seekers of privacy.

Whitewashed houses with the traditional blue trim at Porto Covo, south of Sines

Vila Nova de Milfontes ❷

Road map C6. 🏠 3,200. 🚌 ℹ️ *Rua António Mantas (283-996 599).* 📅 *2nd & 4th Sat of month in Brunheiras.*

One of the loveliest places on Portugal's west coast is where the River Mira meets the sea. The popular resort of Vila Nova de Milfontes, on the sleepy estuary, is low-key and unassuming, but offers many places to stay. Its small castle overlooking the bay once defended the coast from pirates, and is now a hotel. In contrast to the quiet river are the pretty beaches with their crashing waves, a major summer attraction, especially with surfers.

ENVIRONS: To the south about 10 km (6 miles) is the unspoilt beach of **Almograve**, backed by impressive cliffs.

The calm, sunny face of the sandy coast near Vila Nova de Milfontes

Zambujeira do Mar ㉗

Road map C7. 🏛 *1,000.* 🚌
ℹ️ *Rua Miramar (283-96 11 44).*

A NARROW STRIP of sheltered land divides the plains of the Alentejo from the bracing Atlantic. Here lies the solitary village of Zambujeira do Mar, the whiteness of its gorgeous beach enhanced by the dark backdrop of high basalt cliffs. Traditionally, families come here for Sunday beach outings, joined nowadays by campers and more adventurous tourists.

Mértola ㉘

Road map D6. 🏛 *1,200.* 🚌
ℹ️ *Rua Alonso Gomes (286-61 01 09).* 📅 *1st Thu of month.*

P RETTY, WHITEWASHED Mértola is of great historical interest. The whole of this small town is a *vila museu*, a museum site, with discoveries from different eras exhibited in *núcleos*, or areas where a concentration of treasures from that period can be found. The tourist office has details of each *núcleo*.

Mértola's origins date back to the Phoenicians, who created a thriving inland port here on the Guadiana, later enjoyed by the Romans and the Moors. Roman artefacts can be seen

Mértola's unusual Moorish-style church, high above the River Guadiana

at the **Núcleo Romano**, based at an excavation beneath the municipal council buildings.

The post-Roman period in Mértola is on display in the **Núcleo Visigótico** and in an early Christian **basilica** whose ruins adjoin the Roman road to Beja *(see p311)*. The influence bequeathed by several centuries of Moorish domination is seen in Mértola's **Núcleo Islâmico** which houses one of

the country's best collections of Portuguese Islamic art, and includes ceramics, coins and jewellery. The **Igreja Matriz** below the Moorish walls was formerly a mosque, unique in Portugal for being so little altered. Among surviving Arab features are the five-nave layout, four horseshoe arches and a *mihrab* or prayer niche.

Overlooking the town is the crumbling hilltop **castle**, with its keep of 1292, offering lovely views of the river valley.

ENVIRONS: The copper mines at **Minas de São Domingos**, 16 km (10 miles) to the east, were the main employer in the area from 1858 to 1965, when the vein was exhausted. An English company ran the mine under the harshest conditions, with miners' families living in one windowless room. The village's population has now fallen from 6,000 to 800, and the ghost-town atmosphere is relieved only by a reservoir and surrounding lush greenery.

Around Mértola, 600 sq km (230 sq miles) of the wild Guadiana valley is a newly designated **Parque Natural**, home to the black stork, azure-winged magpie and raptors such as the red kite.

THE VERSATILITY OF CORK

Groves of evergreen cork oak *(Quercus suber)* provide the Alentejo with welcome shade and a thriving industry. It was Dom Pérignon, the wine-making monk, who in the 17th century revived the use of cork as a tasteless, odourless seal for wine. Portugal, the world's largest cork producer, has almost 7,000 sq km (2,700 sq miles) under cultivation and turns out some 30 million corks a day. In rural areas, this versatile bark is fashioned into waterproof, heatproof food containers and these decorated boxes are a traditional craft of the Alentejo.

Harvesting cork is a skilled task. Mature trees, stripped in summer every ten years or so, reveal a raw red undercoat until their new bark grows.

The glowing red of a stripped tree in an Alentejan cork grove

ALGARVE

ENCLOSED BY RANGES OF HILLS *to the north, the Algarve has a climate, culture and scenery very different from the rest of Portugal. Its stunning coastline and year-round mild weather, maintained by warm sea and air currents from nearby North Africa, make it one of the most popular holiday destinations in southern Europe.*

The Algarve's fertile soil and strategic headlands and rivers have attracted visitors since the time of the Phoenicians. Five centuries of Arab rule, from AD 711, left a legacy that is still visible in the region's architecture, lattice chimneys, *azulejos*, orange groves and almond trees. Place names beginning with Al are also of Moorish origin; Al-Gharb ("the West") denoted the western edge of the Islamic empire.

When the Algarve was reclaimed by the Christians in 1249, the Portuguese rulers designated themselves kings "of Portugal and of the Algarves", emphasizing the region's separateness from the rest of the country. It was the Algarve, however, that shot Portugal to prominence in the 15th century, when Henry the Navigator *(see p49)* is said to have set up a school of navigation at Sagres, and launched the age of exploration from these southern shores.

The earthquake of 1755 *(see pp62–3)* had its epicentre just south of Lagos, then the region's capital. Virtually all the towns and villages were destroyed or badly damaged, which explains why very few buildings in the region predate this period.

Since the 1960s, when Faro airport was opened, international tourism has replaced agriculture and fishing as the region's main industry. A few stretches of the southwestern seashore are now cluttered with high-rise complexes catering for the yearly influx of tourists. However, the whole western seaboard exposed to the Atlantic and the lagoons east of Faro have been less affected by development. Trips inland, to the pretty whitewashed village of Alte or the border town of Alcoutim in the east, provide a welcome reminder that, in places, the Algarve's rural way of life continues virtually uninterrupted.

Colourful ceramic plates for sale outside a local craft shop in Alte

◁ **Strolling along the sandy Praia da Rocha near Portimão**

Exploring the Algarve

THE ALGARVE IS A DELIGHT to visit all year round. In summer, the coast between Faro and Lagos attracts thousands of visitors; but even near popular resorts such as Albufeira and Portimão it is possible to escape the crowds. Though often by-passed, Faro itself is well worth a visit. Picturesque Tavira is an ideal centre for the lagoons of the eastern Algarve, while from Lagos you can reach the beaches on the rugged southwest coast. Inland, the hillside villages are peaceful, with lush vegetation, both wild and cultivated. The wooded Serra de Monchique is an area of outstanding beauty offering lovely walks.

Wooded slopes around the vast lake created by the Bravura dam, north of Lagos

KEY

▬▬	Motorway
▬▬	Major road
▬▬	Minor road
▬▬	Scenic route
━━	River
☀	Viewpoint

Brightly painted fishing boats in the harbour at Sagres

One of the delightful sandy coves near Albufeira

SIGHTS AT A GLANCE

Albufeira ⑪
Alcoutim ㉔
Aljezur ①
Almancil ⑭
Alte ⑫
Alvor ⑧
Cabo de São Vicente ⑤
Cacela Velha ㉑
Castro Marim ㉓
Estoi ⑯
Faro pp326–8 ⑰
Lagos ⑦
Loulé ⑮
Monchique ③

Olhão ⑱
Parque Natural
  da Ria Formosa ⑲
Portimão ⑨
Sagres ⑥
Serra de Monchique ②
Silves ⑩
Tavira ⑳
Vila do Bispo ④
Vilamoura ⑬
Vila Real Santo António ㉒

GETTING AROUND

The A22 (E1) runs from Albufeira to Spain and has relieved the N125, which can become congested in summer. Roads branch off to beaches, coastal towns and inland villages.

A frequent but slow rail service connects the main towns, but stations are sometimes far from the centre. Reliable buses link coastal resorts and inland towns, though progress can be slow.

| 0 kilometres | 10 |
| 0 miles | 5 |

SEE ALSO

Whitewashed house and lattice-work chimney in Cacela Velha

Commanding view of the countryside from Aljezur's Moorish castle

Aljezur ❶

Road map 7C. 👥 *2,500.* 🚌
ℹ️ *Largo do Mercado (282-99 82 29).*
📅 *3rd Mon of month.*

THE SMALL VILLAGE of Aljezur is overlooked by a 10th-century **Moorish castle**, reached via the old quarter. Although now in ruins, a cistern and towers remain, and there are splendid views towards the Serra de Monchique.

Aljezur's **Igreja Matriz**, much rebuilt after the earthquake of 1755 *(see pp62–3)*, has a fine Neo-Classical altarpiece. Dating from about 1809, it was probably executed in the workshop of José da Costa of Faro.

ENVIRONS: From Aljezur, the wild and deserted beaches of the Algarve's west coast are easily explored, although a car

is essential. Open to the strong currents of the Atlantic, **Praia de Arrifana** 10 km (6 miles) southwest, and **Praia de Monte Clérigo**, 8 km (5 miles) northwest, are sandy, sweeping beaches backed by cliffs. On the Alentejo border, **Praia de Odeceixe** is a sheltered cove that is popular with surfers.

Serra de Monchique ❷

Road map 7C. 🚌 *Monchique.*
ℹ️ *Monchique.*

PROVIDING SHELTER from the north, this volcanic mountain range helps to ensure the mild southern climate of the Algarve. The highest point is **Fóia** at 902 m (2,959 ft). This, however, is less pleasantly wooded than **Picota**, which, at 773 m (2,536 ft), is the second highest peak. An impressive 4-km (2-mile) walk to this peak from Monchique passes among chestnut trees and fields of wild flowers. A spectacular panorama sweeps down to the Ponta de Sagres *(see p320)* and there are stunning views of the rest of the range. Whether you explore the Serra on foot or by car, there is a wonderful variety of vegetation to enjoy with rhododendron, mimosa, chestnut, pine, cork oak and patches of terraced fertile land in the valleys.

In recent years, the increased planting of fast-growing eucalyptus trees has given cause for concern. This highly flammable species is one of the reasons for the serious fires that break out all too often in the Serra.

The 68-km (42-mile) run along the N267 from Nave, just below Monchique, to Aljezur in the west, leads through a beautiful part of the Serra. The landscape is a mixture of woods and moorland, kept fertile by an abundant water supply. Cork oak grows here, home to the nuthatch and lesser-spotted woodpecker.

Monchique ❸

Road map 7C. 👥 *7,000.* 🚌
ℹ️ *Largo dos Chorões (282-91 11 89).*
📅 *2nd Fri of month.*

Manueline portal of the Igreja Matriz in Monchique

THE SMALL market town of Monchique is primarily famous for its altitude, 458 m (1,500 ft), and consequently spectacular views. It is also known for its wooden handicrafts, particularly the folding chairs which are believed to date back to Roman times.

The 16th-century **Igreja Matriz**, on the cobbled Rua da Igreja behind the main square, has an impressive Manueline doorway whose knotted columns end in unusual pinnacles. Above the town is the ruined monastery of **Nossa Senhora do Desterro**. This Franciscan house, founded in 1632 by Dom Pero da Silva, is now only a shell but it is worth visiting for the stunning views across to the peak of Picota.

The mountains of the Serra de Monchique rising above meadows of wild flowers

ENVIRONS: A delightful, tiny spa, 6 km (4 miles) south, **Caldas de Monchique** is set in the foothills of the Serra in peaceful wooded surroundings.

The hot, curative waters have attracted the ailing since Roman times, and even though João II died soon after taking them in 1495, their reputation has remained undiminished. In the summer, people come to be treated for skin, digestive and rheumatic complaints. As well as the wholesome spring water, the bars here offer the local firewater, *medronheira*.

The shady main square has a large, attractive handicraft centre and there are some pretty walks in the woods.

Vila do Bispo ❹

Road map 7C. 🏠 *7,000.* 🚌 ❗ *Sagres (282-624 873).* 🎪 *1st Thu of month.*

THE GRAND NAME of "The Bishop's Town" today refers to a peaceful village, rather remote in feel, which makes the crowds of central Algarve seem very far away. It acquired its name in the 17th century when it was donated to the see of Faro. The town's parish church, **Nossa Senhora da Conceição**, has a delightful interior decorated with 18th-century *azulejos* from the floor up to the wooden, painted ceiling, and a Baroque altarpiece dating from 1715.

ENVIRONS: The beaches in the area are remote and unspoiled. **Praia do Castelejo**, 5 km (3 miles) to the west, is accessible by a dirt road that

Baroque altarpiece inside Nossa Senhora da Conceição, Vila do Bispo

Promontory of Cabo de São Vicente jutting into the Atlantic Ocean

winds up from the village over moorland. The beach, set at the foot of steep cliffs, is large, sandy and surf-fringed. The intrepid can turn off this track for the 6 km (4 miles) journey to **Torre de Aspa**, an obelisk at 156 m (512 ft) marking the spot for spectacular views over the ocean. The road is quite rough, so it is advisable to walk the last 2 km (1 mile).

Cabo de São Vicente ❺

Road map 7C. 🚌 *to Sagres then taxi.* ❗ *Sagres (282-624 873).*

IN THE MIDDLE AGES, this windblown cape at the extreme southwest of Europe was believed to be the end of the world. The Romans called it the *Promontorium Sacrum* (Sacred Promontory), and today, with its 60-m (200-ft) cliffs fronting the Atlantic, it still presents a most awe-inspiring aspect. The ocean waves have created long, sandy beaches and carved deep caves into the cliffs.

Since the 15th century, Cabo de São Vicente has been an important reference point for shipping, and its present lighthouse has a 95-km (60-mile) range, said to be the most powerful in Europe. For even longer it has had religious associations, and its name arises from the legend that the body of St Vincent was washed ashore here in the 4th century. Prince Henry the Navigator (*see p49*) was also reputed to have lived here, but, if so, all traces of his Vila do Infante have disappeared. A number

of important naval battles have taken place off the Cape, including the defeat of a Spanish fleet in 1797 by the British admirals Jervis and Nelson.

Since 1988 the coast from Sines in the north to Burgau in the east has been made a nature reserve, providing important nesting grounds for Bonelli's eagle, kestrel, white stork, heron and numerous other bird species. There is also a colony of sea otters.

Clump of scented thyme near Cabo de São Vicente

FLOWERS OF THE WESTERN ALGARVE

The remote headlands of Cabo de São Vicente and Sagres are renowned in botanical circles for their flowers, which put on a strikingly colourful and aromatic display from February to May. The climate, underlying rock and comparative isolation of these headlands have given an intriguing, stunted appearance to the local vegetation. There is a great array of different species, including cistuses, squills, an endemic sea pink, junipers, lavenders, narcissi, milk-vetches and many other magnificent plants.

The enormous Rosa dos Ventos wind compass on Ponta de Sagres

Sagres ➏

Road map 7C. 🏘 *3,500.* 🚌
ℹ *Rua Comandante Matoso (282-62 48 73).* 🏛 *1st Fri of month.*

THE SMALL TOWN of Sagres has little to offer except a picturesque harbour. Essentially it is a good base from which to explore the superb beaches *(see p286)* and isolated peninsula west of the town. Henry the Navigator *(see p49)* built a fortress on this windswept promontory and, according to tradition, a school of navigation and a shipyard. From here he realized his dream "to see what lay beyond the Canaries and Cape Bojador … and attempt the discovery of things hidden from men". From 1419–60, he poured his energy and the revenues of the Order of Christ *(see p185)*, of which he was master, into building caravels and sending his fear-stricken sailors into unknown waters.

In 1434 Gil Eanes of Lagos was the first sailor to round the dreaded Cape Bojador, in the region of Western Sahara. With this feat, the west coast of Africa was opened up for exploration *(see pp48–9)* and Portugal poised for expansion.

Little remains of Prince Henry's original fortress: the walls that can be seen today are part of a 17th-century fort. Still visible is the giant pebble wind compass, the **Rosa dos Ventos**, 43 m (141 ft) in diameter, said to have been used by Henry. The simple chapel of **Nossa Senhora da Graça** was also built by him. The whole site, looking across to Cabo de São Vicente and out towards the open Atlantic, is exhilarating and atmospheric.

ENVIRONS: The town is also within easy reach of many superb beaches. Some, such as **Telheiro**, 9 km (5 miles) west of Sagres, and **Ponta Ruiva** 2 km (1 mile) further up the west coast, are only accessible by car. Nearer to Sagres, **Beliche** is surprisingly sheltered, **Tonel**, on the tip of the promontory, has wonderful surf and **Martinhal**, 1 km (half a mile) east, has a watersports school offering water-skiing, surfing and wind surfing.

Lagos ➐

Road map 7C. 🏘 *20,000.* 🚉 🚌
ℹ *Sítio de São João (282-76 30 31).* 🏛 *1st Sat of month.*

SET ON ONE of the largest bays in the Algarve, Lagos is an attractive, bustling town. In the 8th century it was conquered by the Arabs, who left

Moorish archway leading onto Avenida dos Descobrimentos, Lagos

São Gonçalo in Santa Maria, Lagos

behind fortifications that were extended in the 16th century. A well-preserved section and archway can be seen near Rua do Castelo dos Governadores, where there is a monument to the navigator Gil Eanes.

The discoveries of the 15th century *(see pp48–9)*, pioneered by Henry the Navigator, whose statue gazes scowlingly out to sea, turned Lagos into an important naval centre. At the same time a most deplorable period of history began, with the first slaves brought back from the Sahara in 1441 by Henry's explorer Nuno Tristão. The site of the first **slave market** in Europe is marked by a plaque under the arcades on Rua da Senhora da Graça.

The city was the capital of the Algarve from 1576–1756. Extensive damage was caused by the earthquake of 1755 *(see pp62–3)*, so that today the centre consists primarily of pretty 18th- and 19th-century buildings. The citizens of Lagos continue to make their living from fishing, which helps the town to retain a character independent of the tourist trade.

The smart new marina on the east side of town provides the first safe anchorage on the south coast for boats coming in from the Atlantic.

⚓ Forte Ponta da Bandeira
Avenida dos Descobrimentos.
📞 *282-76 14 10.* ⏰ *Tue–Sun.* ⬤ *public hols.* 🏛
On the seafront stands the 17th-century fortress which defended the entrance to the harbour. Its imposing ramparts afford far-reaching views over the town and the bay.

🏛 Santa Maria
Praça Infante Dom Henrique.
📞 *282-76 27 23.* ⏰ *daily.* 🏛
The parish church of Lagos originated in the 16th century, and still retains a Renaissance doorway. Of local interest is a statue of São Gonçalo of Lagos, a fisherman's son born in 1360 who became an Augustinian monk, preacher and composer of religious music.

🔒 Santo António

Rua General Alberto Silveira. 🔲 *282-76 23 01.* 🔲 *Tue–Sun.* ● *public hols.*

This 18th-century church is an Algarvian jewel. The lower section of the walls is covered in blue and white *azulejos*, the rest in carved, gilded and painted woodwork, an inspirational and riotous example of Baroque carving. Cherubs, beasts, flowers and scenes of hunting and fishing, surround eight panel paintings of miracles performed by St Antony.

A statue of the saint stands above the altar, surrounded by gilded pillars and arches adorned with angels and vines. St Antony was patron and honorary colonel-in-chief of the local regiment and, according to tradition, this statue accompanied it on various campaigns during the Peninsular War (1807–11) *(see p54).*

Near the altar is the grave of Hugh Beatty, an Irish colonel who commanded the Lagos regiment during the 17th-century wars with Spain. He died here in 1709 and his motto "Non vi sed arte" (Not with force but with skill) adorns the tomb.

🏛 Museu Regional

Rua General Alberto Silveira.
🔲 *282-76 23 01.* 🔲 *Tue–Sun.*
● *public hols.* 🈲

Next door to the church of Santo António, an eclectic ethnographic museum displays local handicrafts and artefacts, traditional costumes and – most oddly – pickled creatures, including animal freaks such as an eight-legged goat kid. The custodian provides an informal guided tour.

Ochre sandstone rocks on the sheltered beach of Praia de Dona Ana, Lagos

ENVIRONS: The promontory, called the **Ponta da Piedade**, sheltering the bay of Lagos to the south has a series of wonderful rock formations, caves and calm, transparent waters. Accessible by road and sea, and most spectacular at sunset, this area is not to be missed. The prettiest beach is **Praia de Dona Ana**, 25 minutes' walk from the centre of town, but **Praia do Camilo**, further round to the tip of the promontory, may be less crowded. The long **Meia Praia** stretches for 4 km (2 miles) east of Lagos; a regular bus service leaves from the centre of town.

A 10-km (6-mile) drive due north of Lagos leads to the huge **Barragem de Bravura** reservoir. It is peaceful and especially picturesque seen from a viewpoint high up.

Alvor ❽

Road map 7C. 🏠 *7,000.* 🚉 🚌
ℹ️ *Rua Dr. Afonso Costa, 51 (282-45 75 40).* 📅 *2nd Tue of month.*

THIS PRETTY FISHING town of white houses is popular with holiday-makers, but in low season retains its charm. It was a Roman port, and later the Moorish town of Al-Bur. By the 16th century it was again a prosperous town, but it suffered much damage in the earthquake of 1755. The town was rebuilt with stone from the Moorish castle, so little of that fortress remains.

At the top of the town the 16th-century church, **Divino Salvador**, has a Manueline portal, carved with foliage, lions and dragons. The outermost arch is an octopus tentacle.

Church of Divino Salvador overlooking the whitewashed houses and the harbour at Alvor

Nossa Senhora da Conceição, Portimão

Portimão ⑨

Road map 7C. 👥 40,000. 🚃 🚌
ℹ️ *Avenida Zeca Afonso (282-47 07 17).* 🎪 *1st Mon of month.*

ONE OF THE LARGEST towns in the Algarve, Portimão is not renowned for its beauty but has plenty of character and a long history as a port. The Romans settled here, attracted by the natural harbour on the wide estuary of the Rio Arade.

Portimão's sprawling outskirts are graced with a new marina and shopping centre. Its 18th-century town centre has excellent shopping as well as a large, bustling market.

The centre lies around the pedestrianized **Rua Vasco da Gama**, with numerous shops specializing in leather goods. Along Rua Diogo Tomé, the church of **Nossa Senhora da Conceição** occupies a low hill. Rebuilt after the earthquake of 1755 *(see pp62–3)*, its 14th-century origins are still visible in the portico with its carved capitals. Inside, there

are 17th- and 18th-century *azulejo* panels. In Largo 1° de Dezembro there are benches adorned with brightly coloured 19th-century tiles. The waterfront is always lively and restaurants serve fresh sardines and sea bass.

ENVIRONS: Just 3 km (2 miles) south lies Portimão's touristic neighbour, **Praia da Rocha**, a series of sandy coves amongst protruding red and ochre rocks. At its east end is the **Fortaleza de Santa Catarina**, a castle built in the 16th century to protect Portimão and Silves. From here there is a superb view of the lovely, sweeping beach backed by 70-m (230-ft) cliffs, and overlooked by a swathe of high-rise hotels. These are multiplying, and visitors will find themselves fighting for space in high season.

Silves ⑩

Road map 7C. 👥 10,000. 🚃 🚌
ℹ️ *Rua 25 de Abril 26–28 (282-44 22 55).* 🎪 *3rd Mon of month.*

SILVES'S COMMANDING position made it the ideal fortified settlement. The Romans built a castle here, but it was under the Arabs that the city flourished, becoming the Moorish capital, Xelb. In the mid-12th century the Arab geographer Idrisi praised its beauty and its "delicious, magnificent" figs.

Silves was renowned as a centre of culture in Moorish Al-Gharb until the Knights of Santiago *(see pp42–3)* took the city in 1242.

Today, the red walls of the castle stand out against the skyline. Next to the castle, the **Fábrica di Inglés** houses a cork museum. the **Museu da Cortiça**, which tells the story of cork production in Portugal.

🏛 Museu da Cortiça
Rua Gregório Mascarenhas. 📞 *282-440 440.* ⏰ *daily.* 📷

Quiet cobbled street in Silves

♣ Castle
Castelo de Silves. 📞 *282-44 56 24.* ⏰ *daily.* 📷 ♿ *(garden only).*
The red sandstone castle dates back mainly to Moorish times, though it has done duty as a Christian fortress and, more recently, as a gaol. It was the site of the Palace of the Verandahs, abode of Al-Mu'tamid from 1053 when he was ruler of Seville and Wali of Al-Gharb.

There are superb views of the town and countryside from the massive, polygonal ramparts. Inside, there are gardens and the impressive vaulted Moorish **Cisterna da Moura Encantada** (Cistern of the Enchanted Moorish Girl).

The castle and town of Silves rising above a fertile valley of orange groves

🔒 Sé

Largo da Sé. ◻ *daily.* ⬤ *public hols.*
Built on the site of a mosque,
the cathedral dates from the
13th century, but has been
much altered over the years.
In the chancel, light falls from
lovely double windows with
stained-glass borders, on a jas-
per statue of Nossa Senhora
da Conceição, believed to date
from the 14th century.

Opposite the Sé, the 16th-
century **Misericórdia** church
has a Manueline side door and
a Renaissance altarpiece.

🏛 Museu Arqueológico

Rua das Portas de Loulé 14. 📞 *282-
44 48 32.* ◻ *Mon–Sat.* 🈺
Situated down the hill from
the cathedral, the Municipal
Museum was opened in 1990.
Its exhibits include Stone and
Iron Age tools, sculpted Roman
capitals, surgical instruments
from the 5th–7th centuries, a
13th-century anchor and items
of 18th-century ceramics. The
museum is built around its
star exhibit, a large Arab
well-cistern of about the
12th century that was
uncovered here in
1980. The staircase
built into the structure
descends 15 m (49 ft) to
the bottom of the well.

ENVIRONS: One kilometre
(half a mile) east of Silves
is the **Cruz de Portugal**,
an ornate 16th-century
granite cross. This may have
been given to the city by
Manuel I, when João II's
body was transferred
from Silves Cathedral to
Batalha *(see pp182–3).*
The faces are intricately carved
with the Crucifixion and the
Descent from the Cross.

Silves's Cruz de Portugal

Albufeira ⓫

Road map 7C. 🏠 *20,000.* 🚉 🚌
🛈 *Rua 5 de Outubro (289-58 52 79).*
📅 *1st & 3rd Tue of month.*

I T IS HARDLY surprising that
this charming fishing town
of whitewashed houses, overlooking a sheltered beach, has
become the tourist capital of
the Algarve. The Romans liked
it too, and built a castle here.
For the Arabs it was Al-Buhar

Colourful fishing boats on the beach at Albufeira

(The Castle on the Sea), and
under them it prospered from
trade with North Africa. The
Knights of Santiago *(see p43)*
took it in the 13th century,
but the consequent loss of
trade almost ruined it. In
1833 it was set on fire by
supporters of Dom
Miguel during the
War of the Two
Brothers *(see p54).*
Much of the town centre
is pedestrianized, including the oldest part around
Rua da Igreja Velha where
some of the buildings still
have original Moorish
arches. The church of **São
Sebastião**, on Praça Miguel
Bombarda, has a Manueline
doorway. Rua 5 de Outubro
leads through a tunnel
to the beach, east of
which is the **Praia dos
Barcos** where the fishermen
ply their trade. From **Praia de
São Rafael**, 2 km (1 mile) west
of Albufeira, to **Praia da Oura**
due east, the area is punctuated by small sandy coves set
between eroded ochre rocks.

Alte ⓬

Road map 7C. 🏠 *500.* 🚉 🚌
🛈 *Estrada da Ponte 17 (289-478
666).* 📅 *3rd Thu of month.*

P ERCHED ON A HILL, Alte is one
of the prettiest villages of
the Algarve. The approach
from the east along the N124

is the most picturesque, with
sweeping views of rolling hills.
The focus of this steep, white
village is the 16th-century
Nossa Senhora da Assunção,
which has a Manueline doorway and baptismal fonts, and
a fine gilded altarpiece celebrating the Assumption. The
chapel of São Sebastião has
beautiful, rare 16th-century
Sevillian *azulejos.*

About ten minutes' walk
from the church, and clearly
marked, is the River Alte, over-
hung with trees, and a water
source known as the **Fonte
Grande**. This leafy setting is
ideal for picnicking. On the
steep slopes, about 700 m (half
a mile) from the village is a
mill (converted into a restaurant) and a 5-m (16-ft) high
waterfall, **Queda do Vigário**.

One of many filigree chimneys
that adorn the rooftops of Alte

Vilamoura ⑬

Road map C7. 🏃 *9,000.* 🚌
ℹ *Praça do Mar, Quarteira (289-389 209).*

THE COAST between Faro and Lagos has effectively become a strip of villa complexes and high-rise hotels. Vilamoura is a prime example of this kind of development and is set to become Europe's largest leisure complex. Its 1,600 ha (4,000 acres) encompass four golf courses, tennis courts, a riding school, fishing and shooting facilities, and indoor and outdoor sports complexes. There is even a small landing strip. Its hotels and apartment blocks are still on the rise, and the already well-established complex is still under construction.

The focal point is the large **marina**, which bristles with powerboats and is fronted by restaurants, cafés and shops. It makes a diverting excursion, attracting many Portuguese visitors, including Lisbon's jet set. Due east is the crowded **Praia da Marina**. You can also visit the nearby Roman ruins of **Cerro da Vila**, which date from the 1st century AD and include a bath complex and a house with mosaics depicting fish.

↟ Cerro da Vila
Avenida Cerro da Vila. ☎ *289-312 153 (museum).* ◯ *daily.* 📷

18th-century tile panels and gilded altar in São Lourenço, Almancil

Almancil ⑭

Road map D7. 🏃 *2,000.* 🚉 🚌
ℹ *Loulé.* 🛍 *1st & 4th Sun of month, antiques 2nd Sun.*

OUTSIDE the undistinguished town of Almancil lies one of the Algarve's gems, the 18th-century **Igreja Matriz de São Lourenço**. Its interior is an outstanding masterpiece of decoration in *azulejo* panels. The church was commissioned by local inhabitants in gratitude to St Laurence, who answered their prayers for water.

The copious blue and white tiles were probably designed by master craftsmen in Lisbon and shipped down. They cover the cupola, the walls of the chancel, nave, and nave vault, to stunning effect. The wall panels depict episodes from the life of St Laurence; on one side of the altar the saint is shown healing two blind men, and on the other, giving money to the poor. The nave arches show the saint conversing with Pope Sixtus II; arguing for his Christian belief with the Roman Emperor Valerian; and refusing to give up his faith. The story culminates in his martyrdom. In the last panel on the right, in which the saint is placed on a gridiron to be burned, an angel comforts him. The nave vault depicts the *Coronation of St Laurence,*

Luxury yachts and powerboats moored at the smart marina at Vilamoura

and the cupola has decorative, *trompe-l'oeil* effects of exceptional quality. The last tiles were put in place in 1730.

The altarpiece, dated around 1735, was the work of Manuel Martins and was gilded by leading local painters. Astonishingly, the 1755 earthquake *(see pp62–3)* only dislodged five tiles from the vault.

Today, Almancil houses a large community of British expats, and is noted for its property agents and holiday and construction-related shops and services. The town is also within striking distance of some of the best restaurants in the Algarve *(see pp419–21)*.

Loulé ⑮

Road map D7. 🏃 *20,000.* 🚉 🚌
ℹ *Edifício do Castelo (289-46 39 00).*
🛍 *Sat.*

LOULÉ IS AN ATTRACTIVE market town and thriving craft centre. Its Moorish origins are still visible in the belltower of the church of São Clemente. The **castle**, on the north side of town, is also Moorish in origin, rebuilt in the 13th century. Remnants of the walls behind the castle afford an overview of the town and the many pretty filigree chimneys, typical of the Algarve.

The heart of the town lies immediately south of Praça da República and encompasses the busy, pink-domed market. On Saturdays the area is particularly lively when gypsies run a simultaneous outdoor market. From Rua 9 de Abril to the Igreja Matriz you can watch handicraft workers carving wood, weaving hats, making lace, decorating horse tackle and painting pottery and tiles.

The 13th-century **São Clemente**, on Largo da Silva, was badly damaged in three earthquakes, the last in 1969, but its triple nave, defined by Gothic arches, has been conserved. There are two beautiful side chapels dating from the early 16th century. The Capela de Nossa Senhora da Consolação is decorated from floor to vault with superb blue and white *azulejo* panels, while the Capela de São Brás, has a Manueline arch and a blue and gold Baroque altarpiece.

Other churches of note are the **Igreja da Misericórdia**, on Avenida Marçal Pacheco, which has a Manueline doorway, and the chapel of **Nossa Senhora da Conceição**, close to Praça da República. Here, the Baroque altarpiece (1745) by Miguel Nobre of Faro is complemented by scenes in blue and white *azulejos*.

ENVIRONS: The 16th-century, hilltop chapel of **Nossa Senhora da Piedade**, adorned with *azulejo* panels, lies 2 km (1 mile) west of Loulé. Behind it stands a modern white church of the same name built to replace the old chapel but which never became a popular place of worship. The spot also affords spectacular views.

Colourful tiled fountain on the terrace of the Patamar da Casa do Presépio, Estoi

Estoi

Road map D7. 🏘 *4,300.* 🚌
🛈 *Faro (289-803 604).* 🗓 *daily.*

THE QUIET VILLAGE of Estoi has two notable sights, separated by a short distance and about 1,800 years. Just off the main square is the **Palácio de Estoi**, an unashamedly pretty Rococo pastiche, unique to the region. The palace was the brainchild of a local nobleman, who died soon after work was begun in the mid-1840s. Another wealthy local later acquired the place, and completed it in 1909. For the vast amount of money and energy he expended on his new home, he was made Viscount of Estoi. The work was supervised by the architect

Domingos da Silva Meira, whose interest in sculpture is evident everywhere.

The palace is now undergoing restoration of its interior – a feast of pastel and stucco – and is to become a *pousada*.

🌿 Palace gardens
Rua do Jardim. 📞 *289-991 620.*
🕐 *Tue–Sat.* 🔴 *public hols.* 🚫

Dotted with orange trees and palms, the gardens continue the joyful Rococo spirit of the palace. (The gardens may be closed during the renovation of the palace: call to check.) The lower terrace features a blue and white tiled pavilion, the Casa da Cascata, inside which is a copy of Canova's *Three Graces*. The main walled terrace above, the Patamar da Casa do Presépio, has a large pavilion with stained-glass windows, fountains adorned with nymphs and tiled niches.

Detail of fish mosaic in the baths of the Roman ruins at Milreu

🏛 Milreu
N2-6. 🕐 *Tue–Sun.* 🔴 *public hols.*

A ten-minute walk downhill from the other end of the main square leads to Estoi's second sight: the Roman complex of Milreu, which dates from the 1st or 2nd century AD. The buildings probably began as a large farmhouse that was converted in the 3rd century into a luxurious villa, built around a central courtyard.

Ebullient fish mosaics still adorn the baths, alongside the living quarters, but most portable archaeological finds are now housed in Faro's Museu Municipal *(see p327)*. The importance of the villa, which may have belonged to a wealthy patrician, is indicated by the remains of a temple overlooking the site. This was converted into a Christian basilica in the 5th century.

Pink Rococo façade of the Palácio de Estoi

Faro ⑰

CAPITAL OF THE ALGARVE since 1756, Faro has been reborn several times over the centuries – following invasion, fire and earthquake. A prehistoric fishing village, it became an important port and administrative centre under the Romans, who named it Ossonoba. Captured from the Moors in 1249 by Afonso III, Faro prospered until 1596, when it was sacked and burned by the Earl of Essex, favourite of Elizabeth I of England. A new city rose from the ashes, only to be badly damaged in the earthquake of 1755 *(see pp62–3)*. Although vestiges of the ancient city walls are still standing, the finest buildings date mainly from the late 18th and 19th centuries.

Statue of Dom Francisco Gomes do Avelar in Largo da Sé

Exploring the Old City

The centre of Faro is attractive and easily explored on foot. It fans out from the small harbour to encompass the compact Old City to the southeast. Partly encircled by ancient walls, this is reached via the

Arco da Vila. The arch was built on the site of a medieval castle gate in the 19th century for the bishop, Dom Francisco Gomes do Avelar, who had taken it upon himself to redesign the city in decline. The portico is originally Moorish, and a statue of St Thomas Aquinas, patron saint of Faro, surveys the scene. At the heart of the Old City, the Largo da Sé is a peaceful square, lined with orange trees and flanked by the elegant 18th-century seminary and **Paço Episcopal** (bishops' palace), still in use and closed to the public. Just outside the walls, through another archway of Moorish origin, the Arco do Repouso, is the 18th-century church of **São Francisco**, impressively decorated with tiled scenes of the life of St Francis. Further north is the 17th-century **Nossa Senhora do Pé da Cruz** with

Azulejo **crucifix in exterior chapel of Nossa Senhora do Pé da Cruz**

fanciful oil panels of stories from Genesis, such as the creation of the sun and stars. At the rear is an interesting exterior chapel or *humilhadero*.

🏛 Sé

Largo da Sé. 📞 *289-80 66 32.*
◯ *daily.* ● *Sat pm, public hols.*
The first Christian church here, built on the site of a mosque, was all but destroyed in the attack by the English in 1596. The base of the belltower, its medieval doorway and two chapels survived, and long-term reconstruction resulted in a mixture of Renaissance and Baroque styles.

By the 1640s a grander building had emerged which included a chancel decorated with *azulejos* and the Capela

Orange trees in front of the 18th-century bishops' palace along the Largo da Sé

de Nossa Senhora dos Prazeres, decorated with ornate gilded woodcarving. One of the cathedral's most dashing and eccentric features is the large 18th-century organ decorated with Chinese motifs. Its range includes an echoing horn and a nightingale's song, and it has often been used by leading European organists.

🏛 Museu Arquológico

Largo Dom Afonso III. 📞 289-89 74 00. ◻ Mon–Sat. ⬤ public hols. 🈀
Since 1973 the Municipal Museum has been housed in the former convent of Nossa Senhora da Assunção, founded for the Poor Clares by Dona Leonor, sister of Manuel I. Her emblem, a fishing net, adorns the portico.

A variety of local archaeological finds are displayed in the museum, partly in the lovely two-storey Renaissance cloister built by Afonso Pires in 1540. The collection contains Roman,

17th-century chancel of Faro's Sé

medieval and Manueline stone carvings and statuary. However, the most attractive exhibit is a huge, Roman floor mosaic featuring a magnificently executed head of the god Neptune (3rd century AD), found near the railway station.

🏛 Museu Marítimo

Rua da Comunidade Lusiada.
📞 289-89 49 90. ◻ Mon–Fri (pm).
⬤ public hols. 🈀
The Museu Marítimo is housed in part of the harbour master's building on the waterfront. Its small and curious collection of maritime exhibits centres on models of boats from the Age of Discovery (see pp46–9) onwards, including the square-rigged nau, prototype of the galleon. One example is Vasco da Gama's São Gabriel, the flagship on his voyage to India in 1498. There are also displays of traditional fishing methods from the Algarve.

FARO CITY CENTRE

Arco da Vila ⑤
Igreja do Carmo ①
Museu Etnográfico ⑩
Museu Marítimo ④
Museu Municipal ⑧
Paço Episcopal ⑥
Palácio Bivarin ③
São Francisco ⑨
São Pedro ②
Sé ⑦

0 metres 250
0 yards 250

KEY

🚂 Railway station
🚌 Bus station
🅿 Parking
🛈 Tourist information
⛪ Church
▬ Railway line
▬ City walls

Exploring Faro

The lively centre of Faro along Rua de Santo António is a stylish, pedestrianized area full of shops, bars and restaurants. Between here and the Largo do Carmo are some fine 18th-century buildings, such as the **Palácio Bivarin**. The early morning market on Largo de Sá Carneiro, to the north, offers fresh produce, clothing and local crafts. From here, a brisk walk uphill to the **Ermida de Santo António do Alto** brings a panorama of Faro with the sea and saltpans to the south.

🏛 Museu Etnográfico

Praça da Liberdade 2. **(** 289-827 610. **○** Mon–Fri. **●** public hols. **⚑ ◎**
The Ethnographic Museum takes a nostalgic look at the Algarve's traditional way of life showing ceramics, looms and decorative horse tackle. Old photographs document peasant farming techniques, with their heavy reliance on manpower, donkeys and oxen. The most charming exhibit is the cart used by the last waterseller in Olhão, in operation until 1974.

Imposing twin-towered façade of the Baroque Igreja do Carmo

⛪ Igreja do Carmo

Largo do Carmo. **(** 289-82 44 90. **○** Mon–Sat. **⚑** to Capela dos Ossos.
The impressive façade of this church was begun in 1713. Inside, the decoration is Baroque run wild, with every scroll and barley-sugar twist covered in precious Brazilian gold leaf.

In sombre contrast, the Capela dos Ossos (Chapel of Bones), built in 1816, has walls lined with skulls and large bones taken from the friars' cemetery. It is a stark reminder of the transience of human life.

Sumptuous Baroque decoration of the main altarpiece in São Pedro

⛪ São Pedro

Largo de São Pedro. **(** 289-80 54 73. **○** daily.
The parish church of Faro is dedicated to St Peter, patron saint of fishermen. Though restored with Italianate columns after the earthquake of 1755, much original Baroque decoration has survived, including the main altarpiece (1689).

Highlights include the chapel of the Santíssimo Sacramento, with a dazzling altarpiece (c.1745) featuring a bas-relief of the Last Supper, and a sculpture of St Anne teaching the young Virgin Mary to read. The altar of the Capela das Almas is surrounded by stunning *azulejos* (c.1730) showing the Virgin and other saints pulling souls out of purgatory.

✡ Cemitério dos Judeus

Estrada da Penha. **(** 282-41 67 10. **○** Mon–Fri (am). **●** public hols. **♿**
At the far northeast corner of town is the Jewish cemetery, created for the Jewish community brought here in the 18th century by the Marquês de Pombal (*see pp52–3*) to revitalize the economy. The cemetery is laid out in the traditional Sephardic way with children buried nearest the entrance, women in the centre and men at the back. It served from 1838 until 1932, during which time 60 families prospered in the area then gradually moved away so that there is no Jewish community in Faro today.

Olhão ⓲

Road map D7. 🏘 *15,000.* 🚌 🚆
🛈 *Largo Sebastião Martins Mestre 6A (289-71 39 36).* 🐟 *daily (fish); Sat (general).*

OLHÃO HAS BEEN involved in fishing since the Middle Ages, and today is one of the largest fishing ports and tuna and sardine canning centres in the Algarve. In 1808 the village was elevated to the status of town, after 17 of its fishermen crossed the Atlantic Ocean without charts, expressly to bring the exiled King João VI, in Rio de Janeiro, the news that Napoleon's troops had been forced out of the country.

Olhão's square, whitewashed houses with their flat roof terraces and box-like chimneys are reminiscent of Moorish architecture. The best view is from the top of the belltower of the parish church, **Nossa Senhora do Rosário**, on Praça da Restauração, built between 1681 and 1698 with donations from the local fishermen. The custodian lets visitors through the locked door leading from the nave. In 1758 the parish priest remarked on the fishermen's great devotion to "Our Lady of the Rosary in their grief and danger at sea, especially in summertime when North African pirates often sail off this coast." At the rear of the church is the external chapel of **Nossa Senhora dos Aflitos**, where women pray for their men's safety in stormy weather.

The narrow, pedestrianized streets of the old town wind down from here to the waterfront, the

Whitewashed chapel of Nossa Senhora dos Aflitos behind the parish church in Olhão

The wide lagoon of the Parque Natural da Ria Formosa

scene of one of the region's most lively and picturesque markets. The noisy covered fish market sells the morning's catch, while on Saturdays outside stalls line the quay, with local farmers selling other produce such as fruit, nuts, honey and live chickens.

Shop selling local basketware in Olhão

ENVIRONS: At the eastern end of the quay, beyond the market, boats take you out to the islands of **Armona** (15 min), **Culatra** (30 min) and **Farol** (45 min). These flat, narrow bars of sand provide shelter to the town, and excellent sandy beaches for visitors, particularly on the ocean side. The islands are part of the Parque Natural da Ria Formosa.

Parque Natural da Ria Formosa ⑲

Road map D7. 🛈 *Centro de Educação Ambiental de Marim (289-70 41 34).* 🚌 *East of Olhão on N125.* ⛴ *from Faro, Olhão & Tavira.*

STRETCHING from Praia de Faro to Cacela Velha *(see p331)*, the Ria Formosa Nature Reserve follows 60 km (37 miles) of coastline. It was created in 1987 to protect the valuable ecosystem of this area, which was under serious threat from uncontrolled building, sand extraction and pollution, all by-products of the massive rise in tourism. The lagoon area of marshes, saltpans, islets and channels is sheltered from the open sea by a chain of barrier islands – actually sand dunes. Inlets between the islands allow the tide to ebb and flow into the lagoon.

The lagoon waters are rich in shellfish, such as oysters, cockles and clams: bred here, they make up 80 per cent of the nation's mollusc exports. The fish life and warm climate attract numerous wildfowl and waders, and snakes, toads and chameleons also live here. Apart from fish and shellfish farming and salt panning, all other human activities which might encroach on the park's ecosystem are strictly controlled or forbidden.

Centro de Educação Ambiental de Marim, about 3 km (2 miles) east of Olhão, is an environmental education centre. Its 60 ha (148 acres) of dune and pinewoods are home to various sights, including a restored farmhouse, a tidal mill, a centre for injured birds, as well as exhibitions and aquariums. The web-footed Portuguese water dog, once much used by fishermen, has been bred back from near-extinction here. At the eastern end of the park are Roman tanks where fish was salted before being exported to the empire.

🦆 Centro de Educação
Quelfes. 📞 *289-70 41 34.* ⏰ *daily.*
⛔ *1 Jan, 25 Dec.* ♿ 📷 🖥

Houses with four-sided roofs, along the river Gilão in Tavira

Tavira ⑳

Road map D7. 🏛 *10,000.* 🚉 🚌
ℹ *Rua da Galeria 9 (281-32 25 11).*
🛍 *3rd Sat of month.*

THE PRETTY TOWN of Tavira, full of historic churches and fine mansions with filigree balconies, lies along both sides of the Gilão river, linked by a **bridge** of Roman origin. This was part of the coastal Roman road between Castro Marim and Faro (*see pp326–8*).

Tavira's early ascendancy began with the Moors, who saw it as one of their most important settlements in the Algarve, along with Silves and Faro. It was conquered in 1242 by Dom Paio Peres Correia, who was outraged at the murder of seven of his knights by the Moors during a truce.

Tavira flourished until the 16th century, after which a slow decline set in, aggravated by a severe plague (1645–6) and the silting up of the

harbour. The town now accommodates tourists, without compromising either its looks or atmosphere.

The best view of the town is from the walls of the **Moorish castle** in the old Arab quarter on top of the hill. From here the distinctive four-sided roofs of the houses that line Rua da Liberdade are clearly visible. These pyramid-like roofs possibly evolved to allow the sudden torrential rain of the Algarve to run off easily. From the castle walls, the nearby clock tower of the church of **Santa Maria do Castelo** also acts as a landmark. The church itself occupies the site of what was once the biggest mosque in the Algarve. Its façade retains a Gothic doorway and windows, and its interior, restored in the 19th century, houses the tombs of Dom Paio Peres Correia and his seven knights. Santa Maria do Castelo and **Igreja da Misericórdia** are the only two of Tavira's 21 churches to be open outside service hours. Below the castle, is the 1569 convent of **Nossa Senhora da Graça**.

Renaissance architecture was pioneered in the town by André Pilarte, and can be seen on the way up to the castle, in the Igreja da Misericórdia (1541–51), with its lovely doorway topped by saints Peter and Paul, and in the nearby **Palácio da Galeria** (open for temporary exhibitions). Rua da Liberdade and Rua José Pires Padinha have a sprinkling of 16th-century houses. The river embankments are graced by a few 18th-century mansions.

Beach on Ilha de Tavira, an island off the Algarve's eastern coast

ENVIRONS: The sandy, offshore **Ilha de Tavira**, provides excellent swimming. A popular resort in summer, it is reached by ferry from Quatro Águas.

Blue and white houses, Cacela Velha

Cacela Velha ㉑

Road map D7. 🏛 *50.* ℹ *Junta de Freguesia de Vila Nova de Cacela (281-95 12 28).*

THIS HAMLET perches on a cliff overlooking the sea, reached via a landscape of fields and olive trees. It has remained untouched by mass tourism, and retains a peaceful atmosphere. Charming blue and white fishermen's houses cluster around the remains of a fort and a whitewashed 18th-century church.

The beach is sheltered by a long spit of sand, and fishing boats are dotted about. The Phoenicians and Moors used this protected site until it was taken over by the Knights of Santiago in 1240 (*see p43*).

Vila Real de Santo António ②

Road Map D7. 👥 *10,000.* 🚉 🚌
ℹ️ *Rua Dr. Teófilo Braga, Centro Cultural António Aleixo (281- 542 100).* 🎪 *3rd Sun of month.*

Bᵁⁱˡᵀ ᵀᴼ ᴬ plan by the Marquês de Pombal in 1774, Vila Real de Santo António is a little like a miniature version of Lisbon's Baixa *(pp81–71)*, rebuilt after the 1755 earthquake also under the auspices of Pombal. The symmetrical grid of fairly wide streets, the equal-sized blocks with similar façades, the well-ordered naming system for the streets, all speak of Pombal's practical and political ideals.

Today, the town is one of the most important fishing ports on the Algarve coast, as well as a border town with its markets geared towards visiting Spaniards. Its centre now seems too grand for its size, all of which makes it an interesting place to drop in on.

Vila Real's Igreja Matriz, famous for its stained glass windows

Castro Marim ②

Road map D7. 👥 *4,000.* 🚌 ℹ️ *Rua José Alves Moreira 2–4 (281-53 12 32).*

Cᴬˢᵀᴿᴼ ᴹᴬᴿⁱᴹ has attracted "visitors" since ancient times. The Phoenicians, Greeks and Romans all made use of its commanding location above the River Guadiana. It was the gateway to the Moorish Al-Gharb and for centuries it was a sanctuary for fugitives from the Inquisition *(see p51)*. The **castle** above the town is of Moorish origin, the outlying walls a 13th-century addition.

Moorish castle and the abandoned Misericórdia church, Castro Marim

Eɴᴠɪʀᴏɴs: The town was also a centre for salt production and the surrounding *salinas* are now home to the wildlife reserve, **Reserva Natural do Sapal**, established in 1975. Extending for 2,090 ha (5,160 acres) south and east of town, this is an area of saltpans and marshes with a large variety of bird species including flamingos, avocets, and black-winged stilts, symbol of the reserve. Group tours may be booked on 281-510 680.

Alcoutim ②

Road map D7. 👥 *1,300.* 🚌
ℹ️ *Rua 1° de Maio (281-54 61 79).*

Tʜᴇ ᵀⁱɴʸ, ᴳᴱᴹ-ˡⁱᴷᴱ, unspoilt village of Alcoutim lies 15 km (9 miles) from the border with the Alentejo, and on the natural border with Spain, the River Guadiana. The drive there along the N122-2, a rough, winding road which sometimes runs alongside the Guadiana, provides stunning views of the countryside and across the river to Spain.

The size of Alcoutim belies its history. As a strategic location and river port, it was seized on by the Phoenicians, Greeks, Romans and, of course, the Moors who stayed until the reconquest in 1240. Here, in 1371, on flower-decked boats midway between Alcoutim and its Spanish counterpart, Sanlúcar de Guadiana, King Fernando I of Portugal signed the peace of Alcoutim with Enrique II of Castile. By the late 17th century, when its political importance had waned, the town had acquired a new reputation – for smuggling tobacco and snuff from Spain.

The walls of the 14th-century **castle** give an excellent view over the small village and its idyllic setting. Near the main square, by the river, is the refreshingly simple 16th-century church of **San Salvador**.

Eɴᴠɪʀᴏɴs: Visitors can take a scenic trip 15 km (9 miles) downriver to **Foz de Odeleite** by fishing boat from the jetty. The boat passes orchards and orange groves and, at Álamo, there is a Roman dam.

View from Alcoutim across the Guadiana to Sanlúcar in Spain

PORTUGAL'S ISLANDS

Portugal's Islands at a Glance

Once REMOTE OUTPOSTS of a maritime empire, today
Madeira and the Azores are easily accessible by
air from mainland Portugal. The fertile islands of
Madeira and Porto Santo, 600 km (375 miles) off the
African coast, are popular holiday destinations, with
subtropical flora and high mountains. The Azorean
archipelago lies further west, close to the Mid-Atlantic
Ridge. The climate here is more temperate and the
active volcanoes have created a fascinating scenery
of moon-like landscapes and collapsed craters.

Terceira *is a relatively flat island
famous for its bull-running festivals,
the "tourada à corda". On the southern
coast, the twin-towered church of São
Mateus, built at the turn of the century,
overlooks the harbour of São Mateus.*

Corvo

Flores

THE AZORES
(See pp358–71)

Graciosa

São Jorge

Faial   Pico

Pico *is the summit of a
steep volcano protruding
from the sea. On the lower
slopes of the mountain
that fall towards the sea,
the fields are crisscrossed
with a patchwork of dry-
stone walls made from
black volcanic basalt.*

◁ **Fertile pastures sloping down to volcanic cones and the sea on the Azorean island of Faial**

MADEIRA
(See pp340–57)

Porto Santo

Funchal *is the capital of Madeira, famous for its flowers. Exotic blooms are sold along the main street, Avenida Arriaga, which is lined with tall jacaranda trees.*

Madeira

Ilhas Desertas

| 0 kilometres | 20 |
| 0 miles | 10 |

Pico Ruivo*, at 1,861 m (6,105 ft), is the highest point on the island of Madeira. The slopes below are dotted with small farms.*

Terceira

| 0 kilometres | 50 |
| 0 miles | 25 |

São Miguel

São Miguel *is popular for its therapeutic spa treatments in hot pools of mineral water. At Caldeira das Furnas, in the east of the island, steaming mud springs bubble from the ground.*

Santa Maria

The Landscape and Flowers of Madeira

MADEIRA HAS A MILD, moist climate which promotes a rich cover of vegetation. At first glance, the flowers and foliage appear to harmonize with the environment. The well-travelled botanist, however, will soon become aware of the strange assortment of flowers from around the world. For example, over the past few centuries, many flowers from South Africa's Cape region and exotic blooms from South America have been introduced, which now thrive alongside indigenous plants.

Pride of Madeira

MADEIRA'S GARDENS

The sub-tropical climate and mixture of indigenous and imported plants combine to produce gardens that are the envy of horti-culturalists all over the world. Gardens such as the Botanical Gardens in Funchal *(see p346)* are awash with colour all year. Here are some of the most striking plants that can be found in Madeira's gardens.

Magnolia in bloom

AROUND THE COAST

In many coastal areas the cliffs are spectacular, such as this stretch at Ponta de São Lourenço *(see p350)*. A rich and varied flora, both native and introduced, can be found along Madeira's coast despite the dry and stony habitat.

AGRICULTURAL AND WAYSIDE GROUND

An irrigation system using man-made channels called *levadas*, such as this one near Curral das Freiras *(see p354)*, allows the islanders to cultivate many otherwise unpromising areas. The margins of agricultural land are often rich with flowers.

Hottentot fig *is a coastal, ground-cover plant originating from South Africa.*

Lampranthus spectabilis *is a South African plant which flowers on the coast between May and July.*

Mimosa trees *grow especially well in wooded parts of Madeira, where they bloom in winter.*

Parrot's Beak *is a large, striking flower that appears in March and April.*

Canary Island date palms *are a familiar sight, especially along the sunny south coast.*

Hibiscus syriacus, *from the Far East, flowers be-tween June and October.*

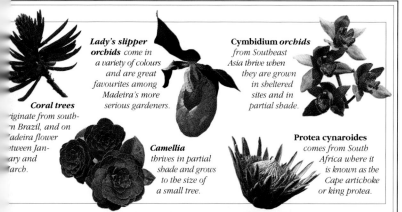

Coral trees originate from south-ern Brazil, and on Madeira flower between Jan-uary and March.

Lady's slipper orchids come in a variety of colours and are great favourites among Madeira's more serious gardeners.

Cymbidium orchids from Southeast Asia thrive when they are grown in sheltered sites and in partial shade.

Camellia thrives in partial shade and grows to the size of a small tree.

Protea cynaroides comes from South Africa where it is known as the Cape artichoke or king protea.

HIGH GROUND

The views from the summit of Pico Ruivo, the island's highest point *(see p354)*, are spectacular. In upland areas, the vegetation harbours a higher proportion of native species than in the lowlands.

TERRACED PLANTATIONS

Plantations, such as this one growing bananas near Calheta *(see p356)*, are made by digging terraces into the hillside. A wide range of crops are grown, for home consumption and export.

Isoplexis sceptrum, known as the yellow foxglove, is a flowering shrub native to Madeira.

Sweet chestnuts grow well in Madeira and produce an abundant autumn harvest.

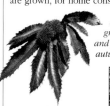

Broom flowers are colourful and popular with pollinating insects.

Pawpaws produce fruit all year round. The plant originates from South America.

Prickly juniper is a hardy, spiny evergreen shrub covered in tough red berries.

Sword aloe has spiky leaves which provide a good physical barrier around plantations.

The Azores: Volcanic Islands Rising from the Ocean Bed

Sᴏᴏᴀᴛᴇᴅ ᴏɴ ᴇɪᴛʜᴇʀ ꜱɪᴅᴇ of the Mid-Atlantic Ridge, the Azores are a result of 20 million years of volcanic activity. As the plates of the earth's crust pull apart, volcanic eruptions form a giant ridge of mountains beneath the Atlantic. In places, the ridge is buckled and cut by perpendicular fractures, known as transform faults. Molten rock (magma) has been forced through these faults to form the Azores. These islands, among the youngest on earth, emerged above the waves less than five million years ago. Their striking landscape tells of their volcanic past and is still shaped by volcanic activity today.

The Mid-Atlantic Ridge is a line of submarine volcanoes that runs the whole length of the Atlantic Ocean.

Corvo

Terceira lies directly above a major transform fault

Graciosa

Flores

Transform fault

The Mid-Atlantic Ridge marks the join where the African, Eurasian and American plates of the earth's crust are being pulled apart.

Faial

Pico

A mantle plume is a mass of partially molten mantle that has welled upwards, pooling beneath the rocky lithosphere. The magma it produces seeks fissures through which to erupt.

São Jorge

São Miguel has several spectacular water-filled calderas and hot springs.

Santa Maria

Vᴏʟᴄᴀɴɪᴄ Rᴇꜱᴏᴜʀᴄᴇꜱ ᴏꜰ ᴛʜᴇ Aᴢᴏʀᴇꜱ

The dramatic formation of the Azores has left the islands with abundant natural resources. Hot springs, strong building materials and, eventually, fertile soil, are all the result of the ongoing volcanic activity. A wet, temperate climate gradually breaks down the volcanic rocks into fertile soils. Older soils support luxuriant vegetation and are excellent for arable farming, but younger soils, like those found on Pico, support little agriculture yet.

These stone cottages on Pico, like many on the islands, make use of the plentiful basalt rock as a durable building material.

Furnas, on São Miguel, is an area of sulphur and hot mud springs used for bathing and for medicinal purposes.

*sing high above the clouds, the still-active
°canic peak of Pico Alto dominates the island of
co, which is itself the top of a giant underwater
°cano. At 2,350 m (7,700 ft) above sea level, Pico
o is the highest peak in the whole of Portugal.*

₁E GEOLOGY OF THE AZORES

e Azores lie along transform fault lines, cracks
the earth's crust which cross the Mid-Atlantic
dge. These faults are weak points through
nich magma can rise. Successive volcanic eruptions have formed hundreds of undersea
mountains on either side of the ridge.
The highest peaks of these
mountains are the nine
islands of the Azores.
Their emergence above
the sea has been aided
by the swelling of the
mantle plume beneath
the ocean crust, which
lifts the sea floor closer
to the surface of the sea.

Thin ocean crust

Atlantic Ocean

The upper mantle is a layer of
dense rock. With the crust above,
it forms the lithosphere, a series
of semi-rigid moving plates.

The lower mantle, or asthenosphere,
is a deep layer of partially molten rock
that surrounds the earth's core.

*₃asalt lava blocks used for dry-stone walls provide
₃helter for vines and protect against soil erosion on
ɪico. Volcanic soil here is of relatively recent for-
₃ation and suitable for few crops except grapes.*

THE FORMATION OF A CALDERA

A caldera is a large crater that forms during or
after a volcanic eruption, when the roof of the
magma chamber collapses under the weight
of the volcano's cone. Water collecting in the
natural bowl of a caldera can form a crater lake.

Caldeira das Sete Cidades on the island of São Miguel

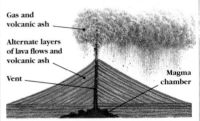

Gas and
volcanic ash

Alternate layers
of lava flows and
volcanic ash

Vent

Magma
chamber

In an active volcano, the magma chamber below
the cone is full of molten rock. As pressure forces
this magma up through the volcano's vent, it is
expelled to the surface as a volcanic eruption.

Exploding
magma

Volcano's
collapsing
cone

Enlarged
magma
chamber

As magma is expelled, the level in the magma
chamber drops. This may cause the volcano's cone
to collapse under its own weight, leaving behind
the characteristic bowl-shaped crater, or caldera.

Caldera lake

Eroded
crater

Residual hot rock

After the volcano has died down and is eroded,
the caldera can fill with water and form a lake.
Residual hot rock near the magma chamber may
continue to heat the surrounding ground water.

MADEIRA

MADEIRA IS A GREEN, SUBTROPICAL *paradise of volcanic origin, its soils formed from lava and ash, completely different in character from the Portuguese mainland. Blessed with an equable daytime temperature that varies only by a few degrees either side of 20° C (68° F), the island has an all-year-round appeal.*

Madeira is a mere dot in the Atlantic Ocean, 608 km (378 miles) from Morocco, and nearly 1,000 km (621 miles) from Lisbon. Despite this, Madeira and Porto Santo appear on a Genoese map of 1351, so there is no doubt that sailors had long known about the islands. They remained unclaimed, however, until 1418 when João Gonçalves Zarco was blown out into the Atlantic by violent storms while exploring the coast of Africa. Zarco counted his blessings at having found safe harbour in Porto Santo, set up the Portuguese flag and returned to Lisbon. A year later he returned on a voyage of discovery sponsored by Henry the Navigator *(see p49)*. Early in 1420, after a winter on Porto Santo, he set sail for the mist-shrouded land on the horizon. He found a beautiful, thickly wooded island (*madeira* means wood), with abundant fresh water.

The bird-of-paradise flower (*Strelitzia reginae*)

Within seven years the island had attracted a pioneer colony and the early settlers exploited the fertile soil and warm climate to grow sugar cane. The islanders grew rich on this "white gold", and slaves were brought in to work the land and create the terraced fields and irrigation channels (*levadas*) that still cling to the steep hillsides. Today, despite the gradients, Madeirans make use of every spare patch of land, growing bananas, flowers and grapes (although tourism is the main industry).

In the late 19th century, Madeira became a popular winter holiday spot for northern Europeans. The start of commercial flights in 1964 introduced the rest of the world to its charms. Today Madeira appeals to keen walkers, plant lovers and sun seekers, although it lacks the sandy beaches of its sister island, Porto Santo.

Triangular-shaped houses, typical of the town of Santana on the north coast of Madeira

◁ **Footpath winding through the spectacular mountain scenery of Pico do Arieiro**

Exploring Madeira

FUNCHAL IS THE ISLAND'S CAPITAL and the only town of any size. This is where most of the museums and historic buildings are to be found, as well as the best hotels, restaurants and shops. Most of Madeira's agricultural crops are grown along the sunny, prosperous south coast. The cooler, wetter north side has fewer settlements and more cattle. Many parts of the mountainous and volcanic interior remain wild, and some are accessible only on foot. Pico Ruivo, the highest peak on the island, is a favourite destination for walkers.

Terraces near Boa Ventura, on the road from Santana to São Vicente

15 PORTO MONIZ

ACHADAS DA CRUZ

R101

PONTA DO PARGO

SEIXAL

R101

PONTA DELGADA

BOA VENTURA

14 SÃO VICENTE

RABAÇAL WALKS **13**

RABAÇAL

PRAZERES

PAÚL DA SERRA **12**

R222

R110

SERRA DE ÁGUA

16 CALHETA

R209

CURRAL DAS FREIR

0 kilometres   5

0 miles   3

R101

PONTA DO SOL

ESTREITO DE CÂMARA DE LOBOS

RIBEIRA BRAVA **17**

CABO GIRÃO

R101

CÂMARA DE LOBOS **18**

Early morning view across the rooftops of Funchal, with the mountainous interior beyond

GETTING AROUND

Madeira's international airport, Santa Catarina, is at Santa Cruz, 18 km (11 miles) northeast of Funchal. Buses operate to all corners of the island from Funchal but are not geared to tourists. Taxis can be used, but for flexibility car hire is best. From north to south the island is 19 km (12 miles) wide and from east to west just 56 km (35 miles) long. Even so, travelling times are magnified by the mountainous terrain. To reach the nearby island of Porto Santo, you can either fly from Santa Cruz or take the ferry from Funchal to Porto de Abrigo (near Vila Baleira). (See also pp444–5.)

PORTO SANTO ⑲

CAMACHA

VILA BALEIRA
(PORTO SANTO)

ILHÉU DE CIMA

ILHÉU DE FERRO

PONTA

ILHÉU DE BAIXO

THE AZORES

MADEIRA

SÃO JORGE

⑦ SANTANA

FAIAL

PORTO DA CRUZ

R103

Ribeira Seca

CURRAL

R108

⑨ PICO DO ARIEIRO

R202

R101

⑧ RIBEIRO FRIO

R109

⑥ CANIÇAL

PONTA DE SÃO LOURENÇO

R108

Ribeira de Santa Cruz

R211

⑤ MACHICO

R101

SANTA CRUZ

R203

R105

MONTE ③

④ CAMACHA

② QUINTA DO PALHEIRO FERREIRO

① ⓷

R229

R101

FUNCHAL

The wild cliffs of Ponta de São Lourenço, near Caniçal

SIGHTS AT A GLANCE

Calheta ⑯
Camacha ④
Câmara de Lobos ⑱
Caniçal ⑥
Curral das Freiras ⑪
Funchal pp344–7 ①
Machico ⑤
Monte ③
Paúl da Serra ⑫
Pico do Arieiro ⑨
Pico Ruivo ⑩
Porto Moniz ⑮
Porto Santo ⑲
Quinta do Palheiro Ferreiro ②
Ribeira Brava ⑰
Ribeiro Frio ⑧
Santana ⑦
São Vicente ⑭

Walks and Tours

Rabaçal Walks ⑬

KEY

▨	Major road
▨	Minor road
▨	Scenic route
〜	River
⚜	Viewpoint

SEE ALSO

- *Where to Stay* pp399–400
- *Where to Eat* pp421–3

Street-by-Street: Funchal ❶

Tiling on Palácio do Governo Regional, Avenida M. Arriaga

THE DEEP NATURAL HARBOUR of Madeira's capital, Funchal, attracted early settlers in the 15th century. The historic core of the capital still overlooks the harbour and boasts fine government buildings and stately 18th-century houses with shady courtyards, iron balconies and carved black basalt doorways. Visitors have justly called Funchal a "little Lisbon" because of the town's steep cobbled streets and overall air of grandeur.

The Igreja do Colégio
(Collegiate Church) was found[ed] by the Jesuits in 1574. The pl[ain] exterior contrasts with the ric[hly] decorated high altar, framed [by] carved, gilded wood (1641–60[...])

Rua da Carreira and Rua do Surdo
have preserved many of their original elegant balconied houses.

São Pedro church

The Museu Municipal
houses an aquarium and is a favourite with children.

Adegas de São Francisco *(see p347)*

The monument to João Gonçalves Zarco, the man who claimed Madeira for Portugal, was created by the sculptor Francisco Franco in 1927.

Toyota Showroom
The building's exterior is decorated with 20th-century tiles depicting various Madeiran scenes including the famous Monte toboggan (see p348).

0 metres   50
0 yards   50

The Palácio de São Lourenço
is a 16th-century fortress housing Madeira's military headquarters.

RUA DAS PRETAS
RUA DO SURDO
RUA DA CARREIRA
RUA S. FRANCISCO
AVENIDA M. ARRIAGA
AVENIDA
RUA DAS FONTES

Yacht Marina
Lined with seafood restaurants, the yacht marina on Avenida do Mar is ideal for an evening stroll. The sea wall around the marina offers good views.

Avenida do Mar

STAR SIGHTS

★ Sé

★ Praça do Município

Câmara Municipal
Funchal's city hall is an imposing 18th-century mansion with a fountain in its courtyard depicting Leda and the Swan. *Inside, a small museum traces the history of Funchal in photographs.*

The Museu de Arte Sacra includes Flemish paintings, embroidered vestments and statues among the displays of religious art *(see p346).*

★ **Praça do Município**
Contrasting black and white stones pave the attractive municipal square. On the northeast side of the square is the Câmara Municipal.

Bus station

Rua do Aljube
Alongside the Sé, flower sellers in traditional costumes offer a colourful array of exotic flowers.

Palácio do Governo Regional

The Alfândega Velha (Old Customs House) was built in 1477 and is now home to the island's regional parliament.

★ **Sé**
São Tiago (St James) is one of many gilded figures that adorn the wonderfully carved wooden choir stalls in Funchal's 15th-century cathedral (see p346).

KEY

– – – Suggested route

Exploring Funchal

Funchal extends in a crescent along the coastline of Funchal Bay, with the Zona Velha or Old Quarter, a warren of former fishermen's houses, at the eastern end and the Hotel or Tourist Zone, dominated by hotels and restaurants, at the western end and beyond. Between these is the heart of Funchal, with its attractive historic centre around the gracious Avenida Arriaga. It has a lively marina and working port, where a small fishing fleet is overshadowed by cruise liners. Only three or four blocks inland, the city begins to fan out in a dense web of red-tiled roofs and subtropical greenery.

Carved Manueline-style lions in the garden at Quinta das Cruzes

🛡 Sé

Largo da Sé. 📞 291-22 81 55.
🕐 daily.

The cathedral is one of the few buildings in Madeira to have survived virtually untouched since the early days of the island's colonization. In the 1490s, King Manuel I (see pp46–9) sent the architect Pêro Anes from the mainland to work on the design of the colony's cathedral. The Sé was finally completed in 1514.

The highlights are the ceiling and the choir stalls, though neither is easy to see in the dark interior. The ceiling of inlaid wood is best seen from the south transept, where enough light filters in to illuminate the intricate patterning. The choir stalls depict saints, prophets and apostles in 16th-century costume. Aspects of Madeiran life feature in the decorative details of the arm-rests and seats: one cherub carries a bunch of bananas, another a goatskin full of wine.

Clock tower of Funchal's Sé

🏛 Museu de Arte Sacra

Rua do Bispo 21. 📞 291-22 89 00.
🕐 Tue–Sat & Sun am.
🔴 public hols. 🖼

Madeiran merchants, who grew rich on the profitable sugar trade, sought to secure their salvation by commissioning paintings, statues, embroidered vestments and illuminated hymn books for their local churches. Hundreds of examples now fill this museum which is housed in the former bishops' palace, a building dating from 1600. There are some masterpieces in the collection, including the late-Gothic processional cross donated by King Manuel I, and religious paintings by major Flemish artists of the 15th and 16th centuries. Some works include portraits of the dignitaries who commissioned them. *Saints Philip and James* is a 16th-century painting showing Simão Gonçalves de Câmara, Zarco's (see p341) grandson.

🏛 Quinta das Cruzes

Calçada do Pico 1. 📞 291-74 06 70.
🕐 Tue–Sun. 🔴 public hols. 🖼

It is said that Zarco, the man who claimed Madeira for Portugal (see p341), built his house where the Quinta das Cruzes now stands. The elegant 19th-century mansion is now the Museum of Decorative Arts, furnished as a wealthy merchant's house with Indian silk wall hangings, Regency sideboards and oriental carpets. In the basement is furniture made from mahogany packing cases used in the 17th century for shipping sugar, and turned into chests and cupboards when the sugar trade died.

The garden is dotted with ancient tombstones and architectural fragments. These include two window frames from 1507 carved with rope motifs, acrobatic figures and man-eating lions in a Madeiran version of the Manueline style of architecture (see pp20–21).

🛡 Convento de Santa Clara

Calçada de Santa Clara. 📞 291-74 26 02. 🕐 daily (ring doorbell).

Opposite Quinta das Cruzes is the Convento de Santa Clara, founded in 1496 by João Gonçalves de Câmara, one of Zarco's grandsons. Zarco himself is buried under the high altar, and Martim Mendes Vasconcelos, his son-in-law, has a tomb at the rear of the church. Precious 17th-century *azulejo* tiles cover the walls.

🌿 Jardim Botânico

Quinta do Bom Sucesso, Caminho do Meio. 🕐 daily. 🔴 25 Dec. 🖼

Opened to the public in 1960, the Botanical Gardens display plants from all over the world. Desert cacti, rainforest orchids and South African proteas grow here as well as native Madeiran dragon trees. There are contrasting sections: formal areas of bedding plants, quiet carp ponds and wild wooded parts.

The intricately patterned formal gardens of the Jardim Botânico

▐ Adegas de São Francisco
Avenida Arriaga 28. █ 291-74 01
10. ○ Mon–Fri, Sat am.
● public hols. ▓ █ compulsory.
In the cobbled courtyards of
the St Francis wine lodge, visitors are greeted by the scents
of ancient wood and Madeira.
Some of the buildings in this
maze of coopers' yards, wine
vaults and sampling rooms go
back to the 17th century when
the site was part of Funchal's
Franciscan friary. It is possible
to sample wines made on the
premises more than 150 years
ago as well as more recent
(and cheaper) vintages. Included in the guided tour is a visit
to the warming rooms where
Madeira is "cooked" by hot
water pipes (see p349).

**Tasting Madeira wine at the
Adegas de São Francisco**

⚱ Mercado dos Lavradores
Largo dos Lavradores. █ 291-22 25
84. ○ Mon–Sat. ● public hols.
The Mercado dos Lavradores is
where flower growers, basket
weavers, farmers and fishermen from all over Madeira
bring their products to market.
The covered market
building, situated on
three floors around an
open courtyard, is full
of the colour and bustle
of island life. Stall-
holders offer slices of
mango or custard fruit
to prove that theirs are
the sweetest and best.
In the basement, marble
tables are draped with
great slabs of tuna and
black-skinned scabbard
fish with huge eyes
and razor-sharp teeth.
On Fridays the mar-
ket spills out into the
back streets of the Zona
Velha (Old Town), the
former fishermen's
quarter and now an
area of small shops

and lively pavement cafés and
bars. The simple, single-storey
dwellings situated at the pedestrianized eastern end of Rua
Dom Carlos I, are said to date
from the 15th century. The
little Corpo Santo chapel was
built by 16th-century fishermen
in honour of their patron, St
Peter, and is said to be the oldest such building in Funchal.

♣ Fortaleza de São Tiago
Rua do Portão de São Tiago. █ 291-
21 33 40. **Museum** ○ Mon–Sat.
● public hols. ▓
Along the seafront is the
newly restored Fortaleza de
São Tiago, built in 1614, with
additions dating from 1767.
The fortress, with its maze of
passages and staircases, commands views over Funchal and
houses a Museum of Contemporary Art and a restaurant.

**Fishmonger chopping tuna into huge steaks in the
basement of Funchal's Mercado dos Lavradores**

House and gardens of the Quinta do Palheiro Ferreiro

Quinta do Palheiro Ferreiro ❷

Sítio do Balançal, São Gonçalo.
█ 291-793 044. ▬ ○ 9am–
12:30pm Mon–Fri. ● 1 Jan, Easter,
1 May, 25 Dec. ▓

T HE QUINTA DO PALHEIRO
Ferreiro is Madeira's finest
garden and a place of pilgrimage for flower-lovers. A French
landscape architect laid out the
gardens in the 18th century for
the wealthy Count of Carvalhal,
who built the elegant mansion
(not open to visitors) overlooking the garden and the Baroque
chapel in the garden itself.
The estate was acquired in
1885 by the long-established
Anglo-Madeiran Blandy family,
hence its English name: Blandy's Gardens. New species
were introduced from
South Africa, China and
Australia, resulting in a
garden that combines
the clipped formality of
late 18th-century layout
with the profusion of
English-style herba-
ceous borders, plus
the combination of
tropical and temperate
climate varieties.
Quite apart from its
horticultural interest,
the garden is a peaceful
wildlife haven, full of
beauty and contrast as
you pass from the for-
mality of the Ladies'
Garden to the tropical
wilderness of the ravine
ominously signposted
"Inferno" (Hell).

The contrasting façade of Nossa Senhora do Monte, created by basalt against whitewash

Monte ❸

🏛 10,000. 🚌 ℹ️ Caminho de Ferro 182, Junta da Freguesia (291-78 25 55).

MONTE HAS BEEN a favourite destination for visitors to Madeira since the late 19th century, when a rack and pinion railway was built to haul cruise liner passengers up the hillside from Funchal. Coming down they would take the famous **Monte toboggan** ride.

An alternative way to get to the Monte is by the new cable car that runs from Jardim do Almirante Reis, below the old town, up to the Caminho das Babosas, by the Monte Palace Gardens. The ascent takes 15 minutes, and the car operates between 10am and 6pm daily. The railway closed in 1939, but the station and a viaduct survive, now forming part of the luxuriant **Jardim do Monte** public gardens. It is a short stroll through the gardens to the church of **Nossa Senhora do Monte**, whose twin-towered façade looks down on the island's capital. The present church was built in 1818 on the site of a chapel built in 1470 by Adam Gonçalves Ferreira.

The Virgin of Monte is Madeira's patron saint and this church is the focal point of the pilgrimage that takes place annually on 15 August (the Feast of the Assumption) when penitents climb the church's 74 steps on their knees. The object of their worship is a tiny statue of the Virgin on the high altar.

Left of the nave is a chapel housing a mortuary chest, containing the remains of the last Hapsburg Emperor, Karl I, who was deposed in 1918. Exiled in Madeira he died of pneumonia in 1922, aged only 35.

Toboggan drivers in straw hats wait for passengers every day on the corner of Caminho do Monte, and they run (for a fee) to Livramento and on to Funchal. From the church steps, past the drivers' corner, a left turn signposted "Old Monte Gardens" leads to the **Monte Palace Tropical Gardens**. These superb gardens, laid out in 1894, will delight children with their maze of pathways and bridges, follies, fountains, cascades and black swans. The gardens extend for 7 ha (17 acres) down a lush valley with areas devoted to Madeiran flora, South African proteas, plants from Japan and China, azaleas, camellias and orchids.

🌺 **Monte Palace Tropical Gardens**
Caminho do Monte 174. 📞 291-78 23 39. 🕐 daily. 📷

One of the skilled wicker workers of Camacha constructing a table

Camacha ❹

🏛 9,000. 🚌 ℹ️ Junta da Freguesia, Complexo de Habitação dos Casais de Além 2 (291-92 24 66).

MOST OF THE wicker products sold in Funchal are made in and around Camacha, and the sole attraction in this otherwise sleepy village is a large shop packed with everything wicker, from picture frames, bedsteads and cradles to peacock-backed armchairs. It is often possible to see weavers at work, bending the pliant stripped willow round a frame to produce a linen basket or plant-pot container. A Noah's Ark full of paired animals is displayed on the middle floor, along with a full-sailed galleon, as an advertisement of the local wicker weavers' skills.

THE MONTE TOBOGGAN

Sliding in a wicker basket mounted on wooden runners, it is possible to cover the 2-km (1-mile) descent from Monte to Livramento in 10 minutes. The trip is made by thousands every year, fascinated by the experience of travelling at speed down a public highway on a wooden sled. Ernest Hemingway once described it as "exhilarating". A cushioned seat softens the ride and passengers are in the safe hands of the toboggan drivers, who push and steer from the rear, using their rubber-soled boots as brakes. Madeiran tobogganing was invented as a form of passenger transport around 1850.

The famous Monte Toboggan ride

Madeira Wine

Wicker-covered Madeira bottle

IN THE 16TH CENTURY, ships stopping at Funchal would take on barrels of local wine. This unforti-fied Madeira often spoiled during the voyage, so shippers started adding spirit to make it better. The wine now seemed to improve after a long, hot voyage, and quality Madeira began to be sent on round trips as an alternative to maturing it in Funchal's lodges. This expensive method was replaced with the *estufa* system, still very much in use today. Large volumes of wine are heated to between 30 and 50°C for a period of three months to a year. The effect is to hurry up the ageing process: the best wines are "cooked" more gently and slowly. The finest Madeirans are heated by the sun, maturing slowly in the attics of the wine lodges.

Most Madeira is made from the Tinta Negra Mole grape, often blended with one of the four noble varieties listed below.

Making barrels for Madeira, Funchal

THE FOUR TYPES OF MADEIRA

Sercial *is made from white grapes grown at heights up to 1,000 m (3,280 ft). Good-quality Sercial is aged for at least ten years, giving it its amber colour. A dry wine – it is mostly drunk as an aperitif or with soup, and is best served chilled.*

Verdelho *grapes are grown in cool vineyards at lower heights than the Sercial. This medium- dry tawny wine is also drunk as an aperitif. Sweeter than Sercial, Verdelho goes well with a slice of Madeira cake (invented by the English for just this purpose).*

The barrels *in the Adegas de São Francisco (see p347), where Madeira is warmed, need fre-quent repair as do the wooden floors that bear their huge weight.*

These casks of Verdelho *are being aged after the addition of brandy to the wine. Vintage wine must spend at least 20 years in the cask and two in the bottle.*

Bual *(or Boal) grapes are grown in lower, warmer condi-tions. Dark, rich and nutty, it is a medium-sweet wine that can be served as an alternative to port. It goes very well with cheeses and dessert, and is best drunk at room temperature.*

Malmsey, *the most celebrated Madeira, is made from Malvasia grapes grown in sunny vineyards backed by cliffs, where the heat absorbed by the rock by day warms the grapes by night. The result is a rich dark wine drunk as an after-dinner digestive.*

Vintage Madeira *from every decade as far back as the mid-19th century is still available for sale. The oldest surviving bottle of Madeira dates from 1772.*

Machico ⑤

🏃 22,000. 🚌 ℹ *Forte de Nossa Senhora do Amparo, Rua da Nossa Senhora (291-96 22 89).*

LEGEND HAS IT that Machico was named after Robert Machim, a merchant from Bristol, who eloped with the aristocratic Anne of Hertford and set sail for Portugal. Caught in a storm and shipwrecked on Madeira, the two lovers died from exposure and were buried. The rest of the crew repaired the boat and sailed to Lisbon, where their story inspired Prince Henry the Navigator *(see p49)* to send João Gonçalves Zarco *(see p341)* in search of this mysterious wooded island.

Main altar in the Capela dos Milagres, Machico

Machico has been Madeira's second most important town since the first settlements, when the island was divided into two captaincies: Zarco ruled the west from Funchal whilst his fellow navigator, Tristão Vaz Teixeira, ruled the east from Machico. However, Funchal's superior location and harbour soon ensured that it developed as the capital of Madeira while Machico became a sleepy agricultural town.

The **Igreja Matriz** on Largo do Município, Machico's main square, dates from the 15th century. Above the high altar is a statue of the Virgin Mary, donated by Manuel I *(see pp46–9)*, as were the three marble pillars used in the construction of the Gothic south portal. Inside, there is a fine example of Manueline-style stone masonry in the Capela de São João Baptista, whose arch shows Teixeira's coat of arms, with a phoenix rising from the flames.

Across the River Machico, on Largo dos Milagres, is the **Capela dos Milagres** (Chapel of the Miracles). The present structure dates from 1815, but it stands on the site of Madeira's first church, where Robert Machim and Anne of Hertford are supposedly buried. The earlier church of 1420 was destroyed in a flood in 1803, but the 15th-century crucifix was found floating out at sea. Machico celebrates the return of its cross with a procession every year on 8 October.

View from Ponta de São Lourenço promontory, east of Caniçal

Caniçal ⑥

🏃 5,000. 🚌 ℹ *(as for Machico) (291-96 22 89).*

CANIÇAL WAS ONCE the centre of Madeira's whaling industry: the whaling scenes for John Huston's film version of *Moby Dick* (1956) were shot here. Whaling only ceased in June 1981, and since then the waters around Madeira have been declared a marine mammal sanctuary, where the killing of whales, dolphins and seals is forbidden. Local fishermen who once hunted whales now work with the Society for the Protection of Sea Mammals, helping marine biologists understand whale migrations.

The old whaling company's office is now the **Museu da Baleia** (Whaling Museum). It shows a 45-minute video on whale hunting with commentaries by retired fishermen.

Caniçal is still a busy fishing port, and the stony beach is used by tuna fishermen to repair their colourful boats.

🏛 Museu da Baleia
Largo Manuel Alves. **C** *291-96 14 07.* **◯** *Tue–Sun.* **◐** *public hols.* 🈲 ♿

ENVIRONS: The easternmost tip of Madeira, the **Ponta de São Lourenço**, is characterized by dramatic wave-battered cliffs plunging 180 m (590 ft) to the Atlantic. Walkers are attracted by footpaths which meander from one clifftop to another, with wild flowers growing in sheltered hollows. The treeless landscape contrasts totally with the island's wooded interior.

On the road from Caniçal to Ponta de São Lourenço, look out for the signpost to the bay of **Prainha**, Madeira's only naturally sandy beach.

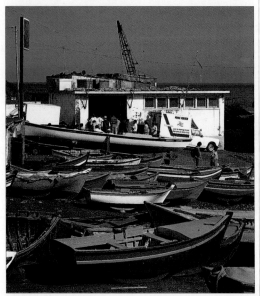

Fishing boats hauled up on the beach at Caniçal

Santana 7

🏠 10,500. 🚌 ℹ️ Sítio do Serrado (291-57 29 92).

SANTANA (named after St Anne, mother of the Virgin) has more than 100 thatched triangular houses, several of which, restored and brightly painted, can be visited by the public. The hillsides above the broad valley in which Santana sits are also dotted with triangular thatched byres, where cows are tethered to stop them from wandering along narrow terrace paths and harming themselves or crops.

The valley is intensively farmed both for fruit and vegetables, and osiers, the willow branches that are the raw material for the wicker workers of Camacha (see p348).

Ribeiro Frio 8

🏠 45. 🚌 from Funchal.

Bridge across a *levada* on the walk from Ribeiro Frio to Balcões

RIBEIRO FRIO is a pretty spot consisting of a couple of restaurants, shops and a trout farm, fed by the "cold stream" after which the place is named.

Surrounding the trout farm is an attractive garden full of native trees and shrubs. This is the starting point for two of the island's best *levada* walks (see p355). The 12-km (7-mile) path signposted to **Portela** (on the right heading downhill past the restaurants) passes through dramatic mountain scenery but is best left to experienced walkers because of the long tunnels and steep drops in places. Far easier is

Sunrise over the mountains, seen from Pico do Arieiro

the 20-minute walk on the left (going downhill) signposted to **Balcões** (Balconies). This viewpoint gives panoramic views across the valley of the River Ametade to Penha de Águia (Eagle Rock), the sheer-sided hill that projects from Madeira's northern coast.

Pico do Arieiro 9

🚌 to Camacha, then taxi. **Pousada do Pico do Arieiro** 📞 291-23 01 10 (reservations: 291-70 20 30).

FROM FUNCHAL it is about a 30-minute drive up the Pico do Arieiro, Madeira's third highest mountain at 1,810 m (5,938 ft). The route leads through steep hillsides cloaked in fragrant eucalyptus and bay laurel. At around 900 m (2,950 ft), you will often meet the cloudline and pass for a few minutes through swirling mists and possibly rain, before emerging into a sunlit landscape of volcanic rocks. At the top, the view is of clouds in the valleys and dramatic mountain ridges with knife-edge peaks. Just visible on a clear day is Pico Ruivo (see p354), connected to Pico do Arieiro by a 10-km (6-mile) path. The Pousada do Pico do Arieiro guesthouse on the mountaintop allows walkers to see a spectacular sunrise.

THE TRIANGULAR HOUSES OF SANTANA

Simply constructed from two A-shaped timber frames, with a wood-panelled interior and thatched roof, these triangular houses are unique to Madeira. They are first mentioned in the 16th century, but most of the surviving examples are no more than 100 years old. Today their doors and windows are often painted a cheerful red, yellow or blue. In the warm year-round climate of Madeira, cooking and eating take place out of doors, and the toilets are placed well away from the house. To the inhabitants, therefore, the triangular houses serve principally as shelter from the rain and for sleeping in. The interior is deceptively spacious, with a living area downstairs and sleeping space up in the loft.

Panoramic view of the mountains from the Pico Ruivo summit

Pico Ruivo ⑩

🚌 to Santana or Faial, then taxi to Achada do Teixeira, then walk.

MADEIRA'S HIGHEST mountain at 1,861 m (6,105 ft), Pico Ruivo is only accessible on foot. The easiest way to scale its heights is via a well signposted footpath which begins at the village of Achada do Teixeira and leads visitors on a 45-minute walk to the top.

Alternatively, follow the walk from the top of Pico do Arieiro *(see p351)* along one of the island's most spectacular footpaths. Awe-inspiring mountain scenery and glorious views can be enjoyed all along the 10-km (6-mile) walk. This takes two to three hours and is really only suitable for experienced, well-equipped walkers. Vertigo sufferers should not attempt the path, as it involves negotiating narrow ridges with sheer drops on either side.

Curral das Freiras ⑪

🏘 3,000. 🚌 🚹 Câmara de Lobos (291-94 34 70).

CURRAL DAS FREIRAS means "Nuns' Refuge" and the name refers to the nuns of the Santa Clara convent who fled to this idyllic spot when pirates attacked Funchal in 1566. The nuns have left now, but the village remains. Visitors first glimpse Curral das Freiras from a viewpoint known as the **Eira do Serrado**, perched some 800 m (2,625 ft) above the scattered village.

The valley is surrounded on all sides by jagged mountain peaks. Until 1959 the only access to the village was by a steep zig-zagging path, but road tunnels now make the journey much easier and allow local people to transport their produce to the capital. Television arrived in 1986.

The sweet chestnuts that grow in profusion around the village are turned into sweet chestnut bread, best eaten still warm from the oven, and *licor de castanha*, a chestnut-flavoured liqueur. Both can be sampled in local bars.

Paúl da Serra ⑫

🚌 to Canhas, then taxi.

Sheep grazing on the wide plateau of Paúl da Serra, east of Rabaçal

THE PAÚL DA SERRA (literally "high moorland") is a large, boggy plateau, 17 km (11 miles) in length and 6 km (4 miles) in width. The plain contrasts dramatically with the jagged mountains that characterize the rest of Madeira.

Electricity for the north of the island is generated here by wind turbines. Only gorse and grass grow on the thin soil, and the sponge-like volcanic substrata act as a natural reservoir for rainfall. Water filters through the rock to emerge as springs which then feed the island's *levada* system.

THE LEVADAS OF MADEIRA

Madeira possesses a unique irrigation system that enables the plentiful rainfall of the north of the island to be distributed to the drier, sunny south. Rainfall is stored in reservoirs and lakes, or channelled from natural springs, and

Levada do Risco, one of many walking routes across Madeira

fed into the network of *levadas* that ring the island. These narrow channels carry water long distances to banana groves, vineyards and market gardens. Altogether there are 2,150 km (1,335 miles) of canals, some dating back to the 1500s. Maintenance paths run alongside the *levadas*, providing a network of footpaths reaching into remote parts of the island inaccessible by road.

◁ **Terraced hillsides around the village of Curral das Freiras**

Rabaçal Walks ⑬

REACHED DOWN a single-track road from the Paúl da Serra plateau, Rabaçal is the starting point for two, equally magical, *levada* walks. One is a simple 30-minute, there-and-back stroll to the Risco waterfall, while the other is a more demanding two- to three-hour walk to the beauty spot known as Vinte e Cinco Fontes (25 Springs).

TIPS FOR WALKERS

Length: These two walks can be combined to create a circular route of 8 km (5 miles), taking around three and a half hours.
Note: The levadas can be slippery and sometimes very narrow. In places the path is only 30 cm (1 ft) wide, but the channel runs at waist height and you can hold on.

Levada da Rocha Vermelha ⑥
Wild, mountainous terrain forms the backdrop to the steep path down to the lower *levada*.

25 Fontes ⑤
A 30-minute walk brings you to a mossy, fern-hung area with a main cascade and many smaller ones.

Ribeira da Janela ④
Cross the bridge and then tackle the steep uphill climb on the left.

Rabaçal ①
The starting point of the walk has a car park and government rest house with picnic tables and views down the secluded valley. Follow the signposted path down to the right to meet the Levada do Risco.

Risco Waterfall ③
At this magnificent spot, a torrent of water cascades from the rocky heights down into the green depths of the Risco valley far below.

KEY

- ▬ ▬ Walk route
- ▬ Road
- ≈ River
- ═ Levada
- P Parking

Levada do Risco ②
The course of the *levada*, which leads to the waterfall, is shaded by tree heathers draped with hair-like lichens.

0 metres 250

0 yards 250

PAUL DA SERRA

Simple stone font in the attractively tiled baptistry of the Igreja Matriz in São Vicente

São Vicente ⓮

🏠 8,000. 🚌 ℹ Câmara Municipal, Vila de São Vicente (291-84 21 35).

THE AGRICULTURAL town of São Vicente has grown prosperous over the years by tempting travellers to break their journeys here as they explore Madeira's northern coast.

To see how the village looked before development began, visit the **Igreja Matriz** (originally built in the 17th century), and look at the painting on the ceiling of St Vincent blessing the town. St Vincent appears again over the elaborately carved and gilded main altar, this time blessing a ship.

Around the church, cobbled traffic-free streets are lined with boutiques, bars and shops selling sweet cakes, including the popular Madeiran speciality

bolo de mel, the so-called "honey cake" (actually made with molasses and fruit).

São Vicente marks the starting point of the coastal road northwest to Porto Moniz, one of the island's most exhilarating drives. The road, little more than a ledge cut into the sheer cliffs, sometimes passes through tunnels, sometimes through waterfalls. The 19-km (12-mile) road took 16 years to build without the aid of machinery.

The only village along this lonely road is **Seixal**. Despite the Atlantic storms that can batter the island's northern coast, Seixal occupies a remarkably sheltered spot where vineyards cling to the hillside terraces, producing excellent wine.

Porto Moniz ⓯

🏠 4,000. 🚌 ℹ Vila do Porto Moniz (291-85 25 94).

ALTHOUGH IT IS only 75 km (47 miles) from Funchal, visitors arriving in Porto Moniz feel a great sense of achievement after the long journey to this remote coastal village, on the northwest tip of Madeira.

Porto Moniz is surrounded by a patchwork pattern of tiny fields. The fields are protected by fences made from tree heather and dried bracken, a necessary precaution against the heavy, salt-laden air that blows in off the Atlantic.

Apart from its picturesque charm, the main attraction at Porto Moniz is the series of natural rock pools joined by concrete paths on the foreshore, where you can paddle or immerse yourself in sun-warmed water while being showered by spray as waves break against the nearby rocks.

Calheta ⓰

🏠 3,500. 🚌 ℹ Câmara Municipal, Vila da Calheta (291-82 02 00).

Bananas, a prolific crop in Calheta

CALHETA STANDS among flourishing vineyards and banana plantations. It is also at the centre of what little sugarcane production survives on Madeira, and the sweet smell of cane syrup being extracted and turned into rum hangs around the village from the **factory** (visitors are welcome; the best time is March to April).

The **Igreja Matriz** looks unpromisingly modern but it dates from 1430 and contains a large ebony and silver tabernacle donated by Manuel I *(see pp46–7)*. There is also a fine wooden ceiling.

🏭 Factory
Vila da Calheta. 🕿 291-82 22 64. 🕐 daily.

ENVIRONS: About 2 km (1 mile) east of Calheta, at **Loreto**, the 15th-century chapel has a Manueline south portal and geometrically patterned ceiling. Outside Estreito da Calheta, 3 km (2 miles) northwest of Calheta, is **Lombo dos Reis**. Here the Capela dos Reis Magos (Chapel of the Three Kings) has a lively 16th-century Flemish altar carving of the *Adoration of the Magi*.

The warm, natural rock pools at Porto Moniz

Part of Porto Santo's splendid sandy beach

Ribeira Brava ⑰

🏠 13,500. 🚌 🛈 Forte de São Bento (291-95 16 75). 🏮 daily.

RIBEIRA BRAVA is a small, attractive resort town, situated on the sunny south coast of Madeira. It has a pebble beach and a fishing harbour, which is reached through a tunnel to the east of the main town.

Overlooking the principal square, **São Bento** remains one of the most unspoiled churches on Madeira. Despite restoration and reconstruction, several of its 16th-century features are still intact. These include a stone-carved font and ornate pulpit decorated with wild beasts such as wolves, the Flemish painting of the *Nativity* in the side chapel, and the wooden statue of the Virgin over the main altar. The church's clock tower has a beautifully tiled roof.

São Bento's clock tower, Ribeira Brava

This is one of Madeira's main centres for catching scabbard fish *(peixe espada)*, which feature on every Madeiran menu. Long lines are baited with octopus to catch these unusual fish that dwell at depths of 800 m (2,600 ft). The fishermen live in single-storey dwellings along the harbour front, and their tiny **chapel** dates from the 15th century, but was rebuilt in 1723. The chapel is dedicated to St Nicholas, the patron saint of seafarers, and is decorated with scenes from the saint's life, as well as vivid portrayals of drownings and shipwrecks.

ENVIRONS: The second highest sea cliff in Europe is **Cabo Girão**, located 10 km (6 miles) west of Câmara de Lobos. It peaks at a dramatic 589 m (1,932 ft) above sea level.

Câmara de Lobos ⑱

🏠 15,000. 🚌 🛈 Câmara Municipal, Largo da República (291-94 34 70). 🏮 Mon–Sat.

VISITORS TO this pretty fishing village are not allowed to forget that it was several times painted by Winston Churchill, who often visited Madeira in the 1950s. Bars and restaurants are named in his honour and a plaque marks the spot on the main road, east of the harbour, where the great statesman set up his easels. The town has not changed greatly since then.

Porto Santo ⑲

🏠 5,000. ✈ 🚢 🛈 Avenida Henrique Vieira e Castro, Vila Baleira (291-98 23 61). 🏮 Mon–Sat, Sun am.

PORTO SANTO, the island that lies 37 km (23 miles) northeast of Madeira, is smaller, flatter and drier than its sister island. It also possesses something that Madeira lacks: a 9-km (6-mile) beach of golden sand, running the entire length of the island's south coast. There is a daily ferry service between Funchal and Porto Santo, which takes 2 hours and 40 minutes. There are also daily flights, shortening the trip to 15 minutes.

Porto Santo is a popular holiday destination for Madeirans, mainland Portuguese and growing numbers of foreign tourists. There are five big, but mostly discreet hotels, and several holiday resorts with villas and apartments. Snorkelling is good here and bicycles can be hired.

The one historic site of note on the island is the **Casa de Colombo** (house of Christopher Columbus), located behind Nossa Senhora da Piedade in Vila Baleira. The restored house is built from rough stone, and contains exhibits that tell Columbus's story, including maps, paintings and engravings.

🏛 Casa de Colombo
Travessa da Sacristia 2, Vila Baleira.
📞 291-98 34 05. ⏱ Tue–Fri, Sat & Sun am.

CHRISTOPHER COLUMBUS ON PORTO SANTO

Historical records vouch for the fact that Christopher Columbus came to Madeira in 1478, probably as an agent for sugar merchants in his native Italian town of Genoa. He went to Porto Santo to meet Bartolomeu Perestrelo, also from Genoa and the island's governor. There he met Filipa Moniz, Perestrelo's daughter. The two were married in 1479, but Filipa died soon after while giving birth to their son. Nothing else is known about Columbus's visit to the island, though this has not prevented local people from identifying his house.

Christopher Colombus by Ridolfo Ghirlandaio (1483–1561)

THE AZORES

F AR OUT IN THE ATLANTIC, *1,300 km (800 miles) west of Portugal's mainland, the nine islands of the Azores are known for their spectacular volcanic scenery, abundant flora and peaceful way of life. Once wild and remote, they are now a popular destination for travellers who enjoy walking, sailing and getting away from it all.*

Santa Maria was the first island discovered by the Portuguese in 1427. The archipelago was named after the buzzards the early explorers saw flying overhead and mistook for goshawks *(açores)*. The islands were settled during the 15th and 16th centuries by colonists from Portugal and Flanders who introduced cattle, maize and vines.

Império **chapel on Pico**

The Azores have profited from their far-flung position in the Atlantic. Between 1580 and 1640, when Portugal came under Spanish rule *(see pp50–51)*, the ports of Angra do Heroísmo on Terceira and Ponta Delgada on São Miguel prospered from the trade with the New World. In the 19th century the islands were a regular port of call for American whaling ships. During the 20th century they have benefited from their use as stations for transatlantic cable companies, meteorological observatories and military air bases.

Today the majority of islanders are involved in either dairy farming or fishing, and close links are maintained with both mainland Portugal and the sizeable communities of emigrant Azoreans in the United States and Canada. Many emigrants return to their native island for the traditional annual festivals, such as the *festas* of the Holy Spirit, celebrated in the colourful *impérios*. With few beaches, a capricious, often wet climate and no large-scale resorts, the Azores have escaped mass tourism. Most travellers come here to explore the green mountains embroidered with blue hydrangeas and relax in quiet ports adorned with cobbled streets and elegant Baroque churches. Once a brave new world of pioneer communities, the Azores are now an autonomous region of Portugal and an exotic corner of the European Union, where life remains refreshingly civil and unhurried.

Small fishing boats on the quayside at Lajes on the southern coast of Pico

◁ **Terceira's walled pastures sloping down to the sea with the two small Ilhéus das Cabras in the distance**

Exploring the Azores

THE ISLANDS OF THE AZORES are spread 650 km (400 miles) apart and fall into three distinct groups. In the east lie Santa Maria and São Miguel, the largest island and home to the regional capital, Ponta Delgada. The main towns in the central group of five islands are Horta on Faial, a popular stop-over port for boats crossing the Atlantic, and Angra do Heroísmo on Terceira, a charming, historic town. From here visitors can travel to the other islands of São Jorge, Graciosa and Pico, the last dominated by a towering volcanic peak 2,350 m (7,700 ft) high. Further west lie the remote, weather-beaten islands of Flores and Corvo.

Transatlantic sailing boat moored in Faial's fine marina at Horta

9 CORVO
Vila Nova do Corvo

8 FLORES
Santa Cruz das Flores
Lajes

Santa Cruz da Graciosa
Praia

4 GRACIOSA

Sights at a Glance

Corvo **9**
Faial **7**
Flores **8**
Graciosa **4**
Pico **6**
Santa Maria **2**
São Jorge **5**
São Miguel pp362–3 **1**
Terceira **3**

Velas
5 SÃO JORGE
Calheta
Santo Antão

7 FAIAL
Capelo
Horta

Madalena
São Roque do Pico
Piedade

São Mateus
6 PICO
Lajes do Pico

Walking among Pico's black volcanic lava rock

| 0 kilometres | 25 |
| 0 miles | 10 |

KEY

━━ Road

━━ Scenic route

❃ Viewpoint

SEE ALSO

• *Where to Stay* pp400–1

• *Where to Eat* p423

GETTING AROUND

São Miguel, Faial and Terceira have international airports and the local airline, SATA, flies between all the islands. Ferry services connect the five central islands several times a week in summer. There is a daily summer service between Flores and Corvo but no service between Santa Maria and São Miguel. All ferry services are subject to the weather. Bus services on the islands are designed for the locals and therefore not always practical for tourists. Car hire is more convenient and available on all islands except Corvo. *(See also p447.)*

THE AZORES

MADEIRA

3 TERCEIRA

Biscoitos

Praia da Vitória

Santa Bárbara

São Mateus

Angra do Heroísmo

Angra do Heroísmo, capital of Terceira

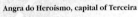

R1-1 Ribeira Grande Porto Formoso R1-1

Sete Cidades

Ponta Delgada

Lagoa

Vila Franca do Campo

Povoação

R1-1

1 SÃO MIGUEL

Ponta Delgada's elegant waterfront, São Miguel

2 SANTA MARIA

Anjos

Santa Bárbara

Vila do Porto

São Miguel ❶

WITH ITS HISTORIC maritime capital, rich green fields and dramatic volcanic scenery, this *ilha verde* (green island) provides a rewarding introduction to the Azores. The largest and most populated of the archipelago's nine main islands, São Miguel is 65 km (40 miles) long and was originally two separate islands. The capital, Ponta Delgada, is a good base from which to make day tours of the rugged coast or visit the volcanic crater lakes and steaming thermal springs in the interior of the island.

The 18th-century city gates leading onto Ponta Delgada's central square

Ponta Delgada

Lined with many impressive churches, convents and trim white houses, the cobbled streets of the Azorean capital recall the wealthy days when the port was a crucial staging post between Europe and the New World *(see pp48–9)*. Its hub is the arcaded Praça de Gonçalo Velho Cabral, named after the first governor of the island in 1444, which looks out onto the seafront. It is dominated by three imposing arches, dating from 1783, that once marked the entrance to the city. To the north, in Largo da Matriz, stands the parish church of **São Sebastião**. Founded in 1533 it has a graceful Manueline portal intricately carved in limestone. The sacristy is decorated with *azulejo* panels and beautiful 17th-century furniture made of jacaranda wood from Brazil.

A short walk west lies the Praça 5 de Outubro, a shaded, tree-lined square overlooked by the **Forte de São Brás**. This Renaissance fortress, built on a spur overlooking the sea, was greatly restored in the 19th century. Also on the square, the immense **Convento da Esperança** becomes the focus of intense festivities when the city celebrates the festival of Santo Cristo dos Milagres on the fifth Sunday after Easter. A statue of Christ, wearing a red robe decorated with sumptuous diamond and gold ornaments, leads the procession through the streets. The statue can be seen in the lower church along with other religious treasures, including reliquaries, monstrances and precious jewels. Colourful tiles, dating from the 18th century, by António de Oliveira Bernardes *(see p22)* decorate the choir.

The principal museum in the Azores, the **Museu Carlos Machado**, occupies the former monastery of Santo André. Its exhibits reflect the fishing and farming industries that have ruled life on the islands. Of particular interest are the paintings by Domingos Rebelo (1891–1975) showing scenes of Azorean life. The natural history wing is packed with an encyclopedic array of stuffed animals, varnished fish, skeletons and a large relief model of the island.

🏛 **Museu Carlos Machado**
Rua João Moreira. 📞 296-283 814.
🕐 *Tue–Sun.* ⬤ *public hols.* 📷

West of the Island

The northwest of São Miguel is punctured by a giant volcanic crater, **Caldeira das Sete Cidades**, with a 12-km (7-mile) circumference. In places its sheer walls drop like green curtains for 300 m (1,000 ft). When not obscured by cloud, the crater is best seen from the viewpoint of **Vista do Rei** from where a walk leads west around its rim. The crater floor contains the small village of Sete Cidades and three dark green lakes separated by a thin strip of land. The crater is believed to have been formed in the 1440s when an eruption destroyed the volcanic peak that had formed the western part of the island. In contrast to the lush vegetation that covers the crater now, the first settlers described the area as a burnt-out shell.

The main town on the north coast, **Ribeira Grande** has a small **Casa da Cultura** (cultural centre) housed in the restored 17th-century Solar de São Vicente. *Azulejos* from the 16th to 20th century are on display and in other rooms the crafts and rural lifestyle of the islanders are recorded, including a period barber's shop rescued from Ponta Delgada.

🏛 **Casa da Cultura**
Rua São Vicente Ferreira 10, Ribeira Grande. 📞 296-47 21 18. 🕐 *Mon–Fri.* ⬤ *public hols.* **Donation.**

KEY

━━━ Main road

══ Other road

🗻 Viewpoint

Turquoise waters of the crater lake, Lagoa do Fogo

VISITORS' CHECKLIST

🏠 125,000. ✈ 3 km (2 miles) W of Ponta Delgada. 🚢 🚌 Avenida Infante Dom Henrique, Ponta Delgada. 🛈 Avenida Infante Dom Henrique, Ponta Delgada (296-28 57 43). 🎉 5th Sun after Easter: Santo Cristo dos Milagres (Ponta Delgada); Festas do Espírito Santo (see p366). 🅦 www.drtacores.pt

East of the Island

The **Lagoa do Fogo**, "Lake of Fire", was formed in the island's central mountains by a volcanic eruption in 1563. On sunny days its remote sandy beach is a tranquil picnic spot.

Further east, the spa resort of **Furnas** is the perfect place to admire the geothermal activity taking place beneath the surface of the Azores (see pp338–9). Scattered around the town are the **Caldeiras das Furnas** where visitors will see the steaming geysers and hot bubbling springs that provide the therapeutic mud and mineral water used for the spa's treatments. In the 18th century, Thomas Hickling, a prosperous merchant from Boston, laid out gardens in Furnas which have now grown into the glorious **Parque Terra Nostra**. Covering 12 ha (30 acres), the gardens have a rich collection of mature trees and plants, including hibiscus and hydrangeas, as well as a bizarre swimming pool with warm, mustard-coloured water.

The volcanic ground on the northern shores of the **Lagoa das Furnas**, 4 km (2 miles) south, is so hot the islanders come here to cook *cozido*

(see p231). The rich meat and vegetable stew is cooked underground for five hours.

The far east of São Miguel is a beautiful area of deep valleys. Two immaculately kept viewpoints, **Miradouro do Sossego** and **Miradouro da Madrugada**, have fine gardens – the latter is a popular spot for watching the sunrise.

🏛 **Caldeiras das Furnas**
Off R1-1. 🛈 🛈 296-584 525.
(The spa: **Central Termal das Furnas**, 296-549 00. ☐ daily.)

Pristine gardens and picnic area of the Miradouro da Madrugada

The wide bay of São Lourenço on Santa Maria

Santa Maria ②

🏠 6,000. ✈ 3 km (2 miles) NW of Vila do Porto. 🚢 Vila do Porto. 🚌 Rua Dr Luis Bettencourt, Vila do Porto. ℹ Aeroporto de Santa Maria, Vila do Porto (296-886 355). 📅 Festas do Espírito Santo (see p366); 15 Aug: Nossa Senhora da Assunção (Vila do Porto). ⓦ www.drtacores.pt

LYING 55 KM (34 miles) south of São Miguel, Santa Maria was the first island in the archipelago to be discovered by the Portuguese around 1427. Though only 18 km (11 miles) long, it has great scenic variety and boasts sandy beaches, tranquil countryside and the warmest climate in the Azores.

Nossa Senhora da Purificação studded with black basalt in Santo Espírito, Santa Maria

The island's capital, **Vila do Porto**, is on the south coast and consists of a long main street that runs down to a small harbour. The west of the island is a dry, flat plateau with a vast airstrip built in World War II. To the north lies the fishing town of **Anjos**, where a statue commemorates a visit made by Christopher Columbus in 1493 on his return from discovering the New World. Next to it, the small, whitewashed chapel of **Mãe de Deus** is the oldest in the Azores.

The highest point of Santa Maria is the central **Pico Alto**, 590 m (1,935 ft) above sea level, which on a clear day offers fine views over the green and hilly east side of the island. Towards the east coast, the village of **Santo Espírito** is worth visiting for the white Baroque façade of its church of Nossa Senhora da Purificação adorned with black lava decoration, while the vine-covered half-crater of **Baía de São Lourenço**, north of here, is a delightful summer beach resort.

Terceira ❸

🏠 60,000. ✈ 3 km (2 miles) NW of Praia da Vitória. 🚢 Angra Alvaro Martins Homem. 🚌 Avenida 1º de Maio, Angra do Heroísmo. ℹ Rua Direita 70–74, Angra do Heroísmo (295-213 393). 📅 Festas do Espírito Santo (see p366); late Jun: Festas de São João. ⓦ www.drtacores.pt

TERCEIRA, MEANING "third" in Portuguese, is so named because it was the third island to be discovered, in 1427. It is the most developed of the five central islands – a result in part of the large American-run airbase that has been operating at Lajes since World War II. Terceira is famous for its unusual form of bull-running, known as the *tourada à corda* (bullfight with a rope), which takes place from spring to autumn. A bull is let loose in the street and taunted while tied to a rope held tight by teams of men. It is also renowned for the brightly painted chapels devoted to the cult of the Holy Spirit *(see p366)*. Terceira's interior is predominantly green pastureland, while the coast has barren areas of black lava.

Taunting a bull with umbrellas during a *tourada à corda*, Terceira

Angra do Heroísmo

This attractive and historic town was declared a UNESCO World Heritage site in 1983, in recognition of the strategic role the port has played in the Atlantic. For over three centuries the town was a stopover point on the routes between Europe, America and Africa. It was here in 1499 that Vasco da Gama *(see p108)* buried his brother Paulo after their pioneering journey to India, and in the early 17th century its harbour glittered with Spanish fleets returning laden with treasure

The 16th-century Sé (cathedral) at the centre of Terceira's capital, Angra do Heroísmo

from the Americas. Maria II gave the town its name for the bravery *(heroísmo)* it demonstrated during the struggles for Liberalism in the early 19th century *(see pp54–5)*. Despite the severe damage caused by an earthquake in 1980, the city's wealthy past is reflected in the pretty streets lined with monumental churches and balconied houses.

The most spectacular view of the harbour is from **Monte Brasil**, a volcanic crater on the western side of the bay. Beside this popular picnic spot stands the fort, **Castelo de São João Baptista**, built during Spain's annexation of Portugal *(see pp50–51)* as a treasure store, and still in military use. A second rewarding viewpoint is from the **Alto da Memória** at the south end of Rua São João de Deus, from where the twin towers of the 16th-century **Sé** (restored after a fire in 1983) are easily seen. A path leads down into the **Jardim Municipal**, the city's restful public gardens. These once formed part of the 15th-century Convento de São Francisco which now houses the **Museu de Angra do Heroísmo**. The museum's exhibits reflect the history of the Azores and the city and include armour, maps, paintings and sculptures.

🏛 **Museu de Angra do Heroísmo**
Ladeira de São Francisco. 📞 295-21 31 47. 🕐 Tue–Sun (Sat & Sun pm only). ♿

Around the Island

Terceira is a large, oval-shaped island with a gentle green interior of forested hills and farmland. Its centre bears witness to its volcanic origins: the **Caldeira de Guilherme Moniz** is an eroded crater 3 km (2 miles) wide, the largest in the Azores. Nearby, the **Algar do Carvão** is a dramatic volcanic blast-hole, thick with dripping moss where visitors can tour an enormous subterranean cave. West of here, the **Furnas do Enxofre** are hot steaming geysers where the heavy sulphur vapours crystallize into brightly coloured formations.

Wooden John the Baptist, Museu de Angra

Two viewpoints overlooking the island can be reached by car: in the west, a road bordered with blue hydrangeas winds up through the **Serra de Santa Bárbara** to a vast lonely crater at 1,022 m (3,353 ft), while the eastern **Serra do Cume**, at 545 m (1,788 ft), overlooks the airport and **Praia da Vitória**. This port has a large bay with a sandy beach. Its name pays tribute to a famous victory in 1581 when the Spanish attempted to seize the island at Baía da Salga, 10 km (6 miles) south, and were thwarted by the release of a herd of cattle onto the shore.

On the north coast, **Biscoitos** (which means biscuits) takes its name from the rubble of biscuit-like lava spread along the shore. Exhilarating swimming pools, popular in the summer, have been created amongst the rocks. The area is also known for its wine, and the land is covered in a chessboard of stone-walled pens *(curraletas)* built to shelter vines. The friendly **Museu do Vinho** explains the simple production methods used to produce the rich *verdelbo* wine that was once exported to the Russian court, and provides an opportunity to taste and purchase today's vintages.

🏞 **Algar do Carvão**
Off R5-2. 📞 295-21 29 92. 🕐 3–5pm daily (Oct–Mar: on request). ♿
🏛 **Museu do Vinho**
Canada do Caldeiro, Biscoitos. 📞 295-908404. 🕐 Tue–Sun.

Patchwork of stone-walled fields in the northeast of Terceira, near Praia da Vitória

The Holy Spirit Festivals

Festivals are a vibrant feature of life in the Azores and have helped foster the deep sense of community that is a hallmark of the islands' culture. Emigrants and relatives from North America and mainland Portugal often return to their native island to celebrate the most popular *festas*.

The islands' most traditional festivals are associated with the Holy Spirit *(Festas do Espírito Santo)*. Brought to the Azores by the first Portuguese settlers, who called upon the Holy Spirit to

A girl wearing the emperor's crown

protect them against natural disasters, the rituals have remained almost unchanged. An "emperor", usually a child, is crowned in the parish church. With a sceptre and silver plate as insignia of the Holy Spirit, the "emperor" presides over the festivities that take place each Sunday for seven weeks after Easter. The seventh Sunday, Whit Sunday, the day of Pentecost when Christ's disciples were filled with the Holy Spirit, is the occasion of a great feast in the village.

The distribution of bread for the Festival of the Holy Spirit originates in the donation of food to the poor introduced by saintly Queen Isabel (see p45). On the last day of celebrations, the seventh Sunday after Easter, a Holy Spirit soup is made from beef and vegetables and is handed out along with bread to everyone outside the local império.

THE IMPÉRIOS OF THE HOLY SPIRIT

Império with Gothic windows in Terra Chã, Terceira (1954)

Flamboyantly decorated *império* in São Sebastião, Terceira (1918)

Simple *império* in Praia da Vitória, Terceira (1861)

The focus of the ceremonies is a small chapel or *império* (empire) which is used for the distribution of the Holy Spirit soup on the seventh Sunday. Here, the emperor's crown, sceptre and plate are displayed on the altar on the last day of the festivities. On Terceira, where the cult of the Holy Spirit is particularly strong, many of the 58 *impérios* are painted in bright colours every spring. Up to 500 islanders gather for a village feast accompanied by dancing, brass bands and lavish floral displays. In many places a *tourada à corda* will be held, where a bull, tied to the end of a long rope, is let loose in the street.

An emperor's crown on ceremonial display in an *império* on São Miguel

Traditional ox-drawn cart on the island of Graciosa

Graciosa ❹

🏠 5,500. ✈ 2 km (1 mile) W of Santa Cruz da Graciosa. ⛴ Praia de São Mateus. 🛈 Praça Fontes Pereira de Melo, Santa Cruz (295-712 509). 🎭 Festas do Espírito Santo; Aug: Santo Cristo. 🌐 www.drtacores.pt

THE "GRACIOUS" ISLAND is one of the most peaceful in the Azores. Only 12 km (7 miles) long, most of its low-lying land is given over to farms and vineyards where ox-drawn carts and ploughs are still in use. The capital, **Santa Cruz da Graciosa**, on the northern coast, has a simple quayside backed by rows of stark, two-storey, whitewashed houses with wrought-iron balconies and oval windows. A small **Museu da Graciosa** recalls life on this sleepy island with a homely miscellany of toys, sea chests, kitchenware, wine presses, furniture and mementoes sent back by emigrants to North America. A building next door houses a whaling boat (*see pp368–9*).

The picturesque Monte da Ajuda that rises behind the town is capped by a 16th-century fortified chapel, **Nossa Senhora da Ajuda**, decorated with 18th-century tiles. Nearby, a small *vigia* (whalers' look-out) faces the sea.

In the southeast lies the island's principal sight, **Furna do Enxofre**, where visitors can descend flights of steps into the bowels of a volcanic crater. At the bottom is a huge cave with a deep, sulphurous lake and peep-holes where bubbling brews of evil grey liquid can be spied beneath the rocks. The best time to visit is late morning when the sun shines through the small cave mouth and lights the interior.

Above the cave, at **Furna Maria Encantada**, a natural tunnel through the rock leads to the edge of the crater. From here there are stunning views over the island. Treatments using the island's geothermal waters are available at the coastal resort of **Carapacho**, at the foot of the volcano.

🏛 Museu da Graciosa
Rua das Flores 2, Santa Cruz. 📞 295-712 429. ⬜ daily (Oct–Mar: Mon–Fri). ● public hols. 🎫

🗻 Furna do Enxofre
2 km (1 mile) E of Luz, follow signs to Caldeira. ⬜ Fri–Wed. 🎫

The rich Baroque interior of Santa Bárbara in Manadas, São Jorge

São Jorge ❺

🏠 11,000. ✈ 7 km (4 miles) E of Velas. ⛴ Velas & Calheta. 🛈 Rua Conselheiro Dr José Pereira 1, Velas (295-412 440). 🎭 23 Apr: Festa de São Jorge; Festas do Espírito Santo; Jul: Semana Cultural de Velas (Velas). 🌐 www.drtacores.pt

SÃO JORGE IS A LONG, thin mountainous island that stretches for 56 km (35 miles) but is only 8 km (5 miles) wide.

On its north coast, sheer cliffs drop 480 m (1,575 ft) to the sea. Over the centuries these cliffs have collapsed in places, creating tongues of land known as *fajãs*. It was on these coastal promontories that the island's Flemish colonists first settled in the mid-15th century.

Today many islanders on São Jorge are engaged in the production of a cured cheese, *Queijo de São Jorge*, exported to mainland Europe. The pace of life is leisurely and most visitors come to enjoy the walking along the paths that climb between the *fajãs*. The most popular route is in the northeast of the island from Serra do Topo 10 km (6 miles) down to Fajã dos Cubres.

Most of the settlements lie along the gentler south coast, including the capital, **Velas**, and **Calheta**, where the small **Museu de São Jorge** displays objects of local history such as the ornate breads baked for the Holy Spirit festival, a honey press, agricultural utensils and religious sculptures. West of Calheta, in the pretty village of **Manadas**, the 18th-century church of **Santa Bárbara** has an atmospheric carved and painted interior. In **Urzelina**, 2 km (1 mile) further west, the tower of a church buried by lava in 1808 protrudes defiantly from the ground. In the west of the island there is a pleasant forested picnic area at **Sete Fontes**, and on a clear day the nearby summit of **Pico da Velha** offers superb views of the central Azorean islands.

🏛 Museu de São Jorge
Rua José Azevedo da Cunha, Calheta. 📞 295-416 323. ⬜ Mon–Fri. ● public hols.

Dramatic cliffs along the north coast of São Jorge

Pico ❻

🏛 15,500. ✈ 8 km (5 miles) E of Madalena. ⛴ Madalena. 🚌 Avenida Machado Serpa, Madalena. 🏢 Rua Conselheiro Terra Pinheiro, Madalena (292- 62 35 24). 🎭 Festas do Espírito Santo (see p366); 22 Jul: Santa Maria Madalena. 🅦 www.drtacores.pt

T HE FULL MAJESTY of Pico, the highest mountain in Portugal, becomes apparent when it is seen from the neighbouring central islands.

Rustic house and well on Pico made from black lava rocks

Only then does one realize how gracefully this volcanic peak soars out of the Atlantic, shooting up 2,350 m (7,700 ft) to form the summit of the greatest mountain range in the world, the Mid-Atlantic Ridge (see pp338–9).

The island's capital, **Madalena**, is a relaxed port that lies opposite Faial's capital, Horta. A regular ferry service crosses the 7 km (4 miles) between the two islands, making a day trip feasible. The entrance to the harbour is guarded by two rocks, Em Pé (standing) and Deitado (lying down) where colonies of birds have made their home.

Many people come to Pico to climb its eponymous peak, which in winter is often snow-capped and at other times can be wrapped in cloud. It is a strenuous climb, best done in

The summit of Pico's volcano

the company of a guide, and permission is required in advance. For further details contact the tourist office.

The other main draw to Pico in summer is whale watching. From **Lajes do Pico** groups are taken out in small boats for three-hour trips organized by the **Espaço Talassa**. They are guided by radio messages

In Pursuit of the Whale

E VERY SUMMER the waters around the Azores are visited by a great variety of whales and dolphins. Until 1984 whaling was a traditional part of Azorean life – in the 19th century American whaling vessels frequently called here to pick up crew for their expeditions, and from the 1870s the Azoreans took up large-scale hunting in their own waters. Flags were waved from clifftop *vigias* (lookouts) giving coded directions so that other villagers would not get to the prize first.

Since whaling was banned in the 1980s, the Azoreans have applied their knowledge gained from hunting to whale watching and conservation.

Scrimshaws are carvings made on the teeth and bones of whales and often depict whaling scenes. This fine example from the Museu do Scrimshaw on Faial (see p370) shows the long, narrow boats called canoas that could hold up to 14 men.

Whale watching today takes place in small boats that allow fast and safe access to the whales. As well as trips out to sea, the whales can be observed from the vigias. These land-based towers afford spectacular views of the whales in their natural habitat. Expeditions run from Pico and Faial (see p370).

from men who scan the sea for a fluke (tail) from the former *vigias* (lookouts). The history of Azorean whaling is recalled at the **Museu dos Baleeiros**, also in Lajes, where boats, tackle and whalebone artefacts are displayed. The whales were processed at an immense factory on the north side of the island at São Roque do Pico. Closed down in 1981, the **Museu da Indústria da Baleeira** has been preserved as a piece of industrial heritage, retaining the boilers where the blubber was turned into oil.

A coastal road encircles Pico, offering a slow but rewarding drive that reveals the charm of this undeveloped island. Minor eruptions in previous centuries have covered parts of its landscape with black mole-hills of lava that the islanders christened *mistérios* (mysteries). The black lava has been used to build houses and grids of stone walls that enclose fields or shelter vines.

In some places, notably around **Cachorro** on the north coast, the eroded lava has formed curious arches in the sea.

Pico's famous *Verdelho* wine, which is similar to the one made in Madeira *(see p349)*, was once regularly exported to mainland Europe. In recent years there has been a revival of viticulture on the island and the production of new reds and whites – such as the much acclaimed *Terras da Lava* – now means visitors have a

refined alternative to the ubiquitous *vinho de cheiro* (wine of smell) traditionally drunk by the Azoreans.

➤ **Espaço Talassa**
Rua do Saco, Lajes. [292-67 20 10.
◯ *daily.* 🌐 🚹
🏛 **Museu dos Baleeiros**
Rua dos Baleeiros, Lajes. [292-67 22 76. ◯ *Tue–Sun am (hols: am).* 🌐
🐋 **Museu da Indústria Baleeira**
São Roque do Pico. [292-64 20 96.
◯ *daily, Sat & Sun am (hols: am).*

West coast of Pico with Faial in the distance

MARINE LIFE IN THE AZORES

Some 20 species of cetaceans can be found in the waters of the Azores. These warm-blooded animals follow the warm currents of the Gulf Stream to feed in the region's abundant, unpolluted waters. Schools of playful and gregarious dolphins are often seen scything through the waves at incredible speeds, but the most impressive sights are sperm whales. These large, sociable animals dive to great depths for giant squid and live in family groups called pods. Like all whales and dolphins they must come to the surface to breathe and this is when whale-watching expeditions make their sightings.

Atlantic spotted dolphins, fast and graceful swimmers

Sperm whales *are huge, tear-shaped creatures, the largest of the toothed whales. They can be seen breaching (diving out of the water), spy hopping (raising their head to have a look around) and socializing by rubbing bodies.*

Pilot whales *belong to the dolphin family and are recognizable from their strong blow of up to 1 m (3 ft).*

Risso's dolphins *have a squat head and light grey colouring. Older ones are often crisscrossed with white scars.*

Bottlenose dolphins *are the best known. These playful animals love to ride the waves at the bow of a moving vessel.*

Loggerhead turtles, *born on Florida's beaches, are frequent visitors to the warm Azorean waters.*

Transatlantic yachts moored in the marina at Horta, Faial, with the pointed summit of Pico in the distance

Faial 7

🏠 16,000. ✈ 10 km (6 miles) SW of Horta. 🚢 Horta. 🚌 Rua Vasco da Gama, Horta. 🛈 Rua Vasco da Gama, Horta (292-292 237). 🎉 Festas do Espírito Santo (see p366); 1st–2nd Sun in Aug: Semana do Mar (Horta). ⓦ www.drtacores.pt

FAIAL WAS SETTLED by Flemish farmers in the 15th century and prospered with the development of Horta harbour as a stopover for ships and – more recently – flying boats crossing the Atlantic. Today it is a fertile island with an international atmosphere and a mild climate, famous as a yachting destination and for the endless rows of colourful hydrangeas that bloom in June and July.

Horta

Stretching around a wide bay, Faial's capital has been a convenient anchorage for caravels, clippers and sea planes over the centuries. Captain Cook commented on Horta's fine houses and gardens when he called here in 1775. Today, visiting crews crossing between the Caribbean and Mediterranean paint a calling card on the quayside and celebrate their safe passage in **Peter's Café Sport**. In the upstairs rooms of the café, an engrossing **Museu do Scrimshaw** exhibits engraved whales' bones and teeth dating back to 1884 (see p368).

In the **Museu da Horta** displays of antique furniture, portraits, nautical memorabilia and nostalgic photographs of the island's port are upstaged by miniature sculptures of liners and scenes of daily life, painstakingly carved from the white pith of fig trees. These virtuoso examples of a traditional island craft are by the Faial-born Euclides Silveira da Rosa (1910–79).

Ship's calling card on the quayside in Horta, Faial

Excursions for dolphin- and whale-watching (see pp368–9) in the waters around the island are organized by the **Espaço Talassa** company.

🏛 **Museu do Scrimshaw**
Peter's Café Sport, Rua T. Valadim 9.
📞 292-292 327. ⬤ Mon–Sat. 🗓
🏛 **Museu da Horta**
Largo Duque D' Ávila e Bolama. 📞 292-293 384. ⬤ Tue–Fri, Sat & Sun pm. ⬤ public hols. 🗓
🐬 **Espaço Talassa**
📞 292-292 067. ⬤ Apr–Oct. 🗓

Barren ash-covered volcanic landscape at Capelinhos, the westernmost point of Faial

Around the Island

Two viewpoints overlook Horta – to its south rises the volcanic peak of **Monte da Guia**, while the northern **Miradouro da Espalamaca** is guarded by a huge statue of Nossa Senhora da Conceição. If the cloud cover permits, it is well worth driving 15 km (9 miles) to see Faial's central **Caldeira do Cabeço Gordo** – a vast green crater 2 km (1 mile) wide and 400 m (1,300 ft) deep. The path winding around its rim takes about two hours to walk and has magnificent views.

Faial's other spectacular natural sight is the **Vulcão dos Capelinhos** in the far west of the island. A volcano erupted here in 1957–8, smothering a lighthouse which can now be seen buried in ash. Around it lies a scorched and barren landscape that has, not surprisingly, been used as the location for a German post-nuclear holocaust film. The story of the eruption is told in the nearby **Museu dos Capelinhos** where photographs and maps trace the area's geological activity, showing how the black land is gradually coming back to life. Also shown are the lava formations created in the eruption.

🏛 **Museu dos Capelinhos**
Canto do Capelo. 📞 292-945 165.
⬤ Tue–Sun. ⬤ 1 Jan, 24, 25 & 31 Dec.

Flores

🚶 2,000. ✈ 1 km (half a mile) N of Santa Cruz. 🚢 Lajes. 🚌 Centro de Saúde, Santa Cruz. ℹ Rua Dr Almas da Silveira 1, Santa Cruz (292-592 369). 🎉 Festas do Espírito Santo (see p366); 24–26 Jun: Festas de São João. (hols: am). 🌐 www.drtacores.pt

OFTEN CUT OFF by stormy weather, the island of "Flowers" is a romantic outpost that was not permanently settled until the 16th century. A notorious hideout for pirates waiting to raid the treasure-laden Spanish galleons on their return to Europe, Flores was the scene of an epic battle in 1591 between the ship of the English commander Sir Richard Grenville and a fleet of Spanish ships. The battle was immortalized in a poem by Alfred Tennyson, *The Revenge* (the name of Grenville's ship).

This westernmost island of the Azores is 17 km (10 miles) long and extremely mountainous. Its name derives from the abundance of flowers growing in its ravines, and the prospect of wilderness draws adventurous walkers here during the summer. The capital, **Santa Cruz**, is enlivened by the enthusiastically run **Museu das Flores**, housed in the former Franciscan convent. Its displays include shipwreck finds, Azorean pottery, furniture and agricultural tools, as well as fishing rods and a guitar made from whalebone. The convent church of **São Boaventura**, erected in 1641, has a beautiful carved cedarwood chancel.

Hydrangeas growing in the mountains of Flores

The southern half of the island is the most scenic. The deep, verdant valleys are punctuated with dramatic peaks and volcanic crater lakes and caves. Yams and sweet potatoes grow in the fertile soil. The tranquil **Lagoa Funda** (Deep Lake), 25 km (15 miles) southwest of Santa Cruz, is a large crater lake at the base of a mountain. Visible from the main road just west of the lake, are the strange vertical rock formations of the **Rocha dos Bordões** formed by solidified basalt.

The winding road continues northwards over the mountains and, as the road descends towards the west coast, there are stunning views of the green valley and village of **Fajãzinha**. The resort of **Fajã Grande**, ringed by cliffs, is a popular base for walkers and impressive waterfalls plunge into the sea from the high cliffs. A short walk north from the town is the **Cascata da Ribeira Grande**, a towering jet of water that divides into smaller waterfalls before collecting in a still pool.

🏛 **Museu das Flores**
Largo da Misericórdia, Santa Cruz.
📞 292-592 159. ⬜ Mon–Fri.
⬛ public hols.

Corvo ⑨

🚶 370. ✈ 🚢 Vila Nova. 🚌 Rua da Matriz, Vila Nova. ℹ Câmara Municipal, Rua J. da Bola, Vila Nova (292-590 200). 🎉 Festas do Espírito Santo (see p366). 🌐 www.drtacores.pt

CORVO LIES 24 km (15 miles) northeast of Flores. The smallest island in the Azores, it has just one settlement, **Vila Nova**, and is blissfully undeveloped, with only two taxis and one policeman. The entire island is the blown top of the marine volcano, Monte Gordo. An ethereal green crater, the **Lagoa do Caldeirão**, squats at its northern end. Its rim can be reached by road, after which there is a steep descent down to the crater floor 300 m (984 ft) below. In its centre, the crater is dotted with serene lakes and islands; a patchwork of stone-walled fields covers part of the slopes.

The island of Corvo seen from the rocky shore of Flores

TRAVELLERS' NEEDS

WHERE TO STAY

PORTUGAL OFFERS a wide range of accommodation, from luxury hotels and restored palaces to family-run hostels and self-catering apartments. The majority of the country's hotels are in Lisbon, Oporto and on the Algarve and Estoril coasts. Elsewhere, outside of the main towns, hotels are relatively scarce. This shortage is made up for by a number of schemes offering accommodation in traditional or historic buildings often set in lovely countryside. These all require advance booking, as rooms are in short supply.

Porter at Lisbon's luxurious Lapa Palace *(see p382)*

Self-catering options include purpose-built apartments in cities and resorts, and converted country villas and farmhouses, all offering flexibility and good value. It is worth remembering that all rooms are cheaper outside high season. Accommodation in Lisbon divides between top-flight hotels and basic lodging with little choice in between. The hotels listed on pages 380–401 have been selected from every price category and represent the best value in each area.

TYPES OF HOTEL

LODGINGS IN PORTUGAL come at all levels of comfort and cost. There are two main types, as classified by the Portuguese tourist authority: hotels and *pensões*. Hotels are distinguished mainly by the fact that they take up an entire building and are often purpose-built. *Pensões* are always housed in shared premises, typically occupying several floors of a residential building. *Apart-hotels* are essentially hotels with self-catering apartments, offering most or all of the services that normal hotels do.

All hotels and *pensões* are meant to provide meals. If they only offer breakfast their name must have *residencial* added to it. It is always best to check, however, as the official regime is often merely

official. There are also plenty of lodgings that operate without classification.

Estalagens (*estalagem* in the singular), are usually located outside of city centres and must have a garden. *Albergarias* are the top category of *pensão*, which means that their facilities are on the same level as 4- or 5-star hotels (see page 375 for information on gradings).

POUSADAS

POUSADAS ARE a special type of lodgings. They come in two categories: regional and historical. Regional *pousadas* are country inns offering a high level of comfort, often located in scenic, sometimes

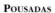

Bedroom at the York House Hotel in Lisbon, a converted 16th-century convent *(see p382)*

remote, areas. Historical *pousadas* are housed in converted castles, convents or palaces and offer excellent service and luxury accommodation as well as memorable historical and architectural surroundings. With the exception of two mountain inns on Madeira that use "*pousada*" in their names, all *pousadas* are state-owned, and are run as a chain by the **Enatur** company.

HOTEL CHAINS

INTERNATIONAL luxury groups such as Le Meridien and Orient-Express are represented in the Algarve and Madeira, as well as in Oporto and the Lisbon area. Smaller luxury groups include **Tivoli Hotels** – with three hotels in Lisbon, two in Sintra, three in the Algarve and one each in Madeira, Oporto and Coimbra – and the **Pestana Group**, with eight hotels in Madeira, five

Hotel Almansor in the resort of Carvoeiro, the Algarve *(see p397)*

◁ **Breakfasting beneath the wisteria at the Pousada de Palmela** in the Algarve, and one each in Cascais, Lisbon and Oporto.

Lower down the scale, **Choice Hotels Portugal** operates a number of hotels in its **Comfort Inn** and **Quality Inn** categories in the Lisbon area and the north of the country, while **Best Western** has 21 hotels countrywide. **IBIS** hotels are also well represented with hotels that are frequently located outside cities and towns, but offer very good value for money.

GRADINGS

THE PORTUGUESE tourist authority rates hotels with one to five stars (five being the top rating) and *pensões* in four categories (*albergaria* is the top rating, followed by 1st to 3rd category). *Apart-hotels* are rated with two to five stars. These ratings are based on a fixed set of criteria which covers most aspects of comfort. They do not, however, take into account more subjective factors such as view, atmosphere or the staff's service-mindedness.

It is important to remember that hotels and *pensões* are rated separately from top to bottom. In other words, a one or two-star hotel will always have a lower level of comfort – and lower prices – than an *albergaria* or even a 1st-category *pensão*. All rated establishments are meant to have a sign by the entrance showing their rating, but as the system has been changed recently, these are not always up-to-date.

PRICES

IN PORTUGAL, establishments are free to decide their own prices, but all tariffs must be clearly displayed at reception and in the rooms. The cost of the room usually includes all taxes and a continental

View from the Seteais Palace, Sintra, now a luxury hotel *(see p386)*

breakfast. Other meals are charged as extras. It is sometimes possible to bargain for a better rate, especially outside the high season. As a rule, the cost of a single room is around 60 to 75 per cent of the cost of a double room.

Tourist areas, such as the Algarve and Estoril coasts, and Madeira and the Azores, can be expensive. But prices drop substantially outside the peak months of the summer. In Lisbon and Oporto however, many business-oriented hotels charge the same rates throughout the year.

Reid's Hotel in Funchal, Madeira *(see p400)*

Pousadas have two rates for low (Nov–Mar except New Year, carnival and Easter) and high (Apr–Oct) season. In Madeira, Christmas and New Year are seen as high season.

BOOKINGS

YOU WILL NEED to book in advance for all tourist areas in the high season. Much of the accommodation in the Algarve and around the Estoril coast is mass booked by tour operators. For Madeira, Lisbon and Oporto, book ahead regardless of the season. Most receptionists speak English so it should not be a problem to book by phone. Deposits are not usually required, but a written confirmation by fax, including a credit card number, may be requested.

Pousadas can be booked through Enatur or at the *pousadas* website, which also has plenty of information. The Portuguese tourist authority, **Direcção-Geral do Turismo**, publishes two official guides which are revised regularly: *Alojamento Turístico*, (Tourist Accommodation) and *Turismo no Espaço Rural* (Tourism in the Country). These list all of the establishments rated by the authority, but only the latter contains any descriptions of individual settings, services or surroundings.

**Casa do Campo, a manor house
in Celorico de Basto (see p393)**

RURAL ACCOMMODATION

THE CHOICE of accommo-
dation in Portugal is vastly
enhanced by the possibility
for visitors to stay in private
manors, country houses or on
farms, usually, but not always,
situated in the countryside
and usually, but not always,
with the owners in residence.

This *Turismo no Espaço
Rural* (Tourism in the
Country) falls into four main
categories: *Turismo de
Habitação* (TH), which are
manors or palatial houses of
recognised historical and/or
architectural value, including
interiors and furnishings;
Turismo Rural (TR), country
houses typical of their region
and located in or near a
village; *Agroturismo* (AG),
houses that form part of a
working farm; and *Casas de
Campo* (CC), country houses
that offer lodging in which the
owners may be in residence.

Most of the grandest *Turismos
de Habitação* are to be found
in the Minho region in the
north. However, there are now
four owner's associations in
Portugal who offer information and a booking facility.

The annual publication
Turismo no Espaço Rural lists
all the houses. Bookings can
be made through agents or
directly through the owners.

RESORT ACCOMMODATION

PORTUGAL'S RESORT
accommodation is
mainly situated along
the Algarve and Estoril
coasts. The most con-
venient way to book
accommodation is to
make prior arrange-
ments through a travel
agent or tour operator.
Hotel prices can drop
considerably outside
high season, and it is
often possible to get a
very good deal at less
popular times of the
year, when there are
also fewer crowds to
contend with.

The tourist village or
Aldeamento Turístico
is a unique feature of
resort areas such as the
Algarve. These self-contained
complexes offer well-furnished
and fitted private apartments
and usually provide a range
of sports facilities, beaches,
pools, restaurants, bars and
sometimes a supermarket.

These complexes are graded
from three to five stars.

Apartamentos Turísticos
(Tourist Apartments) do not
have the hotel-style facilities
of the tourist villages but are
ideal for those who require
flexibility and independence.
They are generally purpose-
built modern buildings in
resort areas that offer self-
catering accommodation.
These Tourist Apartments
also carry quality gradings of
between two and five stars.

**The luxurious Marinotel at the resort
of Vilamoura in the Algarve (see p399)**

BUDGET ACCOMMODATION

YOUTH HOSTELS in Portugal
(*Pousadas de Juventude*)
are mainly dotted along the
coast, and include two in the
Azores. There are 22 in total
and they are open all through
the year, but advance booking
is advisable in the summer.
They require a valid IYHF card
which can be obtained from
any Youth Hostel Association.
Facilities vary greatly, and may
include the use of a kitchen,
bar and swimming pool. Some
also offer facilities for disabled
travellers. Information is available from **Movijovem**, the
head office of the Portuguese
Youth Hostel Association.

Almost as cheap as youth
hostels, and offering greater
privacy, rooms (*quartos*) in
private houses will invariably
cost less than a *pensão*. This
type of accommodation is
often rented out in resorts, and
lists of *quartos* are available
from the local tourist office.

Dining room at Casa de Esteiró, rural lodging in Caminha (see p393)

CAMPING AND CARAVANNING

THERE ARE OVER 100 official campsites in Portugal in total. Most are along the coast, usually in attractive locations. The largest is at Albufeira in the Algarve, but most are small and quiet. There is a national chain of campsites run by the company **Orbitur**.

Generally you pay a rate for the tent and per person, and an extra charge for showers and parking. The Portuguese Tourist Office will provide lists of campsites and information. You will need an international camping carnet, available from motoring organizations or the **Camping and Caravanning Club** in Great Britain. This provides third party insurance cover and entitles holders to some out-of-season discounts.

Provided you show due care and consideration for the environment, it is possible to camp outside official sites in

São Miguel campsite, near Odemira in the Alentejo region

the countryside, except for the Algarve, where it is strictly forbidden to stray from the sites.

CHILDREN

CHILDREN ARE as welcome as adult visitors to Portugal and families are well catered for. Some hotels give children under eight years old a 50 per cent discount on the price of accommodation and meals.

DISABLED TRAVELLERS

HOTELS WITH facilities for the disabled are listed by the Portuguese National Tourist Office, who also produce a leaflet with useful information. Some campsites and youth hostels provide special facilities and these are listed by relevant organizations, and in a guide published by the **Secretariado Nacional de Reabilitação**.

The Pousadas of Portugal

Pousada symbol

THE CONCEPT of the *pousada* dates from the 1940s, when the Portuguese government decided to establish a national network of state-run country inns, offering "hospitality in keeping with the style and tradition of the region". *Pousadas* are often set in remote, scenic locations, and most have fewer than 30 rooms, so visitors can expect friendly, personalized service and a high degree of comfort. This map does not show all of Portugal's *pousadas*, just the 38 that are described in the listings on pages 380–401.

Pousada da Ria near the port of Aveiro has 19 bedrooms, most of which have balconies overlooking the sheltered lagoon of Ria de Aveiro (see p388).

Pousada de São Pedro lies 13 km (8 miles) southeast of the picturesque town of Tomar and was originally built in the 1940s to house engineers working on the nearby Castelo de Bode dam. Overlooking the River Zêzere below the dam, the pousada reopened in 1993 after closing for extensive renovation (see p386).

Pousada do Castelo, in the walled town of Óbidos, is situated in a beautifully restored palace inside the 15th-century castle keep. The pousada combines a medieval atmosphere with all modern comforts and a highly recommended restaurant (see p387).

Pousada de Palmela boasts an elegant interior, commanding hilltop views over the town of Palmela and the Atlantic Ocean, and an illustrious history. It is a thoughtful conversion of a monastery which was the headquarters of the Portuguese Knights of Santiago in the 13th century (see p385).

Pousada do Infante occupies a spectacular clifftop position in the most southwesterly town of Europe, Sagres. The terrace restaurant of this purpose-built pousada has magnificent views over the Atlantic Ocean (see p398).

Va
do N

Vila Nova
de Cerveir

Viana do
Castelo

Condeixa-
a-Nova

Batalha

Ourén

ESTREMADUR
AND RIBATEJO

Queluz

LISBON

THE
LISBON
COAST

Setúb

Alcácé
do S.

Santiago
do Cacém

Santa Clara-
a-Velh

ALGARVE

Pousada de Santa Marinha da Costa, housed in a medieval monastery near the city of Guimarães, is one of Portugal's most impressive and historic pousadas (see p393).

Pousada do Barão de Forrester, named after JJ Forrester, an influential figure in 19th-century port production (see p252), enjoys a peaceful setting among vineyards in the small Douro town of Alijó (see p390).

0 kilometres 50

0 miles 25

INHO

eira do
nho

Bragança **P**

DOURO AND
TRÁS-OS-MONTES

P

marante
P
são
rio

Almeida **P**

mulo

Manteigas **P**

P
Belmonte

P Monsanto

THE BEIRAS

Pousada da Rainha Santa Isabel dominates the town of Estremoz and the surrounding countryside. In the 13th century, the site of the pousada was home to King Dinis and his wife Queen Isabel (see p395).

Marvão **P**

rato **P**
P Sousel

P
P **P** Elvas
Vila Viçosa
P

Pousada dos Lóios in Évora has been converted from a 15th-century monastery. Adjacent to the remains of a Roman temple of Diana, it features an elegant dining room set in the original monastic cloisters and a Neo-Classical façade that dates from the mid-18th century (see p395).

P Alvito

P

P Serpa

ALENTEJO

São Brás
de Alportel
P

Pousada de São Francisco is located in the heart of the old Roman town of Beja at the centre of the sun-baked plains of the southern Alentejo. The building incorporates parts of a former Franciscan convent, dating back to the 13th century. It was opened as a pousada in 1994 (see p395).

Choosing a Hotel

THE HOTELS in this guide have been selected across a wide price range for their good value or exceptional location. The chart gives a brief description of each hotel, highlighting factors which may influence your choice. Entries are listed by price category within the towns with colour-coded thumb tabs to indicate the regions covered on each page.

	CREDIT CARDS	RESTAURANT	GARDEN	SWIMMING POOL	NUMBER OF ROOMS
LISBON					
ALCÂNTARA: *Carlton Palace Hotel* @ carlton.palace@pestana.com €€€€€ Rua Jau 54, 1300-314. **Map** 2 F3. **(** 21-361 56 00. **FAX** 21-361 56 01. This grand hotel is housed partly in the 19th-century Palácio Valle-Flor and retains the palace's gardens. There is a gym and pool as well as business facilities. 🛏 TV 🍴 P	AE DC MC V				44
AVENIDA: *Alegria* €€ Praça da Alegria 12, 1250-004. **Map** 4 F1. **(** 21-322 06 70. **FAX** 21-347 80 70. This basic, good-value *pensão* offers clean and homely rooms. It borders on the red-light district, although the police station is next door. 🛏	AE DC MC V				36
AVENIDA: *13 da Sorte* €€ Rua do Salitre 13, 1250-198. **Map** 4 F1. **(** 21-353 18 51. **FAX** 21-353 18 51. This well located *pensão* is situated close to Avenida da Liberdade and the Jardim Botanico. Breakfast is not included. 🛏 TV 🍴	MC V				22
AVENIDA: *Tivoli Jardim* @ htjardim@mail.telepac.pt €€€€ Rua J. César Machado , 1250-135. **Map** 4 F1. **(** 21-353 99 71. **FAX** 21-355 65 66. This smart hotel has spacious rooms. A round pool graces the garden behind the hotel and there is use of extensive sports facilities. 🛏 TV 🍴 P	AE DC MC V	●	■	●	119
AVENIDA: *Veneza* w www.3khotels.com €€€€ Avenida da Liberdade 189, 1250-141. **Map** 5 C5. **(** 21-352 26 18. **FAX** 21-352 66 78. The ornate staircase decorated with modern murals by Pedro Luiz-Gomes is the highlight of this spacious and comfortable hotel. 🛏 TV 🍴 P	AE DC MC V				30
AVENIDA: *Britânia* @ britania.hotel@heritage.pt €€€€€ Rua R. Sampaio 17, 1150-278. **Map** 5 C5. **(** 21-315 50 16. **FAX** 21-315 50 21. Housed in a building designed by the architect Cassiano Branco in 1944, this delightful hotel has a beautiful marble lobby. 🛏 TV 🍴 P	AE DC MC V				36
AVENIDA: *Lisboa Plaza* w www.heritage.pt €€€€€ Travessa do Salitre 7, 1250-205. **Map** 4 F1. **(** 21-321 82 18. **FAX** 21-347 16 30. Built in 1953, and situated off Praça da Alegria, and Av. da Liberade, with decor by the Portuguese interior designer, Graça Viterbo. 🛏 TV 🍴	AE DC MC V	●			112
AVENIDA: *Sofitel Lisboa* @ h1319@accor-hotels.com €€€€€ Av. da Liberdade 127, 1269-038. **Map** 4 F1. **(** 21-322 83 00. **FAX** 21-322 83 10. The comfortable, modern Sofitel features an attractive piano bar called the "Molière", situated just off the lobby. 🛏 TV 🍴 P ♿	AE DC MC V	●			170
AVENIDA: *Tivoli Lisboa* @ reservas@tivoli.pt €€€€€ Av. da Liberdade 185, 1269-050. **Map** 4 F1. **(** 21-319 89 00. **FAX** 21-319 89 50. This large and elegant hotel has modern rooms and a huge two-level central lobby. The suites are particularly spacious. 🛏 TV 🍴 P	AE DC MC V	●	■	●	329
BAIRRO ALTO: *Pensão Londres* €€€ ua Dom Pedro V 53, 2°, 1250-092. **Map** 4 F2. **(** 21-346 22 03. **FAX** 21-346 56 82. One of the better basic *pensões* in the area, avoiding the worst of the Bairro Alto's night-time noise. 🛏	DC MC V				36
BAIXA: *Beira Minho* € Praça da Figueira 6, 2° E, 1150. **Map** 7 B3. **(** 21-346 18 46. **FAX** 21-886 78 11. The central location of this simple but comfortable *pensão* makes up for the lack of facilities. 🛏					24
BAIXA: *Coimbra e Madrid* €€ Praça da Figueira 3, 3°, 1100-240. **Map** 7 B3. **(** 21-342 17 60. **FAX** 21-342 32 64. A plain and simple *pensão* with rather sparse decoration. Some of the rooms, however, have magnificent views of the Castelo de São Jorge. 🛏	€€				32

| | Price categories | | | | | | | | |

	CREDIT CARDS	RESTAURANT	GARDEN	SWIMMING POOL	NUMBER OF ROOMS
BAIXA: *Duas Nações* €€ Rua da Vitória 41, 1100-618. **Map** 7 B4. **[** 21-346 07 10. **FAX** 21-347 02 06. The "Two Nations" is a friendly place to stay, right in the heart of the Baixa, but the rooms overlooking Rua Augusta can be noisy.	AE DC MC V				69
BAIXA: *Norte* €€ Rua dos Douradores 159, 1100-205. **Map** 7 B3. **[** 21-887 89 41. **FAX** 21-886 84 62. Centrally located near Praça da Figueira, this *pensão* has few facilities and no breakfast but the rooms are neat and comfortable. Good value.	MC V				36
BAIXA: *Internacional* @ reservas@hotel–internacional.com €€€ Rua da Betesga 3, 1100-090. **Map** 7 B3. **[** 21-324 09 90. **FAX** 21-347 86 35. This hotel features modern and spacious rooms. Residents can relax in the hotel's large, comfortable TV lounge and small bar.	AE DC MC V				52
BAIXA: *Portugal* €€€ Rua João das Regras 4, 1100-294. **Map** 7 C3. **[** 21-887 75 81. **FAX** 21-886 73 43. Though plain on the outside, this hotel situated off Praça Martim Moniz has a fairly stylish old-fashioned decor.	AE DC MC V				59
BAIXA: *Vip Eden* @ aparthoteleden@viphotels.com €€€€ Praça dos Restauradores 24, 1250-187. **Map** 7 A2. **[** 21-321 66 00. **FAX** 21-321 66 66. The modern Vip Eden offers apartments and studios, three of which have been adapted for the disabled.	AE DC MC V			●	134
CASTELO: *Ninho das Águias* €€ Costa do Castelo 74, 1100-179. **Map** 7 C3. **[** 21-885 40 70. The simple "Eagle's Nest" *pensão* sits below the castle walls. A stuffed eagle greets visitors on the terrace that has amazing views. No breakfast.			■		16
CASTELO: *Solar do Castelo* W www.heritage.pt €€€€€ Rua das Cozinhas 2, 1100-181. **Map** 7 C3. **[** 21-887 09 09. **FAX** 21-887 09 07. This small, luxurious hotel occupies a recently rennovated 18th-century mansion located within the castle walls.	AE DC MC V		■		14
CHIADO: *Lisboa Regency Chiado* @ regencychiado@madeiraregency.pt €€€€€ Nova do Alameda 114, 1200-290. **Map** 7 B4. **[** 21-325 61 00. **FAX** 21-325 61 61. Stylish, small and central, the Regency Chiado has a privileged location and fabulous views over the heart of Lisbon. Car access can be difficult as there are a limited number of parking spaces.	AE DC MC V				40
ENTRECAMPOS: *Quality Hotel Lisboa* @ quality.lisboa@mail.telepac.pt €€€€ Campo Grande 7, 1700-087. **[** 21-791 76 00. **FAX** 21-795 75 00. A pleasant hotel that caters for the business traveller. Features include a small health club, with a jacuzzi.	AE DC MC V				84
GRAÇA: *Mundial* @ mundial.hot@mail.telepac.pt €€€ Rua Dom Duarte 4, 1100-198. **Map** 7 B3. **[** 21-884 20 00. **FAX** 21-884 21 10. This hotel, located centrally off Praça da Figueira, has plain but comfortable rooms. The restaurant offers marvellous views.	AE DC MC V	●			255
GRAÇA: *Senhora do Monte* €€€€ Calçada do Monte 39, 1170-250. **Map** 7 D1. **[** 21-886 60 02. **FAX** 21-887 77 83. This *albergaria* is somewhat off the beaten track, but it is well worth the effort to find it. The rooms are fairly plain but the views, especially from the rooftop bar and garden, are simply the best in town.	AE DC MC V				28
LAPA: *As Janelas Verdes* W www.heritage.pt €€€€€ R. das Janelas Verdes 47, 1200-690. **Map** 4 D3. **[** 21-396 81 43. **FAX** 21-396 81 44. A delightful *pensão* housed in an 18th-century ivy-covered mansion, once owned by the Portuguese novelist Eça de Queirós *(see p55)*. It has Neo-Classical decor and a peaceful, charming patio.	AE DC MC V		■		29

Price categories in euros for a standard double room per night, including breakfast:
€ under 35
€€ 35–60
€€€ 60–100
€€€€ 100–150
€€€€€ over 150

RESTAURANT The hotel has one or more restaurants open for lunch and supper, sometimes reserved for residents.
GARDEN A garden, courtyard or large terrace for the use of hotel guests.
SWIMMING POOL The hotel has its own indoor or outdoor pool.
CREDIT CARDS Major credit cards accepted: *AE* American Express, *DC* Diners Club, *MC* MasterCard and *V* Visa.

For key to symbols see back flap

Price categories in euros for a standard double room per night, including breakfast:
€ under 35
€€ 35–60
€€€ 60–100
€€€€ 100–150
€€€€€ over 150

RESTAURANT
The hotel has one or more restaurants open for lunch and supper, sometimes reserved for residents.
GARDEN
A garden, courtyard or large terrace for the use of hotel guests.
SWIMMING POOL
The hotel has its own indoor or outdoor pool.
CREDIT CARDS
Major credit cards accepted: *AE* American Express, *DC* Diners Club, *MC* MasterCard and *V* Visa.

	CREDIT CARDS	RESTAURANT	GARDEN	SWIMMING POOL	NUMBER OF ROOMS
LAPA: *Lapa Palace* W www.orient-express.com €€€€€ R. do Pau da Bandeira 4, 1249-021. **Map** 3 C3. 21-394 94 94. **FAX** 21-395 06 65. A gracious and charming hotel located in the city's diplomatic area. Each room in the Palace Wing is uniquely decorated in its own Portuguese style – from 18th-century Neo-Classical to Art Deco.	AE DC MC V	●	■	●	94
LAPA: *York House* €€€€€€ Rua das Janelas Verdes 32, 1200-691. **Map** 4 D4. 21-396 24 35. **FAX** 21-397 27 93. This enchanting *pensão* is housed in the 17th-century Convento dos Marianos. Set around a shady, plant-filled patio, the luxurious rooms have wooden or terracotta floors and elegant antique furniture.	AE DC MC V	●	■		34
MARQUÊS POMBAL: *Castilho* €€ Rua Castilho 57 4°, 1250-068. **Map** 4 F1. 21-386 08 22. **FAX** 21-386 29 10. An excellent-value *pensão* on the fourth floor of a building. Good facilities and comfortable rooms, some with three or four beds.	DC MC V				25
MARQUÊS POMBAL: *Capitol* @ sanaclassic.capitol@sanahotels.com €€€ Rua Eça de Queirós 24, 1050-096. **Map** 5 C4. 21-353 68 11. **FAX** 21-352 61 65. A comfortable hotel just off Avenida de Duque de Loulé. All the rooms are equipped with satellite television and mini bars.	AE DC MC V	●			57
MARQUÊS POMBAL: *Jorge V* W www.hoteljorgev.com €€€ Rua Mouzinho da Silveira 3, 1250-165. **Map** 5 C5. 21-356 25 25. **FAX** 21-315 03 19. This pleasant, comfortable hotel offers good value for the area. Roughly half the rooms have balconies, so request one when checking in.	AE DC MC V				51
MARQUÊS POMBAL: *Nacional* @ hotelnacional@mail.telepac.pt €€€ Rua Castilho 34, 1250-070. **Map** 5 B5. 21-355 44 33. **FAX** 21-356 11 22. This interesting glass-fronted hotel has comfortable rooms and extensive facilities. There are also two suites available.	AE DC MC V				61
MARQUÊS POMBAL: *Diplomático* W www.diplomatico.com €€€€ Rua Castilho 74, 1250-071. **Map** 5 B5. 21-383 90 20. **FAX** 21-386 21 55. The Diplomático has spacious rooms with modern facilities and offers complimentary tea, coffee and chocolate in the rooms.	AE DC MC V	●			90
MARQUÊS POMBAL: *Rex* @ sanaclassic.rex@sanahotels.com €€€€ Rua Castilho 169, 1070-051. **Map** 5 B4. 21-388 21 61. **FAX** 21-388 75 81. The Rex is located close to the Parque Eduardo VII. The top floor conference room has good views.	AE DC MC V	●			68
MARQUÊS POMBAL: *Le Méridien Lisboa* W www.lemeridien-lisbon.com €€€€€ Rua Castilho 149, 1099-034. **Map** 5 B4. 21-381 87 00. **FAX** 21-389 05 05. Overlooking the Parque Eduardo VII from one of the city's seven hills, this hotel has comfortable rooms and spectacular views.	AE DC MC V	●			330
MARQUÊS POMBAL: *Ritz Four Seasons* W www.fourseasons.com €€€€€ Rua R. da Fonseca 88, 1099-039. **Map** 5 B5. 21-381 14 00. **FAX** 21-383 17 83. The legendary Ritz is an elegant, comfortable hotel. Many of the rooms have balconies that overlook the Parque Eduardo VII.	AE DC MC V	●	■		283
PARQUE DAS NAÇÕES: *Tivoli Tejo* €€€€€ Avenida Dom João II, 1990-83. 21-891 51 00. **FAX** 21-891 53 45. @ httejo@tivoli.pt This modern hotel caters to conference and trade fair guests. Its location avoids the traffic congestion of central Lisbon.	AE DC MC V	●		●	279
RATO: *Amazónia* €€€€ T. da Fábrica dos Pentes 12–20, 1250-106. **Map** 5 B5. 21-387 70 06. **FAX** 21-387 90 90. Conveniently close to the city centre, this mid-range hotel has elegant public rooms, large bedrooms and a piano bar.	AE DC MC V			●	192

RATO: *Altis* @ reservations@hotel-altis.pt €€€€€
Rua Castilho 11, 1269-072. **Map** 4 F1. 21-310 60 00. **FAX** 21-310 62 62.
This huge hotel has every expected facility, including a rooftop grill
and well-equipped health club with an indoor pool. 🛏 📺 🍴 P 👤

	AE	●		●	303
	DC				
	MC				
	V				

RESTAURADORES: *Nova Goa* €€
Rua do Arco do Marquês de Alegrete 1100-034. **Map** 7 C3. 21-888 11 37.
FAX 21-886 78 11. Just around the corner from Praça da Figueira, this *pensão*
is like many in the vicinity: clean, comfortable and fairly basic. 🛏 📺

| | | | | | 42 |

RESTAURADORES: *Restauradores* €€
Praça dos Restauradores 13, 4°, 1250-187. **Map** 7 A2. 21-347 56 60.
A very small and fairly basic *pensão* on the fourth floor of a building
with a great location in the busy centre of the city. No breakfast. 🛏

| | | | | | 30 |

RESTAURADORES: *Suíço Atlântico* €€
Rua da Glória 3–19, 1250-114. **Map** 7 A2. 21-346 17 13. **FAX** 21-346 90 13.
In a small side street by the Elevador da Glória, this hotel has large old-
fashioned rooms and public areas with stone arches and wooden beams. 🛏

	AE				90
	DC				
	MC				
	V				

RESTAURADORES: *Florescente* €€€
Rua das Portas de S. Antão 99, 1150-266. **Map** 7 A2. 21-342 66 09. **FAX** 21-342 77 33.
For a *pensão* the rooms of the Florescente are extremely well equipped.
The street is known for its many fine restaurants. No breakfast. 🛏 📺 🍴

	AE				60
	MC				
	V				

RESTAURADORES: *Roma* €€€
Travessa da Glória 22a, 1°, 1250-118. **Map** 7 A2. 21-346 05 57. **FAX** 21-346 05 57.
This simple *pensão* has a fine location just off Avenida da Liberdade, conve-
nient for shops and sightseeing. There is a 24-hour bar service. 🛏 📺 🍴

	AE				24
	DC				
	MC				
	V				

RESTAURADORES: *Avenida Palace* @ hotel.av.palace@mail.telepac.pt €€€€€
Rua 1° de Dezembro 123, 1200-359. **Map** 7 B3. 21-321 81 00. **FAX** 21-342 28 84.
Elegant and luxurious, the Avenida Palace hotel, with its Neo-Classical façade
and enviable location, retains many charming original details. 🛏 📺 🍴 P

	AE				82
	DC				
	MC				
	V				

ROSSIO: *Metrópole* @ sales@almeidahotels.com €€€€€
Praça Dom Pedro IV 30, 1100-200. **Map** 7 B3. 21-321 90 30. **FAX** 21-346 91 66.
This charming and elegant hotel has been renovated in a style reminiscent
of the 1920s. Buçaco wines *(see p210)* are sold here. 🛏 📺 🍴

	AE				36
	DC				
	MC				
	V				

SALDANHA: *Marisela* €
Rua Filipe Folque 19, 1050-111. **Map** 5 C3. 21-353 32 05. **FAX** 21-316 04 23.
A good-value *pensão* with rather basic rooms, in a quiet street between
the gardens of Parque Eduardo VII and Praça do Duque de Saldanha. 🛏 📺

	AE				19
	MC				
	V				

SALDANHA: *Horizonte* €€
Av. António A. de Aguiar 42, 1050-017. **Map** 5 B4. 21-353 95 26. **FAX** 21-353 84 74.
This large *pensão* offers good value for money for this area. The rooms at
the front can be noisy. 🛏 📺 🍴

	AE				52
	DC				
	MC				
	V				

SALDANHA: *VIP* €€
Rua Fernão Lopes 25, 1000-132. **Map** 5 C3. 21-356 86 00. **FAX** 21-315 87 73.
A simple hotel built over shops in a busy part of the city, the VIP is neat
and tidy, although the decor is somewhat old-fashioned. 🛏 📺 🍴

	AE				54
	DC				
	MC				
	V				

SALDANHA: *Príncipe* @ confortprincipe@mail.telepac.pt €€€
Avenida Duque de Ávila 201, 1050-082. **Map** 5 B3. 21-353 61 51. **FAX** 21-353 43 14.
Most of the rooms in this modern hotel have their own balcony.
There is a small bar and lounge just off the lobby. 🛏 📺 🍴 P 👤

	AE	●			67
	DC				
	MC				
	V				

SALDANHA: *Hotel Marquês de Sá* @ marquessahotal@mail.telepac.pt €€€€
Av. Miguel Bombarda 130, 1050-167. **Map** 6 B2. 21-791 10 14. **FAX** 21-793 69 86.
A pleasant hotel located in one of the most elegant areas of Lisbon, and a
short walk from the Museu Calouste Gulbenkian *(see p76–9)*. 🛏 📺 🍴 P

	AE				97
	DC				
	MC				
	V				

SALDANHA: *Real Parque* @ info@hoteisreal.com €€€€
Avenida L. Bivar 67, 1069-146. **Map** 5 C3. 21-319 90 00. **FAX** 21-382 29 30.
This impressive modern hotel, located on a quiet side street, has six
rooms specially designed for the disabled. 🛏 📺 🍴 P 👤

	AE	●			153
	DC				
	MC				
	V				

SALDANHA: *Sheraton Lisboa* €€€€€
Rua L. Coelho 1, 1069-025. **Map** 5 C3. 21-312 00 00. **FAX** 21-354 71 64.
Lisbon's Sheraton offers spacious rooms, a top-floor restaurant and bar with
fine views, a communications centre and a health club. 🛏 📺 🍴 P 👤

	AE	●		●	375
	DC				
	MC				
	V				

<table>
<tr><td>
Price categories in euros for a standard double room per night, including breakfast:

€ under 35
€€ 35–60
€€€ 60–100
€€€€ 100–150
€€€€€ over 150
</td><td>
RESTAURANT
The hotel has one or more restaurants open for lunch and supper, sometimes reserved for residents.

GARDEN
A garden, courtyard or large terrace for the use of hotel guests.

SWIMMING POOL
The hotel has its own indoor or outdoor pool.

CREDIT CARDS
Major credit cards accepted: *AE* American Express, *DC* Diners Club, *MC* MasterCard and *V* Visa.
</td></tr>
</table>

	CREDIT CARDS	RESTAURANT	GARDEN	SWIMMING POOL	NUMBER OF ROOMS

THE LISBON COAST

	CREDIT CARDS	RESTAURANT	GARDEN	SWIMMING POOL	NUMBER OF ROOMS
ALCÁCER DO SAL: *Pousada Dom Alfonso II* [w] www.pousadas.pt €€€€€ Alcácer do Sal, 7850. [C] 265-61 30 70. [FAX] 265-61 30 74. This atmospheric and historic *pousada* occupies a converted castle on a hilltop, overlooking the town and surrounding countryside. ⊟ TV ▤ P &	AE DC MC V	●	▣	●	35
CARCAVELOS: *Praia-Mar* [w] www.almeidahotels.com €€€€ Rua do Gurué 16, 2775-581. [C] 21-458 51 00. [FAX] 21-457 31 30. This delightful hotel overlooks the Estoril coast's largest sandy beach. Modern and elegant throughout, the rooms are spacious and comfortable. The famed wines from Buçaco *(see p210)* are also available. ⊟ TV ▤ P &	AE DC MC V	●	▣	●	158
CASCAIS: *Casa da Pérgola* €€€ Avenida Valbom 13, 2750-508. [C] 21-484 00 40. [FAX] 21-483 47 91. This grand 19th century house has rooms with stucco ceilings and ornate furniture. It is closed from 15 Dec–31 Jan. ⊟			▣		11
CASCAIS: *Cidadela* €€€ Avenida 25 de Abril, 2750. [C] 21-482 76 00. [FAX] 21-486 72 26. A short walk from the town centre, the Cidadela is surrounded by gardens. Most of the rooms have spectacular views over the bay. ⊟ TV ▤ P	AE DC MC V	●	▣	●	113
CASCAIS: *Solar Dom Carlos* €€€ Rua Latino Coelho 8, 2750-408. [C] 21-482 81 15. [FAX] 21-486 51 55. This delightful hotel, the former summer residence of King Carlos I, has a garden, historic chapel and comfortable rooms. ⊟ TV	AE DC MC V		▣		18
CASCAIS: *Baía* €€€€ Avenida Marginal, 2750. [C] 21-483 10 33. [FAX] 21-483 10 95. The modern Baía hotel has a great location between the busy centre of Cascais and the small fishermans' beach. ⊟ TV ▤ P &	AE DC MC V	●	▣	●	113
CASCAIS: *Albatroz* €€€€€ Rua F. Arouca 100, 2750-353. [C] 21-483 28 21. [FAX] 21-484 73 80. Built in the 19th century as a retreat for the Portuguese royal family, the Albatroz sits perched on the rocks directly overlooking the ocean. Inside, the luxurious decoration is matched by excellent service. ⊟ TV ▤ P &	AE DC MC V	●	▣	●	46
COSTA DA CAPARICA: *Praia do Sol* €€ Rua dos Pescadores 12, 2825-386. [C] 21-290 00 12. [FAX] 21-290 25 41. A small hotel, the Praia do Sol offers well-appointed rooms conveniently located close to the beach in this popular resort town. ⊟ TV ▤	AE DC MC V				53
COSTA DA CAPARICA: *Costa da Caparica* €€€€ Av. Gen. Delgado 47, 2829-506. [C] 21-291 89 00. [FAX] 21-291 06 87. This hotel, with an unusual semi-circular entrance, overlooks the beach. It has seven rooms adapted for the disabled. ⊟ TV ▤ P &	AE DC MC V	●	▣	●	353
ERICEIRA: *Vilazul* €€€ Calçada da Baleia 10, 2655-238. [C] 261-86 00 00. [FAX] 261-86 29 27. Only 500 m (550 yds) from the sea, this bright and airy hotel has panoramic views from the terrace and some of the bedrooms. ⊟ TV ▤ P	AE DC MC V	●			21
ESTORIL: *São Cristóvão* €€€ Av. Marginal 7079, 2765-480. [C] 21-468 09 13. [FAX] 21-468 09 13. This charming *pensão* is housed in an interesting old villa. Located on the ocean side of the Avenida Marginal, it offers spectacular views. P			▣		14
ESTORIL: *Amazónia Lennox* €€€€ Rua Eng. A. de Sousa 175, 2765-191. [C] 21-468 04 24. [FAX] 21-467 08 59. Situated in its own lush gardens with panoramic views, this hotel is perfect for golfers. ⊟ TV ▤ P	AE DC MC V	●	▣	●	34

ESTORIL: *Hotel Alvorada* €€€€
Rua de Lisboa 3, 2765-240. (21-464 98 60. FAX 21-468 72 50.
Only a few minutes' walk from the beach and opposite the casino, this hotel offers friendly service and bright, well-appointed rooms. 🛏 TV 🍴 P ♿

AE DC MC V — 52

ESTORIL: *Hotel da Inglaterra* €€€€
Rua do Porto 1, 2765-271. (21-468 44 61. FAX 21-468 21 08.
Some rooms in this impressive early 20th-century mansion have lovely views over the bay of Cascais or the Sintra hills. 🛏 TV 🍴

AE DC MC V ● ■ ● 52

ESTORIL: *Palácio* @ palacioestoril@mail.telepac.pt €€€€€
Rua do Parque, 2769-504. (21-464 80 00. FAX 21-468 48 67.
An elegant hotel located between the sea and the casino. Guests have access to an 18-hole golf course and tennis courts. 🛏 TV 🍴 P ♿

AE DC MC V ● ■ ● 162

GUINCHO: *Estalagem Muchaxo* €€€€
Praia do Guincho, 2750-642. (21-487 02 21. FAX 21-487 04 44.
This rustic *estalagem*, with exposed beams and open brickwork, overlooks the ocean. The sea-water pool is built into the cliffs. 🛏 TV 🍴 P

AE DC MC V ● 60

GUINCHO: *Fortaleza do Guincho* w guinchotel.pt €€€€€
Estrada do Guincho, 2750-642. (21-487 04 91. FAX 21-487 04 31.
Perched on a clifftop overlooking the ocean, this atmospheric hotel with arched ceilings and medieval decor was once a fortress. 🛏 TV 🍴 P ♿

AE DC MC V 29

GUINCHO: *Senhora da Guia* €€€€€
Estrada do Guincho, 2750-374. (21-486 92 39. FAX 21-486 92 27.
Set in its own grounds with a sea-water pool, this charming *estalagem* is housed in a comfortable and relaxing manor house. 🛏 TV 🍴 P

AE DC MC V ● ■ ● 42

MAFRA: *Castelão* €€€
Avenida 25 de Abril, 2640-456. (261-81 60 50. FAX 261-81 60 59.
Convenient as a base when visiting the fabulous monastery in Mafra, this hotel is comfortable and clean. 🛏 TV P

AE DC MC V 35

PAÇO D'ARCOS: *Solar Palmeiras* €€€€
Avenida Marginal, 2780. (21-446 83 00. FAX 21-446 83 99.
Housed in a 19th-century manor house, many of the rooms in the Sol Palmeiras are suites with views over the Tagus. 🛏 TV 🍴 P

AE DC MC V ● ■ 35

PALMELA: *Pousada de Palmela* w www.pousadas.pt €€€€€
Castelo de Palmela, 2950-997. (21-235 12 26. FAX 21-233 04 40.
The fortified walls of this 12th-century castle now enclose a tranquil *pousada* with whitewashed rooms and many plants. 🛏 TV 🍴 P

AE DC MC V ● ■ 28

QUELUZ: *Pousada da Dona Maria I* w www.pousadas.pt €€€€€
L. do Palácio Nacional, 2745-191. (21-435 61 58. FAX 21-435 61 89.
Once used by staff of the marvellous 18th-century Palácio de Queluz, today the "Clock Tower" is an impressive *pousada*. 🛏 TV 🍴 P ♿

AE DC MC V ● 26

SESIMBRA: *Hotel do Mar* €€€€
R. Gen. Humberto Delgado 10, 2970-628. (21-228 83 00. FAX 21-223 38 88.
This hotel, built on different levels on the cliffside, is surrounded by lush gardens. The presidential suite has a private pool. 🛏 TV 🍴 P ♿

AE DC MC V ● ■ ● 168

SETÚBAL: *IBIS Setúbal* €€
Rua Alto da Guerra, 2914-518. (265-77 22 00. FAX 265-77 24 47.
Featuring the usual combination of IBIS comforts and economy, this hotel is surrounded by its own peaceful gardens. 🛏 TV 🍴 P ♿

AE DC MC V ● ■ ● 102

SETÚBAL: *Pousada de São Filipe* w www.pousadas.pt €€€€€
Castelo de São Filipe, 2900-300. (265-55 00 70. FAX 265-53 25 38.
This historic castle, built by Philip II of Spain *(see p50)* in 1590, is an friendly pousada with fine views over the estuary. 🛏 TV 🍴 P

AE DC MC V ● ■ 16

SINTRA: *Central* €€€
Praça da República 35, 2710-625. (21-923 09 63.
Heavy furniture and peeling paint give this hotel an old-fashioned atmosphere. It has an excellent position opposite the Palácio Nacional. 🛏

AE DC MC V ● 10

SINTRA: *Residencial Sintra* @ pensao.residencial.sintra@clix.pt €€€
T. dos Avaleres 12, 2710-506. (21-923 07 38. FAX 21-923 07 38.
Located just east of Sintra town centre in the residential area of São Pedro, this rambling old *pensão* is friendly and full of character. 🛏 P ♿

MC V ■ ● 10

Price categories in euros for a standard double room per night, including breakfast: € under 35 €€ 35–60 €€€ 60–100 €€€€ 100–150 €€€€€ over 150	**RESTAURANT** The hotel has one or more restaurants open for lunch and supper, sometimes reserved for residents. **GARDEN** A garden, courtyard or large terrace for the use of hotel guests. **SWIMMING POOL** The hotel has its own indoor or outdoor pool. **CREDIT CARDS** Major credit cards accepted: *AE* American Express, *DC* Diners Club, *MC* MasterCard and *V* Visa.	CREDIT CARDS	RESTAURANT	GARDEN	SWIMMING POOL	NUMBER OF ROOMS

	CREDIT CARDS	RESTAURANT	GARDEN	SWIMMING POOL	NUMBER OF ROOMS
SINTRA: *Tivoli Sintra* W www.tivolihotels.com €€€€ Praça da República, 2710-616. (21-923 35 05. FAX 21-923 15 72. The modern Tivoli Sintra, tucked away in a corner of Sintra's main square, has wonderful views across the valley, a bar and a boutique. 🔲 TV 🍽 P ♿	AE DC MC V	●			76
SINTRA: *Caesar Park* W www.caesarparkpenhalonga.com €€€€€€ Estr. da Lagoa Azul, Linhó 2714-511. (21-924 90 11. FAX 21-924 90 07. This huge, luxurious complex in the Sintra hills has a 9 and an 18-hole golf course, designed by Robert Trent Jones Jr, and a health club. 🔲 TV 🍽 P ♿	AE DC MC V	●	■	●	177
SINTRA: *Lawrence's* @ info@portugalvirtual.pt €€€€€€ Rua Consiglieri Pedroso 38-40, 2710-550 Sintra. (21-910 55 00. FAX 21-910 55 05. A cosy, family-run luxury hotel that dates back to the 18th century. Lord Byron is said to have stayed here in 1809. 🔲 TV 🍽 P ♿	AE DC MC V	●	■		16
SINTRA: *Palácio de Seteais* W www.tivolihotels.com €€€€€€ Av. B. du Bocage 8, 2710-616. (21-923 32 00. FAX 21-923 42 77. Just outside town, this elegant hotel occupies a delightful 18th-century palace with tastefully decorated interiors and a topiary garden. 🔲 TV P	AE DC MC V	●	■	●	30
ESTREMADURA AND RIBATEJO					
ABRANTES: *Hotel de Turismo* €€€€ Largo de Santo António, 2200-349. Road map C4. (241-36 12 61. FAX 241-36 52 18. This hotel, decorated in bright, classic colours, is found in a very pleasant location surrounded by attractive gardens. 🔲 TV P	AE DC MC V	●	■		40
BALEAL: *Casa das Marés* €€€ Praia do Baleal, Peniche, 2520. Road map B4. (& FAX 262-76 92 55. The family-run "House of Tides" is set on a promontory with dramatic sea views. Breakfast is served on the terrace above a cove. 🔲 TV 🍽 P					12
BARRAGEM DO CASTELO DE BODE: *Pousada de São Pedro* €€€ Castelo de Bode, Tomar, 2300. Road map C4. (249-38 11 59. W www.pousadas.pt Overlooking the River Zêzere, this pleasant *pousada* offers simple but tastefully furnished rooms and excellent regional cooking. 🔲 TV 🍽 P	AE DC MC V	●			25
BARRAGEM DO CASTELO DE BODE: *Estalagem Lago Azul* €€€€ Lago Azul, Ferreira do Zêzere, 2240. Road map C4. (249-36 14 45. FAX 249-36 16 64. The rooms of this *estalagem* are functional but there are tennis courts and sailing boats and the lakeside setting is spectacular. 🔲 TV 🍽 P	AE DC MC V	●	■	●	20
BATALHA: *Pousada do Mestre Afonso Domingues* €€€€ L. do Mestre A. Domingues 6, 2440. Road map C4. (244-76 52 60. W www.pousadas.pt This *pousada* stands next to the town's abbey, Batalha, and is named after its architect. The rooms are traditionally furnished. 🔲 TV 🍽 P	AE DC MC V	●			21
CALDAS DA RAINHA: *Caldas Internacional* €€€ Rua Dr.Figueirôa Rego 45, 2500. Road map B4. (262-83 05 00. FAX 262-84 44 82. Patterned floor tiles in the reception area welcome the visitor to the efficient and modern Caldas Internacional Hotel. 🔲 TV 🍽 P ♿	AE DC MC V	●	■	●	83
CONSTÂNCIA: *Quinta de Santa Bárbara* €€€ 2250-092. Road map C4. (249-73 92 14. FAX 249-73 93 73. A fine 18th-century manor house, the Quinta de Santa Bárbara has been converted into a distinguished hotel, with cosy, rustic rooms. The Gothic stone vaults of the former refectory now house the restaurant. 🔲 🍽 P		●	■	●	7
FÁTIMA: *Dom Gonçalo* W www.estalagemdomoncalo.com €€€ Rua Jacinta Marto 100, 2495-450. Road map C4. (249-539 330. FAX 249-539 335. A delightful *estalagem* that is set in charming, well-kept gardens and woods, and yet is still very close to the sanctuary. 🔲 TV 🍽 P	AE DC MC V	●	■	·	42

FÁTIMA: *Verbo Divino* €€€ DC MC V — 208
Praça Paulo VI, Aptdo 2, 2496-908. **Road map** C4. 249-53 30 43. **FAX** 249-53 22 63.
Built to guarantee a revenue for the Divine Word Missionaries, this is a
large, simply decorated hotel for pilgrims to Fátima. 🚪 TV 🍽 P

GOLEGÃ: *Casa da Azinhaga* @ joao.v.saldanha@clix.pt €€€ — 7
Azinhaga, 2150-021. **Road map** C4. 249-957 146. **FAX** 249-957 182.
This classic manor house, 7 km (4 miles) south of horse-loving Golegã,
offers comfortable rooms in a pleasant ambience. 🚪 P

LEIRIA: *Leiriense* €€ MC V — 24
Rua A. de Albuquerque 8, 2400-080. **Road map** C4. 244-82 30 54. **FAX** 244-82 30 73.
Found tucked away in the narrow side streets of the old area of Leiria,
this *residencial* is clean, welcoming and quite charming. 🚪 TV 🍽

LEIRIA: *Dom João III* €€€ AE DC MC V — 64
Avenida Dom João III, 2400-164. **Road map** C4. 244-817 888. **FAX** 244-817 880.
The modern, well-equipped rooms of this hotel have views to the
splendid *loggia* of the castle and over the River Lis. 🚪 TV 🍽 P

LOURINHÃ: *Quinta de Santa Catarina* @ quinta.santa.catarina@netc.pt €€€ — 5
Rua Visconde de Palma de Almeida, 2530-166. **Road map** B4. 261-42 23 13
FAX 261 41 48 75. This well-kept manor house surrounded by gardens and
farmland is still in the hands of the original owners. 🚪 P

NAZARÉ: *Mar Bravo* €€€€ AE DC MC V — 16
Praça S. Oliveira 71, 2450-159. **Road map** C4. 262-56 91 60. **FAX** 262-56 91 69.
In the heart of Nazaré this *albergaria* has panoramic views over this pic-
turesque town and the beach. All rooms have balconies. 🚪 TV 🍽 P

ÓBIDOS: *Estalagem do Convento* €€€ AE MC V — 31
Rua D. João D'Ornelas, 2510. **Road map** B4. 262-95 92 17. **FAX** 262-95 91 59.
Once a convent, the rooms of this tastefully converted *estalagem* are
traditionally and elegantly furnished. Some have marvellous views. 🚪 TV

ÓBIDOS: *Rainha Santa Isabel* €€€ AE DC MC V — 20
Rua Direita, 2510. **Road map** B4. 262-95 93 23. **FAX** 262-95 91 15.
Enclosed within the walls of this pretty town, the attractive wood-
panelled rooms of this *albergaria* contain lovely *azulejos*. 🚪 TV 🍽

ÓBIDOS: *Pousada do Castelo* w www.pousadas.pt €€€€€ AE DC MC V — 9
Paço Real, 2510-999. **Road map** B4. 262-95 50 80. **FAX** 262-95 91 48.
The novelist Graham Greene stayed in this stunning *pousada*, converted
from a 15th-century royal castle. Book early as it is very popular. 🚪 TV 🍽

OURÉM: *Pousada Conde de Ourém* w www.pousadas.pt €€€€€ AE DC MC V — 30
Largo João Mansur Castelo, 2490 Ourém. **Road map** C4. 249-540 920.
FAX 249-542 955. Set in a restored cluster of medieval houses within the
walled town of Ourém, northeast of the sanctuary of Fátima. 🚪 TV 🍽 P

PENICHE: *Casa do Castelo* €€€ AE DC MC V — 7
N 114 no. 16, 2520 Atouguia da Baleia. **Road map** B4. 262-750 647.
Situated inland from Peniche and built on the ruins of a Moorish castle,
this extended 17th-century manor house is modest and pleasant. 🚪 P

SANTARÉM: *Vitória* €€ AE DC MC V — 25
R. 2º Visconde de Santarém 21, 2000-197. **Road map** C4. 243-30 91 30.
FAX 243-328 202. A modest *pensão* handy for Santarém's main sights, the
Vitória offers small rooms that are cosy and welcoming. 🚪 TV 🍽

SANTARÉM: *Quinta de Vale de Lobos* w www.valedelobos.com €€€ V — 4
Azóia de Baixo, 2000. **Road map** C4. 243-42 92 64. **FAX** 243-429 313.
This restored 19th-century manor house, set among cedar trees, has
traditionally furnished rooms and an inner courtyard. 🚪 P

SÃO MARTINHO DO PORTO: *Americana* €€ MC V — 25
Rua D. José Saldanha 2, 2460-645. **Road map** B4. 262-98 91 70. **FAX** 262-98 93 49.
Conveniently located close to the sandy, sheltered beach popular with
families, this friendly *pensão* offers pleasant rooms. 🚪 TV

SÃO PEDRO DE MUEL: *Mar e Sol* €€€ AE DC MC V — 63
Avenida da Liberdade 1, 2430-501. **Road map** C4. 244-59 00 00. **FAX** 244-59 00 19.
Right beside the ocean and spectacular beach, this neat and unpretentious
hotel offers rooms with sea views in this popular resort. 🚪 TV 🍽 P ♿

For key to symbols see back flap

<table>
<tr><td colspan="2">

Price categories in euros for a standard double room per night, including breakfast:

€ under 35
€€ 35–60
€€€ 60–100
€€€€ 100–150
€€€€€ over 150

</td><td colspan="5">

RESTAURANT
The hotel has one or more restaurants open for lunch and supper, sometimes reserved for residents.
GARDEN
A garden, courtyard or large terrace for the use of hotel guests.
SWIMMING POOL
The hotel has its own indoor or outdoor pool.
CREDIT CARDS
Major credit cards accepted: *AE* American Express, *DC* Diners Club, *MC* MasterCard and *V* Visa.

</td></tr>
</table>

	CREDIT CARDS	RESTAURANT	GARDEN	SWIMMING POOL	NUMBER OF ROOMS
TOMAR: *Hotel dos Templários* €€€ L. Cândido dos Reis 1, 2304-909. **Road map** C4. 249-31 01 00. FAX 249-32 21 91. Overlooking the River Nabão and conveniently located in the city centre, this hotel offers tennis courts, a gym and a health club. ⟐ TV 𝄄 P ♿	AE DC MC V	●	■	●	176
TOMAR: *Santa Iria* €€€ Parque do Mouchão, 2300-586. **Road map** C4. 249-31 33 26. FAX 249-32 12 38. Wonderfully situated on an island park on the River Nabão, this discreetly elegant *estalagem* is near many of the city's sights. ⟐ TV P	AE MC V	●	■		14
VILA FRANCA DE XIRA: *Lezíria Parque* €€€ N1, 2600-246, Povos. **Road map** C5. 263-276 670. FAX 263-276 990. Close to the Lisbon to Oporto motorway (the A1), this attractive hotel has pleasant views over the River Tagus. ⟐ TV 𝄄 P ♿	AE DC MC V	●	■		71
THE BEIRAS					
ALMEIDA: *Morgado* €€ Bairro de São Pedro, 6350-210. **Road map** E2. 271-57 44 12. Found just outside the walls of the fortress at Almeida, this modern *pensão* is clean and comfortable, and very good value. ⟐ TV 𝄄 P					12
ALMEIDA: *Pousada da Senhora das Neves* w www.pousadas.pt €€€€ Rua da Muralha, 6350. **Road map** E2. 271-57 42 90. FAX 271-57 43 20. Inside the star-shaped fortifications that enclose the town, this *pousada* has pleasantly furnished rooms, some with four-poster beds. ⟐ TV 𝄄	AE DC MC V	●			21
AVEIRO: *Arcada* €€ Rua Viana do Castelo 4, 3800-275. **Road map** C3. 234-423 001. FAX 234-421 886. Located in a Neo-Classical arcaded building overlooking the central canal, the Arcada has character as well as all modern comforts. ⟐ TV	AE DC MC V				49
AVEIRO: *Mercure* €€€ Rua L. G. de Carvalho 23, 3800-211. **Road map** C3. 234-404 400. FAX 234-404 401. This hotel was recently modernised and offers every modern amenity while retaining its charming small garden. ⟐ TV 𝄄 P ♿	AE DC MC V		■		45
AVEIRO: *Pousada da Ria* w www.pousadas.pt €€€€ Bico do Muranzel, Torreira, 3870-301. **Road map** C3. 234-860 180. FAX 234-83 83 33. This modern *pousada* has a peaceful location on the banks of the Ria de Aveiro. Most of the rooms have balconies overlooking the lagoon where the local painted boats *(moliceiros)* are moored. ⟐ TV 𝄄 P	AE DC MC V	●	■	●	19
BUÇACO: *Palace Hotel do Buçaco* €€€€€ Buçaco, 3050-261 Luso. **Road map** C3. 231-937 970. FAX 231-93 05 09. This extraordinary Neo-Manueline hotel, set in a luxuriant forest, was built as a hunting lodge for the last Portuguese kings. The grand interior offers attractive rooms, some with decorative *azulejos*. ⟐ TV 𝄄 P	AE DC MC V	●	■,		60
CARAMULO: *Pousada de São Jerónimo* w www.pousadas.pt €€€€ 3475-031. **Road map** C3. 232-86 12 91. FAX 232-86 16 40. This modern *pousada*, covered in ivy, offers well-appointed rooms and a delightful setting high up in the Serra do Caramulo. ⟐ TV 𝄄 P	AE DC MC V	●	■	●	12
CASTELO BRANCO: *Rainha Dona Amélia* €€€ Rua de Santiago 15, 6000-179. **Road map** D4. 272-34 88 00. FAX 272-34 88 08. This pleasant modern hotel has comfortable rooms and an excellent location in the city centre close to the historical sights. ⟐ TV 𝄄 P ♿	AE DC MC V	●			64
CASTRO D'AIRE: *Montemuro* €€ Termas do Carvalhal, 3600-398. **Road map** D2. 232-38 11 54. FAX 232-38 11 12. Located in the mountains between Viseu and the Douro, this modern hotel offers facilities for rafting and canoeing. ⟐ TV 𝄄 P ♿	AE DC MC V	●	■		80

CELORICO DA BEIRA: *Mira Serra* €€
Bairro de S. Eufémia, 6360. **Road map** D3. 📞 271-74 26 04. 📠 271-74 13 82.
As the name Mira Serra suggests, this attractive and pleasant hotel has
stunning views of the Serra da Estrela mountain range. 🛏 📺 🍽 🅿 ♿

AE DC MC V	●	■		42

COIMBRA: *Internacional* €
Avenida Emídio Navarro 4, 3000-150. **Road map** C3. 📞 239-82 55 03. 📠 239-83 84 46.
Conveniently located close to the railway station, and overlooking the
River Mondego, this *pensão* is welcoming but very basic. 🛏 10 rooms. 📺

				27

COIMBRA: *Astória* €€€
Av. Emídio Navarro 21, 3000-150. **Road map** C3. 📞 239-85 30 20. 📠 239-82 20 57.
A charming Art Deco hotel with modernised facilites, the Astória has
stylish rooms with fine views across the Mondego. 🛏 📺 🍽 🅿

AE DC MC V	●			62

COIMBRA: *Bragança* €€€
Largo das Ameias 10, 3000-024. **Road map** C3. 📞 239-82 21 71. 📠 239-83 61 35.
A slightly old-fashioned but very comfortable hotel located in the heart of
Coimbra. The suites have marble bathrooms. 🛏 📺 🍽 🅿

AE DC MC V	●			83

COIMBRA: *Quinta das Lágrimas* €€€€
Santa Clara, Aptdo. 5053, 3041-901. **Road map** C3. 📞 239-80 23 80. 📠 239-44 16 95.
A handsome 18th-century country house, famous for the "Fountain of Love"
where Pedro and Inês *(see p179)* used to meet in secret. 🛏 📺 🍽 🅿 ♿

AE DC MC V	●	■	●	39

COIMBRA: *Tivoli Coimbra* 🌐 www.tivolihotels.com €€€€
Rua João Machado 4, 3000-226. **Road map** C3. 📞 239-82 69 34. 📠 239-82 68 27.
This modern hotel in the heart of the city boasts an excellent health club
with a Turkish bath, massage and gymnasium. 🛏 📺 🍽 🅿

AE DC MC V	●		●	100

CONDEIXA-A-NOVA: *Pousada de Santa Cristina* 🌐 www.pousadas.pt €€€
Rua Francisco Lemos, 3150-142. **Road map** C3. 📞 239-94 12 86. 📠 239-94 30 97.
This modern *pousada*, situated in its own gardens, is a good base for
visits to Coimbra and the Roman ruins of Conimbriga. 🛏 📺 🍽 🅿

AE DC MC V	●			45

COVILHÃ: *Hotel Serra da Estrela* €€€
Penhas da Saúde, 6200. **Road map** D3. 📞 275-310 300. 📠 275-310 309.
Set in the Serra da Estrela, this modern hotel offers lodging in triangular
bungalows and facilities for horse riding and winter sports. 🛏 📺 🅿

MC V	●	■		40

CURIA: *Curia Palace Hotel* €€€
Tamengos, 3780-541. **Road map** C3. 📞 231-51 03 00. 📠 231-51 55 31.
This elegant Art Nouveau palace is set in manicured gardens and features
a tennis court and mini-golf. Open April to October. 🛏 📺 🅿

AE DC MC V	●	■	●	114

FIGUEIRA DA FOZ: *Casa da Azenha Velha* €€€
Caceira de Cima, 3080-055. **Road map** C3. 📞 233-42 50 41. 📠 233-42 97 04.
This *Turismo Rural* is part of a large estate where horses, deer and wild
boar are reared. There is a restaurant a short walk away. 🛏 📺 🍽 🅿

		■	●	6

FIGUEIRA DA FOZ: *Hotel Costa de Prata* €€€
Largo Coronel Galhardo 1, 3080. **Road map** C3. 📞 233-42 66 20. 📠 233-42 66 10.
Overlooking the sea, this hotel is brightly decorated throughout and has a
bar and breakfast room with panoramic views. 🛏 📺 🍽

AE				66

GUARDA: *Solar de Alarcão* €€€
Rua Dom Miguel de Alarcão 25-27, 6300-684. **Road map** D3. 📞 271-21 12 75.
📠 271-21 43 92. This *turismo de habitação* occupies a granite house built in
1686. There is a chapel and the rooms are full of antiques. 🛏 📺 🅿

		■		3

LUSO: *Astória* €
Rua Emídio Navarro, 3050-224. **Road map** C3. 📞 231-93 91 82.
This small *pensão* is a delight. The rooms are simply furnished but
comfortable, and the bar has a friendly atmosphere. 🛏 📺

AE MC V	●			9

LUSO: *Grande Hotel* €€€
Rua Dr. Cid de Oliveira 86, 3050. **Road map** C3. 📞 231-93 79 37. 📠 231-93 79 30.
Dominating the skyline of this attractive spa town, this elegant hotel has
sports facilities as well as access to the spa. 🛏 📺 🍽 🅿 ♿

AE DC MC V	●	■	●	143

MANGUALDE: *Casa d'Azurara* €€€
Rua Nova 78, 3530. **Road map** D3. 📞 232-61 20 10. 📠 232-62 25 75.
Built in the 18th century, today the Casa d'Azurara is a friendly *estalagem*,
set in its own gardens, with many original features. 🛏 📺 🍽 🅿

AE DC MC V	●	■		15

For key to symbols see back flap

<table>
<tr>
<td colspan="2">
Price categories in euros for a standard double room per night, including breakfast:
€ under 35
€€ 35–60
€€€ 60–100
€€€€ 100–150
€€€€€ over 150
</td>
<td>
RESTAURANT
The hotel has one or more restaurants open for lunch and supper, sometimes reserved for residents.
GARDEN
A garden, courtyard or large terrace for the use of hotel guests.
SWIMMING POOL
The hotel has its own indoor or outdoor pool.
CREDIT CARDS
Major credit cards accepted: AE American Express, DC Diners Club, MC MasterCard and V Visa.
</td>
</tr>
</table>

	CREDIT CARDS	RESTAURANT	GARDEN	SWIMMING POOL	NUMBER OF ROOMS
MANTEIGAS: *Pousada de São Lourenço* w www.pousadas.pt €€€€ Penhas Douradas, 6260-200. **Road map** D3. 275-98 24 50. FAX 275-98 24 53. This traditional granite *pousada*, high in the Serra da Estrela, is ideal for hikers and others seeking a secluded retreat. 🛏 TV 🍴 P	AE DC MC V		■		21
MANTEIGAS: *Pousada do Convento de Belmonte* €€€€€ Belmonte 6250. **Road map** D3. 275-91 03 00. FAX 275-91 03 10. w www.pousadas.pt Occupying a 13th-century convent, this *pousada* has well-equipped, modern rooms around the central convent courtyard. 🛏 TV 🍴 P	AE DC MC V	●	■	●	24
MONSANTO: *Pousada de Monsanto* w www.pousadas.pt €€€ Rua da Capela 1, 6060-091. **Road map** D3. 277-31 44 71. FAX 277-31 44 81. A friendly and attractive *pousada* in an ancient and famous village where the hillside houses are squeezed between giant boulders. 🛏 TV 🍴	AE DC MC V				10
SABUGUEIRO: *Casas do Cruzeiro* €€ Apartado 85, 6270-990, Seia. **Road map** D3. 238-312 825. FAX 238-315 282. Tucked away in a village in a Serra da Estrela valley, the granite cottages of the Casas do Cruzeiro offer simple apartments with kitchenettes. 🛏 TV P					30
SÃO JOÃO DE AREIAS: *Solar da Quinta* €€€ Póvoa dos Mosqueiros, 3440-458. **Road map** D3. 232 89 17 08. FAX 232 89 23 82. This chaming 400 year-old house has a large garden with a pond and each room is furnished with antiques. 🛏 P	AE DC MC V		■		5
VISEU: *Hotel Montebelo* w www.grupovisabeira.pt €€€ Urbanização Quinta do Bosque, 3510-020, Viseu. **Road map** D3. 232-42 00 00. FAX 232-41 54 00. This well-equipped business hotel also has good facilites for tourists, including nearby horse-riding and golf. 🛏 TV 🍴 P	AE DC MC V	●	■	●	100

DOURO AND TRÁS-OS-MONTES

	CREDIT CARDS	RESTAURANT	GARDEN	SWIMMING POOL	NUMBER OF ROOMS
ALIJÓ: *Pousada de Barão do Forrester* w www.pousadas.pt €€€€ Rua José Rufino, 5070-031. **Road map** D2. 259-95 92 15. FAX 259-95 93 04. This *pousada* is in the heart of the port wine country and was named after the Englishman, James Forrester (1809–62), an advocate of "pure wine" *(see p252)*. Its sports facilities include tennis courts. 🛏 TV 🍴 P	AE DC MC V	●	■	●	21
AMARANTE: *Pousada de São Gonçalo* w www.pousadas.pt €€€€ Aptdo. 286, 4604-909. **Road map** D2. 255-46 11 13. FAX 255-46 13 53. Set in tranquil pine forests, the unusual semi-circular shape of this friendly *pousada* affords spectacular views of the Marão hills. 🛏 TV 🍴 P ♿	AE DC MC V	●	■		15
BRAGANÇA: *Classis* €€ Av. João da Cruz 102, 5300-178. **Road map** E1. 273-33 16 31. FAX 273-32 34 58. A pleasant, modern and comfortable *residencial* just a short walk from the city centre, the Classis is particularly good value. 🛏 TV 🍴 ♿	AE DC MC V				20
BRAGANÇA: *Estalagem do Caçador* €€€ Largo Manuel Pinto de Azevedo 5340-219, Macedo de Cavaleiros. **Road map** E1. 278-42 63 56. FAX 278-42 63 81. Located in a valley at the foot of the the Serra de Bornes, southwest of Bragança, this friendly and welcoming country inn has a pleasant interior. 🛏 TV P	AE DC MC V	●	■	●	24
BRAGANÇA: *Pousada de São Bartolomeu* w www.pousadas.pt €€€€ Estrada do Turismo, 5300-271. **Road map** E1. 273-33 14 93. FAX 273-32 34 53. This popular *pousada* offers a panoramic view of the city of Bragança. Wooden furniture and stone walls add rustic charm. 🛏 TV 🍴 P	AE DC MC V	●	■	●	28
CHAVES: *Aquae Flaviae* €€€ Praça do Brasil, 5400. **Road map** D1. 276-30 90 00. FAX 276-30 90 10. An impressive hotel that dominates the skyline of Chaves, the modern Aquae Flaviae has health and beauty facilities. 🛏 TV 🍴 P	AE DC MC V	●	■	●	165

CINFÃES: *Casa de Rebolfe* €€€
Porto Antigo, 4690-423 Oliveira do Douro. **Road map** D2. 📞 & 📠 255-56 23 34.
Located east of Cinfães, near Porto Antigo, this 18th-century house beside the
Douro has been converted into a welcoming hotel. 📶 📺

ESPINHO: *Praia Golfe* 🔲 www.praiagolfe.com €€€€
Rua 6, 4500-357. **Road map** C2. 📞 22-733 10 00. 📠 22-733 10 01.
Situated on the wide sandy beach, with views of the ocean, this hotel is
located next to a casino. There is a health club upstairs. 📶 📺 📧 🅿 ♿

AE DC MC V — 133

LAMEGO: *Hotel do Parque* €€
Parque N. S. dos Remédios, 5100-025. **Road map** D2. 📞 254-60 91 40. 📠 254-61 52 03.
Set in a grand whitewashed house next to the Santuário dos Remédios,
this hotel offers rustic rooms overlooking a chestnut forest. 📶 📺

AE DC MC V — 42

LAMEGO: *Quinta de Santa Eufémia* 🔲 www.casasantaeufemia.com €€€
Parada do Bispo, 5100-360. **Road map** D2. 📞 254-32 23 57. 📠 254-33 11 18.
This wine-producing farm also functions as a *Turismo Rural*, and guests
are invited to share family meals in the renovated historic house. 📶 🅿

MC V — 4

LAMEGO: *Villa Hostilina* €€€
Almocave, 5100-192. **Road map** D2. 📞 254-61 23 94. 📠 254-65 51 94.
Housed in a 19th-century farmhouse, Villa Hostilina offers tranquility
and charm and the use of a health club and tennis court. 📶 📺 🅿

— 7

MESÃO FRIO: *Casa d'Além* €€€
Oliveira, 5040-204. **Road map** D2. 📞 254-32 19 91. 📠 254-32 19 91.
Originally a port wine-growing country estate built in the 1920s, this
family-run *quinta* has attractive interiors with original decor. 📶 🅿

AE DC MC V — 4

MESÃO FRIO: *Pousada do Solar da Rede* 🔲 www.pousadas.pt €€€€€
Mesão Frio 5040. **Road map** D2. 📞 254-89 01 30. 📠 254-89 01 39.
Set in an 18th-century manor house and furnished in sumptuous period
style, this *pousada* offers beautiful views of the Douro river. 📶 📺 📧 🅿

AE DC MC V — 27

OPORTO: *Malaposta* €€
Rua da Conceição 80, 4050-214. **Road map** C2. 📞 22-200 62 78. 📠 22-200 62 95.
Tucked away on a quiet side street, and centrally located, the attractive
and modern Malaposta is a friendly, good-value hotel. 📶 📺 📧

AE DC MC V — 37

OPORTO: *Nave* €€
Av. Fernão de Magalhães 247, 4300-190. **Road map** C2. 📞 22-589 90 30. 📠 22-589 90 39.
This modern hotel is conveniently situated ten minutes walk from the
centre of town. The bedrooms have recently been renovated. 📶 📺 📧 🅿

AE MC V — 81

OPORTO: *Pensão dos Aliados* €€
Rua Elísio de Melo 27, 4000-196. **Road map** C2. 📞 22-200 48 53. 📠 22-200 27 10.
This excellent *pensão* with well-equipped rooms is located in the centre
of town in an impressive building recognized as a city landmark. 📶 📺

AE MC V — 45

OPORTO: *Pensão Paris* €€
Rua da Fábrica 27, 4050-274. **Road map** C2. 📞 22-207 31 40. 📠 22-207 31 49.
A characterful old-world hotel in the Baixa area, whose atmosphere,
location and price more than compensate for the fairly basic standard. 📶 📺

MC V — 38

OPORTO: *Boa-Vista* €€€
Esplanada do Castelo 58, 4150-196. **Road map** C2. 📞 22-532 00 20. 📠 22-617 38 18.
Located on the right bank of the mouth of the Douro, the charming Boa-
Vista hotel has superb views over the ocean. 📶 📺 📧 🅿

AE DC MC V — 39

OPORTO: *Dom Henrique* 🔲 www.hotel-dom-henrique.pt €€€
Rua G. de Azevedo 179, 4049-009. **Road map** C2. 📞 22-340 16 16. 📠 22-340 16 00.
Located right in the heart of the city, this hotel has 17 floors – two
designated non-smoking – and a bar with a panoramic view. 📶 📺 📧

AE DC MC V — 112

OPORTO: *Hotel da Bolsa* €€€
Rua F. Borges 101, 4050-253. **Road map** C2. 📞 22-202 67 68. 📠 22-205 88 88.
The "Stock Exchange" hotel has an attractive façade and well-appointed
rooms, and is convenient for both shopping and tourist areas. 📶 📺 📧 ♿

AE DC MC V — 36

OPORTO: *Internacional* €€€
Rua do Almada 131, 4050-037. **Road map** C2. 📞 22-200 50 32. 📠 22-200 90 63.
A curious but pleasing combination of Baroque and modern styles in
the reception rooms make this an interesting place to stay. 📶 📺 📧

AE DC MC V — 35

Price categories in euros for a standard double room per night, including breakfast: € under 35 €€ 35–60 €€€ 60–100 €€€€ 100–150 €€€€€ over 150	**RESTAURANT** The hotel has one or more restaurants open for lunch and supper, sometimes reserved for residents. **GARDEN** A garden, courtyard or large terrace for the use of hotel guests. **SWIMMING POOL** The hotel has its own indoor or outdoor pool. **CREDIT CARDS** Major credit cards accepted: *AE* American Express, *DC* Diners Club, *MC* MasterCard and *V* Visa.	**CREDIT CARDS**	**RESTAURANT**	**GARDEN**	**SWIMMING POOL**	**NUMBER OF ROOMS**

OPORTO: *São José*   €€€
Rua da Alegria 172, 4000-034. **Road map** C2. 📞 22-208 02 61. FAX 22-332 04 46.
One of several hotels in this busy street, close to the city centre, the São
José has a very pleasant style and ambience. 🛗 TV 🍽 P ♿
AE DC MC V — — — — 43

OPORTO: *Holiday Inn Garden Court*   €€€€
Praça da Batalha 127, 47-102. **Road map** C2. 📞 223-39 23 00. FAX 223-39 23 00.
This modern comfortable hotel is conveniently located for sightseeing.
🛗 TV 🍽
AE DC MC V — — — — 113

OPORTO: *Pestana Porto Carlton* W www.pestana.com   €€€€
Praça da Ribeira 1, 4050-513. **Road map** C2. 📞 22-340 23 00. FAX 22-340 24 00.
Housed in a block of carefully restored riverfront buildings, this tastefully
decorated hotel offers gracious living and fabulous views. 🛗 TV 🍽
AE DC MC V ● — — — 48

OPORTO: *Quinta da Granja*   €€€€
Rua Manuel Francisco Araújo 444, 4425-120 Maia. **Road map** C2. 📞 229 71 01 47.
Five km from the city centre in the suburb of Maia, this quiet hotel is
housed in a grand granite 18th-century manor house. 🛗 TV 🍽 P
AE V — ■ ● — 5

OPORTO: *Infante de Sagres* W www.hotelinfantesagres.pt   €€€€€
P. Dona F. de Lencastre 62, 4050-259. **Road map** C2. 📞 22-339 85 00. FAX 22-339 85 99.
This is a beautifully appointed city-centre hotel with public rooms full of
antiques, a refined atmosphere and bedrooms which offer everything a
discerning traveller expects from such a highly rated hotel. 🛗 TV 🍽 .
AE DC MC V ● ■ — — 77

OPORTO: *Porto Palácio* W www.summithotels.com   €€€€€
Av. da Boavista 1269, 4100-130. **Road map** C2. 📞 22-608 66 00. FAX 22-609 14 67.
This elegant hotel, situated in an affluent suburb of Oporto, is only a
short drive away from the beach and the historical city centre. It offers
modern facilities, including a comprehensive health club. 🛗 TV 🍽 P ♿
AE DC MC V ● — ● — 250

OPORTO: *Tivoli Porto* W www.tivolihotels.com   €€€€€
Rua A. L. Vieira 66, 4100-020. **Road map** C2. 📞 22-607 79 00. FAX 22-607 79 45.
The modern Tivoli Porto, situated in the elegant suburb of Boavista, has
comfortable rooms, most of which have a balcony. 🛗 TV 🍽 P
AE DC MC V — — ● — 58

PESO DA RÉGUA: *Hotel Régua Douro*   €€€
Largo da Estação DA CP, 5050-237. **Road map** D2. 📞 254-32 07 00. FAX 254-32 07 09.
Régua's main hotel is geared more to business travellers than to tourists, and
offers the city's best facilities plus a good view of the river. 🛗 TV 🍽 P
AE DC MC V ● ■ ● — 77

PINHÃO: *Quinta de la Rosa* W www.quintadelarosa.com   €€€
5085, Pinhão. **Road map** D2. 📞 254 73 22 54. FAX 254 72 23 46.
This delightful farmhouse offers rooms as well as cottages to rent. The
farm produces excellent port, wine and olive oil. Tours of the property
can be arranged on request, and a shop sells the produce. 🛗 TV 🍽 P
AE DC MC V — ■ ● — 6

PINHÃO: *Vintage House Hotel* @ vintagehouse@mail.telepac.pt   €€€€€
Lugar da Ponte, 5085-034. **Road map** D2. 📞 254-73 02 30. FAX 254-73 02 38.
This elegant hotel, located on the river Douro, is built on the site of an
old port lodge and is surrounded by majestic vineyards. Rooms each
have a private balcony and the restaurant is excellent. 🛗 TV 🍽 P
AE DC MC V ● ■ ● — 43

SABROSA: *Casa de Visconde de Chanceleiros*   €€€
Covas do Douro 5085-201, Sabrosa. **Road map** D2. 📞 254-73 01 90. FAX 254-73 01 99.
This *Turismo de Habitação* occupies an 18th-century manor house and is
tastefully furnished. The house is set among vineyards. 🛗 TV P
AE DC MC V ● ■ ● — 6

TORRE DE MONCORVO: *Brasília*   €€€
5160-287. **Road map** E2. 📞 279-25 42 56. FAX 279-25 86 10.
This neat and tidy *pensão*, offering all modern facilities, is conveniently
located on the main road through town. 🛗 TV P
MC V — ■ ● — 29

VIDAGO: *Vidago Palace Hotel* €€€€ — AE DC MC V — 83
5425-307. **Road map** D1. (276-99 09 00. FAX 276-90 73 59.
This truly magnificent turn-of-the-century spa hotel, surrounded by forest,
has a grandiose façade and a beautiful inside staircase flanked by marble
columns. The bedrooms are also charming. 🖥 TV 🗏 P

VILA REAL: *Casa Agrícola da Levada* @ levada@netc.pt €€ — AE V — 10
Timpeira, 5000-460. **Road map** D2. (259-32 21 90. FAX 259-34 69 55.
Constructed in 1922 by the Portuguese architect Raúl Lino, this charming
Art Deco house has elegant rooms and a lovely rose garden. 🖥 TV P &

VILA REAL: *Mira Corgo* €€€ — AE DC MC V — 166
Av. 1º de Maio 78, 5000-651. **Road map** D2. (259-32 50 01. FAX 259-32 50 06.
The modern Miracorgo is tastefully decorated and has superb views from
the terrace of the deep ravine and river below. 🖥 TV 🗏 P &

MINHO

BARCELOS: *Quinta de Santa Comba* €€€ — 6
Lugar de Crujães, 4755-536 Várzea. **Road map** C1. (253-83 21 01. FAX 253-83 45 40.
A spectacular 18th-century residence with wooden beams and granite
stonework, this manor house has an elegant rustic charm. 🖥 P

BOM JESUS DO MONTE: *Hotel do Elevador* €€€ — AE DC MC V — 22
Praque do Bom Jesus do Monte, 4710-455, Braga. **Road map** C1. (253-60 34 00.
FAX 253-60 34 09. A luxurious hotel that derives its name from the 19th-century
water-operated elevator that still takes visitors up to the sanctuary. 🖥 TV 🗏 P

BRAGA: *Confort Inn Braga* €€ — AE DC MC V — 72
Rua Damiana Maria da Silva 20, Ferreiros, 4700. **Road map** C1. (253-00 06 00.
FAX 253-67 38 72. Located a short distance from the city centre, and convenient
for a quick stopover, this hotel offers the usual amenities. 🖥 TV 🗏 P &

BRAGA: *Dona Sofia* €€ — AE DC MC V — 34
L. São João do Souto 131, 4700-326. **Road map** C1. (253-26 31 60. FAX 253-61 12 45.
Adjacent to a small square with a lovely fountain, this modern hotel
is in the centre of Braga, close to the city's cathedral. 🖥 TV 🗏 P &

BRAGA: *Largo da Estação* €€€ — AE MC V — 51
Largo da Estação 13, 4700-223. **Road map** C1. (253-21 83 81. FAX 253-27 68 10.
Located just outside the town centre, close to the railway station, this
hotel offers some rooms with jacuzzi bathtubs. 🖥 TV 🗏 P &

BRAGA: *Turismo de Braga* €€€ — AE DC MC V — 132
Praceta João XXI, 4710-245. **Road map** C1. (253-20 60 00. FAX 253-20 60 10.
This large hotel dominates a small square in the centre of town. Modern
facilities and panoramic views are on offer here. 🖥 TV 🗏 P

CELORICO DE BASTO: *Casa do Campo* €€€ — AE MC V — 8
Molares, 4890-414. **Road map** D1. (255-36 12 31. FAX 255-36 12 31
A granite gateway welcomes visitors to this early 18th-century country house.
The garden is said to contain the oldest camellia tree in Portugal. 🖥 P

GUIMARÃES: *Casa de Sezim* €€€ — AE DC MC V — 6
Santo Amaro, Apartdo 410, 4801-913. **Road map** C2. (253-52 30 00. FAX 253-52 31 96.
An attractive 18th-century house built around an enclosed courtyard and
furnished with antiques. Vinho verde wine is produced here. 🖥 P

GUIMARÃES: *Hotel de Guimarães* €€€ — AE DC MC V — 116
Rua E. de Almeida, 4810-911. **Road map** C2. (253-42 48 00. FAX 253-42 48 99.
A modern well-equipped hotel in the city centre that boasts a health
club, gymnasium, sauna and massage facilities. 🖥 TV 🗏 P

GUIMARÃES: *Pousada de Nossa Senhora da Oliveira* €€€€ — AE DC MC V — 15
Rua de Santa Maria, Aptdo. 101, 4801-910. **Road map** C2. (253-51 41 57.
W www.pousadas.pt This *pousada* was once a distinguished aristocratic
mansion in the old district of town. Inside, leather armchairs and antique
paintings help preserve the original character of the house. 🖥 TV 🗏 P

GUIMARÃES: *Pousada de Santa Marinha* W www.pousadas.pt €€€€€ — AE DC MC V — 51
Lugar da Costa, 4810-011. **Road map** C2. (253-51 12 49. FAX 253-51 44 59.
This marvellous building, once the 12th-century Santa Marinha da Costa
monastery, has been carefully adapted to house this beautiful *pousada*.
Original *azulejo* decoration adorns the sumptuous rooms. 🖥 TV 🗏 P

For key to symbols see back flap

<table>
<tr><td colspan="2">Price categories in euros for a standard double room per night, including breakfast:
€ under 35
€€ 35–60
€€€ 60–100
€€€€ 100–150
€€€€€ over 150</td><td>RESTAURANT
The hotel has one or more restaurants open for lunch and supper, sometimes reserved for residents.
GARDEN
A garden, courtyard or large terrace for the use of hotel guests.
SWIMMING POOL
The hotel has its own indoor or outdoor pool.
CREDIT CARDS
Major credit cards accepted: AE American Express, DC Diners Club, MC MasterCard and V Visa.</td></tr>
</table>

	CREDIT CARDS	RESTAURANT	GARDEN	SWIMMING POOL	NUMBER OF ROOMS
PONTE DE LIMA: *Paço de Calheiros* €€€ Calheiros, 4990 Ponte de Lima. **Road map** C1. **(** 258-94 71 64. **FAX** 258-94 72 94. Occupying a scenic position on a hillside outside the town, this baroque manor house offers well-equipped apartments as well as rooms.	AE MC V		■	●	15
PÓVOA DE VARZIM: *Mercure Póvoa de Varzim* €€€ L. do Passeio Alegre 20, 4490-428. **Road map** C2. **(** 252-29 04 00. **FAX** 252-29 04 01. An elegant hotel in the centre of Póvoa de Varzim, right next to the casino and overlooking the beach. Guests can make use of the nearby Estrela golf course.	AE DC MC V	●			86
VALENÇA DO MINHO: *Val Flores* €€ Esplanada, 4930. **Road map** C1. **(** 251-82 41 06. **FAX** 251-82 41 29. Located in the new part of town, outside the town's fortifications, this *residencial* is clean, functional and inexpensive.	AE DC MC V				31
VALENÇA DO MINHO: *Casa do Poço* €€€€ T. da Gaviarra 4, 4930. **Road map** C1. **(** 251-82 52 35. **FAX** 251-82 54 69. Inside the Vauban-style fort, this handsome house has a spectacular interior that combines modern decor with antique furniture.	AE		■		6
VALENÇA DO MINHO: *Pousada de São Teotónio* €€€€€ Baluarte do Socorro, 4930-735. **Road map** C1. **(** 251-80 02 60. **W** www.pousadas.pt The traditionally furnished rooms of this small *pousada* have enchanting views of the valley, across the River Minho to Tuy, in Spain.	AE DC MC V	●	■		18
VIANA DO CASTELO: *Calatrava* €€€ Rua M. Fiúza Júnior 157, 4900-458. **Road map** C1. **(** 258-82 89 11. **FAX** 258-82 86 37. Located conveniently close to the old centre of Viana do Castelo, this *pensão* is neat and tidy and has old-fashioned decor.	AE MC V				15
VIANA DO CASTELO: *Casa dos Costa Barros* €€€ Rua de São Pedro 22–28, 4900-350. **Road map** C1. **(** 258-82 37 05. **FAX** 258-82 43 83. This delightful house, which was constructed in the 16th century and has been owned by the same family since 1765, has an elegant interior and handsome stone carvings over the outside windows.	MC V				10
VIANA DO CASTELO: *Hotel Parque* €€€ Praça da Galiza, 4900-476. **Road map** C1. **(** 258-82 86 05. **FAX** 258-82 86 12. A welcoming hotel located just outside the old town within its own attractive gardens, laid out around the swimming pool.	AE DC MC V		■	●	124
VIANA DO CASTELO: *Pousada Monte de Santa Luzia* €€€€ Monte de S. Luzia, 4901-909. **Road map** C1. **W** www.pousadas.pt **(** 258-80 03 70. **FAX** 258-82 88 92. Surrounded by eucalyptus and pines, this luxurious *pousada* has a spectacular vantage point over the town of Viana.	AE DC MC V	●	■	●	48
VIEIRA DO MINHO: *Pousada de São Bento* **W** www.pousadas.pt €€€€ Caniçada, 4850-047. **Road map** D1. **(** 253-64 91 50. **FAX** 253-64 78 67. Set on the edge of the nature reserve of the Peneda-Gerês National Park, and overlooking the River Cávado, this ivy-clad *pousada* was converted from a hunting lodge. The interior retains a rustic style.	AE DC MC V	●	■	●	29
VILA DO CONDE: *Hotel Sant'Ana* €€€ Monte de Sant'Ana, 4480-160 Azurara. **Road map** C2. **(** 252-64 17 17. **FAX** 252-64 26 93. Within easy reach of Oporto airport, this hotel has a magnificent location on the banks of the pretty River Ave, which can be seen from the many rooms with balconies.	AE DC MC V	●	■	●	73
VILA NOVA DA CERVEIRA: *Pousada de Dom Dinis* €€€€ Terreiro, 4920-296. **Road map** C1. **(** 251-70 81 20. **FAX** 251-70 81 29. **W** www.pousadas.pt Built within the walls of the medieval castle at Vila Nova, this tranquil and charming *pousada* has spacious and pleasant rooms.	AE DC MC V	●	■		28

ALENTEJO

ALVITO: *Pousada do Castelo de Alvito* [w] www.pousadas.pt €€€€€
Apartado 9, 7920-999. **Road map** D6. (284-48 53 43. FAX 284-48 53 83.
This elegant *pousada*, housed in a restored 15th-century castle, has stunning Gothic vaulting in the dining room and Manueline details on the windows. Peacocks roam the tranquil gardens.
AE DC MC V — 20

BEJA: *Hotel Melius* €€€
Av. Fialho de Almeida, 7800-395. **Road map** D6. (284-32 18 22. FAX 284-32 18 25.
At the southern edge of the medieval town of Beja, this modern hotel is pleasant and comfortable and offers exceptional value.
AE DC MC V — 60

BEJA: *Pousada de São Francisco* [w] www.pousadas.pt €€€€€
L. Dom N. Álvares Pereira, 7801-901. **Road map** D6. (284-32 84 41. FAX 284-32 91 43.
Originally a Franciscan convent founded in 1268, this attractive white building is now a beautiful and luxurious *pousada*.
AE DC MC V — 35

CASTELO DE VIDE: *Garcia d'Orta* €€€
Estrada de São Vicente, 7320-202. **Road map** D4. (245-90 11 00. FAX 245-90 12 00.
A discreet and attractive hotel with all the modern amenities and a handsome restaurant offering good Alentejan cooking.
AE DC MC V — 53

CRATO: *Pousada de Flor da Rosa* [w] www.pousadas.pt €€€€€
Flor da Rosa, 7430-999. **Road map** D4. (245-99 72 10. FAX 245-99 72 12.
An architecturally outstanding adaptation of the 14th-century Mosteiro de Santa Maria Flor da Rosa houses this elegant *pousada*.
AE DC MC V — 24

ELVAS: *Elxadai Parque* €€€
N4, Varche, 7350-422. **Road map** D5. (268-62 13 97. FAX 268-62 19 21.
A well-equipped complex situated on top of a hill just west of Elvas, with a water park, sports facilities and an equestrian centre.
AE DC MC V — 41

ELVAS: *Quinta de Santo António* €€€
Aptdo. 206, 7350-903. **Road map** D5. (268-62 84 06. FAX 268-62 50 50.
This splendid *estalagem* has elegant 18th-century gardens. The long buildings offer attractive, rustic accommodation.
AE DC MC V — 30

ELVAS: *Pousada de Santa Luzia* [w] www.pousadas.pt €€€€
Avenida de Badajoz, 7350-097. **Road map** D5. (268-63 74 70. FAX 268-62 21 27.
The pleasantly decorated Santa Luzia was the first *pousada* to open, in 1942, and has a pool and tennis courts.
AE DC MC V — 25

ESTREMOZ: *Pousada da Rainha Santa Isabel* €€€€€
Largo Dom Dinis, 7100-509. **Road map** D5. (268-33 20 75. [w] www.pousadas.pt
This grandiose *pousada* has been beautifully integrated into the 13th-century castle in Estremoz. The 17th- and 18th-century style furniture of the rooms includes four-poster beds and coats of arms.
AE DC MC V — 33

ÉVORA: *IBIS Évora* €€
Quinta da Tapada, Muralha, 7000-968. **Road map** D5. (266-74 46 20. FAX 266-74 46 32.
Located just outside the walls that encircle the old town, this modern hotel is basic, but has all of the usual comforts of an IBIS hotel.
AE DC MC V — 87

ÉVORA: *Évorahotel* €€€
N114, Quinta do Cruzeiro, Apartado 93, 7000-171. **Road map** D5.
(266-74 88 00. FAX 266-74 88 06.
On the outskirts of the old town, this is an impressive modern hotel. The well-equipped rooms all have a balcony.
AE DC MC V — 114

ÉVORA: *Solar Monfalim* €€€
Largo da Misericórdia 1, 7000-646. **Road map** D5. (266-75 00 00. FAX 266-74 23 67.
In the heart of the old town, this Renaissance house offers visitors well-appointed rooms and a delightful atmosphere.
AE MC V — 26

ÉVORA: *Pousada dos Lóios* [w] www.pousadas.pt €€€€€
Largo Conde Vila Flor, 7000-804. **Road map** D5. (266-70 40 51. FAX 266-70 72 48.
Originally a 15th-century monastery, the simple rooms in this elegant *pousada* were converted from the monks' cells.
AE DC MC V — 32

MARVÃO: *Pousada de Santa Maria* [w] www.pousadas.pt €€€€
Rua 24 de Janeiro 7, 7330-122. **Road map** D4. (245-99 32 01. FAX 245-99 34 40.
This charming *pousada* is set in a cosy, whitewashed town house with traditional painted furniture and friendly staff.
AE DC MC V — 29

For key to symbols see back flap

Price categories in euros for a standard double room per night, including breakfast:

€ under 35
€€ 35–60
€€€ 60–100
€€€€ 100–150
€€€€€ over 150

RESTAURANT
The hotel has one or more restaurants open for lunch and supper, sometimes reserved for residents.
GARDEN
A garden, courtyard or large terrace for the use of hotel guests.
SWIMMING POOL
The hotel has its own indoor or outdoor pool.
CREDIT CARDS
Major credit cards accepted: *AE* American Express, *DC* Diners Club, *MC* MasterCard and *V* Visa.

Hotel	Price	Credit Cards	Restaurant	Garden	Swimming Pool	Number of Rooms
MÉRTOLA: *Casa das Janelas Verdes* Rua Dr M. Gomes 38–40, 7750. **Road map** D6. **(** 286-61 21 45. A pleasant hotel in a whitewashed Alentejan house in the centre of town. Water-sport facilities are available on the Guadiana River.	€€			■		3
REDONDO: *Convento de São Paulo* w www.hotelconventospaulo.com Aldeia da Serra, 7170-120. **Road map** D5. **(** 266-98 91 60. **FAX** 266-99 91 04. Set in the remote Serra de Ossa, this former 12th-century monastery is decorated with thousands of *azulejo* panels and frescoes in all the rooms. Baroque and Renaissance fountains cool various patios.	€€€€€	AE DC MC V	●	■	●	35
SANTA CLARA-A-VELHA: *Pousada de Santa Clara* Barragem de Santa Clara, 7665-879. **Road map** C7. **(** 283-88 22 50. w www.pousadas.pt Overlooking the vast Santa Clara-a-Velha lake, this peaceful *pousada* is ideal for water sports, hiking and shooting.	€€€€	AE DC MC V	●	■	●	19
SANTIAGO DO CACÉM: *Pousada Quinta da Ortiga* IP8, Apartado 67, 7540. **Road map** C6. **(** 269-82 28 71. w www.pousadas.pt This delightful farmhouse, just north of town and very close to the sea, is surrounded by 4 ha (10 acres) of land with stables.	€€€€	AE DC MC V	●	■	●	13
SERPA: *Pousada de São Gens* w www.pousadas.pt Alto de São Gens, 7830. **Road map** D6. **(** 284-54 04 20. **FAX** 284-54 43 37. A modern *pousada* located high on a hill overlooking the town of Serpa, the São Gens has spectacular views of the wide Alentejo plains.	€€€€	AE DC MC V		■	●	18
SOUSEL: *Pousada de São Miguel* w www.pousadas.pt Cerro de São Miguel, 7470-999. **Road map** D5. **(** 268-55 00 50. **FAX** 268-55 11 55. This modern *pousada* is ideal for those in search of peace or outdoor pursuits. There are facilities for hunting and fishing.	€€€€	AE DC MC V	●	■	●	32
VILA NOVA DE MILFONTES: *Moinho da Asneira* Quinta do Rio Mira, 7645-014. **Road map** C6. **(** 283-99 61 82. **FAX** 283-99 71 38. Rooms in the main house and hillside cottages of this country estate overlook the estuary of the River Mira and are close to the beach.	€€€	AE DC MC V		■	●	20
VILA VIÇOSA: *Casa de Peixinhos* 7160-999. **Road map** D5. **(** 268-98 04 72. **FAX** 268-88 13 48. This castellated 17th-century building with grand rooms is decorated in shades of ocre and red with Baroque statues in the pebbled patio.	€€€	AE DC MC V		■		6
VILA VIÇOSA: *Pousada de Dom João IV* w www.pousadas.pt 7160-250. **Road map** D5. **(** 268-98 07 42. **FAX** 268-98 07 47. Cloisters and a labyrinthine layout characterize this 17th-century royal convent. The restaurant serves well-prepared regional dishes	€€€€€		●	■	●	36

ALGARVE

Hotel	Price	Credit Cards	Restaurant	Garden	Swimming Pool	Number of Rooms
ALBUFEIRA: *Falésia* w www.falésia.com Pinhal do Concelho, Praia da Falésia, 8200-911. **Road map** C7. **(** 289-50 12 37. **FAX** 289-50 12 70. Located by Falésia beach, this hotel has brightly furnished and airy rooms and an atrium decorated with hanging plants.	€€€€	AE DC MC V	●	■	●	169
ALBUFEIRA: *Alfagar* w www.alfagar.com Semina, Santa Eulália, 8201. **Road map** C7. **(** 289-54 02 20. **FAX** 289-54 19 79. On a cliff top overlooking the ocean, this attractive complex offers apartments with direct access to the Santa Eulália beach.	€€€€	AE DC MC V	●	■	●	215
ALBUFEIRA: *Montechoro* Rua Alexandre O'Neil, 8201-343. **Road map** C7. **(** 289-58 94 23. **FAX** 289-58 99 47. A modern and stylish hotel surrounded by its own gardens, this hotel has extensive sports facilities and a health club.	€€€€€	AE DC MC V	●	■	●	362

ALBUFEIRA: *Sheraton Algarve Pine Cliffs* W www.luxurycollection.com €€€€€ — AE DC MC V — 215
Apartado 644, 8200-909. **Road map** C7. 289-50 01 00. **FAX** 289-50 19 50.
The elegant and expensive Sheraton offers *azulejo* decoration on the bedsteads, sports facilities and a lift down to the beach. ⊟ TV ▤ P ⅖

ALJEZUR: *O Palazim* €€ — 12
N120, Aldeia Velha, 8670. **Road map** C7. 282-99 82 49.
This boarding house is in an attractive building with a terrace offering wonderful views. The lounge is decorated with *azulejo* panels. ⊟ TV P

ALMANCIL: *Quinta dos Rochas* @ quintadosrochas@clix.pt €€€ — 6
Fonte Coberta, Caixa Postal 600-A, 8135-019. **Road map** D7.
289-39 31 65. **FAX** 289-39 91 98.
This small *quinta* (country estate) is conveniently situated close to the beach and offers visitors the comforts of home, a friendly welcome and peaceful, rural surroundings. ⊟ TV P

ALMANCIL: *Quinta do Lago* W www.quintadolagohotel.com €€€€€ — AE DC MC V — 141
8135-024. **Road map** D7. 289-35 03 50. **FAX** 289-39 63 93.
This smart hotel has delightful rooms with views over the ocean, a health club, golf concessions, and many other facilities. ⊟ TV ▤ P ⅖

ALTE: *Alte* €€€ — AE DC MC V — 30
Montinho, 8100-012. **Road map** C7. 289-47 85 23. **FAX** 289-47 86 46.
In a peaceful inland location away from the teeming crowds on the coast, the charming Alte Hotel boasts excellent views, pleasant gardens and a shuttle bus that takes residents to the beach. ⊟ TV ▤ P

ALVOR: *Pestana Carlton Alvor* W www.pestana.com €€€€€ — AE DC MC V — 197
Praia dos Três Irmãos, 8500. **Road map** C7. 282-40 09 00. **FAX** 282-40 09 99.
A large, superbly situated luxury hotel complex with gardens that lead directly down to the beach, a heated sea-water swimming pool and easy access to nearby golf courses. ⊟ TV ▤ P ⅖

CARVOEIRO: *Colina Sol* €€€€ — AE DC MC V — 124
Vale de Centianes, Praia do Carvoeiro, 8400. **Road map** C7.
282-35 08 20. **FAX** 282-35 86 51.
This large Neo-Moorish hotel complex with well-equipped apartments is set in its own attractive gardens, overlooking the sea. ⊟ P

CARVOEIRO: *Tivoli Almansor* W www.tivolihotels.com €€€€€ — AE DC MC V — 293
Praia Vale Covo, 8401-911. **Road map** C7. 282-35 11 00. **FAX** 282-35 13 45.
This hotel has a dramatic location perched above a small cove. The secluded beach can be reached by a stairway at low tide. ⊟ TV ▤ P ⅖

ESTÓI: *Monte do Casal* W www.montedocasal.pt €€€€€ — AE DC MC V — 19
Cerro do Lobo, 8005-436. **Road map** D7. 289-99 15 03. **FAX** 289-99 13 41.
The elegant Monte do Casal has separate apartments set in a delightful Mediterranean garden with eucalyptus and bougainvillea. ⊟ ▤ P

FARO: *Residencial Samé* €€ — AE DC MC V — 36
Rua do Bocage 66, 8000-297. **Road map** D7. 289-82 43 75. **FAX** 289-80 41 66.
This quiet hotel, located east of the cathedral, offers clean modern rooms with bathrooms and television. ⊟ TV

FARO: *Alnacir* €€€ — AE DC MC V — 53
Estr. Senhora da Saúde 24, 8000-500. **Road map** D7. 289-80 36 78. **FAX** 289-80 35 48.
A tidy, modern hotel, Alnacir is located on a quiet street close to the centre of this busy town. Some rooms have a terrace. ⊟ TV ▤ P

FARO: *Hotel Eva* €€€€ — AE DC MC V — 148
Av. da República 1, 8000-678. **Road map** D7. 289-80 33 54. **FAX** 289-80 23 04.
A modern and comfortable hotel with a hairdresser and a barber. Ask for a room that looks out over the marina and the ocean beyond. ⊟ TV ▤ ⅖

LAGOA: *Parque Algarvio* €€ — AE DC MC V — 42
Sítio do Carmo, N125, 8400-405. **Road map** C7. 282-35 22 65. **FAX** 282-35 22 78.
Although located alongside the main Algarvian highway, this is a charming and good-value hotel with rooms around the pool. ⊟ TV P

LAGOS: *Rubi-Mar* €€ — 8
Rua da Barroca 70, 8600-688. **Road map** C7. 282-76 31 65. **FAX** 282-76 77 49.
The English-run Rubi-Mar is a friendly hotel overlooking the sea. Generous continental breakfast is served in the rooms. ⊟ TV

Price categories in euros for a standard double room per night, including breakfast:
€ under 35
€€ 35–60
€€€ 60–100
€€€€ 100–150
€€€€€ over 150

RESTAURANT
The hotel has one or more restaurants open for lunch and supper, sometimes reserved for residents.
GARDEN
A garden, courtyard or large terrace for the use of hotel guests.
SWIMMING POOL
The hotel has its own indoor or outdoor pool.
CREDIT CARDS
Major credit cards accepted: *AE* American Express, *DC* Diners Club, *MC* MasterCard and *V* Visa.

	CREDIT CARDS	RESTAURANT	GARDEN	SWIMMING POOL	NUMBER OF ROOMS
LAGOS: *Marina Rio* W www.marinario.com €€€ Av. dos Descobrimentos, Apartado 388, 8600-645. **Road map** C7. (282-76 98 59. FAX 282-76 99 60. Located in the eastern part of Lagos, this *albergaria* is modern and pleasant and has attractive views over the marina. 🛏 TV 🗐 P 🗘	AE DC MC V			●	36
LAGOS: *Quinta das Achadas* €€€ Estrada da Barragem, Odiáxere, 8600-251. **Road map** C7. (282-79 84 25. FAX 282-79 91 62. Small, characterful bed and breakfast away from the bustle of the beaches. Three individually decorated rooms and three self-catering apartments. 🛏 🗐 P	MC V		■	●	6
LAGOS: *Belavista da Luz* W www.belavistadaluz.com €€€€ Praia da Luz, 8600-184. **Road map** C7. (282-78 86 55. FAX 282-78 86 56. The hotel overlooks the sandy Praia da Luz. Facilities include a health club and games room. Closed four weeks during Nov–Dec and three weeks in Jan–Feb. 🛏 TV 🗐 P 🗘	AE DC MC V	●	■	●	45
LAGOS: *Hotel Tivoli de Lagos* W www.tivolihotels.com €€€€€ Rua C. dos Santos, 8600-678. **Road map** C7. (282-79 00 79. FAX 282-79 03 45. This pleasant complex has five restaurants, a health club and, during the summer, barbecues are prepared on the beach. 🛏 TV 🗐 P 🗘	AE DC MC V	●	■	●	329
LOULÉ: *Loulé Jardim* €€€ Praça Manuel de Arriaga, 8100-665. **Road map** D7. (289-41 30 94. FAX 289-46 31 77. This small hotel on a quiet garden square is an appealing conversion of a classic town house, including a discreet rooftop pool. 🛏 TV 🗐 P	AE DC MC V			●	52
MONCHIQUE: *Abrigo da Montanha* W www.abrigodamontanha.com €€€ Estrada da Fóia, 8550-257. **Road map** C7. (282-91 21 31. FAX 282-91 36 60. This *estalagem*, made from wood and bare stone, makes a peaceful retreat and a good base for walks in the Serra de Monchique. 🛏 🗐 P	AE DC MC V	●	■	●	16
MONTE GORDO: *Vasco da Gama* €€€€ Avenida Infante Dom Henrique, 8900. **Road map** D7. (281-51 09 00. FAX 281-51 09 01. Set on the beach, this hotel has spacious rooms, each with its own balcony. There is also a children's pool and playground. 🛏 TV 🗐 P	AE DC MC V	●	■	●	175
PORCHES: *Vila Vita Parc* W www.vilavitaparc.com €€€€€€ Alporchinhos, 8400-450. **Road map** C7. (282-31 02 00. FAX 282-32 03 33. Set along a beautiful stretch of coastline in its own gardens with tropical flowers, this luxurious hotel has direct access to the beach. 🛏 TV 🗐 P 🗘	AE DC MC V	●	■	●	182
PORTIMÃO: *Bela Vista* W www.hotelbelavista.net €€€€ Avenida Tomas Cabreira, 8500. **Road map** C7. (282-45 04 80. FAX 282-41 53 69. An attractive hotel situated above the popular Praia da Rocha, the Bela Vista is tastefully decorated with relaxing sofas and *azulejo* panels. There is also a terrace overlooking the sea. 🛏 TV P	AE DC MC V		■		14
PORTIMÃO: *Le Méridien Penina* W www.lemeridien.com €€€€€ Caixa Postal 146, 8501-952. **Road map** C7. (282-42 02 00. FAX 282-42 03 00. This hotel is a golfers' paradise. Set in a lush garden, it has practice facilities, tuition and three championship courses. 🛏 TV 🗐 P	AE DC MC V	●	■	●	196
SAGRES: *Navigator* W www.hotel.navigator.com €€€ Rua Infante D. Henrique, 8650-381. **Road map** C7. (282-62 02 40. FAX 282-62 43 60. This hotel on the Sagres promontory has spectacular views. The rooms are individual apartments with all modern conveniences. 🛏 TV 🗐 P	AE DC MC V	●	■	●	56
SAGRES: *Pousada do Infante* W www.pousadas.pt €€€€ Sagres, 8650-385. **Road map** C7. (282-62 02 40. FAX 282-62 42 25. Named after Henry the Navigator *(see p49)*, this *pousada* has a superb location overlooking the ocean on the Sagres promontory. 🛏 TV 🗐 P	AE DC MC V	●	■	●	39

SÃO BRÁS DE ALPORTEL: *Pousada de São Brás* W www.pousadas.pt €€€€
Poço dos Ferreiros, 8150-054. **Road map** D7. 289-84 23 05. FAX 289-84 17 26.
This peaceful *pousada* is housed in a country manor north of Faro, with
spectacular views of the hills and the sea.

AE DC MC V — 33

SILVES: *Quinta do Rio* €€
Sítio São Estevão, Aptdo. 217. **Road map** C7. & FAX 282-44 55 28.
Only a few kms from the centre of Silves (see pp332–3), this farmhouse is
still home to the Italian family that grow fruit trees here. Visitors have access
to the big garden and delicious dinners are available on request.

AE DC MC V — 6

TAVIRA: *Convento de Santo António* €€€€
Rua de Santo António 56, 8800-378. **Road map** D7.
281-32 15 73. FAX 281-32 56 32
This charming whitewashed former convent offers elegant rooms around
the shady patio, or pretty rooms converted from the monks' cells.

AE — 7

TAVIRA: *Quinta do Caracol* €€€€
São Pedro, 8800-000. **Road map** D7. 281-32 24 75. FAX 281-32 31 75.
This 17th-century whitewashed country house is surrounded by the spacious
gardens of the *quinta* (estate) that include a tennis court. This is a quiet
and practical base from which to explore the coast and hilly interior of the
eastern Algarve.

AE DC MC V * — 7

VILA DO BISPO: *Os Gambozinos* €€€
Praia do Martinhal, 8650. **Road map** C7. 282-62 01 60. FAX 282-62 01 69.
This attractive hotel, located on the isolated Sagres peninsula, stretches
along the sandy Martinhal beach, popular with windsurfers.

— 17

VILAMOURA: *Atlantis* W www.graopara.pt €€€€€
Apartado 210, 8125 Quarteira. **Road map** C7. 289-38 16 00. FAX 289-38 99 62.
A stylish and modern hotel with views over the sea and extensive
facilities including tennis courts and a horse-riding club.

AE DC MC V — 305

VILAMOURA: *Tivoli Marinotel* W www.tivolihotels.com €€€€€
Aptdo. 65, 8125-911 Quarteira. **Road map** C7. 289-30 33 03. FAX 289-30 33 45.
This large and luxurious hotel boasts an exclusive "Presidential Suite".
The hotel overlooks an impressive marina and the ocean. There is a wide
choice of sporting activities available here, including tennis, golf and
horse riding.

AE DC MC V — 382

VILA REAL DE SANTO ANTÓNIO: *Guadiana* €€€
Avenida da República 94, 8900. **Road map** D7. 281-51 14 82. FAX 281-51 14 78.
A prettily refurbished 19th-century town house, this hotel is right in the
centre of town and has good views over the River Guadiana.

AE DC MC V — 36

MADEIRA

CANIÇO: *Roca Mar* W www.hotelrocamar.com €€€
Caminho Cais da Oliveira, 9125-028. 291-93 43 34. FAX 291-93 49 03.
All rooms at the clifftop Roca Mar have large balconies from which to
enjoy the sea views. The hotel offers lively evening entertainments, as
well as access to sports facilities and a free minibus to Funchal.

AE DC MC V — 100

CANIÇO: *Quinta Splendida* W www.hotelquintasplendida.com €€€€
Estrada da Ponta Oliveira II, 9125. 291-93 04 00. FAX 291-93 04 01.
The rooms of the Quinta Splendida, a villa complex set in the gardens
of a 16th-century mansion, are tastefully furnished.

AE DC MC V — 141

FUNCHAL: *Monte Carlo* €€
Calçada da Saúde 10, 9001-801. 291-22 61 31. FAX 291-22 61 34.
Housed in a graciously ageing building with fine views from the rooms at
the front, this hotel is a steep walk uphill from the centre.

AE DC MC V — 53

FUNCHAL: *Residencial Santa Clara* €€
Calçada do Pico 16b, 9000-206. 291-74 21 94. FAX 291-74 32 80.
A ten-minute uphill walk from the centre of town, this small, quiet hotel
has grand old interiors and splendid views of the city and mountains.

— 14

FUNCHAL: *Residencial Vila Teresinha* W www.pensaoresvilateresinha.com €€
Rua das Cruzes 21, 9000-025. 291-74 17 23. FAX 291-74 45 15.
Housed in a traditional Funchal townhouse, this hotel is in a quiet
residential area and has pleasant rooms and a lovely terrace.

AE DC MC V — 12

For key to symbols see back flap

Price categories in euros for a standard double room per night, including breakfast:

€ under 35
€€ 35–60
€€€ 60–100
€€€€ 100–150
€€€€€ over 150

RESTAURANT
The hotel has one or more restaurants open for lunch and supper, sometimes reserved for residents.

GARDEN
A garden, courtyard or large terrace for the use of hotel guests.

SWIMMING POOL
The hotel has its own indoor or outdoor pool.

CREDIT CARDS
Major credit cards accepted: *AE* American Express, *DC* Diners Club, *MC* MasterCard and *V* Visa.

	CREDIT CARDS	RESTAURANT	GARDEN	SWIMMING POOL	NUMBER OF ROOMS
FUNCHAL: *Quinta da Penha de França* €€€ Rua Carvalho Araújo 1, 9000-022. **(** *291-20 46 50*. **FAX** *291-22 92 61*. This fine traditional mansion sits in a walled garden. There is a modern 33 room extension nearby, next to swimming pools and the sea. 🖼 📺 ▤ 🅿	AE DC MC V	●	■	●	109
FUNCHAL: *Pestana Miramar* Ⓦ www.pestana.com €€€€ Estrada Monumental 182-184, 9000-098. **(** *291-70 61 00*. **FAX** *291-76 39 88*. Built around the old Miramar Hotel, and adjacent to the Pestana village, this hotel has excellent facilities and service. 🖼 📺 ▤ 🅿 ♿	AE DC MC V	●	■	●	152
FUNCHAL: *Quinta Perestrelo* Ⓦ www.charminghotels.com €€€€ Rua do Dr Pita 3, 9000-089. **(** *291-70 67 00*. **FAX** *291-70 67 06*. This mid-19th-century mansion offers luxurious accommodation and is filled with antiques and set in manicured gardens. 🖼 📺 ▤	AE DC MC V	●	■		37
FUNCHAL: *Pestana Carlton Park* Ⓦ www.pestana.com €€€€€ Rua Imperatriz Dona Amélia, 9004-513. **(** *291-20 91 00*. **FAX** *291-23 20 76*. Madeira's liveliest hotel, with a casino, a cinema, cabaret and disco, was designed by Oscar Niemeyer (architect of the Brazilian capital, Brasília). The comfortable rooms have fine views. 🖼 📺 ▤ 🅿	AE DC MC V	●	■	●	375
FUNCHAL: *Reid's Palace* Ⓦ www.reidspalace.com €€€€€ Estrada Monumental 139, 9000-098. **(** *291-71 71 71*. **FAX** *291-71 71 77*. Founded in 1891, this elegant hotel is the haunt of wealthy and famous patrons. Furnished like a stately home, with chandeliers in the dining room, it enjoys prime clifftop views and palm-fringed pools. 🖼 📺 ▤ 🅿	AE DC MC V	●	■	●	164
FUNCHAL: *Savoy Resort* Ⓦ www.savoyresort.com €€€€€ Avenida do Infante, 9004-542. **(** *291-21 30 00*. **FAX** *291-22 31 03*. Unobtrusive service is the hallmark of this luxury hotel with spacious rooms and leisure facilities such as boules and shuffleboard. 🖼 📺 ▤ 🅿	AE DC MC V	●	■	●	337
PICO DO ARIEIRO: *Pousada do Pico do Arieiro* Ⓦ www.dorisol.pt €€€ 9230 Santana. **(** *291-23 01 10*. **FAX** *291-22 86 11*. Located on top of Madeira's second highest mountain, this *pousada* has stunning dawn views for those willing to rise early. 🖼 📺 🅿	AE DC MC V	●	■		25
PORTO MONIZ: *Residencial Orca* €€ Sítio das Poças, 9270-095. **(** *291-85 00 00*. **FAX** *291-85 00 19*. Atlantic waves batter the shore in front of this isolated hotel. Natural rock pools below the hotel are sometimes suitable for bathing. 🖼 📺 🅿	AE DC MC V	●	■	●	12
PORTO SANTO: *Hotel Torre Praia* Ⓦ www.torrepraia.pt €€€€€ Rua Goulart Medeiros, 9400-164. **(** *291-98 04 50*. **FAX** *291-98 24 87*. Mid-sized hotel near all amenities, including the main attraction – the beach, to which it has direct access. 🖼 📺 ▤ 🅿	AE DC MC V	●	■	●	66
RIBEIRA BRAVA: *Brava Mar* €€ Rua Comandante Camacho de Freitas, 9350-209. **(** *291-95 22 20*. **FAX** *291-95 11 22*. An ideal base for exploring the western part of the island, the Brava Mar is a modern hotel with mostly balconied rooms and friendly staff. 🖼 📺	AE DC MC V	●		●	70
SERRA DE ÁGUA: *Pousada dos Vinháticos* Ⓦ www.dorisol.pt €€€ Ribeira Brava, 9350-306. **(** *291-95 23 44*. **FAX** *291-95 25 40*. Book well in advance for this charming *pousada* geared to walkers and set in woodland just below the Encumeada Pass. 🖼 📺 🅿	AE DC MC V	●	■		21
THE AZORES					
CORVO: *Casa de Hóspedes* € Estrada para o Caldeirão, Vila do Corvo, 9980. **(** *292-59 61 30*. Apart from private homes, this is the only accommodation available on the tiny island of Corvo. The rooms are clean but very basic.				■	5

FAIAL: *Quinta das Buganvílias* €€€ — AE MC V — ■ — 8
Castelo Branco, 9900-330 Horta. **(** 292-94 32 55. **FAX** 292-94 37 43.
This family-run *quinta*, near the airport has a rose garden, fruit orchard and commercial greenhouses filled with flowers. ⌂ TV ▤

FAIAL: *Estalagem Santa Cruz* €€€€ — AE DC MC V — ● ■ — 25
Rua Vasco da Gama, 9900-017 Horta, . **(** 292-29 30 21. **FAX** 292-29 39 06.
Overlooking the sea, this 16th-century fort that once protected Horta has been turned into a cosy hotel adorned with antiques. ⌂ TV ▤

FLORES: *Ocidental* Ⓦ www.hotelocidnetal.com €€€ — AE V — ● ■ ● — 36
Sítio do Boqueirão, 9970 Santa Cruz. **(** 292-59 01 00. **FAX** 292-59 01 01.
The main hotel on Flores is a functional block on the outskirts of Santa Cruz. Rooms are plain but most have balconies facing the sea. ⌂ TV P

GRACIOSA: *Santa Cruz* €€ — ■ — 19
L. Barão de Gaudalupe 9, 9880-344 S. Cruz da Graciosa. **(** 295-71 23 45. **FAX** 295-71 28 28.
A friendly *pensão* on a quiet square near the town centre. Accommodation on Graciosa is very limited so book well in advance. ⌂ TV

PICO: *L'Escale de l'Atlantic* Ⓦ www.ciberacores.com/escale €€ — ■ — 5
Morro de Baixo, 9930-212, Piedade. **(** 292-66 62 60. **FAX** 292-66 62 60.
On the eastern tip of the island with views of São Jorge, this is a small, informal hotel with pleasantly decorated rooms. ● Oct–Apr. ⌂ P ♿

PICO: *Pico* €€€ — AE MC V — ● ■ ● — 68
Rua dos Biscoitos, 9950-334 Madalena. **(** 292-62 84 00. **FAX** 292-62 84 07.
A modern, well-equipped establishment offering some rooms with balconies and views of the spectacular blackened peak of the island. ⌂ TV ▤ P

SANTA MARIA: *Praia de Lobos* €€€ — AE DC MC V — 34
Rua M, 9580 Vila do Porto. **(** 296-88 22 77. **FAX** 296-88 24 82.
A smart, efficiently run hotel in the centre of Vila do Porto, the Praia de Lobos offers modern facilities and a friendly welcome. ⌂ TV ▤

SÃO JORGE: *Hotel São Jorge* Ⓦ www.acores.com €€€ — AE DC MC V — ■ ● — 58
Rua Machado Pires, 9800-526 Velas. **(** 295-43 01 00. **FAX** 295-41 27 36.
On the outskirts of Velas, this is the only modern hotel on the island. The attractive rooms have balconies facing the sea. ⌂ TV ▤ P

SÃO MIGUEL: *Casa Nossa Senhora do Carmo* €€€ — ■ — 6
Rua do Pópulo Decima 220, 9500 Livramento. **(** 296-64 20 48 **FAX** 296-64 20 38.
A lovingly restored and secluded *quinta*, just to the east of Ponta Delgada. The rooms are full of antiques and family treasures. ● Dec. ⌂ P

SÃO MIGUEL: *Solar de Lalém* Ⓦ www.acores.com €€€ — ■ ● — 10
Estrada de São Pedro, 9625-332 Maia. **(** 296-44 20 04. **FAX** 296-44 21 64.
An elegant 19th-century manor house on the north coast that has been decorated in a simple style by its easy-going German owners. ⌂ P

SÃO MIGUEL: *Bahia Palace* €€€€ — AE DC MC V — ● ■ ● — 101
Água d'Alto, 9680-365 Vila Franco do Campo. **(** 296-53 91 30. **FAX** 296-53 91 38.
A large, isolated complex on the south coast with sports and conference facilities, the Bahia is often used by business travellers. ⌂ TV ▤ P

SÃO MIGUEL: *São Pedro* €€€€ — AE DC MC V — ■ — 26
L. Almirante Dunn, 9500 Ponta Delgada. **(** 296-30 17 40. **FAX** 296-30 17 44.
Built in 1812 for the American merchant Thomas Hickling, the São Pedro is now a gracious harbourside hotel furnished with antiques. ⌂ TV P

TERCEIRA: *Beira Mar* €€€ — AE MC V — ● — 23
L. Miguel Corte-Real, 9700-182 Angra do Heroísmo. **(** 295-21 51 88. **FAX** 295-62 82 48.
Overlooking the harbour, this hotel has small, basic rooms but is excellently located for exploring the old heart of the city. ⌂ TV

TERCEIRA: *Quinta do Martelo* Ⓦ www.acores.com €€€ — AE MC V — ● ■ ● — 10
Canada do Martelo 24, 9700-576 A. do Heroísmo. **(** 295-64 28 42. **FAX** 295-64 28 41.
An idyllic rural hotel with rooms decorated with island crafts and a restaurant serving Azorean dishes. Price includes car hire. ⌂ TV ▤ P

TERCEIRA: *Quinta da Nasce-Água* Ⓦ www.matosarte.com €€€€ — AE DC MC V — ● ■ ● — 14
Vinha Brava, 9700-236 Angra do Heroísmo. **(** 295-62 85 01. **FAX** 295-62 85 02.
Overlooking Angra do Heroísmo, this is a luxurious modern *quinta* in private grounds with large gardens, tennis and mini-golf. ⌂ TV ▤ P

WHERE TO EAT

ORTUGAL IS the country to feast on all kinds of fish and seafood, from clams, lobster and sardines to tuna, swordfish and *bacalhau* (salted cod), the national favourite. All along the coast are restaurants dedicated to cooking freshly caught fish. The Portuguese are great meat eaters too and justifiably proud of such dishes as roast kid and sucking pig. While meat may be more common in inland regions, fresh fish is available throughout Portugal.

Sign for roast suckling pig at Mealhada *(see p412)*

Most restaurants are reasonably priced, and offer generous portions. Lisbon has plenty of cheap cafés and restaurants, as well as international ones, as does the Algarve. This introduction gives tips on types of eating places, menus, drinks and ordering to help you enjoy eating out in Portugal.

Drinks waiter at the Palácio de Seteais, near Sintra *(see p409)*

TYPES OF RESTAURANTS

EATING VENUES come in all shapes and sizes and at all price levels. Among the most reasonable is the local *tasca* or tavern, often just a room with half-a-dozen tables presided over by a husband-and-wife team. These are often frequented by locals and professionals at lunch time, which is a good lead to follow. The *casa de pasto* offers a budget three-course meal in a large dining room, while a *restaurante* is more formal and offers a wider choice of dishes. At a *marisqueira* (found all along the coast), the emphasis is on fresh fish and seafood. The *churrasqueira*, a very popular concept imported from Brazil, specializes in spit-roasted foods, while a *cervejaria* (beerhouse) is the ideal place to go for a beer and a snack. As a rule, restaurants in the better hotels are generally of good quality. *Pousadas (see pp378–9)*, found throughout the country, offer a network of high-quality restaurants featuring regional specialities.

Sign for Maria Rita's *(see p415)*

EATING HOURS

LUNCH IS USUALLY served between 1 and 3 pm when many restaurants, especially in cities, get very crowded. Dinner is served from 7–10pm in most places, but can be later in restaurants and *cervejarias* in major cities and resort areas such as Lisbon, Oporto and the Algarve. Another choice for a very late dinner would be to combine a meal with a show at a *fado* house *(see pp66–7)*, open from about 9:30pm to 3 or 4am.

RESERVATIONS

IT IS A GOOD IDEA to book ahead for expensive restaurants, and for those in popular locations in high season. Disabled people should certainly check in advance on facilities and access. Special facilities are generally lacking but most places will try to be helpful.

THE MENU

SOME RESTAURANTS, especially in tourist areas, offer an *ementa turística*, a cheap, daily-changing three-course menu served with coffee and a drink (glass of wine, beer, water or soft drink). This provides a full meal at a good price with no hidden costs. Lunch, *almoço*, is often a two-course fixed menu, consisting of a fish or meat main course with potatoes or rice and either a starter or a

The impressive interior of the Cozinha Velha *(see p407)* at Queluz

Sharing the local veal speciality at Gabriela's, in Sendim *(see p413)*

pudding. To sample a local speciality, ask for the *prato do dia* – dish of the day.

Dinner *(jantar)* may be two or more courses, perhaps followed by ice cream, fruit, a simple dessert or cheese. Casserole-style dishes, such as fish or meat stews or *carne de porco à alentejana* (pork with clams), are brought to the table in a pot for people to share, as are large fish such as sea bass, which are sold by weight. One serving can easily be shared by two people and it is perfectly acceptable to ask for the *meia dose* or half-portion. Peculiar to Portugal is the plate of assorted appetizers – olives, cheese and sardine pâté – brought with bread at the start of a meal. These are not included in the menu price, and may add substantially to the bill.

VEGETARIANS

VEGETARIANS WILL not eat as well as fish lovers, although local cheeses and breads can be excellent. In Lisbon or along the Algarve, vegetarians will benefit from ethnic restaurants. Chefs will usually be happy to provide something meatless, though this will probably mean simply an omelette or a salad.

WINE AND DRINKS

IT WOULD BE a shame to visit Portugal without sampling its two most famous fortified wines: port *(see pp252–3)* and Madeira *(see p349)*. Wherever you are, it is safe to order a bottle or jug of house wine to wash down your meal.

Otherwise, ask for the wine list, and choose one of Portugal's many native wines *(see pp28–9)*. Sagres and Super Bock are good beers and the bottled water is recommended. This comes either *com gás* (sparkling) or *sem gás* (still).

Relaxing at a seafront bar at Póvoa de Varzim in the Minho

CAFÉS AND CAKE SHOPS

CAFÉS ARE FUNDAMENTAL to Portuguese daily life and vary from modern white rooms to splendidly decorated, tiled and mirrored places where you can sit and talk or read the paper for hours. Many have tables outside. They make perfect meeting points and usually offer a range of snacks and sandwiches. At any time of the day a café is the obvious choice for a coffee break with a roll, croissant or cake. Do not miss the *pastelarias* (cake shops); the sweet-toothed Portuguese adore cakes, and the selections are excellent *(see pp147, 231 & 289)*.

PAYING THE BILL

IT IS COMMON practice to add a 5–10 per cent tip to bills. Although service is not included, it provides a low wage which the tip is meant to supplement. Note that not all restaurants accept credit cards.

CHILDREN

IN PORTUGAL, children are viewed as a blessing rather than a nuisance, so it is an ideal country for families to eat out together. Children's portions or half-portions at reduced prices are advertised or will be provided on request.

SMOKING

SMOKING IS WIDESPREAD and permitted in all public places in Portugal, unless there is a sign saying *proibido fumar*. No-smoking areas in restaurants are fairly rare.

COFFEE DRINKING IN PORTUGAL

Coffee is widely drunk in Portugal and served in many forms. The most popular is a small cup of strong black coffee like an espresso. In Lisbon and the South this is called *uma bica*; elsewhere ask for *um café*. A strong one is called *uma italiana*; for a weaker version, try *um carioca de café*. *Uma meia de leite* is half coffee, half milk. Strong coffee with a dash of milk is known as *um garoto escuro* (*um garoto claro* is quite milky). If you like your coffee with plenty of milk, ask for *um galão* (a gallon). This is served in a tall glass, and again you can order *um galão claro* (very milky) or *escuro* (strong).

Uma bica   **Um galão**

Choosing a Restaurant

THE RESTAURANTS in this guide have been selected for
their good value, exceptional food or interesting location. This chart highlights some of the factors which may
influence your choice. This chart lists the restaurants by
region; the thumb tabs on the side of the page are colour-
coded to correspond with the regional areas in the guide.

	CREDIT CARDS	LATE OPENING	OUTDOOR TABLES	GOOD WINE LIST

LISBON

AJUDA: *O Nobre* €€€€ | AE MC V | ■ | | ■
Rua das Mercês 71a–b. **Map 2 D3.** (*21-363 38 27*
Worth searching out on a day trip to Belém, O Nobre serves crab soup, game
stew, partridge, fish with olives and roast pork with grapes. ● *Sun; Sat lunch.*

ALCÂNTARA: *Alcântara Café* €€€€€ | AE DC MC V | ■ | | ■
Rua Maria Luísa Holstein 15. **Map 3 A4.** (*21-362 12 26.*
Long the only contemporary restaurant in Lisbon, Alcântara Café is now a
"classic". The 1980s interior is still impressive. ● *lunch.* ▤ &

ALFAMA: *Hua-Ta-Li* €€
Rua dos Bacalhoeiros 109–115. **Map 7 C4.** (*21-887 91 70.*
This is a large Chinese restaurant close to the docks that serves all the
regular rice and noodle favourites. Fast and efficient service. ▤

ALFAMA: *Lautasco* €€ | AE DC MC V | ■ | ● |
Beco do Azinhal 7a (off Rua de São Pedro). **Map 8 E4.** (*21-886 01 73.*
Rustically decorated with wooden panelling and wagon-wheel chandeliers,
Lautasco specializes in typical Portuguese cuisine. ● *Sun; 20 Dec–15 Jan.*

ALFAMA: *Mestre André* €€€ | AE | ■ | ● |
Calçadinha de Santo Estevão 6. **Map 8 E3.** (*21-887 14 87.*
Lively Portuguese restaurant offering delicious pork and fish dishes as well as
excellent *churrasco* (spit-roasted meat) *(see p120).* ● *Sun.*

ALFAMA: *Viagem de Sabores* €€€ | DC MC V | | |
Rua de São João da Praça 103. **Map 8 D4.** (*21-887 01 89.*
Located in a converted fish shop close to the cathedral, this restaurant serves an
eclectic mix of eastern and western cuisines. Great starters. ● *Lunch, Sun.* ▤

AVENIDA: *Ribadouro* €€€ | AE DC MC V | ■ | |
Rua do Salitre 2–12. **Map 4 F1.** (*21-354 94 11.*
On the corner of the Avenida da Liberdade in a long, pointed building. Like
most, this *cervejaria* specializes in seafood. ▤

BAIRRO ALTO: *Bota Alta* €€€ | AE DC MC V | | |
Travessa da Queimada 35-37. **Map 7 A3.** (*21-342 79 59.*
The "High Boot" is an attractive restaurant with original paintings on the
walls. The menu consists of traditional Portuguese dishes. ● *Sat lunch; Sun.*

BAIRRO ALTO: *El Último Tango* €€€ | MC V | ■ | ● |
Rua Diário de Notícias 62. **Map 7 A4.** (*21-342 03 41.*
In this Argentinian restaurant the most popular choice is meat grilled over an
open fire. It also has cocktails. ● *Sun; lunch; 2 weeks in Jun; 2 weeks in Oct.* ▤

BAIRRO ALTO: *Massima Culpa* €€€ | AE DC MC V | ■ | |
Rua da Atalaia 35-7. **Map 4 F2.** (*21-342 01 21.*
This restaurant has a simple, uncomplicated decor with a very Italian atmos-
phere, and offers numerous antipasti and pasta dishes. ● *lunch; Mon.* ▤

BAIRRO ALTO: *Casanostra* €€€€ | AE MC V | | |
Travessa do Poço da Cidade 60. **Map 7 A3.** (*21-342 59 31.*
Within the green, white and black interior of this Italian restaurant you
can choose from a six-page menu full of delicacies. ● *Mon, Sat lunch.* ▤

BAIRRO ALTO: *Pap'Açorda* €€€€ | AE DC MC V | | | ■
Rua da Atalaia 57. **Map 4 F2.** (*21-346 48 11.*
Both Lisboetas and tourists come here for the *açorda de mariscos* (bread stew
and seafood). The menu is traditional Portuguese with some novel touches.
● *Mon lunch; Sun; 2 weeks in Jul; 2 weeks in Oct.* ▤

	CREDIT CARDS	LATE OPENING	OUTDOOR TABLES	GOOD WINE LIST

Price categories are for a three-course meal for one with half a bottle of wine, including cover charge, service and VAT:

€ under 10 euros
€€ 10–15 euros
€€€ 15–20 euros
€€€€ 20–30 euros
€€€€€ over 30 euros

LATE OPENING
The kitchen stays open after 10pm, and you can usually have a meal up until at least 11pm.
OUTDOOR TABLES
Tables for eating outdoors, in a garden or on a balcony, often with a pleasant view.
GOOD WINE LIST
The restaurant will have a good selection of quality wines.
CREDIT CARDS
This indicates which of the major credit cards are accepted: AE American Express, DC Diners Club, MC MasterCard and V Visa.

BAIRRO ALTO: *Tavares* €€€€€
Rua da Misericórdia 35-37. **Map** 7 A4. **(** 21-342 11 12.
Lisbon's oldest restaurant, Tavares, dates from 1784. Its reputation is maintained with dishes such as breast of partridge on toast with *foie gras* and fillets of sea bass *au gratin* with prawn sauce. ● *Sat; Sun lunch.* ▤ &

AE DC MC V — — — ▪

BAIXA: *Paris* €€€
Rua dos Sapateiros 126. **Map** 7 B4. **(** 21-346 97 97.
Open for nearly half a century, Paris offers a delicious mixture of Portuguese and Galician cuisine. Try the swordfish steak or the Alentejan pork. ▤ &

AE DC MC V

BELÉM: *Já Sei* €€€€
Avda Brasilia 202. **Map** 1 A5. **(** 21-301 59 69.
This has a beautiful location, right on the river, so it is pleasant in the summer; the seafood-based menu is good all-year-round. ● *Sun dinner; Mon.* ▤ ♫

AE DE MC V — — ● ▪

BELÉM: *São Jerónimo* €€€€
Rua dos Jerónimos 12. **Map** 1 C4. **(** 21-364 87 97.
São Jerónimo is an elegant, spacious restaurant with 1930s decor. The excellent mixed menu of Portuguese and French cuisine includes skate in peach sauce and duck with nuts in wine sauce. ● *Sat lunch; Sun.* ▤

AE DC MC V — — — ▪

BELÉM: *Vela Latina* €€€€
Doca do Bom Sucesso. **Map** 1 B5. **(** 21-301 71 18.
On the waterfront, this restaurant has a bar and terrace overlooking the Torre de Belém. The speciality is *cataplana rica do mar* (seafood). ● *Sun.* ▤ &

AE DC MC V ▪ ● ▪

CACILHAS: *Atira-te ao Rio* €€€
Cais do Ginjal 69-70. **(** 21-275 13 80.
View Lisbon from the other bank of the Tagus and enjoy the restaurant's Brazilian specialities, including *feijoada à Brasileira* (bean stew). ● *Mon.*

▪ ●

CAMPO DE OURIQUE: *Tasquinha D'Adelaide* €€€€
Rua do Patrocínio 72-4. **Map** 3 C2. **(** 21-396 22 39.
Popular with locals, this small restaurant serves inspired interpretations of classic Portuguese regional dishes. Booking essential. ● *Lunch, Sun.* ▤

AE DC MC V ▪

CAMPO PEQUENO: *Chimarrão* €€
Campo Pequeno 79. **Map** 5 C1. **(** 21-793 97 60.
One of a small restaurant chain specialising in Brazilian food. Try *rodízio* (unlimited amount of grilled meat) with salad, rice and black beans. ▤ ♫

AE DC MC V ▪ — — ▪

CAMPO PEQUENO: *A Gôndola* €€€
Avenida de Berna 64. **Map** 5 B2. **(** 21-797 04 26.
A Gôndola is a charming restaurant offering a wide choice of dishes including Italian as well as Portuguese specialities. In the summer enjoy your meal in the pleasant surrounding gardens. ● *Sun.* ▤

AE MC V — — ● ▪

CAMPO PEQUENO: *António Clara – Clube dos Empresários* €€€€
Avenida da República 38. **Map** 5 C1. **(** 21-799 42 80.
This wonderful old mansion offers a French-influenced menu in dining areas that were once individual rooms in the house. ● *Sun.* ▤

AE DC MC V — — — ▪

CASTELO: *Restô do Chapitô* €€€
Costa do Castelo 7. **Map** 7 C3. **(** 21-886 73 34.
The extensive menu includes a wide range of international dishes. A cheerful restaurant with a bar and fine views over the harbour. ● *Mon.* ♫ *irregularly*

▪ ●

CASTELO: *Casa do Leão* €€€€
Castelo de São Jorge. **Map** 8 D3. **(** 21-887 59 62.
Beneath arched brick ceilings, inside part of Castelo de São Jorge *(see pp78–9)*, this restaurant offers superb service and excellent traditional Portuguese cuisine. Sit outside to enjoy the magnificent views. ▤ ♫ *Wed–Fri.*

AE DC MC V — — ● ▪

For key to symbols see back flap

Price categories are for a three-course meal for one with half a bottle of wine, including cover charge, service and VAT: € under 10 euros €€ 10–15 euros €€€ 15–20 euros €€€€ 20–30 euros €€€€€ over 30 euros	**LATE OPENING** The kitchen stays open after 10pm, and you can usually have a meal up until at least 11pm. **OUTDOOR TABLES** Tables for eating outdoors, in a garden or on a balcony, often with a pleasant view. **GOOD WINE LIST** The restaurant will have a good selection of quality wines. **CREDIT CARDS** This indicates which of the major credit cards are accepted: *AE* American Express, *DC* Diners Club, *MC* MasterCard and *V* Visa.		

	CREDIT CARDS	LATE OPENING	OUTDOOR TABLES	GOOD WINE LIST
CHIADO: *Tágide* €€€€€ Largo da Academia Nacional de Belas Artes 18–20. **Map 7 B5.** (21-342 07 20. An elegant restaurant with 18th-century tiles, a 17th-century fountain and a superb view over the Tagus. Luxurious dishes include marinated salmon, baby octopus in red wine sauce and partridge in port sauce. ● *Sat lunch; Sun.* ▤	AE DC MC V			▨
ESTRELA: *Conventual* €€€€ Praça das Flores 44-45. **Map 4 E2.** (21-390 91 96. Decorated with religious antiques, this restaurant has an interesting menu that includes fried baby eels and ox tongue in egg sauce. ● *Sat lunch; Sun; Mon.* ▤	AE DC MC V			▨
GRAÇA: *Via Graça* €€€€ Rua Damasceno Monteiro 9b. **Map 8 D1.** (21-887 08 30. Via Graça offers some fine views of the castle and the Baixa, and well-presented Portuguese cuisine. ● *Sat lunch; Sun.* ▤	AE DC MC V	▨		▨
LAPA: *Café d'Arte* €€ Rua das Janelas Verdes, Museu de Arte Antiga. **Map 4 D4.** (21-396 09 30. This establishment provides an excellent opportunity to combine lunch with a museum trip in a fantastic riverside setting. ● *Mon; Tue & evenings (closes with museum).* ▤ ♿	AE MC V		●	
LAPA: *Picanha* €€€ Rua das Janelas Verdes 96. **Map 4 D4.** (21-397 54 01. Picanha sells one dish: *picanha*, which is rump steak grilled on an open fire, served with potatoes, rice, salad and beans. ● *Sat; Sun lunch.* ▤		▨		▨
LAPA: *A Confraria* €€€€ Pensão York House, Rua das Janelas Verdes 32. **Map 4 D4.** (21-396 24 35. This delightful hotel restaurant has a varied menu. Sit inside and admire the tiled walls, or outside below a palm in the flower-laden courtyard. ▤	AE DC MC V		●	▨
LAPA: *Sua Excelência* €€€€ Rua do Conde 34. **Map 4 D3.** (21-390 36 14. The owner here can recite the menu in five languages. Classical Portuguese dishes served in a relaxed atmosphere. ● *Sat & Sun lunch; Wed; Sep.* ▤ ♿	AE DC MC V		●	▨
LAPA: *Ristorante Hotel Cipriani* €€€€€ Lapa Palace, Rua do Pau da Bandeira 4. **Map 3 C3.** (21-394 94 34. This restaurant offers modern Italian and Mediterranean food in an elegant setting. There is a non-smoking section. ▤ ♿	AE DC MC V			▨
MARQUÊS POMBAL: *Pabe* €€€€ Rua Duque de Palmela 27a. **Map 5 C5.** (21-353 74 84. Pabe looks like a Tudor house and serves traditional Portuguese food. A medieval atmosphere is accentuated by wooden-beamed ceilings and copper tables. ▤ ♿	AE DC MC V	▨		▨
MARQUÊS POMBAL: *Restaurante 33A* €€€€ Rua Alexandre Herculano 33a. **Map 5 C5.** (21-354 60 79. Offering traditional Portuguese cuisine, this restaurant also has a small lounge with a country ambience and decor to match. ● *Sat lunch; Sun.* ▤ ♪ ♿	AE DC MC V		●	▨
PRAÇA DO CHILE: *Cervejaria Portugalia* €€€ Avenida Almirante Reis 117. **Map 6 E5.** (21-314 00 02. This atmospheric beer hall is the original of a small chain, the restaurant is popular with families and serves excellent shellfish and steaks. ♿	AE DC MC V	▨		
PRAÇA ESPANHA: *Adega da Tia Matilde* €€€ Rua da Beneficiência 77. **Map 5 A1.** (21-797 21 72. Known for its hearty Portuguese cuisine and good regional food. Specialities include *arroz frango* (rice with chicken). ● *Dinner Sat, Sun.*	AE MC V			

Praça Espanha: *O Polícia* €€€ AE MC V
Rua Marquês Sá da Bandeira 112a. **Map** 5 B3. 21-796 35 05.
A pleasant restaurant with an attractive bar, so named because
the owner's grandfather was a policeman. The menu changes
daily. ● *Sat eve; Sun.*

Rato: *Os Tibetanos* €€ AE MC V
Rua do Salitre 117. **Map** 4 F1. 21-314 20 38.
This vegetarian restaurant, in a Tibetan Buddhist centre, has much character
and offers a tasty and inexpensive Tibetan menu. No smoking. ● *Sat; Sun.*

Rato: *Casa da Comida* €€€€ AE DC MC V
Travessa das Amoreiras 1. **Map** 5 B5. 21-388 53 76.
A refined Lisbon restaurant with a charming patio, and an exquisite menu
offering caviar, frogs' legs, goat, duck and pheasant. ● *Sat lunch; Sun.*

Restauradores: *Casa do Alentejo* €€ MC V
Rua das Portas de Santo Antão 58. **Map** 7 A2. 21-346 92 31.
Set in a fine 19th-century house, this restaurant specializes entirely in Alentejan
food such as *açorda alentejana* (coriander and bread soup). ● *1–19 Aug.*

Restauradores: *Lagosta Real* €€€€ AE DC MC V
Rua das Portas de Santo Antão 37. **Map** 7 A2. 21-342 39 95.
Fish, and particularly shellfish, is the order of the day here. Shellfish casserole,
lobster stew and a grilled seafood platter are house specialities.

Restauradores: *Solar dos Presuntos* €€€€ AE DC MC V
Rua das Portas de Santo Antão 150. **Map** 7 A2. 21-342 42 53.
An enticing window display of fish and shellfish draws diners inside. Caricatures
of famous footballers adorn the walls. ● *Sun; 2 weeks in Aug; 1 week at Christmas.*

Restauradores: *Gambrinus* €€€€€ AE V
Rua das Portas de Santo Antão 23. **Map** 7 A2. 21-342 14 66.
Renowned throughout Portugal, Gambrinus is an exceptional and expensive
restaurant. The excellent wine list includes an array of vintage ports. ● *1 May.*

Saldanha: *António* €€ V
Rua Tomás Ribeiro 63. **Map** 5 C3. 21-353 87 80.
This restaurant is a good stop for lunch. The cooking is straightforward,
and includes steak and fries and roast chicken. ● *Sun.*

Saldanha: *Espiral* €€ AE MC V
Praça da Ilha do Faial 14a. **Map** 6 D3. 21-357 35 85.
This vegetarian restaurant, set in a pleasant square, has a plain interior but a large
menu, with fresh juice drinks and organic wine. ● *1 Jan; 1 May.*

Saldanha: *Café Creme* €€€ AE DC MC V
Avenida Conde de Valbom 52a. **Map** 5 B2. 21-796 43 60.
An attractive, open and airy restaurant, Café Creme offers a wide choice of
pastas, salads, cod, beef and grilled dishes. ● *Sat lunch; Sun.*

Santa Apolónia: *Casanova* €€€ AE MC V
Avenida Infante Dom Henrique. **Map** 8 D5. 21-887 75 32.
Housed in a converted warehouse, this is said to be Lisbon's best pizzeria. Italian
standards including pastas and salads are also serverd. ● *Mon, Sat lunch.*

Santa Apolónia: *Bica do Sapato* €€€€€ AE DC MC V
Avenida Infante Dom Henrique, 1100. **Map** 8 D5. 21-881 03 20.
Lisbon's trendiest restaurant serves some of the best modern fish dishes.
Housed in a converted warehouse, the interior is 1970s retro.

Santos: *Kais* €€€€ AE DC MC V
Cais da Viscondessa, Rua da Cintura do Porto de Lisboa. **Map** 4 D4. 21-393 29 30.
Modern Portuguese and Mediterranean cooking served in a converted
engine shed. The interior would not look out of place in a Batman film.
● *Mon.*

Xabregas: *D'Avis* €€€€ AE DC MC V
Rua do Grilo 96-98. 21-868 13 54.
Specialities at this restaurant, located east of the city centre, include cod with
coriander and *migas* (bread dish with spare ribs). ● *Sun.*

Price categories are for a three-course meal for one with half a bottle of wine, including cover charge, service and VAT:

€ under 10 euros
€€ 10–15 euros
€€€ 15–20 euros
€€€€ 20–30 euros
€€€€€ over 30 euros

LATE OPENING
The kitchen stays open after 10pm, and you can usually have a meal up until at least 11pm.

OUTDOOR TABLES
Tables for eating outdoors, in a garden or on a balcony, often with a pleasant view.

GOOD WINE LIST
The restaurant will have a good selection of quality wines.

CREDIT CARDS
This indicates which of the major credit cards are accepted: *AE* American Express, *DC* Diners Club, *MC* MasterCard and *V* Visa.

	CREDIT CARDS	LATE OPENING	OUTDOOR TABLES	GOOD WINE LIST
THE LISBON COAST				
CASCAIS: *Dom Manolo* €€ Avenida Marginal 11. 21-483 11 26. A good-value mixed menu; the house speciality is *frango no churrasco* (spit-roast chicken). *Pastéis de bacalhau* (cod croquettes) are also good. ● Jan. ▤			●	
CASCAIS: *Estrela da India* €€ Rua Freitas Reis 15b. 21-484 65 40. Some distance from the waterfront, this unpretentious Indian restaurant has a good choice of vegetarian dishes and a takeaway service. ● Mon. ▤	AE MC V			
CASCAIS: *Os Navegantes* €€€ Travassa dos Navegantes 13. 21-486 86 31. This Portuguese restaurant is very popular with locals and is famous for its fresh fish and spit-roasted meats. ● Sun.	AE V	▪		▪
CASCAIS: *Buchanan's Café, Bar and Restaurant* €€€€ Travassa da Alfarrobeira 2. 21-484 75 90. Located on the top floor of a building with stunning views over the new marina. High-quality modern European cuisine is served, with a choice of vegetarian dishes and fine wines. The café/bar has a fireplace. ● Mon (Oct–Mar). ▤	AE MC V	▪	●	▪
CASCAIS: *Casa Velha* €€€€ Avenida Valbom 1. 21-483 25 86. With a recomended regional menu and charming rustic decor, Casa Velha also boasts a table always reserved for the president. ● Wed. ▤ 🔊	AE MC V	▪		▪
CASCAIS: *Eduardo's* €€€€ Largo das Grutas 3. 21-483 19 01. Tucked away in a quiet corner, Eduardo's serves a mix of Belgian cuisine and Portuguese dishes, many of which are flambéed at the table. ● Wed.	AE MC V		●	▪
CASCAIS: *Esplanada Santa Marta* €€€€ Travassa do Enviado de Inglaterra 1d, e, f. 21-352 11 94. Known for its wide range of fish and shellfish dishes, as well as for a good choice of traditional Portuguese fare. During the summer the food is also served outside on a small terrace overlooking the sea. ▤ 🔊	AE MC V	▪	●	▪
CASCAIS: *O Pescador* €€€€€ Rua das Flores 10b. 21-483 20 54. A well-known seaside restaurant, decorated with old boats, nets and pictures of famous people who have eaten here. Specializes in seafood. ● Sun. ▤	AE DC MC V	▪	●	▪
ERICEIRA: *O Barco* €€€ Rua Capitão João Lopes 14. 261-86 27 59. O Barco has sea views. The fish specialities include *feijoada de marisco* (seafood and bean stew) and seafood curry. ● Thu; 2 weeks in Jul & Dec. ▤	AE DC MC V			
ESTORIL: *Pinto's* €€€ Arcadas do Parque 18b. 21-468 72 47. Close to the Palácio Hotel, Pinto's is a mix of bar, cafeteria and restaurant. It serves pizzas and pastas, as well as a large selection of shellfish. ▤	AE DC MC V	▪	●	
ESTORIL: *Four Seasons* €€€€€ Hotel Palácio Estoril, Rua do Parque. 21-464 80 00. Exposed beams and leather seats furnish this luxurious restaurant. Try the flambéed prawns with Pernod, cream and hollandaise sauce. ▤ 🎵 🔊	AE DC MC V			▪
GUINCHO: *Estalagem Muchaxo* €€€€ Praia do Guincho. 21-487 02 21. Overlooking Cabo da Roca, Muchaxo offers a good seafood menu. A popular dish is lobster in a tomato, cream and port sauce. ▤ 🎵 Sat & Sun lunch. 🔊	AE DC MC V	▪	●	▪

GUINCHO: *Porto de Santa Maria* €€€€€
Estrada do Guincho. [21-487 94 50.
This is one of the best seafood restaurants in the area. Choose your meal from
the fish tanks and marble table where the best fish is displayed. ● *Mon.* 🍽 🔲

AE	
MC	
DC	
V	

MONTE ESTORIL: *O Sinaleiro* €€€
Avenida de Sabóia 595. [21-468 54 39.
O Sinaleiro serves excellent food and is popular with locals. Try *escalopes à
Zíngara* (in Madeira wine sauce with cream). ● *Wed; 2 weeks in Apr & Oct.* 🔲🍽

AE	
MC	●
DC	
V	

MONTE ESTORIL: *O Festival* €€€€
Avenida de Sabóia 515d. [21-468 85 63.
This delightful restaurant serves an essentially French menu. Try the duck à
l'orange or the sole filled with salmon mousseline. ● *Mon; Tue lunch.* 🍽

AE	▪ ● ▪
MC	
DC	
V	

PAÇO D'ARCOS: *La Cocagne* €€€€€
Avenida Marginal (Curva dos Pinheiros). [21-441 42 31.
One of the best French restaurants in Portugal, La Cocagne has refined decor,
impeccable service, exquisite dishes and magnificent views of the ocean. 🍽

AE	● ▪
DC	
MC	
V	

PALMELA: *Pousada de Palmela* €€€€
Pousada de Palmela, Castelo de Palmela. [21-235 12 26.
The converted refectory of the 15th-century monastery offers such delicacies as
oyster soup or salt cod filled with bacon and coated in corn bread. 🎵 *Fri & Sat.*

AE	● ▪
DC	
MC	
V	

PORTINHO DA ARRÁBIDA: *Beira-Mar* €€€€
Portinho da Arrábida. [21-218 05 44.
Enjoy specials such as *arroz de tamboril* (monkfish rice) and *arroz de marisco*
(seafood rice) in this stunning seaside setting. ● *Wed (Oct–Mar); 15 Dec–15 Jan.*

AE	●
DC	
MC	
V	

QUELUZ: *Cozinha Velha* €€€€
Largo Palácio Nacional de Queluz. [21-435 61 58.
Set in the old kitchens of the Queluz Royal Palace, this spacious restaurant is
famous for its typical Portuguese fare, such as pork with clams. 🍽 🎵

AE	● ▪
DC	
MC	
V	

SESIMBRA: *Ribamar* €€€€
Avenida dos Náufragos 29. [21-223 48 53.
Right next to the sea and offering fantastic views, Ribamar serves some
unusual specialities; try fish with seaweed, or cream of sea-urchin soup. 🍽 🔲

AE	●
MC	
V	

SETÚBAL: *Copa d'Ouro* €€€
Rua João Soveral 17. [265-52 37 55.
A superb fish menu here features *caldeirada à Setubalense* (seafood stew)
and *cataplana de tamboril* (monkfish steamed *a cataplana*). ● *Tue; Sep.* 🍽

AE	▪ ●
MC	
V	

SETÚBAL: *Pousada de São Filipe* €€€€
Pousada de São Filipe, Castelo de São Filipe. [265-55 00 70.
This restaurant is part of a *pousada* that overlooks Setúbal and the Sado estuary.
Its regional dishes include pumpkin cream soup and fried red mullet. 🍽

AE	● ▪
DC	
MC	
V	

SINTRA: *Tulhas* €€€
Rua Gil Vicente 4–6. [21-923 23 78.
This rustic restaurant, decorated with blue and yellow Sintra *azulejos*, serves
superb traditional dishes such as veal steaks in Madeira sauce. ● *Wed.* 🍽

AE	
DC	
MC	
V	

SINTRA: *Lawrence's* €€€€
Rua Consiglieri Pedroso 39–40, Sintra. [21-910 55 00.
Set in the Lawrence's Hotel, this restaurant has a wide-ranging international
and Portuguese menu that changes daily. 🍽 🔲

| AE | ● ▪ |
| V | |

SINTRA: *Panorâmico* €€€€
Hotel Tivoli Sintra, Praça da República. [21-923 35 05.
Overlooking the lush, verdant Sintra valley, this restaurant offers a different
speciality as a main dish each evening, as well as a regular menu. 🍽 🔲

AE	
DC	
MC	
V	

SINTRA: *Restaurante Palácio de Seteais* €€€€€
Avenida Barbosa du Bocage 8, Seteais. [21-923 32 00.
Set in an 18th-century palace, which is now a hotel, this restaurant has a daily-
changing menu of international and traditional Portuguese cuisine. 🎵 🔲

AE	▪
DC	
MC	
V	

VILA FRESCA DE AZEITÃO: *O Manel* €€€
Largo Dr Teixeira 6a. [21-219 03 36.
A family-run restaurant with a good-value menu. Specialities here are cod in
cream sauce and *feijoada de gambas* (seafood and bean stew). ● *Sun; Oct.* 🍽

AE	
MC	
V	

For key to symbols see back flap

Price categories are for a three-course meal for one with half a bottle of wine, including cover charge, service and VAT:
€ under 10 euros
€€ 10–15 euros
€€€ 15–20 euros
€€€€ 20–30 euros
€€€€€ over 30 euros

LATE OPENING
The kitchen stays open after 10pm, and you can usually have a meal up until at least 11pm.
OUTDOOR TABLES
Tables for eating outdoors, in a garden or on a balcony, often with a pleasant view.
GOOD WINE LIST
The restaurant will have a good selection of quality wines.
CREDIT CARDS
This indicates which of the major credit cards are accepted: *AE* American Express, *DC* Diners Club, *MC* MasterCard and *V* Visa.

	CREDIT CARDS	LATE OPENING	OUTDOOR TABLES	GOOD WINE LIST

ESTREMADURA AND RIBATEJO

ABRANTES: *O Pelicano* €€
Rua Nossa Senhora da Conceição 1. **Road map** C4. 🄲 241-36 23 17.
Situated on the busy main square, O Pelicano serves good-value Portuguese food such as *bacalhau à Lagareiro* (breaded cod steak). ▤

| AE DC MC V | | | |

ALCOBAÇA: *Trindade* €€
Praça Dom Afonso Henriques 22. **Road map** C4. 🄲 262-58 23 97.
Located in a beautiful square next to the north wing of the monastery. Specials include *frango na púcara* (chicken stew). ● *2 weeks in May & Oct.* ▤

| AE MC V | | ● | |

ALMEIRIM: *Toucinho* €€
Rua de Timor 20. **Road map** C4. 🄲 243-59 22 37.
A family-run restaurant with a reputation for fine country cooking. Try the home-made bread and the real *sopa de pedra (see p146).* ● *Thu; Aug.* ▤

| | | | |

BARRAGEM DO CASTELO DE BODE: *São Pedro* €€€€
Pousada de São Pedro. **Road map** C4. 🄲 249-38 11 59.
In a *pousada* dating from the 1950s, this restaurant has a regional menu that includes grilled trout and *chanfana* (goat meat stewed in red wine). ▤

| AE DC MC V | | | ▦ |

BATALHA: *Mestre Afonso Domingues* €€€€
Largo Mestre Afonso Domingues. **Road map** C4. 🄲 244-76 52 60.
This restaurant, found in the *pousada* named after the architect of the nearby monastery, serves such regional dishes as fried pork with turnip tops. ▤

| AE DC MC V | | ● | ▦ |

CALDAS DA RAINHA: *A Lareira* €€€
Rua da Lareira, Alto do Nobre. **Road map** B4. 🄲 262-82 34 32.
Located in a pine wood, A Lareira offers typical traditional Portuguese food such as *ensopado de enguias* (eel stew), *perdiz à Lareira* (partridge with chestnuts, fruits and vegetables) and home-made desserts. ▤ 🄳

| DC MC V | ▦ | | ▦ |

CALDAS DA RAINHA: *Supatra* €€€
Rua General Amilcar Mota, 2500. **Road map** B4. 🄲 262-84 29 20.
Once Portugal's only Thai restaurant, *Supatra* still attracts visitors from far and wide. Portuguese dishes are also served. ● *Mon; 2 weeks in May & Dec.* 🄳

| AE MC V | ▦ | | ▦ |

FÁTIMA: *Dom Gonçalo* €€€€
Rua Jacinta Marto 100. **Road map** C4. 🄲 249-53 93 30.
Set in a charming hotel surrounded by its own grounds, not far from the sanctuary. Try the fillet of fish with prawn rice or the braised duck. ▤ 🄳

| AE DC MC V | | | ▦ |

FÁTIMA: *Tia Alice* €€€€
Rua do Adro. **Road map** C4. 🄲 249-53 17 37.
One of the best restaurants in the area. The service is excellent and house specialities are Trás-os-Montes-style rice and duck rice. ● *Mon; Sun eve; Jul.* ▤

| AE MC V | | | ▦ |

LEIRIA: *Tromba Rija* €€€€
Rua Professores Portelas 22, Marrazes. **Road map** C4. 🄲 244-85 50 72.
Well-known throughout Portugal, this restaurant serves excellent starters, including *ovos verdes* (a speciality egg dish), and a variety of *empadas* (pies). Main courses include partridge. ● *Mon; Sun; 2 weeks in Jul.*

| AE MC V | | | ▦ |

NAZARÉ: *Beira-Mar* €€€€
Avenida da República 40. **Road map** C4. 🄲 262-56 13 58.
Beira-Mar has a delightful seafront setting. House specialities include *parrilhada de mariscos* (grilled seafood with garlic, butter and lemon). ● *Dec–Feb.*

| AE DC MC V | | ● | |

ÓBIDOS: *O Alcaide* €€€
Rua Direita. **Road map** B4. 🄲 262-95 92 20.
Try *coelho à Alcaide* (rabbit stew) or *bacalhau à Alcaide* (cod with potatoes and olive oil) at this rustic restaurant with panoramic views of the town. ● *Mon; Nov.*

| AE DC MC V | | ● | |

ÓBIDOS: *Castelo* €€€€
Paço Real. **Road map** B4. 262-95 91 05.
Located in the *pousada*, which is part of the fairy-tale medieval castle,
Castelo serves such regional delights as asparagus with smoked ham,
cabrito (braised kid) and *trouxas de ovos* (egg and sugar rolls).

ÓBIDOS: *Estalagem do Convento* €€€€
Rua D. José D'Ornelas, 2510. **Road map** B4. 262-95 92 17.
Located within the hotel of the same name *(see p387)*, the restaurant serves
both international and Portuguese dishes. Only open for dinner. Sun.

PENICHE: *Estelas* €€€
Rua Arquitecto Paulino Montês 21. **Road map** B4. 262–78 24 35.
Estelas has a large seafood menu and a selection of meat dishes. Try octopus
salad, seafood rice or a monkfish kebab. Wed; 2 weeks in Oct.

PENICHE: *Marisqueira Cortiçais* €€€€
Porto d'Areia Sul. **Road map** B4. 262-78 72 62.
Popular with locals, this rustic restaurant overlooks the beach and specializes
in seafood and shellfish dishes. Wed (Sep–Jul); 2 weeks in Sep.

SANTARÉM: *Central* €€€
Rua Guilherme de Azevedo 32. **Road map** C4. 243-32 23 03.
This Art Deco restaurant has been open since 1933 and is popular with
locals. Try the delicious *bife à Central* (steak in a mustard sauce). Sun.

SANTARÉM: *Mal Cozinhado* €€€
Campo da Feira. **Road map** C4. 243-32 35 84.
Do not be put off by the name, Mal Cozinhado (badly cooked). Dishes include
bacalhau com magusto (baked cod with green broth). Sun.

TOMAR: *A Bela Vista* €€
Fonte do Choupo 3–6. **Road map** C4. 249-31 28 70.
A Bela Vista offers beautiful views of the river and castle, and excellent regional
specialities such as roast kid and *caldeirada* (fish stew). Mon eve; Tue; Nov.

TOMAR: *Calça Perra* €€€€
Rua Pedro Dias 59. **Road map** C4. 249-32 16 16.
This charming restaurant is in the gardens of a 16th-century house in the historic
part of town and specializes in Brazilian dishes. Wed.

TOMAR: *Chico Elias* €€€
Algarvias. **Road map** C4. 249 31 10 67.
A rustic restaurant on the old road to Torres Novas 2 km south of Tomar,
famous for its traditional, regional food. Tue, 1-15 Sept.

TORRES VEDRAS: *O Pátio do Faustino* €€
Largo do Choupal. **Road map** B5. 261-32 43 46.
This rustic restaurant specializes in grilled fish. Decorated with antiques
and Roman-style amphorae, it has a pleasant atmosphere. Sun eve.

VILA FRANCA DE XIRA: *O Redondel* €€€€
Arcadas da Praça de Touros. **Road map** C5. 263-27 29 73.
This restaurant is housed in the elegant arcades of the town's bullring.
Traditional Ribatejo dishes such as *açorda de sável* (bread and shad fish stew)
are served. There is an excellent wine list. Mon.

THE BEIRAS

ALMEIDA: *Senhora das Neves* €€€€
Pousada da Nossa Senhora das Neves. **Road map** E2. 271-57 42 83.
This restaurant, in the *pousada* inside Almeida's star-shaped fort,
serves dishes such as grilled cod in olive oil and braised kid.

AVEIRO: *Cozinha do Rei* €€€
Rua Doutor Manuel Neves 66. **Road map** C3. 234-42 68 02.
The Cozinha do Rei, one of the best restaurants in Aveiro, is often hired out
for functions, so check availability in advance. Dishes include seafood salad,
roast sea bass, and *ovos moles de Aveiro* (egg and sugar sweets).

AVEIRO: *O Mercantel* €€€
Cais dos Mercantéis 13. **Road map** C3. 234-42 80 57.
Offering romantic views over the canal, this restaurant serves speciality sea-
food and shellfish dishes. A good meat selection is also available. Mon.

The payment/credit card column for entries shows:
AE / DC / MC / V for most listings.

Price categories are for a three-course meal for one with half a bottle of wine, including cover charge, service and VAT: € under 10 euros €€ 10–15 euros €€€ 15–20 euros €€€€ 20–30 euros €€€€€ over 30 euros	**LATE OPENING** The kitchen stays open after 10pm, and you can usually have a meal up until at least 11pm. **OUTDOOR TABLES** Tables for eating outdoors, in a garden or on a balcony, often with a pleasant view. **GOOD WINE LIST** The restaurant will have a good selection of quality wines. **CREDIT CARDS** This indicates which of the major credit cards are accepted: *AE* American Express, *DC* Diners Club, *MC* MasterCard and *V* Visa.	**CREDIT CARDS**	**LATE OPENING**	**OUTDOOR TABLES**	**GOOD WINE LIST**

	CREDIT CARDS	LATE OPENING	OUTDOOR TABLES	GOOD WINE LIST
BELMONTE: *Pousada do Convento de Belmonte* €€€€ Serra da Esperança, Belmonte. **Road map** D3. 275-91 03 00. Ambitious local and other regional Portuguese food is served in this historic *pousada*, plus newer dishes such as duck breast with jasmine sauce. 目 ら	AE DC MC V			
BUÇACO: *Palace Hotel do Buçaco* €€€€ Palace Hotel do Buçaco. **Road map** C3. 231-93 79 70. The dining room here is a Manueline fantasy, and the intricately carved balcony is unique *(see p210)*. Dishes include cod *au gratin* with cream and roast sucking pig from Bairrada. Buçaco's acclaimed wines are bottled in the basement. 目	AE DC MC V		●	▪
CARAMULO: *São Jerónimo* €€€€ Pousada de São Jerónimo, N230. **Road map** C3. 232-86 12 91. Found in a small *pousada* south of Caramulo, one of Portugal's leading health spas, São Jerónimo offers hearty fare such as kid stew and grilled octopus. 目	AE DC MC V			▪
CASTELO BRANCO: *Praça Velha* €€€€ Largo Luís de Camões 17. **Road map** D4. 272-32 86 40. Situated in the old part of town, in an old granary transformed by architects and interior designers, Praça Velha offers ambitious cuisine that combines traditional methods and modern creativity in fish and meat dishes. ● Mon.	AE DC MC V			▪
COIMBRA: *Democrática* €€ Travessa Rua Nova 5. **Road map** C3. 239-82 37 84. Hard to find, but worth the effort. The back room has long benches and is a favourite hangout for university students. The house speciality is *arroz de polvo* (octopus rice). Food is served as long as there are customers. ● Sun. 目 ら	AE DC MC V	▪		
COIMBRA: *O Trovador* €€ Largo da Sé Velha 15–17. **Road map** C3. 239-82 54 75. This rustic restaurant, set in the historic part of the town, offers excellent regional dishes such as *chanfana* (kid stew in wine sauce). ● Sun. 目	MC V			
COIMBRA: *L'Amphitryon* €€€€ Avenida Emídio Navarro 21. **Road map** C3. 239-85 30 20. Set in the fine circular dining room of the Astória hotel amid 1920s decor, L'Amphitryon serves traditional French and Portuguese specialities. 目	AE DC MC V			▪
COIMBRA: *Arcadas da Capela* €€€€€ Santa Clara. **Road map** C3. 239-80 23 80. Located in the Quintas das Lágrimas hotel, this restaurant offers excellent, creative cooking including carpaccio of *bacalhao* with basil oil. 目 ら	AE DC MC V			▪
CONDEIXA-A-NOVA: *Santa Cristina* €€€€ Rua Francisco de Lemos. **Road map** C3. 239-94 12 86. A modern restaurant, aptly set in a modern *pousada* close to the famous ruins of Conimbriga. Regional specialities include roast kid with turnip tops, octopus rice and roast chicken with pepper sauce. 目	AE DC MC V			▪
GUARDA: *Telheiro* €€€€ Exit 16, Guarda. **Road map** D3. 271-21 13 56. Well-known for its version of *bacalhao* and seafood rice, this restaurant lies close to the Spanish border. Game is a speciality in season. 目	AE MC V			▪
LUSO: *O Cesteiro* €€ Rua Monsenhor Raúl Mira 76. **Road map** C3. 231-93 93 60. In an attractive setting with pleasant decor, this rustic restaurant serves regional specialities such as *chanfana* (kid stewed in wine), sucking pig and cod. 目 ら	AE DC MC V			
MANTEIGAS: *São Lourenço* €€€€ N232, Penhas Douradas. **Road map** D3. 275-98 24 50. Set in a *pousada* high in the Serra da Estrela, north of Manteigas, it specializes in local dishes such as red bean and cabbage soup and trout in onion marinade. 目	AE DC MC V			▪

MEALHADA: *Pedro dos Leitões* €€€ AE MC V
N1, Sernadelo. **Road map** C3. **(** 231-20 99 50.
A handy stop for travellers. The speciality here is delicious *leitão* (roast sucking pig) roasted in a wood-burning oven and served with chips. ● *Mon; Aug.* ▤ &

MONSANTO: *Pousada de Monsanto* €€€€ AE DC MC V
Rua da Igreja. **Road map** E3. **(** 277-31 44 71.
In a well-preserved village, this traditional restaurant serves regional dishes such as broad bean and coriander soup, wild boar stew and roast kid. ▤

MONTEMOR-O-VELHO: *Ramalhão* €€€€ MC V
Rua Tenente Valadim 24. **Road map** C3. **(** 239-68 94 35.
Dine in a 16th-century manor house surrounded by antiques, and try such local specialities as *ensopado de enguias* (eel stew). ● *Sun eve, Mon; Oct.* &

SORTELHA: *Dom Sancho I* €€€€
Largo do Corro. **Road map** D3. **(** 271-38 82 67.
This rustic restaurant with large open fireplaces serves suitably hearty fare, including game in season. No fresh fish to speak of.

TRANCOSO: *O Museu* €€
Largo de Santa Maria. **Road map** D2. **(** 271-81 18 10.
This rustic restaurant is in the old part of town within the castle walls. Regional smoked meats cooked with cabbage and potatoes are a speciality.

VISEU: *Casablanca* €€ AE DC MC V
Avenida Emídio Navarro 70–72. **Road map** D3. **(** 232-42 22 39.
Situated near the historic city centre, Casablanca is decorated with pretty tiles, and serves a variety of fresh fish and seafood as its specialities. ● *Mon.* ▤

VISEU: *Churrascaria Santa Eulália* €€ AE DC MC V
N2, Repeses. **Road map** D3. **(** 232-43 62 83.
South of Viseu, Santa Eulália is a spacious restaurant with a seafood-based menu. Try the fish kebab or the *feijoada de marisco* (beans and seafood). ● *Thu.* ▤ &

VISEU: *O Cortiço* €€ AE DC MC V
Rua Augusto Hilário 47. **Road map** D3. **(** 232-42 38 53.
This restaurant on two sides of a street in the centre of town serves tasty, rustic food in huge portions. The menu features humorous names for some dishes. Soft easy-drinking house *dão* (wine). ▤

DOURO AND TRÁS-OS-MONTES

ALIJÓ: *Barão de Forrester* €€€€ AE DC MC V
Rua José Ruffino. **Road map** D2. **(** 259-95 92 15.
Located in a *pousada* deep in port wine country, this restaurant has a menu that includes grilled octopus and pears with Muscatel wine. ▤

AMARANTE: *Lusitânia* €€€
Rua 31 de Janeiro. **Road map** D2. **(** 255-42 67 20.
Among the many roast dishes served here is *cabrito assado no forno* (spit-roast kid). Also enjoy splendid views over the River Tâmega. ▤

AMARANTE: *O Almirante* €€€€ AE DC MC V
Rua António Carneiro. **Road map** D2. **(** 255-43 25 66.
O Almirante combines excellent food with a friendly atmosphere. Among the house specialities are lamprey rice and beef with mushrooms. ▤

AMARANTE: *São Gonçalo* €€€€ AE DC MC V
Pousada de São Gonçalo, Ansiães. **Road map** D2. **(** 255-46 11 13.
Northeast of Amarante, São Gonçalo boasts a spectacular view down a long, deep valley, especially at sunset. On the menu are dishes such as trout stuffed with ham and pork with chestnuts, as well as some enticing desserts. ▤ &

BRAGANÇA: *Solar Bragançano* €€€€ AE DC MC V
Praça da Sé 34. **Road map** E1. **(** 273-32 38 75.
Solar Bragançano is housed in an old mansion overlooking the main square. Try the game dishes, such as *perdiz com uvas* (partridge with grapes) or *faisão com castanhas* (pheasant with chestnuts). ● *Mon in winter.* ▤

CHAVES: *Leonel* €€ AE DC MC V
Campo da Roda. **Road map** D1. **(** 276-32 31 88.
Popular with the locals for its superb food. Try *bacalhau au gratin* (baked cod) or *açorda de marisco* (bread and shellfish stew). ● *Mon; 2 weeks in Jul & Nov.* ▤

For key to symbols see back flap

	CREDIT CARDS	LATE OPENING	OUTDOOR TABLES	GOOD WINE LIST

Price categories are for a three-course meal for one with half a bottle of wine, including cover charge, service and VAT:

€ under 10 euros
€€ 10–15 euros
€€€ 15–20 euros
€€€€ 20–30 euros
€€€€€ over 30 euros

LATE OPENING
The kitchen stays open after 10pm, and you can usually have a meal up until at least 11pm.

OUTDOOR TABLES
Tables for eating outdoors, in a garden or on a balcony, often with a pleasant view.

GOOD WINE LIST
The restaurant will have a good selection of quality wines.

CREDIT CARDS
This indicates which of the major credit cards are accepted: *AE* American Express, *DC* Diners Club, *MC* MasterCard and *V* Visa.

	Cards	Late	Outdoor	Wine
CHAVES: *Carvalho* €€€ Alameda do Tabolado, Bloco 4. **Road map** D1. 276-32 17 27. Enjoy fine views from this pretty two-roomed restaurant with a charming garden. Try the local beef or *arroz de fumeiro* (rice with smoked meats). ● Thu. ▤	AE DC MC V	■	■	
CINFÃES: *Varanda de Cinfães* €€ Rua General Humberto Delgado 20–22. **Road map** D2. 255-56 12 36. This cosy informal restaurant serves traditional Portuguese cuisine, and is popular with locals. The house specialities are roast lamb and baked cod. ▤				
ESPINHO: *Terraço Atlântico* €€€ Praia Golfe Hotel, Rua 6. **Road map** C2. 22-733 10 00. Few restaurants have such a wonderful panoramic ocean view as this one. Fish dishes are prominent on the menu, although the meats are not forgotten, and there are both red and white wines from every region of Portugal. ▤	AE DC MC V			■
GIMONDE: *Dom Roberto* €€€€ N218. **Road map** D2. 273-30 25 10. This rustic, stone-walled restaurant is located on the riverside in the small town of Gimonde, 7 km (4 miles) east of Bragança. People come from far and wide to try the excellent game dishes and smoked meats. ▤	AE DC MC V	■	●	
LAMEGO: *O Tonel* €€ Estrada de Arneirós. **Road map** D2. 254-61 21 61. A friendly restaurant popular with locals, O Tonel offers good-value Portuguese cuisine, including baked cod and *espetadas* (meat kebabs). ● Tue pm.		■		
LAMEGO: *Panorâmico Turisserra* €€€ Complexo Turístico Turisserra, Serra das Meadas. **Road map** D2. 254-60 91 00. This charming three-roomed restaurant, set in the tourist village 6 km (4 miles) north of Lamego, serves excellent traditional Portuguese fare. Enjoy the beautiful views of the Douro and surrounding hills. ▤	AE DC MC V			
LEÇA DA PALMEIRA: *Boa Nova* €€€€ Lugar da Boa Nova. **Road map** C2. 22-995 17 85. This modern restaurant overlooking the sea was built by one of Portugal's most famous architects, Siza Vieira. Try the baked sole or sea bass. ● Sun. ▤	AE DC MC V	■		■
LEÇA DA PALMEIRA: *O Chanquinhas* €€€€ Rua de Santana 243. **Road map** C2. 22-995 18 84. The restaurant is set in a large mansion with elegant dining rooms warmed by a cosy fireplace. The fish and desserts are excellent. ● Sun; 3 weeks in Aug. ▤	AE DC MC V	■		■
MIRANDA DO DOURO: *Buteko* €€ Largo Dom João III. **Road map** E1. 273-43 11 50. Set in the centre of town, Buteko's specialities include *posta Mirandesa* (beef) and *bacalhau à Buteko* (cod in the house style). ● Sun (winter); 2 weeks in Jan. ▤	DC MC V			
MIRANDA DO DOURO: *Balbina* €€€ Rua Rainha Dona Catarina 1. **Road map** E1. 273-43 23 94. Well-known politicians sit with locals and Spanish holiday-makers to enjoy dishes such as *bife à balbina*, a steak of local *Mirandesa* beef.				
MURÇA: *Miradouro* €€ Pensão Miradouro, Curvas de Murça. **Road map** D2. 259-51 24 61. The small handwritten menu in this plain restaurant changes daily. Dishes include cod Miradouro, kid and roast sucking pig. ● Tue; 15–30 Sep. ▤	MC V	■	●	
OPORTO: *Filha da Mãe Preta* €€ Cais da Ribeira 40. **Road map** C2. 22-208 60 66. Set into the arches by the river, this restaurant offers superb views and an excellent choice of Portuguese food, including sardines. ● Sun. Sep. ▤	AE DC MC V			■

Oporto: *Adega Vila Meã* €€€
Rua dos Caldeireiros 62. **Road map** C2. [22-208 29 67.
This is a busy, family-run restaurant. There are daily specials, as well as classic
favourites such as baked octopus and roast kid. ● Sun; 3 weeks in Aug. ▤

Oporto: *Bule* €€€ AE DC MC V
Rua de Timor 128. **Road map** C2. [22-617 93 76.
Bule has charming views over a garden sloping down to the sea. The specialities
here include roast duck and home-made pastries. ● First two weeks in Aug. ▤

Oporto: *Casa Aleixo* €€€ AE MC V
Rua da Estação 216. **Road map** C2. [22-537 04 62.
Run by the same family since 1948, this friendly restaurant offers good value.
Traditional dishes include octopus and veal. ● Sun & public hols; 3 weeks in Aug. ▤

Oporto: *Mercearia* €€€ AE DC MC V
Cais da Ribeira 32. **Road map** C2. [22-200 43 89.
Set on two floors in an old building, Mercearia offers Portuguese food, good
service and a pleasant atmosphere. ● Tue in winter. ▤

Oporto: *Peixes & Companhia* €€€ AE DC MC V
Rua do Ouro 133. **Road map** C2. [22-618 56 55.
A pleasant restaurant with a menu offering fish prepared in various ways,
mostly grilled. Meat is only available by prior agrrangement. ● Sun. ▤

Oporto: *Tripeiro* €€€ AE DC MC V
Rua de Passos Manuel 195. **Road map** C2. [22-200 58 86.
Tripeiro – meaning "tripe eater" – is the name for a native of Oporto as well as
this famous tripe-serving restaurant. Seafood is also available. ● Sun. ▤

Oporto: *Dom Manoel* €€€€ AE DC MC V
Avenida Montevideu 384. **Road map** C2. [22-617 23 04.
Set in a mansion with Atlantic views, Dom Manoel offers *parrilbada mista* (fish
and shellfish mixed grill) as well as meat dishes. ● Sun; 3 weeks in Aug. ▤ &

Oporto: *Dom Tonho* €€€€ AE DC MC V
Cais da Ribeira 13–15. **Road map** C2. [22-200 43 07.
This is one of many restaurants on the historic quayside, in the shadow of the
Dom Luís bridge. The menu has a selection of regional Portuguese dishes. ▤

Oporto: *Bull and Bear* €€€€€ AE DC MC V
Avenida da Boavista 3431. **Road map** C2. [22-610 76 69.
One of Portugal's most highly-regarded restaurants. Dishes include octopus
carpaccio and oriental-style tuna. ● Sat lunch & Sun. ▤ &

Oporto: *Portucale* €€€€€ AE DC MC V
Rua da Alegria 598, 13th floor. **Road map** C2. [22-537 07 17.
One of the most famous restaurants in the country with a wide array of
excellent meat, fish and game dishes, and spectacular views over the area. ▤

Peso da Régua: *Varanda da Régua* €€ AE MC V
Lugar da Boavista, Loureiro. **Road map** D2. [254-33 69 49.
Enjoy panoramic views from this friendly, family-run place just north of Régua.
The menu offers superb Portuguese cuisine such as roast kid and baked cod. ▤

Romeu: *Maria Rita* €€€ MC V
Rua da Capela. **Road map** E1. [278-93 91 34.
This homely restaurant in a town house has rustic furniture and stone fireplaces.
Try the spicy sausage soup or the roast turkey. ● Mon; Wed eve. ▤

Sendim: *Gabriela* €€€
Largo da Igreja 27. **Road map** E2. [273-73 91 80.
Gabriela's specialities inclde *posta à Gabriela* (beef steak) and smoked meats.
The restaurant is attractively furnished with wooden panels and an open fire. ▤

Torre de Moncorvo: *O Artur* €€€ AE DC MC V
Lugar de Rebentão, Carviçais. **Road map** E2. [279-93 91 84.
Dishes at this friendly restaurant situated outside Torre include *posta
Mirandesa* (thick grilled beef steak), baked cod and wild boar. ● Mon. ▤

Vila Nova de Gaia: *Presuntaria Transmontana* €€€ AE MC V
Avenida Diogo Leite 80. **Road map** C2. [22-375 83 80.
Located on the riverfront in Gaia this restaurant specializes in hams, smoked
meats and cheeses and is a popular place for an early or late evening snack.

For key to symbols see back flap

Price categories are for a three-course meal for one with half a bottle of wine, including cover charge, service and VAT:

€ under 10 euros
€€ 10–15 euros
€€€ 15–20 euros
€€€€ 20–30 euros
€€€€€ over 30 euros

LATE OPENING
The kitchen stays open after 10pm, and you can usually have a meal up until at least 11pm.

OUTDOOR TABLES
Tables for eating outdoors, in a garden or on a balcony, often with a pleasant view.

GOOD WINE LIST
The restaurant will have a good selection of quality wines.

CREDIT CARDS
This indicates which of the major credit cards are accepted: *AE* American Express, *DC* Diners Club, *MC* MasterCard and *V* Visa.

	CREDIT CARDS	LATE OPENING	OUTDOOR TABLES	GOOD WINE LIST
VILA REAL: *Cozinha do Vale* €€€ Casa de Campeã, Torgueda. **Road map** D2. 259-97 96 04. Set in the scenic Campeã valley, 8 km (5 miles) north of Vila Real, this modern restaurant offers local dishes and a good selection of wines. 🍴 🚻	AE DC MC V		●	▪
VILA REAL: *Espadeiro* €€€ Avenida Almeida Lucena. **Road map** D2. 259-32 23 02. This restaurant offers superbly prepared regional dishes accompanied by local wines. The house specials include *cabrito* (roast kid), cod Espadeiro and roast leg of pork. ● *Mon; last 2 weeks in Sep.* 🍴	AE MC V	▪		
MINHO				
ARCOS DE VALDEVEZ: *Costa do Vez* €€€€ N121, Silvares. **Road map** C1. 258-51 61 22. In a pretty setting just north of Arcos, Costa do Vez serves traditional cuisine such as roast veal and *cozido à portuguesa* (meat stew). ● *Mon; 15–30 Oct.* 🍴	AE MC V DC	▪		
BARCELOS: *Bagoeira* €€€ Avenida Sidónio Pais 495. **Road map** C1. 253-81 12 36. A large and popular restaurant serving Minhoto specialities, *rojões* (fried pork with potatoes) and kid stew, prepared with finesse in generous portions. 🍴	AE MC V			
BARCELOS: *Dom António* €€€ Rua Dom António Barroso 87. **Road map** C1. 253-81 22 85. Dom António's is a stone-walled place with rustic decor in the centre of town. House specials include grilled wild boar. 🍴	AE DC MC V	▪		
BRAGA: *Abade de Priscos* €€€ Praça Mouzinho Albuquerque (Campo Novo) 7. **Road map** C1. 253-27 66 50. Overlooking the leafy square beside the Catholic University, this restaurant offers good value and has a large menu ranging from curried prawns through to rabbit and braised veal. ● *Mon lunch; Sun; public hols & 3 weeks in Jul.* 🍴				▪
BRAGA: *Expositor* €€€€ Parque de Exposições. **Road map** C1. 253-21 70 31. Located in Braga's exhibitions park, this lively family restaurant specialises in regional dishes such as *rojões* (fried pork with potatoes). ● *Tue; 2 weeks in Jun.* 🍴	AE MC V	▪		
BRAGA: *Ignácio* €€€€ Campo das Hortas 4. **Road map** C1. 253-61 32 35. Just outside the city walls, Ignácio is full of character. Enjoy a range of regional dishes amidst artefacts and antiques. ● *Tue; 2 weeks in Apr; 2 weeks in Sep.* 🍴	AE DC MC V			
BRAGA: *São Frutuoso* €€€€ Rua Costa Gomes 168, Real. **Road map** C1. 253-62 33 72. A friendly restaurant just north of Braga which serves superb country food. Try the cod with corn bread or the stuffed veal. ● *Wed; 3 weeks in Aug.* 🍴	MC V		●	
CAMINHA: *Napoleon* €€€€ Lugar de Coura, Seixas. **Road map** C1. 258-72 71 15. Just northeast of Caminha, Napoleon has a high standard of cooking and offers local, national and French dishes. ● *Mon; Sun eve; 2 weeks in May; 2 weeks in Dec.* 🍴	AE DC MC V	▪		▪
GUIMARÃES: *El Rei* €€€ Praça de São Tiago 20. **Road map** C1. 253-41 90 96. El Rei is a cosy place with a good-value menu and a pleasant atmosphere. Try the *bacalhau mistério* (cod surprise) – a house-invented speciality. ● *Sun.* 🍴	DC MC V	▪		
GUIMARÃES: *São Gião* €€€€ Lugar de Vinhas, Moreira de Cónegos. **Road map** C1. 253-56 18 53. Found in a small village just south of Guimarães, São Gião offers tasty dishes such as hare stew, wild boar and marinated partridge. ● *Mon; Sun dinner; Aug.* 🍴	AE V			▪

GUIMARÃES: *Solar do Arco*　€€€€　AE DC MC V
Rua de Santa Maria 48–50. **Road map** C1. 253-51 30 72.
This elegant restaurant is located in a charming mansion in the heart of the city. Specialising in fresh seafood, but with plenty of meat dishes too, it is famous for its *arroz de tamboril* (monkfish with rice). ● *Sun dinner.* 🍴

PONTE DA BARCA: *Bar do Rio*　€€€　AE MC V
Fonte Velha, Praia Fluvial. **Road map** C1. 258-45 25 82.
This is a charming wood-panelled restaurant with stunning views of the River Lima. Try the specials of roast veal or cod *au gratin.* ● *Tue.* 🍴

PONTE DE LIMA: *A Carvalheira*　€€€　MC V
Antepaço, Arcozelo. **Road map** C1. 258-74 23 16.
Just northwest of Ponte de Lima, this restaurant is popular with locals. The house special is *bacalhau com broa* (cod with maize bread). ● *Mon; 2 weeks in Oct.* 🍴

PONTE DE LIMA: *Encanada*　€€€　AE DC MC V
Largo Doutor Rodrigues Alves. **Road map** C1. 258-94 11 89.
This busy restaurant, overlooking the river, offers traditional Minhoto fare such as *rojões à moda do Minho* (pork Minho style) and river trout. ● *Thu; May.* 🍴

PÓVOA DE VARZIM: *O Marinheiro*　€€€€　AE DC MC V
Rua Gomes de Amorim, Estrada Fontes Novas. **Road map** C2. 252-68 21 51.
An attractive restaurant in the shape of a boat and decorated with fishing nets and buoys, O Marinheiro offers a fine seafood-based menu. 🍴 ♿

VALENÇA DO MINHO: *Mané*　€€€€　AE DC MC V
Avenida Miguel Dantas 5. **Road map** C1. 251-82 34 02.
Above a café-bar, this modern restaurant has a wide, and relatively inexpensive, array of fish and meat dishes. ● *Sun eve; Mon (except Aug); Jan.* 🍴

VALENÇA DO MINHO: *Pousada de São Teotónio*　€€€€　AE DC MC V
Baluarte de Socorro. **Road map** C1. 251-80 02 60.
In a *pousada* within the old fort, São Teotónio offers a fantastic view across the Minho valley to Tuy in Spain, and hearty local dishes such as kid stew. 🍴

VIANA DO CASTELO: *Cozinha das Malheiras*　€€€　AE DC MC V
Rua Gago Coutinho 19–21. **Road map** C1. 258-82 36 80.
Enjoy good traditional cuisine in this small and intimate restaurant in a former manor house. The seafood dishes are recommended. ● *Tue.* 🍴

VIANA DO CASTELO: *Camelo*　€€€€　MC V
N202, Santa Marta de Portuzelo. **Road map** C 1. 258-83 90 90.
In a village 1 km (half a mile) from Viana do Castelo, this gem of a restaurant holds monthly festive banquets and offers summer dining under shady vines. Try the *bacalhau à camelo* (house cod speciality). ● *Mon; 2weeks in Jun & Oct.* 🍴

VIANA DO CASTELO: *Casa d'Armas*　€€€€　DC MC V
Largo 5 de Outubro 30. **Road map** C1. 258-82 49 99.
Behind a gracious and imposing façade, the stone and wood-panelled interior of Casa d'Armas is enhanced by medieval-style decor. Expect only the freshest fish and shellfish, and prime quality meats. ● *Mon.* 🍴

VILA PRAIA DE ÂNCORA: *Tasquinha do Ibraim*　€€€€　AE V
Rua dos Pescadores 11. **Road map** C1. 258-91 16 89.
Overlooking the harbour, this cosy place has excellent service and specializes in seafood. Alternatively try the tasty *costeletão* (T-bone steak). ● *Tue.* ♿

ALENTEJO

ALANDROAL: *A Maria*　€€€€　AE DC MC V
Rua João de Deus 12. **Road map** D5. 268-43 11 43.
An enchanting restaurant serving Alentejan dishes that include *cozido de grão* (pork and chickpea stew) and *sopa de cação* (dogfish soup). ● *Mon; Aug.* 🍴

ALVITO: *Castelo de Alvito*　€€€€　AE DC MC V
Pousada do Castelo de Alvito, Apartado 9. **Road map** D6. 284-48 53 43.
A 15th-century castle with beautiful gardens provides the setting for this fine restaurant. Try the cod stewed with herbs or roast lamb with spinach. 🍴 ♿

BEJA: *Dom Dinis*　€€€　AE DC MC V
Rua Dom Dinis 11. **Road map** D6. 284-32 59 37.
Dom Dinis is a country restaurant specializing in grilled food, the most popular dishes being the meat kebabs and veal chops. ● *Wed.* 🍴

For key to symbols see back flap

Price categories are for a three-course meal for one with half a bottle of wine, including cover charge, service and VAT: € under 10 euros €€ 10–15 euros €€€ 15–20 euros €€€€ 20–30 euros €€€€€ over 30 euros	**LATE OPENING** The kitchen stays open after 10pm, and you can usually have a meal up until at least 11pm. **OUTDOOR TABLES** Tables for eating outdoors, in a garden or on a balcony, often with a pleasant view. **GOOD WINE LIST** The restaurant will have a good selection of quality wines. **CREDIT CARDS** This indicates which of the major credit cards are accepted: *AE* American Express, *DC* Diners Club, *MC* MasterCard and *V* Visa.		

	CREDIT CARDS	LATE OPENING	OUTDOOR TABLES	GOOD WINE LIST
BEJA: *Os Infantes* €€€ Rua dos Infantes 14. **Road map** D6. 284-32 27 89. Os Infantes has a beautiful setting, fine decor and a good-value menu. Specialities include traditional Alentejo cuisine, of lamb and hare.	AE DC MC V			■
CAMPO MAIOR: *O Faisão* €€€ Rua 1° de Maio 19. **Road map** E5. 268-68 61 39. This cosy restaurant, with a fire and pictures of local life on the walls, offers a good selection of traditional dishes such as *cozido de grão* (pork and chickpea stew). Alternatively, try the house beef in mushroom sauce.	AE DC MC V	■		
CRATO: *Flor da Rosa* €€€€ Pousada da Flor da Rosa. **Road map** D4. 245-99 72 10. The restaurant is located in this marvellous *pousada* adapted from the monastery which is thought to date from the mid-14th century. Traditional regional favourites are served such as *açorda* (bread stew).	AE DC MC V			■
ELVAS: *Pousada de Santa Luzia* €€€€ Avenida de Badajoz. **Road map** D5. 268-63 74 70. Not far from the Spanish border, the large restaurant of this *pousada (see p395)* is popular with Portuguese and Spaniards alike. They come here to enjoy the large portions of *bacalhau á Lagareiro* and other traditional treats.	AE DC MC V		●	
ESTREMOZ: *Adega do Isaías* €€ Rua do Almeida 21. **Road map** D5. 268-32 23 18. Offering the best of rustic Alentejan cooking in an old wine cellar, Isías serves tender lamb and rabbit from the grill. Good local wine by the jug. ● *Sun; 2 weeks in Aug; Public hols.*				■
ÉVORA: *Cozinha de Santo Humberto* €€€€ Rua da Moeda 39. **Road map** D5. 266-70 42 51. Just off the main square, this is a real delight. A whitewashed cellar is adorned with antiques, and Alentejo dishes and local game are served. ● *Thu; Nov.*	AE DC MC V			
ÉVORA: *Fialho* €€€€ Travessa das Mascarenhas 16. **Road map** D5. 266-70 30 79. One of the most highly regarded restaurants in Portugal Fialho has an exceptional selection of traditional Alentejan dishes. ● *Mon; 1–24 Sep.*	AE DC MC V	■		■
ÉVORA: *O Grémio* €€€€ Rua Alcárcova de Cima 10. **Road map** D5. 266-74 29 31. A wonderful restaurant built into the city's Roman wall. Try the tasty hare stewed with beans. ● *Wed.*	AE DC MC V			■
ÉVORA: *Sâo Rosas* €€€€ Largo Dom Dinis 11. **Road map** D5. 268-33 33 45. In a tastefully rustic setting, Margarida Cabaço cooks regional specialities with flair, including partridge pie and saddle of lamb. ● *Mon.*	AE DC MC V			
MARVÃO: *O Sever* €€€ Portagem. **Road map** D4. 245-99 33 18. A pretty restaurant with excellent river views. The menu offers immaculately prepared regional specialities such as pork with clams and lamb stew.	AE DC MC V	■	●	
MÉRTOLA: *Alengarve* €€€ Avenida Aureliano Mira Fernandes 20. **Road map** D6. 286-61 22 10. This modest restaurant offers good-value regional cuisine such as pork cooked with chick peas and rabbit stew. ● *Wed; 2 weeks in Oct.*	AE MC V		●	
MONSARAZ: *O Forno* €€€ Travessa da Sanabrosa. **Road map** D5. 266-55 71 90. Located near the main square of an attractive hill top town, O Forno serves mainly regional dishes such as lamb stew and pork with clams. ● *Tue.*	AE MC V		●	

PORTALEGRE: *Quinta da Saúde*   €€€ | AE DC MC V

Serra de São Mamede. **Road map** D4. **【** 245-20 23 24.
Part of an *estalagem* (inn) overlooking Portalegre. Good Alentejan food such
as gaspacho, spinach soup with clams and breaded pork. 🍴 ⅛

REDONDO: *Convento de São Paulo*   €€€€ | AE DC MC V

Convento de São Paulo, Aldeia da Serra. **Road map** D5. **【** 266-99 91 00.
Inside a beautiful hotel, this restaurant offers a wonderful array of dishes
such as melon with port and duck with olive sauce. There are also regional
Alentejan dishes. 🍴 ⅛

SANTIAGO DO CACÉM: *O Retiro*   €€€ | AE MC V

Rua Machado dos Santos 8. **Road map** C6. **【** 269-82 26 59.
A charming country restaurant with friendly service. House specialities are
duck rice and *bacalhau com natas* (cod in a creamy sauce). ● *Sun.* 🍴

SERPA: *Molha o Bico*   €€€

Rua Quente 1. **Road map** D6. **【** 284-54 92 64.
A friendly local restaurant where the food is often outstanding. Try the
veal steak or the *cozido de grão* (pork and chickpea stew). ● *Wed.* 🍴

TERRUGEM: *A Bolota Castanha*   €€€ | AE MC V

Quinta das Janelas Verdes. **Road map** C6. **【** 268-65 74 01.
This celebrated Alentejan restaurant serves modern versions of traditional
dishes, including wild boar with chestnut purée. ● *Mon.* 🍴 ⅛

VIDIGUERA: *Vila Velha*   €€€ | AE MC V

Rua do Mal Anda 4. **Road map** D5. **【** 284-43 65 50.
Pleasant restaurant decorated with regional costumes and artefacts, serving
classics such as pig's trotters in coriander sauce and duck rice.
● *Mon; last 2 weeks of Aug, first 2 weeks of Sep.* 🍴

VILA NOVA DE MILFONTES: *Marisqueira Dumas Mil*   €€€€ | AE MC V

Off Avenida Marginal. **Road map** C6. **【** 283-99 71 04.
This highly regarded fish restaurant serves a delicious *arroz de marisco*
(seafood rice) and *caldeirada de peixe* (fish stew). 🍴

ALGARVE

ALBUFEIRA: *Os Compadres*   €€€ | AE DC MC V

Avenida Dr Sá Carneiro, Edifício Cristina Pateo Sá Carneiro. **Road map** C7. **【** 289-54 18 48.
This restaurant has a good atmosphere and friendly, relaxed service. The owner
is always around to offer advice on what to choose. ● *Sun (Oct–Apr); Jan.* 🍴

ALBUFEIRA: *Marisqueira Santa Eulália*   €€€€ | AE DC MC V

Praia de Santa Eulália. **Road map** C7. **【** 289-54 26 36.
Overlooking the beach, this modern restaurant serves typical Portuguese seafood dishes, including grilled monkfish, salmon and clams. ● *Dec–Jan.* ⅛

ALBUFEIRA: *Ruína*   €€€€ | AE DC MC V

Rua Cais Herculano. **Road map** C7. **【** 289-51 20 94.
Set in a restored early 19th-century building, Ruína is one of the best
restaurants in town. Specialities of the house are fresh fish and seafood.
Rooms are set aside for coffee and for listening to *fado.* 🍴

ALBUFEIRA: *Vila Joya*   €€€€€ | AE DC MC V

Praia da Galé. **Road map** C7. **【** 289-59 17 95.
The German chef here concentrates on fish and seafood from nearby
sources, which he scents with basil or serves on rösti. ● *Nov-Mar.* 🍴 ⅛

ALMANCIL: *Ibérico*   €€€€€ | AE MC V

Estrada Almancil, Vale do Lobo. **Road map** D7. **【** 289-39 40 66.
Set near the Vale do Lobo complex south of Almancil, Ibérico's eclectic menu
offers such dishes as smoked swordfish with horseradish sauce. ● *lunch.* 🍴

ALMANCIL: *Ermitage*   €€€€€ | AE DC MC V

Estrada de Vale de Lobo. **Road map** D7. **【** 289-39 43 29.
One of Portugal's top restaurants, Ermitage serves dishes such as guinea fowl
with celery purée. ● *lunch; Mon; 3 weeks in Dec, 2 weeks in Jun/Jul.* 🍴

ALMANCIL: *O Tradicional*   €€€€€ | AE MC V

Estrada da Fonte Santa, Escanxinas. **Road map** D7. **【** 289-39 90 93.
This excellent restaurant, south of Almancil, serves dishes such as crab soup with
bread and sea bass with wild asparagus and rice. ● *lunch; Sun; Dec–Jan.* 🍴 ⅛

For key to symbols see back flap

Price categories are for a three-course meal for one with half a bottle of wine, including cover charge, service and VAT:

€ under 10 euros
€€ 10–15 euros
€€€ 15–20 euros
€€€€ 20–30 euros
€€€€€ over 30 euros

LATE OPENING
The kitchen stays open after 10pm, and you can usually have a meal up until at least 11pm.

OUTDOOR TABLES
Tables for eating outdoors, in a garden or on a balcony, often with a pleasant view.

GOOD WINE LIST
The restaurant will have a good selection of quality wines.

CREDIT CARDS
This indicates which of the major credit cards are accepted: *AE* American Express, *DC* Diners Club, *MC* MasterCard and *V* Visa.

	CREDIT CARDS	LATE OPENING	OUTDOOR TABLES	GOOD WINE LIST

ARMAÇÃO DE PÊRA: *Santola*   €€€€
Largo da Fortaleza. **Road map** C7. ☎ 282-31 23 32.
With panoramic seaside views, Santola has a pleasant atmosphere and is a reliable choice for seafood and shellfish dishes.

AE		●	
MC			
V			

ESTOI: *Monte do Casal*   €€€€
Cerro do Lobo. **Road map** D7. ☎ 289-99 15 03.
The menu at this converted farmhouse restaurant includes a selection of vegetarian dishes and house specialities such as salmon in a white wine and dill sauce, and seafood with Monte do Casal sauce. ● mid-Nov–mid-Feb. 🍽

| MC | | ● | ▨ |
| V | | | |

FARO: *Adega Nortenha*   €€
Rua Leite 8. **Road map** D7. ☎ 289-82 27 09.
This busy, unpretentious place overlooks a pretty square. Daily specials include *feijoada* (bean stew) and *caldeirada* (fish stew). 🍽

FARO: *A Taska*   €€€
Rua do Alportel 38. **Road map** D7. ☎ 289-82 47 39.
Popular with locals, A Taska is a modest but cosy restaurant decorated as an old tavern. Try the eel stew or the pork with clams. 🍽

AE	▨	●	
DC			
MC			
V			

FARO: *Camané*   €€€€
Avenida da Nascente, Praia de Faro. **Road map** D7. ☎ 289-81 75 39.
Camané is a bright and spacious seafood restaurant located by Faro's beach. The house special is fried cuttlefish. ● Mon; 2 weeks in Oct. 🍽 ♿

| MC | ▨ | ● | ▨ |
| V | | | |

FARO: *Dois Irmãos*   €€€€
Praça Ferreira de Almeida 13–14. **Road map** D7. ☎ 289-82 33 37.
One of the most popular restaurants in Faro, the Dois Irmãos offers good quality cooking and efficient service. Seafood specialities include fish or meat *cataplana (see p288)* and a variety of fresh fish dishes.

AE	▨	●	
MC			
V			

LAGOA: *O Lotus*   €€€
Rua Marquês de Pombal 11. **Road map** C7. ☎ 282-35 20 98.
O Lotus offers good Portuguese cuisine such as marinated sardines, octopus and egg salad and arroz de peixe (fish rice). Desserts include chocolate mousse or *morgado de figo* (fig and almond paste cakes). ● Sat. 🍽

AE			
DC			
MC			
V			

LAGOA: *O Castelo*   €€€€
Rua do Casino 63, Praia do Carvoeiro. **Road map** C7. ☎ 282-35 72 18.
Booking is advisable in this cliff-top seafood restaurant surrounded by a pretty garden. Try the monkfish and prawn rice. ● Mon; 10 Jan–10 Feb. 🍽

AE	▨	●	▨
DC			
MC			
V			

LAGOS: *Dom Sebastião*   €€€
Rua 25 de Abril 20–22. **Road map** C7. ☎ 282-76 27 95.
This rustic restaurant has an extensive menu offering traditional Portuguese fare such as smoked swordfish and kid stew in red wine. ● 1–25 Dec. 🍽

AE	▨	●	
DC			
MC			
V			

LOULÉ: *Casa dos Arcos*   €€€
Rua Sá de Miranda 23–5. **Road map** D7. ☎ 289-41 67 13.
Set in Loulé's historic centre, this restaurant is popular with tourists and locals alike. It serves good-quality seafood specialities and meat dishes. ● Sun. 🍽

AE			
MC			
V			

LOULÉ: *Bica Velha*   €€€€
Rua Martim Moniz 17–19. **Road map** C7. ☎ 289-46 33 76.
The oldest house in Loulé, dating from 1816, is the setting for this rustic, family-run restaurant. Specialities include lamb kebab, pork chop with apple sauce, and orange mousse for dessert. ● Sun (except Aug); 2 weeks in Nov or Dec.

AE	▨		
DC			
MC			
V			

OLHÃO: *O Lagar*   €€€
Pechão. **Road map** D7. ☎ 289-71 54 37.
Inland from Olhão, on the road towards Estoi, this simple restaurant serves great Algarvan food, including gaspacho and grilled sardines. ● Wed. 🍽

| | | ● | |

OLHÃO: *O Tamboril* €€€€
Avenida 5 de Outubro 174. **Road map** D7. 289-71 46 25.
Tamboril or monkfish is the speciality here, where you will find it and other
seafood served grilled, with rice or in stews. ● *Sat pm (winter only).* ▤

	AE	■	●	
	DC			
	MC			
	V			

PORTIMÃO: *Cervejaria Lúcio* €€€
Largo Francisco Maurício 33. **Road map** C7. 282-42 42 75.
Overlooking the river, this cheerful, noisy beerhouse is a popular meeting
place for locals and serves mainly fish and seafood dishes. ● *Mon.*

		■	●	

PORTIMÃO: *A Lanterna* €€€€
Rua Foz do Arade. **Road map** C7. 282-41 44 29.
A variety of Portuguese dishes include local clams, a selection of fish, and
grilled duck with honey. ● *Sun; Nov–Dec.*

	MC	■		■
	V			

PORTIMIÃO: *Vila Lisa* €€€€
Rua Francisco Bivar, Mexilhoeira Grande. **Road map** C7. 282-96 84 78.
Run by an artist, this is the most characterful restaurant on the Algarve.
A fixed menu of five dishes includes clam rice. ❑ *Jul–Sep: daily; Oct–Jun:
Fri & Sat only.* ● *lunch.* ▤

QUINTA DO LAGO: *Casa Velha* €€€€€
Quinta do Lago. **Road map** D7. 289-39 49 83.
This elegant restaurant occupies an old farm house within the Quinta do
Lago resort. It has an eclectic menu offering exciting international dishes
such as cod with tomato and ray cooked in milk. ● *lunch; Sun; Jan.* ▤ ♿

	AE	■	●	
	DC			
	MC			
	V			

SAGRES: *Pousada do Infante* €€€€
Pousada do Infante. **Road map** C7. 282-62 42 22.
With stunning views over the cliffs and ocean, this restaurant features
dishes like sole with clams and grilled veal with mint. ▤

	AE		●	
	DC			
	MC			
	V			

SAGRES: *O Telheiro* €€€€
Praia da Mareta. **Road map** C7. 282-62 41 79.
Enjoy the excellent service, and dining room with panoramic views and a
terrace. The house speciality is lobster rice. ● *Tue; 2 weeks in Nov or Dec.* ▤ ♿

	AE		●	
	DC			
	MC			
	V			

SILVES: *Marisqueira Rui* €€€€
Rua Comendador Vilarinho 23. **Road map** C7. 282-44 26 82.
Popular with the locals, this busy town-centre restaurant is open until 2am. Menu
highlights are the seafood rice and selection of fresh fish. ● *Tue; 2 weeks in Nov.* ▤

	AE	■		
	DC			
	MC			
	V			

TAVIRA: *Aquasul* €€€€
Rua Silva Carvalho 11–13. **Road map** D7. 281-32 53 29.
On a small side street on the left bank of the Gilão river, Aquasul serves
Mediterranean-inspired food – salads, pastas and tagines – in an informal setting.

	MC		●	■
	V			

VILAMOURA: *Sirius Restaurant* €€€€€
Vilamoura Tivoli Marinotel. **Road map** D7. 289-30 33 03.
Located in an elegant hotel, Sirius looks out over the marina and serves some
superb international and French-orientated cuisine. Indulge in beluga caviar
and vodka, escargots bourguignon or lobster thermidor. ● *Lunch.* ▤ ♫ ♿

	AE	■		■
	DC			
	MC			
	V			

MADEIRA

FUNCHAL: *Dom Filet* €€€
Rua do Favila 7. 291-76 44 26.
"King Fillet" specializes in beef served Madeiran style (cubed, skewered on a bay
twig and grilled) or char-grilled Argentinian style. ● *Sun.* ▤

	AE	■		
	DC			
	MC			
	V			

FUNCHAL: *O Jango* €€€
Rua de Santa Maria 166. 291-22 12 80.
O Jango is a cosy restaurant in a converted fisherman's house in the old town.
The good-value, fresh food includes bouillabaisse and paella. ▤

	AE	■		
	DC			
	MC			
	V			

FUNCHAL: *Jardim da Carreira* €€€
Rua da Carreira 118. 291-22 24 98.
This fairly basic restaurant offers some of the cheapest eating in central Funchal.
Dishes such as grilled fish and meat skewers are popular with tourists. ▤

	AE		●	
	MC			
	V			

FUNCHAL: *Londres* €€€
Rua da Carreira 64a. 291-23 53 29.
This downtown restaurant has a typically Portuguese daily special, such as
bacalhau (salt cod) with olives or *cozido*, a hearty meat casserole. ● *Sun.* ▤

	AE			
	MC			
	V			

Price categories are for a three-course meal for one with half a bottle of wine, including cover charge, service and VAT:

€ under 10 euros
€€ 10–15 euros
€€€ 15–20 euros
€€€€ 20–30 euros
€€€€€ over 30 euros

LATE OPENING
The kitchen stays open after 10pm, and you can usually have a meal up until at least 11pm.

OUTDOOR TABLES
Tables for eating outdoors, in a garden or on a balcony, often with a pleasant view.

GOOD WINE LIST
The restaurant will have a good selection of quality wines.

CREDIT CARDS
This indicates which of the major credit cards are accepted: *AE* American Express, *DC* Diners Club, *MC* MasterCard and *V* Visa.

	Credit Cards	Late Opening	Outdoor Tables	Good Wine List
FUNCHAL: *Marisa* €€€ Rua de Santa Maria 162. 291-22 61 89. An intimate old town restaurant that feels like a private home, as father and son cook delicious paella or seafood rice and mother takes the orders.	AE DC MC V			
FUNCHAL: *Carochinha* €€€€ Rua de São Francisco 2a. 291-22 36 95. Carochinha calls itself an "English" restaurant, but its eclectic menu includes a wide choice of dishes from various countries. There is roast beef though. ● Sun. ▤ ♿	AE DC MC V			
FUNCHAL: *O Celeiro* €€€€ Rua das Aranhas 22. 291-23 06 22. O Celeiro offers candle-lit dining and a fish-based menu featuring several dishes for two, such as shellfish and lobster *cataplana*, and bouillabaisse. ● Sun. ▤	AE DC MC V			
FUNCHAL: *Dona Amélia* €€€€ Rua Imperatriz Dona Amélia 83. 291-22 57 84. Flambé dishes, grilled fish and *espetadinhas* (small beef kebabs) on baywood skewers are the speciality of this prettily tiled restaurant. ▤	AE DC MC V	■		■
FUNCHAL: *Eatwell* €€€€ Rua Dr. Pita 23a. 291-76 40 20. This small restaurant lives up to its name. The short menu is varied but usually includes such Madeiran fare as skewered beef. ● Sun. ▤	AE MC V			
FUNCHAL: *Marina Terrace* €€€€ Marina do Funchal. 291-23 05 47. One of a run of outdoor restaurants by the yacht marina, this place serves dishes from simple pizza to lobster or grilled fish. ♿	AE DC MC V	■	●	
FUNCHAL: *Mezanino* €€€€ Hotel Ocean Park. 291-76 34 85. Australian chef Anthony Parker provides an eclectic menu including, grilled tuna with couscous and tandoori chicken. ● Sat lunch; Sun; public hols. ▤ ♿	AE DC MC V			■
FUNCHAL: *Quinta Palmeira Gourmet Restaurant* €€€€ Avenida do Infante 17–19. 291-22 18 14. In this fine 19th-century town house traditional Portuguese dishes are presented with flair, and the home-made ice cream is delicious.	AE DC MC V	■	●	■
FUNCHAL: *O Tapassol* €€€€ Rua Don Carlos I 62. 291-22 50 23. Booking is advised at this excellent small restaurant in the old town. Dine on quail, mussels, limpets or rabbit, choosing the indoor dining room for style, or the tiny roof terrace for a fun evening. ▤	AE DC MC V	■	●	
PORTO MONIZ: *Orca* €€€ Residencial Orca, Vila Porto Moniz. 291-85 00 00. Orca is made entirely of wood, apart from the large windows that enable diners to gaze out over the sea. Try the special of scabbard fish with banana.	AE DC MC V		●	
PORTO SANTO: *O Calhetas* €€€ Calheta. 291-98 43 80. This pleasant restaurant at the southern tip of the island serves well-cooked fish such as *arroz de cherne* (grouper rice) as well as the usual meat dishes. A hotel pick-up and drop-off service is available. ▤	MC V	■	●	
RIBEIRA BRAVA: *Restaurante Água Mar* €€€ Vila Ribeira Brava. 291-95 11 48. This informal restaurant offers a wide-ranging menu that includes Portuguese as well as French-influenced dishes. Perhaps the most popular choice is the simply grilled or fried fresh fish and shellfish. ● Mon. ♿	AE DC MC V	■	●	

SANTANA: *Quinta do Furão* €€€€ AE DC MC V ●
Achada do Gramacho. **(** 291-57 01 00.
Sit next to the fireplace among antiques in this cosy restaurant overlooking the sea. Specials include steak in pastry and seafood kebabs. 🍽

THE AZORES

CORVO: *Traineira* €€€ ●
Largo do Porto da Casa. **(** 292-59 62 07.
Currently the only restaurant on Corvo, Traineira is usually busy. The menu concentrates on fresh, locally caught fish. ● *Sun.* 🍽

FAIAL: *Capote* €€€ AE MC V ■
Rua Conselheiro Miguel da Silveira 24, Horta. **(** 292-29 32 95.
A lively and often crowded restaurant at the north end of the seafront, it is popular with both locals and yachties celebrating their return to land. 🍽

FAIAL: *Trovada* €€€€ AE DC MC V ● ■
Rua Vasco da Gama, 9900-017, Horta. **(** 292-29 30 21.
Housed in the Estalagem de Santa Cruz (see p401), some claim that this is the best restaurant on the island. The cooking is of a high quality and uses good local ingredients. 🍽 ♿

FLORES: *Reis* €€€ MC V ■
Rua da Boa Vista, Santa Cruz das Flores. **(** 292-59 26 97.
Up in the hills above Santa Cruz, this is a clean and simple restaurant attached to the *salsicharia* (sausage shop) run by a local butcher. ● *Sun.*

GRACIOSA: *A Coluna* €€€
Largo Barão de Guadalupe 10, Santa Cruz da Graciosa. **(** 295-71 23 33.
The owner of this small, idiosyncratic restaurant spent many years in Brazil and serves *feijoada* (bean and meat stew) and other Brazilian favourites. ● *Sun.*

PICO: *Terra e Mar* €€€ ●
Miradouro do Arrife, Terras, Lajes do Pico. **(** 292-67 27 94.
This small cliff-top restaurant has a windmill and terrace. Serving simple fish and meat dishes, it is a good place to pause while touring the island.

SANTA MARIA: *Candeia* €€€
Cruz Teixeira, Vila do Porto. **(** 296-88 20 63.
A Candeia specializes in hearty Azorean dishes like *sopa de nabos* (meat and vegetable stew) and *alheira e morcela* (garlic sausage and black pudding). Book a day in advance to be asssured of a table at this popular restaurant.

SÃO JORGE: *Manezinho* €€ ■ ●
Furna das Pombras, Urzelina. **(** 295-41 44 84.
A simple seaside restaurant that is popular with locals. Dishes include *ameijoas* (clams) from Fajã da Caldeira de Santo Cristo. ● *Mon.*

SÃO MIGUEL: *Alcides* €€€
Rua Hintze Ribeiro 67–77, Ponta Delgada. **(** 296-28 26 77.
An unpretentious but accomplished restaurant serving robust steak and chips fare, close to the Igreja Matriz de São Sebastião. ● *Sun.* 🍽

SÃO MIGUEL: *Monte Verde* €€€ AE V ■ ●
Rua da Areia 4, Ribeira Grande. **(** 296-47 29 75.
Monte Verde is a small, friendly restaurant with a first-floor dining room decorated with modern *azulejos*. Competent fish dishes include *tigelada de chicharro*, a stew made with thin, sardine-like fish.

SÃO MIGUEL: *Tony's* €€€ AE DC MC V ■ ●
Largo do Teatro 5, Furnas. **(** 296-58 42 90.
Tony's specializes in *cozido (see p231)*. The meat stew is slowly cooked in the hot volcanic rocks found around Furnas. Book at least a day in advance. 🍽

TERCEIRA: *Casa do Peixe* €€€ MC V
Estrada Miguel Corte Real 30, Angra do Heroísmo. **(** 295-21 76 78.
Overlooking the harbour, the city's former fish market has been turned into an atmospheric restaurant with a full menu and friendly service. ● *Tue.*

TERCEIRA: *Quinta do Martelo* €€€€ AE MC V ■ ● ■
Canada do Martelo 24 , Cantinho, São Mateus. **(** 295-64 28 42.
This is the place to go to try rich Azorean dishes like Holy Spirit soup (meat and vegetables in white wine) and *alcatra* (meat stew). ● *Wed.* 🍽 🎵

SURVIVAL
GUIDE

PRACTICAL INFORMATION

PORTUGAL IS an easy country to visit. In the Algarve and the Lisbon area, where most tourists go, the choice of hotels, restaurants and entertainment is vast. English is widely spoken, and visitors are welcomed. But even in the less developed parts

Sign for Tourist Information Office

of the country, visitors will find it easy to deal with friendly locals. And even here, English is widely spoken. Accommodation can be found virtually anywhere, children are always welcome, and food is good. Most towns also have helpful tourist offices.

WHEN TO VISIT

THE COUNTRY'S long Atlantic coast is the single most important factor for Portugal's climate. Coastal regions can be very rainy in winter, and although temperatures don't drop that low, it often feels very cold. The exception is the Algarve, which although it is also on the Atlantic, faces south and is protected from northerly winds by inland hills.

The Algarve, then, is the only year-round destination, with hot to very hot summers and mild winters. Other coastal areas generally have warm to hot summers, with either balmy or windy evenings. Inland areas throughout the country are subject to more extreme conditions, with colder winters even in the Alentejo and hotter summers even in Trás-os-Montes.

Spring and autumn are good times to visit because the weather is mild, but spring in particular may be wet, which contributes to the glory of the country flowers.

CUSTOMS

ON 30 JUNE 1999, the intra-EU Duty and Tax Free Allowances, better known as Duty-free and mainly affecting such items as alcohol, perfumes and tobacco, were abolished. Consulates can generally provide up-to-date information on particular customs regulations. For more details on customs and other tax-related matters, see pages 436–7.

Bottles of port

VISAS

EU NATIONALS only need a valid passport to enter Portugal. If they stay for more than six months they should apply for a residence permit. There is currently no visa requirement for Americans, Canadians, New Zealanders or Australians entering Portugal. Nationals of those countries may stay for up to 90 days and then apply for an extension (usually another 90 days). However, travellers from outside the EU are advised to check with the nearest Portuguese embassy or consulate before going, as visa regulations are subject to change.

TOURIST INFORMATION

THE PORTUGUESE MINISTRY of Tourism divides the country into a number of touristic regions, which are separate from its administrative districts. All major cities or large towns within each touristic region have a **Municipal Tourist Office** (Posto de Turismo), as do the larger towns on Madeira and the Azores. This guide gives details of the relevant tourist information office for each sight. Here, visitors can obtain information about the region, town plans, maps and details on regional events. In some cases they will also sell advance tickets for local shows and concerts. Information about local hotels will be available from the tourist office, although they will not usually book the accommodation.

High season on a beach in the resort of Albufeira, in the Algarve

◁ **Fruit and vegetable stalls at the Mercado dos Lavradores, Funchal**

Signpost in the village of Marvão

Office opening hours vary as each tourist region is organized independently, but generally they follow the same opening hours as local shops. In more rural areas, offices are often closed at weekends, and may not offer the same information and services that can be found in larger towns. There are tourist offices at all the major airports, as well as in all cities and large towns. Visitors can also obtain information prior to travelling, from Portuguese tourist offices abroad. These offices will normally provide visitors planning a trip with a wide range of useful maps, fact sheets and tourist brochures.

Map of mainland Portugal showing the country's six tourist regions

MUSEUMS

THE MAJORITY of Portugal's museums are run by the state, although there are also a number of private ones. In addition to the main national museums and galleries, there are countless regional ones scattered around the country. These cover a range of topics, from the history of a region to the works of local artists.

ADMISSION CHARGES

MOST MUSEUMS in Portugal charge a small entrance fee, which varies from one to three euros. These charges are sometimes reduced or waived altogether (or just in the morning) on Sundays and public holidays. Young people under 14 or pensioners (with proof of age) may obtain a 40 per cent discount. Those under 26 with a *Cartão Jovem* (youth card) or ISIC card (International Student Identity Card) are

Museum tickets

entitled to half-price entrance. Tourists to Lisbon may also buy a Lisboa card, available from the airport, tourist offices, and travel agents. It allows free entry to 26 of the city's museums, and reduced entry to many others, including the Gulbenkian, as well as free public transport for a fixed period. Lisboa cards are valid for one, two or three days.

OPENING TIMES

MUSEUMS ARE usually open from 10am–5pm from Tuesday to Sunday, with many closing for lunch either from noon to 2pm or from 12:30pm to 2:30pm. Smaller and private museums may have different opening times. Museums and some sights close on Mondays and public holidays. Major churches are open during the day without a fixed timetable although some may close between noon and 4pm. Smaller churches and those in rural areas may only be open for religious services and in some cases you may need to find the keyholder for admittance.

DIRECTORY

EMBASSIES AND CONSULATES

United Kingdom
Rua de São Bernardo 33,
1249-082, Lisbon. **Map** 4 D2.
〔 *21-392 40 00.*

British Consulates
Funchal 〔 *291-22 12 21.*
Lisbon 〔 *21-392 41 60.*
Oporto 〔 *22-618 47 89.*
Portimão 〔 *282-41 78 00.*

Australia
Avenida da Liberdade 198, 2º,
〔 *21-310 15 00.*

Canada
Avenida da Liberdade 196-200,
3º, 1269-121, Lisbon. **Map** 5 C5.
〔 *21-316 46 00.*

Republic of Ireland
Rua da Imprensa à Estrela 1, 4º,
1200, Lisbon. **Map** 4 E2.
〔 *21-392 94 40.*

US
Avenida das Forças Armadas,
1600, Lisbon. 〔 *21-727 33 00.*

TOURIST OFFICES

Coimbra
Largo da Portagem, 3000–337.
〔 *239-833 019.*
[w] *www.turismo-centro.pt*

Faro
Avenida 5 de Outubro 18–20,
8001–902, Faro.
〔 *289-80 04 00.*
[w] *www.rtalgarve.pt*

Lisbon
Lisboa Welcome Center,
Rua do Arsenal 15,
1100-038, Lisbon. **Map** 7 A2.
〔 *21-031 27 00; toll free 800-296 296.*
[w] *www.atl-turismolisboa.pt*

Oporto
Rua Clube dos Fenianos 25,
4000–172, Oporto.
〔 *22-339 34 70/72.*
[w] *www.portoturismo.pt*

In the UK:
22–25a Sackville Street,
London W1X 1DE.
〔 *09063-640 610.*

In the US:
〔 *212-220 5772.*

In Canada:
〔 *1 416-921 7376.*

Newspaper stall in the Brasileira Café *(see p90)*

LANGUAGE

Written Portuguese is fairly similar to Spanish, so if you know Spanish you should have little difficulty understanding Portuguese text. However, Portuguese pronunciation is different and spoken Portuguese sounds nothing like spoken Spanish.

The Portuguese are justifiably proud of their own language, and may take offence at being addressed in Spanish. Their own language is widely spoken throughout the world as a result of former colonial ties with Brazil and a number of countries in Africa. A phrase book containing the most useful words and phrases, along with their phonetic pronunciations, can be found on pages 479–80.

ETIQUETTE

Although English is more widely spoken in Portugal than in neighbouring Spain, the Portuguese appreciate visitors' efforts, however small, to communicate in their language. A simple *bom dia* (good day) or *boa tarde* (good afternoon) can work wonders. For any attempts at more advanced communication, be prepared to repeat yourself several times, allowing your listener to suspend his disbelief and adjust to the peculiarities of your pronunciation. Portuguese retains some old-fashioned modes of address which are seen as polite rather than formal, including *o senhor* and *a senhora* where English uses "you". This contrasts with the informality of cheek-kisses, used between men and women as well as between women in most situations except formal and business introductions. Men generally shake hands.

Although dress is generally relaxed these days, arms should be covered up and shorts should not be worn when visiting churches.

NEWSPAPERS AND MAGAZINES

English-language newspapers printed in Europe are available at large newsagents on the day of publication, including the American *International Herald Tribune*. Various other European newspapers and periodicals are generally on sale the day after home publication.

Portuguese dailies and the English APN

Portuguese daily newspapers include *Diário de Notícias* and *Público*. The weekly *Anglo-Portuguese News* (APN) is the Lisbon area's main English-language publication, catering largely to the British expatriate community along the Estoril coast. A similar publication for the Algarve region is the *Algarve News*.

RADIO AND TELEVISION

Portugal has two state-owned television channels, RTP1 and RTP2, and two privately-owned channels, SIC and TVI. Most foreign-language programmes are broadcast in the original language, with Portuguese subtitles. Other European and international broadcasts are available via satellite and cable, and include the usual 24-hour news, music, sports and feature channels. RDP radio broadcasts in English in the summer only.

FACILITIES FOR THE DISABLED

Facilities in Portugal for the disabled are limited at present, although the situation is gradually improving. Wheelchairs and adapted toilets are now available at most airports and the main stations, reserved car parking is becoming more evident and ramps and lifts are gradually being installed in public places. In addition, Lisbon and Oporto have a dial-a-ride bus service. To book, phone and indicate when and where you want to be picked up, and your destination. The operators speak only Portuguese, so you may need to ask your hotel for help. There is a special taxi service in Lisbon, but it has to be booked long in advance.

A dial-a-ride bus for the disabled *(transporte especial para deficientes)*

Women travellers admiring the view from the castle in Lisbon

WOMEN TRAVELLING ALONE

Travelling alone in Portugal is fairly safe for women although common principles, such as keeping to well-lit, public areas after dark, still apply. Some areas of Lisbon, such as the Baixa, Bairro Alto and Cais do Sodré, are best avoided at bar closing time. Resorts on the Algarve and Lisbon coasts tend to be the worst for unwanted attentions. Hitching alone is not safe; use taxis or public transport.

STUDENT INFORMATION

Young people aged 12–25 may buy a *Cartão Jovem*, (youth card), which costs about ¤5,99 and is valid for a year. It offers travel insurance and discounts for shops, museums, travel and youth hostels *(see p376)*. This card is supplied by the **Instituto Português da Juventude** (Portuguese Youth Institute). The International Student Identity Card (ISIC) provides the same benefits as the *Cartão Jovem* and can be bought in your own country.

RELIGION

Roman catholicism is the dominant religion in Portugal. Church services are held most evenings and every Sunday morning as well as on religious holidays. Sightseeing may be difficult (and is not encouraged) while services are in progress. Churches of other denominations, including the Church of England, Baptist, and Evangelical can be found in larger towns and cities. **St Vincent's Anglican Church**, which travels from place to place, holds a number of religious services in the Algarve.

PORTUGUESE TIME

Portugal and Madeira follow Britain in adopting Greenwich Mean Time (GMT) in winter and moving the clocks forward one hour from March to September (as in British Summer Time). In the Azores, clocks are one hour behind GMT in winter and the same as GMT in summer. The 24-hour clock is more commonly used throughout Portugal.

ELECTRICAL ADAPTORS

Voltage in portugal is 220 volts and plugs have two round pins. Most hotel bathrooms offer built-in adaptors for electric razors.

Worshippers leaving a church after mass in Trás-os-Montes

CONVERSION CHART

Imperial to Metric
1 inch = 2.54 centimetres
1 foot = 30 centimetres
1 mile = 1.6 kilometres
1 ounce = 28 grams
1 pound = 454 grams
1 pint = 0.6 litres
1 gallon = 4.6 litres

Metric to Imperial
1 millimetre = 0.04 inches
1 centimetre = 0.4 inches
1 metre = 3 feet 3 inches
1 kilometre = 0.6 miles
1 gram = 0.04 ounces
1 kilogram = 2.2 pounds
1 litre = 1.8 pints

Personal Health and Security

Pharmacy sign

PORTUGAL DOES not have a serious crime problem, but simple precautions should always be taken. Watch out for pickpockets in crowded areas and on public transport, avoid carrying large amounts of cash and don't leave valuables in parked cars. The police are helpful, but bureaucratic. Reporting a crime can be slow but is necessary. For minor complaints, consult a pharmacy.

Police station at Bragança in the Trás-os-Montes region

WHAT TO DO IN AN EMERGENCY

THE NUMBER to call in an emergency is 112. Dial the number and ask for the service you require – police *(polícia)*, ambulance *(ambulância)* or fire brigade *(bombeiros)*. If you need medical treatment, the casualty department *(serviço de urgência)* of the closest main hospital will treat you. On motorways and main roads, use the orange SOS telephone to call for help should you have a car accident. The service is in Portuguese; press the button and then wait for the operator who will connect you.

Motorway SOS telephone

HEALTH PRECAUTIONS

NO VACCINATIONS are needed for visitors, although doctors recommend being up-to-date with tetanus, diptheria and measles jabs. Tap water is safe to drink throughout the country. If you are visiting during the summer, it is advisable to bring insect repellent, as mosquitoes, while they do not present any serious health problems, can be a nuisance.

MEDICAL TREATMENT

SOCIAL SECURITY coverage is available for all EU nationals, although you may have to pay first and reclaim later. To reclaim, you must obtain an E111 form before you travel. This form is available at post offices throughout the UK or from the Department of

Health, with a booklet called *Health Advice for Travellers*, which explains entitlements and how to claim them. The E111 covers emergencies only, so medical insurance is strongly advised. Bear in mind that private health care is expensive in Portugal and get an itemized bill for your insurance carrier.

The **British Hospital** in Lisbon has English-speaking doctors, as do health centres on the Lisbon coast and throughout the Algarve. Details of these can be found in the local English newspapers.

PHARMACIES

PHARMACIES *(farmácias)* in Portugal can diagnose simple health problems and suggest appropriate treatment. Pharmacists can dispense a range of drugs that would

normally only be available on prescription in many other countries. The sign for a *farmácia* is a green cross on a white background. They are open from 9am to 1pm and 3pm to 7pm. Each pharmacy displays a card showing the address of the nearest all-night pharmacy and a list of those with late closing (10pm).

PORTUGUESE POLICE

IN ALL MAIN CITIES and towns, the police force is the *Polícia de Segurança Pública* (PSP). Law and order in rural areas is kept by the *Guarda Nacional Republicana* (GNR). The *Brigada de Trânsito* (traffic police) division of the GNR, recognizable by their red armbands, is responsible for patrolling roads.

PERSONAL SECURITY

VIOLENT CRIME is rare in Portugal, and the vast majority of visitors will experience no problems whatsoever. Nonetheless, a

Traffic policeman

Male PSP officer

Female PSP officer

Fire engine

Ambulance

Police car

few sensible precautions are worth taking: in Lisbon, avoid quiet areas such as the Baixa after dark, and don't stroll alone through Bairro Alto, Alfama or around Cais do Sodré after bars' closing time. In the daytime, be alert to the possibility of pickpockets or bag-snatchers. Similar precautions apply to some of the resorts in the Algarve and to the Ribeira district of Oporto.

It is generally a good idea to ignore any jeering, heckling or other provocations – they are usually not as serious as they can sound. Other precautions include not carrying large amounts of cash and holding on to mobile phones and cameras. If you are robbed, you are advised not to try to resist.

REPORTING A CRIME

IF YOU HAVE any property stolen, you should immediately contact the nearest police station. Theft of documents, such as a passport, should also be reported to your

consulate. Many insurance companies insist that policy holders report any theft within 24 hours. The police will file a report which you will need in order to claim from your insurance company on your return home. Contact the PSP in towns or cities, or the GNR in rural areas. In all situations, keep calm and be polite to the authorities to avoid delays. The same applies should you be involved in a car accident. In rural areas you may be asked to accompany the other driver to the nearest police station to complete the necessary paperwork. Ask for an interpreter if no one there speaks English.

Ladies' toilet sign

Men's toilet sign

DIRECTORY

EMERGENCY NUMBERS

General Emergency (Fire, Police, Ambulance)
📞 *112.*

Assistentes Intérpretes de Portugal
Avenida da República 41 3°,
1050-197, Lisbon.
📞 *21-799 43 60.*

British Hospital
Rua Saraiva de Carvalho 49,
1269-098 Lisbon.
📞 *21-395 50 67.*

Ordem dos Advogados
Largo de São Domingos 14, 1°,
1169-060 Lisbon.
📞 *21-882 3550.*

LEGAL ASSISTANCE

AN INSURANCE POLICY that covers the costs of legal advice, issued by companies such as Europ Assistance or Mondial Assistance, will help with the legal aspects of your insurance claim should you have an accident.

If you have not arranged this cover, call your nearest consulate or the **Ordem dos Advogados** (lawyers' association) who can give you names of English-speaking lawyers and help you with obtaining representation.

Lists of interpreters, if you require one, are given in the local Yellow Pages (Páginas Amarelas) under *Tradutores e Intérpretes*, or can be contacted through the **Assistentes Intérpretes de Portugal**, which is based in Lisbon.

PUBLIC CONVENIENCES

THE PORTUGUESE for toilets is *casa de banho*. If the usual figures of a man or woman are not shown, look for *homens*, *senhores* or *cavalheiros* (men) and *senhoras* or *damas* (ladies).

Toilet facilities are provided at service areas every 40 km (25 miles) and at drive-in rest areas on motorways.

Banking and Local Currency

BPI Bank Logo

Portugal is one of the founding members of the European Monetary Union and one of the countries that launched the euro in 2002. Conversion to the new currency went more smoothly than anyone had dared hope, but in some cases prices may still be quoted in both currencies. Traveller's cheques are the safest way to carry money, but cashing them can be quite expensive, and they are rarely accepted as payment. Credit and debit cards are often a more convenient option. Still, it is always a good idea to arrive with enough euros in cash to cover one or two days' expenditure.

Bank façade in Lisbon

BANKING HOURS

Banks are open between 8:30am and 3pm, Monday to Friday. Some branches stay open for longer, usually until 6pm – enquire at individual banks to find out which these are, as they sometimes change. Banks are closed at weekends and on public holidays.

CHANGING MONEY

Money can be changed at banks, bureaux de change (*agências de câmbios*) and at many hotels. Bank branches are everywhere, but their rates of exchange and commissions vary. Waiting times and bureaucratic practices at banks may also make them a worse option. Bureaux de change charge higher commissions than many banks but offer a more expedient service, as well as longer opening hours (including weekends). As a rule, hotels have the highest rates of exchange. At banks and bureaux de change you may be asked to show your passport or some other form of identification for exchange transactions.

If you are passing through Lisbon, a convenient alternative is to use one of a few currency exchange machines.

CHEQUES AND CARDS

Traveller's cheques are a safe but not very convenient way of carrying money in Portugal. It is rare for shops or hotels to accept them as payment, and cashing them may be quite expensive. In general, bureaux de change are better for this than banks, whose commissions may be high.

Most visitors, however, find it most practical and convenient to withdraw cash from an automatic teller machine (*Multibanco* or MB) using their credit/debit card. *Multibanco* machines are typically found outside bank branches or in shopping centres. Most accept Visa, MasterCard, American Express, Maestro and Cirrus. Bear in mind that transaction fees are always charged when withdrawing cash on a card, and that these are sometimes irrespective of the amount withdrawn. Fewer and larger withdrawals are therefore preferable to many small ones.

DIRECTORY

MAJOR BANKS

Banco Bilbao Vizcaya Argentária
Avenida da Liberdade 222, Lisbon.
(21-311 72 00.

Banco Potuguês de Investimento
Rua Tenente Valadim 284, Oporto.
(22-607 31 00.

Banco Santander
Rua Dr. Joiao Dias 16–17, Faro.
(289-86 08 20.

Barclays Bank
Avenida da República 50, Lisbon.
(21-780 08 77.

Caixa Geral de Depósitos
Rua do Ouro 49, Lisbon.
(21-342 86 09.

LOST CARDS OR TRAVELLER'S CHEQUES

American Express
(800 204 050.

MasterCard
(800 811 272.

Travelex
(01 733 294 451 or 452 (UK).

Visa
(800 811 824.

Fortress-like head office of Caixa Geral de Depósitos in Arco do Cego

THE EURO

TWELVE COUNTRIES have replaced their traditional currencies with a single European currency called the euro. Austria, Belgium, Finland, France, Germany, Greece, Ireland, Italy, Luxembourg, The Netherlands, Portugal and Spain chose to join the new currency; the UK, Denmark and Sweden stayed out, with an option to review their situation. The euro was introduced on 1 January 1999, but only for banking purposes, with notes and coins coming into general circulation on 1 January 2002. Euros can be used anywhere within the participating member states, dispensing with the frequent exchanges in currency that were previously necessary every time you travelled between these countries.

Bank Notes

Euro bank notes have seven denom-inations. The 5-euro note (grey in colour) is the smallest, followed by the 10-euro note (pink), 20-euro note (blue), 50-euro note (orange), 100-euro note (green), 200-euro note (yellow) and 500-euro note (purple). All notes show the 12 stars of the European Union.

5 euros

10 euros

20 euros

50 euros

100 euros

200 euros

500 euros

2 euros   1 euro   50 cents   20 cents   10 cents

Coins

The euro has eight coin denominations: 2 euros and 1 euro; 50 cents, 20 cents, 10 cents, 5 cents, 2 cents and 1 cent. The 2- and 1-euro coins are both silver and gold in colour. The 50-, 20- and 10-cent coins are gold. The 5-, 2- and 1-cent coins are bronze.

5 cents   2 cents   1 cent

Using the Telephone

ONCE NOTORIOUS for its unreliability, Portugal's telecommunications system is now fully modern. The visitor should have few problems using the telephone, with the possible exception of a few old-fashioned telephone booths. The previous monopoly of the state operator, Portugal Telecom, has been broken, and a price war is in full swing. Look out for special offers on phone cards, which are the best option when using a public telephone.

There are three mobile phone operators in Portugal: Telecel/Vodafone, TMN and Optimus. All have good coverage in most parts of the country.

English-style phone box

Post office *cabine* phone

USING A COIN PHONE

1 Lift receiver and wait for the dialling tone.

2 Insert coins into this slot one at a time.

3 The display shows amount of credit. If more money is required the message "*Inserir mais moedas por favor*" appears.

4 Key in telephone number and wait to be connected.

5 To make another call, press the follow-on call button.

6 Replace receiver after call. Unused coins will be refunded.

USING A CARD PHONE

1 Lift receiver and wait for the dialling tone.

2 Insert phonecard arrow side up, or credit card magnetic strip down.

3 The screen will display number of units available, then tell you to key in telephone number.

4 Key in number and wait to be connected.

5 If phonecard runs out in the middle of a call, it will re-emerge. Remove it and in-sert another one.

6 Replace receiver after call. When card re-emerges, remove it.

Phonecards are available in varying amounts

TELEPHONING IN PORTUGAL

PUBLIC PAY PHONES come in both the coin and the card variety, as well as in combinations of the two. They are found in booths in the street as well as in bars, cafés and shopping centres. Coin-operated phones now accept all denominations of euro and cent coins except the one-cent coin. Card operated phones are more common and more convenient, accepting a variety of phone cards available from post offices, newsagents, tobacconists and Telecom company outlets. Some also accept credit cards, although that incurs a small extra charge.

The cheapest way to use a payphone is with a phone card. The main operator, PT Comunicações (previously the monopoly holder and still the owner of the network), charges about three European cents per minute for a local call. International calls and calls to mobile phones are more expensive again, but there are special cards and deals to be had. An alternative is to phone from a post office, without having either change or card. You simply step into a free booth, make your call, and pay the cashier afterwards. The cost per unit is relatively low. Some cafés, restaurants and bars also have a units meter connected to their phone and calculate the cost of your call. They charge more than the post office but less than hotels.

For international calls and calls to mobile phones in particular, bear in mind that rates are lower between 9pm and 9am and at weekends and on public holidays.

REVERSE CHARGE CALLS

REVERSE CHARGE calls can be made from any telephone. Dial the *Directo* number listed at the front of the telephone directory, after the country and city dialling codes or dial 179 and ask for the *Directo* number to the country you wish to call. This number will put you in contact with an operator in the country you wish to call. For some countries, including the USA, there is a choice of carriers (eg AT&T or MCI).

A coin telephone covered by a shelter in Oporto

DIALLING CODES

- To make a call within each town or region, and also to call from one town or region to another, simply dial the nine-digit number that you require.
- To phone Portugal from abroad dial the Portugal country code (+ 351), and then the nine-digit local number that you require.
- To call abroad from Portugal, dial 00 and then the country code and local number you require. The telephone country code for US and Canada is 1; Ireland is 353; UK is 44; Australia is 61; and New Zealand is 64.
- Portugal's directory enquiries number is 118. For international directory enquiries dial 177.

Postal Services

Correios (postal service) logo

THE POSTAL SERVICE is known as the *Correios*. It is reasonably efficent: a letter sent to a country within the EU should take five to seven days, and a letter sent to the USA or further afield should take about seven to ten days. The *Correios* sign features a horse and rider in white on a red background.

SENDING A LETTER

FIRST-CLASS MAIL is known as *correio azul* and second-class mail is called *normal*. First-class letters are posted in blue postboxes and second-class post in red ones. At post offices there may be separate slots for national and international mail. There is also an express mail service called EMS, and for valuable letters, a recorded delivery service *(correio registado)* is available. Stamps *(selos)* can be bought from post offices or from any shop displaying the red and white *Correios* sign, and also from vending machines. These are found in airport terminals and in railway stations, as well as on the streets of large towns.

Portuguese stamps

POSTE RESTANTE

A MAIL-HOLDING service *(posta restante)* is also available at most major post offices. The envelope should carry the name of the recipient in block capitals, underlined, followed by *posta restante* together with the postcode and the name of the destination town. To collect the mail, take your passport and look for the counter that is marked *encomendas*. A small fee is charged for this service.

POST OFFICES

POST OFFICES are usually open from 9am until 6pm from Monday to Friday. Central post offices in major cities have different opening times. These are 8am–10pm from Monday to Friday and 9am–6pm on Saturdays.

PORTUGUESE ADDRESSES

PORTUGUESE ADDRESSES often include both the storey of a building and the location within that floor. The ground floor is the *rés-do-chão* (r/c), first floor *primeiro andar* (1°), the second floor is expressed as 2°, and so on. Each floor is divided into left, *esquerdo* (E or Esq^{do}), right, *direito* (D or D^{to}).

Portugal's Postboxes
First-class letters should be posted in blue (Correio Azul) boxes and second-class letters in red boxes.

Information on collection times | First-class postbox

Second-class postbox

Shops and Markets

TRADITIONAL ARTS and crafts have not been lost as a result of Portugal's modernization. Pottery, ceramics and tiles *(azulejos)* are produced everywhere with differing styles from town to town, while lace and embroidery are particularly good from Madeira. Cheeses, cured hams, sausages and wines can all be bought from local shops and markets; port, Madeira and spirits from wine shops or direct from the producer. Portugal is not an expensive country when compared with the rest of Europe, and prices are likely to be very reasonable for traditional craftwork and produce, especially away from the cities.

Serra cheese from the Serra da Estrela

produce, it also sells pottery, lace, rugs, and clothes. At the regional markets throughout the country a range of local produce is on sale such as cheeses, breads and hams. In this guide, the market days are given in the information that precedes each town entry. Where a regular date is given, but that date happens to fall at a weekend, the market is held on the nearest weekday.

Choosing fresh, locally grown vegetables and fruit at a typical roadside stall in the Alentejo

main square; ask for the *mercado* or *feira* if in doubt. Most markets sell a wide range of goods from food to household items and clothes, but you will also see sites devoted to antiques and local crafts. Roadside stalls are common, often selling produce from smallholdings. Most markets are held in the morning only, but in tourist areas they may go on until late afternoon.

Perhaps Portugal's largest and best-known market is the one in Barcelos *(see p273)* in the Minho, which is held every Thursday in the main square. As well as selling a vast range of household goods and local

RECLAIMING VAT

VALUE ADDED TAX (IVA) can be reclaimed by non-EU residents who stay for less than 180 days. Ask for an *Isenção de IVA* form or invoice in triplicate, describing the goods, quantity, value and buyer's identity (best done where you see the "Tax Free for Tourists" signs). Present the forms at customs on departure.

OPENING HOURS

SHOPS OPEN at 9 or 10am and close at 7pm and smaller shops or those in quieter areas close for lunch between 1pm and 3pm. Large shopping centres, which may include a supermarket, restaurants and banks, have sprouted all over Portugal recently. Opening times for shopping centres are usually from 10am until 11pm daily (including Sunday).

MARKETS

A SOCIAL AND commercial occasion, the street market is integral to Portuguese life. It is usually held in the town's

CERAMICS

IN MOST CITIES you can buy as well as commission ceramic tiles and panels. Portugal has a long-standing tradition in ceramics, both for decorative purposes and for home use *(see pp24–5)*. Styles range from elegant Vista Alegre porcelain to simple but classic terracotta crockery. Antique *azulejos* are highly sought after and very expensive, but you can buy reproductions of well-known historic designs at places such as Lisbon's Museu Nacional do Azulejo *(see pp122–3)*.

OTHER CRAFTS

PORTUGAL IS well known for its delicate embroidery and fine lace, and the best-known source is the island of Madeira. On the mainland, the best lace and embroidery comes from towns in the Minho such as Viana do Castelo, also famous for its brightly printed shawls. Embroidered bedspreads are sold in Castelo Branco in the Beira Baixa, and colourful carpets, such as those from Arraiolos *(see p301)*, are sold throughout the Alentejo.

Prices are very reasonable for knitwear, and woollen fishermen's sweaters from Nazaré *(see p180)*, which are often hand-knitted, can be good value.

Ceramics at the market in Barcelos *(see p273)*

Filigree jewellery *(filigrana)* from the Minho is typically worn at festivals and is sold locally. Gold and silver threads are worked into fine, intricately designed brooches, earrings and pendants. In theory, all the gold sold in Portugal must be at least 19 carats.

Wickerwork is another speciality of Madeira that is produced in large quantities. Colonial-style garden chairs are much sought after. Woven baskets are produced throughout the country and make delightful souvenirs. Cork from the Alentejo *(see p313)* is used to make articles, such as mats and ice buckets.

Embroidered handkerchiefs and table mats in Caldas do Gerês, the Minho *(see pp270–71)*

Locally-made baskets for sale in the Beiras region *(see p195)*

REGIONAL PRODUCE

I N PORTUGAL every region has its specialities and it is best to buy fresh items in the region where they are made, although most of the better-known regional produce can be found throughout the country. Cured ham *(presunto)* from the north of the country is particularly good in Chaves *(see pp256–7)*, and spicy pork sausages *(linguiça)* are a speciality of Oporto *(see pp236–41)*.

Regional cheeses include the delicious ewe's cheese Serra, which is produced from May to October in the Serra da Estrela *(see pp218–19)*, Ilha is a stronger, hard cheese from the Azores, and Queijinhos are small white cheeses produced in Tomar and the surrounding region *(see pp184–5)*.

WINES AND SPIRITS

W HILE IT MAY be best known for fortified wines such as port *(see pp228–9)* and Madeira *(see p349)*, Portugal also has a wide and varied range of excellent table wines *(see pp28–9)*. Some of the most characterful wines, particularly reds, are made in the Douro region, where port is also made. More approachable reds (and increasingly, whites) are made in the Alentejo, whose wines are much loved by the Portuguese themselves.

Home distilling is common throughout Portugal. Besides distilled wine *(aguardente)* and grape skins *(bagaço or bagaceira)*, various liqueurs are made with cherries *(ginjinha)*, almonds *(amêndoa)*, and figs *(figo)* – both commercially and in garages. A speciality of the Algarve is *medronheira*, a firewater made from the fruit of the strawberry tree *(see p289)*.

CLOTHING AND SHOES

P ORTUGAL HAS a thriving textile industry, but much of the country's production in clothes and shoes goes to supply well-known designer brands abroad. These clothes are not usually available in the shops. Some excellent-value seconds are on sale at local markets everywhere; a particularly well-known one is at Carcavelos between Lisbon and Estoril. However, beware of fakes, especially of upmarket labels. Leather goods such as shoes, gloves, belts and bags can be good buys, but prices will reflect the quality of the product.

Shopping for gloves in the Chiado area of Lisbon *(see pp92–3)*

SIZE CHART

Australia uses both British and American systems.

Women's dresses, coats and skirts

Portuguese	34	36	38	40	42	44	46
British	8	10	12	14	16	18	20
American	6	8	10	12	14	16	18

Women's shoes

Portuguese	36	37	38	39	40	41
British	3	4	5	6	7	8
American	5	6	7	8	9	10

Men's suits

Portuguese	44	46	48	50	52	54	56	58 (size)
British	34	36	38	40	42	44	46	48 (inches)
American	34	36	38	40	42	44	46	48 (inches)

Men's shirts

Portuguese	36	38	39	41	42	43	44	45 (size)
British	14	15	15½	16	16½	17	17½	18 (inches)
American	14	15	15½	16	16½	17	17½	18 (inches)

Men's shoes

Portuguese	39	40	41	42	43	44	45	46
British	6	7	7½	8	9	10	11	12
American	7	7½	8	8½	9½	10½	11	11½

Sporting Holidays and Outdoor Activities

ALTHOUGH IT IS A SMALL COUNTRY, Portugal offers an amazing variety of terrain, with sports and activities to match. Golf and tennis facilities have been well established for many years, and in the south the mild climate means that both sports can be enjoyed all year round. Other activities such as walking, cycling, riding and water sports are also widely enjoyed and easily arranged. Events are often organized on a local basis, so contact the regional tourist offices for the most up-to-date information on sporting facilities and events.

Walkers on the summit of Pico Ruivo in Madeira *(see p354)*

Windsurfing at sunset, Viana do Castelo *(see pp274–5)*

WATER SPORTS

SURFING, WINDSURFING and sailing are extremely popular along Portugal's 500 miles of coastline and around the Atlantic islands. The best beaches for surfing are on the Lisbon Coast at Ericeira *(see pp152–3)* and at Guincho *(see pp162–3)*. However, the ocean breakers are only suitable for experienced surfers. More moderate conditons can be found in the Algarve, where windsurfing boards and sailing dinghies can be rented and lessons easily arranged. In the Algarve, the marinas at Lagos and **Vilamoura** are important yachting centres.

For information on scuba-diving centres in Portugal, including Madeira and the Azores, contact the **Federação Portuguesa de Actividades Subaquáticas**.

Canoeing and kayaking are popular on many of the country's rivers, especially the Mondego, the Zêzere and the Cávado. For further details, contact the **Federação Portuguesa de Canoagem**.

WALKING AND CYCLING

BOTH THE PARQUE NATURAL de Montesinho *(see p260)* and the Parque National da Peneda-Gerês *(see pp270–71)* are good areas for walkers, but some of Portugal's best walks are on Madeira and the islands of São Miguel and São Jorge in the Azores. In Madeira you can walk alongside the *levadas* (irrigation channels), some of which date back to the 15th century *(see p354)*.

Portugal is well suited to mountain biking, although the country's hilly terrain may deter the less fit. Bikes can be hired in the Parque Nacional da Peneda-Gerês, which has many scenic mountain routes.

TENNIS AND GOLF

TENNIS COURTS are found practically everywhere in Portugal and certainly alongside most tourist facilities. In the Algarve, most of the courts in tourist complexes are hard, although elsewhere many are clay. The larger

GOLF COURSES IN THE ALGARVE

The majority of Portugal's best golf courses are concentrated in the Algarve, which has gained a reputation as one of Europe's prime golfing destinations. The climate ensures that games can be enjoyed year round, and many courses have been designed by leading professsionals such as Henry Cotton. Some of the top courses insist that players demonstrate a reasonable degree of proficiency, while others welcome golfers of any ability and provide excellent coaching. Serious golfers might consider booking a specialist holiday.

Golfers enjoying a game at Vale do Lobo in the Algarve

Algarve resorts and a few other places offer tennis coaching holidays.

Portugal's resorts are famous for their golf courses, which include some of Europe's best. Many offer coaching for golfers of all abilities and specialist holidays are easy to arrange. Most courses are in the Algarve and the Lisbon area, but there are good facilities elsewhere. Despite its rocky, mountainous terrain, Madeira has two fine courses: Santo da Serra in the east of the island and Palheiro Golf, high above Funchal. For comprehensive information on golf courses throughout Portugal go to the useful website www.portugal-info.net. For detailed information on Algarve courses try www.algarvegolf.net.

FISHING

ALONG THE COASTS and rivers of Portugal are plenty of opportunities for the fisherman, from deep sea fishing off the shores of the Algarve, Madeira and the Azores, to angling in the mainland rivers for trout. You will need to obtain a licence, available from the **Instituto Florestal**.

HORSE RIDING

PORTUGAL ENJOYS a famous riding tradition as a result of the country's fine Lusitano horses. In the Algarve, **Quinta dos Amigos** and **Vale de Ferro** are well-known riding schools. Other popular locations include the Alentejo, and the Peneda-Gerês National Park in the north of Portugal.

Immaculate fairway at Vilamoura

11 Pine Cliffs *(289-500 113)*.
12 Vilamoura *(general: 289-310 333)*.
   Laguna *(289-310 180)*.
   Millennium *(289-310 188)*.
   Old Course *(289-310 341)*.
   Pinhal *(289-310 390)*.
13 Vila Sol *(289-300 522)*.
14 Vale do Lobo
   Ocean Course *(289-353 465)*.
   Royal Course *(289-353 465)*.
15 Quinta do Lago
   Pinheiros Altos *(289-359 910)*.
   Quinta do Lago *(289-390 700)*.
   Ria Formosa *(289-390 700)*.
   San Lorenzo *(289-396 522)*.
16 Benamor *(281-320 880)*.
17 Quinta da Ria and Quinta de
   Cima *(281-950 580)*.
18 Castro Marim *(281-510 330)*.

1 Parque da Floresta *(282-690 054)*.
2 Boavista *(282-782 151)*.
3 Palmares *(282-790 500)*.
4 Penina *(282-420 200)*.
5 Alto Golf *(282-460 870)*.
6 Gramacho *(282-340 900)*.
7 Pinta *(282-340 900)*.
8 Vale do Milho *(282-358 953)*.
9 Salgados *(289-583 030)*.
10 Balaia *(289-570 442)*.

TRAVEL INFORMATION

PORTUGAL, MADEIRA and Porto Santo, as well as the major Azorean islands, have airports served by TAP, the national airline. European and other airlines fly to the international airports of Lisbon, Oporto, Faro and Funchal, which all get busier during the holiday season. Charter flights, which may or may not be part of a package deal, are often the cheapest alternative. Portugal's mainland rail network is fast and modern on busy lines such as Lisbon-Oporto and slow on provincial lines. Trains are inexpensive, especially if you are eligible for any of the discounts. Buses are sometimes faster and generally offer a wider choice of departures than the rail network. Car rental is not cheap (pre-arranged package deals are often the best value), but obviously offers the greatest flexibility. Diesel costs less than petrol, while motorway tolls can be expensive. Road users should also be aware that Portugal has one of Europe's highest road accident rates.

Logo of TAP Air Portugal

---

flights from London (three from Heathrow and two from Gatwick) to Lisbon and one to Oporto (from Heathrow), plus several weekly ones. It is worth checking the internet for bargains (TAP auctions flights online every Thursday, under "virtual auction" on www.tap.pt).

Faro is the usual Portuguese destination for charter flights and low-cost airlines, particularly during the holiday season. Many fly to Lisbon as well.

Funchal and Porto Santo are also package holiday destinations, which means that charter flights may be available. The Azores are becoming a more accessible holiday destination, in terms of flights and prices (see p441).

Check-in at Lisbon Airport

ARRIVING BY AIR

LISBON, AND TO A lesser extent Oporto, have regular scheduled flights from European capitals and major cities, including London, Paris, Madrid, Rome, Munich, Frankfurt, Zurich and Milan. Most of these are daily, and in many cases there are several daily connections. **TAP**, Portugal's national carrier, currently operates five daily

Signs at the airport for visitors' facilities

LONG-HAUL FLIGHTS

TRAVELLERS FROM North America will usually have to change at some European hub. **Delta** flies to Lisbon via Paris (using a partner airline) daily or twice daily. TAP's only direct flights from the US are out of Newark. South America is better served thanks to Portugal's ties with Brazil: TAP has direct flights to and from several Brazilian destinations, as does the Brazilian national carrier, **VARIG**.

There are no direct flights to mainland Portugal from Canada, Australia or New Zealand. London is the usual hub for flights from these countries.

AIRPORT	ℹ INFORMATION	DISTANCE TO CITY CENTRE	TAXI FARE TO CITY CENTRE	PUBLIC TRANSPORT TO CITY CENTRE
Lisbon	21-841 35 00	7 km (4 miles)	€7–10	🚌 20 minutes
Oporto	22-943 24 00	20 km (12 miles)	€15–20	🚌 30 minutes
Faro	289-80 08 00	6 km (4 miles)	€8	🚌 15 minutes
Funchal	291-52 49 41	18 km (11 miles)	€18–24	🚌 30 minutes
Ponta Delgada	296-20 54 00	3 km (2 miles)	€6	🚌 10 minutes
Horta	292-94 35 11	10 km (6 miles)	€7–8	🚌 15 minutes

North Americans wanting to visit the Azores will find a greater choice of direct connections, due to the large Azorean communities in the US and Canada. The same is true of the ever-popular Madeira.

AIR FARES

CHARTER FLIGHTS are available to Lisbon and Faro, particularly during the summer months. Tickets always have fixed outward and return dates, but as they are often cheaper than a regular one-way ticket, many passengers only use the outward flight. Some charter companies now re-sell empty return seats at very competitive prices.

Major low-cost airlines such as easyJet and Ryanair fly weekly or several times a week to Faro – Ryanair currently only from Dublin, while easyJet flies from Luton, Stansted, East Midlands and Bristol. bmibaby is another low-cost airline with a weekly flight to Faro, from East Midlands.

Shuttle service stop, Lisbon Airport

Much the best way of getting a cheap ticket is to check websites such as www.cheapflights.com which offer an overview of currently available deals. These are not necessarily on low-cost airlines, as regular airlines sell quotas of low-cost seats or unsold ones via a network of agents.

PACKAGE DEALS

SPECIALIST HOLIDAYS are now a popular option in Portugal. These include stays in manor houses and *pousadas*

TAP Air Portugal aircraft on the tarmac at Lisbon Airport

(see pp378–9), short breaks to Lisbon and Oporto, tennis and golfing holidays in the Algarve especially, and walking holidays in the Minho. These, together with package deals including hotel, villa or apartment accommodation, will often provide inclusive bus service to your destination from the airport. Fly-drive deals are also available, to the Algarve especially, that mean you spend less time at the airport dealing with paperwork. Car hire, when booked as part of a package deal, may be very reasonable. Travel agents sell these holidays but a list of companies specializing in them on the mainland and the islands is available from **ICEP**, the National Tourist Office.

INTERNAL FLIGHTS

TAP ALSO FLIES, between major domestic destinations, including Lisbon, Oporto, Faro and Funchal. **Portugália**, Portugal's privately owned second airline, has an extensive domestic network (and a growing European one). In

partnership with **SATA**, **TAP** flies daily from Lisbon and Oporto to Funchal and from Lisbon to São Miguel, Terceira and Faial in the Azores.

DIRECTORY

ARRIVING BY AIR

British Airways
London ☏ 0845-77 333 77.

TAP Air Portugal
London ☏ 020-87 62 73 76.
Dublin ☏ 01-679 88 44.
Lisbon ☏ 707-205 700.

LONG-HAUL FLIGHTS

American Airlines
US ☏ 800-433 73 00.

Continental Airlines
US ☏ 800-525 17 00.

Delta
US ☏ 800 221 1212.

SATA
Boston ☏ 508-677 0555.
Toronto ☏ 416-515 71 88.

PACKAGE DEALS

ICEP
Portuguese Trade & Tourism Office,
22–25a Sackville Street,
London W1X 2LY.
☏ 09063-640 640.

INTERNAL FLIGHTS

Portugália
Lisbon ☏ 21-842 55 00.

SATA
Ponta Delgada ☏ 296-20 97 27.

TAP shuttle bus waiting to leave for central Lisbon

Travelling by Rail

THE PORTUGUESE STATE RAILWAY, Caminhos de Ferro Portugueses (CP) provides an inexpensive, country-wide network. Quality of service can vary considerably, however, and much modernization to the system is still in the planning stage. The Alfa train between Lisbon and Oporto, via Coimbra, is fast and efficient, but for some other long journeys, such as Lisbon to Évora, it may be quicker and more comfortable to take the bus.

Carved arch over entrance to Lisbon's Rossio station *(see p82)*

ARRIVING BY TRAIN

THERE ARE TWO main routes into Portugal by train. The first is to travel from Austerlitz station in Paris, changing at Irún on the French-Spanish border, then continuing on to the Portuguese border town of Vilar Formoso in the north. The train splits near Coimbra, heading north for Oporto and south for Lisbon, coming into Santa Apolónia station. The entire journey from London to Lisbon, using the Eurostar to reach Paris, takes 30 hours.

The alternative route is to travel on the overnight train from Madrid, passing through Marvão and Santarém, then on to Lisbon. Travel from Madrid into Lisbon takes 10 hours. This train, called the "hotel-train", has luxurious carriages, some of which have showers.

TRAVELLING BY TRAIN

MOST AREAS of Portugal are served by rail, although the more remote lines, such as Mirandela to Bragança, have sadly been made obsolete as new roads are built. A bus service covers any gaps in the system, although it is wise to confirm that the service you require exists before setting off.

There are several categories of train in Portugal. The most comfortable and quickest is the modern, high-speed Alfa, which travels between Lisbon, Coimbra and Oporto. The Rápido Inter-Cidades (IC), is only marginally slower, although less luxurious, and connects most important towns and cities. Most smaller

Logo for Caminhos de Ferro Portugueses

towns and villages throughout the country are served by the Regional and the Inter-Regional lines. As you would expect, these local lines are considerably slower than the Rápido and Alfa, and the trains are less comfortable, with fewer facilities. However, they stop at a great many more stations.

High-speed Alfa train at Santa Apolónia Station in Lisbon

CITY STATIONS

LISBON HAS FOUR rail termini. Santa Apolónia station, on Avenida Infante Dom Henrique to the east of the Alfama district, serves the north and all international destinations. A new station, **Oriente**, by the Expo site, Parque das Nações, and on the same line as Santa Apolónia, was opened in 1998. For routes south and east you must cross the Tagus by ferry to catch the train from **Barreiro** station. The ferry departs from the terminal next to Praça do Comércio. West of here is the **Cais do Sodré** station, from where trains leave for Estoril and Cascais. The trip to Cascais takes around 30 minutes.

Rossio station, near Praça dos Restauradores, serves Sintra, about 45 minutes away, and stations north along the coast as far as Figueira da Foz. Care should be taken on the Lisbon to Sintra line at night.

Coimbra has two mainline stations: trains from Lisbon and Oporto stop at **Coimbra B**, a five-minute shuttle ride from the central **Coimbra A**.

Oporto has two mainline stations: international and long-distance trains come into **Campanhã**, to the east of the city and regional and sub-urban trains come into **São Bento** in the centre. From here there is a shuttle service to **Campanhã** station. The former rail station at Trindade will become a Metro station.

Exterior of station at Santiago do Cacém with *azulejo* decoration

Time Destination Platform Type of train Other remarks

Departures board in Santa Apolónia Station, Lisbon

FARES

FARES WITHIN PORTUGAL are fairly cheap in comparison with other European countries, and there are numerous discounts available. Children

PORTUGAL'S PRINCIPAL RAILWAY LINES

under the age of four travel free, and those from four to twelve pay half-fare. There are also discounts for groups, students and pensioners.

First-class travel on Portugal's trains is 40 per cent more expensive than second class, and second-class travel, while fairly basic on some lines, is usually sufficiently comfortable.

Visitors who intend to do much travelling by train might consider buying a tourist ticket *(bilhete turístico)*. This is valid for an unlimited number of journeys for 7, 14 or 21 consecutive days, and can be used on all the different types of train.

Families can save money by using the *cartão de família*, which gives good discounts, but only on journeys over 150 km (90 miles). It works as follows: one member of the family pays full fare, other members over 13 years of age pay half the full fare, and those under 13 pay a quarter of the fare.

An Interrail pass for young people under 26 gives unlimited travel on all European trains for a month, so will allow travel both to and within Portugal (if it is bought outside the country). The slightly more expensive Interrail 26-plus pass does not allow travel in Spain. For journeys within Portugal only, the Eurodomino pass offers unlimited travel for three, five or ten days, with a reduced rate for those younger than 26.

BUYING TICKETS

TICKETS FOR Alfa and Rápido (IC) trains can usually be booked up to 20 days ahead, although some services only offer 10-day advance bookings, so it is important to check first. Reservations can be made at stations or travel agents. If you want to buy a ticket the day you travel, arrive early as long queues at the ticket office are normal, especially during peak hours and holiday periods. It is important that you buy a ticket before boarding, otherwise you are liable to be fined on the spot by the conductor.

Comboios de amanhã e dias seguintes

Sign at ticket office showing where to buy advance tickets

Só para Comboios de hoje

Sign at ticket office showing where to buy tickets on day of travel

TIMETABLES

MAIN STATIONS in Portugal provide a complete rail timetable, the Guia do Horário Oficial. This has details of all routes for IC, Inter-Regional and Regional trains, and a section in Portuguese only which details the tickets and discounts that are available.

Driving in Portugal

Automóvel Clube de Portugal logo

PORTUGAL'S ROAD NETWORK includes an expanding motorway system, but some older main roads may be in need of repair, while minor roads can be very rough and tortuous. Traffic jams are a problem in and near cities. Never attempt driving in the rush hour, and be wary of reckless Portuguese drivers. Always carry your passport, licence, log book or rental contract, and car insurance. Failure to produce these *documentos* if the police stop you will incur a fine.

A steep road near Gouveia in the Serra da Estrela *(see pp218–9)*

Disembarking at Setúbal after crossing on the car ferry from Tróia

ARRIVING BY CAR

THE QUICKEST ROUTE is to cross the French-Spanish border at Irún and then take the E80 via Valladolid to Vilar Formoso in Portugal. To go to Lisbon or the Algarve, turn off at Burgos, head for Cáceres and then on to Badajoz.

Taking the car ferry to northern Spain from the UK reduces time on the road, but crossings are extremely long: 24 hours to Santander and 35 hours to Bilbao. **Brittany Ferries** travel to Santander leaving from Plymouth (March to November), and from Portsmouth (November to January). **P & O**'s Portsmouth-Bilbao line runs all year round, and all routes operate twice-weekly. There are no ferries travelling to Madeira or the Azores.

Driving time may also be reduced by using the Motorail link from Paris Gare d'Austerlitz to Lisbon, a twice-weekly service. Drivers load their cars one day, travel by passenger train the next, and pick up their cars on the third day. **French Railways** in the UK will supply information.

CAR HIRE

CAR HIRE AGENCIES may be found at Lisbon, Faro and Oporto airports and in main towns. Local firms usually offer better rates than international ones, but you should check the condition of the car more carefully before you accept it, as well as the insurance coverage. You must have an international driving licence, be over the age of 23 and have held a licence for at least one year.

TRAVELLING AROUND BY CAR

MAJOR ROADS include EN *(Estrada Nacional)* roads, many of which have been upgraded to either IP *(Itinerário Principal)* or IC *(Itinerário Complementar)* roads. IP roads are much used by heavy goods lorries avoiding motorway tolls, and can be slow as a result.

Always fill up with petrol in town before setting off, as petrol stations can be scarce in remote areas. The best road maps are by Michelin or the Portuguese motoring organization, the ACP *(Automóvel Clube de Portugal)*.

PARKING

FINDING A PARKING space in cities can be difficult. Most parking spaces in Lisbon and Oporto are now pay-and-display during the working week. A simpler and safer, if more expensive, alternative is one of the many new underground car parks. Follow the blue signs with a white P.

PETROL

PETROL IS RELATIVELY expensive and generally the same price countrywide. Diesel *(gasóleo)* is cheaper than petrol, both leaded and unleaded. Some pumps are self-service and colour-coded: green for unleaded, red for leaded and black for diesel.

Traffic queueing to pass over the Ponte 25 de Abril, Lisbon

RULES OF THE ROAD

TRAFFIC DRIVES on the right hand side, continental rules of the road apply and the international sign system is used. Unless there are signs to the contrary, traffic from the right has priority at squares, crossroads and junctions. Cars on roundabouts travel anticlockwise, and have priority over waiting traffic. There is very little advance warning of pedestrian crossings.

Seat belts must be used and the alcohol limit is 0.05 per cent. Speed limits are 60 kph in towns and 90 kph on other roads (37 mph and 55 mph), and 120 kph (74 mph) on motorways. Breaking the speed limit incurs an on-the-spot fine.

ESTORIL

SUL-PONTE

SETE RIOS

Signs in Lisbon for the coast, south via the Ponte 25 de Abril, and zoo

MOTORWAYS AND TOLLS

PORTUGAL'S EXPANDING motorway network (*see map on back endpaper*) links Lisbon with Braga and Guimarães in the north, and Oporto with Amarante. Another section goes from Lisbon to Torres Vedras, and a cross-country stretch runs east to the Spanish border at Elvas. Apart from some sections near Lisbon and Oporto, all motorways have

A motorway toll – the left lane reserved for users of the Via Verde system

two lanes. Tolls are payable on motorways and on Lisbon's bridges, the Ponte 25 de Abril and the new Ponte Vasco da Gama. Do not use the Via Verde (green lane) at tolls; this is only for the use of drivers who subscribe to an electronic system allowing them to pay automatically.

BREAKDOWN SERVICES

THERE IS a reciprocal breakdown service between **ACP** and other organizations. To qualify, drivers should take out European cover with their own organization. Motorways have SOS phones, and if you use them, state that you are entitled to ACP cover. For drivers without cover, most towns have a garage with breakdown lorry.

CYCLING

THE SOUTH IS the best area for cycling, but in summer the Alentejo can be too hot. If you plan on doing a lot of cycling, **Instituto Português de Cartografia e Cadastro** sells good large-scale maps.

ROAD NUMBERS

Roads in Portugal may have up to three different numbers. Thanks to a building and upgrading programme, former EN or *Estrada Nacional* roads can also be IP (*Itinerário Principal*) roads. A road with an E (*Estrada Europeia*) number indicates that it is also a direct international route.

The Bragança-Oporto road is now the IP4, part motorway (A4) and part dual carriageway.

IP 4

210

E 82

The road's original EN number (*Estrada Nacional*)

The E82 is an international route, ending in Spain near Valladolid.

Travelling by Coach

The logo of EVA, one of the country-wide coach companies

SINCE THE PRIVATIZATION of Portugal's bus network, the Rodoviária Nacional (RN), coach companies have multiplied and some routes are now even operated by foreign companies. Regional operators compete with each other to offer better services to more destinations, and as a result, many coach journeys, such as Lisbon to the Algarve, are quicker and often more comfortable than the equivalent train journeys. Coaches also cover the increasing number of defunct sections of railway, such as Mirandela-Bragança and Beja-Moura.

offers daytrips running from Lisbon to Évora and Coimbra, a cruise on the Tagus and a trip lasting three days to the Algarve. Pick-up points are at the main hotels or central locations. It is also possible to arrange longer trips to areas of historical or scenic interest.

In the Algarve, there are frequent coach trips to places of interest such as Loulé, Silves and Monchique, the southwest and the River Guadiana, and further afield to Évora and Lisbon. Tourist offices, hotels and travel agencies can help with these, and pick-up points are the main coastal hotels.

A Rodonorte coach, which covers the far north of the country

GETTING TO PORTUGAL BY COACH

TRAVELLING TO PORTUGAL by coach is cheap but very time-consuming. **Eurolines** runs a weekly summer service from Victoria Coach Station in London to Oporto, avoiding Paris. Passengers change in Valladolid in central Spain, and the journey takes 31 hours in total. The London to Lisbon service, which runs all year, takes even longer. Passengers change in Paris and spend two nights on the coach.

TRAVELLING AROUND BY COACH

COACH OPERATORS in Portugal include **Renex**, who link Faro, Lisbon, Oporto and Braga, and **EVA** which focuses on the Algarve. **Rodoviária de Lisboa** connects Lisbon with Estremadura. In Vila Real, **Rodonorte** covers the extreme north, and **Rede Expressos**, based in Oporto, covers the inland areas of Portugal.

There is no central coach station in either Lisbon or Oporto as companies are private and operate separately, but the main coach terminus in Lisbon is on Avenida Casal Ribeiro. In Oporto, the main departure and arrival points are at Rua das Carmelitas and

Praça Dona Filipa de Lencastre. Information on routes and prices is available from tourist offices and travel agencies.

COACH TOURS

BUS AND COACH tours around Lisbon and Oporto are plentiful. **Citirama** runs sightseeing tours of Lisbon and its coast, and daytrips to sights such as Batalha, Sintra and Mafra. It also offers a night-time tour of the city, taking in the Jerónimos monastery and then dinner with a *fado* show. From Oporto, it runs tours of the Minho and Douro valleys, and a six-day trip to Lisbon. **Gray Line**, part of Citirama, also

A Cityrama coach on an excursion along the Lisbon coast

Travelling Around the Islands

O N THE ROCKY, MOUNTAINOUS ISLANDS of Madeira and the Azores, the pace of transport is necessarily slow, and some places are only accessible on foot. Driving needs care and patience, and you may find organized trips by coach or taxi are more relaxing and rewarding.

Inter-island aircraft on the runway on Pico

ISLAND HOPPING

T AP FLIES SEVERAL times a day between Funchal and Porto Santo in the Madeira group, and on the Azores, flights are operated by SATA *(see p441)*. Flights to Flores and Corvo are often disrupted by adverse weather conditions, so for extensive island hopping it is a good idea to insure against delays. SATA flights should be confirmed at least 72 hours before take-off.

Logo of the Azorean airline

The most useful ferry connections are between the five central islands of the Azores, especially the Faial-Pico run.

AROUND MADEIRA

B USES OPERATE throughout Madeira, but cater mainly for islanders' needs. However, companies such as **Intervisa**

and **Blandy** organize coach trips around the island. Taxis can be hired by the day or half-day, but car hire offers the most flexibility *(see p444)*. Book well ahead and allow plenty of time for journeys: roads are steep, tortuous and full of potholes. The new road along the south coast was finally finished in 1999, but many places are still accessible only on foot.

AROUND THE AZORES

C ARS CAN BE HIRED on all the Azores except Corvo, from firms such as **Ilha Verde Rent-A-Car**. Charges are high compared to the mainland and the roads are precipitous, so it may be more restful, at least on the smaller islands, to take a tour by taxi. Many drivers speak English, and they often make memorable companions. Before setting off on a day trip, you should agree a price, itinerary and return time. You should also offer to pay for the driver's lunch. Check the weather beforehand: if the mountains and calderas are concealed by clouds, there is no point setting out. Buses are cheap but, as on Madeira, of little use to visitors. Tourist offices can supply information on coach trips by **Agência Açoreana de Viagens** and others, and also on boat trips along the coast. Bicycles can be hired, but the mountainous terrain makes cycling difficult. On the smaller islands you can usually hitch a lift with ease.

The best way to enjoy the Azores is on foot. Taxi drivers are willing to drop visitors off at the start of a route and pick them up further on. Detailed maps of the Azores are hard to find, so try to acquire one prior to arrival. Some routes are described in the specialist guidebooks sold locally.

DIRECTORY

MADEIRA

Blandy
Avenida Zarco 2,
Funchal.
291-20 06 91.

Intervisa
Avenida Arriaga 30, Funchal.
291-22 56 41.

AZORES

Agência Açoreana de Viagens
Lado Sul da Matriz 68–9,
Ponta Delgada, São Miguel.
296-28 54 37.

Ilha Verde Rent-A-Car
Praça 5 de Outubro 19,
Ponta Delgada.
296-28 52 00.

THE AZORES: INTER-ISLAND FLIGHTS AND FERRIES

KEY

_ _ Flight routes

.... Ferry routes

Corvo

Flores

Graciosa

São Jorge

Terceira

Faial

Pico

Ponta Delgada

São Miguel

Santa Maria

0 kilometres 100

0 miles 50

Travelling within Cities

Sign for Metro in Lisbon

THE INTERESTING parts of most towns and cities in Portugal – generally the *centró histórico*, – are small and eminently walkable, if you have both the time and inclination. In hilly cities such as Oporto and, particularly, Lisbon, the steep climbs can be avoided by using a choice of options such as centenarian tram, funicular or lift. Other cities are well served by buses, trolleybuses and taxis. Transport of any kind should be avoided during rush hour (8–10am and 5:30–7:30pm).

BUSES

BUSES ARE A PRACTICAL way to travel round and see the main cities, and Lisbon has an extensive network. When boarding the bus, enter at the front door and exit by the central door.

Tickets may be bought from the driver on boarding and are clipped by the *(obliterador)* machine near the driver. However, it is cheaper to buy tickets beforehand, usually for two journeys. Travelling without a valid ticket, if discovered by roaming inspectors, will incur a hefty fine. Every bus *(autocarro)* displays its destination *(destino)* at the front and most bus stops *(paragens)* have information about the route that the bus will take.

LISBON METRO

LISBON'S METRO network currently has four lines, mainly on the north-south axis, and is the most efficient way to get around, particularly during the rush hour (8–10am and 5:30–8pm approximately) when the city is full of traffic. The network is set to expand further north and west.

Tickets are bought in machines or from ticket offices at the stations. They must be validated on entering the platform area and on leaving the station. In most stations, there are now gates that open on insertion of a valid ticket, or there is a small stamping machine to use. Fines for travelling without a valid ticket are severe. The Metro operates between 6am and 1am.

No. 15, Lisbon's new longer, streamlined tram

Antique red tram operating the Linha do Tejo tour in Lisbon

BUS TOURS

IN OPORTO, **Gray Line** runs city tours at least twice a week, and more often in summer. They include a visit to a port lodge with tasting *(see p247)*. Tickets are sold at the Gray Line office, and the tourist office in Praça Dom João I, from where the buses depart. Citirama runs a once-weekly tour of Coimbra. They have no office there, but the tourist office can take bookings and enquiries, and the bus departs from just outside.

TRAMS AND FUNICULARS

FUN WAYS of exploring Lisbon are by tram *(eléctrico)*, funicular or lift (both *elevador*), while Oporto has one short tram route along the waterfront. In Lisbon, **Carris** runs a "hill tour" *(Linha das Colinas)* by antique tramcar.

Single trip Metro ticket   **Discounted Carris ticket**

TICKETS IN LISBON

Buses, trams and funiculars accept the same tickets, which can be bought from Carris kiosks around the city. The basic multi-trip Carris ticket is for two journeys. They are valid for an unlimited number of days. Other options are 1 and 3-day tickets. The Metro has its own ticket system. The choice is between a single-trip or a two-trip ticket, or a ten-trip ticket valid for an unlimited number of days. There are also 1, 7 or 30-day passes, and combined Carris/Metro 1-day tickets. Tourist Passes are valid for 4 or 7 days on both Carris and the Metro. Visitors may require ID to buy them.

Lisbon's Elevador da Glória ascending to the Bairro Alto

Funiculars offer wonderful views over Lisbon (as well as saving tired legs) and there are a variety that ascend from river level up to the Bairro Alto: the Elevador da Bica starts near Cais do Sodré station and the Elevador da Glória goes from Praça dos Restauradores. Although the lifts in the Elevador de Santa Justa remain open to visitors using the café at the top, closure of the walkway for works means the lift does not currently link the Baixa with the Bairro Alto *(see p86)*.

The Elevador da Lavra climbs from Praça dos Restauradores up to the Hospital São José.

TAXIS

TAXIS HAVE traditionally been black with a green roof, but these have been phased out in favour of a beige livery. They are relatively cheap and if you share the cost it sometimes works out cheaper than a bus or tram. Vacant taxis have their rooftop "taxi" signs switched on, but it is sometimes difficult to see if they are lit. From behind, they glow counter-intuitively red. The green lights indicate that the taxi is taken; two green lights mean that the higher rate is being charged (10pm–6am, weekends and public holidays), one that the normal rate applies. A flat rate

of €1.50 is charged for any luggage placed in the trunk.

The starting rate for a taxi hailed in the street or taken at a taxi rank is €1.80. A telephone callout from a firm such as **Autocoope** costs an extra €0.75. The meter should always be used, although the driver might suggest agreeing on a price beforehand for very long trips.

LISBON'S METRO SYSTEM

Falagueira
Alfornetos
Pontinha
Carnide
Colégio Militar/Luz
Laranjeiras
Jardim Zoológico
Praça De Espanha

Alto dos Moinhos
São Sebastião

Quinta das Mouras
Campo Grande
Telheiras
Cidade Universitária
Entre Campos
Campo Pequeno

Ameixoeira
Lumiar
Alvalade

Odivelas
Senhor Roubado
Roma

Oriente
Cabo Ruivo
Olivais Sul
Chelas
Bela Vista
Olaias

Areeiro

Saldanha
Picoas
Marquês De Pombal
Rato
Avenida
Restauradores
Cais do Sodré

Parque

Alameda
Arroios
Anjos
Intendente
Martim Moniz
Rossio
Baixa-Chiado
Terreiro do Paço
Santa Apolónia

KEY

— Linha azul
— Linha amarela
— Linha verde
— Linha vermelha
— Under construction

General Index

Acknowledgments

DORLING KINDERSLEY would like to thank the following people whose contributions and assistance have made the preparation of this book possible.

CONSULTANT
MARTIN SYMINGTON was born and brought up in Portugal. A freelance travel writer, he is the author of *New Essential Portugal* (AA), and contributed to *Eyewitness Great Britain* and *Eyewitness Seville and Andalusia*. He writes extensively on Portugal and is a regular contributor to the *Daily Telegraph*, *Sunday Telegraph* and other British national newspapers.

CONTRIBUTORS
SUSIE BOULTON studied history of art at Cambridge. She is a freelance travel writer and author of *Eyewitness Venice and the Veneto*.

CHRISTOPHER CATLING is a freelance travel writer and author of *Madeira* (AA) and *Eyewitness Florence & Tuscany*. He also contributed to *Eyewitness Italy* and *Eyewitness Great Britain*.

MARION KAPLAN has written for a wide range of magazines and newspapers. She has lived in Portugal and wrote *The Portuguese* (Viking/Penguin 1992). She also contributed to the *Berlitz Travellers Guide to Portugal*.

SARAH MCALISTER is a freelance editor and writer for *Time Out* guides and has spent much time in Lisbon and the surrounding area.

ALICE PEEBLES is a freelance editor and writer and has worked on several *Eyewitness Travel Guides*.

CAROL RANKIN was born in Portugal. As an art historian, she has lectured extensively on most aspects of Portuguese art and architecture and has acted as consultant for various cultural projects.

JOE STAINES is a freelance writer and co-author of *Exploring Rural Portugal* (Helm).

ROBERT STRAUSS is a travel writer and publisher. He worked for the Luso-British Institute in Oporto and has written several titles for Lonely Planet and Bradt Publications including the Portugal sections for *Western Europe* and *Mediterranean Europe* (Lonely Planet 1993).

NIGEL TISDALL is a freelance journalist who has written many articles on the Azores. He also contributed to *France*, *Spain* and *California* in the Eyewitness Travel Guide series.

EDITE VIEIRA has written many books on Portuguese food including *The Taste of Portugal* (Grub Street). She is a member of the Guild of Food Writers and broadcasts regularly for the BBC World Service.

ADDITIONAL CONTRIBUTORS
Dr Giray Ablay, Gerry Stanbury, Paul Sterry, Paul Vernon.

ADDITIONAL ILLUSTRATIONS
Richard Bonson, Chris Forsey, Chris Orr, Mel Pickering, Nicola Rodway.

DESIGN AND EDITORIAL ASSISTANCE
Gillian Allan, Douglas Amrine, Gillian Andrews, Vivien Crump, Joy FitzSimmons, Paul Hines, Esther Labi, Kathryn Lane, Michelle de Larrabeiti, Felicity Laughton, Helen Markham, Rebecca Mills, Robert Mitchell, Adam Moore, Helena Nogueira, David Noonan, Alice Peebles, Marianne Petrou, Andrea Powell, Tom Prentice, Andrew Ribeiro-Hargreave, Alison Stace, Amanda Tomeh, Tomas Tranaeus, Fiona Wild.

INDEX
Hilary Bird.

ADDITIONAL PHOTOGRAPHY
Steve Gorton/DK Studio, John Heseltine, Dave King, Martin Norris, Roger Phillips, Clive Streeter, Matthew Ward.

PHOTOGRAPHIC AND ARTWORK REFERENCE
Steven Evans, Nigel Tisdall.

SPECIAL ASSISTANCE
Emília Tavares, Arquivo Nacional de Fotografia, Lisboa; Luísa Cardia, Biblioteca Nacional e do Livro, Lisboa; Marina Gonçalves and Aida Pereira, Câmara Municipal de Lisboa; Caminhos de Ferro Portugueses; Carris, Lisboa; Enatur, Lisboa; Karen Ollier-Spry, John E. Fells and Sons Ltd; Maria Fátima Moreira, Fundação Bissaya-Barreto, Coimbra; Maria Helena Soares da Costa, Fundação Calouste Gulbenkian, Lisboa; João Campilho, Fundação da Casa de Bragança, Lisboa; Pilar Serras and José Aragão, ICEP, London; Instituto do Vinho de Porto, Porto; Simoneta Afonso, IPM, Lisboa; Mário Abreu, Dulce Ferraz, IPPAR, Lisboa; Pedro Moura Bessa and Eduardo Corte-Real, Livraria Civilização Editora, Porto; Metropolitano de Lisboa; Raquel Florentino and Cristina Leite, Museu da Cidade, Lisboa; João Castel Branco G. Pereira, Museu Nacional do Azulejo, Lisboa; TURIHAB, Ponte de Lima; Ilídio Barbosa, Universidade de Coimbra, Coimbra; Teresa Chicau at the tourist office in Évora, Conceição Estudante at the tourist office in Funchal and the staff at all the other tourist offices and town halls in Portugal.

PHOTOGRAPHY PERMISSIONS

DORLING KINDERSLEY would like to thank the following for their assistance and kind permission to photograph at their establishments: Instituto Português do Património Arquitectónico e Arqueológico (IPPAR), Lisboa; Fundação da Casa de Alorna, Lisboa; Instituto Português dos Museus (IPM), Lisboa; Museu da Marinha, Lisboa; Museu do Mar, Cascais; Igreja de Santa Maria dos Olivais, Tomar and all the other churches, museums, hotels, restaurants, shops, galleries and sights too numerous to thank individually.

PICTURE CREDITS

t = top; tl = top left; tlc = top left centre; tc = top centre; tr = top right; cla = centre left above; ca = centre above; cra = centre right above; cl = centre left; c = centre; cr = centre right; clb = centre left below; cb = centre below; crb = centre right below; bl = bottom left; b = bottom; bc = bottom centre; blc = bottom left centre; brc = bottom right centre; bra = bottom right above; bla = bottom left above; br = bottom right; d = detail.

The work illustrated on page 120 tl, *Reclining Figure, 1982*, is reproduced by kind permission of the Henry Moore Foundation; the work illustrated on page 121b, *Terreiro do Paço* by Dirk Stoop, is reproduced by kind permission of the Museu da Cidade, Lisboa.

The publisher would like to thank the following individuals, companies and picture libraries for permission to reproduce their photographs:

MAURÍCIO ABREU: 33t/cr, 145tr, 338bc/br, 358, 360t, 364b/c, 365b, 366ca, 367c, 368tr/ca/cb, 370t, 371t, 399b; AISA: 38tr, 39tc, 39br, 56br, 106b; PUBLICAÇÕES ALFA: 186b. ALGARVE TOURIST OFFICE: 286tr; ALLSPORT: Mike Powell 57crb; ARQUIVO NACIONAL DE FOTOGRAFIA-INSTITUTO PORTUGUÊS DE MUSEUS, Lisboa: Museu Nacional de Arte Antiga/Pedro Ferreira 98t, 99t; Francisco Matias 49tl; Carlos Monteiro 46cla; Luís Pavão 39tl, 52clb, 53c, 60t, 96bl/br, 97b, 99c; José Pessoa 20bl, 21tr, 45c, 49tr, 50tr, 51t/clb, 96tl/tr, 97t/cr, 98b, 99b; Museu Nacional do Azulejo: *Painel de azulejos Composição Geométrica*, 1970, Raul Lino-Fábrica Cerâmica Constância 23tr; Francisco Matias 22b; José Pessoa 22cra/23cb/bl; Colecções Arquivo Nacional de Fotografia/San Payo 39tr; Igreja de São Vicente de Fora/Carlos Monteiro 39bl; Museu Nacional dos Coches/José Pessoa 39bc, 103bl, 144br, 145b; Henrique Ruas 104b; Museu Nacional de Arqueologia/José Pessoa 40t, 41ca/cb, 105c; Museu Monográfico de Conímbriga 41tl; Museu de Mértola/Paulo

Cintra 42cl; Igreja Matriz Santiago do Cacém/José Rubio 43tl; Museu Nacional Machado de Castro/Carlos Monteiro 44tl; José Pessoa 45tl; Biblioteca da Ajuda/José Pessoa 44cla; Museu de São Roque/Abreu Nunes 47tl; Museu Grão Vasco/José Pessoa 48bl; Universidade de Coimbra, Gabinete de Física/José Pessoa 52tr; Museu de Cerâmica das Caldas da Rainha/José Pessoa 54 cla; Museu do Chiado 55tl; Col. Jorge de Brito/José Pessoa 62/3tc; Col. António Chainho/José Pessoa 66b; Arnaldo Soares 66tr, 67tl; Museu Nacional do Teatro/Arnaldo Soares 66cl; Luisa Oliveira 67tr; Museu de Évora/José Pessoa 303 cra; TONY ARRUZA: 282–3, 38c, 44bl, *Portrait of Fernando Pessoa* by Almada Negreiros © DACS 1997: 56tr; 57br, 62/3c, 145ca.

JORGE BARROS S.P.A.: 226cr; INSTITUTO DA BIBLIOTECA NACIONAL E DO LIVRO, Lisboa: 37b, 46bca/b, 47crb, 50cb, 51br, 53br, 165bl, 183b; 283 (inset); GABRIELE BOISELLE: 144bl; BOUTINOT PRINCE WINE SHIPPERS, Stockport: 228br; THE BRIDGEMAN ART LIBRARY, with kind permission from Michael Chase: *Landscape near Lagos, Algarve, Portugal* by Sir Cedric Morris (1889–1982), Bonhams, London: 8–9; By permission of THE BRITISH LIBRARY, London: *João I of Portugal being entertained by John of Gaunt* (d), from de Wavrin's *Chronicle d'Angleterre* (Roy 14E IV 244v) 46/7c; © Trustees of THE BRITISH MUSEUM, London: 43cla, 48br, 54bl.

CÂMARA MUNICIPAL DE LISBOA: 51crb, António Rafael 62cl; CÂMARA MUNICIPAL DE OEIRAS: 52clb; CENTRO EUROPEU JEAN MONNET: 57tr; CEPHAS: Mick Rock 28crb, 29c; CERAMICARTE: 24bl; CHAPITO: 64tr; COCKBURN SMITHES & CIA, S.A. (an Allied Domecq Company): 228crb; COMPANHIA CARRIS DE FERRO DE LISBOA: 448cr; CORBIS: Peter Wilson 236br; CTT, CORREIOS: 434cr, 435cr.

DIÁRIO DE NOTÍCIAS: 55cl; MICHAEL DIGGIN: 334t/b, 359t/b, 360b, 361t, 365t, 369t; DOW'S PORT 229cr.

EMPICS: Steve Etherington 32c; ESPAÇO TALASSA: Gerard Soury 368b; ET ARCHIVE: Naval Museum, Genoa 357b; Wellington Museum 193b; EUROPEAN COMMISSION: 433, 434cl; GREG EVANS INTERNATIONAL: Greg Balfour Evans 287br; MARY EVANS PICTURE LIBRARY: 51bl, 63tr, 161b, 210b; EXPO '98: 57cra.

FOTOTECA INTERNACIONAL, Lisboa: Luís Elvas 33cl, 144tl/tr/cr; César Soares 27t, 38bl; LUÍZ O FRANQUINHO/ANTÓNIO DA COSTA: 337bla; FUNDAÇÃO DA CASA DE BRAGANÇA: 298t/c/b, 299bl; FUNDAÇÃO CALOUSTE GULBENKIAN: 64b; FUNDAÇÃO DA CASA DE MATEUS: Nicholas Sapieha 254b; FUNDAÇÃO RICARDO DO ESPÍRITO SANTO SILVA, MUSEU-ESCOLA DE ARTES DECORATIVAS PORTUGUESAS 72c.

JORGE GALVÃO: 57clb; GIRAUDON: 48c. ROBERT HARDING PICTURE LIBRARY: 13b; KIT HOUGHTON: 32b; 145cb.

THE IMAGE BANK: Maurício Abreu 30bl; Moura Machado 19t, 361b, 371b; João Paulo 31cb, 227cl, 363t; IMAGES COLOUR LIBRARY: 226b.

MARION KAPLAN: 144cl, 227t/cr.

LUSA: António Cotrim 67c; André Kosters 93t; Manuel Moura 56bc, 357t; Luís Vasconcelos 92b.

JOSÉ MANUEL: 63br; ANTÓNIO MARQUES: 296c, 297b; ARXIU MAS: 50tl; METROPOLITANO DE LISBOA: 448cr; METROPOLITANO DE LISBOA, Paulo Sintra: *Four Tiles from Lisbon Underground Station* (Cidade Universitária), Maria Helena Vieira da Silva © ADAGP, Paris and DACS, London 1997, 56tl; JOHN MILLER: 21b; MUSEU CERRALBO, Madrid: 42tl; MUSEU CALOUSTE GULBENKIAN, Lisboa: *Enamelled Silver Gilt Corsage Ornament, René Lalique* © ADAGP, Paris and DACS, London 1997, 116ca; 116t/ca/cb/b, 117t/ca/cb/b, 118c/b/t, 119b/t/c; MUSEU DA CIDADE, Lisboa: António Rafael 62tl/bl/br; 63c/bl; MUSEU DA MARINHA, Lisboa: 38br, 56cl, 108b.

NATIONAL MARITIME MUSEUM, London: 50ca; NATIONALMUSEET, Copenhagen: 48tr; NATURE PHOTOGRAPHERS: Brinsley Burbidge 336br, 337br; Andrew Cleave 336clb/bl, 337bl; Peter Craig-Cooper 329crb; Geoff du Feu 329b; Jean Hall 336bcr; Tony Schilling 336bcl; Paul Sterry 319c, 337bra/blc; NATURPRESS: Juan Hidalgo-Candy Lopesino 32tl, 33br; Jaime Villanueva 24t; NHPA: Michael Leach 369crb; Jean-Louis le Moigne 329cra. ARCHIVO FOTOGRÁFICO ORONOZ: 38bc, 42/3c, 43b, 46lb, 179br. Fotografia cedida y autorizada por el PATRIMONIO NACIONAL: 42cb; THE PIERPONT MORGAN LIBRARY/ART RESOURCE, New York: 37t;

POPPERFOTO: 55b; POUSADAS DE PORTUGAL: 378t/cla; POWERSTOCK PHOTOLIBRARY: 203t.

DIAS DOS REIS: 121tl, 432t; NORMAN RENOUF: 374b, 379b; RCL, PAREDE: Rui Cunha 30t, 31cl, 32tr, 65t, 332–3, 336cra, 337cra, 339tr, 365c, 366t/b, 377; REX FEATURES: Sipa Press, Michel Ginies 57bl; MANUEL RIBEIRO: 22t; RADIO TELEVISÃO PORTUGUESA (RTP): 54t, 55clb, 56cr.

HARRY SMITH HORTICULTURAL PHOTOGRAPHIC COLLECTION: 337cla; SOLAR DO VINHO DO PORTO: 252b; SPECTRUM COLOUR LIBRARY: 236cl; TONY STONE IMAGES: Tony Arruza 30ca; Shaun Egan 286b; Graham Finlayson 41crb; Simeone Huber 284b; John Lawrence 31b; Ulli Seer 317t; 426b; SYMINGTON PORT AND MADEIRA SHIPPERS: Claudio Capone 29cl, 229t/cla/bc/br.

TAP AIR PORTUGAL: 441t; NIGEL TISDALL: 339tl , 362, 363b, 364t, 367t/b, 370c/b, 447t; TOPHAM PICTURE SOURCE: 57ca; ARQUIVOS NACIONAIS/TORRE DO TOMBO: 36, 44bla, 267b; TOMAS TRANAEUS: 432b; TURIHAB: Roger Day 376tl; 376b.

NIK WHEELER: 314; PETER WILSON: 30br, 31tr, 56bl, 68, 84tl, 87br, 93b, 226tl/r/cl; WOODFALL WILD IMAGES: Mike Lane 169b; WORLD PICTURES: 287tc/bl.

JACKET
Front - DK PICTURE LIBRARY: crb; Linda Whitwam clb; GETTY IMAGES: Hans Peter Merten main image; HORIZON: Adina Amsel bc. Back - DK PICTURE LIBRARY: Linda Whitwam t; Paul Harris b. Spine - GETTY IMAGES: Hans Peter Merten.

Front Endpaper: All special photography except MAURÍCIO ABREU tl; NIK WHEELER br; PETER WILSON blc.

All other images © DORLING KINDERSLEY. For further information see www.DKimages.com

Phrase Book

IN EMERGENCY

Help!	Socorro!	soo-**koh**-roo
Stop!	Páre!	**pahr'**
Call a doctor!	Chame um médico!	**shahm'** ooñ meh-dee-koo
Call an ambulance!	Chame uma ambulância!	**shahm'** oo-muh añ-boo-**lañ**-see-uh
Call the police!	Chame a polícia!	**shahm'** uh poo-**lee**-see-uh
Call the fire brigade!	Chame os bombeiros!	**shahm'** oosh bom-**bay**-roosh
Where is the nearest telephone?	Há um telefone aqui perto?	ah ooñ te-le-**fon'** uh-**kee pehr**-too
Where is the nearest hospital?	Onde é o hospital mais próximo?	ond' eh oo ohsh-pee-**tahl'** mysh **pro**-see-moo

COMMUNICATION ESSENTIALS

Yes	Sim	seeñ
No	Não	nowñ
Please	Por favor/ Faz favor	poor fuh-**vor** fash fuh-**vor**
Thank you	Obrigado/da	o-bree-**gah**-doo/duh
Excuse me	Desculpe	dish-**koolp'**
Hello	Olá	oh-**lah**
Goodbye	Adeus	a-**deh**-oosh
Good morning	Bom-dia	boñ **dee**-uh
Good afternoon	Boa-tarde	boh-uh **tard'**
Good night	Boa-noite	boh-uh **noyt'**
Yesterday	Ontem	oñ-**tayñ**
Today	Hoje	**ohj'**
Tomorrow	Amanhã	ah-mañ-**yañ**
Here	Aqui	uh-**kee**
There	Ali	uh-**lee**
What?	O quê?	oo keh
Which?	Qual?	**kwahl'**
When?	Quando?	**kwañ**-doo
Why?	Porquê?	poor-**keh**
Where?	Onde?	**oñd'**

USEFUL PHRASES

How are you?	Como está?	**koh**-moo shtah
Very well, thank you.	Bem, obrigado/da.	bayñ o-bree-**gah**-doo/duh
Pleased to meet you.	Encantado/a.	eñ-kañ-**tah**-doo/duh
See you soon.	Até logo.	uh-**teh loh**-goo
That's fine.	Está bem.	shtah **bayñ**
Where is/are . . . ?	Onde está/estão . . . ?	ond' shtah/shtowñ
How far is it to . . . ?	A que distância fica . . . ?	uh kee dish-**tañ**-see-uh **fee**-kuh
Which way to . . . ?	Como se vai para . . . ?	**koh**-moo seh vy puh-ruh
Do you speak English?	Fala inglês?	**fah**-luh eeñ-**glehsh**
I don't understand.	Não compreendo.	nowñ kom-pree-**eñ**-doo
Could you speak more slowly please?	Pode falar mais devagar por favor?	**pohd'** fuh-**lar** mysh d'-va-**gar** poor fuh-**vor**
I'm sorry.	Desculpe.	dish-**koolp'**

USEFUL WORDS

big	grande	**grañd'**
small	pequeno	pe-**keh**-noo
hot	quente	**keñt'**
cold	frio	**free**-oo
good	bom	**boñ**
bad	mau	**mah**-oo
quite a lot/enough	bastante	bash-**tañt'**
well	bem	**bayñ**
open	aberto	a-**behr**-too
closed	fechado	fe-**shah**-doo
left	esquerda	**shkehr**-duh
right	direita	dee-**ray**-tuh
straight on	em frente	ayñ **freñt'**
near	perto	**pehr**-too
far	longe	**loñj'**
up	para cima	pur-ruh **see**-muh
down	para baixa	pur-ruh **buy**-shoo
early	cedo	**seh**-doo
late	tarde	**tard'**
entrance	entrada	eñ-**trah**-duh
exit	saída	sa-**ee**-duh
toilets	casa de banho	**kah**-zuh d' **bañ**-yoo
more	mais	mysh
less	menos	**meh**-noosh

MAKING A TELEPHONE CALL

I'd like to place an international call.	Queria fazer uma chamada internacional.	**kree**-uh fuh-**zehr** oo-muh sha-**mah**-duh in-ter-na-**see**-oo-**nahl'**
a local call.	uma chamada local.	oo-muh sha-**mah**-duh loo-**kahl'**
Can I leave a message?	Posso deixar uma mensagem?	**poh**-soo day-**shar** oo-muh meñ-**sah**-jayñ

SHOPPING

How much does this cost?	Quanto custa isto?	**kwañ**-too **koosh**-tuh eesh-too
I would like . . .	Queria . . .	**kree**-uh
I'm just looking.	Estou só a ver obrigado/a.	**shtoh** soh uh vehr o-bree-**gah**-doo/uh
Do you take credit cards?	Aceita cartões de crédito?	uh-**say**-tuh kar-**toinsh** de **kreh**-dee-too
What time do you open?	A que horas abre?	uh **kee oh**-rash **ah**-bre
What time do you close?	A que horas fecha?	uh **kee oh**-rash **fay**-shuh
This one	Este	**ehst'**
That one	Esse	**ehss'**
expensive	caro	**kah**-roo
cheap	barato	buh-**rah**-too
size (clothes/shoes)	tamanho	ta-**man**-yoo
white	branco	**brañ**-koo
black	preto	**preh**-too
red	vermelho	ver-**melh**-yoo
yellow	amarelo	uh-mah-**reh**-loo
green	verde	**vehrd'**
blue	azul	uh-**zool'**

TYPES OF SHOP

antique shop	loja de antiguidades	**loh**-juh de añ-tee-gwee-**dahd'sh**
bakery	padaria	pah-duh-**ree**-uh
bank	banco	**bañ**-koo
bookshop	livraria	lee-vruh-**ree**-uh
butcher	talho	**tah**-lyoo
cake shop	pastelaria	pash-te-luh-**ree**-uh
chemist	farmácia	far-**mah**-see-uh
fishmonger	peixaria	pay-shuh-**ree**-uh
hairdresser	cabeleireiro	kab'-lay-**ray**-roo
market	mercado	mehr-**kah**-doo
newsagent	kiosque	kee-**yohsk'**
post office	correios	koo-**ray**-oosh
shoe shop	sapataria	suh-puh-tuh-**ree**-uh
supermarket	supermercado	soo-**pehr**-mer-**kah**-doo
tobacconist	tabacaria	tuh-buh-kuh-**ree**-uh
travel agency	agência de viagens	uh-**jen**-see-uh de vee-**ah**-jaynsh

SIGHTSEEING

cathedral	sé	seh
church	igreja	ee-**gray**-juh
garden	jardim	jar-**deeñ**
library	biblioteca	bee-blee-oo-**teh**-kuh
museum	museu	moo-**zeh**-oo
tourist information office	posto de turismo	**posh**-too d' too-**reesh**-moo
closed for holidays	fechado para férias	fe-**sha**-doo puh-ruh **feh**-ree-ash
bus station	estação de autocarros	shta-**sowñ** d' oh-too-**kah**-roosh
railway station	estação de comboios	shta-**sowñ** d' koñ-**boy**-oosh

STAYING IN A HOTEL

Do you have a vacant room?	Tem um quarto livre?	tayñ ooñ **kwar**-too **leevr'**
room with a bath	um quarto com casa de banho	ooñ **kwar**-too koñ **kah**-zuh d' **bañ**-yoo
shower	duche	**doosh**
single room	quarto individual	**kwar**-too een-dee-vee-doo-**ahl'**
double room	quarto de casal	**kwar**-too d' kuh-**zahl'**
twin room	quarto com duas camas	**kwar**-too koñ **doo**-ash kah-**mash**
porter	porteiro	poor-**tay**-roo
key	chave	**shahv'**
I have a reservation.	Tenho um quarto reservado.	**tayñ**-yoo ooñ **kwar**-too-re-ser-**vah**-doo

EATING OUT

English	Portuguese	Pronunciation
Have you got a table for . . . ?	Tem uma mesa para . . . ?	tayñ oo-muh meh-zuh puh-ruh
I want to reserve a table.	Quero reservar uma mesa.	keh-roo re-zehr-var oo-muh meh-zuh
The bill please.	A conta por favor/ faz favor.	uh kohn-tuh poor fuh-vor/ fash fuh-vor
I am a vegetarian.	Sou vegetariano/a.	Soh ve-je-tuh-ree-ah-noo/a
Waiter!	Por favor!/ Faz favor!	poor fuh-vor fash fuh-vor
the menu	a lista	uh leesh-tuh
fixed-price menu	a ementa turística	uh ee-mehñ-tuh too-reesh-tee-kuh
wine list	a lista de vinhos	uh leesh-tuh de veeñ-yoosh
glass	um copo	ooñ koh-poo
bottle	uma garrafa	oo-muh guh-rah-fuh
half bottle	meia-garrafa	may-uh guh-rah-fuh
knife	uma faca	oo-muh fah-kuh
fork	um garfo	ooñ gar-foo
spoon	uma colher	oo-muh kool-yair
plate	um prato	ooñ prah-too
napkin	um guardanapo	ooñ goo-ar-duh-nah-poo
breakfast	pequeno-almoço	pe-keh-noo-ahl-moh-soo
lunch	almoço	ahl-moh-soo
dinner	jantar	jan-tar
cover	couvert	koo-vehr
starter	entrada	eñ-trah-duh
main course	prato principal	prah-too prin-see-pahl'
dish of the day	prato do dia	prah-too doo dee-uh
set dish	combinado	koñ-bee-nah-doo
half portion	meia-dose	may-uh doh-se
dessert	sobremesa	soh-bre-meh-zuh
rare	mal passado	mahl' puh-sah-doo
medium	médio	meh-dee-oo
well done	bem passado	bayñ puh-sah-doo

MENU DECODER

Portuguese	Pronunciation	English
abacate	uh-buh-kaht'	avocado
açorda	uh-sor-duh	bread-based stew (often seafood)
açúcar	uh-soo-kar	sugar
água mineral	ah-gwuh mee-ne-rahl'	mineral water
(com gás)	koñ gas	sparkling
(sem gás)	sayñ gas	still
alho	al-yoo	garlic
alperce	ahl'-pehrce	apricot
amêijoas	uh-may-joo-ash	clams
ananás	uh-nuh-nahsh	pineapple
arroz	uh-rohsh	rice
assado	uh-sah-doo	baked
atum	uh-tooñ	tuna
aves	ah-vesh	poultry
azeite	uh-zayt'	olive oil
azeitonas	uh-zay-toh-nash	olives
bacalhau	buh-kuh-lyow	dried, salted cod
banana	buh-nah-nuh	banana
batatas	buh-tah-tash	potatoes
batatas fritas	buh-tah-tash free-tash	french fries
batido	buh-tee-doo	milk-shake
bica	bee-kuh	espresso
bife	beef	steak
bolacha	boo-lah-shuh	biscuit
bolo	boh-loo	cake
borrego	boo-reh-goo	lamb
caça	kah-ssuh	game
café	kuh-feh	coffee
camarões	kuh-muh-roysh	large prawns
caracóis	kuh-ruh-koysh	snails
caranguejo	kuh-rañ-gay-joo	crab
carne	karn'	meat
cataplana	kuh-tuh-plah-nuh	sealed wok used to steam dishes
cebola	se-boh-luh	onion
cerveja	sehr-vay-juh	beer
chá	shah	tea
cherne	shern'	stone bass
chocolate	shoh-koh-laht'	chocolate
chocos	shoh-koosh	cuttlefish
chouriço	shoh-ree-soo	red, spicy sausage
churrasco	shoo-rash-coo	on the spit
cogumelos	koo-goo-meh-loosh	mushrooms
cozido	koo-zee-doo	boiled
enguias	eñ-gee-ash	eels
fiambre	fee-añbr'	ham
fígado	fee-guh-doo	liver
frango	frañ-goo	chicken
frito	free-too	fried
fruta	froo-tuh	fruit
gambas	gam-bash	prawns
gelado	je-lah-doo	ice cream
gelo	jeh-loo	ice
goraz	goo-rash	bream
grelhado	grel-yah-doo	grilled
iscas	cesh-kash	marinated liver
lagosta	luh-gohsh-tuh	lobster
laranja	luh-rañ-juh	orange
leite	layt'	milk
limão	lee-mowñ	lemon
limonada	lee-moo-nah-duh	lemonade
linguado	leeñ-gwah-doo	sole
lulas	loo-lash	squid
maçã	muh-sañ	apple
manteiga	mañ-tay-guh	butter
mariscos	muh-reesh-koosh	seafood
meia-de-leite	may-uh-d' layt'	white coffee
ostras	osh-trash	oysters
ovos	oh-voosh	eggs
pão	powñ	bread
pastel	pash-tehl'	cake
pato	pah-too	duck
peixe	paysh'	fish
peixe-espada	paysh'-shpah-duh	scabbard fish
pimenta	pee-meñ-tuh	pepper
polvo	pohl'-voo	octopus
porco	por-coo	pork
queijo	kay-joo	cheese
sal	sahl'	salt
salada	suh-lah-duh	salad
salsichas	sahl-see-shash	sausages
sandes	sañ-desh	sandwich
santola	sañ-toh-luh	spider crab
sopa	soh-puh	soup
sumo	soo-moo	juice
tamboril	tañ-boo-ril'	monkfish
tarte	tart'	pie/cake
tomate	too-maht'	tomato
torrada	too-rah-duh	toast
tosta	tohsh-tuh	toasted sandwich
vinagre	vee-nah-gre	vinegar
vinho branco	veeñ-yoo brañ-koo	white wine
vinho tinto	veeñ-yoo teeñ-too	red wine
vitela	vee-teh-luh	veal

NUMBERS

	Portuguese	Pronunciation
0	zero	zeh-roo
1	um	ooñ
2	dois	doysh
3	três	tresh
4	quatro	kwa-troo
5	cinco	seeñ-koo
6	seis	saysh
7	sete	set'
8	oito	oy-too
9	nove	nov'
10	dez	desh
11	onze	oñz'
12	doze	doz'
13	treze	trez'
14	catorze	ka-torz'
15	quinze	keeñz'
16	dezasseis	de-zuh-saysh
17	dezassete	de-zuh-set'
18	dezoito	de-zoy-too
19	dezanove	de-zuh-nov'
20	vinte	veent'
21	vinte e um	veen-tee-ooñ
30	trinta	treeñ-tuh
40	quarenta	kwa-reñ-tuh
50	cinquenta	seen-kweñ-tuh
60	sessenta	se-señ-tuh
70	setenta	se-teñ-tuh
80	oitenta	oy-teñ-tuh
90	noventa	noo-veñ-tuh
100	cem	sayñ
101	cento e um	señ-too-ee-ooñ
102	cento e dois	señ-too ee doysh
200	duzentos	doo-zeñ-toosh
300	trezentos	tre-zeñ-toosh
400	quatrocentos	kwa-troo-señ-toosh
500	quinhentos	kee-nyeñ-toosh
700	setecentos	set'-señ-toosh
900	novecentos	nov'-señ-toosh
1,000	mil	meel'

TIME

English	Portuguese	Pronunciation
one minute	um minuto	ooñ mee-noo-too
one hour	uma hora	oo-muh oh-ruh
half an hour	meia-hora	may-uh-oh-ruh
Monday	segunda-feira	se-goon-duh-fay-ruh
Tuesday	terça-feira	ter-sa-fay-ruh
Wednesday	quarta-feira	kwar-ta-fay-ruh
Thursday	quinta-feira	keen-ta-fay-ruh
Friday	sexta-feira	say-shta-fay-ruh
Saturday	sábado	sah-ba-doo
Sunday	domingo	doo-meen-goo